Classical Psychoanalysis And Its Applications:

A SERIES OF BOOKS
EDITED BY ROBERT LANGS, M.D.

THE TECHNIQUE OF

Psychoanalytic Psychotherapy

VOLUME I

The Initial Contact

Theoretical Framework

Understanding the Patient's Communications

The Therapist's Interventions

ROBERT LANGS, M.D.

Clinical Assistant Professor of Psychiatry,
State University of New York, Downstate Medical Center

THE TECHNIQUE OF

Psychoanalytic Psychotherapy

JASON ARONSON, INC., NEW YORK

To my wife, Joan

*No one who, like me, conjures up the most evil of those
half-tamed demons that inhabit the human breast,
and seeks to wrestle with them, can expect to come through
the struggle unscathed.*

FREUD *(1905)*

Brief
Table of Contents

Comprehensive
Table of Contents

THE TECHNIQUE OF

Psychoanalytic Psychotherapy

VOLUME I

The Initial Contact

Theoretical Framework

Understanding the Patient's Communications

The Therapist's Interventions

Preface

This book grew largely out of my experiences as a supervisor of psychotherapy at the Hillside Hospital Division of the Long Island Jewish—Hillside Medical Center in Glen Oaks, New York. I went there trained in psychoanalysis and experienced in psychoanalytically-founded psychotherapy. I went knowing that there were many other ways of doing therapy besides my own, and fully expecting to find, as I worked with psychiatric residents and postgraduate fellows in psychotherapy who had been taught these other techniques, that I would learn something of the elements common to sound psychotherapy, whatever its orientation. Much to my surprise, I discovered something quite different. I found that the therapeutic work that I supervised fell into two main groupings: sound and unsound. In the former, psychoanalytic principles were utilized; the therapy itself went well; and the patient improved clinically. In the latter, analytic principles were ignored or violated; the therapy itself was stormy and the therapist often under direct attack; and clinically, the patient did poorly.

As a result of these observations, I began to focus on and refine the psychoanalytic concepts and principles of technique that were applicable to the psychotherapeutic situation. I found that I had to develop many of these concepts directly from my own observations, since the literature available in this area fell short in many ways.

Nowhere could I find an exposition of the major issues that was thorough enough and up-to-date; and nowhere could I find a detailed study that began with the daily problems my supervisees and I were facing and concluded with well-established principles of technique that were both basic and directly useful.

In consequence, I began to sharpen my own observations and to develop a method of clinical study that was predictive. This enabled me to generate hypotheses of technique that I could subsequently test. I leaned heavily on the model of supervision described by Arlow (1963b), one that I had the good fortune to experience directly in a most helpful experience in analytic supervision with him. In essence, this supervisory method is modelled on the therapy session itself. It consists of the supervisor's listening to material from the patient as presented in sequence by the therapist, formulating an intervention or an hypothesis about the meaning of the material, and looking to the remaining material from the patient, and the therapist, for validation. Validation of this kind, based on agreement between myself and the therapist presenting the material to me, is clearly open to bias and a search for affirmation, and I make no pretenses regarding the rigorously scientific qualities of this work (Langs, 1972). It clearly is not controlled research, but it is a methodology that offers an advance from uncontrolled or random clinical observations. The patient as a human being becomes the basic field of observation and the material from him is the source of hypotheses, as well as the basis for their confirmation.

Out of this work, which included many detailed observations, hypotheses, revised hypotheses, reconsiderations, and reformulations, have come the principles of technique presented in this book. Since the clinical observations were replete with daily therapeutic problems, the book explores many basic clinical issues and their management. And since I had at hand hundreds of documented clinical vignettes, the discussions of those problems are presented in work-book form, with several hundred detailed illustrations in which I report to the reader, for his own appraisal, the material as it was presented by the patient to the therapist and to me.

In all, then, I hope to cover the fundamental problems and issues of psychotherapy in this work. With such ambitious goals, however, I must say at the outset that I am well aware of the many hazards and problems with which I am faced. A book of this scope, written by a working and learning analyst such as myself, can only be a statement of present insights and delineations. My ideas are in a constant process of revision and change, I hope toward fuller understanding. By now, however, there appears to be a sound core to them, while peripherally, shifts in subtle or more major ways of viewing matters continue to provide new insights. I believe that I have reached a juncture where the basic principles have proved durable and sound, and that I have sufficient data on which to base meaningful and definitive formulations. But I am well aware that I am discussing matters of great complexity and that flexibility, within limits, must prevail.

While I hope to cover the field thoroughly, it is one of so many intricacies that I cannot possibly discuss every variation and nuance. Essentially, I have tried to establish a set of basic principles complete enough so that the therapist is prepared for the inevitable new twists that his patients will find. I know, too, that there is much controversy about some of the principles that I shall describe; I can only state that each one has been empirically based and tested, and has been found to be sound and useful. All are open to revision if new observations demand such changes. I have tried wherever possible to define the theoretical underpinnings and implications of these findings and formulations. While psychoanalytic theory has undoubtedly greatly influenced my selection of observations and the conclusions I have drawn from them, I have attempted to reverse this process whenever possible, by reformulating and retheorizing on the basis of my data.

This, then, is the spirit of this book: an attempt to be as empirical and definitive as possible, to take firm stands where experience dictates the need for them, to discuss clearcut alternatives where they seem to exist, and to define the limits and freedom of sound technique. I have tried to establish the boundaries of psychotherapy, and, within these empirically-founded lines, to promote flexibility and creativity in the therapist.

This entire undertaking rests on the ultimate foundation of an extensive psychoanalytic literature and many years of direct learning. Since this is a book derived primarily from empirical observations, it has not been feasible for me to return extensively to the literature to trace the roots of my ideas in the writings of others. I shall allude to major sources in the text, but here I want to acknowledge the contributions of the many psychoanalytic investigators to whom I shall not be able to refer directly. In addition, I want to single out as particularly influential for the development of this book three psychoanalytic writers who, in addition to Sigmund Freud, especially inspired my thinking: Jacob Arlow, Michael Balint and Ralph Greenson.

However, my gratitude to those who taught me about psychotherapy, and who stimulated my clinical and scientific interests in this field, goes back many years, to Dr. Richard Silberstein and his psychiatric staff, with whom I worked as an intern at the Public Health Service Hospital on Staten Island; to Drs. Milton Rosenbaum and Morton Reiser and the many others from whom I learned as a resident and research fellow at the Albert Einstein complex in the Bronx; and to the many fine instructors at the Downstate Psychoanalytic Institute at Brooklyn where I was a candidate and graduate. Among these last, I should like to single out for their special influence Drs. Jacob Arlow, Frank Berchenko, Mark Kanzer, William Neiderland, Robert Savitt, and Melitta Sperling. And finally, my years at the Research Center for Mental Health under the aegis of Drs. Robert Holt, Leo Goldberger, and the late George Klein were of inestimable help in developing my senses of observation and theorizing. The distillation of these influences and the entire responsibility for the material and discussions in this book are, of course, mine entirely.

My main appreciation for the inspiration for this book belongs ultimately to the residents and postgraduate fellows at Hillside Hospital, who came to me to develop their skills as psychotherapists, who presented their work to me with dedication and eagerness, and who suffered with me the inevitable and necessary disappointments and gratifications of learning. To my own patients, I acknowledge a special sense of appreciation for the wisdom and maturity working with them has afforded me. I am also deeply indebted to my friends and colleagues who critically reviewed this work, especially Drs. Peter Giovacchini and Leonard Barkin, who read through the entire manuscript, and Drs. Harold Blum, Joseph Coltrera and William Console, who read portions of it. I was greatly assisted by the editing of Mrs. Jan Blakeslee and Ms. Catherine Wilson, who also served as overseer for the publication of the book. My secretary, Judith Caccavale, proved to be an untiring worker and my publisher, Dr. Jason Aronson, has been helpful in countless ways. Lastly, my wife, Joan, and children, Charles, Bernard, and Sandra, were the source of considerable faith and support throughout this undertaking.

I think of this book as being open-ended, and had even hoped that it could be published as a looseleaf edition to which sections could readily be added. I have no doubt that my own patients, students, colleagues, and readings will point me in new directions and toward further understanding. I believe that the heart of this book will prove sound and lasting; beyond that, I hope to refine and revise it as I continue to work and write. It is my greatest hope that the reader, too, will be inspired by what is to follow to develop a similar core of sound working principles of technique, that he will utilize them in his own individual way, and that he will on his own revise and elaborate upon them, thereby advancing his work with his patients and the field of psychoanalytic psychotherapy yet another step toward greater efficacy.

Robert J. Langs, M.D.
Roslyn Heights, N.Y.
April, 1973.

I

INTRODUCTORY

COMMENTS

1 Why This Book Was Written: Its Scope and Goals

BASIC CONCEPTS

This is a book written out of frustration and need. In my work—supervising and practicing psychotherapy—I was repeatedly confronted with problems and issues for which no significant literature existed, either on a practical or theoretical level. Therefore, I have been collecting data over the past ten years in an effort to fill this void and develop a comprehensive compendium of predictable and practically confirmed principles of technique that are based on a sound clinical methodology. This book is the outcome of this work.

I will be dealing with insight-oriented psychoanalytic psychotherapy, which I define as a relationship between two persons—a patient who is suffering with emotional problems and a therapist who has the professional skills to aid in their resolution. This relationship is characterized by a definitive body of explicit and implicit ground rules that create an exquisite interaction and setting in which the patient can achieve the goals of symptom-resolution by positive inner change. This is accomplished through the patient's free and open verbal and nonverbal communication with the therapist and through the latter's stance and verbal interventions, especially his interpretations.

In addition, the therapist practicing psychotherapy uses definitive, scientific principles and rules of technique; beyond these boundaries, one must speak of either parameters (i.e., therapeutically indicated deviations in technique; see Eissler, 1953) or technical errors. Many of the technical principles are borrowed from psychoanalysis and they are modified only when necessitated by the nature of the patient's pathology or the limits of the psychotherapeutic modality. Such therapy includes analytic work in the generic sense of exploration, interpretation, and working through. However, it is done in a more limited fashion than in psychoanalysis.*

The following table lists the main dimensions of psychotherapy and contrasts them with those of psychoanalysis (see Wallerstein, 1969; and the pioneering papers of Alexander, 1954; Bibring, 1954; Fromm-Reichman, 1954; Gill, 1954; Rangell, 1954; and Tarachow and Stein, 1967).

DIMENSIONS	PSYCHOTHERAPY	PSYCHOANALYSIS
GOALS	Symptom resolution; adaptive stability; structural and personality changes—all within limits	*Revision of the total personality*
AIMS	Exploration of presenting symptoms, unconscious fantasies, and genetic development—in a focal way	*Full exploration of these dimensions*
TECHNIQUES	Interpretation of primary importance among nondirective interventions. Confrontations often used.	*Interpretation of primary importance, used in greater depth*
METHODS	Approximation of free association	*Free association*
PATIENTS	Entire range of psychopathology	*Those with the capacity to be analyzed*
FOCUS	The patient's life situation; secondarily, the patient–therapist relationship	*Primarily the patient– therapist relationship and the analytic situation; secondarily, the patient's life situation*
DISCOVERY	Limited exploration of core conflicts; greater study of derivative conflicts	*Maximal work with core conflicts*

---

* I will use the term "analyze" throughout this book in the generic sense, meaning the process of obtaining associations, exploring, interpreting, working through, and resolving intrapsychic conflicts with resultant inner structural change, all within the limits possible in psychotherapy.

TIME	More time-bound and immediate; less time before intervening	*Less time-bound; seems endless and permits longer delays before the therapist intervenes*
CHARACTERISTICS	Face-to-face; one to three times weekly	*Use of couch; analyst out of sight; four to five times weekly*
REGRESSION	Embedded in reality; some modification of defenses; circumscribed periods of regression	*Many regressive pressures; deprivations; modification of defenses; and greater shifts toward primary process thinking*
PATIENT–THERAPIST RELATIONSHIP	Clear boundaries; deprivation of extratherapeutic gratifications; intensity of the relationship is limited for both persons	*More restrictive and with a greater intensity to the relationship between patient and therapist*

Since this is primarily a workbook and one that will focus on problems of technique, I will not discuss these distinctions between psychoanalysis and psychotherapy here, nor explore their implications for the latter mode of treatment. The table outlines some of the main features of psychotherapy and the intricacies of its use, and its characteristics will unfold in the body of this book. Within this framework, the main goals of this book are as follows:

To update, clarify, and systematize the conceptualization of insight-oriented psychoanalytic psychotherapy.

• To define the symptom-ameliorating aspects of this therapeutic modality in terms of its verbal and nonverbal dimensions.

• To investigate and clarify the patient-therapist interaction, including its role in achieving symptom-relief for the patient.

• To study the role of the therapist's verbal interventions in imparting insights that foster the resolution of intrapsychic conflicts.

• To define correctly the supportive aspects and interventions of this therapy.

To present the practical applications of the relatively new developments in psychoanalytic theory, and particularly those in the area of ego psychology.

• To reconceptualize the complementary role of reality and such intrapsychic factors as conflicts and conscious and unconscious fantasies and memories in the development of neurotic behavior and symptoms. To review the implications of this interplay for the technique of psychotherapy.

• To delineate the contribution of the adaptive metapsychological viewpoint to the understanding of symptom-formation and the technique of psychotherapy.

• To provide an understanding of the role of working with unconscious fantasies and memories in psychotherapy and clarify the role of working with ego dysfunctions.

To specifically select and explore recurrent pitfalls and problems which are seldom discussed in the literature, although failure to deal adequately with these difficulties can undermine the entire therapy.

To present a more scientific and valid predictive approach to psychoanalytic psychotherapy, one which will enable the therapist to listen properly, understand the basis for his interventions, and recognize the verbal and behavioral consequences of these interventions.

To document the differences between sound and unsound psychotherapy, in terms of both the short- and long-range consequences of specific correct and incorrect interventions.

• To explore the role of countertransference problems in disturbances which occur during treatment and clarify the technical principles for dealing with such errors.

To translate psychoanalytic theory into concrete principles and concrete interventions which can be used directly in the practice of psychotherapy.

• To provide an opportunity for the reader to formulate case material and therapeutic principles for himself before studying the discussions in the book.

• To present a source book for reviewing specific problems in psychotherapy, a book that addresses itself to the needs of the novice and the experienced clinician, alike. To this end, an index of clinical vignettes listing all of the case material related to each of the major problems discussed has been established.

To demonstrate the scientific validity of insight-oriented psychoanalytic psychotherapy as a means of predicting human behavior, and of understanding, revising, and ameliorating the realities, conflicts, anxieties, and conscious and unconscious fantasies on which such behavior is based.

These are extensive goals. However, psychoanalytic psychotherapy is an effective and maturing form of psychiatric treatment, and one that is well suited for modification of the psychopathology seen in the patients of our times. Furthermore, there is much more specificity to this work than is generally acknowledged. There are, for example, definitive indications for therapeutic interventions that are correctly timed and subsequently validated; and valid interventions lead to symptomatic relief and ego maturation and development. The goal of this book is to define the specific techniques for achieving such sound clinical results. While this may sound potentially dogmatic, it is primarily intended to convey the conviction that there are valid basic principles of psychotherapy. Beyond these lie errors with predictable consequences which can be detected in the material from the patient, and rectified. Therefore, the definitions will be tempered with the understanding that these tenets are open to further revision based on fresh observations. The principles thus defined must be used creatively and flexibly, in the service of the patient's needs and the therapist's style of work.

The treatment of most non-psychotic syndromes, including the neuroses, character disorders, perversions, and borderline syndromes will be the primary concern of this book; more rarely, it will consider the problems of ambulatory schizophrenic patients. These principles are applicable to any frequency of psychotherapy sessions, though most of the vignettes will be drawn from twice-weekly treatment. All of the clinical material in this book is drawn from the psychotherapeutic situation. The greater percentage of the material comes from my observations as a supervisor of psychiatric residents and fellows who were working with patients in clinics (see Arlow, 1963b). This is supplemented by references from my own work in private practice and from that of colleagues. In all cases, the basic data is derived from process notes made immediately after—or rarely, during—the therapy session. All reports made to me in supervision were in strict sequence, enabling me to generate hypotheses and predictions and to seek their confirmation, or their lack of confirmation. This decision was based on agreement between myself and the therapist presenting to me and there was seldom any disagreement in this regard. Therefore, the principles of technique presented in this book come from correctly predicted, clinically confirmed hypotheses and formulations (see Langs, 1972).

I have attempted to insure the anonymity of the patients discussed through disguising identifying information and by not indicating when more than one vignette refers to the same patient. Further, I have occasionally used clinical material drawn from the same sessions in different contexts and chapters, generally without attempting to refer back to its previous application. While some insights may have been lost in this way, I doubt that any significant drawback will result and, in my view, the guarantee of anonymity for these patients takes precedence.

THE GOALS OF INSIGHT-ORIENTED PSYCHOANALYTIC PSYCHOTHERAPY

In essence, psychotherapy is aimed at the alleviation of emotional problems that are reflected in symptoms, disturbed affects, and behavior problems (see Chapter 8). These are the outcome of unresolved intrapsychic conflicts, ego dysfunctions, and failures in adaptation. One distinction of psychoanalytic psychotherapy is that it endeavors to produce these alterations primarily through structural changes in the patient, that is, the alleviation of symptoms through strengthening and maturing of the ego, modification of pathological ego mechanisms, constructive change in the superego, and modifications of pathological instinctual drives. Essentially, the patient's intrapsychic conflicts and his methods of resolving them must be discovered and defined, with special attention given to the ways in which these methods have failed. With balanced attention to reality and intrapsychic factors including conscious and unconscious fantasies, the material from the patient is explored so that the ego can consciously scrutinize as much of the conflict situation and its genetics as is feasible, and develop new and less costly solutions or adaptations to these problems.

Beyond these structural changes, which are achieved within the limits of the technique, the goal of psychoanalytic psychotherapy is to help the patient effect an alteration and maturation of his total self or way of being a person. He is offered a "new beginning" (Balint, 1968) or an opportunity to go through new self-experiences (Khan, 1972), thereby releasing processes that are directed toward more mature integrations and relatedness.

These goals are accomplished in two ways, through the relationship between the patient and the therapist and through the interventions of the therapist. The former establishes the therapeutic alliance and atmosphere necessary for the patient's basic development and for his investment in the therapy and in the communications from the therapist. The latter fosters the resolution of specific intrapsychic conflicts through insight and structural change, thereby creating new adaptive resources.

THE REQUISITES AND REWARDS FOR A PSYCHOTHERAPIST

There is considerable validity to the investment of one's abilities and interests in the challenge of sound psychotherapy. There is an unfortunate tendency in some quarters to devalue it vis-à-vis psychoanalysis, but it has its own challenges and rewards and can provide legitimate therapeutic satisfactions for both participants. Some therapists see psychotherapy as the illegitimate child of psychoanalysis, and they turn to it for relief from the rigors of the analytic setting, permitting themselves a loose and undisciplined therapeutic stance that is untenable and detrimental to the patient. Creative use of the technique of psychotherapy is to be differentiated from unprincipled therapy.

There are many special requisites and rewards for those who practice psychotherapy (see also Greenson, 1966 and 1967). Among the former is the need to accept the unusual nature of the psychotherapeutic situation as a deeply meaningful interaction in which certain deprivations and special awarenesses must prevail. The therapist and patient both must forego gratifications beyond the therapeutic relationship and accept the necessary frustrations and boundaries that are essential to the patient's revealing himself and revising his pathology. The therapist must maintain his integrity and honesty as a model for new identifications for the patient and as his part of a sound therapeutic alliance through which the patient's forbidden and inappropriate wishes and needs can be frustrated and rechanneled. The therapist must be neutral but not indifferent; he must be tolerant, yet not foster acting out; he must be warm but not seductive; he must be concerned and empathic, yet not overly involved. His role is that of a clinical assessor and interpreter of the patient's material who does not participate in the patient's neurotic fantasies and behavior, nor morally judge them. Along the way, however, the therapist must always be prepared for his inevitable errors and countertransference problems, and in a position to recognize and revise them. He should be comfortable during the unavoidable periods of regression and chaos and patiently wait to understand and intervene. In all, he should be capable of creating a therapeutic atmosphere and alliance which facilitates the resolution of the patient's ills.

For himself, the therapist must expect long hours with few breaks and relative isolation. He must be able to work in the absence of direct appreciation and immediate gratification, allowing inner knowledge of a job well done to suffice. He must refrain from discussing his patients with others and have the capacity for maintaining full confidentiality and for controlling any tendency to use his patients for neurotic, exhibitionist, or self-assuring needs.

These are some of the requisites for those who choose to work in psychotherapy. They are ideals which every therapist strives for and endeavors to not consciously violate; to meet them brings considerable gratification and reward. Among the major satisfactions of being a sound psychotherapist is the sense of accomplishment in helping human beings revise the neurotic aspects of their personalities. Success brings a highly individual kind of achievement which bears a unique, personal stamp for each psychotherapist. The practical result is a stable practice and a good income. In addition, one earns the respect and silent gratitude of his patients, and achieves a strong and appropriate sense of self-esteem. With these requisites and rewards in mind, let us begin our study of the technique of psychotherapy.

II

THE
INITIAL CONTACT
WITH THE PATIENT

2 The Office and the Setting of Treatment

Before the first contact with a patient can be made, the therapist must have an office and a telephone. Although it serves as the crucial physical setting in which therapy unfolds, the office is seldom discussed in the literature. It is well known that the layout and decor of the therapist's surroundings inevitably reflect his personality; many dimensions of these arrangements need not, however, be left to his "unconscious" or to chance.

A therapist's office can be located in a professional building. This promotes the image of medical or professional treatment for emotional illnesses, a concept which I support (see Greenson, 1967), and encourages referrals from colleagues in the same building. General office or apartment buildings that offer space to professional people seem to offer little advantage or disadvantage. Finally, the therapist's office may be located in his apartment or home. It is my impression that this setting has the potential for creating complications. It may generate discomfort and anxiety for the therapist's family, causing them concern about meeting patients and reacting properly; this is a particularly difficult matter for children to handle, both in reality and in their fantasies. The personal setting also creates some difficulties in analyzing transference resistances that interfere with the progress of treatment. This is true because many patients, particularly those who are borderline, will cling to the real aspects of the situation rather than explore their underlying fantasies, which they often keep secret. These patients frequently attempt to make the therapist a person who will, in reality, offer nontherapeutic gratifications (see Chapter 20). Actually being in the therapist's home may stimulate such fantasies and desires, leading to serious obstacles for the therapy and problems that are difficult to resolve. While this setting can nontheless prove workable, the selection of one's home for the office must be accompanied by a special alertness to the realities of the situation. Such awareness is, of course, vital in any setting, and must include an understanding by the therapist of the real and fantasied meanings of his particular location for himself, as well as for his patients.

A brief vignette is illustrative of some of the complications which can arise with a home–office setting:

> Mrs. D.R. was a borderline woman in therapy for depressive episodes and marital problems. Her therapist, Dr. S., had recently purchased a home with an attached office which had a separate entrance and path set off from his living quarters, but did not preclude a view of much of the house itself.
>
> Early in her therapy, it became clear that Mrs. D.R.'s depression had become especially severe two years earlier after her mother had died. As she explored this loss and her entire relationship with her mother, primitive and intensely ambivalent fantasies of wanting to both possess and destroy her were evident. In this context, the patient began to express a vague interest in the therapist and his private life. At this juncture in her treatment, the therapist went into his waiting room after one session with Mrs. D.R. and found his three-year-old son under a waiting room chair.
>
> In addition to the disturbance for the therapist and his family evoked by this incident, Mrs. D.R., who had seen the child, became intensely curious about him and his family. A period of chaos followed as the patient developed erotic fantasies toward the therapist and expressed direct hopes for their gratification. She

repeatedly drove past his home for glances at his family, and it was only with great difficulty that the patient produced material that enabled the therapist to interpret this behavior as related to Mrs. D.R.'s efforts to re-create a symbiotic alliance with the therapist similar to one she had had in her early childhood with her mother. Even then, the fantasies toward the therapist did not fully abate, and they have proven difficult to resolve.

While the nature of this patient's psychopathology, conflicts, and adaptive efforts contributed to this sticky, erotized transference, the location of Dr. S.'s office in his home intensified Mrs. D.R.'s fantasies about him, provided some real basis for them, and made her extra-therapeutic wishes toward him particularly difficult to resolve. Therapeutic work is not impossible in such a setting, but it demands considerable insight and skill in the therapist; at times, it may prove unresolvable after the occurrence of accidental incidents between severely disturbed patients and members of the therapist's family.

The office should be comfortably furnished and efficiently sound-proofed. A lavatory in the office is preferable to using a public or semi-private lavatory in an office building, since this can lead to inadvertent, difficult-to-analyze meetings between the patient and his therapist in the bathroom. Again, these real incidents which often prompt intense fantasies in the patient (and therapist) are difficult to explore and resolve in psychotherapy because of the limitations in the availability of the derivatives of unconscious fantasies and transference expressions in this therapeutic modality. There are therapists who have bathrooms in their office which they alone use, providing a key so their patients can use the public lavatory. Such an arrangement has real hostile and deprecatory implications and should therefore be avoided.

There are two major furniture arrangements for psychotherapeutic consultation rooms with and without a desk. Using a desk conveys a formal and professional atmosphere, but it may also be misused, providing the unduly anxious therapist with an artificial barrier between himself and the patient. Thus, some therapists conceal themselves behind the desk, thereby communicating to the patient their inappropriate need for protection from him. The use of two comfortable chairs without a desk but with a table between the two chairs is an arrangement many therapists now prefer. The table serves as a place for ash trays or a small lamp and as a reminder of the appropriate and realistic boundaries between the patient and the therapist, but it is not essential. Eye-to-eye contact must be feasible between the two parties and must not be precluded by the office setting. All furniture arrangements will evoke fantasies and feelings in both the patient and the therapist, and the latter must be well aware of the implications of the arrangement for himself. He must be comfortable with it and be prepared to analyze his patient's fantasies regarding it, should they become focal or a vehicle for resistances. Consideration of the office arrangement may come into play during therapy.

> Mrs. D.S., an ambulatory schizophrenic woman, sat at her therapist's desk; it brought her quite close to him. During one period of her treatment, she became pre-occupied with her fantasies about the therapist. In the face of unusual cruelty on her husband's part, intense and guilt-ridden longings for closeness and intimacy with the therapist were hinted at. At this point, she moved away from the therapist's desk to a chair in a far corner of his room, refusing to look directly at him. She spoke of her intolerance for the physical proximity and related it to her general tendency to withdraw from people when anxious. This physical separation was a focal point of considerable exploratory work with this patient's fears of losing control of her impulses and fantasies, her magical attempts at protecting herself, and her phobic attitudes.

Some therapists share a waiting room with colleagues, usually of the same speciality. This is a workable arrangement, but it is one that fosters displaced transference fantasies and other conscious and unconscious fantasies in the patient. The therapist should be alert to such derivatives in the associations and reactions of his patients. He, in turn, should be well aware of the meanings of this arrangement for himself and be at ease with them.

For example, the colleague may unconsciously become the omnipotent sage for the patient. He may also be the all-giving provider, the chaperone, the malevolent intruder, or the oedipal rival. Much of the working through of such fantasies depends on the therapist's ability to be comfortable with such material, and to treat it as he would any other communication from the patient. Some patients will have friends in treatment with the co-tenant and they will attempt to play out fantasies of rivalry and favoritism. As long as the therapist does not personally join in, such material is grist for the therapeutic mill.

Having established our office, let us now turn to the logistics of the telephone. A therapist must have his own telephone, preferably with a full-time answering service, which is entirely separate from his home phone. Therapists who follow the current trend of using a recorded message state that they find no disadvantage in this method. However, it has an impersonal quality and may also make it more difficult for the therapist to be reached in an emergency. The patient who calls in a crisis and receives a recorded answer may well become even more anxious; the sense of distance from, and unavailability of, the therapist is bound to be enhanced. Particularly if one treats psychotic, borderline, or suicidal patients (and it is hard to imagine the therapist who does not), such a system may have drawbacks. If it is used, the therapist must be comfortably prepared to explore his patient's reactions and fantasies regarding it.

Whether one answers the telephone during the course of therapy sessions is a matter of personal preference, although repeated calls are disturbing and should not be answered. In the past, I did not find it disruptive to answer an occasional telephone call except at an important moment in a session. I did so by picking up the phone, giving my name, and then listening very briefly. I rather quickly informed the caller that I was in session with a patient, asked for their telephone number if I needed it, and let them know when I would be free to return their call.

However, I do not currently answer the telephone during sessions and have instructed my answering service accordingly. I prefer to create a therapeutic atmosphere in which my full attention is devoted to the patient in the session. This fosters a maximal sense of care and trust, and is part of my offer of an ideal therapeutic "hold" to the patient (see Chapter 8). The patient in the therapy session will seldom directly object to or resent the telephone interruption and the lack of concentrated concern about him which is reflected in this diversion; it will create a silent undercurrent of distrust, however. I therefore allow five minutes between sessions in order to check with my answering service after the telephone has rung and to call back anyone who has tried to reach me. I also instruct my answering service that, in the event of an emergency, the patient should be advised to call back immediately and the service should allow him to ring through; I then answer such a call.

When I am not at home, I let my answering service know where I can be reached. I have instructed my service that, if they call me at my home and find that I am out, they should not give the message to any member of my family but simply leave word that they have a message for me. This is in keeping with a most important point— the practice of psychotherapy is a very special and sensitive profession in which the patient's right to total privacy is essential.

CONFIDENTIALITY

Let us expand on this matter of confidentiality. There should be no third party to the therapeutic relationship, with the sole exception of a supervisor (see Chapter 6). One should never discuss patients with friends or family, even if names are not used; all too often, I have heard of situations in which information was revealed which led to correct, though inadvertent, identification of an unnamed patient. Such violations of confidentiality are not only destructive to the patient, they also give the field of psychotherapy a poor and questionable reputation. Beyond this, such remarks are unnecessary and usually reflect unresolved problems in the therapist. In fact, most discussions of patients between therapists and their professional colleagues are motivated by neurotic needs rather than constructive ones. These inappropriate, unconscious motivations include the need for reassurance through the phallic exhibitionism of successes, and masochistic, guilty, punishment-seeking reporting of failures. Such discussions may also reflect grandiosity, insecurity, hostility toward one's patients, or an erotization of one's work.

Even telling one's wife about one's patients, a common form of leakage, is an unnecessary burden and source of confusion for her. It often prompts her to be indiscreet—along with her therapist-husband.

It should be clear from all of these examples that discretion and silence must prevail. Reflection regarding patients must be private and accomplished through self-analysis or with the help of one's own supervisor or therapist. At times the loneliness of this work proves to be a difficult burden, but each of us must work through this problem for himself. Misusing one's patients or violating their right to total confidentiality is destructive on every level.

3 The First Contact with the Patient

THE FIRST TELEPHONE CALL IN PRIVATE PRACTICE

Once a professional practice is established, referrals may be expected from such sources as therapists and related professionals, physicians of varying specialties, and a variety of lay persons. This leads us to the initial telephone call—what it reflects, the problems which can arise in its course, and how they should be handled.

DATA AVAILABLE TO THE THERAPIST

Mr. A.K. called a psychiatrist, stating that he was planning to divorce his wife and she had insisted that he consult a psychiatrist first. So he wanted an appointment. He asked what the doctor's fee was, and he mentioned that he worked long hours and hoped he could be seen on a Saturday. What can we immediately glean from these opening remarks?

Initially, we can be certain that Mr. A.K. is a reluctant and resistant patient. His motivation for treatment appears to be minimal, while the pressures from his wife seem maximal; not only can we realize how little commitment he has for therapy, we can anticipate that he will be inclined to use the consultation against his wife. In fact, therapy may well be—for both of them—a weapon in their quarrels. Therefore, we should be prepared to deal with expressions of these serious resistances in the initial interview with Mr. A.K.

The prospective patient is probably inclined toward serious acting out and manipulativeness. Rather than internalize and control his impulses, he appears to live them out—a situation reflected in the tone of the divorce. He probably uses reality to rationalize excessive demands on his part, as in his request for the Saturday session. He is making the consultation difficult to arrange and is already looking for a way out of therapy, a fact which may be seen in his inquiry regarding the fee. Note that questions about fees during the initial call are often an ominous sign.

These impressions are not loose speculations, but are implications readily available from the patient's brief comments during his first telephone call. In the main they were all borne out: Mr. A.K. did indeed have extremely strong resistances against treatment which had to be dealt with in his initial session; he also tended to act out extensively and to manipulate others.

The Therapist's Basic Stance

Let us pause briefly before answering Mr. A.K.'s questions, and delineate our findings to this point in terms of some basic principles:

1. *Understand that the initial telephone call reveals important aspects of the patient's anticipatory attitudes toward therapy and the therapist.* This includes the preformed generalized transference.

2. *Listen to these calls with an ear for diagnosis, dynamic conflicts, and in particular, be alert to signs of strong resistances.*

3. *Respond to questions with these resistances, and reality, in mind.*

How then, would we reply to Mr. A.K.'s question regarding the fee? The possibilities range from suggesting that the fee be discussed in the first session, to stating a flat fee or range of fees, to asking the patient why he asks. However, it is generally best to be brief and not discuss fees on the telephone, since many patients will use such information to foster their already intense resistances and anxieties. Furthermore, it is not usually possible to clarify any other potential misuse of the fee issue in an initial phone conversation. I generally suggest to the patient that we discuss the fee when I see him, partly because I have a range of fees (see Chapter 5). However, if he persists, I tell him this range, while making a mental note that this pressure suggests possible financial problems, a sense of mistrust, considerable hesitancy, and/or some special degree of demandingness.

Finally, Mr. A.K.'s request for a Saturday hour—another demand and a severe limitation—must be responded to. Such requests are often the cloak, but also the clue, for strong inner resistances. The response must be made with this in mind and still be in accord with the reality of the therapist's own time schedule. If the time requested by the patient is available, offer it; if it is not open, describe what time you do have available to see him and let him decide if he can work it out. The therapist may even make a brief intervention in such a situation, to the effect that the patient seems to be rather hesitant about the consultation, a fact that indicates noticeable reluctance (not "resistance"; avoid technical terms). This may help the patient bring his resistances into focus and recognize that the therapist is in tune with his problems.

CONSULTATION OR IMMEDIATE REFERRAL

There are a number of facts which should be determined in the first telephone call. The first of these relates to whether the therapist's schedule and that of the patient will permit a consultation and/or arrangement for ongoing therapy if it is indicated. Practices vary in this regard. Some therapists will not see a patient unless they have hours available for continuing therapy, believing that a proper therapeutic stance should include definite continuing availability. Others prefer to tell the patient they are available for only a single consultation hour—or two at most, since there can be no justification for developing an ongoing relationship under such circumstances, and let the patient decide whether he will accept this arrangement or would prefer to see someone else who has therapy-time available. This stance is partly justified by the fact that the referring physician often prefers to have his own consultant see the patient initially. Furthermore, some patients will not enter therapy if the highly recommended consulting therapist does not see them. On the other hand, most patients who are seen under these conditions maintain some expectation that the therapist will find a way to continue with them and are traumatized when this is not feasible. In such an instance, it can happen that they will not accept referral to another therapist, using the reality circumstances to fortify their resistances.

The therapist should be flexible in this regard and follow his own preferences, while heeding the relevant clues from the patient. My own practice is to establish by telephone whether I can work out therapy hours with a patient. If I cannot do so, I tell him this and offer to send him to a competent therapist who has suitable available time. For this purpose, I keep on hand the names of colleagues with open time. I do not give a patient long lists of names, nor do I disregard his often urgent search for a therapist. I consider it my responsibility to assist him, and it is rare that a patient is anything but grateful for this kind of response.

Let me clarify the basis for this attitude and approach. There are few justifications for a psychiatric consultation when you cannot offer therapy to a patient yourself. Some therapists do so, as I said, in the belief that they are helping the patient develop his motivation for treatment, promoting recognition of his need for therapy, aiding him in finding the proper therapeutic modality (psychoanalysis, psychotherapy, etc.), and/or insuring as much as possible that he reaches an available therapist. I do not believe that such goals justify this kind of a consultation unless the patient is hesitant or insists on it. If the referral to a colleague is handled properly, this serves the patient best in the long run and time and money are not spent with minimal (if any) return.

The therapist who receives the initial call should be as sensitive as possible to the patient's needs and preferences. Failure to do so will only reinforce major resistances and may, indeed, prompt the patient to abandon his efforts at seeking help. Any insensitivity is bound to make the patient feel rejected and deserted by an uncaring therapist, and this may reinforce his preformed negative fantasies and anxieties. Calling colleagues for the patient or directly referring him to a specific available therapist counteracts these obstacles and any feelings of rejection evoked by the therapist's not seeing the patient himself. In fact, the caller will appreciate the therapist's honesty and interest.

The essential principles are:

1. *Show concern and be of assistance.*

2. *If only consultation is possible, inform the patient of this and explain what you can offer him through it.* Remember to keep such consultations to a minimum, confining them to patients where there are clear indications for their necessity.

3. *If you decide on direct referral to a therapist with available time, refer the patient to someone that you know has open time or make the calls yourself so that he will be more likely to follow through.*

4. *In regard to every aspect of the initial phone call, be a therapist and be therapeutic; treatment has already begun.*

Some Common Problems

Having established initial concepts regarding the handling of the first telephone call, let us deal with frequent problems which arise in the course of these calls.

Suicidal Patients

Mrs. A.L. called a psychiatrist, stating that she had just seen her internist who had given her his name and told her to call him immediately. She felt like crying a lot and rather confused. Did he have any time to see her?

There can be only one answer to a patient of this kind; any hint of depression or suicidal trends must be detected and investigated immediately. This is a crucial factor in setting up a consultation; emergencies should be picked up and acknowledged in the initial call and a prompt consultation arranged in response to any possible urgent need.

Thus, the doctor asked Mrs. A.L. just how badly she

was feeling. She responded that she had thoughts of killing herself, but she knew that she really did not have the
courage to do it. However, she thought it best to have a
consultation, since her internist was so concerned. When
could she be seen?

The therapist must take every reference to suicide seriously and
not accept the patient's assurances that he will not attempt to take
his life. This is one of the few psychiatric emergencies and it is the
therapist's responsibility to sense it, define it, and then arrange to
see the patient as soon as possible, but certainly on the same day.
The therapist must be prepared to find anything from a schizophrenic who is seriously in danger of killing himself, to an hysteric
who is being manipulative, hostile, and demanding. In any case,
the therapist must assume the responsibility of making sure that the
patient is seen promptly. In principle, then:

1. *Be alert to indications of severe depression and manifest or
implied (concealed) suicidal thoughts and impulses as they are revealed or hinted at in the first phone call.*

2. *Take them seriously as emergencies, and arrange to see the
patient that day—and as soon as possible.*

Calls from Relatives of the Patient

A common variation on the problem of the depressed patient is
the following:

Mr. A.M. called stating that his wife seemed depressed
and disturbed. Could he make an appointment for her?
If a spouse calls for an appointment for his mate, do
you arrange an hour with him, do you ask to speak to the
prospective patient, or do you suggest that the mate call
you directly when she wishes to do so?

I adhere to the principle that the therapist should accept a patient
on any reasonable terms by which he agrees to be seen. Therefore,
I would make the appointment as requested or, at most, ask if the
prospective patient is there and can talk to me. In addition, I would
make a mental note of the implications of the call. I would suspect
that, in this case, Mrs. A.M. is a very passive and dependent woman,

probably rather resistant to treatment, and quite frightened. I would expect to deal with these problems in the first hour or later. Too many hesitant, yet urgently needy, patients are lost to therapy by a therapist's insistence that they take responsibilities and overcome fears which they actually may not be able to handle without his help. Remember, too, that Mrs. A.M. may be suicidal. This calls for seeing her in any legitimate way possible.

In principle, then:

1. *To whatever extent it is possible, accept the patient initially on his own terms.*

2. *If someone else makes the first call and the patient is not available, make the first appointment with him.*

3. *Learn what you can directly and implicitly from such a call, and be prepared to deal with the resistances and problems it reflects in the first hour.*

Calls Regarding Adolescents

Calls regarding adolescents have certain characteristics which merit separate consideration.

> Mrs. A.N. called, saying that her daughter was not doing well at school and might be on drugs. She had found two capsules of some kind in the girl's purse. Could she or her daughter make an appointment? It was urgent, but they were planning a vacation in a week—so, the consultation might have to be postponed.
>
> The therapist asked, as a matter of routine, how the caller had obtained his name. Mrs. A.N. responded that she had forgotten to mention it, but the therapist's sister was her close friend and had recently mentioned that he had just opened his office. In any case, should she tell her daughter about her phone call and how should she tell her about treatment?

With an adolescent, does one see the parents? (I will confine myself here to patients who are at least fifteen years of age, and not deal with younger adolescents or children.) In my training, I was taught to see one or both of the parents initially. This was done to get a full picture of the background of the problems and establish with the parents just what could be offered the patient in terms of frequency of visits and possible length of therapy. The support of the parents for the therapy was thus obtained and, if possible, they were enlisted as allies. In addition, the therapist could determine— and hopefully work through—their resistances, objections, and anxieties about treatment for their child. Finally, seeing the parents provided an opportunity to first establish the ground rules, setting, and the mode of therapy. It was reasoned that once this was done, the therapist worked primarily with the adolescent, seeing either parent as needed. It was claimed that the therapist did not encounter problems of mistrust on the part of the patient because he had seen the parents first. It was made clear to all concerned that everything mentioned by the parents that related to the patient would be shared by the therapist with him but that the reverse road would be closed, all that the patient shared with the therapist remaining completely confidential. Only in an emergency, was it arranged to see the patient first.

However, years of clinical experience and heightened sensitivity to important nonverbal and mothering aspects of the patient– therapist relationship have led me to abandon such a commonly used practice in favor of seeing the adolescent exclusively. I have observed many situations where seeing the parents, despite all of the therapist's verbal guarantees, generated unresolvable mistrust in the patient and fostered a destructive image of a misalliance between the therapist and the parents directed against the patient. Beyond this, the sense of exclusive care and concern is lost and a sense of betrayal fostered. The constructive, ego-building therapeutic atmos- phere in which the patient is responsible for his therapy, and for the handling of problems that his parents have in regard to it, is also undermined. Finally, little that is positive and effective is really accomplished in seeing the parents, and nothing is done that cannot be done better by a different therapist who can see the parents if necessary, and in a therapeutic atmosphere which is proper and facilitating for them.

Thus, I believe that the therapist should make the first appoint- ment with the adolescent directly, if possible, or with the parent if his child is not available at the moment. Depending on the questions asked, the therapist can explain to the parents on the telephone (or briefly in the first hour with the adolescent present) his fee and pertinent ground rules. He must make clear that it will be the adolescent's therapy, adding that, to make it as helpful as possible, he will deal only with the patient. From there, all inquiries and problems from the parents and all ground rules from the therapist are funnelled through the patient. In situations of difficulty, the parents are referred to a colleague.

In principle, then:

1. *With all patients, the therapist should convey on the telephone his interest in arranging the initial appointment directly with the patient, but should not insist on it if it is not feasible.*

2. *He should communicate at the outset the fact that the therapy will be the exclusive, totally confidential, domain of the patient and all problems or questions regarding treatment should come through him.*

Mrs. A.N.'s request for help in introducing her daughter to treatment is not uncommon. It is best to answer this question simply and directly; one can suggest that the teenager be told that his parents are concerned and want him to get professional help. The parent should be firm and insist on at least a consultation; on this basis, many reluctant adolescents can be helped to enter therapy.

Another problem reflected in Mrs. A.N.'s call related to the family's pending vacation; this situation speaks for major resistances in the parents and probably the adolescent. However realistic it is, it implies delay and flight. The therapist should perhaps see this adolescent quickly to deal with these resistances before they solidify into an escape from therapy. A relaxed, covering-over-the-problems rest can very well promote such a negative occurrence. Be alert to such hints; the therapist's first job is to help needy patients actually enter treatment.

WHO THE THERAPIST SHOULD NOT TREAT

While there are inevitably gray areas, definite guidelines regarding the persons a therapist should accept into treatment can be established. It is wise to lean in the direction of referring to a colleague any patient with whom some uncertainty exists. I will begin my discussion with the situation posed by Mrs. A.N. In this instance, the source of the referral was the therapist's sister, a close friend of Mrs. A.N., who undoubtedly knew the prospective patient as well. Should the therapist accept such a referral?

I think it is best not to do so. I have found that adolescents (and adults) often mistrust such an arrangement and worry about leaks of information, despite all verbal assurances to the contrary. Therefore, consciously or unconsciously, the patient may conceal a good deal. In this particular case, the patient's real relationship with the therapist's sister will strongly influence and interfere with both the transference and the therapeutic alliance in her work with the therapist. Actual extraneous complications (e.g., a destructive act by the sister) that cannot be controlled by the therapist may also occur. As long as other therapists are available (and they usually are), such patients are best referred. Psychotherapy is taxing enough without unneeded difficulties that can silently—or loudly—undermine the therapy.

> The therapist actually agreed to see Mrs. A.N.'s daughter in consultation. The session was strained; the young lady was very guarded. The therapist asked her if she knew his sister and if she felt that this was interfering with their interview. The patient said that she did know her and did feel quite uncomfortable talking to the relative of someone she knew; she had come to see him only because of the pressures of her parents. On the basis of her response, the therapist referred her to a colleague and the patient appeared relieved and appreciative. This patient was able to directly verbalize her discomfort only after the therapist sensed it and asked her about it. Often, such feelings and fantasies are avoided by both parties and remain an unspoken, undermining facet of the therapy.

Where to draw the line in accepting a referral from one's own relatives is a matter of individual judgment. If the relationship between the therapist's relative and the prospective patient seems sufficiently distant, and the therapist does not know the person himself, the patient can be accepted. He must then be alert to the implications of this mode of referral and prepared, when derivatives appear, to interpret the conscious and unconscious meanings for the patient. These will often relate to early, critical resistances which should be quickly detected and analyzed. To do this, the therapist must also be in touch with the meanings of such a referral to himself. This is never a simple matter for the patient or therapist and it requires considerable sensitivity.

Let us now attempt to define some basic general principles regarding who a therapist should exclude from therapy with himself:

1. *Close and distant relatives of the therapist cannot obtain unbiased and uncontaminated therapy, and should be referred to a colleague.*

2. *The same is true of close and even distant friends.*

3. *Do not treat anyone with whom there has been a prior relationship, either between yourself or between a close relative of yours and the prospective patient.*

REFERRALS FROM THE THERAPIST'S PATIENTS

Referrals from patients that are, or have been, in treatment with the therapist are a source of much debate. My analytic and psychotherapeutic experience indicates that, without exception, such referrals are an attempt to seduce, demean, and/or act out with the therapist. Some therapists, prone to an unconscious search for extratherapeutic gratifications from their patients, attract such referrals; such a tendency should be detected within oneself and resolved.

There are two basic principles to observe in such instances:

1. *Analyze the conscious and unconscious meanings of the referral for the patient who has made it.*

2. *Refuse the referral at an appropriate point in the session after it has been explored.* An offer to directly assist the person in need of treatment to find an available therapist can then be made.

It is important to listen to the patient and attempt to understand the *context* in which the referral is offered. Thus, the therapist can understand its unconscious meanings and interpret them to the patient. Such meanings are often concealed by the patient's insistence that he merely admires and respects his therapist. Among the more common unconscious reasons is the desire on the part of the referring patient to flee from therapy and offer a substitute in his place. He may also be motivated by guilt over destructive behavior and sadistic fantasies toward the therapist and attempting to alleviate this guilt by a real gift, rather than through analysis of the behavior and its accompanying fantasies. The fear of actual retribution may be a factor, or the acting out of seductive fantasies and longings to be sexually involved with, or mothered by, the therapist may be involved. Such a referral could be an attempt to act out pregnancy fantasies with the therapist through the birth of referred patients. Incestuous oedipal and sibling fantasies are sometimes acted out through an unconscious misalliance in which the referred patient becomes the incestuous or sibling child. Very often such offers are made when there is an intense need to bypass and deny a separation from the therapist, for example, a pending vacation or termination of treatment.

Variations on these themes are infinite. However, these few possibilities indicate how such a referral may be an acting out of unresolved conflicts and fantasies and/or an attempt to deal with anxieties and depressive affects through denial, undoing, and other defensive means. Should the therapist gratify such acting out, whether it is interpreted to the patient or not, he will only serve to reinforce the patient's inappropriate and pathological attempts to solve underlying conflicts. If the therapist accepts the referral under such circumstances, work toward insight will become impossible and further acting out will be encouraged. At the same time, the therapist should establish the meaning of the referral for himself. Such referrals can then be analyzed and refused, so that the patient's therapy is not undermined by a mutual acting out on the part of both patient and therapist. Such a dual stance of not accepting these referrals and analyzing their meanings has, in my experience, always been confirmed in the subsequent material and responses from the patient. The patient who offers the referral unconsciously hopes that it will be refused and his associations indirectly reflect his appreciation of the therapist's integrity, exclusive interest in him, and capacity to maintain an optimal therapeutic atmosphere. These principles, incidentally, are comparable to those we apply regarding any gift offered by the patient to the therapist (see Chapter 5).

When the patient making the referral is no longer in therapy, the problem may seem more difficult. The principles should be essentially the same, however, since this may nevertheless be a way of assuaging unanalyzed guilt, testing the therapist, inviting him into a mutual acting out or betrayal, or undoing a successful therapeutic outcome (see Chapter 25).

We must also recognize that such avenues of referral will have significance for the patient being referred. He may feel manipulated and sense the unconscious acting out to which he is being made a party. If he accepts, it may well be for his own neurotic needs, to the detriment of his own therapy.

The principles regarding patient referrals should now be clear:

1. *In evaluating them, consider and analyze the underlying dynamics, defenses, and fantasies for the patient· and for yourself.*

2. *Assess the real implications for the present and anticipated treatment.*

3. *Since there is always a potential for disrupting or seriously complicating both therapies, refer the prospective patient to a colleague.*

INITIAL CONTACTS WITH PATIENTS IN CLINICS

Many clinics leave the arrangements for initial interviews to secretaries or social workers and use social workers to screen patients and collect data, including interviewing other family members. In such instances, it is often overlooked that whoever answers such initial calls should be competent to assess and handle emergencies, detect any urgent problem, and have the means of responding appropriately to it. Such a person will usually make an intake or initial interview appointment for the patient, but the fewer personnel with whom a patient must deal, the better (see Chapter 7).

The guidelines as to whom a therapist accepts as a patient in a clinic should be based on the principles already defined for private practice. This is especially pertinent in terms of the treatment of other staff members. If there is any level of past or present personal contact between a potential patient and a given therapist, the patient should not be seen by that therapist. In fact, it is best for all

such patients to be treated at another clinic or privately by a therapist not associated with the clinic. I have observed several such
treatment situations and they all proved disastrous. The patient has
intense reality and transference fears of betrayal. There is also fear
of the incompetence of a therapist known to be in training, a great
frequency of displaced transference reactions, and many distorted
beliefs regarding the therapist based on contacts with him outside of
treatment or impressions derived from his close colleagues. In short,
the contaminations and obstacles are enormous and usually prove
to be unresolvable.

The Assessment Portion
of the First Session

INITIAL PRINCIPLES OF TECHNIQUE

The first hour presents a unique and crucial situation that has problems and pitfalls distinctive to this session. It, therefore, requires the application of special techniques and principles. Let us turn directly to the opening fragment of a first session to orient ourselves to the tasks it presents for the therapist.

Mrs. A.O. had called Dr. Z. stating that she was extremely depressed and frightened, and worried about killing herself. She sounded agitated and Dr. Z. questioned her in some detail, ascertaining that she was not seriously suicidal. He decided from the conversation that she was rational and able to control herself. She seemed reassured when Dr. Z. offered to make an appointment for the next day. He told her to call back sooner if her upset or suicidal feelings became too overwhelming for her.

At the appointed hour, Dr. Z. met the patient in the waiting room, greeted her with a handshake, and introduced himself. He escorted her into his consultation room and allowed her to find her way to the chair next to his desk. He started the session by asking her to tell him about her problems and she began to cry, saying how depressed and suicidal she felt. She spontaneously went on to describe her unhappy marriage to a cruel, unfeeling man who constantly attacked her, both physically and verbally, and did little to gratify her sexually. She spoke volubly and at length—with many details—about their childless, frustrating, infuriating life together.

Before we deal with the immediate problems of Mrs. A.O.'s suicidal feelings and the possible resistances reflected in her focus on her husband, I want to establish some basic principles of technique for the therapist's first moments with the patient. Within the context of the uniqueness of each initial hour, we can develop the following general guides to the steps taken by the therapist in this first meeting with the patient:

1. *Greet the patient in the waiting room with a handshake, while introducing yourself and identifying the patient by name, unless there are others present in the waiting room.* From the outset, be warm, cordial, and polite. The initial nonverbal impressions that are conveyed to the patient are important factors in the therapeutic alliance, and can evoke trust and comfort or mistrust and anxiety, depending on your demeanor.

2. *Start collecting impressions immediately, but do not over-value or overdefine these initial observations.*

3. *Escort the patient to the consultation room and let him find his way to the chair used for the interview, directing him only if necessary.* In this way, you immediately discover clues to his degree of self-reliance or dependency. This is simultaneously an expression of your preference for not controlling and for allowing the patient his freedoms where possible.

4. *The interview should be conducted face to face (see Chapter 6).*

5. *You need note paper to record the patient's name and address, but do not do this until the end of the hour.* Take as few notes as possible—preferably none—until after the session so you can give the patient your full attention and not direct his flow of associations through his response to what you do and do not write.

Crucial names and dates can be noted or, better still, remembered and recorded later.

Extensive note taking or use of a tape recorder is primarily defensive on the part of the therapist, despite its common usage. Remember that the patient's anxiety in meeting you—a strange, unknown, and possibly dangerous therapist—has its counterpart in your own anxiety at meeting a new patient. Work through such anxieties on your own part so they are minimal and do not interfere; and do not use techniques which will frighten the patient and heighten his mistrust of you. I recommend not taking notes at all during subsequent sessions so you can fully attend the patient and are free to react on all levels. Therapists vary in regard to recording notes after the sessions: there are those who dictate or write a lengthy résumé (which is of questionable value), those who write monthly or yearly notes, and those who keep no notes at all. This is a matter of individual preference with only two basic considerations: first, you must be able to maintain a fresh and full picture of recent sessions, particularly the last one or two; and second, in keeping with your medical and/or professional responsibilities, you should maintain some type of brief record to document the treatment of a patient.

6. *Once the patient is seated, the session can be set in motion.* There is a range of methods, from those who say nothing at all and wait for the patient to speak to those who make elaborate introductory remarks. I prefer a brief question to orient the patient and set the tone. I ask: "What can I help you with?" or "What problems have you been having?" I thereby immediately communicate my medical orientation as a physician vis-à-vis a patient and my role as an expert in helping the patient to alleviate his emotional suffering.* Nonmedical therapists can communicate a similar stance.

7. *Having asked the patient about his problems, the therapist's next job is to listen to the patient.* This is a task that can only be understood in the context of the goals of this first session.

---

* Empirically, this setting is effective and workable. I will subsequently make it clear to the patient that we will be working together on his problems and that this type of help differs from the usual medical model in that each of us have an active, albeit different, responsibility. Initially, however, the patient is seeking help and I am offering it to him; the rest will unfold later.

THE THERAPIST'S GOALS
IN THE FIRST HOUR

There are a number of important goals for the therapist in the first session. Each should be kept in mind, though some will be more successfully achieved than others, depending on the therapist's skills and the ways in which the patient communicates and defends. I consider the following to be the primary goals for the first hour:

Definition of the patient's emotional problems and establishment of a diagnosis.

Ascertainment of the background of these problems.

Determination of how the patient copes and assessment of his assets.

Definition of any acute problems.

Clarification of the major resistances toward treatment.

Assessment of pre-formed attitudes and transference fantasies toward the therapist and therapy.

Assessment of the patient's capacity to work in therapy.

Recommendations to the patient.

Establishment of the therapeutic alliance.

DEFINITION OF THE PATIENT'S EMOTIONAL
PROBLEMS AND ESTABLISHMENT
OF A DIAGNOSIS

Of prime importance in the initial assessment of the patient is a diagnostic evaluation. The therapist listens for the patient's symptoms, character structure (its assets and pathology), level of ego functioning, and current dynamics. It is important to obtain a picture of the nature of the patient's ongoing emotional problems, the stresses which precipitated his present symptoms, the environment in which he is currently functioning, and his intrapsychic conflicts. Since we want to establish a clinical and dynamic diagnosis, the factors that prompted the patient to seek therapy at the present time are especially important.

ASCERTAINMENT OF THE BACKGROUND
OF THESE PROBLEMS

To the extent that time permits, the therapist learns about the patient's current life and its influence on his emotional problems, and determines how much the people and circumstances surrounding him will support or oppose treatment. In addition, the genetic history—the study of the early life of the patient—must be elicited. In this area, one might best focus first on the relationship between the patient and his parents and siblings, including the detectable pathology in the parent–child relationship—a major clue to the patient's pathology, object relationships, and level of adaptation. Secondly, we want to hear about the patient's early adjustment and childhood symptoms, if any. Finally, we search for any major traumas in his childhood and adolescence; these, if significant, often share with the precipitating situation the initial focus of therapy (see Chapter 23).

DETERMINATION OF HOW THE PATIENT
COPES AND ASSESSMENT OF HIS ASSETS

It is necessary to assess how the patient copes with his conflicts and anxieties and how well he is functioning overall. Does he internalize his conflicts or act them out, inflicting pain on others rather than suffering within himself? How adequate are his object relationships and on what level do they operate? What are his major defenses and how successfully are they being used? Is the patient significantly anxious, depressed, inhibited, or uncontrolled? Broadly assess his ego strengths and weaknesses, the intensity of his instinctual drives, and the nature of his superego function—his conscience, values and ideals, regulation of self-esteem, controls, extent of self-punitive attitudes, and guilt.

DEFINITION OF ANY ACUTE PROBLEMS

Do not fail to respond to emergencies and to search out fully any serious or dangerous symptoms by bringing them into sharp focus in this first hour. The major items here are suicidal and/or homicidal risks and the potential for such acute decompensations as psychotic depressions and severe schizophrenic regressions.

With suicidal patients, one must recommend hospitalization if there is any serious doubt that the patient or those about him cannot clearly cooperate with the therapist and insure full control. A firm and reliable therapeutic alliance must be established immediately with the patient (and if necessary, his relatives) for office therapy to make sense. Since suicidal impulses occur in patients with a wide range of diagnoses such as schizophrenia, depressions (psychotic and neurotic), hysteria, and impulse character disorders, it is vital to determine the underlying pathology and to what extent it seems modifiable. While medication always deserves consideration in any acute situation, the therapist should not rely too heavily on drugs and should avoid their use whenever possible (see Chapter 6). A strong therapeutic alliance with the patient, indications that you understand and can help him, and making yourself available if needed are the best tools that you, as a therapist, have for helping such patients.

With suicidal or homicidal schizophrenic patients, you must determine if there is danger to themselves or others, whether they are delusional or have other disorders of thinking, just how paranoid they are, and how severely their reality testing and object relationships are impaired—or the extent to which these and other functions are intact. Assess such issues as: Can the patient work with you in therapy or does it seem difficult to relate to him? Does he show any capacity to reconstitute and recover? How available and workable are his assets? Sparing patients the trauma of hospitalization should be weighed against the risks involved in attempting office therapy.

Acute anxiety and panic may require both medication and support through the therapeutic alliance. Discovery of the immediate precursors of the symptoms and insight into their meanings may be possible even in the first hour, and clarifying these factors will go a long way toward setting a workable therapeutic tone and alleviating the acute symptoms.

Clarification of the Major Resistances
Toward Treatment

It is important to detect early resistances to therapy as quickly as possible, since working with and interpreting such resistances may enable patients who might otherwise leave therapy to remain in treatment. Many therapists allow themselves to be overwhelmed by the patient's early attempts to flee treatment or else simply ignore them. However, if one is alert to manifestations (derivatives) of such flight tendencies, they often provide the opportunity for the therapist's first interventions and/or interpretations. They may even take place in the first session (see Chapter 23).

These initial resistances form serious obstacles to treatment. They may emanate primarily from the patient or from such significant people in his environment as a parent or a spouse. Ultimately, they reflect some resistance within the patient regardless of the external realities to which he ascribes them. Thus, the therapist must explore and analyze such resistances to enable the patient to deal with the interfering third person himself. If the problem is a major one, confrontation of the patient's reluctance to begin treatment and his apparent motives is indicated in the first session. In fact, alertness to indications of major resistances against therapy and interventions regarding them are among the most important goals of the therapist in the beginning hour, since, with some patients, the entire possibility of treatment is at stake.

If relatives, especially those who control the payment of the fees, are in frank opposition to the therapy, some therapists will see them in consultation, with or without the patient present. While a dire emergency such as a suicidal patient may justify this procedure, I have found that it disturbs the therapeutic alliance and atmosphere, has seductive and infantilizing qualities, and seldom proves helpful in a lasting way. Therefore, it is preferable to convey to the patient his responsibility for dealing with his parents or spouse, and to allow him to work it out with them. In the meantime, as they emerge from his associations, the therapist should explore and interpret the patient's own resistances to therapy, his wishes to introduce a third party into the therapeutic relationship, his own use and unconscious promotion of the other person's resistances, his manipulativeness and/or his passivity and dependency, and other meanings and fantasies reflected in this situation. Unless the patient resolves his own resistances and deals unambiguously with the interfering third person, there is little chance that a viable psychotherapy will unfold. Early resistances are a vital and often overlooked problem. Some illustrations will orient us.

> Mr. A.P. was in his early fifties and sought treatment for multiple phobias and inhibitions, particularly a fear of returning to his job. Six months earlier, he had suffered a myocardial infarction. In his first session, his anxiety mounted as he described his physical and emotional illnesses: his fears of death, his fears of leaving the safety of his home, and his anxiety about any stress lest he have another heart attack.

The therapist should quickly sense that this patient is expressing derivatives of an intense dread of therapy and that his main defense is avoidance. In fact, with so much open anxiety, the therapist should be prepared for a very early attempt to flee or avoid treatment. In such a situation, a very early intervention is essential; the indications for it are the acute symptoms and marked resistances. A confrontation is suggested; the patient should be told rather candidly that it appears that he is also frightened of the possible stresses of therapy. Thus, he is shown that the therapist understands him and appreciates the source and extent of his anxiety. Then it should be pointed out that it would be wise for him to keep an eye on this fear so that he can master it and not leave treatment. To this can be added that, by dealing with this fear, eventually he will be able to face his other fears and work them out as well. In this manner the therapist has offered the patient models for motivation, adaptation, delay, and exploration.

> Unfortunately, the therapist in this case missed the importance of this patient's mounting anxiety, and the underlying resistances, and did not comment on it. The patient became more and more panic-stricken and, after about thirty minutes of this initial session, he stood up

and said he did not want treatment and walked out. He did not return when the therapist called after him.

This is a highly dramatic example of an acute resistance and ultimate flight from therapy. The therapist failed to recognize the impending crisis, and the consequence of the missed intervention was the loss of the patient (see Chapter 19). Rationalization that this was a borderline patient can only be an unfortunate and ill-founded defense and denial on the part of the therapist. As such, it prevents the opportunity to learn from a mistake.

> Mr. A.Q. came for a consultation at the behest of his wife and the therapist had detected considerable reluctance regarding therapy in the initial phone conversation. In the first interview, Mr. A.Q. reported that he had been having affairs for the past three years and now wanted to leave his wife and son. He found his wife cold and unresponsive and described her problems in some detail: she was abusive, frigid, a nasty mother, and a poor partner. She suspected his affairs and he spent little time at home with her and his son. There had been several previous separations, but none of his other relationships with women ever worked out. He would become severely depressed and return to his wife. His son was doing poorly in school and this bothered the patient. He felt justified in leaving, but he described the gnawing sense of guilt and doubt that had led him to the therapist, whom he hoped would understand his dilemma and offer some advice. The problem seemed to be his wife's, and he was only reacting. Was there a way he could leave in peace?
>
> The therapist diagnosed Mr. A.Q. as an immature, impulsive character disorder with considerable acting out tendencies. He had anticipated from the call strong resistances against therapy, brought about by the patient's impaired capacities to delay and to think through. This was confirmed by the unfolding of the session. Mr. A.Q.'s life-style was so embedded in acting out and manipulating—the affairs and separations—and defensive denial

and projection of his own conflicts, problems, and disturbing affects of guilt and depression that the therapist felt a prompt confrontation was indicated. It was further felt that the patient had come to the therapist as part of a manipulation by which he was seeking a misalliance wherein the therapist would reinforce his acting out and pathological defenses, rather than assist him in resolving his inner conflicts and their influence on his life situation and behavior. If there was to be any psychotherapy at all, confrontations with these impressions was essential; perhaps then the patient could mobilize other, more constructive, viable motives for treatment. If all his acting out was ignored, he would eventually be disappointed and enraged, and leave.

Thus, when the session was about two-thirds over, the therapist verbalized his impressions of the patient and made his recommendations. He pointed out that Mr. A.Q.'s life was one of doing and running. He noted that this way of living had not produced contentment for him, thereby addressing himself to the adaptive aspect of his symptoms and pointing out the cost to the patient for the maladaption he had made (see Chapters 13 and 16). Mr. A.Q. could continue to run and hide, the therapist went on, or he could hold still for once and use therapy to find out about himself and effect some changes from within. Once this was accomplished, Mr. A.Q. could then decide on a life course which might prove genuinely gratifying. In addition, the therapist pointed out the specific manipulation being made of therapy—the attempt to use it to deny his guilt and destructiveness, and to bypass his conscience. It had to be realized at the outset that this could not be considered treatment. However, if Mr. A.Q. really wanted help with his problems, the therapist could offer that to him. In fact, he strongly recommended therapy.

The extent of these comments were considered necessary in this situation. These and similar later confrontations, along with the interpretation of their genetic and dynamic aspects, enabled Mr. A.Q. to both remain in treatment and learn a great deal about himself and his intrapsychic problems; and he changed considerably.

We can see that the concept of resistance is not an ivory-towered, hypothetical construct, but a reference to real threats to therapy, quite alive and dangerous in its manifestations. I will briefly list some of the major resistance that must often be dealt with in the first hour if the patient is to return, and describe how one might deal with them in principle (see also Chapter 23):

Blaming Others

Establish, for the patient, the means by which he provokes others. Demonstrate to the patient his own problems in such situations.

Mistrusting and Having Paranoid Feelings

Initially, show the patient how he suffers with such feelings. Make yourself an honest ally. Later, you can delineate to the patient how he provokes attack.

Acting Out

Indicate the cost of such behavior to the patient and others. Gently stir up realistic guilt which helps motivate the patient toward insight therapy. Be a model of incorruptibility, delay, and thoughtful consideration. Present therapy as an opportunity to change from within.

Using a Spouse or Parent Who Opposes Treatment

Show the patient how he is using the other person to express his own doubts, and how he shares in or promotes the opposition. Have the patient recognize his responsibility to deal with the situation.

Denying Emotional and Intrapsychic Problems

Listen carefully and delineate those inner problems which the patient indirectly reveals; they are always there. Detect his role in creating the situations which brought him to therapy. Tactfully confront the patient with these observations and his need for inner change if they are to be modified. Patients who use this form of resistance focus on real, external-life problems, to which their intrapsychic conflicts are not a major contributor. Detect less rational problems and expressions of inner conflicts and demonstrate them to the patient.

Having Financial or Time Problems

Work out a realistic fee and hour or arrange an appropriate referral. Do not deny the existence of these problems, but seek out the underlying resistances which the realities serve and explore them.

Fearing Treatment and the Therapist

Confront the patient with the expressions of these anxieties and attempt to explore their basis. Unfortunate experiences with a previous therapist, emotional problems in other family members and the treatment they have received, fears of going crazy or of being hospitalized, and a wide range of fears of inner fantasy life and of the therapist may be involved. Seek these out, explore them, and begin to resolve them.

Other indications of strong, often latent resistances—however effectively they are rationalized through reality factors— include lateness to the first session, many silences, and difficulties in arranging hours or a suitable fee. In principle, maintain an alertness for manifestations of resistances in the initial session and be prepared to investigate them, lest the patient avoid direct mention and exploration of them, then elaborate upon them in his inner fantasies, and leave therapy prematurely.

Basically, then, there are two potentially urgent problems in the first session which dictate active interventions by the therapist: acute symptomatic crises and major resistances against therapy. While most of the initial session is devoted to learning about the patient and establishing the framework for the therapy, these two jobs cannot be overlooked or the patient may never return. The following two vignettes illustrate some of these issues:

> Mrs. A.R. was a young, separated woman, who came to the therapist because she was seriously depressed. She arrived twenty minutes late for her first session, blaming it on her babysitter's tardiness. She began by describing in detail how her husband was jobless, inadequate, and attacking. The therapist eventually intervened, pointing

out that she was not describing her own problems. The patient responded that she was very depressed and not taking care of her children. She had attempted suicide two months before, after finding her husband with another woman. She described this incident fully, emphasizing her sense of despair and her fear of leaving her children to their father. The therapist then asked about her early relationship with her husband, and Mrs. A.R. described their courtship and marriage. She spoke especially of a time when her son had had a convulsion and her husband panicked and was totally unable to handle the emergency.

A patient's lateness to the initial hour, except for extraordinary reality obstacles (in this case, it is not clear how much, if at all, the patient contributed to her lateness), is a serious sign of resistances to treatment. It should immediately alert the therapist to search for them.

In this vignette, the patient initially avoided her own emotional problems and focused on reality concerns to which it might seem that her intrapsychic conflicts did not significantly contribute. The therapist correctly confronted her with this avoidance and the patient confirmed the value of this intervention by revealing her suicide attempt. As this material unfolded, the therapist then shifted the patient away from this topic onto less crucial facts about her early marriage.

In supervision, the therapist's defensively-motivated deflection of focus was discussed with him, and he actually recognized it before it was pointed out. While he had correctly dealt with the patient's early resistances, he had ignored and taken her away from her acute symptoms of serious depression and a serious suicide attempt. This is a technical error; the patient's suicidal episode and her current depression and suicidal potential should have been explored as fully as possible in this first hour. There was confirmation of this failure to respond to the acute crisis from the patient's material in her criticism of her husband's failure to deal with an immediate crisis (see Chapters 19 and 22).

Another vignette is relevant here:

Mrs. A.S. was referred by her internist to a psychiatrist, after a detailed medical examination failed to turn up a basis for a series of vague physical complaints. In her initial session, she was very guarded and spoke primarily of her physical symptoms. As she began to fall silent for long periods, the therapist asked a number of questions about her life circumstances when the symptoms began, her present life situation, and her past history. In response, she dated her problems to a sudden stroke suffered by her father, and spoke of her own excessive dependency on others and her overriding concern with neatness and details; she eventually recalled that, when she was ten, her father had made a suicide attempt, was hospitalized, and received shock treatments. The therapist suggested that her guardedness with him must be related to that experience and the many anxieties and fears it generated in her. The patient agreed and added that she was very frightened that she, too, was crazy. She said that she felt relieved in mentioning this fear to the therapist and subsequently agreed to enter therapy.

This patient's recalcitrance was handled by active questioning which proved valuable, in that it enabled her to reveal the main source of her resistances to treatment. At the same time some data regarding the underlying factors in her symptoms, namely their relationship to her conflicts and fantasies toward her father, were brought to the surface. The therapist made a general interpretation of the source of her anxieties, and it was confirmed by the patient, thus clearing the way for Mrs. A.S. to enter treatment.

This patient had intense anxieties and disturbing fantasies in anticipation of her first session with the therapist. Therefore, let us now consider dealing with this aspect as a separate goal for the therapist in the first session.

ASSESSMENT OF PERFORMED ATTITUDES AND TRANSFERENCE FANTASIES TOWARD THE THERAPIST AND THERAPY

All patients come to their initial hour with conscious and unconscious fantasies, expectations, and feelings which we term "pre-formed transferences." There are two main sources for these fantasies: the telephone conversation with the therapist; and the patient's direct and indirect previous experiences with the caring figures in his life, especially his mother, and with all types of medical and other assisting figures, including therapists.

Before the initial telephone call, the second of these factors is maximal, although it is already influenced by what the patient has been told about the therapist by the referring source. Added to this is the fact that some statement the therapist makes or does not make, something in his tone, or his stance on the phone can prompt fantasies and reactions in the patient. If the therapist can only see the patient in consultation—a reality frustration not evoked by a technical error on his part—or if he is gruff and impatient—a reality hurt evoked by a technical error, the patient's fantasies will be mobilized along negative lines in keeping with these realities. Such fantasies will have genetic precursors but can only be correctly understood in light of the precipitating factor (see Chapters 20 and 22).

If the therapist has been considerate and nontraumatizing on the phone, the patient's preformed negative transference fantasies are mobilized almost entirely by the anticipation of seeing any therapist. Warmth can evoke positive feelings and fantasies based on genetic links to good mothering figures, and this will facilitate the develop-ment of a strong therapeutic alliance. On the other hand, this may be overshadowed by mistrustful and anxiety-provoking feelings and fantasies which contribute to crucial resistances and misalliances. These latter are most often based on poor mothering experiences and on specific traumatic incidents with physicians. In regard to the latter, the death of a family member when the patient was a child and experiences with previous therapists are notable. If the patient has had previous psychotherapy or analysis, it is important to ask about it and to detect any negative effects it is having on the present consultation. Learning why the patient left his previous treatment and/or why he did not return to his former therapist at the present time is especially helpful. Important, potentially disruptive, negative transference fantasies that can be detected from the material of the session are worth mentioning to the patient. Such confrontations both help him recognize the source of his resistances and demonstrate your understanding of him; often this latter is in contrast to his previous experience (see Chapter 20).

ASSESSMENT OF THE PATIENT'S CAPACITY TO WORK IN THERAPY

The assessment of the patient's capacity to work in therapy is one that the therapist makes as he listens to what the patient says and does not say throughout the session. These are capacities that can be worked on and developed during treatment. The therapist tunes in on many dimensions: the patient's ability to communicate; to trust; to imagine, fantasize, and dream; to cooperate; to accept interventions; and to introspect. On the other hand, he must observe how guarded and secretive the patient seems or make note if the patient is too open and the material too blatant, reflecting poor defenses and controls. These factors indicate the ease or difficulty with which treatment will unfold. Our initial impressions regarding the patient's capacities to communicate, express himself, regress in a controlled manner, and form a therapeutic alliance are important at this point.

In this context, the therapist hopes to collect impressions regarding the patient's past and present life situations, but should feel no special pressure to do this in an overly thorough manner. Instead, he should observe how the patient tells about himself and what he reveals and avoids. The therapist should elicit enough information to enable him to make a tentative diagnosis and specific recommendations. If this is not feasible, he should see the patient in a second consultation session.

As the patient's story unfolds, an alertness should be maintained for indications of acute emotional crises, regressions, and serious and major resistances to therapy. They should not be sought out with questions unless there are clues from the patient. However, when derivatives of these kind appear, they should be investigated thoroughly. The principle of analyzing resistances first applies to the initial hour and then to every session in therapy.

RECOMMENDATIONS TO THE PATIENT

Once the therapist has collected impressions, made initial formulations to himself, and possibly commented on some crucial resistances, he must make his all-important recommendations to the patient. In principle, this should include the following basic considerations:

1. *The therapist should begin with a brief formulation to the patient, in the latter's own idiom, regarding the essentials of his difficulties.* This should be done as succinctly and as simply as possible, and entirely without technical terms.

2. *Next, the therapist should indicate the type of treatment he feels will best help the patient with his problems.* The kind of psychoanalytic psychotherapy being developed in this book, which addresses itself equally to unconscious fantasies and dynamics and to ego functioning and reality, is applicable to virtually all ambulatory syndromes. The limitations of this therapy fall into two broad areas: first, it cannot be used with those syndromes requiring hospitalization and somatic therapies, such as the psychoses; or, second, with those syndromes for which psychoanalysis is indicated. This latter includes those patients with relatively strong egos, internalized symptoms, and the capacity to tolerate intensive analysis; financial factors and the patient's motivations may also play a role. The therapist should review the literature on the criteria for analyzability and develop his own concepts in this regard (see Waldhorn, 1960; and Greenson, 1967). If he does not do analysis himself, he should learn when to refer patients for it, if it is available.

3. *If psychotherapy is recommended, the therapist should state clearly that he feels he can be of help to the patient.* He should then suggest the number of sessions per week that he feels is optimal. This generally should be at least two weekly hours, or three sessions per week if the therapist feels that more extensive inner change is possible or is confronted with serious acting out potential. Financial factors are often relevant in this determination (see Chapter 5).

4. *The therapist should let the patient know that treatment is a long-term process which requires months and probably years.* He should not pretend to know the duration more precisely than that.

5. *Where such obvious obstacles to treatment exist as major*

tendencies to act out or major opposition within patient or others, the therapist should address himself to them and anticipate them for the patient. This may help forestall a precipitous termination. In acting-out patients, such a discussion is aimed at creating a split in the ego so that the patient begins from the outset to observe his behavior and, later, his fantasies. This may help prevent his living them out blindly.

6. *Once this is done, the therapist should ask the patient if he has any questions and try to answer them as honestly, directly, and briefly as possible.* This includes questions regarding training, which should be answered directly here but analyzed in regard to timing and meaning later on, and a frank appraisal of the patient's prognosis.

7. *The therapist must deal with complicating factors such as medication, other therapists that the patient may be seeing, and other physicians who are treating the patient.* I prefer to deal with such problems after I have established the ground rules of therapy (see Chapters 5–7).

Once these recommendations have been presented in whatever order or degree of completeness that is appropriate for the particular patient, we may expect him to accept therapy. In those instances where the patient asks for time to consider your recommendations, recognize this as a likely resistance, and attempt to explore the basis for it, interpreting it on some level if you have sufficient material. In addition, arrange a definite second appointment for further discussion; in this way the patient is more likely to continue with you.

ESTABLISHMENT OF THE THERAPEUTIC ALLIANCE

I have left this goal for last because, in many ways, it is an aspect of every one of the other goals of the initial hour. Everything that the therapist does in this first session conveys his concern, competence, and interest in helping the patient. In this way, he offers the patient a therapeutic alliance, a partnership designed to resolve his emotional problems. Directly and indirectly, consciously and unconsciously, the therapist communicates this offer to the patient and even indicates, to some extent, what his role in this alliance will be—and that of the patient as well.

On the patient's part, his wish for help, with its conscious and unconscious meanings, forms the basis of his contribution to this alliance. His realistic expectations from the therapist and his concepts of his role in therapy are also pertinent. However, not all therapeutic relationships are alliances in the positive and constructive sense usually implied in the term "therapeutic alliance" (Zetzel, 1956) and "working alliance" (Greenson, 1967). In this book, I will refer to alliances that are not based on mature and realistic wishes for symptom relief through inner change and do not foster the patient's resolutions of intrapsychic conflicts as "antitherapeutic alliances" or "therapeutic misalliances." Such misalliances arise out of the patient's neurotic needs to continue to suffer, to manipulate others rather than change himself, and to maintain his symptoms, and/or out of the therapist's neurotic needs toward the patient— his countertransference problems. Usually both factors are involved. Seldom is a therapist drawn into a misalliance by a patient simply out of ignorance; and, likewise, seldom is the patient an innocent victim of the therapist without complementary needs of his own. The therapist, however, has a greater and more fundamental responsibility to create a proper therapeutic alliance and to analyze any of the patient's efforts in other directions.

In the initial hour, major resistances from the patient pose the most serious threats for the development of a sound therapeutic alliance. Patients who are unable to trust and who are filled with fear are unlikely to ally themselves with anyone. Fantasies regarding unrealistic and neurotic expectations from the therapist also interfere and lead to narcissistic and magical misalliances if the therapist joins in with the patient. The search for such neurotic gratifications as a person to vent rage at, to seduce, or be punished by can also lead to antitherapeutic alliances if the therapist is unwary and participates.

In the first hour, the therapist is alerted to the patient's wishes for such misalliances if they are present. If they pose major threats to the treatment, they must be dealt with in the context of the patient's material. Beyond that, the exploration of these problems is a major focus in the opening phase of therapy (see Chapter 23).

Therefore, the therapist must gently confront the patient with his unrealistic wishes regarding therapy and his fears of the therapist and treatment. He also must be certain that he does not consciously or unconsciously participate in, or offer to the patient, an antitherapeutic alliance. He establishes clear ground rules and defines the relationship verbally and nonverbally so that a proper therapeutic atmosphere prevails and everything is directed toward the exploration and resolution of the patient's neurosis. Failures in this regard will appeal to the patient's neurotic needs and will almost always lead to antitherapeutic alliances which ultimately result in therapeutic failure (see Chapters 19 and 22).

TRIAL INTERPRETATIONS

There are many therapists who make it a practice to offer so-called "trial interpretations" (tentative interpretations from the material) to patients in the initial interview. They do so, they state, in order to assess both the patient's ability to work psychologically and his depth of understanding. Such interpretations range from those related to the motives behind symptoms and conflicts to elaboration of possible unconscious fantasies and genetic interpretations. I object in principle to such interventions and to any concept which suggests that the patient is on trial and being tested. These interpretations are almost always premature and evoke all of the negative consequences of such ill timing (see Chapter 19). It is naïve to think that they are without potential detrimental consequences. Only interventions related to resistances and acute regressions are indicated in the initial hour. Two brief, but rather typical, vignettes will illustrate these points.

> Mrs. A.T. was seen in consultation on referral from a neurologist for a mild, right-sided, flaccid hemiparesis that was diagnosed as hysterical. She did not feel that she had any significant emotional problems but nothing else had helped her, so she had agreed to a psychiatric consultation. In addition to other material, her history included the fact that her mother had had a right-sided stroke when the patient was ten. The patient emphasized how her parents had never been happy together, but her mother's illness had enslaved her father. The patient also

described some marital conflicts between herself and her husband.

The therapist, feeling this patient was not particularly psychologically minded and hoping to generate her interest in treatment, decided to make a trial interpretation. He pointed out to the patient that her mother seemed to have "resolved" her marital conflicts through her illness, and that the patient seemed to be doing the same thing with her own husband. Mrs. A.T. responded that she had no wish to enslave her husband or make him suffer as her mother had done with her father. She went on to mention her dislike of her husband's frequent speaking out of turn. The therapist incorrectly concluded that there was little hope for insight therapy.

Later in Mrs. A.T.'s treatment, after a period of supervision and change in the style in which her therapist worked, it became clear that the interpretation, while somewhat correct in its content, was ill-timed and had been offered at a moment when the patient was not prepared for it. Furthermore, it did not touch upon the central fantasies involved in the symptom, which related much more to the death of a brother and to rage at her mother. On the other hand, it did touch directly upon an extremely sensitive area of conflict for this patient; the therapist was unaware at the time that the patient was very anxious over being helplessly dependent upon her husband. Later in her treatment, Mrs. A.T. mentioned that she had felt that the therapist's intervention that first hour had seemed arbitrary to her.

In discussing this vignette, I want to emphasize these points:

1. *Trial interpretations in the first session are actually not a means of a assessing treatability or psychological-mindedness.*

2. *Interpretations of unconscious fantasies and conflicts are open to inevitable error and often generate antagonism in the initial hour.* There cannot possibly be sufficient data on which to base them nor sufficient knowledge of what the interpretation touches on or will set off in the patient. They may be entirely incorrect and even

anxiety-provoking. As a result, they often serve as detriments to establishing an effective therapeutic alliance. They may seem wild, unfounded, and arbitrary to the patient, and—correctly so—they may frighten him away. They cannot be integrated by the patient into some total picture and worked through and, therefore, have no therapeutic value.

The case of Mrs. A.T. demonstrates the lack of value of these interventions. The patient's unconscious awareness of the therapist's inappropriate comment is seen in her reference to her husband speaking out of turn. Her failure to accept these essentially erroneous comments did not reflect any prognostic dimension, unless it indicated her positive capacity to critically evaluate the interventions offered to her by the therapist.

3. *The risks in interpretations of this kind far outweigh their value.* In situations of acute anxiety and with sufficient pertinent material, the therapist may offer an interpretation which has reassuring aspects to it, but such moments are very rare.

On the other hand, brief confrontations or interpretations of major resistances to treatment which appear in the first session are indicated and can be helpful, as the following case demonstrates.

> Mr. A.V., a man in his early twenties, had told his therapist on the telephone that he was living with his parents and calling for an appointment only at their insistence. In the initial session, he described difficulties in holding a job, extensive drug usage, and many affairs with women. A previous therapist had encouraged him to live freely. His parents, while voicing objections, lent him their car, ignored indications of his drug usage, and supported him "royally" when he was out of work.
>
> The therapist endeavored to accomplish two major tasks in this first hour, both related to his goals of making a proper assessment and establishing a therapeutic alliance. First, he indicated to the patient that he appeared to have some fairly serious emotional problems that, with the support of both his parents and his previous therapist, he had been denying. This was a confrontation with a crucial defense-resistance shared by the patient

and others close to him. It had to be clarified, even in the
first session, if therapy was to unfold. Second, he pointed
out that the patient tended to act and live out, rather than
to think and reflect, and that this was not working out too
well for him. The patient acknowledged his awareness of
this and confirmed it by adding that he was often anxious
and had some vague fears of homosexuality. The therapist then went on to describe how things could be worked
out differently through the kind of treatment he was
offering, one in which talking and exploring would take
precedence over acting. In light of the patient's parent-
supported style of living-things-out and not-sticking-with-
things, the therapist went on, such treatment would
undoubtedly be difficult for him to adhere to. Therefore,
he should anticipate wanting to leave and be prepared to
explore it thoroughly before doing so. This intervention
served as an anticipation of the defense-resistance of
acting out in the form of abruptly terminating treatment.
It was an effort to prepare the patient for such a moment,
to encourage the splitting of his ego (self) so that observations of his own behavior would begin to take place and,
eventually, controls over such behavior developed. It also
made clear that an alliance through mutual acting out
would not be the *modus vivendi* of this therapy, as it had
been with the previous therapist.

Thus, the interventions made to this patient related
to major defenses and behavior which endangered the
continuation of therapy. It was even possible in this case
to make an immediate general genetic link to the patient's
parents. Subsequent material further confirmed these
interventions and their validity.

In advising such an approach, I must add a word of caution.
Acting out is so much a part of the life-style of such patients that
the therapist must adopt both a firm interpretive stance against such
behavior and yet tolerate some degree of it initially. Strategically,
one deals with the most dangerous and treatment-disrupting acting
out first and other manifestations later. Hopefully, these will ulti-

mately be given up by the patient himself. There is a delicate balance here in which firmness is combined with patience and tolerance. It is a balance which must be maintained, since either extreme will be detected by these very sensitive patients and exploited.

One last point regarding trial interpretations should be made here. The astute clinician should have more than enough clues in ascertaining the patient's degree of psychological-mindedness, potential workability for insight therapy, and resistances in his observations of the patient's spontaneous comments in the first hour. This can be accomplished by noting, among other trends, the extent of the patient's frankness, his spontaneity, his grasp of his own problems and their sources, and the degree of cohesiveness of the present and historical picture offered. On the negative side, the therapist should assess the extent to which the patient is inclined to act out, deny, conceal, somatize, rationalize, intellectualize, and present himself in a disorganized manner. In time, one can establish a reliable initial impression in this regard without resorting to a risky and questionable interpretation which may frighten the patient and make therapy seem arbitrary.

THE LEVEL OF THE THERAPIST'S ACTIVITY

I want to conclude this discussion of the goals of the initial hour with some comments regarding the level of activity on the part of the therapist as he strives to achieve them. Each first session is a truly unique experience and a singular patient–therapist interaction. There are, however, a few basic principles which can serve as guides to the role of the therapist in this hour.

1. *Let the patient determine the unfolding of the material and the extent of your activity; be flexible.* With a verbose patient, say little, but enough to get the essential data you need for a proper assessment and set of recommendations. With a halting, relatively reserved patient, do not hesitate to guide the interview if necessary.

2. *Be active enough to obtain sufficient data.* Do not, however, attempt to cover every possible facet. Be silent if the patient is con-

cise. On the other hand, interrupt a diffuse, uninformative patient
and ask specific questions.

3. *Keep in mind the tone that you are setting: professional,
honest, helpful, thoughtful, and free—yet patient.* Show concern,
but do not become solicitous or overly involved.

4. *Do not press the patient or challenge his defenses.* Do not
overly investigate an area to which the patient is especially sensitive, such as sexual difficulties, a traumatic life event, or a source of
guilt. Such pursuits may evoke anxiety and flight.

Generally, the therapist's goal is to facilitate his understanding
of the patient and to create a sound therapeutic alliance. Consider
this as you elect to intervene or remain silent. Keep your activity to
the minimum that is necessary; the more that you know about the
patient, the more appropriate, valuable, and less disruptive will your
interventions, including your questions, be. Until matters are clear,
judicious silence proves wisest. Balanced against this is the need to
work with important resistances from the outset and to create a
genuinely warm and concerned image as a therapist. The first
session is always a delicately balanced interaction and experience;
sensitivity to the patient's needs is among the therapist's most
valuable assets in assuring a satisfactory conclusion to this hour.

5 The Ground Rules of Psychotherapy: Fees and Responsibility for the Sessions

Once the patient has agreed—upon the therapist's recommendation—to enter therapy, it is essential to succinctly present the main ground rules of treatment to him. These guidelines, some stated and some implied, are an essential part of the framework of therapy and form the working agreement between the therapist and the patient. In the closing minutes of the first hour, these ground rules should be presented to the patient simply and directly, providing a description of how the therapy will be conducted. They are then clarified and explicated in this and subsequent sessions only when they become an issue or problem. The patient's conception of, and response to, the ground rules sometimes becomes the vehicle for important resistances, transference fantasies and reactions, and realistic responses to the therapist (see Chapters 20 and 22). Therefore, as a matter of course, the therapist must always be silently on the alert for such reactions and prepared to analyze them should they arise. Failure to do so at a crucial moment will seriously undermine an entire therapy; disturbances in this area generally take precedence when they occur. Furthermore, since patients are highly sensitive to these ground rules, handling them requires considerable skill and self-confidence on the part of the therapist.

The following are the major areas which should be dealt with in establishing this understanding. One approaches their presentation flexibly, covering such essentials as the hours and the fee, and alluding to other aspects only as indicated. They are:

The frequency of the sessions.

The setting of the fee.

The responsibility for the sessions on the part of both the patient and the therapist.

The making of major decisions during therapy.

The fundamental rule of free association.

Other implicit and explicit fundamentals for the establishment of a suitable therapeutic milieu and alliance.

Let us now consider each of these in detail.

THE FREQUENCY OF THE SESSIONS

There are specific indications for the different number of therapy sessions per week. Once-weekly psychoanalytic psychotherapy is a very limited modality. It is indicated with patients for whom there is minimal expectation of inner change, and who primarily need support or medication. This includes those who are rigid or non-psychologically minded and certain depressed, borderline, or schizophrenic patients for whom restricted goals are set. It is also used when there is a financial problem which limits the frequency of sessions. It can nonetheless be the vehicle for the achievement of slow ego-building and the development of gradual circumscribed insights into critical major conflicts. In situations where there are extremely strong environmental or inner resistances to treatment, one may begin with once-weekly sessions in the hope of shifting to a more frequent arrangement once some of the patient's resistances are worked through. The attempt should be made to increase the number of weekly sessions as soon as possible, using leads developed from the patient's material and not by threatening or cajoling the patient. Often, references to the need for more help or allusions to the long period between sessions will enable the therapist to introduce this subject at a time when the patient is receptive.

Twice-weekly treatment is a suitable vehicle for insight and ego-enhancement in virtually any ambulatory, workable patient. In those with marked acting out or regressive tendencies such as psychotic breaks, panic episodes, and other decompensations, it is advisable to consider three sessions per week. On the other hand, patients with strong egos—good capacities for delay, insight, relating, fantasizing, etc.—should also be considered for three-times-weekly therapy or psychoanalysis if it is feasible and available.

THE SETTING OF FEES

Clinical experience as a therapist and supervisor has made it clear to me that this is usually one of the most sensitive aspects of the ground rules, and thus filled with many pitfalls. The real, transference, and countertransference implications—conscious and unconscious—for both the patient and therapist are virtually limitless. I will, therefore, discuss many aspects of this matter as it pertains to both private practice and clinics.

FEES IN PRIVATE PRACTICE: ESSENTIAL TENETS

Let us begin with a few basic principles:

1. *Once you have established the need for treatment and the patient has indicated an interest in following your recommendations, tell the patient your fee per session and indicate that the time will be put aside exclusively for him and you expect him to be responsible for his hours.* Having stated this as simply as possible, continue on to the other ground rules. Do not offer an explanation regarding possible exceptions to this responsibility nor any clarification as to why this is the way in which you work unless the patient questions it. Then answer only his specific queries and leave other possible problem areas to be handled when they actually arise.

2. *Your fee should reflect your training, years of experience, and competency.* It must be fair to both yourself and the patient, so as to not form a basis for dispute, conflict, and disruptive fantasies. The fee should also be in keeping with the standards of the community of fellow therapists in which you are practicing.

3. *A single, ongoing fee should be stated directly, and the patient should be allowed time to react.* If the patient has already

indicated concern in this area, you should refer to this and consider it fully in your discussion.

4. *If the patient feels he cannot afford the stated fee, you should have a lower one ready to offer him.* Indicate that such a fee is acceptable to you and open to exploration, both in regard to the realities of the patient's finances and the multiplicity of intrapsychic conflicts and fantasies such a reduced fee evokes. If you prefer not to have a range of fees, you must explain this to the patient and offer to refer him to someone who will accept a lower fee.

5. *Finally, indicate that you will bill the patient at the end of each month for the sessions of the month.* I do not state how soon I expect to be paid after receipt of the bill; I leave this question open and explore it only if delinquency becomes a problem. I prefer handing the bill directly to the patient so that this aspect of our relationship is not isolated from the rest of treatment.

These matters seem simple enough, and sometimes need virtually no subsequent elaboration, clarification, or analysis. Very often, however, complications follow, and these must be both analyzed for meanings and intrapsychic implications, and resolved in reality. The most common foci of issues related to the fee are the request for a reduced fee, delayed payment of fees, increasing fees, insurance policies, the offer of special arrangements regarding fees, missed sessions and vacations, and gifts. Each merits a separate discussion.

THE REQUEST FOR A REDUCED FEE

Mr. A.U. was seen in consultation. He was involved in an affair and was seeking therapy because his life had been disrupted by this involvement. In the initial session he agreed to treatment, but felt that the thirty-five-dollar fee asked by the therapist for each of the two sessions per week was beyond his means. He was an engineer with a limited income and had a wife and three children to support. He said that he might be able to manage sixty dollars per week for a while, and asked the therapist if he would accept such an arrangement.

The therapist agreed to the reduced fee as it was within his range. He then added that the patient should also understand that the matter would remain open to further exploration, both realistically and in terms of whatever meanings it had for him. In addition, he cautioned the patient to carefully consider the long-term cost of a therapy which might extend over a number of years and to be certain that he could realistically afford such extended treatment, even with the lower fee.

In subsequent sessions, it became clear that the reduced fee was a realistic necessity for Mr. A.U. However, some months later, dreams prompted by the therapist's vacation portrayed the therapist as a provider of boundless supplies of food, and associations revealed that the patient unconsciously viewed the reduced fee as a gift from a mother-figure who would gratify his every need. This meaning of the lowered fee was interpreted to him and was confirmed by the patient's recollection of other memories regarding his mother's over-indulgence and overtly seductive attitudes toward him.

This leads us to our first set of supplementary principles regarding fees:

1. *Be as certain as possible from the outset that the fee agreed upon is a realistic one for the patient.* It must also be one he can handle on a long-term basis.

2. *Deal with requests for a reduced fee directly in the initial hour.* Always leave room for further exploration on all levels.

3. *Be alert for any indications (particularly in dreams and acting out behavior) of concealed assets or income.* While such manipulating is rare, it does occur and must be analyzed and resolved if treatment is not to be totally depreciated and undermined. Do not, however, be accusatory or chronically suspicious of your patients.

4. *The granting of a reduced fee must subsequently be dealt with on two levels.* Of first consideration is the basis for it in reality. Then the meanings for the patient in his fantasies and its relationship to his intrapsychic conflicts must be constantly considered.

This latter aspect should be analyzed when the material from the patient permits or necessitates it. These fantasies must be explored and resolved when they contribute to resistances, disturbances in the therapeutic alliance, and other fantasies related to the patient's unresolved pathology. Such an arrangement may foster pronounced passivity in the patient or undue dependency on the therapist, particularly if such propensities exist in the patient beforehand. Reduction of the fee may be seen as seductive and can promote excessive denial of angry feelings toward the therapist by the patient. This reality also evokes conscious and unconscious fantasies of being a privileged and special patient. However, if the arrangement is a realistic one, the derivatives of its meanings for the patient should not interfere with the treatment. The therapist's responsibility is to keep this arrangement in mind as a context for listening to the patient's associations, and to interpret its implications when indicated.

> With Mr. A.U., this material lay dormant until his therapist went on vacation some four months after his treatment began. At this time, as I indicated, he dreamt directly of the therapist who was giving him a huge supply of food. Associations indicated that the patient was attempting to deny his separation anxieties and sense of loss, linked genetically to a hospitalization of his mother when he was a young child. He had used the fact that the therapist had reduced the fee as a reality on which to build fantasies of the therapist as an omnipotent, ever-giving, and ever-present mother. Interpretation of these fantasies, particularly their defensive and genetic aspects, led to a reduction in the defensive use of denial with which the patient was responding to the vacation. This, in turn, was followed by a working through of aspects of his separation anxiety.

PATIENTS WITH INSURANCE

Currently, in some areas of the United States, many patients have insurance policies which cover payment of some percentage of the cost of treatment. Many problems that may be critical to the outcome of therapy arise in this regard. I will consider those that are most common and attempt to develop principles with which these and other variations can be handled (see Halpert, 1972a and b). We can begin with a clinical experience which relates to this issue; it will also permit further study of reductions in fees and introduce the subject of increasing fees.

> Mr. L.N. was a young man with a severe character disorder and perversions who had been in treatment for seven months when the themes of concealing and having secrets appeared indirectly in the material he was discussing. Inquiries by the therapist revealed the fact that Mr. L.N.'s treatment was covered in part by an insurance policy, and that he had recently received the first check from them. In this instance, no report from the therapist was required (in itself, a remarkable, but not uncommon, fact) and Mr. L.N. had avoided mentioning it. His conscious reason was that initially he had planned not to use the policy for fear that he would be fired from his job if it was discovered that he was in psychotherapy. As this matter was explored, it became clear that an important unconscious factor in his decision was based on the fact that the therapist had agreed to treat Mr. L.N. at a reduced fee because of his limited income. The patient wanted desperately to have some reality basis for maintaining the fantasy that the therapist would be a giving, protecting mother–father figure for him. Indulgences of this kind had been prominent in his parents' handling of him as a child, and had contributed significantly to his psychopathology.
>
> Exploration indicated that the patient's behavior in regard to the insurance reflected his poor impulse control, his propensity to act out, the corruption of his superego, and his insistence on unlimited gratifications from others and pathogenic idealizations of them.

The therapist has two responsibilities here. The first is to reassess the patient's financial capabilities in light of the insurance available to him. The second is to explore the dynamics and meanings of what the patient has done and to work through the implications.

Through these two measures, the proper climate of treatment and a mature therapeutic alliance can be established and important fantasies and pathology modified. Both jobs are essential. The therapist has to decide whether the fee should be increased, and whether such an increment should be retroactive or simply commence as of the session in which the patient revealed his coverage.

Since this particular patient was in his seventh month of treatment at the time, this was a particularly difficult problem. Asking him to pay an additional sum for approximately fifty sessions would create considerable financial hardship and probably generate unresolvable rage. On the other hand, failure to respond to the patient's deception would leave him with the feeling that he had duped the therapist and corrupted the entire treatment. In addition, the situation, with its attendant guilt-punishment themes, was fraught with feelings of humiliation and narcissistic mortification for the patient; it called for the utmost sensitivity and tact on the part of the therapist.

In keeping with this, the therapist followed an extremely useful principle applicable to such situations. He presented the problem to the patient and asked him to share the responsibility for deciding the manner in which the dilemma should be resolved, all the while recognizing his own ultimate responsibility in the matter. He then listened to the patient's response for manifest and latent clues that could be used in deciding how to deal with the issue and interpreting its meanings for the patient.

After considerable exploration, it was decided that the patient could afford the therapist's regular fee which was to be charged, as they had agreed when they first began to study the problem, as of the session in which the insurance was first revealed. Associations then indicated that, for a time, the patient considered the lower fee for the first seven months to be a gift from—and a successful deception of—the therapist. However, reality exploration revealed that the patient actually was not financially able to pay a larger fee for that period, particularly since there was a large deductible amount to the insurance policy which the patient had to pay on his own.

As these real issues were being resolved, the meanings of the patient's deception and insistence on a lower fee unfolded. Once it was established that he would pay the higher fee, his reaction to this increase was also explored. That this was a very sensitive issue for the patient is revealed in the fact that he spent more than two months exploring its repercussions. In his fantasies, the therapist's increase in fee was seen as a corruption and likened to the dishonest merchant who increases the price of his furniture when a wealthy customer comes along (his father was in the furniture business). As this fantasy unfolded and was interpreted to the patient, the therapist also returned repeatedly to the reality on which the decision was based so that the patient became aware that the fantasy was actually unfounded. This led to the revelation that the patient had once lied to a doctor regarding a whiplash injury, in order to receive unwarranted insurance benefits. The physician, on his part, had charged the patient a fee that was larger than usual because it was an insurance case. The fantasy that the higher fee was a mutual corruption was interpreted to the patient and led to considerable genetic material regarding his corrupt interaction with his parents. They had often unconsciously sanctioned the patient's petty thieveries and sex play with his sisters by ignoring all evidence of them.

As the patient began to recognize that there was a real basis for the increase in his fee, his rage mounted because he felt that he was losing his favored status with the therapist. He became depressed as he expressed, worked through, and renounced his fantasies of being united with the therapist. Eventually, he recognized his ability to be responsible for the therapist's regular fee and this led to a greater sense of independence and ego enhancement. This was confirmed and solidified when the patient described the overindulgent father of a friend, who had "created" a helpless drug-addicted child. In this context, the therapist was able to show the patient his own awareness of the disadvantages of an indulgent and corrupt misalliance.

Several principles emerge from this vignette, to which I will add some additional basic points:

1. *Insurance should not influence the therapist to charge a larger-than-usual fee.* This is an exploitation that will corrupt and undermine the entire treatment. Insurance should be considered as a resource only when a patient cannot otherwise afford the therapist's usual fee.

2. *Insurance may be used by the patient as a real basis for resistances that can undermine the therapy.* It is my impression that in most instances of psychotherapy insurance does not become a major obstacle, though one must be alert to it at all times. When it does form the core of a resistance or therapeutic misalliance, it must be analyzed and explored on every level. As a third party to therapy (see Chapter 6), insurance may be used to reinforce strong defenses against involvement in therapy and the quest for inner change. It may represent the bountiful mother, whom the patient possesses and who gratifies his neurotic needs, or it may be experienced as a barrier between the patient and the therapist. With the real gratifications supplied in this way, the insurance may prove an insurmountable obstacle. While this is rare, we must consider this possibility if the therapy of such patients becomes stalemated.

3. *Insurance is the responsibility of the patient and is his resource.* The therapist should not, if possible, receive his fees directly from the insurance company, since this reinforces the resistance and neurotic gratification aspects, especially the patient's dependency, passivity, and remoteness.

4. *As is true regarding any real and not-in-itself inappropriate aspect of the relationship between the patient and the therapist, insurance may simply be part of the silent background of treatment unless it becomes a vehicle for focal, psychopathological fantasies or resistances to therapy.* At such times, it must be dealt with in terms of any real obstacles that it is creating (in a sense, the "ego" and "reality" aspects) and the related fantasies. Since unresolved realities of this kind create unmodified fantasies that support the patient's

neurosis and interfere with resolution of his conflicts, in selected, rare cases therapy may be unfeasible unless the insurance is given up.

5. *The quest for insurance coverage after a patient has begun therapy should be considered a serious form of acting out.* Such insurance is often obtained dishonestly through lying about when treatment began, and therefore serves to really corrupt the treatment and render it ineffectual. It must be thoroughly analyzed, and the destructive and deprecatory aspects, as well as the grandiose implications, demonstrated to the patient. Patients who will not give up such acting out when its various conscious and unconscious meanings are demonstrated to them usually have such strong and serious resistances to therapy that they may be untreatable. They are usually psychopathic, narcissistic, grandiose, and sometimes borderline (see Kohut, 1971). Their pathology is usually reflected in their entire style of working in the sessions. It is striking for its negativism, restriction of material to the surface and to reality problems and concerns, acting out, and other detrimental behavior. Such patients continue to see the therapist only if they can maintain their ill-gotten, antitherapeutic alliance with him. It may be rarely necessary, as a last resort, to confront such a patient with his massive resistances, manipulativeness, and lack of motivation for self-change, and ultimately work toward a choice between his blatant acting out, including the dishonest insurance payments, and possible inner change via treatment.

However, the main danger here, is a primarily moralistic or judgmental attitude in the therapist and a loss of empathy for the patient's needs, rather than a maintainance of an analytic stance. Such corruptions communicate major aspects of the patient's fantasies and pathology, and should be explored like any material from the patient. Only when the patient's associations reflect his unconscious awareness of the detrimental aspects—the narcissism and corruption—of his behavior should he be confronted with its negative consequences for himself and his therapy; to this should be added interpretations of the context and unconscious meanings of this behavior and its genetic roots.

6. *The acceptance of offers of devious fee arrangements corrupts the entire therapy and should be responded to with an*

intervention which directs the patient to explore his suggestion thoroughly. While refusal to participate is implicit in this attitude, direct refusal should seldom be necessary. Suggestions of this kind, for instance, asking the therapist to report a higher fee than he is actually charging the patient and then splitting the extra money obtained in that way, reflect important aspects of the patient's pathology. They should not be condemned or responded to in a moral way. They merit full analysis in the expectation that the patient will, through insight, give up his offer. However, as the analysis is being carried out, the therapist must be certain that he does not agree to the idea in any way since this would undermine the exploratory efforts and possibly the therapy.

7. *When the patient passes on insurance forms to be filled out, do so in as brief and simple a manner possible.* Be certain to have the patient's written permission before releasing any information. Feel free to return such forms directly to the patient, and to discuss and explore the information you have given. Make your written diagnosis as simple as possible.

ON INCREASING FEES

Since the vignette regarding Mr. L.N. is still fresh, let us turn now to these additional questions. Are there any indications and justifications for increasing fees during therapy? If so, what principles should guide us? This is an enormously sensitive issue, and one that poses real dangers to the outcome of treatment. The main indication for a higher fee is a significant increase in the patient's income. However, such a change in the fee, no matter how appropriate, will always generate considerable rage, hurt, and resistance in the patient, often to the point of seriously disrupting therapy. Therefore, the therapist should be quite clear regarding this indication for such a move and not abuse the privilege of treating patients and of setting fees; he must recognize that the patient is particularly vulnerable in this regard.

Only rarely can a general increase in one's fees be justified. As part of the ground rules, the therapist has agreed in principle to accept a specified fee from the patient from the beginning of treatment. If the particular patient is initially paying an unusually low fee and there is clear indication later that he can pay a higher fee, the therapist is entirely justified in increasing his fee. On the other hand, if the therapist raises his fee scale for other patients subsequent to the beginning of treatment with a given patient, this does not justify increasing the latter's fee. Wherever possible, the therapist should maintain the agreed-upon fee as part of the realistic and reliable arrangements that he has made with the patient. Only if a treatment has gone on for many years and living costs have increased markedly (and one should always question such a longstanding therapy), should the therapist even consider raising the fee in the absence of a marked increase in the patient's income.

The therapist should never charge patients who come into considerable wealth fees that go beyond his usual fees. There can be no justification for such a stance; it is selfish, manipulative, and destructive, and will provide the patient with a real basis for strong resistance to treatment through appropriate negative feelings. Furthermore, nonverbally and unconsciously, it gives the patient permission to act out and indulge himself, based on the model offered by the therapist. An unconscious therapeutic misalliance ensues and proves unresolvable since the therapist has, in reality, participated in it.

Whenever an increase in fee is considered completely justified and presented to the patient, it should be explored thoroughly in regard to its real justification and its meanings to the patient. The narcissistic hurt implied often evokes vengeful rage and threats from the patient that he will leave therapy. These responses must be analyzed in terms of their present source and their specific genetic underpinnings. The delineation of the patient's conscious and unconscious fantasies is a particularly important task in this regard. At the same time, the "cost" in suffering to the patient for any of his efforts at gaining revenge on the therapist and the reality factors which justify the increased fee must be clearly delineated to him. In this way, he can be helped to adapt to the increased fee in a less damaging and healthier way and to work through the conflicts and transference disturbances it has evoked.

DEVIOUS FEE ARRANGEMENTS

Empirically, it proves necessary to discuss offers of devious fee arrangements made by patients to their therapists. Many therapists are either unwary in this regard or rationalize and deny the repercussions of the acceptance of such offers, while others inappropriately condemn them without analyzing their meanings. Devious arrangements include insurance manipulations and payments made in cash so that the therapist need not report them as income; in return, the patient's fee is lowered. More subtly, patients offer payments in stock or investment opportunities for the therapist in return for reduced fees. In some cases, they even make these gifts without asking for special consideration from the therapist.

The therapist who accepts such offers rationalizes that the treatment will be unaffected or mysteriously enhanced by this response. We know, of course, that this is not the case. Clinical findings as well as theoretical understanding have established that this creates a corrupted antitherapeutic alliance. It is clear that such an arrangement offers the patient support for his pathological grandiosity and license for corruptions, acting out, and gratification of his forbidden instinctual wishes. The therapist can no longer expect the patient to accept the painful need to honestly face his illness and the pathology within himself, nor can he expect the patient to be motivated to revise such pathology if it is being supported.

Many subtle and not-so-subtle, conscious and unconscious, attempts to corrupt the therapist occur during the course of psychotherapy. The therapist who personally has problems in this area will fall prey to these manipulations. While it is certainly possible to make errors and to initially miss a subtle corruption, the therapist is bound to discover it if he follows the material from the patient, for it will inevitably point to it. However, conscious participation by the therapist in the patient's corruption is one of the few contaminants of psychotherapy that usually necessitates referral of a patient to another therapist. If the therapist has inadvertently participated and then detected his error, it may be worked through with the patient. If it is done intentionally and in consort with the patient, even though its implications are realized subsequently, it often cannot be undone and will leave its mark throughout the treatment.

The struggle with the patient's neurosis centers around the establishment of appropriate and incorruptible avenues of gratification and related renunciations, and a shift from narcissistic behavior based on fantasies of omnipotence to a more realistic concept of oneself and others. Therefore, only a totally honest background can serve for the unfolding of insight and inner change. This is one issue without ambiguity; be alert to its more subtle, but crucial, manifestations.

Technically, then, if the therapist is offered a deviant fee arrangement, he must first explore its meanings and implications fully with the patient. Care must be taken to not become moralistic and critical. The therapist's own position of analytic interest, combined with implicit lack of corruptibility, will provide the climate in which the exploration of such offers can be made. Empathic understanding of the patient's need for the corruption must be combined with an absence of participation in the offered misalliance (see Kohut, 1971). In this way, considerable additional material will unfold that otherwise would remain concealed and never be worked through.

The attempt to corrupt the therapist and therapy may extend beyond fee arrangements into subtle or blatant efforts to have the therapist sanction acting out of all kinds and to have him deviate from his neutral therapeutic stance. In general, it is an effort to promote mutual acting out and evoke external coercion in the place of analysis and the search for inner change. Involved is an attempt to seduce the therapist and have him share an antitherapeutic alliance and reliving of the past and to sanction or condemn the patient's neurotic adjustment. This sharing of a seriously pathological defense inevitably leads to an undermining of the total treatment. Therefore, it must be dealt with by an implicit refusal on all levels and a thorough exploration of the patient's material, leading to meaningful working through. The result will be not only a proper therapeutic atmosphere and alliance, through which the unfolding of the critical aspects of the patient's neurosis can occur, but also considerable maturation and ego development within the patient. Such offers are not uncommon in narcissistic patients with psychopathic traits, and their analysis provides a rich avenue for the exploration of the pathology in these patients (Kohut, 1971).

I will conclude this discussion with a vignette which demonstrates the importance of analyzing and resolving devious fee arrangements and indicates the far-reaching effects on the therapeutic alliance and the course and outcome of the entire therapy.

Mrs. H.D. had been in therapy in a clinic for phobic anxieties and a severe characterological disturbance for about ten months when her therapist began to present her case to me in supervision. She had been exploring her reactions to a recent biopsy of a breast nodule which showed possible early malignant changes and which had been sent to several pathologists for evaluation. Early reports were somewhat encouraging, but not definitive.

She came to a session at this time with a cup of coffee that she drank as she spoke. She had been sleeping poorly; her husband was away on a sales trip. She discussed the biopsy and, for the first time, reported that she had been avoiding intercourse with her husband. She did not fully trust the doctors in charge of her breast problem; they were clinic physicians and in training. She was afraid of being alone; her husband refused to allow a girlfriend and her lover to stay with her while he was away. Her son had a nightmare that there was a strange man in his room.

She began the next hour by mentioning that she had driven another patient home after the previous session. She described a premonitory dream of her mother's in which the mother's apartment was robbed; it then actually had happened. The patient was planning to move because her husband was receiving a promotion; she had quarreled with her mother about the move. Her father is becoming blind. Her mother thinks that she (the patient) keeps secrets, for instance, about money and sex. She does have a large bank account which is a secret from everyone because of tax evasions that are related to it; even the clinic does not know about it. If they did, they would increase her fee. (In this clinic, the intake social worker sets and collects the fee, not the therapist. Mrs. H.D.'s therapist knew of the hidden money earlier in therapy, but had never explored it with the patient and it had not been mentioned in some months.)

Mrs. H.D. next spoke of her husband's suspicions that she had a boyfriend in his absence. She had fallen badly after the last session and had imagined that there was a black hand on her front door when she got into bed and dozed. Was she right or wrong in waking her son?

At this point, we might pause briefly to formulate the material and to make some predictions. To touch upon only the main points, it was felt in supervision that, in the absence of the patient's husband and in the face of her bodily anxieties (the adaptive contexts), erotic fantasies regarding the therapist had been stirred up and were being expressed in derivative form in the material, especially in the references to other men and the patient's driving another patient home. But the most crucial point was that the therapist, by not exploring the patient's devious fee arrangement, had silently sanctioned and participated in it; and it came up at this time because the patient unconsciously viewed the therapist as corruptible and seducible. Thus, her erotic fantasies were especially terrifying because the patient's doubts about the therapist's integrity made them especially dangerous. It was therefore suggested that this infraction of the ground rules be non-judgmentally analyzed and worked through. Without such work, a major disruption in the therapeutic alliance would be continued and would interfere with the analysis of the patient's phobias which were known to be based, in part, on fears of losing control of her sexual impulses as the patient had done many years previously. A corrupted misalliance had to be resolved.

In the next session the patient reported a brief episode of fainting after the last session. Her landlady planned to sue her for breaking her lease and moving away. In return, the patient said that she would report her fire violations. Mrs. H.D. believed that she could not be sued since they have nothing in their name—it's all hidden away. She had flirted openly at a party; her husband, who was back now, wanted her to quit therapy. She had dreamt of a man breaking into her house and of a dog, dead in the street. Her brother had attacked her sexually in her childhood and she had fainted. She had been treated for passing out after intercourse several years ago by a doctor with whom she subsequently had an affair. Her husband had discussed their finances and offered to come to the session in the patient's place. As the hour ended, Mrs. H.D. took out a picture of herself in a bathing suit to show the therapist how she had once been very sexy.

The next hour contained references to money problems and a dream in which the patient was with a cousin who goes crazy and is institutionalized. The patient had had an affair with her cousin's husband. She mentioned again her mistrust of her other doctors.

It was in the next session, as the patient spoke of a past sexual liaison with a neighbor and of her dislike of collusion, that the therapist pointed out the patient's deception of the clinic regarding her fee and suggested that they explore it, adding that his silence on the matter seemed to be viewed by the patient as collusion on his part. In brief, the patient indicated that she had expected all along that the therapist would question her about the fee, and then she rationalized her acknowledged deception. She wondered if the therapist taped the sessions and insisted on seeing him like a computer. She spoke of deceiving her husband and wondered if it all did not somehow relate to her fears.

In the remaining hours of her therapy, which was terminated soon after these sessions because the patient did leave the area, Mrs. H.D. seemed angry and spoke of regretting her deceptiveness. In reviewing the fee problem again, she said that she feared her husband because they were dishonest with each other; she hadn't been fully honest with the therapist because she felt that he had not been honest with her—he never answered her questions. She next thought of times when she had wanted to run out of the therapist's office and recalled his checking up on her fee payments when she had been delinquent, relating it to her feelings that he had been dishonest with her. She had hidden a lot from the therapist, she realized. Now, she somehow felt brave and could be more open.

In the last session, she recalled once deceiving her boss when she worked, and always regretting it. Her brother is corrupt, she went on; as a physician in a clinic, he used to do minor surgery just for the practice. She recalled deceptions on the part of her parents during her childhood, extending into the facts about her real family name and background. In some way, being corrupt interfered with her being the whole person she hoped to be. Maybe if she continued her therapy after her move, she could start all over. Or would she lie again? She didn't know.

I have described this material in some detail to show how the unanalyzed, silently sanctioned, deception of the clinic by the patient contributed to a tainted and mistrustful therapeutic misalliance. This fostered an unanalyzed erotic transference and, by being an unresolved sharing of the patient's pathology, interfered with the possibility of helping her analyze and give up her symptoms. Since these effects are so far-reaching, it follows that the noncritical exploration of such issues must take precedence over virtually all else in the therapy.

THE THERAPIST'S RESPONSIBILITY
FOR THE SESSIONS

A vignette will serve to begin this discussion.

Miss A.W., a young woman with an hysterical character disorder, was in twice-weekly psychotherapy. At the time of a series of schedule changes made at her request, she missed a session and did not call. In the next hour, she stated that she had been to the therapist's office at an hour other than the time he had expected her, but he was not there. She felt that she must have made a mistake and had not called. The therapist checked his appointment book and discovered that Miss A.W. was right; it was actually he who had been in error. The patient then said that she had thought so, but somehow had just blamed herself. She said that she had attended to some long over-due errands with the free time and was glad to have had the chance; she then talked about how people often leave her unexpectedly. She thought of this because her mother had recently taken an unannounced trip and had broken her arm in a fall. No one told the patient about it at first and she accidentally found out from her cousin. She said she would not help take care of her mother now; she's too nasty and it doesn't pay to get involved. She hated her mother and would just stay away from her. She went on to say how inconsiderate people are. A man had nearly hit her with his car while she was driving to the session; he might have killed her and she wanted to murder him.

The therapist intervened to point out to the patient that he had mistakenly missed a session and now she was talking about people disappointing her and making her angry. The patient responded by denying that she had any anger at the therapist. She thought instead of her cat who was so loving and how she was unable to respond since it might die and leave her. When her father died, she was given a dog, but her mother eventually gave it away when she was not at home one afternoon. With this, the session ended.

In supervision, once the therapist's intervention had been reported and assessed as far too inadequate, it was predicted that confirmation through validating associa-tions (see Chapters 18 and 19) would not follow—all of this was borne out in the session. A myriad of unanalyzed fantasies and reactions were present in this hour and they continued to be expressed, unabated, in the following two sessions. Themes of rejection, loss, hurt, and affront abounded. The therapist again meekly attempted to sug-gest that this material was related to the missed hour, but the patient continued to deny it. At the end of the second session, Miss A.W. told the therapist that she had a sur-prise for him; she had gotten engaged the night before to a man she had known only a few weeks.

This is a poignant episode in an unfortunately handled treatment. Let us learn what we can from it. The therapist's task in this situation was actually threefold: to clarify and correct the reality of the situation; to explore its meanings for the patient on every level, including her reactions in fantasy and behavior; and to examine on his own his countertransference difficulties (see Chapter 22). Thus, the first order of business—one that was completely overlooked by this therapist—was an apology for the error and probably some indication to Miss A.W. that he was endeavoring to understand the reasons for his oversight. Then, a makeup session should have been offered as a deserved compensation for a real hurt, leaving the decision to accept or reject such a session to the patient.

Next, the therapist should have initiated his interpretive remarks by alluding to the main defenses the patient was using to handle her hurt and rage, namely, denial and displacement. The maxim of giving the interpretation of defenses and disturbances in the therapeutic alliance prime consideration is a sound and basic one. He should have pointed out the themes of feeling hurt, slighted, and attacked by someone who either hates her or ignores her feelings and endangers her. Then he should have quickly pointed out that rather than express these feelings and fantasies directly toward him for what he had done, she was denying them and shifting focus onto other less immediate and, in part, less personal hurts.

A genetic tie to both the loss of her father and the destructiveness of her mother could then have been made. However, this should not have been treated as an isolated or irrational and unjustified, primarily transference-based fantasy, but as a genetically-founded response to the therapist's actual behavior (see Chapter 22). His action resembled the many hurts that the patient had suffered from her mother, and it also created a moment which was not unlike the sudden loss of the patient's father. Thus, the intervention should have included an acknowledgement of the real hurt evoked by the therapist's error and then have moved on to demonstrate the conscious and unconscious fantasies and memories with which the patient was responding.

There are basic human elements to such a total response by the therapist: brief acknowledgement of his error and in this case, an apology; an offer to appropriately correct the hurt; and the interpretations of the patient's responses in a manner that accepts the responsibility for evoking these reactions, yet resumes the work of the therapy by helping the patient achieve insight. In all, these human qualities accompanied by correct interpretations will reestablish a healthy therapeutic alliance and foster a full working-through of the trauma. At such moments, patients are grateful for candid, concerned, and helpful interventions by their therapist. If properly handled, these errors can often be converted into moments of very moving and meaningful therapeutic work and insight.

The patient's reaction to the therapist's poorly worded and incomplete interventions was, in no way, confirmatory. Actually, Miss A.W. continued to deny any direct feelings about the incident, which nonetheless, as we see from the material, hurt her deeply. The implications of the fantasies and memories related to the harm and deprivation caused by her mother are clear, as are those of being attacked and of losing her father. The defensive use of denial was also reflected in her reaction to her mother's injury, and in her acting out, through her sudden engagement, to repair her sense of loss and avenge herself on the therapist. This latter was foreshadowed in the patient's reference to replacing her father with a dog and probably could have been forestalled with correct interventions. Another defense that should have been interpreted was the patient's blaming herself for what had happened. In this way she denied her rage at the therapist, this time by displacing it onto herself. The self-abasement and denial continued, in part, because the therapist promoted it by not acknowledging his full responsibility for initiating what had happened and by not attempting to compensate for it. The patient had continued reason to feel devalued and this also contributed to her sudden engagement.

There is a definite need for the therapist to explore his conscious, and to get to the unconscious, reasons for his oversight; it must be emphasized that such errors should not be rationalized or ignored. Behavior of this kind can, with proper technique, be worked through with the patient to an adequate degree, but it is based on significant difficulties within the therapist. Only self-analysis and working through to a resolution of these problems will ensure that they are neither repeated nor reflected more subtly in the therapist's subsequent behavior and comments. Repeated behavior of this kind could undermine the entire therapy, just as the therapist's failure to properly handle the incident with Miss A.W. did so (see also Chapters 19 and 22).

We can see from this vignette that the therapist has a critical and vital responsibility to the patient to be present for the sessions. Patients are extremely sensitive to deviations from this responsibility. Two additional clinical experiences will further document this for us, as well as add to our understanding of how such occurrences are to be handled.

> Dr. Y. awoke one morning, ill with a fever. He was faced with six appointments with patients in the clinic at which he worked and realized that he had to miss these sessions since he was exhausted and had considerable malaise. He elected to call his secretary at the clinic and asked her to cancel his hours, feeling that the six telephone calls would be a tremendous burden for him in his condition. His secretary did as he requested. One of the patients whose session Dr. Y.'s secretary cancelled was Mr. A.X. He came in later that week for a session.

It was possible in supervision to make several predictions before hearing the material from this session. It must be expected that the cancellation will be one of the central issues and contexts in this hour (see Chapter 9). This constitutes a real event within the treatment that prompts conscious and unconscious fantasies, defenses, conflict, behavior, and feelings within the patient. Therefore, it is the job of the therapist to listen to the material of the session in this context. On this basis, he will be able to interpret the specific meanings to the patient of the cancellation and his methods of responding to it and dealing with it. While patients are inevitably infuriated by sudden cancellations—such an experience brings out feelings of helplessness, rejection, and vulnerability—the rage in this specific instance was likely to have been heightened because the therapist did not cancel his sessions personally. This constitutes a disregard for the feelings of the patient and a real trauma; it will evoke a reality-based reaction with ties to the patient's past, similarly traumatic, experiences. He will be doubly angry and will have real reasons for this anger. The expectation, therefore, was that the patient would directly or indirectly communicate considerable rage in the subsequent session. The therapist's avoidance (not calling the patient himself) was also expected to promote similar avoidance and denial in the patient.

> In his session, Mr. A.X. was quite ruminative, remotely recounting a series of recent seemingly trivial experiences in which he came upon a number of cold, indifferent, and unfeeling people. The therapist did not detect this underlying theme which was clearly a derivative of how the patient felt toward him at this time, and he failed to intervene in any way.
>
> In the next session, the patient reported the following dream: he was sleeping and his parents did not wake him; he raged at them because he had missed his session. In association, the patient avoided the obvious references to the missed session, and instead spoke of his anger at his parents for being lazy, cold, and inconsiderate. The therapist suggested that the patient was angry about the hour that had been cancelled, but the patient denied such feelings.

We will not follow this vignette further, except to note that later material—and more perceptive and accurate use of it—enabled the therapist to help the patient work through this trauma. That Dr. Y.'s failure to call him directly particularly angered Mr. A.X. became clear not only through the dream noted above but also through an incident several weeks later. At that time, the patient was ill and he had his mother call Dr. Y. to cancel the hour.

With the material available to us, particularly the relatively undisguised dream with its few associations and context, we can establish some salient points. Dr. Y. implicitly abdicated his responsibility for the session and for cancelling it, so in the dream Mr. A.X. did the same; both shared the same defenses and avoidance. The rage at Dr. Y. was displaced onto Mr. A.X.'s parents, and this was fostered by real similarities in behavior. The sleep in the dream refers both to the patient's passive-aggression, denial, and blindness, and also to that of the therapist. It is again based on an identification with the therapist because the latter failed entirely to deal with the problem in the session after the cancellation. The outcome is a mutual misalliance for the moment.

It has been my repeated observation that when such hurts and fury as this unresolved reaction to the therapist remain uninterpreted, they prompt more and more blatant expressions of the underlying feelings and fantasies, and often culminate in destructive acting out.

In principle, then, the therapist in this case has the same three basic therapeutic responsibilities that I described regarding the session overlooked by Miss A.W.'s therapist. These principles apply to the therapist's handling of any technical error that he makes, and we vary the specifics of the response to suit the particular situation. Here, the therapist's oversight in not cancelling the hour himself should have been acknowledged and an apology offered. Next, from the patient's material, the responses to the error should have been interpreted, dealing first with his defenses and then with his conscious and unconscious fantasies and the genetic ties. Lastly, self-exploration regarding the insensitivity reflected in not directly calling the patient should be carried out by the therapist. Often, unresolved hostility and/or fears of closeness to the patient are factors here (see Chapter 22).

Let us contrast this vignette with another in which the therapist cancelled his sessions directly with his patients. Despite this, they reacted strongly, each in his own way.

> Dr. x. had to cancel his hours for an entire day when a sudden death occurred in his family. He called the patients involved and told them he had to cancel the session due to an emergency. He intentionally stated this ambiguously for two reasons: first, to maintain his anonymity and not involve his patients in his personal life; and second, to maintain a therapeutic field in which there would be sufficient opportunity for each patient to both fantasize and react.

When the cancellation is due to the therapist's illness, this should be succinctly reported to the patient. Beyond that, the therapist should refer to "urgent matters" or "emergencies" as reasons for his pending absence. When cancelling in advance for one or two days, so as to go to a professional meeting or for some comparable reason, he should simply state that he will not be having hours (or that he will not be in his office) on those days. The response of Dr. x.'s patients to this situation will illustrate some typical reactions to, and basic tenets regarding, single sessions missed by the therapist.

The first observation is that every single patient reacted significantly to this abrupt interruption; it is a traumatic separation that must be worked through. Usually, this can be done briefly with a perceptive interpretation of the specific meanings of the absence to the patient, the patient's method of coping with the separation and the anxieties and conflicts it evoked, and its genetic roots. Often, the therapist is only partially successful in clarifying each of these aspects, but some degree of working through is crucial and if the major response is touched upon, this will prove sufficient.

In brief, these were the reactions of Dr. x.'s patients:

> Mrs. A.Y.: She had dreamt of a threesome—man, woman and baby—and spoke of feelings of being alienated from her husband, and of thoughts of an affair and of getting pregnant. Dr. x. pointed out her avoidance of any reference to the missed session. The patient then expressed directly her resentment and the therapist linked this to her feelings of alienation and to the dream, which expressed her wish to undo the separation by having a baby with him.
>
> Mrs. A.Z.: She had dreamt that her child's teacher had committed suicide. The teacher had been absent yesterday and the patient wondered if she had cancer. Associations unfolded along two lines: the patient's murderous rage at her brother, which was related to her fear that his recent lung illness might be cancer and cause his death; and her fears of her own guilt-ridden, suicidal impulses. The overwhelming sense of loss and the rage against the therapist because of the cancelled session, turned against herself in

part because of her guilt, were interpreted to her and confirmed.

Miss B.A.: She had dreamt of missing several days at work, and of being accused of lying. She planned to visit a boyfriend who was away, and recalled a man who had been seductive. The therapist noted her implied mistrust of his unspoken reason for his absence (the lying in the dream), and she then revealed many suspicions in this regard. She later dreamt that Dr. x. was gone and she was ill, and linked it herself to the missed session and to earlier longings in her childhood for her sick and absent mother.

Mr. B.B.: He was worried that his fly was open as he came in (homosexual longings and possible fellatio fantasies). He had dreamt of caring for his sister's children. Associations were to longings to be close to his remote mother and to an early homosexual experience with a friend, previously identified as both a father figure and a giving mother-substitute. The therapist tied it all to the missed hour.

Mrs. B.C.: She dreamt that her daughter was on her lap. Then she was in a harem and the men were being executed. She next was dating a psychiatrist named David (the therapist's first name). Associations were to both parents, with expressions of both longings for, and rage against them in response to various hurts. These were particularly directed toward her father who had deserted their family. This patient was a borderline woman who expressed her reaction to the separation in these, and a number of other, relatively undisguised dreams, fantasies, and genetic links.

Mr. B.D.: He was late and immediately saw it as his revenge on the therapist. He had dreamt of a man being mutilated and associated it both to his wife's miscarriage and his rage at the therapist. After the therapist's call, he had acted out and picked a fight with his wife because she had wanted to leave him and go to a movie with a girlfriend.

Mrs. B.E.: She was mostly silent and this was interpreted as a response to the missed session. She then reported that she had lost her wallet while shopping and had been enraged at a friend whom she felt didn't care enough or show sufficient concern for her. She linked this now to the missed hour, saying that she felt that the cancellation meant that the therapist had more concern for others than for her. She wondered if a patient had attempted suicide or needed hospitalization, or if there had been a personal crisis (similar speculations were reported by most of the other patients). She ended the session by recalling a dream; the friend with whom she had quarreled had moved and her sense of loss was intense.

The material is relatively clear and virtually speaks for itself. The separation evoked a distinctive reaction that was in keeping with the character structure, personality, conflicts, genetics, and unconscious fantasies of each patient. The therapist's responsibility was to listen to the material from the patient in the context of his absence and interpret it accordingly, also recognizing that other intervening traumas might have occurred and have also evoked significant reactions in the patient. In such instances, he would analyze the material using both contexts; typically, the patient himself condenses and merges such a pair of adaptive tasks. In virtually every instance, the therapist's relatively brief and pointed interventions sufficed to promote the necessary working-through, and the focus of the treatment was able to move on to other issues.

Having established the importance of the therapist's attendance at all scheduled sessions, let us elaborate on this principle. The therapist should not cancel sessions frivolously, without serious thought and clear need, and should not do so too often in any case. Last minute cancelations should be avoided unless there is a dire emergency. With anticipated cancellations, two- to three-weeks notice should be given to the patient so that the separation reaction can be fully analyzed.

If the therapist is ill, he (and no one else) should call the patient and explain the reason for the cancellation, doing so in a general way. Under no circumstances should the patient be charged for the missed session. No replacement session should be offered, nor should it be arranged if the patient requests it, unless there is an emergency. A make-up session would foster undue dependency in the patient and undermine his autonomy. It might also seem greedy and promote in the patient unreported fantasies of anger and being abused.

THE THERAPIST'S LATENESS

The therapist's lateness to sessions should be avoided whenever possible. If it occurs, the patient's responses to it must be analyzed and worked through using the same principles as those which apply to cancelled sessions. Clinical observations indicate that reactions to both of these experiences are comparable and may be quite intense.

Miss B.F. was a teenager in psychotherapy for recurrent depressions and a poor social adjustment. She had a rather infantile character structure, with relatively poor impulse control, and was exceedingly dependent. In the seventh month of her treatment, her therapist was inadvertently delayed by traffic and arrived at their session five minutes late. He apologized to the patient for his lateness and she accepted the apology without commenting upon it directly. In the session, she spoke of various ways in which she took revenge upon her brother when he provoked her. She related a dream in which she exposed herself to a boyfriend whose name resembled that of her therapist. Associations led to the lack of privacy in her parental home, and the problem of the therapist's lateness was not alluded to again by either the patient or the therapist. The latter did not extend the hour to permit a full session since another patient was waiting.

The patient arrived five minutes late for the next session. She had had a dream about leaving a boyfriend's house; the time of her departure was confused and she became enraged with this fellow and began to beat him. Miss B.F. went on to explain her lateness; her mother had been late in picking her up to drive her to the session.

She associated her anger in the dream to her resentments against her brother. She then spoke of copying answers on a recent examination and how she got away with stealing small articles of clothing in a department store. She next returned to the matter of her lateness and realized that she had known where her mother was, and could have called her and made the session on time.

It was at this point that the therapist intervened. He made his comments on two levels. First, he discussed the dynamics and genetics of Miss B.F.'s reaction to the lateness that he had failed to make up, including her handling of the reaction. Next, his comments were directed to the real problem that he had created. In regard to the first, the interpretation referred to the patient's rage at the therapist for his lateness, which she had experienced as a rejection and hurt reminiscent of those that she had suffered from her brother. In regard to the second, he noted the inappropriateness of his failure to make up the lost time for which she was charged, and offered to extend the current session by five minutes if it was agreeable to the patient. He then related his own "dishonesty" to that of the patient and pointed out that she seemed to inappropriately take it as a sanction to be dishonest herself and to live out her anger directly, alluding at this point to her own lateness to the sessions.

The patient responded by acknowledging her anger and hurt directly. The reference to her use of the therapist's lateness and handling of it as license for her own corruption reminded her of previously unreported memories of stealing from local stores and leaving the items around the house, then seeing her mother ignore this provocation. Once the therapist had in reality corrected his inadvertent "dishonesty," his interpretations provided both insight and an opportunity for the patient to change. The developing misalliance was modified and corrected.

Let us now summarize the most salient principles we have evolved for handling single absences and lateness on the part of the therapist:

1. *Listen to the material of the subsequent session or sessions with this context in mind.*

2. *Recognize that single absences and latenesses very often evoke significant reactions and resistances in the patient.* Thus, they almost always require interpretation; be prepared to do this. Usually all that is required is a single, succinct, as-complete-as-possible intervention.

3. *Among the most common reactions to these experiences are rage, narcissistic hurt, rejection, and loss of mothering.* Longings for closeness in various ways often follow. Among the most common defences are denial, displacement, and acting out.

4. *The therapist's behavior, since it is an action, is often taken as sanction for corrupt and uncontrolled behavior by the patient, even when nothing dishonest has been done.* It is this critical aspect which is most often overlooked and not worked through. Acting out is thereby inadvertly promoted and will persist until this dimension is clarified and repudiated by the therapist.

5. *With lateness and forgetting a patient's session, recognize the real wound to the patient, and acknowledge and correct it as far as possible.* Be sure to explore your countertransference problems in these matters.

6. *In conclusion, take your responsibility for the sessions seriously.* Failure to do so will set a model of irresponsibility that will undermine therapy. Chaos is bound to prevail to the detriment of the concerned and consistent atmosphere in which proper treatment can unfold.

THE PATIENT'S RESPONSIBILITY FOR THE SESSIONS

The patient's responsibility for his sessions is not as simple to define and maintain as it might seem. Many patients use this area to express highly rationalized resistances and both transference-based and reality-based hostile and erotic fantasies about the therapist. They also employ it to test out the therapist's honesty, consistency, and fairness. I will select some of the most common problems in this area and discuss each one.

ILLNESS OF THE PATIENT

The patient's responsibility for sessions that he misses because of illness is a perennially debated issue among therapists. Stances range from never charging for such absences—though this runs the risk of fostering frequent interruptions in the therapy, somatic expressions of unconcious fantasies, and the use of physical illness for maladaptive conflict resolution and communication—to charging for all missed sessions regardless of the length of the illness, though this may appear punitive and greedy. Some therapists explore the context of, and associations to, such occurrences and do not charge for those absences which do not, in their clinical judgment, serve pathological unconscious fantasies and acting out propensities. This risks seeming arbitrary, judgmental, and punitive on the one hand and rewarding somatically-based acting out on the other. Despite these varying attitudes, it is possible to arrive at a sound stance in this regard, one that is in the best interests of both the patient and the therapist.

Empirically, there is a direct ratio between the therapist's propensity toward errors and countertransference problems, and illnesses in his patients; in a well-run practice of psychotherapy, such occurrences are rare. Careful observation indicates that virtually every illness that occurs during therapy serves the total personality as a means of expressing unconscious fantasies related to unresolved intrapsychic conflicts and reflects resistances on some level. Therefore, illnesses are a nonverbal means of acting out; they interfere with verbalized insight and directly adaptive responses. Thus, it is a disservice to the patient to reward these maladaptive responses by not charging a fee for absences. Such a position reinforces expressions-through-illness and weakens the therapist's position to analyze such maladies and, therefore, his capacity to help the patient modify their usage. This creates a "somatic-expressions-are-favored" kind of misalliance between the patient and therapist, and undermines the therapy.

For the therapist's part, his hours are by appointment and set aside for the patient; if he does not fill an hour to which a patient is committed, he is entitled to charge a fee for it. To do otherwise is to sacrifice unnecessarily for the patient and to foster his inappropriate gratitude and, at times, guilt. Such behavior also proves to be overly seductive and ultimately destructive to the therapy.

Based on these considerations, it is recommended that the ground rules related to the patient's responsibility for all scheduled sessions not be modified for illnesses and that the therapist maintain this stance, with some flexibility for special exceptions. In adopting this position, the therapist should be mindful of the hostility and other negative responses this can evoke in the patient, especially when the illness is heavily invested in by the patient as a means of expression. Thus, when an illness occurs, we must be prepared for the dual task of analyzing its unconcious meanings and uses for the patient, and exploring, to the extent necessary, the patient's reactions to being charged a fee for the missed time. For a therapist convinced of the bilateral soundness and fairness of this attitude, there will be little difficulty in conveying to the patient the ways in which his position serves the therapy, and the fact that it is not taken out of greed or misuse of the patient. Interpretation of the patient's reactions to all aspects of the illness situation, including its resistance dimensions, will be facilitated and the outcome will be insight-producing for the patient. I have not seen acting out or other regressive responses to the proper application of these principles, though I have seen repeated maladaptive and manipulative use of illnesses when they are not used.

Some patients, and some parents of adolescents, attempt to use the fee issue under these circumstances to rationalize and justify their negative feelings toward treatment and the therapist. Exploration will always clarify this misuse of the situation and the underlying resistances, which can then be interpreted to the patient. Even very negativistic patients and parents do not want to overtly impair the therapeutic setting or foster pathological maladaptations and misalliances. A brief, non-defensive explanation of these factors as an introduction to an interpretive intervention is a useful tool when needed. Many patients readily understand the unconscious meanings of their illness from their associations to it and from its context and timing. They can then accept the therapist's interpretations of exactly what is involved, and respect the therapist for his position.

It is best to not discuss these issues on the telephone with the patient who calls to cancel his hour because he is ill, and to not offer him a make-up session on the telephone. If the patient asks directly about his responsibility for the hour, simply remind him of your mutual agreement and add that he can discuss it further at the next session. In the session, maintain the usual technique of first listening fully to the patient's direct comments—or lack of them—about the problem and especially to his indirect associations, which will reveal the specific unconscious fantasies involved. Questions should not be answered initially, though you should, if asked, explain that it is best to explore the patient's thoughts and fantasies before commenting.

In principle, such absences should not be made up since this also rewards the unhealthy uses of illnesses by the patient and engenders undue dependency and denial. It is important for him to face and accept the responsibility for his hours and for his use of this somatic means of expressing himself. Requests for substitute time must be analyzed along with the other dimensions of the situation.

The following vignette will illustrate some of the meanings and uses of illnesses during therapy:

> Mrs. B.G. was a young woman with a severe character disorder and depression. After a year of once-weekly therapy, the therapist took a vacation. The patient was depressed, and derivatives of sexualized longings for closeness with the therapist emerged and appeared to be related to a guilt-ridden, erotized relationship with her father. Upon the therapist's return, she reported a dream of being seriously ill and her associations related it to her wishes that her therapist would nurse her. The next hour was cancelled by the therapist because of a legal holiday and the patient had an episode of fainting which was interpreted from her associations as a costly way of living out her dream and as a means of expressing her anger with the therapist. The latter then reminded the

patient that because of another legal holiday, the following hour would also be cancelled, and the patient's indirect expressions of anger and feelings of emptiness were then expressed and analyzed.

In her next session, Mrs. B.G. reported a dream of being reunited with her lost Siamese cat. As associations linked this to her longings for the therapist, she announced that she would miss the next hour because of a vacation arranged for herself and her husband by his parents. She caught her slip of the tongue; she was actually to miss the session two weeks hence. Interpretation was made of the talion revenge on the therapist through her slip of the tongue and her actual plan, along with the therapist's acknowledgement that he might have checked the calendar before his vacation and better prepared Mrs. B.G. for the past two missed hours. It was also pointed out that the patient was inappropriately using this oversight as a sanction for living out her revenge on the therapist. Links to similar experiences with both parents then unfolded, as did her longings to possess the therapist as she had possessed her dolls in her childhood; the patient's vacation was also interpreted as a flight from these longings and an expression of her grandiose needs.

The patient cancelled the next hour because she had a throat infection and missed the following session because of her trip. She was late for the next hour and had felt suicidal. She reviewed her depression and spoke of her mother, who had been away. The therapist eventually asked what came to mind about her absences and the relevant realities were reviewed by the patient. She then spoke of a man who had attempted to seduce her and her flight from him. When this was related to her recent fearful fantasies about the therapist and her absences were seen as a flight from them, she spoke of her problems with her husband, with whom she was alternately close and uninvolved. She then reported that she had dreamt of an indifferent surgeon who gave her heart to someone else. Associations were to her therapist whom she felt was distant and uninvolved. She recalled her previous therapist who talked to her father after every session; she never told him anything except the things she wanted filtered back to her father. Her mother had been in treatment and her therapist would pat her on the back and give direct advice; that was crazy too. In response to a query as to what Mrs. B.G. might be concealing from her own therapist, she spoke of two of his colleagues whom she had met socially and had never mentioned in her treatment. She had spoken to them about her fee; she was worried about the therapist's competence since he was seeing her at a reduced fee. They had reassured her.

The therapist interpreted the patient's illness and absence as an attempt to create distance from him at a time when her longings to be one with him had intensified, and he linked this to her difficulties with her husband. He also pointed out how her reduced fee had heightened these longings.

This vignette illustrates the ways in which illnesses are generated and used to express feelings of depression, narcissistic hurt, rage, intense longings, and a series of overdetermined unconscious fantasies. These range from total union with the therapist in sickness to talion, vengeful fantasies of desertion and attack. For the therapist to effectively interpret such expressions, he must not sanction them nor in any way unconsciously reinforce their use.

This vignette also illustrates some basic principles that I have already developed in previous sections:

1. *Patients are exceedingly sensitive to sessions cancelled for any reason by their therapists.* The therapist should anticipate holidays and remind the patient of them a week or two in advance so that reactions to them can be adequately explored and worked through.

2. *If the therapist makes an error in this regard, the error and its role in the patient's response should be acknowledged in the interpretation of the patient's reaction to the situation.* Any attempt by the patient to misuse the error to sanction his own acting out or misuse of illness should also be interpreted.

3. *A reduction in fee must be remembered as a potential source of fantasies about the therapist, and its meanings must be interpreted when the material permits.* For Mrs. B.G., it was seen as a seduction by the therapist and fostered erotized longings for him; it also led her to question his competence. These fantasies emerged a year after the beginning of her treatment in the context of the cancelled hours.

After this brief detour, let us return to some supplementary issues which may arise in connection with patients' illnesses.

HOSPITALIZED PATIENTS

Occasionally, patients are hospitalized for psychiatric and medical reasons; in psychiatric cases, your own practice regarding whether you are able to continue to see hospitalized patients must prevail, although continuity is generally best for the patient. Depending on this, you may continue with the patient, see him occasionally, or refer him to a psychiatrist associated with the hospital. In the latter two instances, you must decide in advance if you will see the patient again on his discharge. If you plan to do so, you should maintain some responsibility for, or liaison with, the in-hospital treatment program.

Medical hospitalizations are another difficult problem. Does the therapist visit the patient or not? Does he volunteer to do so, or do so only in emergencies? In principle, with neurotic patients and character disorders, the therapist should not make it a practice to visit them while they are in the hospital unless a psychiatric emergency arises. With psychotic patients, one must be more flexible and visit them if they or their family, with good cause, request it. This can provide crucial support for such patients at a time when they are under great stress, experiencing considerable anxiety, and prone to regress (factors which, for example, foster complications after surgery). As with any deviation in technique or parameter (Eissler, 1953), the therapist must first do a serious bit of self-analysis and be certain that the visit is indicated solely in terms of the patient's needs and does not reflect inappropriate needs within himself. When the patient is well and is again being seen in the therapist's office, the therapist must listen to the material and understand the meanings of his visit for the patient. He must then be sure to analyze and work through any fantasies, conflicts, and neurotic gratifications it has created. As always, this is best done by waiting for direct and indirect references to the hospital visit in the patient's associations; these will always turn up. If necessary, the therapist must be prepared to introduce the topic himself and to point out the patient's defensive omission of references to the experience. This type of avoidance and denial may occur with borderline or psychotic patients who want to preserve the real gratification—and the fantasy extensions of it—provided by the visit, rather than work these through and renounce them. In such instances, symptomatic relief through fantasies of the therapist's omnipotent care can become the preferred means of dealing with emotional problems, and this will inevitably interfere with the development of the patient's own capacities to cope.

LONG-TERM ILLNESSES

Another difficult problem arises in regard to patients who are seriously ill and must miss a large number of sessions. Here again, flexibility seems essential. With a patient who is coming once or twice weekly, there is no justification for suggesting that the patient accept the responsibility for the fee for these sessions so that he can secure these hours for his return. I believe this imposes an unnecessary burden upon the patient and it should be possible for any therapist, even if he fills the time with another patient, to offer at least one weekly hour to the sick patient once he is well. If nothing else is available, it would be appropriate to add an extra hour to one's schedule as a temporary measure. The underlying principles involve the need for the psychotherapist to be in reality a reasonably available, non-seductive, non-punitive, and not overly-demanding individual. This is important not only for the unfolding of the material necessary for successful treatment but also for the therapist to be a positive model of identification for the patient. In addition, the therapist's stance should be one that fosters trust and promotes a strong therapeutic alliance; if not, unanalyzable resistances and rage will undermine the therapy.

In principle, then, if the context and timing of a patient's illness lasting two to three weeks points unmistakably toward the expression of unconscious fantasies and resistances, the therapist must not feel guilty or destructive in charging for such missed hours upon the patient's return if the time has been reserved for him, and after a full exploration. Some therapists will make an exception to the full-responsibility rule when prolonged illness occurs and there are no manifest or latent indications of maladaptive usage. There is a risk, however, of missing an important dimension of the relevant intrapsychic conflicts or of having the patient unconsciously repress material which would lead to such a charge for the sessions. It therefore seems best to maintain the basic ground rules in regard to all illnesses, and to release the patient and yourself from the hours involved if he is to be out for a prolonged period; in such a case, new hours should be arranged once the patient is well.

FUNERALS, LEGAL AND RELIGIOUS HOLIDAYS, AND OTHER UNUSUAL CIRCUMSTANCES

Occasions such as the death of a close relative and the funeral and mourning period call for compassion and flexibility in the therapist. I prefer to not charge for such absences, and to make up the lost sessions if my schedule permits. It is best to arrange an alternate hour when the patient feels that he should attend any funeral. These are constructive, ego-building activities which merit indirect support from the therapist.

Less well defined, however, are those situations which arise, for example, when a mother in treatment has a seriously ill child or claims that she realistically cannot get someone to stay with the child. Here one must listen very carefully to both the reality and the meaning of the situation for the patient. The determination regarding responsibility for the fee should be made in the following session and not on the telephone. It should be made on the basis of the reality, regardless of the unconscious gratification to the patient. Should it prove to have been a necessary absence for which the patient is not charged, and one finds that the patient has fantasies of being indulged, duping the therapist, or having her narcissistic needs gratified, the therapist must interpret these gratifications and bring the patient back to the reality on which the decision was based. In the situation of a sick child, one must recognize the mother's investment in the welfare of her child and not take a stance that might reflect criticism of such concern or create conflicts regarding it. In general, it is best to give the patient the benefit of the doubt in such situations and to listen carefully to the subsequent material since it will reflect any error you might have made. This will enable you to analyze and correct it, if it turns out that the patient should have been responsible for the session. Here, too, if the therapist's schedule permits, making up such a missed session after it has been explored, thereby bypassing this issue, is a useful alternative.

Another variation on this theme is that of religious holidays. The therapist should not charge patients for such absences as long as they are truly observing the holiday religiously. Should this not be the case, the therapist must detect this in the course of the treatment and raise questions regarding the patient's decision to miss the session. Those patients who are not observing the holiday, but simply using it as a means of avoiding a session, should have their responsibility for the session spelled out to them considerably in advance so that all of the repercussions can be explored. In this way, acting out can be prevented, or at least not sanctioned by the therapist.

Major legal holidays should be days on which the therapist does not work. Such missed sessions should not be made up; doing so only fosters undue dependency and anxiety in the patient, and is seductive and greedy. The following vignette is representative of the problems this can create:

> Mrs. B.H. was in therapy for four months for phobic symptoms and a severe character disorder. She began one session by describing her anxieties about treatment and how she felt transparent to her friends. The therapist immediately related this to her fears of himself, and the patient responded by asking him if he would be missing the session a week hence because of a pending religious holiday. The therapist responded that she was also worried about separation from him.
>
> Mrs. B.H. then bitterly attacked her husband for being

aloof and never answering her questions, and she went on in this vein with mounting rage. The therapist said that he actually would miss the hour next week, and offered a make-up session. The patient said that she was not sure that she could arrange it.

In the next session the patient felt well, and described her unnecessary visit to a doctor for her son who had only a mild cold. She recalled a friend with a facial scar who was laughed at by others and ended up in a state hospital. She herself feared going crazy. She could not arrange the make-up session; did the therapist not think that she could make it on her own, she asked.

Briefly, the offer of a make-up hour when there was no emergency need for it evoked in Mrs. B.H. the image of an unnecessarily overprotective therapist-parent who was afraid she might go crazy without his constant care. The patient had sufficient belief in her own capacities, and undoubtedly fears of the therapist's attempt to bind her to him, to refuse the offer; she did well without the hour. Thus, what seemed like a friendly and supportive gesture by the therapist turned out to be anxiety-provoking for the patient because of the seductive and fearful elements in the offer (see Chapter 16).

Note too that this therapist intervened much too soon in the first hour described here, and evoked justified rage when he did not answer the patient's appropriate question regarding the holiday. Then he failed to detect in the material from the patient in the second session the indications that he had erred in offering a make-up session, and did not interpret the fantasies it had evoked in the patient (see Chapters 19 and 22).

PATIENTS' VACATIONS AND BUSINESS TRIPS

At times, patients wish to take vacations during ongoing treatment. There are a number of possibilities as to why such a request will come up. One problem is the patient who cannot get a vacation time which coincides with that of the therapist, often simply because his (or a spouse's) firm has a set vacation policy that leaves him no flexibility. In such instances, after investigating both the reality of the situation and the patient's fantasies, the therapist should accept this reality and not charge the patient for the sessions missed during such a vacation. These sessions can be made up if possible. In fact, sometimes patients who are in such a position are afraid to take a vacation at all and the avoidance must be picked up by the therapist and analyzed. It reflects such problems in the therapeutic alliance as unnecessary dread of the therapist, unrealistic concepts of treatment, and, often, underlying paranoid trends or excessive dependency. Responses to such explorations are usually quite positive and go a long way toward promoting a firm therapeutic alliance.

Another common question for you to consider comes up when a patient simply wants to take time off during the therapy year when you, as the therapist, have no such plans. In my experience, such vacations have always proved to be an acting out against treatment and a reflection of serious resistances and disturbances (often latent) in the therapeutic alliance. For this reason, it is your responsibility in such instances to pursue the analysis of such requests, including their timing and context. This usually reveals the underlying anxieties, conflicts, and hostilities which have set off the wish to temporarily flee treatment. Such vacations are often strongly rationalized and defended in part through some use of reality. Clearly, in such situations, there is no realistic basis on which to forego the patient's responsibility for the sessions; and further, it is necessary to charge for such sessions so that there is no direct or indirect sanction of, or participation in, the acting out involved. This is a crucial principle since patients who use acting out in order to maladaptively "resolve" their conflicts by outer changes, thereby avoiding their inner anxieties and fantasies, have not developed the superego functioning or capacity for delay that is necessary for more adaptive and less destructive resolutions of their problems. Further, they will not learn to do so if the therapist reinforces or gratifies acting out behavior.

Thus, while a therapist may fill an hour when a patient is absent for an unavoidable vacation agreed upon in the ground rules well in advance, he should never fill an hour missed by a patient who is acting out against treatment. To do so is to share in the patient's acting out, inappropriate gratification, and corruption, thereby fostering an anti-therapeutic alliance between the patient and therapist. As a result, the critical analysis and/or confrontations necessary for change in this regard will not occur. Alliances of this kind provide a detrimental narcissistic gratification to the patient and often result in deceptive flights into health and apparent "cures" that cannot prove to be lasting. Ultimately, the underlying guilt and satisfaction over having duped and corrupted the therapist will promote rage at him for permitting or sanctioning such behavior and regression. As a result, further destructive acting out and symptoms will appear.

I have already illustrated the acting out dimensions of vacations taken during ongoing therapy in the vignette regarding Mrs. B.G. Such vacations are typically a response to either the therapist's appropriate absences for holidays or vacations, or the therapist's errors or countertransference-based interventions which hurt, frighten, or are seductive. Quite rarely, they are a flight from emerging unconscious fantasies and memories that terrify the patient.

Thus, it is important to search out the context and unconscious reasons for the announcement by the patient of such vacation plans. The therapist should especially search for his own role in pre-cipitating such acting out, and interpret this factor along with its specific meanings, links to the past, and current misuses that the patient is making of the total situation (see Chapters 21 and 22).

At times, events such as weddings necessitate an out-of-town trip by a patient and the occasional realistic problem of having to miss a session. This is rare except for Saturday hours. In these circumstances, it is advisable to listen carefully to the reality situation and, if there is no detectable acting out, to arrange an alternate hour.

Two brief, but typical, clinical illustrations will demonstrate some of the consequences of not using sound principles of technique and appropriate ground rules to deal with absences of this type:

> Mr. J.H. was a college student who sought therapy because of a multitude of fears and anxieties; he was diagnosed as a severe character disorder with obsessions and phobias. He had been extremely anxious about

therapy, having done poorly with two previous therapists. In his first session he had reported a dream of
missing his hour and of turning, instead, to a newspaper
columnist who gave advice to people with emotional
problems. His fears of the therapist remained intense
during the first month of treatment and he was preoccupied with thoughts that he would not be helped.
The therapist had then made some headway with these
anxieties and the patient calmed down.

After six weeks of treatment the therapist announced
that she would miss an hour the following week and
offered to make an alternative time available to the
patient. He accepted the offer and went on to ruminate
about his anxiety during his sessions and how unsafe he
felt. His mother told him he could terminate if it did not
get better. The therapist seemed too impersonal to him.

In the next hour, he reported fears that a burglar
would shoot him; he was afraid of dying. He was planning
a vacation with his parents for the following week and
would have to miss a session. The therapist offered to
see him on another day and he agreed. He then spoke
of fears of being helpless and unprotected. The therapist
suggested that his feelings related to the therapy, and
Mr. J.H. said that he felt that this therapy situation was
an intrusion on him in some way; in contrast, he felt
uninvolved with his prior therapists. He ruminated about
fears of involvement with his present therapist and of
things ending, including his life.

In the next hour, the session before the one to be
made up for the patient's trip, he reported a dream that
two people had died, one of whom—a public figure—had
actually passed away after the dream. When people leave
him, he fears that they are dead. Again, he spoke of fears
of involvement with the therapist who linked these fantasies and anxieties to her recent absence. The patient
said he felt derailed, confused. If the therapist was wrong,
it would be awful; he thought that she would be angered
by his pending absence.

Mr. J.H. did not come in for his make-up session, nor did he call the therapist. In the next hour, he said that he had forgotten the appointment until it was too late. He was anxious and guilty over having wasted the therapist's time; he expected her to be mad at him. He was afraid that his absence had been a slight to the therapist. His fears of burglars and intruders had intensified and the therapist said that he seemed to see her making up the missed sessions as trapping him and had reacted by distancing himself. The patient said this could be so; he had felt that she had been pursuing him of late.

In this vignette, both make-up sessions seemed to have enhanced the patient's anxieties and fears of the therapist who was seen as an intruder and attacker who would trap and destroy him. As a result, Mr. J.H. acted out and missed the session offered in lieu of his regular hour. Here, the therapist should have explored his trip with his parents as a possible acting out of revenge for her own absence and flight from the anxieties evoked by the therapist's failure to simply cancel the hour she had to miss. The acceptance of this probable acting out and the seductive reward with an alternate hour evoked so much anxiety and fears of being trapped, that the patient resorted to acting out and missing the session in response. Thus, the make-up session was obviously not viewed with gratitude and acceptance.

The therapist's interpretation of the patient's fantasies after these experiences did, however, help to restore calm. In the following hour, further working-through occurred and the paranoid fantasies evoked by these technical errors were traced out and alleviated (see Chaper 22).

Here is another clinical vignette that is related to these issues:

Mrs. J.I. had been in therapy for about one year because of marital problems which had led to a divorce and periods of depression; she had a moderate character disorder. In her agreement with her therapist, she was not held responsible for vacations regardless of when they were taken. There had been an episode with her therapist in which he had accidently brushed against her, and it had evoked considerable anxiety and mistrust over several subsequent sessions, with thoughts of affairs with other men. While the therapist eventually—and quite tentatively—related this material and other disturbing fantasies to his inadvertently touching the patient, the therapeutic situation remained tense.

The patient then cancelled a session because of her job, though the reason seemed vague. In the next hour, she expressed feelings of guilt especially since she had decided to take her son and go on vacation with her present boyfriend, rationalizing that her boss had encouraged her to take some time off. She went on to criticize her boss for his ignorance and his failure to stick to the rules. She was afraid that the therapist would be angry. When the therapist related her vacation to his having broken the rules of therapy, the patient could not see it. When he specifically spoke of his having touched her and how upset she had been, she alluded to her great fears of being touched, even by her father. She gets sexual feelings when she is touched and fears that they are crazy. Recently, she had had a fantasy of marrying a psychiatrist. Her fears were excited when the therapist had touched her; she hadn't been honest with her boyfriend lately. When the therapist becomes so real, she must become unreal.

Briefly, in the session after her vacation, Mrs. J.I. said that she had been anxious on her trip; she had had many thoughts that she couldn't tell the therapist and considered stopping treatment. While away, she had had many fears similar to those she had experienced after the therapist had touched her. She felt especially neglectful of her son, as if she didn't care what happened to him.

In addition to the erotized transference and anxieties evoked by the therapist's physical contact with the patient (see Chapters 6 and 22), this vignette illustrates how vacations that are based on the acting out of unconscious fantasies and resistances to therapy do, indeed, frequently arise in the context of technical errors by the therapist. Mrs. J.I.'s vacation was prompted by the therapist's inadvertent physical contact with her and by his slowness in analyzing her anxious and erotized responses to it based on a father-transference (her father had been openly seductive in her childhood). This culminated in a series of sexual fantasies, and the acting out of a defensive flight from the therapist and from her own inner fantasies.

The therapist's failure to establish ground rules that would not sanction such maladaptive responses in the patient contributed to her acting out. Unconsciously, Mrs. J.I. saw this as neglectful and disinterested "mothering" and as a reflection of the therapist's inability to handle his own problems and those of the patient. This compounded his difficulties in analyzing the entire incident for some weeks and led the patient to feel that she, in turn, had seduced the therapist and fooled him.

An even more difficult problem of this kind, one that is often rationalized very intensely, relates to business trips. Repeated experience has taught me that patients in phases of resistance can very cleverly use and manipulate reality to provide themselves with seemingly unquestionable facades for acting out their resistances against treatment. In principle, one must not forego the fees for such sessions, since this will support the acting out aspects of such business trips to the detriment of the development of insight and the capacity for renunciation. It is also necessary to explore carefully the timing of such travelling, though always with the awareness that it may actually be unavoidable. In interpreting the underlying resistances and fantasies, the therapist should acknowledge the reality where it is present, and then emphasize the way in which the patient is using it. In principle, patients are very often met half-way by reality as they search for means to act out unconscious and conscious fantasies and resistances. However, careful attention to the patient's associations during such times will lead to an understanding of the particular fantasies which are being acted out at the moment.

Some businessmen come to their first session knowing that they will have to travel during certain periods of each year. They expect to either forego the fee for sessions missed in this way, or make up such hours. The therapist must be prepared to be flexible here and not accept such a patient if it appears that he will miss too many sessions or that make-up hours will not be feasible. However, in agreeing to such an arrangement, the therapist must then explore the realities and unconscious fantasies related to each missed session.

A brief vignette will illustrate some of these points:

> Mr. B.I. was a young man in therapy because of marital problems and a series of unsatisfactory affairs. After a long period of treatment, he came to a session and declared that he had to present a series of new products to an important out-of-town client and would miss his two sessions the following week. Since it was the first time this had ever happened, he asked the therapist to excuse him from these hours.
>
> The therapist simply asked the patient to explore it all further. What emerged were associations indicating that the patient was seriously considering another affair at this time and that this was related to the fact that the therapist was planning a vacation. The affair and the business trip were planned as a means of acting out of a number of feelings and fantasies in response to the desertion the patient anticipated. Both revenge and replacement were involved. Later material tied this reaction to the patient's responses to his father, who often left his family for business trips. Correct interpretation of the material led the patient to realize that an affair would be pointless, and that he could actually make his selling trip over a four-day weekend and not miss any sessions if the therapist could shift one hour. Further exploration made this last request appear entirely reasonable and the therapist complied. This served to foster ego growth in the patient by showing him that while neurotic acting out is not supported, realistic and necessary business needs are recognized. No acting out followed and important new material unfolded in subsequent sessions; this confirmed that the situation had been dealt with in an appropriate manner.

Having discussed various issues related to the patient's responsibility for attending sessions, I will now pull together the major principles which have emerged:

1. *Deal with questions of a missed session on two levels.* First, the reality of the cause for the absence and, second, the dynamic aspects related to the conscious and unconscious fantasies, conflicts, genetics, and meanings for the patient. Do this both for the actual absence and for the patient's response to your way of dealing with it.

2. *Decide on responsibility for the hour based on the ground rules mutually agreed upon by the patient and therapist.* Be flexible where reality calls for it, but do not make an exception to the ground rules (a parameter) without careful self-scrutiny and a full exploration with the patient; often these prove to be technical errors unless the situation is entirely unambiguous.

If an exception is indicated and made, explore the meanings of it for the patient and work them through. Be especially wary of sanctioning acting out and creating misalliances through exceptions to the ground rules. When in doubt, do not make a decision in advance; instead, explore the matter with the patient and let the manifest and latent material assist you in recognizing the correct solution. If the therapist discovers that he has erred in making an exception to the fee arrangements, he should explore this finding and be prepared to right the mistake.

3. *Patients who act out via missed sessions must be held responsible for such hours.* The therapist must therefore not see another patient in that time slot since he is not entitled to two fees for a given hour.

4. *The therapist must be alert to countertransference problems in dealing with absences.* These range from unconscious sanctions of acting out that are seductive and corrupt the therapy to punitive charges for those rare hours that the patient must miss without choice.

5. *These problems should be anticipated beforehand by the therapist whenever possible and the patient helped to renounce any acting out along these lines.* This is best done by being constantly on the alert for such behavior and by using the specific material at hand to develop insight and controls. This must be accomplished

through correct interpretations of the underlying fantasies and the inappropriateness of dealing with such fantasies, and the conflicts they reflect, through acting out. Such behavior usually reflects major characterological pathology and constitutes a prime threat to the continuation of treatment; it must take precedence in the therapeutic work, must not be overlooked, and must be thoroughly analyzed. More minor instances can be briefly interpreted so that therapy can return to its usual focus on major life problems.

In analyzing these problems, the therapist must get to specific current and genetic meanings, and not rely on generalities. The context of the acting out is an important clue to its meaning (see Chapter 9). Among such contexts, the therapist must not fail to recognize his own possible contribution to the acting out, whether it was through an error or his correct behavior and/or interventions. This often proves to be a vital part of what precipitates such behavior in the patient; failure to recognize this factor can undermine the exploration and resolution of such problems.

6. *The honest, nonjudgmental, uncorruptible, fair, empathic, and insightful working through of these problems can provide the patient with a strong therapeutic alliance, a step toward renunciation and appropriate controls, a stronger superego, and a model of a "good" therapist with which to identify.*

RECURRENT ABSENCES AND LATENESSES

The principles needed to deal with the problem of recurrent absences or latenesses may be gleaned from the following vignette:

> Mr. B.J. was a young man with a borderline diagnosis in psychotherapy because he was failing in college and tended to date provocative, destructive girls. He also took a variety of drugs with some frequency. From the outset, he was late to his sessions and occasionally absent without justifiable reasons. Initially, the material in his sessions revealed that this behavior reflected conscious reluctance regarding therapy. It also related to his tendencies to act out and to be passively aggressive. In time, the absences clustered around the therapist's vacations,

and the patient ultimately associated it to his mother's illness with rheumatic heart disease when he was three. It emerged that when she had been hospitalized at that time for six months, Mr. B.J. was profoundly depressed and helplessly enraged. This experience also evoked a series of paranoid fantasies that some unknown person was trying to destroy him. Specific interpretations linking his fear of, and rage against, the "deserting" therapist helped to resolve this acting out. Another related factor in this regard was his fear of becoming aware of his inner fantasies, including his murderous, devouring fantasies toward his mother.

We can see that chronic lateness and absence reflects deep characterological problems and responses to critical genetic experiences. Often, it is also based on an identification with a parent who tends to act out or be passive–aggressive and is fostered by unconscious parental sanction which must not be continued by the therapist. Underlying such behavior are specific sources, meanings, and uses for each patient. In general, the therapist should be on the alert with such patients for tendencies to act out, fear of closeness to others, fears of inner fantasies and therapy, difficulties in object relatedness, unresolved narcissistic problems, and paranoid trends that emphasize mistrust of the therapist.

In principle, such behavior constitutes a major resistance and disturbance in the therapeutic alliance and major pathology in the patient. It therefore requires early and repeated interpretations before other therapeutic work can be done. These should be made from the material of each session related to its occurrence. Through this, the specific present usage and meanings of the behavior and its specific genetic roots can be clarified. Included in this working-through are direct, non-moralizing confrontations with the patient's ego and superego dysfunctions and lacunae, including his poor controls, inadequate frustration tolerance, corrupted values, and impairments in relating to others with due consideration for their needs. This work proves essential if the therapy is to succeed. Exploration and modification based on an in-depth understanding of such patients can lead to considerable structural change within the patient and effect the outcome of both his treatment and his life.

Along with the problem of recurrent absences, we may consider the problem of the patient who fails to appear for a given session or two, and does not call. In principle, it is best to not attempt to contact a patient who misses a single session. If a second session is missed, it is advisable to call the patient to clarify the situation and encourage him, should he not want to return at all, to come in for at least one more session to explore his reasons for terminating. In the subsequent session, both the absences or decision to terminate and the patient's reaction to the telephone call must be explored and analyzed. Such occurrences reflect a major rupture in the therapeutic alliance and great resistances; both aspects must be resolved if treatment is to continue. This will prove feasible only if the therapist listens for the context, and manifest and latent content, of the acting out before he intervenes. Unconscious fantasies are crucial determinants of such behavior. Countertransference problems and errors by the therapist often play an important role in such situations; they should not be overlooked (see Chapters 19 and 22). Once the patient is absent, countertransference anxieties, anger, and seductive needs are mobilized in some therapists. These should be recognized and controlled. No attempt should be made to cajole, threaten, or seduce the patient into continuing his therapy. This decision should remain the privilege and right of the patient. The therapist's role is to understand and interpret the conscious, and especially the unconscious, fantasies and reasons on which it is based.

Some therapists feel that a telephone call to an absent patient at any time is seductive and detrimental to the therapeutic alliance and setting. This is undoubtedly true for some patients and, in such cases, a letter notifying the patient of your plans to terminate with him and to use his hours for other purposes is preferred. With others, a telephone call offers the patient an opportunity to reconsider his acting out, and may enable him to continue treatment. Any seductive or dependent fantasies evoked by the call can be subsequently analyzed since the therapist has invoked a parameter. Since it has been done in response to the pathology and needs of the patient, and is justified in reality, analytic resolution of its meaning is potentially feasible.

REQUESTS TO CHANGE HOURS;
LAST-MINUTE CANCELLATIONS

At times, and for varying reasons, patients will request a change in their hour. Sometimes, this will be done well in advance, while at other times, it will be a last-minute request. The following vignette is related to these problems:

> Mrs. L.O. was a depressed woman who was separated from her husband and had a moderate character disturbance. She began one session with a request to change her hour the following week so she could participate in a peace march in Washington, D.C.
>
> The therapist intervened immediately by stating that treatment should be more important to her than the march. The patient responded by becoming angry and then dismissed the topic. She soon shifted to fantasies of being seduced by her boyfriend and ruminated about her annoyance with her children. She then missed the session in question despite the therapist's stance. Her subsequent associations linked her behavior to the material of the two previous sessions, which both she and her therapist had completely avoided. This related to a disturbing part of the patient's neurosis, the current manifestations of her attraction to sadistic men who ultimately hurt her. This had been brought into focus partly through her relationships with her present boyfriend and partly because of provocative, countertransference-based interventions by the therapist—not unlike his response to her request.

In principle, the therapist should have suggested initially that the patient further explore her request for a different hour. He should have then used the time himself to filter through the context in which it was brought up, searching out indications in the recent material for motives to act out and run away from therapy. Simultaneously, he should have considered the appropriateness of the conscious-reality aspects of the reasons offered for the requested shift in the hour. He also should have observed the contiguously associated material that followed this direct discussion by the patient. This latter would have provided clues to the unconscious meanings of the request. His response to it ultimately should have depended on the reality of the need, the extent to which the request seemed to be determined by acting-out motives, and the flexibility of the therapist's schedule.

In this instance, interpretation of the patient's flight from the therapist, who had been inadvertently provocative and was being viewed as sadistic, might have modified the patient's intentions. If not, and the material from the patient indicated that her plans were for a cause that she was strongly and constructively invested in, it would have been best to offer an alternate hour.

Instead the therapist seductively argued with this patient, adding to her motives for flight. He thereby shared in the patient's acting out and no insight was achieved. Even after the absence, some understanding could have been salvaged if the therapist had interpreted the intrapsychic factors contributing to the patient's absence. At the same time, he should have acknowledged his role as a partial evoker of the response. He should also have dealt with her responsibility for her maladaptive use of action to deal with her conflicts; with the resistances, defenses, and other fantasies reflected in the absence; and with the reality of her interest in the march itself, which was then used as a vehicle of these many expressions.

In contrast, consider this brief vignette:

> Mrs. B.K., a borderline woman, cancelled her session by telephone on the day prior to its occurrence. The therapist accepted the cancellation, but only after ascertaining that the patient had unavoidably been given a conflicting appointment by another physician. In the following session, the therapist allowed the patient to further explore the reality of her request. She spontaneously recognized that she could have actually shifted the other appointment. She then searched out the reasons for her behavior. She realized that she had been terrified of the sadistic fantasies which had emerged during the

previous week. The therapist then also pointed out the hostile aspects of the cancellation—in effect, the acting out of sadism. There was no question that the patient was responsible for this missed hour.

It should be rare for a patient to act out after the emergence of previously repressed unconscious fantasies. Mrs. B.K., however, was a borderline woman who tended to act out, and continued to do so despite work with this problem in her treatment. Actually, this episode was part of a turning point in her therapy. The previous work with her acting out enabled her, on this occasion, to observe and then explore what she had done. She was no longer totally involved in such behavior, simply living out, but now began to think about it. She was gratified by the understanding she achieved and this led to considerable improvement in her controls.

In principle, if a patient has a realistic need to change an hour, this should be done whenever possible. Brief attention to the meaning for the patient of this gratification—or frustration, if it is not possible to shift the hour—should follow. Be flexible, realistic, and alert to meanings for yourself and the patient.

The principles for dealing with last-minute cancellations can be gleaned from the following clinical experience:

> Miss B.L. was a borderline teenager in therapy for six months because of poor controls in many areas and periods of depression. She did not come to her second session one week and called her therapist during the hour, frantically apologizing for her absence which she said was unavoidable. The therapist said that he would see her at the next appointed session. Miss B.L. said that she had gotten a job and would not be able to make it. The therapist then offered to see her early the next day.
>
> The patient began that session by describing how she had thought that the therapist had just now made a mistake and was not in his office at the agreed-upon time. It turned out that she had arrived early and was mistaken herself. She then inquired seductively about an attractive male therapist she had seen outside her therapist's office.

A response to an inquiry from the therapist revealed that the patient had missed her session because of a long talk with a girlfriend and could have arrived late, but did not attempt it. She had not expected the make-up session. She then spoke of how she felt that the therapist was often affected by her comments about him, and how she had inadvertly left a letter from a married man out on her desk where her mother had discovered it. She then recalled once seducing an old boyfriend who later jilted her. The therapist said that he felt that the patient was angry at him and behaving destructively.

The following week, the patient allowed herself to be sexually seduced by a therapist at a clinic attended by a girlfriend.

In principle, the therapist should never change an hour at the last minute or after the time has already arrived. Except for dire emergencies which are exceedingly rare, there can be no justification for such a move. Even if the patient's reason for the absence is entirely justified—a flat tire, a sudden illness, or an emergency—he must learn to accept his responsibility for scheduled hours and not be treated as an exception lest this stance undermine the therapy. Many of these cancellations are not justified in reality, but blatantly serve acting-out impulses. This was clearly the situation with Miss B.L., whose absence had been prompted by an intensely erotized transference which the therapist was finding difficult to interpret and resolve, and which he had stimulated to some degree by behavior of the kind reported here. By adding to this transference, the real seduction of providing the make-up hour proved disastrous (see Chapter 22).

Notice that the patient began her replacement session with the theme that the therapist had erred. Her sexual fantasies were then expressed in displaced form; they had been so aroused by the therapist's offer that she had unconsciously found a derivative means of alerting her mother to the situation. She correctly sensed that the therapist was reacting inappropriately to her and had permitted her to seduce him.

Unfortunately, none of this was interpreted to the patient, nor was the error partially corrected by charging the patient for both sessions and using the make-up hour as a substitute for the next session. Failure to acknowledge the error and deal with its many meanings and repercussions for the patient contributed to her subsequent, blatant acting out. For this patient, the therapist's unresolved seductiveness became license for further uncontrolled behavior on her part, in which she remarkably lived out in almost undisguised form the mutually seductive antitherapeutic alliance which had developed in her therapy.

EXCEPTIONS TO THE PATIENT'S RESPONSIBILITIES FOR THE SESSIONS

Basically, any agreement which modifies the patient's total responsibility for the hours set aside for him (or any other aspect of the ground rules) invites flaws in the therapeutic alliance, resistances, and acting out. They are therefore to be avoided. Rarely, as I discussed above, a therapist may agree to be flexible with a patient who must travel for business. This will often be misused by the patient and the acting out will prove difficult to analyze and resolve. Other requests for exceptions prove even less tenable. I will illustrate:

> Mr. B.M. was a borderline single man in his twenties who was depressed and was struggling to not return to active homosexuality, as he had done in the past. He had been in treatment with a therapist who had charged him for all missed hours and there were many, apparently because of the patient's business responsibilities. He had terminated partly because of this issue. In his initial interview with his new therapist, he said that he would enter treatment only if he was not charged for sessions cancelled in advance. The therapist, wanting to provide much-needed therapy for this patient, agreed to this arrangement without exploring its ramifications.
>
> The patient was not absent during the first few months of therapy. After the therapist took his vacation, Mr. B.M. had to cover for vacationing personnel in his

firm and began to miss many hours. Occasionally, he simply overslept.

In the session after both the therapist's vacation and the patient's first cancellation, the patient spoke of the deaths of two friends and his own fears of being old and alone. He had thoughts of traveling to South America with a male friend. When he was forced to take responsibilities at work, he functioned well; in contrast, when his mother let him sleep in the morning, he would miss half a day at work. He was afraid of getting close to people; his homosexuality might be detected.

This excerpt, which contains latent threads both predicted in supervision and repeated in subsequent sessions, reveals some of the unconscious meanings of the deviant ground rules for this patient. It was a means of combating his separation anxieties through denial of need and a repetition of the infantilization and seduction that the patient experienced from his mother. Primarily, it was a defense against latent homosexual transference fantasies which were thereby never confronted and analyzed. In discussing, in supervision, his reasons for agreeing to this arrangement, the therapist alluded to his own anxieties in treating a homosexual patient; this suggests that the therapy was structured in this way as a defense for both parties. This was a misalliance and it prompted repeated absences and chaos.

In principle, the therapist had two choices: to not accept the patient on such a basis, explaining that resolution of the patient's emotional problems would be impossible under such circumstances; or preferably, to suggest that this request, which had so many conscious and unconscious motivations, be fully explored and analyzed before a mutual decision was made as to its feasibility. This would enable the patient to enter therapy and give the therapist ample opportunity to demonstrate the unconscious meanings of the request. The patient could then reasonably understand why such a deviation in the ground rules was not in his best interests. On that basis, and because the therapist understood his anxieties and fantasies, it was likely that the patient would accept treatment on proper terms.

Generally, then, we adhere to the basic ground rules without exceptions; empirically, any other stance courts disaster.

DELINQUENT PAYMENTS

The problems of financially delinquent patients is often a difficult one for the patient and therapist alike. The income of the therapist is involved, posing a real concern and, at times, a real threat for him. Since this is the case, it provides the patient an avenue through which he may really frustrate, annoy, or "harm" the therapist. The resultant real and countertransference problems for the therapist are considerable.

I will begin my discussion of this topic with my own viewpoint and policies in this area. I give my bills for a month's sessions to the patient in the first session of the following month. At one time, I mailed my bills and have found little apparent difference in patient's responses to the two methods. However, I prefer handing the bills to the patient because it is more direct and personal, and avoids any indication on my part that I want to isolate issues related to fees. There are those who do not bill their patients at all, and leave the calculating to the patient; I have no experience with this method, although I see no special problem with it.

I generally expect payment within a few days up to three weeks of billing, and consider anything beyond a month to be tardy. I automatically observe the timing, the manner in which the patient pays me (directly or by mail), and the material from the patient for anything that might relate on any level to the fee. For most patients, payment is a matter of course and does not become part of the therapeutic material or of any significant transference or real conflicts, despite the fact that fantasies about fees are universal. With delays in payment I generally will not bring the problem up if the patient has not alluded to it, unless payment has not been made within a month. I then try to deal with it in the context of the patient's material and without recrimination. Very often, when there have been failures in paying bills, the patient will explain why directly or his associations will clearly relate unconsciously to the problem and to the factors involved on various levels. If the patient is having realistic financial difficulties, I will accept a delay of a month or two, but feel that any extension beyond this point is seductive, unrealistic, overly permissive on my part, and bound to create difficulties for the treatment and for myself. The absence of financial difficulties points to the acting out of serious resistances regarding treatment and to problems in the therapeutic alliance. These must take precedence over other therapeutic contexts, and be explored and then resolved through insight; only then can other aspects of the treatment proceed. As always, these must be investigated in terms of their specific meanings and genetic background for the patient. Most often, such delays reflect a serious disregard for the needs of the therapist (and therefore serious narcissistic problems and difficulties in relating to others), strong tendencies to act out, psychopathic traits, unresolved aggressions, and serious reservations about therapy.

When the parents of adolescents and spouses delay payment, I explore this problem with the patient and expect him to deal with it. This is in keeping with the principles that the therapy should be the responsibility of the patient, and that all resistances and problems which arise through third parties should be his to deal with and resolve. To do so is both ego-building for the patient and constructive in working out problems that he has with the other person; it proves helpful to the latter, as well. The therapist must also endeavor to detect ways in which the patient is promoting or using this recalcitrance in other people and analyze this aspect of the situation. Such difficulties should be exceedingly rare in a well-conducted therapy. When they do occur, the therapist should always check for countertransference problems, even though the patient does not appear to be the person directly involved in the issue.

In principle, the therapist should not call the third person or endeavor to reach him in any other way. This is seductive and infantalizing to the patient and will not have the desired result of prolonging treatment on a sound basis; such maneuvers will actually undermine treatment. There can be no substitute for the patient's responsibility to arrange for and maintain his therapy.

If any payment to the therapist is overdue by two or three months, it is likely that the psychotherapy has not been undertaken on a realistic financial basis. In this situation, there are clear reasons for discontinuing treatment until the patient can afford it or referring the patient to a suitable clinic where he can obtain therapy at a realistic cost. Such an intervention requires very careful exploration on all levels, in regard to the reality problems and to the conscious and unconscious fantasies involved. Adequate time must be allowed for working-through so that such a termination occurs without undue detrimental effects (see Chapter 25). Such terminations are always traumatic and should be extremely rare. They can be prevented by a realistic review of resources in the initial session, especially with those patients with marginal incomes. For patients who have suffered an unexpected diminution of income, hopefully temporarily, the therapist should be prepared to reduce his fee. As we might expect, this real gratification must then be analyzed and fully worked through, but there should be room for such contingencies in everyone's practice.

Mr. B.N. characterizes the type of patient who often gets into difficulties regarding payment of fees. He came to treatment because of numerous affairs that were getting out of hand and a guilt-ridden desire to flee the responsibility of his marriage. Diagnostically, he was considered to be a severe character disorder with acting-out tendencies.

He had requested a reduced fee in his consultation, and examination of the realities had led the therapist to agree to this request. In fact, his ability to handle the lower fee was questioned and explored because of his low income, but he insisted that he could manage it.

During his therapy, he was chronically late in paying his bill. In those periods where this occurred for extended durations, he would avoid direct reference to the problem. Despite this, the themes of his sessions, including his dreams and associations, would repeatedly lead indirectly into this area and enabled his therapist to use the material as a vehicle for exploring the problem and helping him work it through.

In one such instance, he was two months behind in his payments when he dreamt that a waiter spilled liquor on his jacket and in response, the patient demanded compensation. He was then in a casino; he thought he'd like to play dice if he had the money. Associations were to his insatiable wishes to be fed in various ways and to his recurrent avoidance of responsibilities in his marriage. Other associations related to his feeling privileged, and even "the exception" in various situations, and to his interests in gambling.

At this point the therapist intervened using this material and that from previous sessions. He confronted the patient with his most recent failure to pay his fee, suggesting that he felt somehow entitled to free treatment, and that he questioned the value of therapy and saw it as a gamble which he preferred to take without much personal risk.

The patient responded by acknowledging his greed and skepticism, by thinly rationalizing his delay in paying his bill, and by denying that he wanted to provoke the therapist into termination so that he could then feel free to do as he pleased. It was easy to demonstrate the truth contained in this last denial.

In subsequent sessions there emerged, through several dreams, a series of transference fantasies related to each of his parents with whom he felt, and was in reality, severely deprived on many levels. Beneath this was revealed his murderous, vengeful hatred of them. In failing to pay his fee, both his longing for endless gratification and his enormous rage were acted out.

Repeated confrontations of this kind, which included both exploration, interpretation, and the actual setting of limits, beyond which failure to pay his fee would lead to termination of the therapy, helped this patient considerably. As might be expected, his parents had failed to set proper limits for him as a child and adolescent. The therapist's firm stand in this area provided the patient with new controls. His interpretations offered insight which led to new ways of adapting. The total experience was corrective, though not in the sense of "corrective emotional experience" as used by certain psychoanalysts, since this implies role-playing and consciously adopted corrective attitudes. Here the therapist maintained his usual therapeutic stance which happened to differ (as it usually will) from that of the patient's parents, and this helped the patient to modify his behavior. The stance itself was supplemented by correct interpretations; without these, little lasting inner change would occur. In all, the patient developed insight into his manipulation of, and disregard for, others, and developed better capacities to tolerate frustration and to accede to the demands of reality. He paid his bills in time, became more tolerant of his family, and his acting out was markedly curtailed.

Since the variations on this problem are infinite (patients can find incredible rationalizations for delinquent payments), I will conclude this discussion with a brief résumé of the basic principles to be used in dealing with a delinquent payment of fees:

1. *If payment is past due by a month, listen to the material from the patient with this problem in mind as a context for the material.*

2. *From this material, introduce the problem and explore it with the patient.* Beyond a certain point, such as four weeks after billing, this should be done regardless of the material.

3. *This exploration should be on two levels.* It should be conducted in terms of the reality on which the delinquency is based, and in terms of the conscious and unconscious meanings and ramifications for the patient.

4. *Flexibility should prevail regarding realistically founded delays in payment.* If the therapist temporarily forgoes payment, the meaning of his stance for the patient should be understood and interpreted from his associations.

5. *Realistic limits beyond which it is detrimental to both the patient and therapist for the bill not to be paid must also be established when necessary.* Failure to set such a limit (for example of two or three months' fees where it is clear that the financial problem is a temporary one or one or two months, if there is no clear sign of possible resolution) provides such inappropriate gratifications for the patient as indulgence, lack of proper limits, permission to manipulate and act out, disregard for the demands of reality, the fulfillment of pathological grandiose fantasies, and sadistic gratifications. It is also an inappropriate sacrifice on the part of the

therapist which has overtones of self-demeaning submission, a need to suffer, guilt over what he is offering to the patient as a therapist, the need to seduce or be overly-permissive, an inappropriate need for the patient, a need to be the all-giving mother-breast and to share with the patient unconscious neurotic fantasies of this kind, and fears of being strong or appropriately aggressive. Limits should be set firmly and in a kindly manner, and the patient's reaction to them explored. Often, the patient's associations offer expressions of his recognition of the need for such limits and the consequences of not establishing them (for example, a dream of a dishonest cop who ignores a traffic violator). Be alert to these and use them to show the patient his own awareness of the implications of what he is doing and his understanding of your response to it.

6. *Be on the alert for countertransference reactions in these situations.* Often, there is considerable conscious or unconscious hostility toward such patients, as well as specific anxieties and vulnerabilities set off by delayed payment of fees. Stay in tune with such responses so that they are not acted out with the patient.

GIFTS FROM THE PATIENT TO THE THERAPIST

The offer of gifts or compensation beyond the therapist's fee on the part of the patient may occur during the course of treatment, although it most often comes up at the time of termination (see Chapter 25) and with patients who are seen in clinics. These gifts range from subtle conscious or unconscious verbal presents of material sought out by the therapist to concrete objects offered to him. The former are to be detected, explored, and analyzed. As to the latter, let us begin our discussion of such gifts during ongoing treatment with three clinical vignettes:

> Mrs. B.O. was a borderline woman in therapy for episodes of anxiety and depression. After three months of intensive therapy, there was evidence of an erotized transference, with guilt and rage at her therapist and herself. At a time when her mistrust of doctors was being traced to several early medical traumas and to her fears of her mother, she came to a session with a magazine

which contained an article on psychotherapy. Rather than accept the patient's suggestion that she give it to him so that he could read it, the therapist suggested that Mrs. B.O. explore her offer. She was annoyed at first, but then spoke of not being able to give of herself; the magazine was a substitute for her. It was a way of holding onto the therapist's hand. The therapist pointed out that the patient could tell him about the article and thereby avoid the inappropriate contact involved, and the patient felt angry and hurt.

In the next hour, Mrs. B.O. reported that she had dreamt of a food market near the therapist's office. In the dream, she filled her basket with too much food. Then, the manager insisted that she borrow money from him.

The patient linked the dream to her offer of the magazine and said that she felt relieved that the therapist had refused to take her crap and be manipulated by her. She then went on to explore her feelings of emptiness and reviewed some of her painful childhood deprivations.

Acceptance of this gift would have meant to this patient that she was viewed by the therapist as empty and as a sexual object. If he had accepted the patient's "feeding," he would have been indebted to feed her in return. A misalliance would have been created and no modification of these inappropriate needs or the patient's pathological self-image could follow.

Miss H.E. was a young woman in therapy for six months because of episodes of depression and a sense of not being able to establish a lasting relationship with a young man. Her therapy had been characterized by many periods of rumination on her part which the therapist had not been able to analyze or modify; there had also been a ruminative preoccupation with what the therapist thought of her. There had been little sense of movement.

In one session as Christmas drew near, the patient spoke of not wanting to come for her hour, of feeling depressed, of relating only to people who reach out for her, and of feeling remote. The therapist related her distance to his having pressured her the previous hour and she denied feeling upset about him. His usual silences were like those of a judge, and she felt angry but shouldn't; it all was nothing.

The patient came to the next session with a sketch of a warm, personless sunset by the water that she had done; it was a gift for the therapist. The therapist suggested that Miss H.E. explore her offer and she spoke of the holidays and wanting to give him a present; he takes a lot of crap from her. She is always tense; the painting shows her calm side. One of her girlfriends gave her a gift with a love note; the patient was confused by it, like she is in her sessions. Her mother is overly critical and creates doubts in her about herself. Love bonds make worries go away.

The therapist said that he saw the gift as an attempt to bypass the problems that they were having in therapy, but the patient disagreed and did not want to take the gift back—it would be a rejection of herself. The therapist said that he felt it would be incorrect for him to accept the gift and suggested that she take it with her or explore it further. Miss H.E. left without the painting.

The sketch was on the therapist's desk at the beginning of the next hour. The patient was still undecided about taking it back, but had felt that the therapist had cared about her in the last session. She understood his reasons for not accepting the sketch and weighed them against her feelings of rejection. She recalled a former boyfriend, who was now married, and wondered about having an affair with him; would he sleep with her? The therapist linked these thoughts to the offer of the painting, saying it seemed like a romantic offer, and the patient responded that his comment made sense and maybe she would take it back next time.

In the next hour, she described for the first time in her therapy the development of a positive and gratifying relationship with a relatively new boyfriend. She had decided to take her painting back. It was too much like the way she used to make deals with fellows to get them to show that they cared for her. She felt that the therapist had showed more concern for her by not accepting the gift than if he had done so. She left with the painting.

In this vignette, we see how the offer of the gift was associated with inappropriate seductiveness and attempts to appease a rejecting mother. Refusal of the gift fostered an analysis of its unconscious meanings and when these were interpreted to her in part, the painting was accepted back. The positive effects of conveying an acceptance of the patient for herself and no expectation of special compensation is reflected in the integrative dimension of the patient's relationship with her new boyfriend.

Consider, in contrast, the following situation:

Mrs. B.P. was in once-weekly psychotherapy because she wanted to kill herself and was having difficulty controlling that impulse. Her marriage was very poor and offered her virtually nothing but recurrent battles, but she was too terrified to leave her husband. As a child, her mother had once attempted unsuccessfully to kill herself and her entire family. The patient was diagnosed as an ambulatory schizophrenic, who, at times, lost all motive for living. When her therapist worked with her on the absurdity and destructiveness of maladaptively attempting to "solve" her problems by killing herself, Mrs. B.P. would attack him verbally or withdraw and attempt to not listen, trying to provoke him into giving up on her. She often stated that she could not trust him or anyone. She tried to goad him into being the destructive mother figure whom she could then hate and use to further condemn herself. At the same time, she feared any closeness with the therapist; to trust him would lead to betrayal. Despite this, she gradually came to understand that he really wanted her to live and really could be trusted, and this sustained her through several life crises.

There was a period of intense suicidal preoccupation

in which she was seriously on the verge of attempting to kill herself. The therapist's work on the underlying factors and the unreality of her "resolution" was met with many verbal assaults. After a while, however, the patient brought the suicidal impulses under control, and discarded some of the pills she had collected for this purpose. At this point, she brought her therapist a cigarette holder, since he smoked during the sessions. When asked, she refused to discuss it other than to say that she realized it was a peace offering and an expression of gratitude over the therapist's persistent belief that she deserved to live.

The therapist accepted the gift despite the fact that further exploration was impossible at the time. He kept the gift in mind as a context for his listening to the patient in subsequent sessions, mindful of the fact that he had permitted a parameter which eventually had to be explored, analyzed, and resolved to whatever extent feasible (Eissler, 1953). Material from later sessions indirectly indicated that the patient viewed the therapist's response as an acceptance of herself and support for that part of her personality that wanted to live. Other material suggested that rejection of the gift would have been viewed as a condemnation and total rejection, and equated with the responses of her mother who wished to kill her. It was felt, and confirmed, that this patient needed concrete evidence of the therapist's acceptance of her, without which she might not survive.

All three of these decisions by the therapists treating these patients proved sound. How can we reconcile them and establish some working guidelines? The following is an attempt to do so:

1. *With certain specific and rare exceptions, an offer of a gift from a patient should be handled by delay of acceptance and analyzing its meaning and implications for the patient.* Hopefully, this will lead the patient to withdraw the offer; if not, the gift ultimately should be refused and the patient's reactions to this explored. Most often, the initial exploration makes it clear to both the patient

and therapist that it is inappropriate to accept the gift, and insight into the specific timing, context, and meanings of the offer is achieved.

2. *Accepting the gift will have real consequences and meanings for the patient and therapist.* (See Chapter 25, where termination gifts are discussed and many of these meanings are further documented.) The accepted gift is a denial of the appropriate boundaries of therapy and an acceptance of a special gratification. In reality, this means that the patient is not expected to renounce inappropriate and forbidden instinctual drive wishes and is granted sanction to bypass or violate such appropriate controls and limits; he may, therefore, as an exception, gratify all such needs. Thus, in treatment, he need not analyze but may act; in real life he need not accept limits, but may do as he pleases. The unconscious fantasy related to this meaning of the accepted gift is often that of a violation of the incest barrier and a gratification of incestuous wishes; more primitive oral, anal, and phallic level fantasies are also involved. In terms of the ego, it is a failure to renounce or find suitable, conflict-free avenues of gratification; it therefore promotes immediate discharge in terms of narcissistic needs without regard for the object.

The accepted gift is a shared corruption (patient and therapist deny the appropriate enforcement of superego sanctions). It is also a shared defense which usually includes a denial of rage, a denial of an appropriate degree of separateness, and a denial of the appropriate therapeutic relationship, including the agreed-upon fee.

The accepted gift is an attempt to form a pathological narcissistic misalliance and union, usually with a mother-figure, or a symbolic attempt to live out pregnancy fantasies, rather than resolve the related separation anxieties. It undermines the basic model and climate of therapy which should be an endeavor to move toward insight, verbalization, inner change, and ego maturation. It is a regressive gratification in mutual acting out; one can hardly expect the patient to afterwards attempt the far more difficult tasks of delaying gratification of needs and facing himself. Furthermore, attempts to repeat such gratifications inevitably follow. Lastly, since such problems are always related to the patient's symptoms, resolution of these is unlikely or impossible under such conditions.

Beyond these general meanings and consequences, the therapist must find the specific meanings and genetic roots of such offers for each patient. A common genetic factor is an overtly seductive or rejecting parent who never set appropriate limits for the patient. For example, Mrs. B.O.'s father had bathed her well into her late childhood and had been seductive in other ways, while her mother had been extremely rejecting and punitive. The gift that she offered to her therapist was both something her father would readily accept, and something that she longed to share with her mother.

3. *No "rule" can be enforced rigidly.* The situation with Mrs. B.P. called for the therapist to accept the gift. For this patient, there was a risk of suicide should the therapist not accept the gift. Such a risk is unjustified in these circumstances. Refusal of the gift would be equated in a very real sense to this schizophrenic patient with rejection, not as an abstract concept, but as a concrete rebuff and narcissistic hurt, meaning to her that the therapist hated her and wished her dead.

Since this is a patient whose mother in reality attempted to kill her, it follows that, at times of crisis, she must be responded to with evidence of acceptance by the therapist, within appropriate limits. This is often true of schizophrenic and borderline patients. However, such acceptance should, as a rule, be restricted to verbalized and feeling-based interventions. Only such emergencies as the dire risk of suicide can justify deviation from this stance, lest the therapist become too seductive and overly gratifying. Severe psychopathology per se is not a justification for a deviation from the ground rules and, in fact, can create chaotic misalliances and regressions in the patient.

This patient could not experience the realization that the therapist was not angry with her and did not hate her without concrete evidence. The gift itself was a token one. Later, when the patient could tolerate it, some of the meanings of the gift were explored and analyzed, as they must always be in such a situation. During the session, the therapist explored his own feelings and fantasies in response to the offered gift. He detected no countertransference need for the gift, felt he could tolerate the added closeness implied, and decided that, in reality, acceptance was indicated. Nothing in his or the patient's associations indicated otherwise. This is an essential step if a deviation in technique is to be undertaken.

4. *If gifts are offered more than occasionally, the therapist must look for some hidden problem which is not being analyzed, including countertransference difficulties.*

In closing this discussion, let me reiterate that gifts can be accepted only in extraordinary circumstances. The fact that a patient is borderline or schizophrenic, and thinks and experiences concretely, is not an indication for acceptance. Actually, not accepting a gift and working through the entire experience can provide crucial models of controls, appropriate distance, self-worth, and of frustration tolerance, and aid the patient in accepting more abstract indications of concern from the therapist and others. Finally, as previously discussed in Chapter 4, the offer of a referral by a patient should be viewed as a proposed gift, and dealt with in accordance with the principles developed in this section.

GIFTS FROM THE THERAPIST TO THE PATIENT

Except in the treatment of children, which is beyond the province of this book, concrete gifts should never pass from the therapist to the patient. More subtle gifts are reflections of countertransference problems. Gifts from the therapist to the patient for birthdays, weddings, and other special events are seductions, mutual acting out, inappropriate narcissistic gratifications, symbolic babies and representations of union, and denials of depressive affects and appropriate, necessary boundaries and limits. They are a direct counterpart of gifts from the patient to the therapist, but the corruption and undermining of therapy is even more intense because it is the therapist who has initiated the offer and created the misalliance. They are a firm reminder that everything that the therapist does in his relationship with the patient has significance, and that certain behaviors on his part undermine all hope of insight therapy and inner change for the patient. If the therapist is a real model of corruption and inappropriate gratification and involves his patient in such antitherapeutic alliances, the painful and frustrating search for self-knowledge will be discarded in favor of acting out. While there may be an initial elation in the patient (and therapist) in response to such presents, rage, regression, depression, and ultimate failure to resolve problems in a lasting way are bound to follow.

Certain types of borderline patients, severe acting-out characters, and psychopaths have a knack of challenging one or more of the ground rules and of finding some reality with which to do so. One must be alert to such potential seductions. Most often they are expressed through some rationalized request to borrow a book or magazine. Unconsciously, a loan is equated with a gift and carries with it all that the latter implies.

> Mrs. B.Q. was in therapy at a clinic and tended to act out. She finished her session with her therapist and, upon leaving, discovered that she lacked carfare home. She asked to borrow a dollar from the clinic receptionist, who lent the dollar to her.
>
> In the next session the patient mentioned the incident and then reported a dream: the receptionist and she were feeding and fondling each other. Associations related to the borrowed dollar and Mrs. B.Q.'s mother who had, in contrast, been cold and punitive, especially at meal times.

The principles for dealing with situations of this kind have already been established. The therapist must first assess the reality of the need, including the consequences for therapy if it is granted, and if it is not. Then he must analyze with the patient the request itself, both in regard to its meaning and the reactions to his handling of it. If possible, this should be done before he makes his decision and certainly, after that decision has been made. At such times, every effort must also be made to tune in on any possible countertransference reactions and problems in handling the matter or, at times, contributing to its occurrence. These may occur in either direction, in tending to be too giving and prone to discard necessary boundaries and limits, and in being unnecessarily and unrealistically restrictive.

As for the situation under discussion, if confronted with such a last-minute request, I would recommend the following: Inquire as to the reality of the need and the possibility of alternative solutions. Then, an interpretation should be made based on the material of the session, on the timing, and on the conscious and unconscious meanings of the request. This would include references to the dynamics of the conflict involved, as well as the "ego aspects," the patient's waiting until the last minute to make the request, her placing the therapist in a damned-if-you-do and damned-if-you-don't situation, the bypassing of the exploration of the request, and the fact that something (perhaps already defined) was being acted out instead of controlled and analyzed. The disadvantages of "acting-out solutions" as compared to other solutions which rely on thought and delay also deserve mention; undoubtedly, the therapist could remind the patient of examples of the unfortunate consequences of such behavior from previous work in the therapy.

In principle, unless the situation is urgent and the patient's plight severe, it is best to adhere to the ground rules and not gratify such requests. In exceptional circumstances (and these should be rare), the therapist may have to accede to it, lest he be unduly sadistic and turn away from the patient who is in a crisis situation. In doing so, however, he must let the patient know that the meanings and repercussions of this experience will have to be explored thoroughly since it could otherwise jeopardize treatment. In the following sessions, it would be urgent to listen to and interpret the material in terms of the incident. In particular, its current meanings in regard to the treatment and the transference would receive primary consideration; the genetic roots and ties to outside problems would then follow.

Returning to Mrs. B.Q., her therapist unfortunately confined his intervention to an interpretation of her longings to convert the receptionist into a mother figure. This simplistic use of dynamics failed to deal both with the transference meanings of the event and its maladaptive aspects. Furthermore, it promoted both a split in the transference, dividing it between the therapist and the receptionist (a "misuse" of clinic personnel), and a perpetuation of unanalyzed transference fantasies and acting out.

Actually, the context and timing of this behavior by the patient indicated that the therapist had also failed to recognize that she was attempting to deny the impact of a pending vacation that the therapist had announced to her. The patient's attempt to deny her sense of depression and loss by possessing a part of the therapist, through his secretary, should have been interpreted to her, along with the confrontation that the patient lived out these needs directly.

The therapist on his part seems to have been defensively deflecting the focus away from himself and sharing with the patient the denial of the pending separation and her transference and reality-based feelings and fantasies toward him.

In general, then, the therapist must think quickly and on several levels when the patient requests something beyond the therapist's verbal interventions. Direct or indirect requests to extend a session are another common expression of this kind. It must be handled with the same principles developed for other types of gifts; with refusal and analysis.

Some final remarks on this subject:

1. *Some offers and requests are more common in psychotic and borderline patients who wish to make the therapist "a real object."* That is, they wish to obtain gratifications from him that extend beyond those appropriate to his role as a therapist. These represent attempts to concretize the constantly threatened positive aspects of the relationship and to deny any underlying hostility and sense of separateness. Participation by the therapist, however mistaken, confirms the need for extraordinary gratifications on the part of both participants, and fails to help the patient find more suitable means of reassurance and relatedness, and to work through and resolve his rage and mistrust.

2. *The presentation of a gift from a patient to a therapist can almost always be prevented by detecting such an intention from the material and analyzing it in advance of the offer.* The narcissistic hurt is always greater when a gift at hand, rather than in thought, is involved. Failure to anticipate such events and difficulty in dealing with them suggest countertransference problems.

3. *Ancillary personnel should be taught to consider these maneuvers on the part of patients as an integral part of treatment.* Whenever possible, they must allow the therapist to handle it and keep him informed of all such incidents.

4. *The inappropriate gratifications in gifts serve as a reminder of the appropriate gratifications available to the patient and therapist in therapy.* For the former, this includes above all the lasting resolution of his emotional problems and, for the latter, the satis-

faction of significantly contributing to such an outcome and an appropriate fee for his services (see Chapter 22).

With these comments, I conclude my discussion of issues related to fees, gifts, and responsibility for the sessions on the part of the patient and therapist. The complexity of the therapeutic problems which can arise in these connections, the difficulties that they present for both parties and the readiness with which they become the vehicle for transference and countertransference expressions, their pervasive influence on the therapeutic alliance and the entire therapy, and the manner in which they reflect the patient's pathology have all been documented. The analysis of deviations in these dimensions of the ground rules takes precedence over virtually all other therapeutic tasks and is especially paramount when the therapist has contributed to them; this is vital to the restoration of a proper therapeutic atmosphere.

Having dealt with these aspects of the ground rules, we can now turn to the other facets of this basic understanding and explore their implications for psychotherapy.

6 The Ground Rules of Psychotherapy: Additional Considerations

MAJOR DECISIONS DURING THERAPY

The patient's handling of major decisions which arise in the course of his therapy is a vital aspect of the basic therapeutic agreement, one that lays the foundation for handling acting out during treatment and creates a most important model of delay and scrutiny for the patient. In structuring treatment toward the end of the initial hour, the therapist should tell the patient that he is now entering a therapy where everything should be explored and analyzed, and that this will particularly apply to major life decisions.

This tenet is basic to insight therapy. Here I shall concern myself with the reasons for this, and the main problems that arise. The following points are salient:

1. *Many patients seen in psychotherapy today have significant tendencies to act out.* That is, they deal with anxieties and intrapsychic conflicts by seeking "solutions" in behavior—action—that is often not thought out in advance, nor based on conscious deliberation, analysis, and decision. Such acting out is usually destructive to the patient and those around him (that is, it is maladaptive), and to insight therapy too. Further, it reflects difficulties in secondary-process, reality-oriented thinking and functioning, in which the capacity for adequate delay and full consideration of reality is

central. These essential functions are impaired to some extent in every neurosis; in therapy, we attempt to create a setting which will promote their development in every possible way. Thus, we invoke this rule first, as a model for the patient and in an effort to help him develop these capacities.

2. *By introducing this rule we create a necessary frustration that limits the motoric discharge of unconscious fantasies and thereby enhances the likelihood that the patient will bring into consciousness verbalized derivatives of these impulses and wishes—fantasies that he might otherwise conceal or avoid.* Acting out, repression, and denial go hand-in-hand. These avoided fantasies and impulses are therefore of two kinds: those that are blatantly acted out without full awareness of their meanings, and those that the patient cannot mention in therapy for fear of living them out, these will emerge only when controls are assured. For example, a seemingly devoted wife who is nonetheless unhappy with her marriage might conceal her discontent and her thought of an affair or divorce for fear of doing something which might be destructive, disruptive, and anxiety- and guilt-provoking. On the other hand, a more action-prone woman might quickly live out such fantasy-impulses and find a lover, much to the detriment of her life and therapy. Of course, other unconscious factors, including transference and genetically determined fantasies, also contribute to such behavior. The requirement that such notions and plans must be analyzed before they are acted upon enables both kinds of patients to face these feelings and fantasies with the knowledge that they will be assisted in not acting prematurely and will not be encouraged to act.

3. *This rule promotes verbalization of conflicts and fantasies, thereby permitting exploration, insight, resolution, renunciation, and working through.* It tends to diminish those forms of acting out that undermine the constructive aspects of treatment. Further, at critical moments in the patient's life or in the therapy, the patient is encouraged to explore, analyze, and ultimately resolve, rather than to live out as he might otherwise do. As a result, the conscious and unconscious meanings of the particular situation, including the underlying fantasies and genetics, are all likely to be revealed, and the patient is actually in a strategic position from which to resolve the problem at hand. Crucial inner change through insight will be

a major part of this type of resolution, fostering this major goal in treatment.

4. *Acting out may also be viewed as an attempt at self-cure; it is, therefore, disruptive to the therapeutic alliance and alien to insight-oriented therapy.* Acting out is most commonly seen in psychopathic patients, who are particularly manipulative, and in borderline, narcissistic, or psychotic patients, who have poor controls. With such patients, the therapist must be especially alert to these problems and prepared to deal with them as a central issue if they arise; their resolution is essential for a proper therapeutic atmosphere.

Several cautions are essential in explicating this ground rule:

5. *The patient's autonomy, his right to make his own decisions, and the vital necessity that he learn to do so, must be accepted and protected by the therapist.* The latter should not use the exploration of major decisions to direct or guide the patient into a particular path or to control the patient in any way. Unless dire outcomes are probable—and these should be interpreted first before other measures are taken—the patient should find his own way. Attempting to manipulate a patient is a common pitfall, one that is bound to be destructive since it deprives him of his relative independence. If we are to foster the patient's ego development and constructive potential, and if we do not wish to infantilize him or use him to gratify our own narcissistic needs, we must never make these important life decisions for him. To do so promotes helplessness, dependency, and feelings of being used, and involves a kind of seductiveness that can only undermine insight psychotherapy and the patient's quest for optional adaptive functioning. Beyond this, making such decisions for the patient creates a situation where the therapist is, on the one hand, vulnerable to the patient's well-deserved rage should the decision he imposes be a poor one; on the other hand, he makes his patient unrealistically indebted to him if the decision works out.

The therapist must be essentially unbiased and prepared to explore and analyze all sides of a decision. In this context, he can, when the material and reality warrants it, point out the various major risks and consequences of a particular choice that the patient is considering. Mainly, however, his job is to interpret from the patient's material the conscious, unconscious and genetic meanings of each course under consideration; he should not make the ultimate choice for the patient, nor should he even suggest what it might be.

6. *Certain kinds of nondestructive acting out have adaptive and constructively experimental aspects to them.* The therapist must not encroach upon the patient's right to, and need for, such behavior; he must interpret its pathological dimensions and leave the rest to the patient. There is a delicate balance here between interpretation and appropriate license, and the therapist should, in general, permit the patient as much freedom and lack of encroachment as feasible without entailing the risks of behavior that will endanger the patient, others, or the therapy.

7. *Such actions are to be viewed as meaningful communications —a facet that must not be overlooked.* Their implications, often grandiose, seductive, or destructive, are to be understood and eventually integrated into the patient's understanding of himself.

8. *Some patients abuse this rule—any of the ground rules may be misused or utilized for resistance—by delaying critical life decisions beyond all reasonable time for exploration in therapy.* This too must be detected, explored and interpreted. Failing to act or decide is itself a decision, and is often a form of passive-aggression and resistance, directed at both the therapist and others.

With these principles in mind, let us turn to two brief vignettes which exemplify their application:

> When he entered treatment, Mr. B.R. was considering one of several affairs, the possibility of divorce, and a move to another country. Diagnostically, he suffered from a severe character disorder with psychopathic trends. These alternatives were all in the direction of external, environmental change and entailed the potential acting out of various unresolved conscious and unconscious fantasies. His only conscious reason for seeking treatment was that he was becoming aware that in the past, such efforts had failed to resolve his anxieties and conflicts. At every critical turn in his treatment and with every revelation regarding his underlying, anxiety-ridden fantasies, he was ready to act out and leave treatment in favor of one of his external "solutions." But following the ground rule

of exploring major decisions, the patient realized very
early in his therapy that this tenet was there to aid him
in delaying instances of acting out that could be catastrophic. Each time he recognized a little more clearly the
need to hold still and to explore his inner motivations and
fantasies, and new insights into himself emerged. For
example, from derivatives which emerged in dreams and
his associations, he soon became aware that underneath
his intense love for the various women in his life was a
whole series of sadistic fantasies in which he imagined
himself raping and murdering them. This insight enabled
him to understand that no matter where he fled, if he
failed to resolve his underlying sadistic fantasies (which
were later traced in part to primal scene experiences and
to unresolved rage against his mother), his life would be
an unendurable series of destructive episodes.

Mrs. B.S. came into treatment with extreme feelings
of depression, primarily because her marriage was un-
successful and there were constant fights with her husband. She was a borderline patient with depressive
features. During the course of her treatment, she recognized as one source of these battles the fact that the had
an entirely depreciated and inadequate self-image, and
allowed her husband to demean her in every conceivable
way. As she began to wish for a more adequate relationship with a man, she faced the problem of whether she
should work things out with her husband or get a divorce.
Initially, the decision was an unbearable one for her, with
much ambivalence and conflicting arguments. She repeatedly attempted to manipulate her therapist into
making the decision for her. Through his steadfast insistence that his role was to help the patient analyze every
aspect of her relationship with her husband and every
dimension of her decision, conscious and unconscious,
present and past, the patient gradually came to realize
that it was a choice that she could make for herself. This
meant, she realized, that she was not as inadequate and

helpless as she had believed. Furthermore, the need to make this decision led her to explore many previously unreported factors in her emotional illness, especially genetic dimensions related to her conflicts with her father, and a number of previously unreported unconscious fantasies related to her husband and other men, such as her view of men as rapists and murderers. With the added insight into the way her past experiences and inner fantasies were influencing her, she was able to arrive at a decision which she then explicated over the ensuing months.

This material demonstrates the ways in which delay accompanied by analysis of major decisions is essential to the discovery of the critical unconscious factors in the dilemma and in the patient's neurotic behavior and symptoms. This ground rule also assists in the creation of a therapeutic atmosphere and alliance through which such work becomes feasible. It must be reinforced by the therapist's conscious and unconscious unconflicted utilization of these principles of technique.

Failures to properly explicate this ground rule usually stem from the therapist's own unresolved propensities for acting out. These lead him to support the patient's flights into behavior and to difficulties in helping the patient verbalize. Premature termination of therapy is a not uncommon outcome (see Chapter 25).

THE FUNDAMENTAL RULE OF FREE ASSOCIATION

In this case, "free association" refers not to some idealized concept of a patient talking without resistances or restraint—a situation that probably does not ever occur—but to the therapist's expectation that the patient will say everything that comes to his mind in his therapy sessions, without exception.

This whole topic is a source of considerable confusion. In psychotherapy, free association evokes the greatest possible number of derivatives of unconscious fantasies and memories, and the clearest expressions of the patient's intrapsychic conflicts. While there are

those who view psychotherapy as conversational rather than oriented to free association (see Wallerstein, 1969, for a discussion of this
question), I believe that it is feasible for patients to approximate this
latter manner of communicating and that this produces the most
effective analytic work and best therapeutic results.

The therapist need not spell this rule out—to the effect that the
patient says everything that comes to mind—in the initial session,
particularly with a verbal patient. With tactiturn patients, however,
in the first and in subsequent early hours, at moments of silence or
other impediments in the flow of material, he can delineate this
rule to the patient and eventually, if necessary, analyze the sources
of any interference in the patient's capacity to comply with it (see
also Chapter 23). I prefer putting it something like this: "In therapy,
say everything that comes to mind, regardless of what it is." Later,
I may add that "Saying everything insures that we will get to know
you most fully and it will provide us with what we need to understand your problems." It may also prove useful to comment on the
need to avoid censoring, and to note that one can never tell in
advance what will prove to be meaningful.

Once the patient understands this, recurrent silences, conscious
concealing, perseverance of one type of material, and frequent
omission of certain kinds of material (e.g., present realities, past
experiences, fantasies, and dreams) must be considered crucial
resistances and reflectors of impairments in the therapeutic alliance; they must, as material permits, be brought into focus and
analyzed. Each leaves a serious void in the therapeutic work and
reflects important pathogenic unconscious fantasies, defenses, and
character traits. Each is overdetermined, consciously and unconsciously, and is based on a multitude of transference, real, and
genetic factors, and should be worked through on all levels. I shall
briefly discuss each of these impediments to a free flow of material
from the patient.

SILENCES

The following vignette brings this problem into focus.

> Miss B.T. came for consultation under pressure from
> her parents, who were upset at her inability to hold a job

and her erratic social life. She planned to go to another city with her current boyfriend, but agreed to see a therapist because she was troubled by her inability to get along with her parents. In the initial hour, she was silent for long periods, insisting that the therapist talk or ask her questions.

The therapist became more active, but the patient remained withdrawn, critical of him, and relatively silent. He attempted also to empathize with her deep mistrust and the fear of him she had especially when he was silent. He also emphasized that he could not guess where the patient's problems lay and that what he could tell her depended on what she told him. The session ended on an uncertain note but the patient returned, and the initial phase of her therapy centered on clarifying her own use of silences. Briefly, the following proved most central: first, a dread of revealing herself, including a dread of her initially unreported symptoms, such as severe bowel and digestive disturbances, and multiple phobias; a great fear of her primitive inner fantasy life; a deep mistrust of the therapist (her parents were often sadistically silent, extremely destructive, and unpredictable); intense denial of her problems; and a deep narcissistic disturbance.

Silences in patients are a complex problem and have been the subject of considerable psychoanalytic study (see the recent paper by Blos, 1972, and Chapter 11). The specific roots and meanings of silences must be traced out with each patient; here I will offer some broad general guidelines:

1. *Since they are often both a major resistance and nonverbal form of expression, silences should be brought into focus as early in treatment as possible.* If they are frequent, the therapist should listen to the material from the patient with the context of the silences in mind, and then try to interpret their meanings and uses.

2. *Silences serve both as gratifications and defenses, and reflect a hierarchy of unconscious fantasies.* With Miss B.T., for example, the silences expressed in addition to the resistive and aggressive meanings, a fantasy of blissful union with the therapist, expressed in

terms of a mother-transference. Thus, silences may express fantasies as diverse as sexual union or aggressive combat. There are always specific life experiences at the roots of silences, and these must be clarified along with their current uses and meanings.

Defensively, silences, by breaking the flow of free associations, conceal unconscious links and fantasies as well as conscious thoughts, and serve to deny the need for the therapist and treatment.

3. *Silences are most often utilized by borderline, narcissistic, and more severely disturbed patients, those with fragile egos and weak defenses, and those who tend to act out.* They often reflect intense mistrust and paranoid trends, poor object relationships, and intense wishes for aggrandized ties; they also suggest severe traumatization in the past. They may be related to aggressive and sexual fantasies about the therapist, and often indicate an instinctualization of the therapeutic relationship which contains strong aggressive or sexual elements for the patient (see Chapters 20 and 21). The fantasies of such patients about treatment and the therapist are intensely colored by conscious destructive or sexual fantasies, and these are defended against, and gratified, by the silences so that the constructive aspects of the therapeutic alliance are seriously impaired. In these patients, silence is also often used as a primitive defense against anxiety-provoking and guilt-related needs for condemnation and punishment.

4. *Silences are often a stubbornly maintained resistance.* It is, therefore, vital that the therapist be patient, empathic, and understanding of them, that he not react countertransferentially with anger, condemnation, directives, or by talking too much. With silent patients, the therapist must be relatively more active and prepared to communicate nonverbally, but the primary responsibility to talk must be the patient's. Modification of the use of silences by a given patient as a result of growing trust of the therapist, insight, working through, and inner change is often accompanied by considerable personality and symptomatic change as well.

5. *Many paranoid and narcissistic patients see the therapist's relative silence as primitively destructive, and reflecting omnipotent annihilating powers.* Their own silence is, in part, a talion revenge and in part, a defensive withdrawal. Other patients dread any moment of silence and see it as a malevolent desertion; they babble

on about trivia in fear of any pause. These problems must be detected and analyzed.

CONSCIOUS CONCEALING

Conscious concealing may be considered a form of silence. A brief example will illustrate the problems involved:

> Miss B.U., a late adolescent with poor controls, diagnosed as borderline, had been in twice-weekly psychotherapy for about ten months and had resolved her main emotional problems. As termination of the therapy approached, the therapist, aided in part by dreams with apparent sexual implications, pointed out in several sessions that the patient was avoiding any reference to her sexual experiences and fantasies, and that she had done so throughout her treatment. In addition to these confrontations, he also commented that her dreams indicated considerable sexual anxiety, which the patient would not have an opportunity to work through if she avoided the topic. Miss B.U. then admitted that she had purposely circumvented the entire subject, and then revealed her intense conscious conflicts about her sexual behavior with boyfriends. She went on to describe a long history of masturbation, with violent fantasies in which she was attacked, beaten, and hurt. Her concealment proved to be a desperate attempt to avoid her sexual conflicts and her anxious, guilt-ridden sexual fantasies; there were hints that erotic fantasies about the therapist were another factor in this omission. Fears of losing control of her sexual impulses, humiliation over the fantasies, and some mistrust of the therapist were also involved.

In principle, then, the therapist must be alert to areas of real and fantasy life which are absent for long periods from the patient's associations. In time, the patient should be confronted with these voids, and, while not cajoled to discuss them nor condemned for the gaps, aided to explore the motives for such omissions and to work them through. In doing so, the dynamic understanding should be supplemented by ego building, that is, helping the patient forego the use of such primitive defenses by developing confidence in his ability to face things and cope with them.

At times, such concealing reflects dishonest and psychopathic trends, and underlying grandiose fantasies which must be analyzed and resolved for therapy to unfold properly.

UNCONSCIOUS CONCEALING

The recurrent absence of one or another aspect of possible material from treatment, done without conscious awareness or intention on the part of the patient, leaves a particular dimension out of treatment and is almost always deeply motivated, requiring exploration and analysis. To give general examples: omissions of current reality are often an attempt to keep treatment remote and unrelated to present life problems; omissions of the past relate to avoiding traumatic and anxiety-provoking recollections that are needed in therapy to demonstrate the development of, and genetic basis for, present conflicts and character traits; avoidance and repression of dreams are often related to fears of conscious and unconscious fantasies and of one's entire inner fantasy life. Some patients steer clear of all references to the therapist, while others become preoccupied with him, excluding other material. In all, significant omission of any aspect of reality or intrapsychic fantasies and memories represents an important resistance that must be worked through.

PERSEVERANCE OF ONE TYPE OF MATERIAL

Some patients defensively confine themselves to one type of communication to the virtual exclusion of other material. I shall briefly allude to several types, each of which must eventually be brought to the attention of the patient, explored, and resolved. If these defensive styles are not modified, the outcome of therapy will be severely limited.

Preoccupation with the trivial details of daily life is one such resistance. The patient obsesses on the surface of his current reality problems and very little of dynamic import or of his inner conflicts and fantasies emerges. Dreams are usually absent; the rare dream which is reported is close to reality in its content, while associations revolve around reality factors. The motives for his own behavior are experienced by this type of patient in terms of reacting to others and not as internally-founded. In all, this style of communicating reflects serious resistances that are often based on severe narcissistic pathology, paranoid fantasies and massive use of defensive denial. Acting out is also frequent in these patients (see Kohut, 1971; and Searles, 1973).

Another pathological cognitive style of communicating in sessions reflects a resistance of a different kind: a propensity to be preoccupied with fantasies of all types, to the relative exclusion of reality events and problems. This style is common in certain borderline and narcissistic patients who report many dreams, and ruminate at length about their content, but seldom link the material to reality circumstances or direct these communications to the therapist as a separate person. Other patients of this type weave elaborate fantasies which are often vague and without focus. Technically, the therapist should not pursue these fantasies even when the dynamics are of utmost fascination; instead, the resistance and narcissistic defenses must be analyzed first, and worked through. Only then will there be an effective therapeutic relationship with material from the patient which has balance and is affectively meaningful.

There are, of course, many other styles of associating and relating to the therapist that involve major resistances. These must be understood, responded to appropriately, analyzed, and worked through as early in treatment as possible. As I will develop in Chapter 23, one main goal in the opening phase of treatment is to work through resistances in the patient to balanced communicating so that the interplay between the therapist and patient, reality and fantasy, and present and past, unfolds in a meaningful workable manner.

OTHER FUNDAMENTAL GROUND RULES OF PSYCHOTHERAPY

Of the many implicit and explicit ground rules of psychotherapy, I shall briefly discuss the following: the face-to-face mode, the one-to-one relationship, confidentiality, proper boundaries and limits, the basic stance of the therapist, and the handling of medication.

THE FACE-TO-FACE MODE

My clinical experience and theoretical understanding both have convinced me that psychotherapy should be done in a face-to-face setting and not with the patient on the couch. As far as I know, empirical research into this variable has not been reported, and certainly is necessary before any definitive statement can be made. Lacking such data, I shall confine my remarks to the principles I believe to be involved in this issue.

The rationale for the use of the couch is the hope that it will promote freer expression of "deeper" id or unconscious material on the part of the patient. In addition, the couch is sometimes used to help a patient talk freely about a subject that he is embarrassed to discuss while looking at the therapist. This kind of thinking, however, is largely related to older models of therapeutic work where the goal was the pursuit of deep fantasy content or the so-called "repressed unconscious," and on remembering the forgotten past. There is a relative disregard in such thinking for the crucial role of work with the patient's ego in psychotherapy—modifying pathological defenses and strengthening his synthetic and adaptive capacities. It also reflects an inadequate concept of working through and of the need to integrate the patient's understanding of his present conflicts and adaptations with that of his past life experiences and their influence on his present behavior. Therefore, uncovering is not the primary goal of therapy, but one of many avenues toward symptom resolution. As part of a gradual unfolding, it is a vital part of treatment; as an uncontrolled or poorly modulated upsurge, it can be quite disruptive.

Placement on the couch can promote such disruptive regressions as overwhelming anxiety, loss of reality-testing capacities—especially in the relationship with the therapist—and abrupt terminations. The patient may experience overly-intense sexual fantasies, feelings of submissiveness, dependency, vulnerability, mistrust and other paranoid fantasies, and a lessening of his reality orientation with consequent primitivization of all experiencing. In all, the risks are considerable, and adverse reactions are difficult to modify when sessions are widely spaced and, compared to the four or five weekly visits of the analytic patient, relatively infrequent. An inadequately trained therapist in particular will find himself unprepared for the complications which often arise. A multitude of reality-based, non-transference and transference-based fantasies may remain concealed from the therapist or promote untoward and unworkable obstacles to the unfolding of therapy. The result is often a treatment in which anxiety or a sense of unreality prevails, or an endless, unresolved rumination regarding fantasies about the therapist is carried on. Instead of the unfolding and working-through of the patient's problems, the therapist may be confronted with a therapist-evoked disturbance for which the patient is justifiably angry.

The specific use of the couch to ease discomfort in discussing certain material avoids analysis of the sources of this discomfort and bypasses the opportunity to strengthen the capacity of the patient's ego to tolerate anxiety and to resolve its sources. It may promote an intensification of resistances and defenses which leads to a closing off of important material at all levels. Further, it may represent a defense on the part of the therapist who is himself uncomfortable in the face-to-face mode. Seductive and hostile motives, and needs to make the patient unduly subservient, may exist in such a therapist. These are difficult to detect and distinguish from any possible therapeutic advantage that the couch may have. Until proven otherwise, the many possible dangers and disadvantages of the couch appear to outweigh any possible value its use may have.

The face-to-face setting actually provides the patient with an anchor in reality and helps reduce the likelihood of untoward regressive episodes, especially of an iatrogenic nature (see Chapter 22). It will not, in patients prone to regress, prevent such experiences, but it does enable the therapist to create a therapeutic setting where he can deal with them more readily and where unanalyzed fantasies about him are less likely to disrupt the therapeutic alliance. It aids the patient in reconstituting object-relatedness and other ego functions, including reality testing and contact, when this is needed. At the same time, this setting amply permits the appearance and analysis of regressive material. It may limit the depth of such work, but not to the extent that the outcome of therapy is endangered. Its useful aspects seem to outweigh any possible limitations.

The following clinical example, which was detailed to me some time after its occurrence (so that my data is somewhat incomplete), will illustrate some of the dangers inherent in the use of the couch.

> Mrs. B.V. was a young woman who came into treatment because she was having an affair, felt that she had an unsatisfactory marriage (she constantly fought with her husband), and was suffering with anxiety and depression. She was assessed as having a moderate character disorder with acting out tendencies. Early in her treatment, because the patient was very verbal, had clearcut problems, and was working hard to resolve them, the therapist decided to put her on the couch and continue her twice weekly treatment in that mode. He felt that this would enable the patient to provide him with more fantasy and transference material with which he could then better help her resolve her difficulties.
>
> From the little we already know about the patient, we might anticipate some of what followed. To make the matter clearer, I can add a little of the patient's history pertinent to this particular problem. She was the only child in an unhappy marriage. Her father had many affairs without taking the trouble to conceal them from his wife or daughter. Her mother was a promiscuous woman who also carried on openly in front of her daughter, often involving her directly in her sexual escapades. As a result, Mrs. B.V. had poor controls and was prone to sexualize relationships and situations.
>
> In her second session on the couch, Mrs. B.V. became extremely anxious and agitated. The source of the anxiety and the material from the patient was not clear to her therapist, who therefore offered only some words of reassurance. Within a couple of weeks, her anxiety reached panic proportions and she was unable to speak and actually left one session early. She was then shifted back to the face-to-face mode.

Some months later, Mrs. B.V. revealed that she had developed intense sexual desires for the therapist, while on the couch, and had become terrified by them. It indirectly became clear from her associations that being placed on the couch had led her to expect that the therapist actually intended to seduce her and that she was going to once more experience a situation similar to the uncontrolled sexual scenes of her childhood. She was unable to believe that this would not occur and her panic mounted as she anticipated what was for her an inevitable seduction. She had not verbalized her anticipations because on one level, she welcomed being seduced, although on another level, she dreaded it. Based on this reaction and additional material which emerged after it, the therapist reassessed Mrs. B.V. as borderline, a diagnosis that seems to be correct.

In this instance, being placed on the couch promoted an unanalyzable regression prompted by a mixture of realistic and transference reactions to the therapist (see Chapters 20 and 22), which were experienced by the patient essentially as a conviction that she was about to be seduced. She was unable to work through the subsequent panic reaction. The therapist, without adequate material from the patient, and possibly out of his failure to understand the implicit content of her associations because of his countertransference problems, was unable to help the patient resolve her anxieties and had to return her to the face-to-face mode. The outcome of treatment was probably seriously impaired through this experience, which later required months of working through that was only partially successful.

The number of uncontrolled variables in this clinical episode is so great that we must not attempt to draw any firm conclusions from it. It can only serve to promote caution in considering the use of the couch in psychotherapy. Those who choose to do so should make a careful assessment of the patient in question so that borderline and other severely disturbed patients who are most prone to disruptive regressions are not so placed. They should also be prepared to explore carefully with the patient his reaction to the couch, and to do so on all relevant levels. They should have competency with this mode of treatment, and be aware of its implications, risks, and their reasons for using it, in terms both of apparent indications for the patient and any conscious and unconscious meanings it has for them as therapists. In particular, they should have resolved any neurotic or inappropriate meanings or uses of the couch for themselves. In all, it is a move not to be taken lightly, best not made at all, and one that is open for research study.

THE ONE-TO-ONE RELATIONSHIP

In times when group and family therapy and even the use of multiple therapists are in vogue, a few words about the special values of one-to-one psychotherapy, the damage resulting from violations of this private relationship, and its implementation as a means of helping other family members are in order.

The Basic Value of One-to-one Therapy

Briefly, the one-to-one mode provides the therapist with the maximal opportunity for exploration of every aspect of the patient's personality, his real and fantasied life and self and, as a result, the best opportunity to help him to achieve lasting inner structural change. The motives for conscious and unconscious concealing are minimal in such a setting, and, if present, usually readily detectable and analyzable. The patient is free to reveal not only his deepest unconscious fantasies, but also his conscious secrets; and he may do so in a setting where no one is harmed by such revelations. I have seen, on an individual basis, a number of patients who had been seen by a therapist in the presence of others; in every instance, conscious or unconscious concealing significantly limited the outcome of the previous therapeutic work.

On the therapist's part, individual treatment provides him with a setting in which he can focus his entire efforts on the patient. He is free to interact with him and to tune in on every possible level and nuance reflected in the patient's associations because he is not hampered by the presence of, or interruptions by, others. He is able to make direct and frank confrontations and interpretations which need not be modified because of others who are listening. Both consciously and unconsciously, his capacity to listen and intervene are at their highest levels.

In addition to these technical considerations, an exclusive two-person relationship offers an opportunity for a therapy situation in which trust, empathy, sole interest, appropriate and necessary concern and gratification and, at times, a nonpathological sense of oneness are maximally available to the patient. Impairments in the patient's constructive use of these important aspects of his relationship with the therapist are open for analysis, which will enhance the patient's adaptive capacities and lessen his neurotic propensities. These unique qualities of the one-to-one relationship offer a therapeutic alliance to the patient in its fullest sense. Reactions to encroachments to this aspect of the therapeutic contract are usually quite intense, as I shall illustrate in the next section of this chapter. For many, if not all, patients, their exclusive relationship with the therapist offers as close to a primary-love relationship as is feasible (Balint, 1968); on that basis, the setting for deep inner growth—a new beginning—is established. By-and-large, any modification of this ground rule is a technical error that impairs the therapy both in regard to the therapeutic alliance itself, and the patient's communication of derivatives of unconscious fantasies; both will curtail the extent to which inner change can be achieved by the patient unless the deviation is exclusively analyzed and resolved for both parties.

The Application of Individual Therapy for Family Pathology
Let us begin our consideration of this problem with a vignette:

> Mrs. B.W. was unhappy in her marriage. Her husband was critical, nasty, and at times impotent. She, on her part, was aloof, provocative, and tormenting. Early in her treatment, when her seductiveness with her children was under scrutiny, she focused on her husband's problems and asked that the therapist see him, or at least tell her what to do about the ways in which he upset her.
>
> The therapist responded to Mrs. B.W.'s request in several ways. He let her know, in context, and without criticism, that the responsibility for changing her relationship with her husband was largely hers since it was she

who was in treatment. He went on to analyze the material at hand, which revealed several unconscious motives for her current attack on her husband. First, she did it to shift the focus away from her growing awareness of her own seductiveness with her children. Attacking him was a displacement of her rage at herself for being an inadequate mother; it was also a defensive attempt to deflect responsibility from herself.

Later in treatment, her anger at her husband was clarified in depth. Briefly, it was tied to her rage at her father who had deserted her family when she was four. It also was related to unconscious masochistic fantasies in which she achieved closeness with her father by being raped and attacked by him; she was thereby simultaneously united with, punished by, and revenged on her father. With these insights, Mrs. B.W. became able to resolve her needs to battle with, punish, and be punished by, her husband; and their relationship, his behavior, and his potency all improved. The patient had turned to her children for gratifications that she lacked with her husband. She had been seductive and they had responded with symptoms of bed wetting, poor controls, and hostility. Analysis of these problems by Mrs. B.W. brought considerable renunciation on her part and striking changes in her children.

This is a rather typical series of sessions in psychotherapy and it will enable us to develop some principles of technique.

1. *The patient in therapy has the responsibility to effect change in other disturbed family members.* This can be done only within certain limits that are wider than most therapists seem to realize; beyond these, the disturbed member should be in therapy himself. Initially, unless the pathology in the spouse or child is quite severe, the patient should be responsible for attempts at modifying his relationship with the other person and at helping the latter become aware of, and modify, his neurotic needs. The results can be quite significant.

2. *This responsibility to modify psychopathology in others close*

to him can be carried out only if the patient analyzes and works through his own role in evoking the other person's disturbed behavior, and his need for that behavior. It may serve to gratify or punish him or aid him with inappropriate defenses.

It is thus necessary to approach this problem along two major avenues. The first is to make the patient aware of his responsibility to work with the others in his family. The second is to analyze the patient's own investment in the neurosis of these family members so that he can modify his needs for such behavior. If the family member's pathology proves to be too severe for sufficient modification in this way, work should be done to help him get into treatment with another therapist.

The same principles apply to adolescent patients and their parents, although the area of possible modification is generally more limited. Their relationship should be dealt with largely by the patient himself; the therapist should intervene only in a dire emergency.

The following vignette is illustrative:

> Miss B.X. was an asthmatic teenager. She was impulsive and tended to act out, was doing poorly as a sophomore in college, and lived at home. Two weeks before a vacation planned by her therapist, she showed evidence of struggling with intense separation anxieties and fantasies of replacing her soon-to-be-absent therapist through promiscuous relationships with several boys whom she knew. She controlled these impulses and was analyzing them when she began a session by reporting that she had wheezed badly the previous night. She had flirted with a new fellow at school and had accepted a gift of a book from him. It had been exceedingly hot that night and one of her teenage brothers asked if he could sleep in the other bed in her room, since only her bedroom had an air conditioner. At the insistence of her parents, she had agreed and then had many conscious sexual fantasies about him, reflecting primarily a great need to possess and somehow have his whole being for herself. She felt awful having such thoughts.

The asthma was interpreted by the therapist as an expression of these fantasies of taking her brother into herself, and was linked to the pending separation from the therapist; the guilt-evoked punishment, smothering herself with asthma, was also touched upon. Lastly, the therapist pointed out how much the patient suffered through seeking such guilt-ridden replacements for himself and how she went along with her parents' failure to provide her brothers with air conditioners (they were well off financially) by never discussing her negative feelings when her brothers had shared her room because of the heat. He also noted how she had accepted her brother into her room to satisfy her own disturbing needs. The patient responded by elaborating upon her fears of losing some part of herself in losing the therapist and then expressed a sudden fear of fainting in the session if she realized and felt the truth in his comments. She also said that she could not influence her parents, who had always pushed her toward excessive closeness to her brothers.

In the next hour, Miss B.X. reported that she had had a long discussion with her parents about herself, and her need for privacy and better boundaries between herself and her brothers. She had directly asked her parents to buy an air conditioner for them (they shared a room) and they did so that very day.

Miss B.X. was well along in her therapy and had a good grasp of her separation anxieties and incestuously-tinged incorporative responses, including their relationship to her asthma. Her use of this symptom was decreasing and her parents were aware of the positive changes in her. She was eager to control both her acting out and her asthma. Her parents were also in the process of revising the loose and open way in which they had raised their children, and were, through the patient's comments and behavior, realizing the consequences of their practices. They therefore readily accepted their daughter's suggestion. This was part of a long and difficult struggle for all concerned toward modifying the pathological interactions within the family, and the success of the outcome was based primarily on the therapist's work with Miss B.X., who then influenced the situation at home.

THE INTRODUCTION OF THIRD PARTIES INTO THE PATIENT-THERAPIST RELATIONSHIP; CONFIDENTIALITY

The introduction of a third party on any level into the patient-therapist relationship is a deviation in the ground rules that has major consequences for the patient and the therapy. Often, this is done by either party in a strongly rationalized or unwary manner, and the consequences go unnoticed. The people most commonly brought in as third parties by patients are relatives and friends, insurance companies, draft boards, and other similar agencies. This may be done directly or indirectly; in person, by telephone or by letter. For the therapist's part, third parties whom he introduces include assistant therapists, psychologists who test the patient, supervisors, colleagues, and more rarely, his own family and friends.

The principles we need for dealing with problems in this regard can be developed through a series of vignettes:

> Mr. B.Y. was a borderline, young, homosexual man in therapy because of his perversion, episodes of depression, and periods of disorganization. After several years of treatment, he had resolved his symptoms and was preparing to terminate his treatment. At this time, soon after the therapist had been on vacation, he came to a session with his college room-mate. While no longer acting out homosexually, the patient was still struggling with homosexual fantasies about his friend. These had intensified with the recent separation from the therapist and with the anticipation of termination. In the previous hour, this had been explored, interpreted, and corroborated in some detail.
>
> Thus, when the patient appeared with his room-mate and asked the therapist to see him, the therapist suggested

that they explore the request first. Mr. B.Y. agreed and then described how he had confessed his past homosexuality to his friend who had been terrified. He feared losing his friendship and being exposed as a homosexual by him. Associations led back to situations in which the patient's father had intervened in an overprotective way when the patient got into difficulties. The entire episode was interpreted by the therapist as an attempt to create a crisis through which he would draw the therapist into an involvement similar to those with his father in the past, involvement that would gratify his homosexual fantasies and undo the pending termination and separation. The patient acknowledged these intentions and his responsibility to handle the situation himself, and the therapist did not see his friend.

In the next hour, the patient had resolved the matter and had made his first date with a girl in several weeks. He felt that the therapist was right in not seeing his friend. He went on to describe how his married brother wanted money from his parents and how he (the patient) opposed this indulgence; if they granted it, he would never learn to take responsibility for his life.

Some important principles follow from this vignette:

1. *Basically, the therapist must not be seduced into agreeing to see a third person introduced by the patient into the treatment in any way.* This includes parents of adolescents, spouses, and all others regardless of the patient's rationale. The responsibility for dealing with the third party must remain entirely the patient's, with only rare exceptions (see below), lest he gratify the patient's inappropriate seductive and defensive fantasies and needs, and promote a countertransference or error-based erotized reaction in the patient toward himself or any other type of misalliance (see Chapter 22).

Often, a patient will bring a companion who will wait for him in the waiting room. This, if noticed or reported, must be analyzed during the session. If the therapist does not bring it up when the patient fails to do so, he is sanctioning the unconscious fantasies on which the behavior is based, and participating in their acting out;

a shared defense and anti-therapeutic alliance will follow until it is undone by proper therapeutic exploration.

Among the most common aspects of intrapsychic conflict and fantasies reflected in bringing a third person into the therapeutic situation are:

• Undoing the sense of loss and depression of a pending separation from, or termination with, the therapist.

• Defensive use of the third person as a barrier and protector against the patient's erotic or hostile wishes toward the therapist. These fantasies may be repressed, denied, or projected onto the therapist, evoking fears of attack and seduction in the patient. The companion serves as a protector on this level as well.

• Gratification of pregenital merger and oedipal, incestuous-based fantasies, through a break in the boundaries of the relationship with the therapist. These fantasies range from those of fusion and omnipotent care to sexual wishes on all levels. Some hostility toward the therapist is always an additional factor.

• Attempts to disturb, rupture, and realign the therapeutic alliance. This has a defensive element and may be a flight from emerging material, especially from fantasies about the therapist. It also represents an effort to create a misalliance and achieve extra-therapeutic (so called "real") gratification from the therapist (see Chapters 20 and 21).

These needs, all of which are related to unresolved conflicts and pathological unconscious fantasies, must not be gratified by the therapist. They must be frustrated so that he remains a nonparticipant and is in a position to help the patient analyze the behavior in terms of its specific context and definitive meanings for him.

2. *Among the most common precipitates of such behavior are necessary and unnecessary (technically erroneous and countertransference-based) hurts from the therapist.* These should be considered whenever efforts to introduce third parties arise from the patient.

3. *Certain exceptions to nonparticipation with third parties to the therapy are inevitable though, as parameters, they must always be subsequently analyzed and resolved to whatever extent is feasible. Inevitable third-party participants include:*

• Insurance companies where forms must be filled out; the meanings of this factor for the patient should be analyzed (see

Chapter 5). Stubbornly held unconscious resistances can arise in this context; they may limit the outcome of therapy.

•   With a suicidal patient, in an emergency, and with the patient's permission (preferably, too, in the presence of the patient), it may be necessary to see a relative. The specific occasions for this include any crises where it is vital for the relative to be completely cooperative, where the therapist must rely on the relative's observations regarding suicidal possibilities, and where the relative must of necessity offer vital protection, understanding, and support to the patient. Only when the assistance of a reliable adult is to be preferred to hospitalization should this be done. It is not routine with a suicidal patient, since it undermines the patient's sense of responsibility for himself. It can be justified only in dire circumstances, and analyzed and undone as much as possible later on.

•   Some therapists will see the parent of an adolescent or a husband who threatens to terminate the patient's therapy. If a suicidal risk exists, this may be justified. Otherwise, the therapist should adhere to the principles established here, and insist that the patient be responsible for his therapy and for his relationships with others. The manipulativeness, seductiveness, and infantilizing qualities, the breach of boundaries, and the defensive usage of such interviews with family members almost always negate any positive aspects for the patient.

These principles can be expanded to include any other type of third party introduced by either the patient or the therapist into their relationship, and may apply especially to the therapist himself, and with a greater degree of responsibility. In essence, except for a supervisor and rarely for a secretary, he should not introduce any third parties on any level into the therapeutic relationship, lest he destroy its boundaries and thereby foster such reactions as mistrust, regressions, instinctualized reactions toward himself, and acting out. Such behavior ruptures the basic therapeutic alliance and creates misalliances in which maladaptive defenses and inappropriate gratifications prevail.

To highlight the exquisite sensitivity that patients have in this regard, consider the following clinical material:

Mr. J.C. was a married man in his thirties whose main

problems related to his seductive touching of young girls. While he functioned well in many areas, his poor impulse control and judgment regarding his sexual impulses suggested a borderline diagnosis.

He was late to one session and his therapist had left the door to his office open and waited for him. A young secretary, who worked in the clinic in which the patient was being seen, came by and sat down in the patient's chair; she wanted to discuss a problem regarding another patient with the therapist. As he was discussing the problem and telling her that he was expecting a patient, Mr. J.C. arrived. The secretary got up and left quickly.

In the session, the patient was remote and ruminative and spoke of some relatively minor problems about doing his job properly. The therapist asked him how he felt about the girl who had left the office as he had arrived. Mr. J.C. said that he had noticed that she was built well, but had no other thoughts about her.

In the next hour, Mr. J.C. described a long talk about his emotional problems with a friend. There was a man in his neighborhood who was molesting little girls and Mr. J.C., with some guilt, described some of his own seductive experiences. The therapist, he now realized, reminded him of a short, scared teenager who worked in his office for whom everyone was always arranging blind dates. The girl who had been in the therapist's office last session had large breasts. The patient recalled having once been a nude model for an art class.

In the following session, Mr. J.C. described how, on the previous day, he had violated a confidentiality given to him by his boss and had gotten himself into serious trouble. He berated himself, and then described how a young girl at work had asked him to go to bed with her and he had refused. Once, a bisexual young man had been upset at work and the patient had tried to help him; the man attempted to seduce him in return. At times, the therapist confuses him with the comments that he makes. As the hour ended, the patient put the therapist's desk in order, saying that the latter should not have things out of place.

As predicted in supervision at the beginning of this presentation, the reactions of this patient relate strongly to the inadvertent introduction of the young lady who was in the patient's chair—during the time set aside for him—when he arrived. As we have seen, patients are, as a rule, extremely sensitive to even seemingly minor deviations in the ground rules, and this experience proves to be no exception. Mr. J.C.'s associations indicate that the situation led him to unconsciously view the therapist as a molester, an inadequate man sexually, an exhibitionist, a violater of his confidentiality, and a bisexual seducer who had best set his own house in order. While these fantasies stem from the patient's own intrapsychic needs, conflicts, and set, they may also reflect on some level correct unconscious perceptions (see Chapter 22).

In the main, the problem here is not so much in the inadvertent presence of the third person, as in the therapist's failure to interpret the patient's reactions to it in fantasy and behavior. The latter may have been intensified because of the absence of interventions in this area. On the other hand, such work, when done correctly, is usually most rewarding and helpful since the patient's reactions to such experiences are usually related to fantasies central to his main inner conflicts. These are almost always connected on some level to deviations in the ground rules, and the insights gained in this way are very productive. The experience of being understood at such times is also important and helps maintain the therapeutic alliance. Since these deviations are of prime importance to the patient, failure to explore his reactions to them will disrupt this alliance for some time.

The patient is aware of some third parties brought into therapy by certain therapists: secretaries, psychologists, and cotherapists; and he is unaware of others: supervisors, colleagues, and friends and relatives of the therapist. As an example of the pitfalls in introducing such people into the relationship on any level, I have already demonstrated the detrimental effects of the therapist's use of secretaries to cancel his appointments when he is ill and shall discuss this topic further in delineating abuses by therapists of clinic personnel (Chapter 7). Beyond this, we must recognize that reporting to a

supervisor is a complication of therapy which, while it is not discussed with the patient, must be recognized as such by the therapist;
he must be aware of its implications for, and effects on, himself and
the treatment. Supervision is often strongly implicit in therapy
carried out in a clinic, and should the patient ask about it, the therapist should explore the context and meaning of the inquiry, and
respond frankly—emphasizing his own ultimate responsibility for
the therapy.

Some of the unconscious meanings of the presence of a supervisor in a case are reflected in the following vignette in which the
therapist misapplied the principles being developed here:

> Mr. E.I. had been in therapy for two months for a
> severe characterological and narcissistic disturbance, and
> problems in functioning. He was divorced, not working,
> and drifting along with the use of various illicit drugs.
>
> He was fifteen minutes late for one session and spent
> most of the time in his hour ruminating about his inaction
> and plight. The therapist eventually interrupted him and
> pointed out that Mr. E.I. had been repeating himself in
> his recent sessions and that he had not done anything
> different in his outside life either. The patient agreed, and
> then criticized himself, spoke of how annoyed he was in
> general, and ended the hour stating, "Something has to
> happen or I'll get kicked out of my apartment on my ass."
>
> He missed the next session without calling and began
> the following hour by saying that he had stayed away
> because he had had nothing important to say. He detailed
> his continued drug taking and lack of constructive func-
> tioning. He spoke of his father's laziness and of how one
> of his brothers was living off a prostitute; he wished he
> could have that kind of arrangement. He thought of hav-
> ing his sessions taped and resented the therapist's occa-
> sional note-writing which, he felt, reflected a lack of
> interest in him.
>
> The therapist responded by informing the patient that
> he was a supervised case, and that the notes were made
> to be clear about the content of the sessions. The patient

nodded without comment and said that he himself had to find work.

In the next session, Mr. E.I. described how he would not allow his drug-addict, prostitute-dependent brother to stay with him, stating, "He's a leech who just wants to suck off me." He recalled that when he was about five years old, he was humiliated by a doctor who told his mother that his penis was very small. He shifted his train of thought again: a friend had called him last night and offered his wife for sexual relations to the patient, who had refused the offer. He then spoke of wanting to get a job, but said he would not return to his previous career as a dancer because of all of the homosexuals he had to be around.

The therapist here gratuitously and incorrectly volunteered the information about his supervisor out of some defensive and countertransference need of his own. At the time, the patient had become critical and angry with the therapist, and the correct intervention seems to have been an interpretation of this anger and the missed session as a response to feelings that the therapist had criticized and pressured this patient in the previous session—the most likely context for these associations.

Once the supervisor was introduced by the therapist, the patient's response was dramatic and filled with striking latent fantasies, a common reaction to the therapist's technical errors (see Chapter 22). The patient seems to have seen the therapist as a helpless leech and a doctor who would expose the patient's frailties to others. He unconsciously now viewed the therapy as a *ménage-à-trois* and experienced homosexual anxieties regarding his relationship with the therapist. While the patient's pathology contributed to these fantasies and to the patient's unconscious perceptions of the situation, these reactions were prompted by the therapist's mistake, which actually had, on some level, many of the meanings that the patient unconsciously sensed.

All of this should have been analyzed as a response to the therapist's disclosure, by acknowledging the inadvertent error and then interpreting the unconscious conflicts and fantasies that it had evoked in the patient (see Chapter 22). Such work following errors in technique has a most salutary effect.

Even when unknown to the patient, the introduction of a third party such as a colleague, friend, or relative into the patient–therapist relationship by discussing the case with him also creates complications for the therapy. Here, countertransference-based, destructive, exhibitionistic, defensive, and other neurotic needs are a factor. The therapist must control such inappropriate misuses of his patients, and analyze and resolve them within himself. I would include here discussions of the therapist's own patient with a colleague who is treating a close relative of that patient. This not uncommon practice, which is carried out with or without the patient's knowledge or permission, is detrimental to the therapy in the same ways as any other breach of confidentiality.

The therapist-patient relationship is subject to total confidentiality. In fact, there are those who feel with some justification that there is no such thing as an informed consent to release information regarding therapy. For now, in most instances, most therapists will release information with the consent, in writing, of the patient, or the parents of an adolescent; in this latter case, consent should also be obtained from the adolescent himself. Confidentiality is a cornerstone of therapy; it is essential to the therapeutic alliance and setting which fosters the unfolding of the patient's problems and fantasies on every level.

In the initial hour, the therapist should make it clear to the patient that confidentiality will prevail. When requests arise to release information to responsible parties (e.g., to insurance companies, draft boards, and schools), the therapist should fill out the form or write the letter with these principles in mind: be brief, honest, accurate, prepared for possible misuse of the information, and do not unduly expose the patient. Give the patient an opportunity to read and clarify the letter. (He will often get to the letter in a clandestine way and then feel confused, betrayed, guilty, and motivated to conceal his discovery.) Whenever possible, send the letter directly to the party to whom it is addressed, though insurance forms may be returned to the patient for disposition if necessary.

The following vignette illustrates the responses in patients when confidentiality is violated:

> Miss L.P. was a teenager in treatment for depression and serious episodes of acting out. During a difficult period in the therapy, she missed two consecutive sessions. The therapist elected to call her to investigate and found that she was out, but that her mother was in. When the mother complained of her daughter's misbehavior and of having sent her to her sessions with little results, the therapist said that she had actually missed her recent hours.
>
> In the next session, the patient was immediately angry with the therapist for not asking her questions and not helping her. She then spoke of how she came to him for help in finding a lost boyfriend and all he wanted to do was to discuss her parents. She teased him sexually and wondered how he would react if she took off her clothes; she also chided him for not believing her. The therapist then mentioned his call to her mother and connected it with Miss L.P.'s anger with him. She responded that she knew of the call, and went on to talk of her mother's loving her regardless of what she did and of sharing her mother's bed with her. Serious acting out followed.

The patient's fury can be traced here in part to the therapist's violation of her confidentiality, which is mirrored in her thoughts of undressing and sharing her mother's bed. Considerable regression and acting out ensued partly because she modeled herself on the therapist who had, himself, acted out, and mainly because the patient's reactions to this technical error were not subsequently analyzed. The damage to the therapeutic alliance caused by this infraction proved difficult to repair.

Let us turn now to the most common third parties whom unwary therapists introduce or allow into the patient-therapist relationship. Two brief vignettes will guide us:

Mrs. B.Z. was a woman with a severe character disorder, who was depressed as she struggled over whether to divorce her husband. As she began to lean toward separation, her husband asked to see the therapist, hoping to influence her decision. This interview was arranged with the patient's permission, and following it she became acutely suicidal, dreamt of being pursued and expelled from a seat into which she had fled for safety, and recalled how she had been betrayed and hurt by family members in her childhood.

Another patient, Mrs. C.A., had been seen by her therapist with her husband. They had discussed with him their disputes in disciplining their son, though the patient had not alluded to her doubts about his paternity, which she had discussed when alone with the therapist. The husband said that she treated their son like a stepchild and the patient silently panicked. In her next session, she was suicidal, afraid to confide in the therapist, and afraid that he would put her in a state hospital; she asked to see him privately rather than in the clinic.

These vignettes are typical, and indicate the disruptive and detrimental effects of the therapist's acceptance of a third party into treatment. In principle, this is to be avoided—including psychological testing during ongoing therapy. Such a practice is of questionable value and undermines the patient's image of the therapist; it often evokes an iatrogenic paranoid syndrome and other negative responses. This next clinical experience is representative:

Mr. C.B. was a borderline adolescent who was doing poorly in school and showed paranoid trends. After two years of therapy with much improvement, he was considering college. At his parents' request, the therapist referred him for psychological testing to help with this decision. The patient agreed but, soon after, he fell silent in his sessions. The testing essentially provided no new information, and the patient began to talk of termination despite new, acute and bizarre symptoms. He had fantasies of being stabbed, of his brain being transplanted, and expressed fears that his identity would be changed. The incident left the patient more suspicious of his therapist than before, and while termination was accomplished on a positive note, the therapeutic alliance remained compromised to the end.

The implications of this vignette are clear: The therapist's use of testing evoked an iatrogenic regression and paranoid disturbance in the patient which was—on the patient's part—in keeping with his latent psychopathology. It is clear that the two-person ground rule should be followed without exception in almost all psychotherapies and that infractions come primarily from the therapist's deficient understanding of proper principles of technique and from his countertransference difficulties.

Now let us briefly consider the introduction of added therapists by either party:

Mr. C.C. was a borderline young man who had been in therapy for several months with problems involving drug abuse and disturbing homosexual fantasies. His treatment was muddled and was not going well. In one session, he alluded to intentions to attend a group therapy meeting at a center for drug addicts. The therapist missed associations which related this to his own pending vacation, and did not intervene. The patient attended the group session and described how close he felt to the others, especially to the man who led the group. He had fantasies of getting closer to this man. The patient had had a dream: someone shot him in the stomach but he felt nothing. He in turn stabbed a man at a blackboard. The patient said that the dream probably related to his therapist, and then described homosexual fantasies about the group leader.

This vignette is typical of those few situations that I have observed where a therapist permits the patient to see another thera-

pist concurrently with himself. Such requests for additional therapeutic help generally come up only in a therapy that is being handled
poorly by the therapist, and that is chaotic and bilaterally disturbing.
The patient involved is usually prone to act out, does not tolerate
anxiety well, and is prone to instinctualize relationships, while the
therapist generally has not resolved his own countertransference
difficulties.

The latter is often threatened by the one-to-one relationship with
the patient, and he consciously or unconsciously permits or fosters
the entry of the other therapists to protect himself and to gratify his
own neurotic fantasies. Unconsciously, the patient is often in tune
with the situation and with the therapist's—and his own—contributions to it (see Chapter 22). This is reflected in Mr. c.c.'s dream:
both the patient and therapist are indeed behaving destructively and
without adequate feeling and awareness. The second therapist serves
as a buffer, as a defense against the erotized relationship with the
first therapist, and as a real and fantasied gratifier of the patient's
inappropriate needs. A misalliance in which acting out prevails and
insight is unattainable is the result. Most often, premature termination is the eventual outcome.

The necessity of a single therapist for a given patient was
validated most eloquently by the patient in the following vignette in
which this issue was more adequately handled by the therapist:

> Mr. F.P. was a college student who lived at home and
> was in therapy for depressions and poor schoolwork.
> After he had been in treatment for six months, his parents
> decided to enter family therapy with their other two
> children, and asked the patient to join them. He was un-
> certain, and in the session in which this was reported, he
> reviewed the relevant issues: it could open things up
> between himself and his parents, and help organize the
> family, but he would have to talk about confidential
> matters and maybe it would affect his present therapy.
> After much rumination along these lines, he fell silent
> and the therapist confronted him with the way in which
> he was keeping to the surface of the problem. Mr. F.P.
> then said that he had been thinking about the lyrics of a

song, "You can't please everyone," and about a baseball player recently traded to the New York Yankees. To the first of these thoughts, he associated the idea that his parents would be pleased to have him in the family therapy situation, but his present therapist would be displeased. With the second thought, he recognized the inner meaning of the added therapist for himself: it meant leaving his present treatment since a baseball player cannot play for two teams or two managers at one time.

Unconsciously, this patient correctly understood that a second therapist meant the end of his meaningful relationship with the first. He crystalized this inner truth with a striking metaphor which could be revealed in his therapy because the thrapist had not participated in or sanctioned the dilution of their relationship, but instead adhered to his commitment to the patient and an analysis of the problem. In this way, the treatment continued as structured.

I have documented breaches of the ground rules regarding the two-person relationship in detail because infringements are quite common and their implications are often missed. Such deviations impair necessary therapeutic intimacy, and for both parties foster and reflect acting out, defend inappropriately against loss and closeness, express erotic and aggressive fantasies without movement toward insight, and destroy the therapeutic alliance, atmosphere and progress. Even their most subtle expressions should be avoided. When the patient moves in such a direction, the therapist should, to whatever extent possible, frustrate any real gratification of this kind and help the patient to analyze and resolve these inclinations, which are always related to his symptoms and maladaptations.

SET HOURS

The therapist should work with fixed appointments for which he and the patient are responsible. Otherwise, their relationship is too tentative and a proper therapeutic "hold" and climate is not established. As a result, therapy has an arbitrary, easily evaded, and unstructured quality which fosters acting out and defensiveness. Treatment needs a firm foundation as a model for the patient's ego development and a setting in which the patient's intrapsychic conflicts and fantasies can unfold. In exceptional circumstances, such as "as-necessary" supportive therapy, this rule may be modified.

SET LENGTH OF SESSIONS

In insight therapy, the length of sessions should be fixed and maintained at 45 or 50 minutes, for the reasons given above. At times, patients will attempt to extend a session or the therapist will want to do so. Let us turn to a few brief clinical vignettes to explore this problem.

> Mrs. C.D. was caught in traffic and was 20 minutes late to her session. She was upset and had a lot to discuss; she offered to pay an additional fee if the session could be extended. The therapist suggested that she explore her request. The associations that emerged were related to the patient's lack of closeness with others and to seductively-tinged longings to be closer to the therapist. This provided the answer for the patient; extending the hour would be a seduction by both the patient and the therapist. In addition, the failure to set firm limits would not encourage the patient, by example, to accept traumatic realities and develop an adequate frustration tolerance. Patients gain much from the experience of frustrating endings of hours, which can provide opportunities to work through their separation anxieties and rage at the necessarily nongratifying aspects of the therapist's role.

> Mrs. C.D. was a seriously suicidal borderline patient. In her session, she had expressed suicidal intentions. As the hour ended, she had not resolved these feelings. In this instance, there is an emergency. The therapist extended the hour, focusing entirely (as he had for most of the session) on the decision to hospitalize the patient if she did not genuinely get her suicidal impulses under control.

The latter proved feasible and in subsequent sessions the meaning of the extension was analyzed (in keeping with the rule to eventually analyze and resolve the effects of all parameters to whatever extent feasible; see Eissler, 1953). Primarily, the patient viewed the extension as a reflection of the therapist's serious concern for her life and found it reassuring; she had actually used it as a basis on which to rebuild her own desire to live and to establish her controls. It also had a seductive meaning for her; this was resolved particularly by demonstrating the reality on which the extension was based.

Maintaining firm limits—within a minute or two—about the length of sessions helps the patient to accept the restrictions of reality, tolerate the frustration of its necessary boundaries, and accept inevitable separations. It avoids untoward seductiveness on the part of either the patient or the therapist. Manipulativeness on either part is also controlled and therapeutic change is fostered. Any anger evoked in the patient by these boundaries can be readily explored, analyzed, and used for insight and ego maturation. The patient's grandiose fantasies and his wishes to have the therapist behave in an omnipotent and all-providing manner are reasonably frustrated, thereby fostering their verbal expression and possible analytic resolution.

NOT TOUCHING THE PATIENT

With all the current inner and outer pressures to rationalize and excuse touching patients by therapists in a psychotherapeutic setting or, conversely, the touching of therapists by patients, one must be clear about the source of these pressures and the reasons why touching is contraindicated and anti-therapeutic.

The longing for closeness and touch is a universal one, and is related to fantasies on virtually every possible level. These range from longing for union and fusion to incestuous sexual desires. They include denial of aggressive and murderous fantasies and their symbolic gratification as well. Beyond these instinctual-drive and defensive aspects, for the ego, touching entails loss of vital controls, failure to tolerate crucial frustrations, and expression through action rather than through verbalization or thought. In terms of the super-ego, touching represents corruption and a failure of appropriate renunciation. Touching can also signify controlling the therapist, becoming an exception, gratifying omnipotent fantasies, and depreciating and demeaning the therapist.

In all, touching gratifies the heart of the patient's neurotic needs and undoes the very core of insight-directed therapy. Such needs must be renounced and worked through by both the patient and the therapist. This is so fundamental to the therapeutic relationship and setting that without it, the essential renunciation of forbidden, pathogenic instinctual drives and development of new, non-neurotic solutions, so critical to the resolution of any neurosis, cannot occur.

If touching occurs at the instigation of the therapist, and as a seductive gesture, insight therapy is at an end; it has been replaced by unilateral or mutual acting out. If initiated by the patient, it represents a serious problem. The overture must be firmly, though not destructively, rejected. Its meaning, genetics, and reflection of ego-control disturbances must be thoroughly analyzed. Often such behavior on the part of the patient is a response to serious counter-transference problems in the therapist. These are often manifested in his failure to detect and analyze indications of erotic fantasies and desires in the patient long before the overt behavior occurs. Needless to say, such incidents call for intense self-scrutiny and self-analysis on the part of the therapist. If he is unable to work through these difficulties both with the patient and within himself, he should refer a patient of this kind to another therapist. If he, himself, has initiated the contact, referral is mandatory, as is seeking therapeutic help for himself.

There are, of course, legitimate moments for touch between patient and therapist, and these deserve mention. A handshake before and after the first meeting with the patient is quite appropriate, as it is at the time of a new year, before and after a long vacation, and at termination.

Occasionally, a patient will continue to offer his hand before or after sessions at the beginning of treatment. Such a practice usually reflects special needs for closeness, unconscious sexual fantasies, the need to undo possible aggressions, and uncertainty in relating to others. When this occurs early in treatment, it is best not to interpret it because of the anxiety and sense of humiliation and rejection this may engender. Usually, when the therapist does not initiate such handshakes, the patient stops this practice. If not, simply and tactfully asking the patient about it is often enough to call it into question and the patient will desist. If he persists, the therapist can eventually interpret its use in the context of the material at hand, emphasizing, since it is early in treatment, the defensive aspects of this behavior.

Beyond these handshakes, there should be no physical contact between the patient and therapist. Should an emergency call for touching the patient or should it occur accidentally, it must then be thoroughly analyzed on all possible levels. The following vignette will help to establish this basic therapeutic principle:

> Mrs. H.Y. had been in therapy for about eight months because of a recent divorce, periods of depression and moments of loss of interest in her work; she had a moderate characterological disturbance. The events to be described here occurred after the anniversary of the death of her father, which had stirred up many memories, especially feelings of guilt over having neglected him while he was ill and over his seductiveness toward her then and in the past.
>
> The patient was then ill and missed a session; in the next hour she ruminated apologetically about her sickness. She recalled her grade school days when she was often ill and was absent from class. She also detailed a number of obsessive fears from that era, especially of losing various objects. When single, she had been a clerk at a medical clinic and was upset when she saw patients whose hands and legs were crushed or otherwise injured. As a child she had injured and slightly deformed her hand, and was still self-conscious about it. The hour ended, Mrs. H.Y. rose to leave and the therapist went to open the door—as he did routinely. The patient suddenly exclaimed that her foot was asleep and started to fall; the therapist, standing at her side, reached out and grabbed

her arm, breaking her fall. She then sat back in her chair, recomposed herself, and left.

In the next session, the patient first said that she was puzzled over her fall the last hour. She went on to describe other times in her life when she was physically ill and focused on a marked fear of heights and escalators that she had developed while in grade school. Her mother had especially frightened her by warning her to be careful and hold on tightly to the rail while on an escalator—detailing how a little girl had been caught in one and had had her hand lacerated. She would try to hide her fear of heights and her impulses to jump off high ledges, and the therapist commented that her mother may actually have brought out fears that the patient already had worried about.

In the next hour, the patient reported feeling unusually well and talking up to her boss for once. She recalled a period in her childhood when her father was away and a psychotic uncle was hospitalized. She was also critical of her mother, for a variety of reasons.

In the following session, Mrs. H.Y. said that she had actually been very anxious the previous hour—she was often not in touch with herself. She next discussed a variety of recent physical symptons. She criticized her boss's methods and spoke again of hassles with her mother. She had been thinking of leaving therapy and the therapist related it to problems that Mrs. H.Y. was having in expressing angry feelings. She responded that she felt that too often she simply told the therapist what he wanted to hear and recalled how, in her childhood, her parents frequently were unaware of how she felt—especially when she felt hopeless. As she left, her foot was asleep again; on this occasion, the therapist withdrew to his chair, suggesting that the patient sit for a moment.

In the next session, the patient began by saying that she was still bothered by the time she had fallen when her foot was asleep. She then spoke of her difficulties in expressing anger and her tendency to avoid problems. Her former husband had taken her three children to a resort and driven very recklessly. The therapist then pointed out that the patient must have been avoiding her angry feelings about his having grabbed her to break her fall, and must have felt that he had been reckless in doing so. It seemed to have frightened her, he went on, and she subsequently felt misunderstood by him and therefore thought of leaving treatment.

Mrs. H.Y. responded that she had been pleased that her therapist had sat down last time; being assisted made her feel weak and helpless, and she spoke again of her criticisms when her boss was inept.

I have described this vignette in some detail because it demonstrates the consequences of a therapist's failure to analyze a deviation in the implicit ground rules and some of the conscious and unconscious meanings for the patient of being touched. To comment briefly:

1. *It seems best to allow patients to find their own way out of the therapist's office.* This contributes to the resumption of their total autonomy and avoids incidents like this one.

2. *The therapist's touching a patient at a time of seeming emergency may prove necessary, but should be avoided if possible.* If the emergency does occur, it must subsequently be explored, analyzed, and resolved to whatever extent possible.

3. *For some patients, being touched intensifies their strong bodily anxieties and fears of losing control.* The therapist can be viewed as threatening and, when he fails to comment on such an episode, he is also seen as not understanding them and as out of touch with himself.

4. *The nonverbal intervention of not touching the patient when her leg once again went numb enabled her to bring the matter up again directly.* This finally alerted the therapist sufficiently so that he was able to intervene regarding it; he then received a positive response from the patient.

5. *Note that the matter remained unresolved for the patient until it was dealt with by the therapist.* The material in her sessions was filled with derivatives of her conscious and unconscious fan-

tasies regarding it. All other therapeutic work stopped and was not resumed until this problem was actively analyzed by the therapist. Direct and indirect references to this incident subsequently appeared for many months, especially when the therapist erred again.

Subtle and displaced forms of touching may also come up during therapy and must be recognized and analyzed. The following incident is illustrative; I will report it as it unfolded in supervision:

> Mrs. C.F. was in her first month of therapy, which she sought because of marital problems and episodes of acute anxiety. Initially, fears of treatment and of revealing her guilty secrets were prominent.
>
> She began one session by describing ways in which she hurt her husband. She then spoke of her adolescence when she falsely played the "good girl" to please her mother and went with undesirable boys on the sly. She would keep people happy at her own expense. She never went to church because she hated confession. Underneath, she felt furious.
>
> In the next hour, she spoke of seeing the therapist in the hall and wondered how she would react to him if she met him on the street. Often, she didn't know what was real. She encouraged abuse of herself and kept hidden supplies of clothes to appease her husband who complained when her things were not perfect. She often thought of running off and had some hidden money. Her husband thought so little of her because she was easily led. She enjoyed her sessions and dressed up for them. She worried about her therapist's reactions, such as in the last session, when she dropped her sweater and he picked it up. She confessed that she had seen it fall and had not picked it up herself.
>
> In the next hour, the patient reported the first recurrence of her anxiety symptoms since she had begun therapy. The main theme in the session was her recollection of the way her husband would engage in sexual foreplay with her and then masturbate himself, leaving her

feeling helpless and used. She was attracted to gentle-appearing men who then always deceived her. Sometimes she could stay in her therapist's office all day.

This therapist intended to be courteous; he failed to recognize the special qualities and necessary boundaries of the therapeutic relationship and the unconscious meanings of the sweater (and all clothes) as extensions of the bodily self. Thus, the correct response by a therapist to a fallen article of clothing is to point it out to the patient, and not to pick it up himself. He can then interpret the seductive fantasies involved if they appear. If he inadvertently participates in such an interaction, he must recognize it, explore to himself his inner reasons for doing so, and analyze the patient's responses. From the material, we see an intense reaction in Mrs. C.F., ranging from seductive longings for the therapist, to rage at being used by him to gratify his own needs, to an exacerbation of her symptoms. Here, too, treatment was disrupted and regression prevailed until the therapist brought up the problem and explored its many facets with the patient (see Chapter 22).

There are those who believe that the therapist can do almost anything with a patient, as long as it is then analyzed. This present topic provides us with an opportunity to show that this is not so. Participation by the therapist in acting out with his patient gives the patient license to act out and to maintain his neurotic maladaptations. Such sanction cannot be undone through verbal criticisms of such behavior as long as the therapist has joined in. At times, unfortunately, only referral to another therapist can offer the patient an already impaired opportunity for healthy inner change.

IMPLIED BOUNDARIES

The many implied boundaries to therapy include when and where the patient and therapist should talk and interact, what the therapist does and does not talk about (e.g., he does not talk to the patient about himself and his personal views), and how the patient behaves in the sessions.

A brief clinical vignette will exemplify the meaning and consequences of extending one of these boundaries and will enable us to delineate some basic principles.

The therapist came for Miss C.G., a moderately depressed young woman, in the waiting room of a clinic and escorted her down a long hall to his office. During the walk to the office, the patient engaged the therapist in a seemingly innocuous lengthy, bilateral conversation. In the session, the therapist failed to explore the meaning of the content of their discussion or the fact that they had talked at length outside the session, or allude to the conversation at all. That evening, the patient dreamt of having intercourse with her father. Associations in the next session indicated that one of the critical day residues for this dream was the unanalyzed conversation with her therapist. The manifest dream, in this context, revealed the unconscious meaning of their extratherapeutic talk: it was a gratification of incestuous longings. Further, with this material unanalyzed, the patient acted out sexually during the following weekend.

It should be clear, then, that nothing that occurs between the patient and therapist is innocuous or without significant meaning for both participants on conscious and unconscious levels. As this vignette so clearly illustrates, even subtle and permissible violations of the appropriate boundaries between these two parties to treatment can constitute, unconsciously, incestuous gratification and sanction to act out derivatives of such longings. Renunciation is ignored and acting is fostered at such times. Minor and human interactions outside the boundaries of therapy are inevitable (Stone, 1961) and even necessary for the therapeutic relationship. They are not to be overdone, however, lest they become the source of resistances and misalliances. When something outside of the usual boundaries of the therapeutic relationship does occur, it should be explored, analyzed, and resolved as fully as possible. Repeated extratherapeutic gratifications (so-called "real" or "transference" gratifications) should be avoided.

In this vignette, the therapist should initially have simply inquired about the patient's thoughts about their conversation; this would suffice to diminish any inappropriate gratification in the incident. Having missed that opportunity, he should then have interpreted the unconscious fantasy gratified by the extratherapeutic conversation by demonstrating the context of the patient's dream, possibly also helping the patient's ego by showing her how easily she was stimulated into having such incestuous fantasies and thereby confronting her with her weak defenses.

The main boundaries which should prevail, to a greater or lesser degree, between the patient and the therapist are:

1. *Interaction and talk between the patient and therapist should be confined to the therapist's consultation room.* Occasional innocuous remarks should the two meet, for example, in the elevator on the way to the therapist's office are permissible since, within the limits defined here, it is essential for the therapist to be warm and human. However, he must then be alert to the unconscious meanings of such encounters for the patient—and himself—and analyze the relevant fantasies. No other meetings should be planned between them. If this does happen by chance (on the street or even at a social function), a courteous greeting and appropriate detachment should prevail. In the subsequent sessions, the experience must be analyzed for the patient.

2. *The therapist's contributions in sessions should be confined to interventions designed to enlighten the patient about his psychic conflicts and neurosis, and to foster the resolution of them through inner change.* Gratuitous remarks, especially if frequent, almost always reflect unresolved countertransference problems, and on some level, the patient will sense it. Comments that are entirely inappropriate include those related to the patient's attractiveness, or other seductive remarks; references to the therapist's own inner fantasy life, including fantasies about the patient and other persons whom the latter is discussing; allusions to the therapist's personal views on any matter; references to the therapist's personal life in any way; and comments which involve the patient in any way in matters other than treatment as defined here. Dreams and fantasies about his patients can be used by the therapist to work through, on his own, countertransference problems with the patient, but should not be shared with him. This is solely the therapist's responsibility and should not become the patient's burden.

Minor deviations in such limits are analyzable, but must first be detected by the therapist. Recurrent deviations or major ones are, as noted, indications for seriously considering referral of the patient to another therapist unless self or therapeutic analysis by the therapist enables him to resolve his difficulties.

3. *A patient may behave in ways that extend beyond the boundaries of treatment, that are intended solely for his gratification and that are unrelated to therapeutic change.* Such behavior usually reflects narcissistic, borderline, and psychotic pathology. These actions include touching the therapist with seductive or destructive intentions. Even verbalization primarily designed for the patient's gratification without thought of self-understanding must be viewed similarly. Such material is acceptable as fantasies, regardless of the content, as long as they are analyzed by both the patient and therapist. The behavior itself must be understood as a communication and explored without condemnation of the patient. If, over a number of sessions, this fails to produce self-scrutiny in the patient and to initiate some modification of the disruptive behavior, it may prove necessary to confront the patient with the inappropriateness of his actions and wishes. Any subtle participation or sanction on the part of the therapist, however, will contribute to the perpetuation of the behavior, constitute a failure to define appropriate limits for the patient, and undermine treatment. Confrontations must be done without moralizing or anger, yet it may be essential if inner change is to be achieved by the patient. If allowed to continue, this behavior reflects the existence of an antitherapeutic alliance.

There are more subtle abuses of the therapeutic setting that must be detected, analyzed without rancor, and resolved. Some patients attempt to manipulate the therapist in various ways; others use treatment to vent their impulses and gratify their needs without making any serious effort to analyze them or strive for inner change. Such resistances must be brought into focus when the patient's associations permit or if the behavior is interfering with the therapeutic work; if all else fails, confrontation with this behavior and its maladaptive consequences is essential or treatment will fail.

THE BASIC STANCE OF THE THERAPIST

The therapist is an expert, a healer, an aide, a model, and an "analyst." His goal is to modify the patient's emotional problems through an honest pursuit of understanding and inner change, including honest and searching self-appraisal. He is tolerant and accepting, but not to be made ridiculous or to be abused. He is neither hostile nor seductive, and respects the necessary boundaries between himself and the patient. In all, he attempts to create a setting in which trust and respect prevail. He offers optional "mothering" as a catalyst for the patient's search for growth and not as a gratification in itself.

In all, the therapist operates in a setting of relative abstinence, as Freud (1915) termed it. By this, we mean that he offers warmth and neutral, insight-oriented interventions, but essentially no gratifications beyond those. This is a vital part of his stance; neurotic maladaptations are perpetuated by extratherapeutic gratifications and the patient will not seek nonsymptomatic adaptions if his neurotic needs are satisfied by the therapist. The clinical material of this chapter demonstrates that gratifications which extend beyond the appropriate boundaries of the patient-therapist relationship; are detrimental to the patient's quest for healthy inner change. Unless these seemingly minor facets of therapy are handled in a fundamentally sound manner, the entire process of psychotherapy will be undermined a misalliance will prevail.

Relative abstinence must be bilateral for therapy to progress. Some therapists smoke or drink coffee and eat during sessions. While it seems too stringent to suggest that smoking be avoided, certainly self-gratifications which go beyond that practice should not occur during the patient's hour. To do so is to create an aura of self-interest, poor capacity for delay and frustration, and an emphasis on inappropriate drive gratification, which can disturb all other efforts toward aiding the patient develop his capacities for adequate controls.

MEDICATION

In this age, questions regarding medication are common in the initial hour. Patients are often already on drugs prescribed for them by some other physician, and some are taking drugs prescribed for a relative. Others have simply heard of the reputed wonders of psychotropic drugs and want their share of them. Despite his relative lack of knowledge regarding the patient, the therapist's handling of these requests for medication, or of the administration of drugs that the patient is already taking, is a delicate issue, and one that is often pivotal in setting the early tone of therapy. Let us turn to three clinical vignettes to clarify the implications and management of medication in insight psychotherapy and the principles we need to handle the problems that arise in this connection.

Mr. C.H. was a young man who had experienced symptoms of derealization and depersonalization during and after several trips with LSD. He was seen by his college physician, placed on Mellaril, and referred for psychotherapy. He was assessed as borderline and showed serious suicidal thinking. Upon beginning his treatment, he said that the medication seemed to be helpful and that he wanted to continue taking it.

Mr. C.H.'s therapist elected to continue the medication as prescribed. He told the patient that this was merely an adjunct to treatment, which would give him some immediate relief; it would not spare him the need to resolve his inner problems through understanding and control.

A positive working relationship and insight into the dynamics of his suicidal feelings unfolded very early in the therapy. The patient's depression and suicidal thinking lessened as he realized that his wish to destroy himself was prompted by impulses for revenge on a girlfriend who had jilted him, and who, unconsciously, represented his mother, who had "deserted" him by being hospitalized when he was very young. Once this was clarified, the patient hesitantly mentioned to the therapist that he really felt that the medication was not helping him at all. The therapist had been waiting for some indication of this kind to provide him with a lead toward reducing the Mellaril. He quickly agreed, noting how helpful understanding had been for the patient, and then gradually reduced the dosage of the drug until it was phased out. The patient tolerated this procedure quite well, and during this period he had a dream of his mother being sick. His associations related to the ways in which he, as well as his mother, utilized illnesses to manipulate others. The therapist linked this to his present symptoms; they were a costly way to force love and care from his mother. Additional associations made it clear that the medication itself represented to him a substitute for the mother from whom he had received almost no gratification. Furthermore, once the medication was stopped, the patient, for the first time, revealed his fear of the revelatory aspects of psychotherapy. He then experienced considerable rage at a friend and controlled it adequately—something he had been unable to do previously. This helped him to understand that he had utilized the medication as some type of magical substitute for his own controls, rather than relying on his own inner resources. Here, too, his struggle with his rage at his mother was a crucial factor in what had disturbed him.

From this vignette, we can derive the following initial principles regarding medication in insight psychotherapy:

1. *The psychotherapist must assume full responsibility for all medication related to the patient's emotional problems.* If he is not a physician, he must familiarize himself with these drugs and work closely with a physician in regard to medication, assuming as much responsibility as possible.

2. *If there is risk of suicide or homicide, the therapist should continue medication until these dangerous impulses are under control.*

3. *In insight psychotherapy, the goal must ultimately be to eliminate medication so that the patient assumes full responsibility for the handling of his problems, thereby building up his ego's capacities and their effectiveness.* This is best done by waiting for clues from the patient's material that lead the way toward his renouncing the so-called support, magic, and pharmacological aid that drugs offer. Premature withdrawal of medication or prolonged unnecessary continuation of it only disrupt the therapeutic alliance and treatment. Tact and use of derivatives from the patient that

reflect his preparedness to give up the drug—or the fact that he no longer really needs it—are important here.

4. *Once drug reduction is initiated, the meaning of the medication should be further explored and analyzed.* The patient may then be expected to provide material which can be used to reinforce the value of insight and inner controls as a replacement for reliance on drugs.

5. *In seriously depressed patients, particularly involutional psychotics and acutely psychotic individuals, drugs may have to be a vital part of the initial phase of therapy if the patient is to survive and reconstitute.* Each therapist must learn to recognize pathology that calls for the adjunctive use of medication and must not fail to utilize drugs where they are a necessity. One does not endanger the life of a patient in the name of "pure" therapeutic work. On the other hand, the use of drugs can undermine the quest for insight, internal change, and ego development. Their use when not truly indicated can reflect serious inadequacies and countertransference problems in the therapist which lead him to avoid the struggle with the patient for understanding and ego-building through confrontations with, and interpretations of, fantasies and intrapsychic conflicts. Aside from the acute psychoses, severe depressions, and selected panic-states, drugs should be used extremely rarely. Even in these conditions, once the patient is well into treatment and a firm therapeutic alliance is established, work which fosters insight, ego controls, and frustration tolerance should be adequate for most crises.

At times, withdrawal from drugs is a difficult matter which meets with considerable resistance and requires much patience and analysis. At other times, the patient is quick to provide an opportunity to eliminate drugs, and the therapist should not fail to use it. For example:

> Mr. C.I. was referred for therapy by an internist who had placed him on librium because of anxiety symptoms; he had a moderate character disorder. The therapist initially pointed out that the medication could only serve as a temporary adjunct and that it could not replace the patient's need to understand his inner self and develop

his own abilities to handle his problems. In one of his first sessions, the patient referred to the way in which he utilized other people to supply him with the controls that he felt were lacking within himself. Associations led to the medication and enabled the therapist to relate this reliance on others to the patient's use of drugs. Mr. C.I. responded that he was already considering stopping the medication. The therapist agreed with this step, and pointed out that the patient could readily use his own controls. Mr. C.I. promptly stopped the drug entirely and experienced no relapse in his symptoms or loss of control.

In addition to the constructive aspects of Mr. C.I.'s decision to forego the medication, there may have been a need to please the therapist. If this was related to undue passivity or to inappropriate fantasies, they could subsequently be analyzed and worked through from his associations.

An example of the misuse of drugs will help us conclude this section.

Miss L.Q. sought treatment because of recurrent depressions and an inability to find a satisfactory career. Socially, she was unable to form lasting relationships with men and found sexual intercourse unpleasant. She was diagnosed as having a severe character disorder.

Early in her treatment, she reported episodes of confusion at work that did not seriously disrupt her functioning, but left her rather unhappy. As these came into focus in treatment, associations in one session led to thoughts of her seeking out a new boyfriend and there were indirect indications that this was related to sexual fantasies regarding the therapist, based on a brother transference. There was considerable rumination and resistance at this time, exemplified by the fact that the patient waited to the very end of the session to report a dream in which she was sitting in an anatomy class.

In the following session, the patient referred again to her anxieties at work and the therapist considered giving her medication. The clues regarding the erotic transference were not followed up by the therapist, who seemed to be disregarding them because of his own anxieties and sharing with the patient the defenses of denial and avoidance. Despite the fact that the patient suffered no further disruption in her functioning, at the next mention of anxiety, the therapist selected to give her medication. This decision came more from his own anxieties about the latent material of the sessions and his inability to understand the patient than out of any therapeutic indication. The patient responded to the medication not by an alleviation of her symptoms, but by concerns that she would be unable to function at all. The intended support had failed and the use of the medication soon led the patient to wonder if the therapist could help her at all, and whether she was going crazy (see Chapter 16).

If a therapist truly believes in the powers of insight and the healthy resolution of conflicts, in ego-strengthening and the fostering of inner controls, in his patient's ability to develop these capacities —and in his own skills to aid the patient in doing so, he will seldom find need for medication. In the flurry of excitement and escape offered by drugs, we forget too quickly the deep satisfactions and inner growth generated by the patient's ability to resolve an acute situation successfully through his own resources. We forget too the very marked limitations, risks, and antimaturing factors in drug usage. There is no substitute for the patient's ego and resources.

7 Concluding Comments on the First Session

In bringing this discussion of the first session to a close, I will concentrate on some special problems that arise in clinic settings. I will then present several condensed descriptions of representative first hours, thereby summarizing the basic principles regarding this crucial aspect of psychotherapy.

FIRST SESSIONS IN CLINICS

The clinic setting tends to promote certain pitfalls in the handling of the first contacts with the patient. Among them, I have selected for discussion the splitting of responsibilities for the treatment of the patient, the problems of being a psychiatric resident, and gifts from clinic patients.

INITIAL CONTACTS WITH PATIENTS IN CLINICS

Many clinics leave the arrangements for initial interviews to secretaries or social workers, and then use the latter to screen patients and collect data, including interviews with other family members. After an assessment meeting on some level, the patient is assigned to a staff member or trainee for therapy.

However, it is often overlooked that whoever answers such initial calls should be competent to assess emergencies and, wherever possible, the same therapist should assess the patient and conduct the therapy. Failure to do this invites splitting of the transference object for the patient and of the clinic's responsibilities to him, both to the detriment of the therapy. Such a division in feelings and fantasies is often concealed in the ongoing treatment, while tenaciously being maintained by the patient. Derivatives of the conscious and unconscious fantasies involved and their influence on the life of the patient and the psychotherapy itself are difficult to detect, and even more difficult to convincingly interpret to the patient. They thereby become the basis for strong resistances and impairments to the therapeutic alliance, undermining treatment.

The patient will often project onto the evaluating therapist hostile and seductive fantasies which are used to deny reactions to the treating therapist. On another level, such an arrangement may promote feelings in the patient that he has been forced upon the final therapist and that the latter is not responsible for the therapeutic contract. Since reactions along these lines are often justified in reality, they are extremely difficult or impossible to resolve. These seemingly subtle facets are often crucial to the outcome of treatment. If the therapist listens carefully to the early sessions of patients who have gone through such a transfer, he will detect references which make it clear that it forms the basis for many unconscious fantasies which color the entire therapy.

For the therapist, too, not evaluating his own patient has important unconscious and conscious meanings and consequences. Some therapists, reluctant to deal with erotic or hostile transference feelings or with their patient's direct reactions to them, welcome the division of responsibilities. They then promote the patient's displacement of these fantasies onto the evaluating therapist and other clinic personnel, thereby joining the patient in his defenses. Then neither party is confronted with the impact of the transference and real feelings the patient has for his therapist.

This separation of responsibilities creates other problems for the therapist, since he may disagree with the recommendations of the evaluating psychiatrist and present conflicting ideas to the patient. He may also resent the patient because he feels that the prognosis is poor or that there should be a different form of treatment. Such resentments are inevitably communicated on some level to the patient and will derail the treatment, particularly if the therapist is not aware of them or does not work them through. This arrangement also encourages the therapist to bypass full responsibility for the patient's treatment. At times, the treating psychiatrist himself splits off part of his countertransference feelings toward the patient onto the referring psychiatrist, and this defense can lead to chaos for the therapy. The working therapist must be alert to such real and countertransference problems and keep them under control.

One last complication is that evaluating personnel have a way of making careless comments to the patient that are superfluous and detrimental, and such comments are often secretly guarded by the patient, who nurtures the wounds caused by these remarks. This reminds us that therapists must consciously be alert to the nature of their communications to the patient and must avoid unnecessary or provocative comments. No aspect of the patient–doctor relationship in a psychotherapeutic setting is insignificant; everything is meaningful on a conscious and unconscious level.

In principle, then, the same therapist should assume total responsibility for evaluating and treating a given patient. This serves to create an optional therapeutic alliance, foster respect for the therapist, and place the focus of the patient's inevitable transference and realistic feelings about the therapist directly onto him alone. It also provides a clear and total commitment on the therapist's part for the treatment of the patient. In all situations, therapists must maintain an awareness of the transference, countertransference, and realistic implications of any shift of patients from one therapist to another.

The therapist should make all of the appointments with the patient, including the first one. He should establish all of the ground rules of therapy, and handle all missed sessions and fees. Failure to do so is an abdication of basic responsibilities to the patient, invites splitting of reactions in the patient, and undermines the therapeutic alliance and the therapy. It also opens the way for uncontrollable errors by others. Generally, it invites loss of respect for the therapist and appropriate feelings of rejection and rage on the part of the patient.

ON BEING A PSYCHIATRIC RESIDENT
OR TRAINEE

In these times, most patients who come to a clinic have some awareness that they will be seeing a therapist who is in training. Therefore, the therapist himself must be aware of this fact and not shy away from it should it come up. If the patient communicates derivatives related to his fantasies regarding being in treatment with a trainee, they must be analyzed and traced out as would any other communication. The material would undoubtedly be related to the patient's current conflicts, to some event in therapy, and/or to aspects of his past life. Most often, this issue comes up directly at times of rage and resistance, usually after an error or provocation by the therapist (see Chapter 22).

If questioned about his trainee status early in the treatment, the resident–therapist should simply acknowledge that this is his status, adding that he is a licensed physician, has undertaken full responsibility for the treatment, and is competent to do so. This proves far more viable for the therapy than uncomfortably concealing this fact that is relevant to the therapeutic setting. The therapist's honesty helps set a positive tone. This is not an extra-therapeutic, personal revelation of the kind that cannot be made to the patient and a simple, direct reply seems best. If the trainee issue comes up later in treatment, it usually must be analyzed without direct response. If the therapist feels unduly vulnerable in this regard, he may unnecessarily avoid or overemphasize this question, and on some level the patient will attempt to exploit it. As a result, the entire treatment may be depreciated and, if this is not analyzed and worked through, therapy will ultimately fail.

There is no need for the therapist to bring this matter up himself, since such an action is detrimental to the therapeutic alliance and can only reflect countertransference conflicts and anxieties (see Chapter 6). If the patient asks about supervision, the therapist should again acknowledge its use and emphasize his capacity to help the patient and his ultimate responsibility for the treatment. He should never lie to the patient about this—or anything else—and should be certain to subsequently focus on why the patient brings it up at any given moment. The therapist should move slowly in working through this area, giving it as much insightful thought as possible; it is bound to be a topic laden with anxiety for him. He must therefore be aware of the conscious and unconscious meanings of his status to himself. If he is not, the patient is likely to exploit the situation and attempt to place the therapist on the defensive. Acting out and denial often prevail at such times, and they should be detected and analyzed.

GIFTS OFFERED BY CLINIC PATIENTS

The problem of gifts tends to come up more in clinics than in private practice, largely because of the relatively imperfect skills of the therapist, and the feelings of guilt and indebtedness generated in the patient by the lowered fee charged in the clinic. The therapist may have countertransference feelings which synchronize with the fantasies of the patient, and feel that he is entitled to additional compensation. To act out with the patient on the basis of such shared fantasies will inevitably prove detrimental to therapy. Such behavior also reflects a mutual denial of hostility. It is based on a breach in the therapeutic alliance and creates a misalliance and transference gratification that encourages acting out, use of pathological defenses, and collusion and corruption. The therapist must analyze such offers and renounce them as he also assists the patient to do the same—in order to convey his acceptance of the therapeutic agreement as it stands and of the patient as he is. Failure to do so gratifies and perpetuates the patient's neurosis (see also Chapter 25).

BASIC PRINCIPLES REGARDING THE FIRST HOUR—SUMMARIZED

I will conclude this chapter with abbreviated descriptions of four initial interviews, in order to summarize the main principles that I have developed in this regard. Consider now, this first session:

> Miss C.J., a woman in her twenties, was referred to Dr. W. by her internist after she had discussed with him

her discontentment with her life. She called Dr. w. her-self to make the initial appointment, telling him who had referred her and saying that she hoped she could be seen quickly. Dr. w. had open time and made an appointment for the consultation later that week. He inquired and was told that there was no immediate crisis, and there was no further discussion on the telephone.

Dr. w. greeted Miss c.j. in the waiting room, intro-duced himself and shook her hand, asking if she were Miss j. He escorted her to his consultation room and they each took appropriate chairs at his desk. Dr. w. then asked how he might be of help to her, what problems was she having? Miss c.j. responded at length, speaking freely and with some sense of pressure.

She was working as a research biologist but was unhappy because she was living at home and couldn't make the break from her parents. Her mother was harsh and attacking, and favored the oldest of the patient's two sisters, both of whom were married and out of the house. Miss c.j. was closer to her father, a medical laboratory technician, who openly wished for the son he never had. He treated the patient as a boy in many ways, and despite their relative closeness, he was remote and non-giving.

Miss c.j. was depressed and smoked pot or tripped with acid to alleviate these feelings. In response to Dr. w.'s query as to just how depressed she became, she stated that she was not suicidal or anything like that, just very unhappy. Socially, she dated and had had inter-course with several men, but always found the relation-ship empty and usually chose men with major hang-ups. In her teens, she had had several affairs. Both of her parents suspected this and criticized her for it, but neither did very much to alleviate her obvious confusion at the time.

Dr. w. listened attentively to what the patient had to say, occasionally asking for a few details in regard to an ambiguous piece of history. He made a mental note of what was omitted, such as references to her childhood and her two sisters, but did not make specific inquiries into these areas since the patient was describing other important aspects of her life, and a reasonably broad picture was unfolding. The patient was clearly motivated for therapy and there were no obvious resistances or thoughts of flight to explore or interpret.

In the last ten minutes of the session, Dr. w. spoke; he had gathered sufficient material for an initial diagnosis and could make his recommendations to the patient. He considered her to be a severe character disorder with depressive features. He first stated that he agreed with the patient: she did have significant emotional problems, and he thought that through therapy he could help her to resolve them. He recommended two or three 50-minute sessions per week, depending on her financial resources. He mentioned his fee and the patient said that she could afford to come only once or twice a week. Dr. w. recommended that she be seen at least twice weekly if she was going to work through her problems and achieve significant and lasting change; he suggested that she try to work it out. He did not suggest a reduced fee at this juncture, but decided to allow the patient to explore her resources first. Should a reduction realistically seem necessary, he was prepared to suggest this possibility at their next session.

Dr. w. went on to explain how they would work: she would be expected to say whatever came to her mind much as she had in this session, and they would take it from there (with this type of verbal patient, this "rule" may be omitted initially). The time for her sessions was being put aside for her and he expected her to be responsible for them. She would be billed at the end of the month for the sessions of each month. Dr. w. added that he took his vacation during the month of July each year and that he expected Miss c.j. to arrange her vacation to coincide with his, if at all possible.

Pointing out the patient's tendency toward action, Dr. W. also said that he wanted the patient to understand that in psychotherapy all important decisions are explored thoroughly before being carried out. He then asked her if she had any questions, and she did not. He therefore arranged the hours of the sessions with her and told her that time was up. They shook hands goodbye and he said that he would see her at the next appointed time.

Consider this first session critically. What, if any, are its flaws, and what are its positive aspects in regard to technique? Actually, it is an essentially sound first hour and it will serve as a basis for a review of some basic principles.

1. *Listen carefully during the first telephone call, and begin to collect impressions, information, and data from the outset.* Be alert from the start for signs of resistances. Be aware that everything you do vis-à-vis the patient has conscious and unconscious meaning for both of you. Yet, be relaxed, cordial, appropriately concerned, and understanding. If you detect any hints of suicidal proclivities, explore them on the telephone and make an early appointment if any doubt exists.

2. *In your office, greet the patient warmly. Begin the session by asking about the patient's problems and then listen.* Allow the patient to speak freely, making inquiries only when really necessary. If the patient is having difficulty in talking spontaneously, ask questions and lead the way until he takes over or the resistances are understood. With marked silences, explain to the patient that your ability to help him depends largely on his talking about himself and what is on his mind.

3. *Get enough data to make an initial diagnosis and dynamic assessment, and to determine the treatment of choice.* This is your primary task in the first hour, and your interventions should relate to this goal. Unnecessary pursuit of details can often provoke anxiety and flight, and should be avoided. Be alert to resistances or indications of a possible quick departure from therapy. Be sure to deal with them if treatment seems at all in jeopardy. Be alert to any

suicidal risk and acute symptoms, and deal with them. Ascertain whether the patient is on medication and begin consideration of its use in the first session, however briefly it may be done.

4. *If time permits, fill in the most critical voids left by the patient in his anamnesis.* Most pertinent usually is the determination of what prompted the present onset of the patient's symptoms and why he is seeking treatment now.

5. *In the final minutes or so of the session, inform the patient, very briefly and in simple language, as to your impression of his problems.* Be frank in recommending therapy and do not understate the seriousness of the patient's problems. Indicate your honest belief that you can help him—as long as this is so. If you anticipate serious difficulties it is well to indicate these impressions. Make your recommendations regarding the type and frequency of therapy. Include here some comment as to anticipated duration and your fee.

6. *Once treatment is accepted, succinctly spell out the remaining ground rules.* Arrange specific hours, discuss responsibility for the sessions, describe your billing style, refer briefly to how you will work in the sessions, and note the need to explore all major decisions. Ask the patient if he has any questions and answer, as simply as possible, those which are professional and not personal.

7. *Conclude the session cordially, usually with a handshake and a reference to the next appointment.*

8. *Be flexible!* Follow leads from the patient wherever possible and do not resort to any rigid sequence other than that of listening before recommending.

With these basics in mind, consider the problems in the following initial hour:

> Mr. C.K. was a young man seen by Dr. V. in a clinic. He had been assessed by another psychiatrist and twice weekly psychotherapy had been recommended. He was assigned to Dr. V., who had two specific hours open, and the clinic secretary had called Mr. C.K. and made the first appointment for him. She also informed him of the fee that the clinic had set and how payment would be made.
>
> At the appointed hour, Dr. V. was introduced to the patient by the secretary. In his office, he began the

session by asking the patient what his problems were. Mr. C.K. spoke haltingly. He wasn't too sure; somehow his life seemed aimless and he didn't know where he was heading. He paused and, as he did throughout much of the session, Dr. V. asked him to go on. Mr. C.K. continued by saying that he wasn't a homosexual, but he worried about becoming one; he was in graduate school and couldn't seem to finish the dissertation required of him. Also, when he walked around campus, he somehow felt stared at and was uncomfortable.

Dr. V. asked him when these problems began, and the patient went on to detail his background, including his parents' recent divorce, something of their personalities and problems, and a bit about his years at home. He described an inability to get close to girlfriends, though he slept with them, and more about his social hang-ups. Dr. V. closed the hour by reminding the patient when the next session would occur.

The reader may be ready to criticize the handling of this session on several counts and, in addition, might wish that certain pertinent questions had been asked. I will briefly list my major comments and the reader can return to the relevant sections in the previous chapters for the principles involved.

It would have been best for the treatment if Dr. V. had assessed Mr. C.K. and recommended the therapy without someone else screening the patient. He should also have called the patient himself and handled the fee. He should not have encouraged splits, distance, impersonality, and an image of not being in charge and fully responsible for the therapy.

Dr. V. correctly intervened to help this patient since he was having difficulty in presenting his problems. This fostered the development of a sound therapeutic alliance. However, there were pertinent questions that the therapist might have asked to clarify this patient's diagnosis. Clarification of his more ominous presenting complaints—his feelings of being watched, for instance—done with tact so that undue anxiety was not generated, could have taken precedence. Asking about his homosexual fears was indicated only if the therapist was still uncertain about the diagnosis (and secondarily, unsure as to his ego strengths and weaknesses). Actually, subsequent data confirmed the therapist's initial impression that this patient had a borderline syndrome with prominent latent homosexual and paranoid problems.

The ground rules were inadequately presented. The therapist's recommendations should have begun (regardless of what had gone on before) with a brief indication that Dr. v. felt that the patient had significant emotional problems and that twice-weekly psychotherapy was, indeed, indicated. This would have established Dr. v.'s own commitment to treat the patient and offered a therapeutic alliance to him. The fee and method of payment should have been reiterated by the therapist. Reference should have been made to the need for the patient to sap everything that comes to his mind and a clear statement made that he explore all major decisions in therapy before acting on them. If there was a time limit to the therapy, it should have been mentioned here. Lastly, the patient should have had an opportunity to ask questions and to have these clarified.

Unfortunately, I cannot take the space to trace out the consequences and repercussions of these omissions as they were reflected in subsequent sessions. They fostered, among other problems, acting out by the patient against the therapy and in his outside life, deprecatory fantasies about the therapist, and splits in the transference and real reactions to Dr. v.

Let us now turn to another, condensed vignette for a clearer discussion of the consequences of a mishandled initial hour.

> Mrs. c.l. arrived at her first appointment ten minutes late. She began to talk to Dr. u. as she went from the waiting room to his consultation room. She spoke rapidly and in a scattered manner. Asked why she sought treatment, she rambled on about being divorced, the trials and tribulations of her recent marriage, her battles with her ex-husband and her rage at him as an ineffectual man, her inability to control her impulses both sexually and with regard to spending money, her ex-husband's inability to satisfy her sexually or to be firm with her in setting

limits, her inexplicable ties to her mother, and her two accidental pregnancies.

Dr. U. sat nonplussed and listened. He finally interrupted the patient to tell her that her time was up. Mrs. C.L. asked when her next appointment would be and he indicated the time. As she departed, the patient added that she had so much more to say; fifty minutes wasn't fair, and she hadn't really been told what to do with her new boyfriend or anything.

The reader can criticize this initial interview on almost every count. Dr. U. failed to follow sound basic principles and the hour was characterized by, and ended in, chaos. Before selecting a few salient issues for brief comment, let us be reminded of the difficulties, anxieties, and sense of being overwhelmed that patients like Mrs. C.L. can create for therapists. The need to have a good grasp on proper principles and a firm command of the session could not be more vividly portrayed.

The main points I want to establish from this vignette are as follows:

1. *Let your patient talk spontaneously, but only to a point.* Then ask the questions necessary to establish the diagnosis, type of treatment, extent of initial resistances, and other vital matters.

2. *Slowly and tactfully intervene in a manner that indicates you are not someone who can be "snowed under" by the patient's avalanche of words and impulses.* This offers him a secure therapeutic alliance and an opportunity for inner change, rather than a repetition of his neurotic interactions.

3. *Be certain to allow sufficient time for your assessment statement to the patient and the establishment of the ground rules.*

4. *When a patient is late to the initial hour, think of serious resistances and be prepared to address some comments to this problem.* Further indications for such an intervention with this patient included her marked tendency to act out by not sticking with any undertaking, her obvious misconceptions regarding exploratory therapy, and her wish for direct advice from the therapist. Dr. U. might well have explained and defined insight psychotherapy to

this patient. He also should have pointed out that delaying, exploring, and thinking through were clearly alien to her style of living, adding that only efforts of this kind could aid her in handling her problems, and finding new and less costly ways to resolve her conflicts.

Mrs. C.L. subsequently continued to test out and act out directly against her therapist by being late, missing sessions, and involving him with other family members. The unfortunate tone set in the initial hour therefore continued, for some time, without the development of any insight or inner change. Such difficulties must not be perpetuated by the therapist since they constitute both a sharing of such defenses as denial, displacement, and flight, and a mutual acting out. These resistances undermine therapy at its core; they must therefore be dealt with from the outset and consistently thereafter until they are worked through, so no misalliance prevails.

In present practice, we all see patients who come for consultation under duress and with great reluctance. This includes those who are pressured by spouses, parents, schools, and employers. Such conditions should be detected as early in the first session as possible. In such circumstances, the focus must be on this major resistance or the patient will probably not return. Enough material should be collected for a diagnostic assessment and for recommendations to the patient regarding therapy; the rest of the session must be geared to tuning in on the pressures the patient is under and why the patient is so set against treatment. These efforts are made to establish a basis for treatment and a therapeutic alliance.

Consider now this first session. How would you have proceeded?

Miss C.M. was a tweny-year-old young woman who called Dr. T. and said that she had just spoken with her internist, who had strongly recommended that she call him; she was in a great hassle with her parents. Perhaps Dr. T. could tell her what to do about it.

In the session, Miss C.M. said immediately that she saw no point in coming. Her parents were crazy; they beat her, often locked her in her room, and were in a rage that she was now living with a fellow whom they detested. Perhaps Dr. T. could tell her how to get along with them. Beyond that, she had nothing to say and sat in silence.

At this point, the therapist has a number of critical problems. What are they, and how would you pursue them?

> Dr. T. first asked several questions in the hope of obtaining some impression of the patient's current problems and a bit of historical material. The patient was very taciturn: she had left college because it was a drag, had a good job now, and that was about it. Dr. T. explained that the patient had given herself this opportunity to gain some insight and had sought this for some reason. He suggested that she use the time for this purpose, and that much would depend on what she told him. Silence prevailed.

Let us pause here. Many patients will make an appointment under such circumstances with either unrealistic hopes (for Miss C.M. this was, "Tell me how to live with my parents"—an impossible task) or with some unconscious or half-conscious realization of a need for professional help which is then denied in the session. This may be due to excessive anxiety, great suspiciousness and mistrust, and/or feelings of vulnerability and fears of mortification. If the therapist can detect any motive for the silences, it should be interpreted. In addition, the reality of the situation must be established and the indications for therapy be presented to the patient for him to consider directly. Thus, confrontation and interpretation of any dynamic aspect of the resistances is supplemented with realistic confrontation with the need for treatment and the patient's denial of it. Such patients are often seriously depressed and paranoid, lack basic trust, and resist any offer of a therapeutic alliance. They are difficult to engage in therapy.

At times, therapeutic work sufficient to enable the patient to reveal a bit more about himself or to agree to return for another session is possible; only rarely do these patients accept therapy and they usually do so in a tentative manner. If the patient decides not to return, the therapist should spell out his assessment of the situation and leave the door open for the patient to call him when he is ready. Now to return to our vignette:

> Dr. T. had little to go on. There was the patient's intense mistrust, her fear of her punitive and blatantly destructive parents that he suspected was the key to this mistrust, her own propensity to act out provocatively, and a strong suspicion that Miss C.M. was concealing severe pathology. He told the patient about each of these impressions, particularly the latter, stating that in the face of all the patient had endured and in light of her intense withdrawal in the session, he suspected that she had significant problems which she was not revealing or facing. (To himself, he considered borderline pathology with paranoid trends.) Should she want to deal with these problems at any time, he added, Miss C.M. should call him.
>
> The patient responded that she couldn't see that anything was to be gained by this kind of session, and left on that basis. The following week, however, she called Dr. T. and made another appointment. She then revealed her previously concealed, manifest pathology; she suffered from intense anxieties, multiple phobias, and a severe eating disorder. She also described a series of blatant traumas at the hands of her parents, filled with brutality and temporary desertions. In particular, silence had been used by them as a major punitive weapon. On the basis of these revelations, though in the face of continued denial that was, however, less intense now, therapy was arranged.

The principles I want to emphasize in regard to reluctant or blatantly resistant patients are as follows:

1. *Be tolerant and patient with such persons, and listen for hints as to their real inner problems.* If the therapist is angered or threatened, he confirms the unconscious or conscious link in the patient's mind between him and the patient's dreaded parents or other punitive figures. That is, the transference fantasy would thereby be confirmed in reality, and the patient would be sure to leave treatment.

2. *Ask questions and attempt to establish a diagnosis, and get at some of the roots of the blatant resistances.* While these may be due to the patient's fears of treatment and fear of his own fantasies and memories, it is often out of fear of the therapist and what he represents. Beyond this, such patients usually have been manipulated into the consultation as a means through which the other person is attempting to harm or control them in some way. Being in treatment may mean, then, that the patient is "at fault" in the situation or the "sick one," leaving the others blameless. More directly, treatment is sometimes used to prepare the way for a spouse or parent to leave his partner, to prepare a law suit against the patient, or to influence and control him in some way.

These are harsh realities and the therapist must not be a party to them. If he and the patient do not establish a clear basis for a therapeutic alliance and for treatment as a means of alleviating the patient's suffering, therapy cannot succeed.

3. *Be alert to such problems, and openly and honestly define them for the patient.* Face the reality of such issues with him and convey any dynamic understanding of them which you discover. This may enable the patient to reveal his own inner need for therapy and recognize a sound basis on which it can begin.

4. *These patients most often use defenses of denial (there is nothing wrong with me), displacement (they—the parents or spouse—are the ones with the problems), and acting out (to vent their rage and to keep their fantasies and pathology from surfacing).* They are most often borderline with strong paranoid trends, and have been strikingly traumatized in their early life. These patients are difficult to confront and reluctant to the end. However, they can sometimes be helped to face themselves and to change.

With these comments, I conclude my study of the first hour. Having arranged psychotherapy for the patient, the therapist next has the task of listening to and understanding him, so that he may intervene in an effective manner. Therefore, I will turn next to the theoretical concepts which are the foundation for our clinical work.

III

THEORETICAL
FRAMEWORK

8 Psychoanalytic Concepts of Psychopathology and Psychotherapy

Clinical observations of patients in psychotherapy and psychoanalysis and direct observations of infants, children, and adults have provided us with a basis for conceptualization of the nature and development of psychopathology, and of the therapeutic relationship and techniques. An outline of these concepts will prepare the way for the clinical explorations which lie ahead of us. In contrast to the rest of this book, this presentation will be essentially theoretical. It will be highly selective and, of necessity, incomplete, but it will be concluded with the practical aspect of exemplifying vignettes from psychotherapeutic situations.

I will begin with a definition of psychopathology, will trace out developmentally its roots and bases, and finally touch upon the implications of these observations and formulations for the psychotherapeutic situation. It is not possible for me to specify the vast bibliography on which this presentation is based, but some of the main references are included.

WHAT IS PSYCHOPATHOLOGY?

Psychopathology may be defined as psychological emotional disorders of adaptation to the inner and outer environment. Developing out of intrapsychic conflicts and dysfunctions, the manifestations are characterological, symptomatic, and behavioral.

The following are the main syndromes of psychopathology (listed roughly in the order of decreasing severity):

The psychoses, including schizophrenic and psychotic depressive reactions (see Jacobson, 1971). These are characterized by major impairments in ego functioning—object relationships, reality testing, synthesizing, and thinking; in self-boundaries; in instinctual drive expressions; and in superego functioning.

The borderline states and severe character disorders that are characterized by a maintenance of self-boundaries or brief impairments in them; major disturbances in various ego, id, and superego functions; and by acute regressions with rapid reconstitution (see Kernberg, 1967 and 1971; and Boyer and Giovacchini, 1967). Their manifestations also include pervasive symptoms such as uncontrolled anxiety, poor impulse control, major disturbances in affect regulation, perversions, severe phobias or obsessions, and the use of primitive defenses such as avoidances, denial, splitting, and projection.

The narcissistic disturbances, in which the regulation of self-esteem is impaired and object relationships are basically in terms of the patient's needs, with little regard for others who are used as "self-objects" (see Kernberg, 1970a; Kohut, 1971).

The moderate and mild character disorders characterized by recurrent behavioral disturbances of a moderately or mildly disruptive kind, moderate phobic or obsessive symptoms, moderate anxiety, and considerable maturation of the psychic macrostructures (see Kernberg, 1970b).

Psychosomatic syndromes, which usually occur in severely or moderately disturbed character disorders and borderline or psychotic patients.

Symptom neuroses such as phobias, obsessions, and anxiety states which may be the surface manifestations of severe or moderate character disturbances.

These are the main syndromes with which the therapist is confronted in patients who come for psychotherapy. To understand how these problems come to be, we will have to go back to the beginnings of life, trace the avenues of development and discuss what can go wrong along the way.

THE NEWBORN

ENDOWMENT

There are variations in intrauterine existence and experience, as influenced by the total inner environment provided by the mother, that in turn are affected by her significant external life experiences and illnesses. These set off sequences with ultimate psychological and psychophysiological effects. The effects of this period on the endowment of the child, and on his subsequent psychopathology, are considerable, but their specific influences on the life of the individual are still a matter for study.

Birth, with its role in separating the infant from the mother and the nature of the experience itself varies along qualitative and quantitative dimensions. There is a wide range of normalcy in this regard, as well as the potential for specific birth traumas which predispose to psychopathology.

Each individual is born with an innate endowment of instinctual drives and needs, and operative ego functions and nuclei. This endowment has inherent weaknesses and strengths, and a multitude of characteristics. This is the core of the autonomous ego apparatus which will evolve into the relatively conflict-free sphere of ego functioning (Hartmann, 1958). There is a normal range of these endowments beyond which the seeds of psychopathology are sown.

RELEVANCE TO PSYCHOPATHOLOGY

In my discussion of the relevance of each particular phase to the development of psychopathology, I will consider three main dimensions: the kinds of possible danger situations that the person may experience during the phase; the resources available to him for coping with these dangers and resolving them; and the possible outcomes.

Intrauterine stresses may occur through illnesses in the mother, unusual physiological changes from various causes, and traumas experienced by the mother. The infant's resources for handling these dangers are minimal and the outcome ranges from miscarriage and death to effects on basic endowments of the newborn. These factors can play an indirect role in the subsequent development of psychopathology. These are experiences not subject to recall directly and I suspect that indirect recall is also not feasible (see also Greenacre, 1952; and Winnicott, 1958). Their relevance in psychotherapy is entirely on an indirect basis.

The birth experience itself may be traumatic, leading to effects ranging from death and major injuries to overwhelming anxiety and psychophysiological disruptions. The infant's resources are still minimal and basically physiological. The effects of such traumas may leave permanent consequences in the subsequent life of the newborn, including psychophysiological disturbances of his drive endowment and ego development which thereby contribute to the development of psychopathology.

There is also a wide range of pathological, psychophysiological disturbances in endowments at birth which have lasting consequences for the life of the newborn and indirect effects on his psychopathology and therapy. Among these are impairments in ego apparatus and functions, and congenital defects of all kinds. In addition, there may be malfunctioning of the stimulus barrier and other innate protective and need-achieving functions. Excessive needs themselves may also pose dangers for the newborn and make meeting them adequately a difficult task.

The newborn's resources for dealing with such traumas and stresses are entirely innate, psychophysiological, and primitive; his need for assistance from others is maximal and vital for his survival. His mode of experiencing and responding is massive, global, and ill-defined.

These traumatic situations, arising from internal and external disturbances to which the newborn is subject, and his responses as they are supported by those available to assist him, form one basis for further developmental problems and psychopathology.

THE FIRST FOUR YEARS

This period comprises those years before the infant and young child has begun to solidify his personality and the structures within it into lasting and mature forms. It is a phase with its own distinguishing maturational sequences, modes of functioning and resources, state of the psychic structures, object relatedness, self-feeling and self-concept, and adaptational tasks (see for example, Spitz, 1957 and 1965; and Winnicott, 1958). It also has its own characteristic kinds of dangers, methods available for coping with them, and outcomes, be they successful or maladaptive.

This period has been called pre-oedipal or pregenital, preverbal (in part), and the period of the basic fault by Balint (1968). He wrote of it as the period of primary love, a time when the basic two-person interaction with its sense of a "harmonious mix-up" predominates and centers on the child's needs and their gratification. It is a period that has been studied in detail by Mahler (1968) and others, who have emphasized the problem of gradual separation from the mother and the establishment of individuation. It is also the period in which major psychotic, narcissistic and borderline disturbances have their main roots. It is, in all, a most fascinating and crucial period of life; let us study it briefly and get some feeling for it.

NORMAL DEVELOPMENT

Maturational Sequences

These refer to the biologically- and psychophysiologically-based inner thrusts toward development and maturation. They are directed toward specificity of functioning, which is built out of the potential endowments within each newborn. These maturational sequences rely on an adequate and facilitating environment in which mothering plays the central role and which shapes their unfolding in a sensitive and exquisite interaction (see Winnicott, 1958). Included here is the unfolding of ego capacities, instinctual drive expressions, superego anlage, and self-feelings (see Erikson, 1950; and Balint, 1968). This unfolding is quite complex, though it is usually described in terms of central drive expressions and needs such as those related to feeding. This is the oral phase, in which needs for physical closeness and other kinds of warmth and stimulation are also important. Other drive expressions involved are the development of motility and impulses toward mastery; the evolution of bowel functions and related instinctual drive expressions— the anal phase; the early, primitive genital stirrings and expressions—the phallic phase. Aggression comes into play as an extension of thrusts toward mastery and as a basic response to frustrations and hurt.

In all, these maturational sequences contribute to the capacity of the child to express his needs, develop as a person, respond to the environment, and deal with stresses and traumas.

Role of the Environment

For the newborn and infant, the mothering figure is the heart of the environmental matrix and, initially, there is a minimal differentiation between the two, and a maximal dependence and influence on the infant by the mother and others. Interactions are essentially two-person and the mothering figure channels, fosters, shapes, and determines the infant's development and styles of adaptation. This two-person interaction is undoubtedly experienced by the infant as some kind of oneness in his earliest days, in which the inner and the outer, and self and the nonself are confused and merged into a global unity. It is a oneness in which "good" and "bad," "me" and "not-me," "satisfied" and "frustrated" may be used as ill-defined terms to characterize vague feeling states out of which a gradual differentiation of the self as separate from others will unfold.

The mother-child matrix involves more than "good" or "bad" mothering, or a "good-enough" or facilitating environment (see Winnicott, 1958). There is a whole, complex interaction which is conscious, preconscious, and unconscious in different ways for each of the two persons, and in which the mother not only nurtures, nourishes, prohibits, and controls in a particular constellation of ways, but responds to many other needs and behaviors of the infant in her own selective fashion. As a result, the infant experiences his mother in a variety of ways which are initially fragmented and separate, and only later integrated as referring to a single person. Each of her responses has special qualities: need-caring, calm, reassuring, anxious, aggressive, disturbing, readily-available, seldom-available, and the like. Furthermore, the mother encourages and reinforces certain aspects of the infant's functioning and repertoire of behavioral, emotional, and psychological thrusts and responses; fails to respond to or reinforce other reactions of her child; and actively discourages, is angered by, or punishes still other affects and behaviors. In all, there is a constant feedback between the mother and child, their respective needs and responses, and the cumulative effects they have on each other.

In addition to this ongoing interaction with its cumulative nurture and traumas (see Khan, 1963), in which so much of the mother's repertoire, personality, and psychopathology play a role, there is a second environmental aspect of critical importance—that of major traumatic events. These are disruptive experiences that evoke a range of disturbances in the infant and lead to various responses related to hurtful effects and attempts at adaptation and mastery. As the child develops, there is an increasing degree of selective reaction to, and toleration of, a potentially disturbing experience without it being traumatic. There is also an increasing degree of sophistication with which he can respond to such events and deal with them behaviorally and intrapsychically.

Modes of Functioning and Repertoire of Resources

SELF AND NOT-SELF; OBJECT RELATIONSHIPS. The infant experiences his environment and his developing self in a global, poorly-distinguished, primitive way. He views himself as a bodily-dominated self who eventually develops a capacity for primitive thinking. He experiences an undifferentiated union or "good me" between himself and a nurturing, gratifying mother, and some kind of dysphoric non-union or "bad me" with a hurtful, non-gratifying mother. Only gradually does the infant develop a feeling of separateness from her, a complex process of separating one's "self" from the "not-self" and developing self boundaries with their varying degrees of permeability and flexibility. Identity development, self-concept, and self-experiencing all evolve from this matrix.

Object relationships begin as global, separate-in-time, unintegrated experiences in which the mother is part of the self one moment and a separate object at another.

Another important dimension relates to the infant's narcissism, his self-centeredness and self-love, his wish that his needs alone be gratified, and his experience of others as extensions of himself or as objects whose sole interest should be the gratification of his needs. Self-aggrandizement is also involved, and this later extends to idealization of others who are experienced at this stage as "self-objects" or extensions of the psychological self (Kohut, 1971). This period, with its non-adult-like features forms the core within every person. If we are to understand and communicate with all of our patients, we must be in touch with and responsive to this part of them.

MODES OF THOUGHT. There is a preverbal period, which lasts for some months, that is probably dominated by image and immediate experience. Speech and thought comes initially in concrete, isolated groupings, and is animistic, inner and wish-dominated, primitive, often affect-laden, not realistic or reality-tested, magical, omnipotent, and primary-process-dominated.

An important aspect of imaging and thinking is fantasizing, much of it expressed in early imaginitive play that is gradually more internalized into thought and daydreams. Under the influence of inner and outer stimuli, needs, and demands, such fantasizing has an important adaptive role, particularly in regard to the working over and resolution of traumas and intrapsychic conflicts. Much of this fantasizing has a crucial unconscious component (only partly related to repression), and is best described as unconscious fantasy activity (see Freud, 1908; Beres, 1962; and Arlow, 1969). This inner fantasy activity occurs in various forms, consciously and unconsciously, and much of it relates to matters which are largely outside of the person's direct awareness. The derivatives of this unconscious fantasy activity are expressed and worked over in disguised form. These fantasies are crystallizations of every aspect of experiencing, and of important traumas and their intrapsychic repercussions.

The early, global, poorly structured, primitive kind of fantasizing that develops in these early years is in keeping with the kind of thinking and perceiving-experiencing predominant in this period. It forms the deepest level of the hierarchical layering of unconscious fantasies and memories within the psyche.

INNER STRUCTURE BUILDING AND DEFENSES. There is a gradual

buildup of inner structures, largely in accordance with the infant's innate assets and liabilities, and the mother's directing and facilitating. The infant incorporates into his self-structure aspects of the mother's functioning and ways of being, relating, perceiving, testing out inner and outer reality, and defending.

On the most primitive level, this process is conceived of as incorporation and we speak of the result as good and bad introjects. We later speak of this process as one of identification as the infant becomes more aware of the separateness and complexity of others. These mechanisms play a crucial role in the child's psychic development and operate on both a conscious and unconscious level.

Another basic building process which also lends itself to defensive use relates to the infant's experiencing something within himself as "not me," a process of externalizing or projecting. Often this process is used to deal with unpleasant and disturbing inner feelings and thoughts, and destructive, threatening impulses and needs.

Other primitive defenses are modeled on the physical reflex of withdrawal and the basic psychological defense of shutting out. These lead to primitive repressive mechanisms and denial, and to early separations within the self, in which anxiety-provoking aspects are split off and denied.

In all, these intrapsychic mechanisms are qualitatively and quantitatively different from those which develop later in the more mature and structured child and adult.

In addition to the defenses which are directed toward anxiety-provoking instinctual drive expressions, other important structures and functions developed in these early years include object- and self-representations, executive apparatus, means of modulating and channeling instinctual drives for appropriate expression and discharge, behavioral and affective controls, and structures related to modulating affective responses, such as anxiety, into controlled signals. Anxiety is a response to instinctual drive wishes which pose various kinds of threats or are forbidden in some sense; it is to be distinguished from fear, which is a response to primarily external dangers (see Freud, 1926; Schur, 1953; and Arlow, 1963a). Other affects, such as sadness and depression, happiness and joy, and rage and fury have developmental vicissitudes of their own (Jacobson, 1971). In general, affects have a more massive, undifferentiated, bodily-embedded quality in these early years than they do later on. There is also a tendency to respond somatically (psychophysiologically) to a wide range of stimuli in this early period, far more so than in later years.

There is also a gradual organization of instinctual drive components into characteristic and repetitive patterns and need expressions. Initially self-directed and autoerotic on the one hand, and mother-directed on the other, these drives and needs unfold around oral, anal, and phallic-vaginal components. In addition, superego precursors in the form of early ideals and prohibitions also develop.

Kinds of Adaptive Tasks and Dangers

ADAPTIVE TASKS. The newborn infant is faced with many specific adaptive tasks. They begin with the postnatal establishment of a capacity to breathe, take in nourishment, evoke care, and, generally, survive. The unfolding and maturing of the self is another critical task for the infant, as is developing a broad capacity to relate and gratify his expanding needs. Resolving special environmental demands, such as those related to feeding and toilet training, is also important.

One special adaptive task relates to developing a separate self by giving up the symbiosis with the mother, and separating and individuating (see Mahler, 1968). The handling and outcome of this complex behavioral, emotional, and psychological process plays an important role in all subsequent development.

DANGER SITUATIONS. Freud (1926) presented us with a hierarchy of traumatic and danger situations. For this phase, he defined these as birth, helplessness in the face of non-gratified needs, the loss of the mother (separation), and the loss of her love (see also Schur, 1953; and Arlow, 1963a). At present, we recognize that matters are more complex. Early, primitively conceived dangers of bodily harm may confront the infant from within and without. Loss of the mother may include her total loss (absence or death), loss of her affectively (depression, flatness, lack of empathy), or the loss of specific aspects of her role in caring for the infant. The mother's reprimands and condemnations also constitute early external dangers of a kind related to later superego functioning. These external dangers generate inner warning signals related to the anticipation, and possible prevention, of traumatic situations. Another source of potential danger arises from within in the form of excessive instinctual drives and needs which may intensify beyond possible mastery or gratification (see A. Freud, 1946).

These dangers are assessed and perceived in terms of the modes of conceiving and experiencing available to the infant. Thus, they are experienced globally and in terms of primitive fears of total annihilation (Winnicott, 1958). At this stage, external traumas imposed on the infant have a great impact psychophysiologically and create major intrapsychic disturbances. The ultimate link-up of these traumas with instinctual drive wishes proves crucial to the development of psychopathology.

RESPONSES TO DANGERS. In keeping with the repertoire of the infant, his responses to traumas and danger situations are crude, massive, somatically oriented, and built around his primitive capacities and defenses. His adaptive resources are limited and his mastery of inner conflicts and anxieties requires considerable maternal support.

RELATIONSHIP TO PSYCHOPATHOLOGY

Character Development and Its Pathology

Briefly, character may be defined as the individual's usual, repetitive, largely ego-syntonic, characteristic way of reacting, behaving, defending, and gratifying himself. It develops out of innate givens and their specific unfolding under the influence of, and in interaction with, his environment. Specific traumas which evoke a need for repetitive reworking also leave their mark on the personality of the infant.

Pathological character formations are repetitive, maladaptive, ego-syntonic patterns. They evolve in these early years out of disturbances in such basic factors as innate endowment (id or ego), impairments in the mothering, and major traumas. The more severe characterological disturbances that we see clinically in adults are based on disruptive influences in these early years and their effects on the growing infant and child, including his continued efforts to master these disruptions.

Severe characterological disturbances, then, are the outcome of

aberrant endowment and development, and disruptive outer influences. These become apparent in distorted personality patterns.
Such disturbances also reflect the efforts of the impaired personality
to repair the disruptive influences in some lasting way. They are not
simply defects of one sort or another, but complex formations in
which conscious and unconscious intrapsychic conflicts play a
crucial role. These conflicts are represented in unconscious fantasies and memories that reflect the entire pathogenic situation in
terms of the prevailing imagery and thinking.

While schizophrenic and other psychotic character disturbances
are embedded in the disturbances of the earliest months in this
period, I will not elaborate upon them here. The pathology of the
borderline personality arises in the later months of this phase and
is characterized by the following: a primitive conceptualization of
danger; global and massive-anxieties, with fears of annihilation;
basic ego dysfunctions in thinking, perceiving, controlling, defending, relating, etc.; intense and relatively blatant instinctual drive
expression; and a primitive superego and aberrant ideals and aspirations. Self-experience and self-boundaries are tenuous and disturbed,
though the basic self and not-self distinction is maintained. Unconscious fantasy systems are characteristically primitive and structured primarily in the modes of the infant, focusing on two-person
and survival conflicts.

Another group of character disturbances embedded in this
period are the narcissistic disorders (Kernberg, 1970a; and Kohut,
1971). These are evidenced in a distorting influence evoked by the
continued investment of the self and then others in grandiose and
omnipotent terms, and in relating to others almost entirely in terms
of one's own needs with little concept of separate, nonself persons
with needs of their own. There are also serious disturbances in self-
esteem, ideals, goals, and aspirations, and there is often a deep mistrust of others. The lack of basic trust is founded in disturbances of
early mothering and in the mother's own narcissistic problems, as
they affect the infant. These persons tend to respond with intense
and primitive rage when they are frustrated. Intrapsychically,
intense, unconscious conflicts and primitive, grandiose and vengeful fantasies prevail, resulting in gross personality disturbances.

Also arising during this period are such severe affective disturbances as non-psychotic manic and depressive states (Jacobson, 1971), addictive characters, and anxiety-ridden characters. They are based on fixations in this phase which evolve from gross over-gratifications and excessive frustrations, or failures to meet the infant's needs. Once established, these intrapsychic aberrations and primitive conflicts contribute to later dysfunctions and pathology. The resultant personality structure is uneven and vulnerable, with considerable continuation of conflicts that are usually covered over and mastered, but accompanied by primitive ego, id, and superego expressions. Under later stresses, these primitive layers show through quite clearly. Such troubled adults even learn to rely on these regressive mechanisms for adaptive responses when under outer and inner pressure.

SYMPTOMS

Symptoms are defined here as painful, intrapsychic maladaptations and aberrations. Their structure is different from that of symptoms derived from difficulties in later childhood and thereafter. Basically, emotional symptoms seem to appear when the characterological endowments and efforts at adaptation are overtaxed and fail to resolve the intrapsychic stresses with which the infant is faced. The following are among the characteristic sources of symptoms during this early period.

Cumulative Disturbances

There are symptoms derived from this period in which inner conflict plays less of a role than do innate aberrations in endowment, major early traumas, and/or gross distortions in the ongoing mothering. Each of these has massive effects, directly and indirectly, on the infant. Such influences operate primarily on ego functioning and development, and lead to so-called ego defects or dysfunctions, and to the basic fault, a psychobiological deficiency described by Balint (1968). It is my impression that such symptoms are not simply defects or faults, but complex, overdetermined, conflict- and fantasy-related intrapsychic disturbances with complicated structures of their own. They are embedded in the early two-person, need-gratifying, intrapsychic conflicts related to primitive instinctual drives and in aberrations in the ongoing relationship with the mother, whose own pathology creates repetitive disturbances in relating to and caring for her child and in insuring his proper psychological development. To illustrate some of the symptoms in this grouping:

INNATE IMPAIRMENTS IN THE STIMULUS BARRIER, SYNTHETIC CAPACITIES, AND FRUSTRATION TOLERANCE. All of these are complex, primitive, interrelated ego functions and impairments will lead to such early symptoms as excessive anxiety, and sleep, feeding, and motility disturbances. These basic dysfunctions contribute to later impairments in the developing ego functions and, intrapsychically, contribute to impairments in defensive operations and synthetic capacity.

INNATE DISTURBANCES IN DRIVE ENDOWMENT. Whether these cause excesses or insufficiencies, they may also disrupt development and lead to early and later symptoms regardless of the adequacy of the mothering. Excessive oral needs, for example, can lead to anxiety, and sleeping and eating disturbances, and form a basis for later symptom-formation. Such aberrant drive manifestations also have an effect on intrapsychic fantasy-formations that contributes to later psychopathology.

DISTURBANCES IN THE MOTHERING. These disturbances produce still another group of symptoms. The earliest of these aberrations probably precede, and blend into, the dysfunctions caused by primitive two-person conflicts, since they occur when the child lacks a concept of others and is immersed in himself and his own needs. These disturbances are often referred to in oversimplified terms as being caused by maternal over-stimulation, excessive frustration, and failure to respond adequately to the child's needs. Failures in mothering can create excessive vulnerability to anxiety and disrupt adequate defensive development.

Narcissistic disorders have their roots in these disturbances in the ongoing relationship with the mother—and later the father—in these early years (Kohut, 1971). Failures in empathy and in meeting the child's narcissistic needs, often related to narcissistic pathology in the mother, are important here. Basic defects in self-image, self-esteem, and in the resolution of grandiose self-feelings and exaggerated idealizations of others are the outcome.

These primitive difficulties with the mother can also generate intrapsychic conflicts based on early, two-person relating and the resultant global, ill-formed conscious and unconscious fantasies. For example, such early conflicts are experienced in terms of threats to survival represented by fears of being devoured and fears of the infant's own devouring impulses. In a more general way, disruptive mothering interferes with the formation of basic trust and creates a deep sense of mistrust (see Erikson, 1950) that is linked to later paranoid and depressive character traits and symptoms. In all, early one-person-experienced (narcissistic) anxieties and fantasies soon give way to two-person conflicts which lead to primitively experienced intrapsychic conflicts. Failure of primitive defenses to resolve these inner conflicts may then lead to symptom formation, including those that are psychosomatic and those that involve impairments in self-boundaries, reality testing, and other basic ego functions.

Whether psychological symptoms occur solely as the result of ego defects that are innately caused or caused by bad-mothering, or whether there is always some degree of anxiety caused by primitive and terrifying instinctual drive wishes that the primitive ego fails to adequately resolve, is a moot point. In psychotherapy, these basic defects virtually always become crystallized around moments of acute trauma, and the intrapsychic anxiety, conflict, and fantasies that such major traumas evoke. Therefore, in treatment the therapist must offer two avenues of repair: an opportunity for new growth and development; and insight into the pathogenic conflicts and unconscious fantasies (see below). However, in these early years, the intrapsychic conflicts are experienced differently than later on, the anxieties are more terrifying, and the defenses more primitive. Global fears of being annihilated, devoured, defecated, masticated, and the like are characteristic. The instinctual drive wishes which evoke such anxieties are poorly defined oral, anal, and early phallic incorporative and expulsive fantasies, represented in the magical and primitive mode of visualizing and fantasizing available to the infant. When the infant's primitive defenses (denial, splitting, projection, etc.) against such wishes fail, symptoms will develop. This is a crude and relatively unstructured intrapsychic struggle that, in later years, becomes considerably more specific and well defined.

Acute Traumas

In addition to the many complex repercussions of ongoing, cumulative traumas in the infant's interaction with his mother, acute traumas play a critical role in symptom formation even in these early months and years. Such traumas may tax the immature psyche beyond its resources and evoke anxieties, conflicts, and fantasies that are not adequately mastered and resolved. For example, there may be a sudden loss of the mother, the birth of a sibling or a miscarriage, or the infant may become seriously ill. Such acute dangers are perceived in primitive terms and evoke primitive fantasies as the infant endeavors to understand and master the overwhelming anxiety that the experience has evoked. Such traumatic experiences, in turn, may stimulate primitive instinctual drive wishes in the infant, causing additional anxieties and conflicts. Primitive defenses are mobilized to ward off these anxiety-provoking impulses, and failure of these defenses will lead to symptom formation.

The entire experience is registered in terms of various conscious and unconscious fantasies, and new efforts at reworking these conflicts—at adaptation—will be made whenever a later experience touches upon the early, acute trauma. In the psychotherapy of patients where such pathogenic traumas have occurred, it will prove crucial to reconstruct or recover these early traumatic experiences in order to understand and resolve the symptoms to which they contribute (see Arlow, 1963a; and Freud, 1912).

LATER SYMPTOM FORMATION. These disturbances in the early years contribute to later symptom formation in several additional ways.

They contribute to basic disturbances in object relationships which promote later outer and inner conflicts and maladaptations. They cause fixations onto pathological means of resolving conflicts, including the use of pathological defenses that later are inherently maladaptive and symptomatic (e.g., splitting, denial and projection). Later coping capacities are thereby impaired. They create an inherent vulnerability to certain kinds of stresses, to the reawakening of disturbing unconscious conflicts and fantasies, and to specific adaptive failures (symptoms) and regressive tendencies. The effects of these earlier disturbances on later ego, id, and superego development is considerable, limiting and distorting it, and directing it toward pathogenic channels.

They impair the resolution and integration into the self-concept of grandiose and over-idealized images of the self and others, and unrealistic ideals, goals, and aspirations. These contribute, in turn, to problems in the development of adequate drive controls and ego-ideal formation.

RELATIONSHIP TO THE PSYCHOTHERAPEUTIC SITUATION

The main implications for the technique of psychotherapy of this phase of development are as follows:

Therapeutic Atmosphere and Therapeutic Alliance

The prevalence of pathology derived from these earliest years makes it imperative that realistic techniques be adapted to help modify such disturbances. We must offer to the patient a therapeutic alliance and atmosphere through which he can develop basic trust, and express his problems at this level and be truly understood and reached.

Since many of these problems are preverbal, they will be accessible to change largely through nonverbal attitudes in the therapist and verbalizations which are in keeping with the patient's needs as derived from this period. The therapist's basic stance is among the most crucial of his nonverbal communications to the patient. Without its being properly expressed, all work on the verbal level, regardless of how precisely it is done, will have little positive effect on the patient. In addition, initial responses to the patient's narcissistic needs, which are expressed either as idealizations of the therapist or by using him as an extension of the patient who is expected to admire and understand him at all times, are designed to create an empathic bond with the patient so that he feels understood rather than threatened (Kohut, 1971).

This overall therapeutic stance is best conceived as being a "good-therapist-mother," though its specific definition is complex: good mothering means offering to the patient, in terms of his needs and his pathology, a proper "fit," a flexible but firm environmental "hold" or protective barrier, and a facilitating influence.

Good-therapist-mothering means acceptance, tolerance, trustworthiness, and gratification of the patient's realistic needs for therapeutic help, but not his primitive needs. This is a special kind of mothering, appropriate to the therapeutic situation and the realistic hopes for inner change that it offers. Gratifications of the patient's wishes that go beyond the appropriate boundaries of the therapeutic relationship make the therapist an indulgent, over-stimulating, over-gratifying mothering figure, and thereby a bad therapist-mother. The goal is to foster basic trust, an atmosphere for inner growth, and a sense that it is safe to regress in the search for new adaptations. Inappropriate gratifications foster regressions for the sake of indulgence and need-satisfaction, that is, malignant regression (see Balint, 1968), and are antitherapeutic.

Proper therapist-mothering has at its core understanding the patient, gratification only within therapeutic boundaries, and fulfillment of the therapist's role by correctly responding and interpreting. It requires a natural stance and not one of role playing; it must be genuine and relatively free of conflict for the therapist. It is not overindulgence of the insatiable patient, though it includes understanding his needs and responding to them within the limits of the therapeutic relationship.

Good-therapist-mothering at times means gently confronting the patient with his excesses or his attempts to ridicule or undermine therapy. Often, therapists mistakenly accept ridicule, derision, or destructive acting out by the patient, as if this indulgence demonstrates acceptance. While one must not respond unduly with anger, but with consistent understanding, good-therapist-mothering does not mean being abused or seductive, thereby permitting inappropriate gratification at the therapist's expense.

Finally, "good-therapist-mothering" means offering a sense of closeness and empathy to the patient, while respecting the necessary distance and boundaries of the relationship. Sensitivity to timing, to frequency of interventions, to the nonverbal aspects of comments that lead to their being experienced primarily as hurts or gratifications, and to silences are among the means of creating a proper therapeutic atmosphere for such patients.

Understanding the Patient

Patients with psychopathology derived from these early years require a special kind of listening, understanding, and relating. While difficult to describe in adult words (see Balint, 1968), it begins with experiencing the patient as an infant-child cloaked in adult trappings. The therapist must be truly empathic and non-verbally in tune with the patient. It is necessary that he be antici-patory, understand the patient's language on the primitive level at which it is meant, and understand the patient intuitively as well as intellectually. It is listening globally and primitively, and to the patient's communications as expressions of need-gratifying demands to which his—the therapist's—responses will be experienced primarily as gratifying or frustrating with little regard for their con-tent. It is listening in a two-person framework and with free access to his own unconscious fantasies and primary processes. The child-in-him and intuitive-mother-in-him listens to the child-in-the-patient at this level. The therapist's goal is to begin with this kind of com-municating and eventually elevate it to a more adult level, thereby promoting the growth of the infantile parts of the patient.

Therapists vary in their propensity and capacity to experience and relate in this way. For some, it is all too easy and, as a result, sometimes difficult for them to promote maturation and adult-level functioning. For others, this level is an enigma and too primitive, mysterious, and frightening for them. They prefer mature, logical thinking and communicating and tolerate this level poorly. In fact, this level, with its primitive threats and fantasies, can be quite anxiety-provoking for many therapists. They consciously or uncon-sciously steer their patients away from such material or refuse (and are unable) to communicate with them in these terms.

Put in other terms (see Kohut, 1971), the therapist initially accepts the patient's narcissistic and infantile needs, and, while not gratifying them beyond measures appropriate to the psychothera-peutic setting, he does not unduly frustrate or reject them. To do so is to lead the patient to experience the therapist as need-frustrating, alien, and destructive; this will disrupt the therapeutic relationship. These early unmet needs must be provided with empathic gratifica-tion in a relationship and an atmosphere in which they can be fully expressed; only then, can they be subsequently modified.

Influences on the Relationship Between the Patient and Therapist

We may characterize the relationship between the patient and therapist at this level as the primal transference (Stone, 1961) or the primary relationship. It has distinctive characteristics for the patient and is evoked by special aspects of the therapist's stance. The therapist is an important, real person to the patient. These patients often make demands on their therapist for extra-therapeutic gratifications ranging from seductions and condemnations to special kinds of care. Their own needs prevail and the therapist is omnipotently expected to gratify them regardless of their content. Frustrations are poorly tolerated, but gratification of their inappropriate needs only calls for further demands; they are insatiable.

The therapist's feelings and fantasies often are readily detected consciously, and especially unconsciously, by these patients. They respond noisily when the therapist is having difficulties regarding them. Primitive transferences to the therapist of feelings and fantasies related to early mothering figures is usually prominent. Problems in differentiating the therapist from these past figures and in seeing him realistically in the present are also evident. These transferences, while at times idealized and glorified, have an underlying terrifying tone and are primitively destructive in content; they are also tenaciously held. The wishes for symbiotic unity are often perceived as ultimately devastating more often than gratifying and elating. Countertransference reactions are readily evoked by these patients because of their incessant demands, their primitive pathology, their tendencies to regress, their excessive idealizations of the therapist, and the kind of anxiety they experience. They create pressures toward intense and intimate relationships and the therapist is often taxed to keep his distance—and not feel overwhelmed.

The nonverbal and primitive verbal interactions with the therapist are especially crucial to the outcome of each session and the entire treatment. The content of interpretations is less important than their tone, latent implications, and gratification or frustrating aspects. When disturbances at this early level prevail, interpreting adult language aspects of later conflicts apparent in the patient's associations will evoke negative responses in him, since he correctly feels misunderstood and suffers from "bad-therapist-mothering."

The goal in the therapist–patient relationship is to satisfy the patient's basic needs for an understanding and empathic therapist-mother. Thereby, he is gradually helped to build verbal insights that lead to more mature adaptations and to a predominance of the secondary therapeutic relationship (mature transference; Stone, 1961) based on more adult-like experiencing and relating.

With narcissistic patients, primitive idealizations of the therapist may predominate, or a grandiose self-image holds sway and the therapist must tolerate wishes for merger or total adulation (Kohut, 1971). Frustrations evoke primitive rage and are experienced as coming from an omnipotently destructive parent-like therapist. Special pressures are on the therapist to tolerate these attitudes in the patient and to allow their full expression.

Responding and Interpreting to the Patient

The therapist's nonverbal responses—his tone, timing, attitude, patience, honesty, sincerity, and the like—and the unconscious aspects of his communications are very crucial at this level. The patient's responses to these dimensions of the therapist's behavior often outweigh those that he has to its adult-verbal content.

In his use of language, the therapist must recognize that the patient is not, at the moment, functioning or receiving communications on an adult level, but primarily on an infantile one. His conceptual framework and his understanding must be geared accordingly. If the therapist speaks to the patient with the language, word-affect-groupings, and need-fantasy-language that prevail in the patient, he will be correctly understood.

Sensitivity to the ego defects and other dysfunctions arising from this period will enable the therapist to address himself to these impairments and foster the maturation and development of these inadequate functions. This must include interpretation of the primitive unconscious fantasies and repressed memories which underlie these dysfunctions. Since separation anxieties and ego-dysfunctions related to inadequate emotional separation from the mother are characteristic sources of psychopathology at this level, proper understanding of, and responses to, separation issues during the therapy are vital. The reworking in therapy of the cumulative traumas in relationship with the mother and of the chronic lack of appropriate and necessary narcissistic gratification must be supplemented by analysis of the acute traumatic experiences from this early period and their intrapsychic consequences.

Indications of Communications at This Early Level

Many aspects of this period from birth to the fourth year are reconstructed from highly condensed earliest memories, stories told to the patient, dreams in context and with associations, observations of present parental interaction, conscious fantasies, and the direct verbal and nonverbal interaction with the therapist. Among the hallmarks of the influence of this period on relationships and fantasies are primitive and magical experiences, uncontrolled anxieties and primitive fears of disintegration, primitive dreams and conscious fantasies, and other primary-process-dominated material (see also Balint, 1968; and Kohut, 1971). Often, the material in the sessions is self- and two-person oriented, and conflicts are poorly defined and relate more to survival and narcissistic gratification than to three-person conflicts which are more clearly defined, logical, and structuralized intrapsychically. The patient may make excessive demands to be gratified at all cost. The meaning of words becomes secondary to their barrenness or their demanding-angry qualities. Silences are also used to communicate. Ordinary language and logical words do not reach or affect the patient or alter his mood, fantasies, or behavior. Intense mistrust of the therapist may dominate the scene and is often difficult to resolve. The patient may become depressed, detached, or argumentative and seemingly thick-headed. Acting out may become rampant. Particularly significant is the absence of any communication of derivatives of unconscious fantasies. The material becomes flat and hollow, and interpretation of this emptiness as a resistance is met with hurt and rage. In all, the therapist feels lost, angry, confused, and out-of-touch. Only a shift to proper tuning in can turn the tide and reinstate a therapeutic alliance.

In summary, then, the relating and experiencing of many adult patients is intimately related to their functioning in their earliest years of life. This level is different in many critical respects from the adult level of functioning. As a result, the psychotherapeutic factors which prove curative for emotional problems evolving from disturbances in these earliest years are distinctive. In particular, modifications of these problems are possible only through a therapeutic stance which entails actual "good-therapist-mothering" and is in tune with the patient's needs. This is eventually supplemented by interventions that enable these needs and interactions to reach higher levels of expression and provide verbalized insights that promote new adaptive responses and resolutions of early inner conflicts in the patient. In addition, the therapist must understand the patient's nonverbal communications and respond to them with nonverbal responses of his own. These will include properly phrased and dosed out interventions in which content is necessary, but only supplemental. The therapist must attempt to bring these nonverbal responses of the patient into the verbal realm. He must also explore and reconstruct the recurrent traumas in the critical relationship between the patient and his mother, and the acute traumas that occurred during these earliest years. Understanding and interpreting must be in the primitive images and language of that era. Lastly, in such therapies, there is a special emphasis on, and sensitivity to, the relationship between the patient and therapist, especially in regard to its most primitive and immediate (primary) dimensions. As already noted, proper response to, and acceptance of, the patient's narcissistic needs and pathology is also essential.

THE YEARS FROM FOUR TO ADOLESCENCE

I will continue to be brief, sketching in the main features of this extended period. It is generally more familiar to the reader than the earlier period and has been covered in detail elsewhere (see, among others, Freud, 1923 and 1926; Erikson, 1950; Arlow, 1963a; Langs, 1972).

NORMAL DEVELOPMENT

Maturational Sequences

Under the decreasing influence of environmental figures, which now include important others beyond the mother, inner development continues to proceed toward maturation. During the years from four to six, genital development and sensations become accentuated. This is followed by a period of relative quiescence, or latency, from ages six to nine or ten. Then follows the prepubertal, pubertal, and adolescent biological thrusts toward the development of secondary sexual characteristics and sexual maturity, including the capacity to procreate. This culminates in the maturation of the instinctual drives and their coalescence under genital primacy with contributions from derivative needs of all kinds. Their overall modulation and control is achieved through a combination of biological maturation and environmental factors. Maturation of ego functioning, the superego, and self is also achieved. The specific outcome of these developments has an effect on the level of the person's experiencing, thinking, fantasizing, adapting, and relating.

The Role of the Environment

The mother continues to play a central role in the child's development, though her sphere of influence begins to diminish and shift, and the extent to which it is an unmodifiable factor also lessens. Specific areas of vulnerability may emerge for a given mother or father, in that certain periods, such as the oedipal one or adolescence, pose special problems for them with a given son or daughter. Sex differences, which were a lesser factor in the early years, now loom larger. This may contribute to a conflicted parent–child interaction that can affect the child's character structure or lay the groundwork for symptoms.

The mother–child interaction continues to influence the child on both a conscious and unconscious level, and to be affected by all facets of the mother's personality, psychopathology, and conflicts. However, the relationship becomes more circumscribed, definable, limited in its effects, reality-attuned, and specific.

In adolescence, a second major psychological, and eventually physical, separation from the mother must be effected, leading to maximal autonomy and the optimal development of outside relationships. During these years, the father, siblings, other members of the extended family, and then peers and non-family adults (society) play an increasingly important role in the development of the child and adolescent. Such three-person relationships as the oedipal one and sibling rivalry become important. They take on a whole range of conscious and unconscious meanings and are strongly influenced by instinctual drive needs, ego capacities, and superego responses.

In addition to the family atmosphere and the tone of other relationships, acutely traumatic events during these years also exert a strong influence on the development of the child. Their importance depends on their nature, his age at the time, his previous development and experiences, the nature of his ongoing conflicts and unconscious fantasies, and many other factors. While the growing child becomes more capable of dealing with actual and potential traumas, their influence on his psyche remains considerable and they often become focal points for disruptive developmental sequences and psychopathology.

Modes of Functioning

SELF AND NOT-SELF; OBJECT RELATIONSHIPS. The self and not-self delineation is generally well established through these years, except in special circumstances, such as orgasm in intercourse. The evolution of a mature and stable sense of identity and self-concept is one of the important accomplishments of this period, though it is fraught with difficulties and steeped in crucial unconscious factors.

Object relationships become increasingly complex and the capacities to empathize, sympathize, and consider the needs of others evolve. From primarily need satisfying object relationships, there is a widening of the basis for relating to include those for various special sexual and aggressive needs; for survival and developmental assistance; and for such derivative needs as friendship, helping others, and education. Out of this, the capacity to love and to sacrifice for another person emerges.

Modes of Thought

Thinking matures and the capacities for symbolization and abstract thinking blossom; thought is less tied to the immediate external situations and inner needs than before. Problem solving through thought, conceptualizing, and anticipating all develop. The capacity for reality-oriented, logical, adaptive, secondary process thinking unfolds during these years and comes to predominate even when inner needs intensify. Daydreaming (conscious fantasizing) and night dreaming are other important adaptive kinds of thought. These extend into unconscious fantasizing in which the child reworks derivatives of intrapsychic conflicts as part of his ongoing adaptive efforts to resolve inner and outer traumas, conflicts, and anxieties.

Inner Structure Building and Defenses

It is during these years that the relatively stable and lasting personality structures, channels of instinctual drive discharge, conscience, ideals, self-concept, and self-boundaries are more or less finalized and solidified. These become the hallmarks of the person's character structure and determine his habitual modes of behaving, thinking, responding, defending, and functioning.

Among the important structures that are developed in relatively permanent form during this period is the superego. It grows out of initial primitive fragments and precursors related to early parental prohibitions, rewards, values, ideals, limits, and the like; and out of the child's early inner stirrings of both a libidinal and aggressive nature. This structure then crystalizes from the resolutions of the oedipal period that provides a more mature contribution in terms of the three-person, parental relationship. Latency and adolescent experiences also make important contributions to this structure both in terms of its prohibitive and punishment aspects, its ideals and goals, and its rewarding and self-esteem dimensions. The roots of the superego are close to the instinctual drives and have many unconscious dimensions; it therefore becomes a powerful source of guilt and anxiety even when the person is not entirely conscious of the intrapsychic conflicts, fantasies, and behavior that are evoking the disturbance.

With the aid of the ongoing maturational processes, the intrapsychic defenses which develop and prevail during these later years are more specific, effective, and thought-dominated than before. They are also relatively less global, less costly to the total personality, and less instinctualized. Repression, the exclusion of mental contents from conscious awareness, becomes the primary defense and—as is true for all defenses—has great adaptive value. It becomes more selective with the years, and is aided by other higher level defenses, many of which rely on the person's growing intellectual capacities. These include isolation, intellectualization, reaction formation, undoing, more effective identifications such as those with aggressors, and more mature forms of projection and externalization. Displacement also plays a crucial role as a defense.

While these defenses operate in a more selective and logical manner than those adopted in the earlier years, we may expect to discover that they have primtive qualities since they have roots in the first years and largely operate unconsciously. There is, then, a hierarchy of defenses, ranging from those that are primitive, primary-process, and drive-dominated to those that are mature, secondary-process, and reality-adaptive.

Many other structures develop to maturity and relative stability during these years. These include those related to affect-expression and the development of signal affects such as signal anxiety, controls, capacity for delay, appropriate channels for instinctual drive discharge, and a whole variety of cognitive controls and functions.

ADAPTIVE TASKS AND DANGERS. There is a whole sequence of major adaptive tasks, quite different from those in the earliest years, which confront the person at this time. They include mastery of the parental and sibling interactions and the development of peer and adult relationships culminating in career and marriage. Puberty and adolescence, with the maturation of sexual characteristics and the upsurge of instinctual drives, are very trying periods. The necessity of separating from the nuclear family is also a major task for these years. Each may become the source of anxiety and conflict, of maladaptation, and of subsequent difficulties.

Danger situations, the way in which they are perceived and assessed, and the reactions to them are also characteristic for this period and different from the earliest years. The aggressive and libidinal instinctual drives, experienced as conscious and unconscious wishes and fantasies, increasingly become the major source of intrapsychic danger.

These danger situations include fears of excessive drives per se, of loss of the mother and others, of the loss of love, and of disapproval; bodily fears of harm often characterized as castration anxiety; and the internal disapproval of the superego. Three-person situations are often focal, and acute traumas generate intrapsychic anxiety primarily through the arousal of forbidden instinctual drive impulses. The assessment of these dangers, while both conscious and unconscious, matures and although links to repressed memories and past anxieties are present and influential, the person's capacity to discriminate and respond selectively is greatly improved. The ultimate resolution of the danger situation is based on relatively mature defenses and resources, and is largely intrapsychic rather than behavioral and somatic.

RELATIONSHIP TO PSYCHOPATHOLOGY

Characterological Problems

While much of the person's character is established in the first three years, this later period plays a role in refining it and may contribute to major characterological changes. Character pathology in these years evolves out of recurrent higher level intrapsychic conflicts that are resolved through repetitive attitudes, defenses, and behavior patterns of an ego syntonic nature. It is here that the more mature obsessional and hysterical characters may be categorized.

Symptoms

It is at this level that the classical formulations regarding symptom formation apply (see Freud, 1912, 1926; and Arlow, 1963a). In essence, these symptoms (and neurotic disturbances) are prompted by traumatic reality situations which create intrapsychic conflicts that tax the ego beyond its adaptive capacities. Experiences such as the birth of a sibling, the loss of a parent or sibling, a surgical procedure, an accident, or a seduction evoke direct fears, intrapsychic anxieties, and conscious and unconscious fantasies (Greenacre, 1956). The latter are laden with instinctual drive wishes of sexual and aggressive nature. These wishes evoke anxiety because they are seen as dangers (as "forbidden") that will lead to personal harm (bodily damage, loss of love, condemnation, etc.). This anxiety prompts the ego into action, primarily through intrapsychic defenses, in an effort to ward off these dangerous id wishes and to repress them. If these defenses are successful, a constructive synthesis of all the claims placed on the person (his ego) will result. This constitutes an adaptive response and no symptoms will appear.

On the other hand, if the ego's defensive and synthetic capacities are overtaxed, a compromise which includes mental representations from the external reality, id, superego, and ego (primarily defenses) will be made. This compromise is the symptom.

Let us be clear on the distinction between real and neurotic (symptom-evoking) conflicts. While the two kinds of conflicts often intermingle, they are conceptually and clinically different. Real conflicts stem from realistic problems in living and relating to others. They are the product of actual, external dangers and create realistic, appropriate anxiety (commonly called "fear") and call for outer-directed adaptive responses. A real attack or dispute, real starvation, and inappropriate seductive overtures are examples of such dangers. To deal with them, the individual calls upon various coping resources which are externally directed, such as feeling angry, physically defending himself, attacking back, seeking food, or not permitting himself to be seduced. While they evoke affective, thoughtful, fantasy and behavioral responses, the intrapsychic component serves adaptation. Further, the threat itself is responded to in terms of a consensually valid assessment of the danger, and not in terms of any idiosyncratic, unrealistic, fantasied elaboration of it. Neuroses are not the direct result of such dangers or failure to adapt to them; what can evolve is real hurt, real pain, and even such disasters as starvation and death. Such traumas can affect character development and become the key to symptom formation only when they evoke intrapsychic conflicts caused by the forbidden instinctual drives mobilized by such events.

Thus, intrapsychic conflict is the central etiological factor in symptom-formation. In this instance, the real event or trauma evokes intrapsychic responses that include instinctual drive expressions which initiate the sequence already described for symptom-formation. Here, anxiety as a response to an instinctual drive wish that is assessed as potentially dangerous is crucial, as are intrapsychic defenses. Symptoms occur when these inner conflicts are not resolved in more adaptive ways.

While some aspects of these intrapsychic conflicts are conscious, most are repressed and unconscious. Symptoms and neurotic behavior are inherently irrational and inappropriate to the external reality. They can only be understood by insight into the repressed fantasies which are evoking them. There is an ongoing attempt by the total personality to resolve such intrapsychic conflicts through improved defenses, renunciation, behavioral changes, influences on others, and other means. These efforts are directed toward either inner or outer changes, and the latter is generally less successful.

Among these adaptive efforts is unconscious fantasy activity, in which the child or adult attempts to represent and rework the entire conflict, its sources, and his efforts at resolving it. Such fantasy activity takes place through the working over of displaced, derivative expressions that are disguised representations of the underlying intrapsychic conflicts. It is these derivatives that we detect in exploring symptoms and interpreting them. In unconscious fantasies, we find representations of all aspects of the intrapsychic struggle (the reality trauma; the id, ego, and superego expressions). Thus, when the repressed content of the instinctual wishes, the defenses against them, and the condemnation-punishment for them are made conscious, the patient can then directly assess the nature of his disturbing impulses, his conflicts, his maladaptive resolution, and the cost to his total personality. Only then can he consider new, less costly adaptations, create new and more effective defenses, and effect necessary renunciations. Such resolution of neurotic conflicts from within promises to be far more lasting and successful than pseudo-resolutions produced by manipulating the environment. Unconscious fantasies are the key to neuroses, and their derivatives must be detected and analyzed if genuine symptom-relief through intrapsychic change is to occur.

Once the original traumatic event and its intrapsychic consequences, especially the multitude of unconscious fantasy responses, have occurred and been experienced by the child at the level of functioning prevalent at the particular age, they create an intrapsychic set and vulnerability. Thus, subsequent events are viewed and experienced in terms of the previous trauma and the repressed-fantasied versions of it. In addition, specific experiences are sought out based on these fantasies as part of further adaptive efforts. Unconscious fantasies and memories are powerful determinants of behavior.

Unconscious fantasies are also ultimately quite specific and personal. Though there are many shared human experiences and traumas and, therefore, many shared and general unconscious fantasies at superficial levels, each person will ultimately experience a given trauma based on his own personal prehistory. Therefore, each individual has his own, personal, specific, repressed versions of such a total experience. This specificity is a crucial point for psychotherapeutic technique.

Each time a subsequent event resembles the original traumatic experience or mobilizes some aspect of it, there is a new working through of the original trauma and the related unconscious fantasies.

Each of these repetitions at a new level of functioning can lead to a new inner and outer resolution and a new set of unconscious fantasies and memories; this contributes to a hierarchy that represents the repetitive external traumas and the intrapsychic reworking of them.

With each fresh situation that repeats a past trauma, part of the person's assessment of it will be in terms of his repressed memories and fantasies. The present intrapsychic danger is therefore regressively assessed and the instinctual drives, ego and superego responses are regressively activated. When this interplay, which is largely unconscious, taxes the defenses and adaptive resources of the person, symptoms will occur. Thus, symptoms are precipitated by reality events that are a version of a prior conflict-evoking trauma.

RELATIONSHIP TO THE PSYCHOTHERAPEUTIC SITUATION

Therapeutic Atmosphere and Alliance

It is from the development and evolution of these years that much of the patient's mature and realistic relationship with the therapist is derived. Irrational elements related to the conflicts from this period may also contribute to this relationship. The patient's recognition that he is suffering from emotional problems and has come to an expert-therapist for assistance in resolving his difficulties is based largely on relationships and functioning developed during these years, as are the more realistic ideas of the patient as to how this help will be offered to him. These are added to his primitive and magical wishes for help from an omnipotent, immediately-relieving therapist, a product of the feelings from his earliest years.

The aspects of the therapeutic alliance that are derived from the later years include cooperation, trust, and hard work. Communications are mainly verbal and well-delineated, and the object relationship with the therapist is relatively adult. The mistrust, anxieties, and neurotic unconscious fantasies directed at the therapist prove to be accessible to verbal communication and to resolution through verbalized insight.

Psychotherapy with patients who function in these later levels often proceeds smoothly and is focused on the search for current stresses and traumas, and their links to repressed memories and fantasies on the one hand, and the patient's symptoms on the other. When some occurrence in or outside of therapy evokes reactions and fantasies toward the therapist, they have a core of reality to them and are based on highly structuralized conflicts and unconscious fantasies. The instinctual drives mobilized, and the superego and ego responses to them, stem from oedipal and post-oedipal experiences and conflicts. They tend, therefore, to be readily expressed in verbal derivatives and directly workable.

Certainly, not all positive elements in the patient's relationship with the therapist come from these later phases. For example, the basic trust derived from the earliest years forms the nucleus of the positive therapeutic alliance, while paranoid fantasies derived from the oedipal period or depressive responses from a major latency loss may promote a strong interference. However, resistances and disruptions derived from later-stage conflicts generally prove far more verbally analyzable than those derived from the earliest years. In particular, separation reactions are generally not as disruptive to the therapeutic alliance when the earliest years have been negotiated relatively successfully, and oedipal and post-oedipal conflicts prevail.

The therapist's stance in dealing with problems from these years is one in which basic honesty and concern is conveyed but does not generally become a central issue. As a relatively neutral observer (see Chapter 22), the therapist listens patiently, tolerates the impulses and fantasies expressed by the patient toward him, and strives to understand the derivatives of the patient's intrapsychic conflicts and unconscious fantasies. He can expect reasonable frustration tolerance in the patient and has the time to listen and understand. His main job is to intervene correctly in regard to timing, content, and consideration of the therapeutic alliance. The initial focus will be on conscious and unconscious defenses, and their unconscious meanings and uses. This leads directly into the repressed memories and fantasies related to the patient's symptoms and ultimately to their interpretation.

In addition, the therapist serves as a model for mature and structuralized identifications regarding instinctual drive controls and channeling, adaptive ego functioning of all kinds, honesty, mature object-relating, and superego functioning. His major responsibilities are to be perceptive regarding unconscious conflicts and fantasies, to time and pace his interpretations properly, to help modify pathological defenses and foster healthier adaptations, and to become gradually less active in the therapy, turning over more responsibility to the patient.

Listening to and Understanding the Patient

Proper listening is based on an accurate understanding of symptom-formation at this level. We begin by ascertaining the current primary adaptive task (the reality problem or context; see Chapter 9) and its intrapsychic repercussions, and assessing the patient's adaptation to it. The therapist's task is to detect derivatives of the unconscious dimensions of this ongoing struggle and to interpret verbally the nature of the fantasies that are evoking the patient's symptoms. This leads to lasting intrapsychic change through insight and working through.

By no means will every relevant unconscious fantasy be made conscious in an effective psychotherapy, nor is this necessary for effective resolution of symptoms. The working through of selected, crucial versions of the unconscious fantasies related to the key conflicts involved in producing the symptoms will suffice. This takes months and sometimes years of work, primarily with unconscious defenses and their content-meaning. This gives access, first, to higher-level and, then, to deeper, unconscious fantasies. Current realities also play an important role in the timing of what emerges and can be dealt with. With proper therapeutic work, as each new event occurs, the patient's reactions deepen and the unconscious aspects become more accessible. Once the critical level of repressed fantasies is reached, a reworking and readaptation will occur, and relief of symptoms will follow.

Influence on the Patient–Therapist Relationship

The therapist is realistically viewed as an ally and assistant to the patient, and this relationship becomes part of the relatively silent backdrop of the therapy. Real, extra-therapeutic demands of the therapist for inappropriate gratification seldom are made since inner controls and reality testing are usually adequate. When such needs are expressed, more primitive roots will usually be found.

Countertransference problems with material from this level usually are related to specific conflicts in the patient which evoke circumscribed, inappropriate reactions in the therapist. These are based on parallel or complementary neurotic problems that occur in both the patient and therapist, and on the therapist's unresolved reactions to the patient's conflicts and fantasies. Such problems are modifiable through self-exploration by the therapist and may also be detected from the patient's material in the sessions, since the latter is often unconsciously aware in some way of these mistakes (see Chapters 19 and 22).

Responding and Interpreting to the Patient

I have already discussed aspects of this problem, and will add here only that the therapist, in dealing with problems on this level, may feel confident in addressing the patient with adult language and concepts, and in terms of adult-level object relationships and functioning.

Indications of Communications at this Level

Material from this period is relatively more accessible through conscious recollections, the various verbalized sources of derivatives, current relationships, and the interaction with the therapist than that from the earlier years.

Among the hallmarks of this level are clear-cut object relationships with definite boundaries between the patient and others; such three-person relationships as rivalries and impulses toward one person with fears of another; evidence of such definitive superego functioning as guilt, themes of punishment, ideals, and standards; themes related to libidinal and aggressive strivings toward others, with an awareness of their separateness; and themes embedded in social situations. Indications of a maintenance of the self and not-self distinction and reflections of maturation in thinking, conceptualizing, and functioning are present. However, only a full consideration of the context of the material from the patient will permit a final decision as to the main level of his functioning.

Patients who are communicating at these levels generally report material that is full of unconscious fantasy derivatives of a definable-in-words nature. In contrast, patients working on problems from the first years of life convey material with either poorly defined or global unconscious fantasies of a primitive kind, or they shut out all unconscious fantasy expressions that are possible to verbalize.

From this discussion of neurotic disturbances, it is apparent that assessing whether a given conscious fantasy or behavior is neurotic or not is a complicated problem. I want to emphasize here the extent of the therapist's participation in such decisions. His own healthy psyche, psychopathology, unconscious fantasies, conscious values, and judgment all play a role in this regard. Every neurotic disturbance is an attempt at adaptation; what is pertinent is the cost, to the patient's total personality and to others, in pain and suffering.

SOME ILLUSTRATIONS

I will illustrate the ideas and distinctions offered in the preceding sections through brief clinical vignettes that will provide a "feel" for how they are manifested clinically.

SYNDROMES DERIVED PRIMARILY FROM THE EARLIEST YEARS

Miss c.n., a late adolescent, sought treatment because of a series of episodes in which she felt "spaced" and "out of it all" after her parents had left on a long trip. She had been very depressed about their leaving and had, typically for her, "latched onto" a young pharmacist in her area, spending hours "rapping" with him at his store.

When her parents returned, she refused to talk to them. She developed a severe migraine headache which lasted several days. She dreamt of going down a river which had many rapids, but she was not sure she was in a canoe. Soapsuds filled the river, contaminating everything and overturning the canoe.

Her mother had been severely depressed after her birth. Miss C.N., as a newborn, had sleep difficulties and also vomited a great deal. She soon became hysterical whenever her mother left her room, and this kind of reaction to being left continued on and off throughout her childhood, when she began nursery and grade school, etc.

In her psychotherapy, she sat on the floor and immediately complained of the time limitations of the sessions, and that the therapist was not sufficiently active and did not reveal enough about himself to her. She was often silent or blatantly angry without clear provocation. She formed intense attachments to several friends and teachers, and talked on and on about herself to them, rather than to her therapist. She thought of running away from home and treatment, and barely controlled her impulse to do so. Interpretations and confrontations regarding her longings for limitless closeness or union with others, her rage when this desire was frustrated, her overall poor frustration tolerance, and her intense demandingness were met with silence and further resentment. Her dreams were of searching through rooms and of houses getting larger and smaller as she looked for a perfect place. When sessions ended, she would leave angry; mistrust and direct complaints grew.

Within the first two months of therapy, a session was cancelled for a legal holiday and another for a professional commitment of the therapist. Miss C.N.'s reaction was catastrophic. She refused the therapist's offer to make up the second missed session and turned a deaf ear to his efforts to tune in on, and verbalize, her sense of loss and hurt, and her rage and need for revenge. It was all to no avail and she eventually refused to return to therapy. The real hurts could not be repaired in any way.

Mrs. C.O. sought therapy because she had had several recent affairs and feared that her sexual impulses were uncontrolled. She felt panicky, confused, and depressed. Initially, she had seriously thought that an affair with her therapist might be helpful and she considered it as a real possibility. As her sexual feelings intensified, she imagined that her therapist, who had not responded to her seductive remarks, was the devil. However, she quickly brought this image under control.

Her father had been blatantly seductive in her early childhood and her mother strangely aloof. In the last two years, her father had been seriously ill and her parents had moved far away. Whenever she saw her father, he was still quite involved with her. Her mother, on the other hand, was uninvolved, self-suffering, complaining, and demanding; they had never related well.

She came to one of her sessions early in treatment and found the door to the therapist's office locked. Although the therapist was not late, she was furious that she had to wait for him. It reminded her of his relative silence and she wanted to terminate her treatment. When it happened a second time, she felt that he was doing it to her on purpose, to provoke her. Exploration of her impatience, self-centeredness, and demands led to little verbalized insight, though it modified her attitude and enabled her to continue her therapy—albeit, bitterly. In fact, only when the therapist returned to his office a little earlier than was usual for him, so that the patient did not have to wait for him, was this issue settled. Though he never verbalized his decision, it was clear that the patient recognized it, since, on the few occasions where Mrs. C.O. was especially early and had to wait for the therapist, it was no longer an issue for her.

Early in therapy, she would become anxious and imagine that the therapist's office was a motel and that he shared with her the sexual fantasies which flooded her thinking. Her first dream was of her therapist lying with her on the floor of his office in the presence of her mother and his wife. Associations revolved around intense and ill-defined longings for closeness with her aloof mother and seductive father.

Before one of the therapist's vacations, she suddenly felt depressed and self-accusatory regarding her own problems as a mother. She cried inexplicably for days and felt suicidal. She dreamt a series of confused dreams including one where she had no image when she looked into the mirrored surface of a lake; a dream of the therapist's bed; and a dream in which her young son touched her small breasts. In the latter dream, she was ashamed that her breasts were so small but his small hands fit just right—it was a perfect fit between mother and child.

Mr. C.P. was a young man in his early twenties who panicked every time he left his home overnight. He sought treatment after failing to stay on as a counselor at a camp. In his initial sessions, he described his mother as an angry, irrational, unhappy woman who constantly criticized and attacked him. His father was described as withdrawn, uninvolved, inane, and unable to take a stand with his wife; later in therapy, it emerged that he would lose control irrationally when provoked.

The patient seldom dated and had never been close to a girl. He had a couple of boyfriends, who infuriated him with minor slights and with whom he was not very close. When he began therapy, his college work was erratic and he was having difficulty passing his courses.

In his initial session, Mr. C.P. pleaded for help but, oddly enough, constantly interrupted his therapist when the latter spoke. In subsequent sessions, he quarreled with virtually everything told to him and would often claim that he knew what the therapist was thinking. In recalling a previous session, he would often confuse what he and the therapist had said. After sessions when the therapist was relatively silent, the patient would ask for his money back and complain about not having been helped. A dream of a tarantula crawling on him led to associations to his mother and the therapist, and was followed by a period of incessant rage at the therapist.

After considerable therapeutic patience and work, the patient took a different stance. He spoke quietly, said little of any depth, and was content to come for his sessions and accomplish virtually nothing. He was not especially anxious, as he had been previously, and was functioning much better in school; but he never spoke seriously of leaving his house overnight. Derivatives of unconscious fantasies were no longer detectable in his associations.

Miss C.Q. was in her early twenties and suffered from asthma. Early in her therapy, whenever her therapist was to leave on vacation, she would begin to wheeze and was hospitalized once. At such times, she would come to her sessions with candy to eat; with cigarettes but no matches, asking the therapist to provide them; or with a nasal discharge for which she took handfuls of the therapist's kleenex home with her.

PSYCHOPATHOLOGY DERIVED PRIMARILY
FROM THE LATER YEARS

I will now turn more briefly to the psychopathology derived from the later years of life. I will outline the highlights of the therapy of a patient whose earliest years were essentially stable and whose mother offered her a good and facilitating maternal experience.

Mrs. C.R. was a married woman, with two daughters,

who sought therapy because of episodes of anxiety and a recurrent tightening in her throat. She had many friends and related well to her children and husband, though they had disagreements because of his aloofness.

In her therapy, the patient was cooperative, rational and spoke freely. She formed a strong therapeutic alliance, accepted without much reaction the inevitable interruptions during the course of her treatment, directed very little toward her therapist except for occasional transference fantasies, and worked primarily with her life problems and their intrapsychic repercussions.

Over a period of two years, the following salient information unfolded. The patient's symptoms began when her friend's sons began to celebrate their entry into manhood (Bar Mitzvahs). Mrs. C.R. had lost a stillborn son with congenital defects. She had never given up her wish for a son and resented her husband's refusal to have more children. Initially, she was only vaguely aware of the feelings and fantasies evoked by this situation.

In time, events prompted dreams, conscious fantasies, and other material that revealed many unconscious fantasies and memories related to her symptoms. For example, she began to question her internist about his children and whether he had any sons. Associations to the therapist pointed to an unconscious wish to have a son with him, a transference fantasy (see Chapter 20). A dream of flushing a mouse down a toilet led to the working out of previously repressed fantasies of devouring her husband's penis, both to castrate and punish him, and as an imagined oral impregnation. The throat symptoms emerged here as a talion punishment of the patient by the incorporated penis for her impulses against her husband's phallus.

This led to the unfolding of experiences in the patient's childhood. There were current dreams of frightening mice and noisy machines that led to the recall of sharing hotel rooms with her parents and the reconstruction of primal scene experiences and her attendant fantasies. These were largely that her mother was being attacked and harmed, and of replacing her mother with her father.

Another line of recollections led to the birth of the first of her two sisters, when the patient was four, and her reaction of anger and wishing that she could be rid of her rival for her parents' love. Fantasies of her mother dying in childbirth then emerged, reflecting both a wish and a fear. Another response was to wish for a child from her father and to imagine presenting him with the son that her mother had failed to give him.

Next, her mother's hospitalization for the removal of a vocal cord tumor was recalled; this occurred when the patient was eight. More sophisticated versions of the patient's fantasies upon the birth of her sisters emerged. She recalled the details of preparing meals and keeping house for her father while her mother was in the hospital. She imagined her mother dying of a post-operative hemorrhage, choking to death. Her throat symptoms were, on this level, a talion punishment for these wishes, and a gratifying identification with her mother as her father's bedmate.

As a final development in her treatment, the patient remembered later primal scenes in her home and this led to specific additional fantasies regarding her parents' intercourse. In these, detailed fantasies of rape and harm to her mother predominated. Once these were worked through, for the first time in many years, the patient remembered additional fantasies from these childhood years in which she, herself, was tied to a bed, raped, and hurt physically by robbers.

I have not described the fluctuations in her symptoms, their exacerbation and remission, and the work with her defenses of repression, identification, and isolation. Nor will I attempt to detail the overdetermined complex layers of readily-verbalizable, conscious and unconscious fantasies, and current and genetic conflicts that determined this patient's symptoms. Suffice it to say that, with the working through of these last fantasies and the connections to recent conflicts with her husband, her symptoms were resolved and her disputes with her husband were worked out. A dream late in her therapy is pertinent to this resolution. In it, the father of one of Mrs. C.R.'s girlfriends asked her to go to bed with him and have relations. She wanted to, but felt that it would be wrong and refused him.

I have tried to establish not only that the syndromes with which we work in psychotherapy cover a wide range of differing manifestations and etiologies, but also that the proper therapeutic response to them also varies significantly, depending on the main period from which they stem. With this as a framework, we are now ready to proceed with our in-depth study of the psychotherapeutic process.

IV

UNDERSTANDING

THE PATIENT'S

COMMUNICATIONS

9 The Framework for Understanding the Communications from Patients in Psychotherapy

Simply and ideally, a psychotherapy session has the following basic structure. Its foundation lies in the previous session and the reality experiences that have occurred since then. The session itself begins with the patient talking about whatever is on his mind, thereby developing the major theme of the hour, and defining his current primary adaptive tasks and his reactions to them on all levels. These initial communications are both verbal and nonverbal. The therapist listens to the manifest and latent content, formulates, and checks out these assessments as the patient goes on, revising his hypotheses accordingly. At an appropriate moment in the session, the therapist makes an intervention. The patient responds verbally and nonverbally, and associates further, either confirming the intervention or failing to do so.

In these sections of the book, I will explore these dimensions of the therapy sessions in detail. I will begin with the basics of therapeutic listening (see also Langs, 1972), since the therapist must first and foremost develop to the fullest a capacity to identify neurotic conflicts and manifest and latent content, and learn how to organize the patient's associations correctly and in meaningful patterns.

OBSERVING THE PATIENT

The therapist's observations of the patient should not be a random matter. While they should be flexible and many-leveled, they cannot lead to proper interventions without some eventual integration by the therapist. This develops out of his basic framework for listening, by which I mean both auditory and visual observing, and a complex mental set that should eventually become rather automatic and integral to his therapeutic stance. To assist us in conceptualizing this task of listening to and comprehending the patient, I shall present a condensed sequence of two sessions.

Miss c.s. had been in therapy for nearly two years for asthma, poor sexual controls, and difficulties with her schoolwork. In the session before the hours to be detailed, she had spoken of returning to college, from which she had dropped out a year earlier. Since her other symptoms had been fairly well resolved, she also brought up the idea of termination. It was explored both as a flight from unresolved fantasies and conflicts about her father, and from a realistic vantage point: the patient's symptom alleviation indicated that it was a sensible step to consider.

In the next session, Miss c.s. described a fight with her boyfriend, who had tried to tell her how she should feel, and reported that she had felt panicky and then experienced wheezing for a brief period. She had been infuriated by errors she had made in her after-school job. She detailed her boyfriend's lack of feelings and consideration for her, and then spoke of mental patients who were a menace and who were allowed to run loose by unwary therapists. She had begun classes at school, and had had a dream: she is in the college auditorium selling tickets from a booth in the center of a theater-in-the-round; a rock singer comes in and she thinks of giving him a free ticket, but sells him one instead. She went on to associate: the singer had died of an overdose of drugs; one of her friends had had intercourse with him and had also died of an overdose. She feared having to perform and yet was studying theater. She had a sense of safety in the booth.

How might we organize and understand the patient's communications in these therapy hours? To enable us to move beyond random guesswork, I will now systematically study the observing portion of the psychotherapy session.

The therapist must listen both comprehensively and selectively, as directed by the flow of the patient's material, for information on many levels. In unraveling the intricate material from each session, he needs a point of departure from which to explore the deeper associations. There are two main contexts which serve this purpose: that related to the primary trauma or adaptive task to which the patient is responding intrapsychically and behaviorally—this I will term the "adaptive context;" and the symptomatic disturbance, which is the current manifestation of the patient's neurosis and which the therapist will endeavor to analyze in the session, that I term the "therapeutic context."

THE PRIMARY ADAPTIVE TASK

Perhaps the first job for the therapist is to identify those responses in the patient that are inappropriate to outer reality—neurotic responses by locating the primary adaptive task and the various indicators of neurotic problems.* To ascertain the former, the therapist must understand the role of human adaptation in neurotogenesis; to recognize the latter, he must distinguish neurotic difficulties from problems that are realistic or physical.

Functioning, responding, and adapting by the patient are set off by environmental alterations. These may be inner or outer changes, but I shall primarily use outer stimuli as models in this discussion. This environmental stimulus may, in general, be positive and supportive or negative and traumatic; it will, in any case, have a wide range

---

* I shall use the term "neurotic problems" in the broad generic sense to mean any kind of emotional disturbance, including those that reflect borderline, narcissistic, and psychotic pathology.

of specific qualities and conscious and unconscious meanings for the patient, and sets off in him a series of multi-leveled responses, both behavioral and intrapsychic. Most crucial for the development of neurotic disturbances are the intrapsychic responses to traumatic stimuli. It is these major, currently disruptive stimuli, which have the potential to set off inappropriate or maladaptive (neurotic) responses, that I have identified as "the primary adaptive task" (Langs, 1972). This term emphasizes that while all events require adaptive responses, certain events are traumatic and become central to the patient's intrapsychic adaptive responses. They thus constitute the main job of adjustment for the person at the moment.

The concept of the primary adaptive task and context is akin to that of the day residue (Freud, 1900; and Langs, 1972), the reality event which sets off the intrapsychic responses which culminate, in part, in a dream. While the day residue has been thought of as less important for understanding dreams and symptoms than its intrapsychic consequences, it nonetheless proves to be an essential part of every intrapsychic sequence; without it, the inner response cannot possibly be understood (see also Sharpe, 1937; and Arlow, 1969).

The idea of the primary adaptive task is a crucial one in living, and for psychotherapy. In each session the therapist must search for the central issues and problems in the patient's current life. These are the initiators of psychological responses, be they non-symptomatic and adaptive or symptomatic and neurotic. Those adaptive tasks which evoke maladaptive responses based on intrapsychic disturbances—that is, on conscious and unconscious conflicts and fantasies, and ego dysfunctions—and the defenses erected to cope with these disturbances—are the heart and focus of the meaningful therapeutic session.

In defining the primary adaptive task as a traumatic event, I want to reiterate that I am speaking broadly to include both inner and outer experiences. While the latter predominate as stimuli for neurotic responses in patients in psychotherapy, the former—in the form of physical or physiological changes and powerful fantasies—may also be the main adaptive problem for the patient at a given time.

Further, this conceptualization includes the fact that we are addressing ourselves here to reality as perceived by the patient, psychic reality. This may be strongly influenced by his unconscious fantasies and past experiences so that adaptive tasks are sometimes a highly individual matter; however, they are often enough consensually agreed upon traumas. In keeping with the influence of conscious and unconscious fantasies on the patient's assessment of inner and outer reality experiences, we must also recognize that these same factors may prompt him to search out or evoke reactions in others and situations through which he can live out or justify his disturbing inner conflicts and fantasies.

Lastly, not every apparent trauma will prove to be the source of intrapsychic conflict for a given patient at a given time. While it is actually rare for patients to adapt well to disturbances which are potentially pathogenic, they may do so temporarily when preoccupied with another more pressing source of conflict or when they are well defended.

In all, then, while the concept of the primary adaptive task is a complex one, I will endeavor here to simplify its use in order to facilitate its application to the clinical situation.

If we return to the clinical vignette regarding Miss C.S., we can identify two interconnected central adaptive tasks for her in the sessions described: her return to college and the termination of her treatment. It is her intrapsychic responses to these actual and anticipated events that unfold in the second hour described. Her return to college aroused conflicts related to unconscious fears of being harmed, and the question of termination produced conflicts related to rage at the therapist for permitting her to leave and fears of annihilation without his protection.

Thus, proper listening begins by identifying the primary adaptive task with which the patient is currently faced. From there, we follow its intrapsychic repercussions on every level. But, to recognize those reality precipitates that evoke the anxiety-provoking and conflicted instinctual drives and needs that in turn generate neurotic disturbances, the therapist must undertake his initial observations in the framework of the previous session and the subsequent reality events; the primary adaptive task usually lies somewhere within these two experiences.

THE ROLE OF THE PREVIOUS SESSION
AND SUBSEQUENT REALITY EVENTS

We can now establish the initial framework and mental set with which the therapist begins each hour. There are three interrelated contexts.

The Previous Session

The manifest and latent content, verbal and nonverbal, of the previous sessions, and especially the last one, is an integral part of the context of a current session. This recalls where the patient stood, the primary adaptive task which occupied his conscious and unconscious attention at that time, and the conflicts, fantasies, and ego dysfunctions that this day residue had evoked. It also brings to mind the therapist's interventions or lack of them, which may have traumatized the patient and evoked responses in him. In remembering that hour, the therapist accents those elements which he feels were most crucial, though he should be prepared to learn that other incidents set the patient off as well.

For instance, in the case of Miss C.S., the therapist, upon entering the second hour, had in mind that the patient was anticipating both her new classes and termination. Out of this matrix, he felt that his agreement to consider termination would be especially traumatic to her since he had never done so before and he knew of her great sensitivity to loss. This was borne out in her associations, especially in the derivatives related to her rage at her insensitive boyfriend and her allusion to therapists who allow the mentally ill to be on the loose without treatment.

Adaptive struggles often continue over several sessions, in which the patient alternates between revealing derivatives of his intrapsychic fantasies, and turning to defensive withdrawal and concealment. It is vital to our understanding of the patient to trace such sequences of shifting responses to any given problem over a series of sessions.

The Prevailing Trauma

This second context is related to the first, though I want to consider it separately. While a given adaptive task may not have been in focus in the previous hour or two, either because of the patient's defensiveness or because another trauma became central for the moment, any major, ongoing external stimulus-event must be part of the context at the beginning of the session.

Thus, if the patient has recently lost a family member or has suffered a major personal trauma of any kind, or the therapist is going on vacation or has disrupted therapy—a fact that may be perceived consciously or unconsciously by the patient and/or therapist—such events must be included in the framework for listening to the hour at hand.

For example, Miss C.S. subsequently to the two sessions already described, had some difficulties in school, and dropped all direct and indirect references to termination for several sessions. Once these school problems, and the conflicts and symptoms they evoked, were resolved, her associations latently clustered around conscious and unconscious fantasies related to termination once again, despite her temporary manifest avoidance of the subject.

The Intercurrent Reality Events

The therapist is also prepared to listen for major reality traumas, and the adaptive tasks they evoke, which have occurred since the last session. This is the part of his initial mental set that is unknown to him; it is important for him to ascertain whether there has been a significant change in the context of the material to emerge from the patient, or whether those problems which prevailed during the previous session are still primary.

As I will demonstrate later, many patients attempt, consciously and unconsciously, to conceal the primary problem, so the therapist must listen carefully for clues. Some patients extend this to a major resistance in which dreams and fantasies are presented repeatedly without a context. Such a resistance must be analyzed and interpreted since therapeutic work undertaken without a clear contextual thread is bound to be unproductive; all effective psychotherapeutic work ultimately begins with the reality precipitate and ends with its intrapsychic repercussions.

I will briefly present another sequence of sessions to illustrate the ways in which the previous hour, the overall adaptive task, and the intervening realities serve as indicators of the initial context of a current session.

Mrs. C.T. was faced with her therapist's pending vacation. She was a young woman with a severe character disorder who had a very traumatic childhood, and was being seen once weekly. Here is the sequence of two sessions before the interruption in therapy.

In the hour previous to these two, she had thought primarily of quitting her job as revenge on her husband, who was not earning very much himself. The therapist had interpreted these thoughts as a response to the coming loss of his support and her angry protest against it.

In the first session in this sequence, she reported leaving her job and then returning to it; she had been in a rage over the favoritism that her boss showed to the others at work. She wanted to avoid reporting a nightmare which had left her terrified, and then described it: a television repairman whom she knew seduced her away from her husband. She went on to reaffirm her love for her husband, and described the man in some detail, emphasizing actual overtures which she had recently rebuffed, but to which she had repeatedly exposed herself. She linked the manifest dream to her mother's many affairs during her childhood. The therapist interpreted both the patient's intense feelings of desertion by him and her need for actual retribution in some form, and her intense longings to possess or be possessed by him. He then linked these fantasies to her anxiety.

Mrs. C.T. was late for the next session and, in beginning her hour, she recalled her absences before previous vacations of the therapist. She again spoke of being unfavored at work and described a dream of an affair with an unsavory friend. She had once had a crush on him, but now hated him. She described having quarreled with her husband and her mother, and then linked the dream to her conflicts regarding the therapist's leaving.

The therapist's vacation was for this woman, who had often been deserted in her childhood, the primary adaptive task at this time. With this as background, each previous session then served as a specific context for the following one, and for the unfolding of the patient's fantasied and symptomatic responses to the pending separation. The intervening realities served more as vehicles for the form of these reactions than as new traumas. Thus, her husband's neglect fostered displacement of the rage against the therapist onto him, and a chance meeting with the repairman promoted his use as a displacement for her sexualized longings for closeness with the therapist. Thus, day residues may serve as traumas or as a means of enabling the patient to respond and adapt to these traumas. Often there are both facets to any event that comes up in therapy, but it is essential to select the primary trauma from the rest or a correct formulation of the patient's behavior and fantasies will not be possible.

INDICATORS OF NEUROTIC PROBLEMS

There is a second prime task in listening to the manifest content or surface of the patient's communications: that of detecting indications that a neurotic problem exists. We must learn to become sensitive to the signs of these difficulties. Work in psychotherapy actually begins with such indicators, since they establish the need for treatment; unless we can identify a neurotic problem, there is no basis for psychotherapeutic work. Further, as shown in Chapter 8, we must constantly distinguish between real, external problems and the intrapsychic conflicts which may be evoked by such events.

Inappropriate behaviors and responses must be distinguished from those that are in keeping with external realities. A woman whose husband wants a divorce has a real problem. She may agree to it or attempt a reconciliation; these are externally directed adaptations. If she develops asthma, a nonphysical numbness of a limb, a phobia, or beats her son, these illogical responses are indications that intrapsychic conflicts have also been set off and that they have not been properly resolved. These latter are, then, indicators of neurotic problems and are reactions inappropriate to the reality situation.

A previous definition of indicators will serve our needs here:

Indicators are communications that inform the therapist that a significant neurotic problem exists, without conveying the unconscious meaning of the problem or the underlying fantasies. They relate primarily to the manifest content or surface of the material. Indicators may pertain to impaired ego functioning, resistances, neurotic symptoms and conflicts, and characterological disturbances, though they do not offer information as to the specific unconscious fantasies and genetics involved. Thus, indicators tell us something is amiss, without telling us the underlying unconscious meaning and basis. They are exemplified in psychotherapy in absences; empty ruminations; inappropriate anger, anxiety, or depression; thoughts of leaving treatment; symptoms; and other manifestations of this kind (Langs, 1972, p. 7).

Of particular interest are those indicators that reflect ego dysfunctions such as poor controls, impaired object relationships, poor reality testing, low frustration tolerance and impaired capacity for delay. Another group reflect unresolved intrapsychic conflicts in the form of symptoms, and inappropriate and maladaptive reactions to external events, such as excessive anger, inability to tolerate a separation from an inessential person, disturbances in state of consciousness, and the like.

Another set of important indicators relates to the signs of conflict resolution and improved functioning leading to the modification of symptoms and neurotic problems. These take various forms, such as dreams of renunciation, lasting changes in behavior which reflect improved adaptation, or improved controls and relationships.

There is considerable confusion regarding the clinical distinction between real and intrapsychic problems. Although I have already discussed this issue from several vantage points (see Chapter 8), it is probably best clarified through clinical vignettes. I will briefly present three and discuss each.

> Mr. L.R. was a borderline, phobic young man who had been in therapy about eighteen months. In the last six months, he had resolved his major problems with his job and in relationships with others, so that he felt relatively comfortable as long as he did not date or attempt to sleep outside of his house. His sessions were repetitious and monotonous. For example, he reported in one hour that one of his friends had ignored him, and Mr. L.R. was

angry and wouldn't call him. His mother had attacked him irrationally for using the kitchen stove to make his lunch, and he had answered her back and sulked. He recalled earlier quarrels with her when he was a child.

In another session, he spoke at length of defecating after smoking and wondered why this happened. He thought of reaming out a dog's rectum. He spoke with a friend and justified his own behavior. He complained that his therapist was too silent.

When he finally slept away from home one night, he fantasied that his boyfriend and the latter's mother would seduce him sexually. For the first time, he revealed pervasive homosexual fantasies and conflicts, especially fantasies of fellatio performed on a huge, powerful penis. He also recalled his mother's exposure of her nude body to him several times during his childhood.

In the early sessions described here, there is no neurosis-related primary adaptive task and no therapeutic context. The material relates to reality problems and issues, adapting to them, and memories connected with them. Fantasies emerge without a context and are therefore isolated and lead nowhere.

Once the phobic defense was modified, intrapsychic conflicts and fantasies, some previously repressed, and all expressing derivatives of further repressed fantasies and memories, emerged in the context of the patient's sleeping away from home. The anxieties evoked by this experience are neurotic, as is the phobic symptom. This material related to the patient's intrapsychic conflicts: his fantasies, anxiety, and behavior are not in keeping with outer reality and can only be understood through a grasp of his inner stirrings.

Another example will illustrate this further:

Mrs. c.u. had found out that her husband was having an affair. She became angry and depressed, and was in conflict about a divorce because of her previous love for her husband and her concern for her young child. She cried, discussed the issues with her husband, gave him an ultimatum and retracted it, and finally decided to stay with him. For several sessions, she described these conflicts and attempts to resolve them.

These are reality conflicts and relatively appropriate reactions; they are not primarily influenced by unconscious fantasies and are not related to neurotic difficulties for the moment. They are not in the realm of insight psychotherapy, since all that could be offered to the patient is advice, environmental manipulation, and second-hand opinions, interventions that are unrelated to structural intrapsychic change. Material of this kind does not lend itself to such modifications. It is only when such realities lead to unresolved intrapsychic conflict that neurotic problems follow, and then psychotherapy can play a role in effecting inner change.

With Mrs. c.u., there were indications of neurotic problems early in her therapy, when she reported fears of going crazy and of self-destructive loss of control. In one session, she described becoming deeply depressed. She had impulsively threatened to jump out of the window when her husband had ignored her. She had dreamt of her youngest brother, who had died of pneumonia in childhood. In the dream, her own face appeared distorted. She went on to describe her attachment to this brother and recalled times when she took care of him and would hit him and feel guilty. She felt that if her husband deserted her, in her ugliness, she would perish.

The patient's reality situation has evoked here several maladaptive and symptomatic responses based on her unresolved intrapsychic conflicts (e.g., depression and suicidal impulses). Unresolved rage and guilt, genetic links to her relationship with her brother, and some related difficulty with her own body image also emerged. These are neurotic problems; they can be resolved only by reaching and analyzing the unconscious fantasies and memories on which they are based. This is the realm of psychotherapy.

Lastly, consider this briefly summarized therapy session:

Mrs. c.v. had a severe character disorder. After

several months of treatment, her therapist had gone on vacation. She began the session upon his return by saying that her phobic symptoms, her many anxieties, and her battles with her husband were all gone, and she thought of stopping treatment. The therapist recommended exploring this idea and she went on to describe in detail how well she was feeling and functioning. She had been upset by a visit to her mother, however. They had quarreled over the patient's not visiting her often enough. Mrs. C.V. was furious with her mother, and in response to questions from the therapist, described the details of their quarrel. She then spoke of how self-centered her mother had been, of the latter's many successes in business at the expense of her children, and of how well they had turned out despite their mother. The patient despised her mother for this. An aunt had taken care of her; she would do almost anything to spite her mother.

In this session, the therapist dealt with the patient's anger with her mother, a real and not a neurotic problem. It certainly had intrapsychic repercussions, including conscious and unconscious fantasies, which are not however always related to psychopathology, but it did not lead to an unresolved intrapsychic conflict. There was a real problem with a neglectful, insensitive mother, and the patient dealt with it by seeing less of her.

On the other hand, the neurotic problem in this hour is the patient's wish to stop therapy. Though it is couched in terms of being well, there is every reason to believe that it is actually inappropriate and constitutes a flight into health or so-called transference cure (see Chapters 20 and 23). The reality precipitate is the therapist's vacation, to which the response—feeling he is not needed, and anger—is inappropriate, in part. Thus, the quarrel with the patient's mother is secondary, a real problem and day residue which lent itself as a vehicle for the displacement of, and defense against, the patient's reaction to the separation from the therapist. Here, the reality situation and memories of the mother convey derivatives of unconscious fantasies regarding the therapist's departure, and the inner conflicts and memories it evoked. In essence, Mrs. C.V. unconsciously identified the separation with the frequent times her mother had left her, and her reaction was to feel well and deny the need for her therapist-mother; she would spite him by proving that he did not help her—she helped herself.

The therapist, in failing to focus on the neurotic problem and inquiring into the patient's real difficulties, lost sight of the ultimate focus on intrapsychic conflicts and fantasies in psychotherapy. He also sought after irrelevant content when faced with a resistance and rupture in the therapeutic alliance. The search for elements inappropriate to reality in the patient's fantasies and behavior must always be to the forefront of psychotherapy.

Recognizing the distinction between real and intrapsychic conflicts is linked to the question of intervention. Real problems are often used as a defensive covering for neurotic ones and this is a defense that the therapist should not participate in. Therapists who prefer to focus on real conflicts tend to stick to manifest content and the surface of the material in the sessions. They ask direct questions regarding these real issues and encourage conscious, reality-oriented thought in the patient. Their own interventions are similarly reality-oriented and direct, rather than interpretive. In contrast, therapists who are interested in intrapsychic conflicts value indirect associations as the "royal road" to repressed fantasies and the conflicts on which symptoms are based. They will allow their patients to go on about seemingly unrelated matters, expecting to reap the rewards of rich, displaced fantasy material. When the main neurotic problem or its precipitate is not clear, such a therapist will listen to the patient's associations in the hope of discovering these vital clues. His questions will not be reality-focused, but will be directed toward the search for derivatives of the repressed. He will not neglect ego dysfunctions, but will constantly search for their underpinnings. The distinction between real fear and neurotic anxiety is a guidepost for his endeavors (see Freud, 1926).

A successful application of the understanding of these distinctions occurred in the following clinical situation:

> Mr. F.P. is the college student to whom I referred in Chapter 6. Briefly, we may recall that his parents independently sought family treatment for themselves and their

family, including the patient and two other sons. Mr. F.P. described this invitation at the beginning of his session with his individual therapist and then spoke of his curiosity about a family therapy experience. He then spoke of a variety of issues this would entail: the violations of the confidentiality of his sessions with his present therapist, the ways in which it could help his family, and the other risks to his present treatment. His parents, he added, seemed annoyed and were stricter with him about the neatness of his room and his jobs around the house. He really mistrusted them.

After the patient then fell silent, the therapist pointed out that by not revealing all his thoughts, Mr. F.P. was trying to restrict exploration of these problems to the surface and realities of them. The patient then said that he had actually thought of a baseball player who had just been traded to the New York Yankees. Asked to link this association to the prospect of family therapy, Mr. F.P. said that it must mean that he saw it as a replacement for his present treatment. The therapist agreed, adding that it was obvious that a ballplayer cannot play for two teams simultaneously.

The adaptive and therapeutic context of this hour is the prospect for the patient of entering group therapy, a move which would undermine his work with his present therapist (see Chapter 5). For most of the session, the patient spoke of the reality details of this step. He did bring up issues of confidentiality, but these also related to real rather than intrapsychic conflicts.

The important latent content of Mr. F.P.'s thoughts was revealed only after a confrontation with his defensive concealment of his free associations. His communication then conveyed in disguised form an unconscious fantasy that was rendered immediately intelligible by the context in which it was embedded. The therapist could now interpret the patient's inner conflicts and fantasies. Without the association, he could only allude to the real problems that he, himself, felt would be created by a second therapist.

MANIFEST AND LATENT CONTENT

In approaching the implied or deeper levels contained in his patient's communications, the therapist always begins with the surface of the patient's associations, and his apparent functioning and adaptations. Thus, he listens for the patient's manifest responses to stimuli as they are reflected in his conscious thoughts, his day and night dreams, and his behavior. He wants to know his conscious feelings and his conscious conflicts, and his surface concerns and responses to them. He may even trace out some of the genetics of such responses, though they seldom relate to neurotic conflicts, simply to define the genetics of his current adaptations to reality.

In listening to manifest content, the therapist also assesses the patient's level and strength of ego functioning—his logic, reality testing, conscious defenses, and object relationships; his conscious superego responses—values, guilt, primitive trends, ideals, etc.; and his consciously permitted or forbidden instinctual drive manifestations—sexual and aggressive needs and responses. He may also learn about the past as the patient consciously remembers it, and its apparent current influence on him. He determines the patient's range of conscious awareness and fantasies. In all, on this level, manifest content reflects many dimensions of the ongoing functioning of the patient and his response to current, surface traumas.

But the manifest content of the patient's associations is also the source of something else crucial for the understanding of neurotic disturbances: latent content. The words and behavior, and the free associations and the nonverbal communications from the patient, contain disguised derivatives or expressions of the repressed, unconscious conflicts and fantasies that are the sources of neurotic reactions and symptoms—and are the key to their secret, irrational (primary-process) logic. These derivatives reflect the causes of such reactions and open the way to their hidden meanings and their modification.

Thus, another major task for the therapist in each session is the job of detecting derivatives of unconscious fantasies. These can take many forms: the direct breakthrough of previously repressed fantasies or memories, or of fantasies which underlie resistances and ego dysfunctions; the recall of specific genetic and current traumatic experiences; indirect allusions to unconscious conflicts and derivatives of the functioning of each of the macrostructures (id, ego and superego); and expressions of the adaptational resolutions of these neurotogenic forces (see also Langs, 1972, p. 7).

In all, then, our framework in listening is to have an ear for reality stimuli and indicators of real problems on one hand, and for intrapsychic anxieties, conflicts and fantasies on the other. The model we use is one of stimulus and response, of external stimulus and adaptive intrapsychic reaction, including drives and defenses. The instinctual drives in turn evoke anxiety and further defenses, and it is this sequence that we seek out.

DETECTING LATENT CONTENT

If repressed fantasies and conflicts are the key to neurotic symptoms, we must be able to detect their expressions in the material from the patient. These disguised representations of unconscious fantasies—derivatives—are latent to the manifest meanings intended by the patient. The patient's efforts to adapt to reality events and traumas, and the intrapsychic conflicts and fantasies they evoke, include fantasy activity (see Chapter 8). From anxiety, feelings of helplessness and pride, fears of punishment and humiliation, a patient will tend to deny aspects of an intrapsychic conflict access to awareness. He will, nevertheless, make repeated attempts to resolve the conflict, imagining at one moment the dangers involved, while at another a possible resolution, while still later on pushing the entire problem aside. This fantasy activity may be mature or primitive, reality-oriented or quite unrealistic. It will emerge at the surface of the patient's thinking and behavior in various disguised and displaced forms, which range from symptoms to neurotic behavior to conscious day and night dreams (see below).

In psychotherapy, we begin with the surface result of this inner work of defense, disguise, and expression: manifest content; and we attempt to understand what the material contains in distorted and concealed form: the latent content. We also seek manifestations of the processes, the disguises and defenses, which transform the repressed content into the manifest material. We endeavor to collect enough clues in a given session from the manifest content itself (by detecting themes, sequences, and contexts) to discover the latent content despite the camouflage. There are elements common to manifest and latent content, bridges between the two (see Langs, 1971a). Manifest content screens or conceals, but also reveals some of what lies beneath it. Often, the key to the latent content is found in tuning in on the proper level of general meaning, the correct metaphor, or the correct level at which the manifest and latent content share imagery and meanings.

Only attention to all levels of communication, the surface and the depths as expressed verbally and nonverbally, can result in properly balanced and successful psychotherapy. It is all too easy to fall into the trap of overemphasizing superficialities and reality, or the reverse: overexploring unconscious fantasies and neglecting the real events which prompt them and make them understandable. Let us now turn to the various ways that the therapist detects latent content.

Inherent and Implicit Latent Content

Inherent latent content refers to all of the underlying, potential meanings in a particular communication. Mention of a given person or event contains a multitude of unspoken memories and fantasies that are both conscious and unconscious. At any given moment and in each specific context, a particular cluster of associations will be active and relevant. Often the patient will allude in passing to a specific incident which, upon inquiry, contains many important latent dimensions. Here is a brief example:

> Mrs. c.w., a woman with a borderline syndrome, had an acute anxiety episode. She reviewed the antecedents and said that she had quarreled with her daughter, had had a discussion with her husband about their marriage, and had spoken to her mother about the latter's illness. She shrugged off each of these as irrelevant to her distress. When the therapist suggested that there must be more to these incidents, Mrs. c.w. described each in detail. The argument with her daughter involved a number of issues, especially the patient's unresolved rage at her. The dis-

cussion with her husband related to sexual problems they were having and evoked guilt-ridden, sexual fantasies in the patient. The call from her mother aroused further issues between the patient and her parents, especially terrifying, murderous rage against her mother, over which Mrs. c.w. feared losing control.

Here, we see how three passing references to incidents prior to the patient's anxiety each inherently contained a host of latent material. Direct inquiry or interpretation of the avoidance defense will often lead to the revelation of such latent material. Sensitivity to incidents which are likely to contain important underlying material is helpful.

Implicit latent content refers to behavior and thoughts which are meant to convey indirectly or by insinuation other concealed feelings and thoughts. A patient may say one thing while implying another through his tone or attitude. Communications designed primarily to get another persons' love or attention, or to manipulate or provoke him, are also of this kind. In these instances, the manifest behavior or thought has latent in it another content and purpose which can be understood only through an assessment of the entire context.

Here is a brief illustration:

Mr. c.x. was depressed. After several sessions of rumination, he spoke of clinging to his parents like a child in order to feel safe and protected. The therapist interpreted his coming to the sessions as a further effort to seek safety rather than inner change and, in response, Mr. c.x. spoke of a teacher to whom he would go to talk when upset.

In the next two sessions, the patient recalled in some detail a series of earliest memories and dreams which did not crystalize around any central theme or conflict. When Mr. c.x. spoke of trying to give others what they want in order to placate them, the therapist asked if this referred to his recent efforts at remembering his past and his dreams. The patient said that he had felt criticized by the therapist and was, indeed, trying to talk about things the therapist seemed to want to hear.

The main latent content of this material was the implicit wish to please the therapist. At times, such nonverbal meanings are more important than the content of the material itself.

Sequence

It is a long-established therapeutic principle that associations that follow one another in a session may have some hidden, repressed link to each other. This may be extended to the thesis that every communication in a given session will have one or more unconscious links. Further, each sequence of sessions may also be linked by one or more repressed fantasies and conflicts. However, I shall demonstrate that all elements in a sequence are not of equal importance, accent, and meaning, and that it is crucial to separate out the day residue (primary adaptive task) from the response (here, unconscious fantasies) in each sequence. Let us first develop a clear picture of the way sequence in itself helps us to detect derivatives of what is repressed.

Sequences are especially helpful in clarifying themes and ideas that are consciously and unconsciously connected. The nature of the relationship and the relevant unconscious fantasies usually become clear only with the aid of the thematic content and context, but repressed connections between events, past memory-experiences, fantasies and behavior are revealed by sequential links and continuity within a session or between sessions.

In the clinical material that follows, I will utilize only sequences in which a hypothesized unconscious link or latent meaning reflected by a sequence was independently confirmed by subsequent material from the patient (see Chapter 18). Since methods for detecting latent content are so closely related to each other, the supplementation of sequential clues by thematic threads and context will be apparent.

> Mrs. c.y. entered the therapist's office and sat in a chair away from his desk. She reported that she had felt empty all week, sexually hungry. She had been thinking of her

therapist's coming vacation. She had dreamt that she was at his office with her husband, but told the others in his waiting room that she did not know the therapist. She then hid from him behind a comic book when he came for her.

Mrs. C.Y. went on to say that she recognized that she was trying to laugh off the expected loss of the therapist. Her husband should come for therapy; she no longer needed it. She had also dreamt that her mother had died and that she looked through her mother's possessions and took nothing.

She went on to criticize the therapist and a stand he had taken recently that had prevented her from attempting to hurt herself. She had been depressed and suicidal all week. Her father was not well and she was worried about him. She then condemned herself for being a destructive mother. She read of a woman who had killed her own child. A friend had said that therapists never help you and would never see you without a fee. As she left the session, she asked if she could take a magazine home from the waiting room so she could finish an article in it.

If we look at the essence of this sequence, we might hypothesize that Mrs. C.Y.'s sexual hunger was linked in some way (unconsciously) to her therapist's vacation, which is connected with her dreams of him. On the surface, the dream reflects attempts to deny both her need for the therapist and her depression over his anticipated loss. The sequence reveals that all this is related to her mother in some way, and to the theme of death and mementos to remember her by. Then it is connected with concern about her father and his health. Next is direct anger at the therapist and anger at herself for being a bad mother. This is linked with mothers who kill their children and with criticisms of psychotherapists. Last in the sequence is the request for the therapist's magazine.

By noting these sequential interrelationships on a manifest level, we begin to sense latent content. The sequence might be condensed as follows: empty and hungry—therapist's vacation—not knowing the therapist—comic book—not needing therapy—mother's death —criticizing therapist—father's health—condemning herself—criticizing therapists—taking the therapist's magazine.

If we recognize that the material of the session revolves around the therapist's pending vacation (the context), the remainder of the sequence can be seen to reflect a variety of inner conflicts, fantasies, defenses, and transference responses to it.

Consider now the sequence in this vignette.

> Mrs. C.Z. was late to her session. She had an anxiety attack coming to it. She thought of the therapist's couch, and reported fantasies and fears of being seduced by him. She wanted a child and her husband could not impregnate her. She read that the husband is often responsible for sterility in the wife. Her father never told her the facts of life, even in her childhood when her mother was ill. She had thought of taking an overdose of sleeping pills.

Here, the essential sequence is: lateness—anxiety—fears of being seduced by the therapist—her wish for a child and blaming her husband for not having one—her father—her mother's illness— and thoughts of suicide. We may postulate, then, that there are latent links between the patient's lateness and symptoms, her fantasies about the therapist, and her childlessness. Genetic links to her father at a time when her mother was ill are tied in, as are her suicidal thoughts. We may readily suspect that a guilt-ridden wish for a child, expressed in a father-transference and related to fantasies that the patient had when her mother was ill, is the source of the patient's anxiety and intrapsychic conflicts.

Often, the most fleeting mention of a past event or a person as part of a sequence of this kind offers a vital clue to a genetic or dynamic dimension of the material in which it is embedded. These are important to detect and explore.

One last example:

> Mr. D.A. was a young man with a severe character disorder who sought therapy because of depressions, problems in establishing lasting relationships with women, and

difficulties in settling on a career for himself. He had missed several sessions because of a vacation that he took for a rest; this clearly reflected, among other things, a wish to disrupt and flee his therapy. Upon his return, he described his uncertainty about continuing and ruminated about his life problems with little depth or insight.

After missing another hour, he began the next session by describing how he had tired of two of his friends and wanted to drop them. One of them would like to be in therapy. Mr. D.A.'s stomach had been upset. One of his teachers had asked a favor of him and he took care of it so he could get closer to him. A patient in the therapist's office building thought he (Mr. D.A.) was a doctor. He'd been thinking about a girlfriend whom he had impregnated and who had had an abortion. He'd been furious with her, but felt awful after reading about how terribly women suffer after an abortion.

The therapist pointed out near the end of this session that the patient had avoided any mention of the hour that he had missed and that these absences were seriously disrupting his therapy. The patient said that he recognized that this was so; he was always uncertain about the things in his life. He would try to not miss another session.

This sequence begins with a series of missed sessions, an hour characterized by intense defensiveness, and another missed session. In the session which was abstracted, the manifest sequence is the following: dropping friends — therapy — stomach upset — getting closer to a teacher—being a doctor—a girlfriend whom the patient impregnated and who aborted and suffered—the therapist's confrontation regarding the missed hour—and the patient's resolve not to miss further sessions.

We can sense a continuity over this series of sessions in which the sequence itself suggests a central problem regarding the therapy. Missing a session is related to dropping friends which is connected to a gastrointestinal disorder and impregnation and abortion. While latent connections are needed to understand the meanings of this sequence, with its reference to possible allusions to fears of harmful penetration or forced incorporation, the clues provided by the temporal connections themselves are important in showing where the unconscious links lie.

Let us return to the vignette and develop the material further:

> In the next session, the therapist arrived five minutes late, and apologized; the patient said that it was "O.K." He had waited in the therapist's office but then left it, fearing that the therapist would think he was too curious. He spoke about past boy and girlfriends and how he was uncertain of his relationships with them. He had either to quit therapy or commit himself to it. He was repairing his car and had had a thought: if gasoline got into his mouth and he got cancer, he wouldn't let any surgeon operate on him. He then recalled a camping trip into the woods: he had climbed a fire tower without fearing that it would fall.
>
> The therapist pointed out that the patient seemed to see him as a dangerous surgeon and tied it to previous fantasies and dreams in which the patient was being attacked and mutilated by animals who had been seen, in context, to represent the therapist. He also said that he suspected that the patient feared some terrible discovery in his treatment.
>
> Mr. D.A. responded that he was aware of his mistrust of the therapist. The woods represented nature and safety to him; if the tower had collapsed, he would have had nothing meaningful left to him. He remembered that he had been very anxious before the session. He could begin to sense a real need to continue his therapy; something was really disturbing him.

The sequence in this hour is: therapist's lateness—excused by patient—patient alone in office—uncertain relationships and therapy —repairing car—fantasy: gasoline in his mouth, cancer, no surgery —woods and no fear—therapist's interpretation—remembering of anxiety before the session.

The mapping of the sequential aspects of the session indicates the areas of underlying connections. There are sufficient clues to support the hypothesis that the material in this session is related to that of the previous hour. The context remains anxieties about treatment, and the suspected theme of harm through penetration—incorporation is elaborated upon. The patient's fear of the therapist is expressed in less and less disguised derivatives as well. Thus, sessions which follow each other are to be considered connected beneath the surface on one or more levels, and should be attended to with such potential relatedness in mind. Usually, the material in contiguous sessions deals with the same problems until they have been partially resolved, or a new trauma intervenes and mobilizes the patient's responses and inner stirrings along new lines. Therapeutic technique which is characterized by a lack of consistent focus upon major issues over a period of time, but instead jumps about from theme to theme, is bound to be poor. Attention to temporal sequence helps prevent such loose and isolated therapeutic endeavors. Our patients communicate through sequence, and we must work with them accordingly.

But, by now, the reader must recognize that sequence alone does not reveal the full latent content of the patient's communications. Sequence comprises manifest themes and contents and these, in themselves, provide clues to what lies beneath the surface. After studying this thematic aspect of latent content, and that of context, we will be able to return to these vignettes and extract the latent conflicts and fantasies more readily.

Thematic Threads and Clusters

Tuning in on clusters of thematic content is not simple; there are many ways in which repressed fantasies are expressed. Despite this, it is possible to learn to listen to the material from patients (associations and nonverbal communications) in a flexible manner so that different levels of images and metaphors, and the multitude of potential meanings, all register freely. At first, in a given session, there is either ready organization around a prominent thematic axis, or more often than not, chaos in which the thematic threads appear to be in flux. Most often, as further associations unfold, the implicit and explicit content will coalesce around one or two central themes. Unhindered listening, as free as possible from inner bias and defensiveness in the therapist, is essential. As his focus shifts about easily from one level and cluster to another, he formulates various unifying threads, examines how well they fit and clarify the material, and decides whether they help to identify a main intrapsychic conflict and the patient's response to it. He also searches for related manifest and latent themes, and for obvious and disguised organizers. When one thread, an aspect of conscious and unconscious fantasy, seems to fit several associations, he makes note of it and listens for further associations for confirmation (further fit), or lack of it, which then redirects his listening.

Consider the following:

> Mrs. D.B. began her session by stating that she didn't want to awaken that morning.

Listening to first communications is especially important; they may contain verbal and nonverbal clues to the entire session. The therapist silently responds immediately to the patient's associations, within the context of the previous session or two, and runs through various possible latent meanings of each unfolding image. While some of his associations undoubtedly will be idiosyncratic, the more that he is in tune with the patient, the more likely it is that this process will reflect possible latent thematic threads intended by the patient. Thus, Mrs. D.B.'s therapist might see this initial comment as a surface wish to be asleep and possibly to be unaware. He might wonder if it implies the patient's wish to flee her inner fantasies or the treatment, or a wish to be a child. It could reflect a sexual fantasy or might even be a reference to childhood or recent experiences in bed. All of this is considered as the patient continues and clusters of content are sought from among the further associations.

To return to the vignette:

> In the previous session, Mrs. D.B. had begun to recognize that in her childhood she had had disguised and even relatively undisguised sexual fantasies about her father, and that they had been evoked by seductiveness on his part.

With this added information, we might wonder if the patient's wanting to sleep reflected a wish to escape from this new material, or was related in some way to the content of her emerging sexual fantasies. We also should consider whether something else happened since the previous hour that would give another latent meaning to her thought.

> To continue: She had been thinking about her father and had dreamt that her dishwasher was overflowing; she put her ear to it.

Dishwasher and listening: how do they connect to sleeping? Is it hearing or not hearing? Cleaning and washing? Is the water a reference to birth or bed wetting? Are there concerns over losing control? Is this somehow related to the past and to auditory primal scene experiences? Her fantasies regarding her father appear to be the context for these associations, but how can we unify these apparently disparate threads?

> In the session, after ruminating about a recent repair to her dishwasher, Mrs. D.B. recalled listening at the wall of her parents' bedroom as a child and hearing them talk. She then spoke of her childhood fears of burglars and added a recollection not previously reported in her therapy: she had wet her bed as a child.

Thus, the manifest thematic threads here run something like this: sleep—dishwasher overflowing—listening—childhood listening to parents in bedroom—fear of burglars—bed-wetting. These are supplemented by directly implied latent themes such as withdrawal —loss of control—curiosity about her parents—stealing—overexcitement. The entire cluster revolves around her father and reflects derivatives of repressed sexual fantasies and memories regarding him. Actually, this sequence of associations culminated in the following sessions with the recall of previously repressed recollections of primal scene observations, and expressions of unconscious fantasies of stealing and devouring her father's penis.

In this series of sessions, the associations and clusters of images and ideas coalesced, and culminated in the revelation of previously unconscious fantasies related to the patient's symptom of a choking in her throat. This productivity may be contrasted with other sessions where the material is flat, disconnected, and does not coalesce, and in which the sequence is not definitive.

Another vignette will further demonstrate the difficulties in detecting thematic trends related to repressed conflicts and fantasies:

> Mrs. D.C., a phobic woman with a severe character disorder, had been in therapy for a year. Termination was approaching because the therapist was going to leave the area. At the time of the session, the patient had undergone a dilatation and curettage that showed some suspicious cells, and laboratory studies were pending.
>
> She began one session while drinking coffee by saying that her husband was out of town on a business trip. She had been sleeping a lot and was waiting to hear further about the pathologist's findings. She had not mentioned in treatment a recent vaginal infection which might account for the cell changes. She had to abstain from sex and it "drove her up a wall." Her brother-in-law had been in the city and left; she had had an affair with him a few years before. Her husband and father had been discussing death before the former left; it depressed her.
>
> The therapist related her fear of death to the biopsy, and Mrs. D.C. said that she was angry at her husband for leaving, especially since he wouldn't let a girlfriend and her lover stay with her. Her son had been afraid that a man had broken into the house; she didn't want to give him her fears.

The thematic threads seem diffuse and do not jell. They may be summarized as follows: drinking coffee in session—husband away —biopsy—vaginal infection—abstinence and anxiety—brother-in-law and affair—husband, father and death—therapist's intervention —anger at husband's absence—girlfriend and lover not staying with her—son's fears of man in house—her own fears. While sexual fantasies are in evidence, their specific nature is unclear. Anxiety about the biopsy may be involved and her husband's absence may also be playing a role. It is best to wait for clarification at such times.

In the next hour, Mrs. D.C. said that she was glad that the therapist, in coming to get her for her session, had rescued her from a young girl who was in therapy with another therapist at the clinic in which both were being treated. Mrs. D.C. had given her a ride home the previous week and the girl was pestering her. She wondered if her therapist believed in ESP. Her sister had dreamt that a boy had taken her car apart and stolen it, and then her car was actually stolen. Her mother has ESP too. She fought with her mother who questioned her about sex and money. The patient and her husband have a secret bank account and the clinic must not find out or it would increase her fee. (This had come up before and had not been dealt with.) Her husband called and suspected jokingly that a man was there. After the last session, the patient had fallen badly. She had then gone home and imagined that a man had followed her. She felt dizzy at this point in the hour. She didn't know how to handle her mother: did she do right or wrong in refusing to sleep at her house?

Here, we have these themes: giving another patient a ride—ESP and sister's premonitory dream of the car theft—fight with mother over sex and money—money secret—therapist shouldn't tell the clinic—husband suspicious—fall after previous session—fantasy of man following her—dizziness—mother and doing right or wrong. The material appears to cluster around infractions of boundaries and limits, and the sharing of a secret corruption with the therapist. The sequence suggests erotic fantasies regarding him and anxiety evoked by these wishes. In displaced form, these forbidden and repressed instinctual fantasies are gratified by driving a patient home and seducing the therapist into participating in the concealment of resources from the clinic.

Briefly, in the next hour, themes of financial secrets, fire violations, flirting with men and enraging her husband who had said she was getting heavy, fears of men breaking into her apartment, an episode of near-fainting after a recent session, and intercourse with a former lover culminating in the patient's showing a picture of herself in a bathing suit to the therapist to prove that she was still slim.

This is a typical sequence of theme and variation in which multiple derivatives of sexual fantasies toward the therapist are expressed verbally, nonverbally, and in behavior. Listening to these threads, the therapist endeavors to grasp and regroup the elements until a major constellation emerges and is subsequently reinforced. The manifest elements, expressing as they do one or another facet of the underlying fantasies and conflicts are, in themselves, clues to the repressed. Ordering them directs the therapist to their implicit content.

The threads in a given cluster are not of equal prominence or strength. Some are heavily laden with latent meanings and others are only weakly so. Some lie at the center of the cluster and others are more peripheral. Some are related to the precipitating traumas and others to the patient's real and intrapsychic responses. A means of organizing these clusters is very helpful; this the context provides (see below).

Having developed a concept of latent content and the means available to the therapist to detect its presence in derivatives in the associations from patients, let us briefly focus on the nature of these derivatives. They are the expressions of unconscious fantasies and memories, defensively disguised in various ways through displacements, condensations, symbolizations and other modifications. Perhaps most important from the vantage of technique is the fact that these disguised manifestations of unconscious fantasies may be generally classified into those that are very strongly modified and distorted representations—I will term these "distant or remote derivatives"; and those that are relatively less altered versions of the unconscious content—these I will refer to as "close derivatives."

In the main, the therapist endeavors to work with the patient's resistances and defenses to foster the gradual expression of unconscious fantasies and memories by means of less and less disguised representations. Interpretations of unconscious fantasies are generally best made with close rather than distant derivatives, since the patient is more receptive and less defensive at such moments (see Chapter 14). To illustrate this distinction, let us consider two vignettes in which I will select out of the patient's associations over several sessions the unfolding derivatives of a central unconscious fantasy.

Mr. J.J. was a depressed and apathetic teen-ager in psychotherapy for about six months. He had a younger brother and sister, and in the context of his brother's birthday and a recent vacation by his therapist, he began to recall a few memories related to the birth of each sibling. It had been clear from the outset of his therapy that their arrival and the deep sense of lost closeness with his mother was a central determinant of his symptoms.

I suggest that the reader try to determine the latent, unconscious fantasies in the material which follows.

In the first session from this period he reported a dream of three pairs of boots planted in his lawn; he was watching their roots. Associations led to a quarrel with his sister over food which ended when the patient hit her.

In the next hour, he reported a dream of a chinchilla outside of his window which was eating smaller animals and throwing them off the roof of their garage. On a television screen, Mr. J.J. watched with his father as the animal somehow bored its way into the patient's room and ran off. In another dream, he was doing a flying somersault. Associations were to a weekend away with a group of children, a movie in which a scorpion bit someone, thoughts of vampires biting, and recollections from his early childhood of animals he owned and took care of.

In the next session, he spoke of people who were injured in car accidents, and other themes of illness and injury followed. Associations related this primarily to his therapy and his fears of treatment were interpreted to him.

He began the next hour with another dream: there is a rat in his kitchen. His mother is holding it and he is afraid it will bite him. He wants to kill it, but his mother says it is too small. In associating, he recalled a series of memories from the year that his brother was born: his interest in small animals; his fantasies of snakes and monsters hidden in the bed of a river near his house, and his fears that they would eat him up; and his fight with a little boy as they waded in that river. As he thought of holding the rat, he suddenly remembered a moment when his mother told him to hold his brother soon after the latter's birth; he was afraid he might drop him.

In the next few hours, many memories and fantasies about his mother's pregnancies and deliveries, and his efforts to remain close to her, unfolded.

In this sequence, we see at first well-disguised, remote derivatives of the patient's fantasies about his mother's pregnancies, the fetus in utero, the process of birth, and his reaction to the arrival of his siblings. With only a little help from the therapist who mainly interpreted a brief period of anxious resistance, the patient spontaneously expressed these fantasies in a variety of ways and eventually worked through some of his own defenses to directly acknowledge that the associations related to his siblings. The dream of holding the small rat is somewhat less disguised than the chinchilla dream, and modification by the patient of his own defenses led to direct recognition of the latent meaning of the rat dream. I will not detail here the various unconscious fantasies which could then be pieced together from these dreams and associations.

Turning now to the other vignette:

Mrs. J.K. had been in therapy for a year-and-a-half because of phobic anxieties and hypochondriacal symptoms; she showed evidence of a borderline syndrome. She had improved considerably and was considering termination. Here are the derivatives of a set of unconscious fantasies as they appeared over several sessions:

The patient dreamt of being chased by an Arab wearing white (she is Jewish). She then spoke of being annoyed with her husband and feeling that therapy was futile. In another session, she reported dreaming of men volunteering for an experiment in which a needle is placed into their genitals to draw blood. In a different dream, her decorator—a man—visits her unexpectedly; she then follows him to his house. Associations were to the death of her father and medical articles that she had read. She had thought of asking her therapist to see her husband; was she too dependent on therapy, she wondered?

In the next hour, she dreamt that her daughter was kidnapped and a detective helped Mrs. J.K. find her. She again alluded to her anger with her husband and suddenly reported an odd thought that she had had: maybe she was in love with her therapist.

In this vignette, well disguised, distant derivatives expressed various aspects of this patient's unconscious, fantasied longings to be closer and united with her therapist. In time, these disguised fantasies became more like the actual fantasies involved, and eventually one aspect of this fantasy-system was expressed directly.

CONTEXT: THE PRIMARY ADAPTIVE TASK

Of all of the means of detecting and decoding clusters of latent content and unconscious fantasies, and correctly understanding other aspects of the patient's behavior, context is the most crucial. We already know that human beings function basically by reacting and adapting to stimuli; only if we correctly ascertain the stimulus (and it is not always easy to do so), can we correctly understand their responses on any level.

Intrapsychically, it follows that when a patient is responding to a trauma or disturbance, his thoughts and fantasies will define it and relate to all of its dimensions. Wherever the surface of his thoughts and fantasies may go, there is an underlying link to the central context. Listening in context to these seemingly unrelated, though unconsciously most definitely relevant, wanderings—associations—will reveal the repressed fantasies and conflicts evoked in the patient by the dangerous situation.

Context defines the problem with which the patient is dealing, the reality event (or internal upheaval) which has prompted the patient's adaptive responses, behaviorally and intrapsychically. When we know this central problem, we can attain a true understanding of what the patient is communicating. At times this is relatively easy to do (for example, after a major trauma), and at other moments this can be quite difficult, since it is often defensively and unconsciously concealed by the patient. Context, then, is—as I have said—a concept akin to the day residues of dreams, and its usage is modeled on the relationship between day residues and the dreams they prompt.*

This vignette will illustrate:

> Mrs. A.H., a young married woman, began this session with a dream. She is in a hospital bed, asleep; then she awakens within the dream and sees a nurse and a doctor. They have a wheel and are going to gas her. They do it twice and then she actually awoke. In the session, she went on to talk about death, funerals, and being embalmed. She had had severe abdominal cramps the night of the dream and they were worse after the dream. She was having problems with her son's poor eating habits and her daughter's lying. She had been furious with them and screamed at them; she had also quarreled with her husband. The dream reminded her of the death of her father; had God placed her in the hospital that day to show her that he died in peace or to punish her? She had worn the shoes that she had put on for his funeral for several weeks after. The gas was like the Rubin's test, in which the doctor had put air into her some years back, in order to see if she had any diseases of her reproductive organs which could account for her infertility at that time.

In this session we can sense thematic references to rage and punishment, to death and separation, and to impregnation. But we cannot really define the specific issues and conflicts with which the patient is dealing and the specific unconscious fantasies which are involved. The main problem with which the patient is dealing is unclear.

---

* The material on pp. 312–316 is based upon Langs, 1972, pp. 14–19. For a fuller discussion of the vignette that follows, the reader is referred to that article.

One can hypothesize several possible primary contexts for this session:

The patient was in the process of terminating therapy. Thus, one might say that the termination was unconsciously being equated with being harmed by the doctor and with the death of her father, and was evoking guilt-ridden rage and longings to remain united with the therapist-father, expressed through unconscious fantasies of union through impregnation. The gastrointestinal pain would there-fore represent the regressive, somatically-expressed gratification of her wish for a child from the therapist-father and the punishment for the wish. It would also represent rage against the deserting, hurting father-therapist and talion punishment for fantasies of attacking and penetrating him.

The patient was considering divorce because of her husband's cruelty. In this context, one would then interpret the material and symptoms in still another way, focusing on the conflict with her husband and its intrapsychic repercussions. Thus, we would think of the rage at her husband as central and displaced onto her father, and as prompting her longings for the latter. The separation anxiety and related pregnancy fantasies would then be a reaction to the thoughts of leaving her husband, and the transference implications would be secondary and displacements that would have to be under-stood in this context.

In fact, this patient's father had recently died and there was little question that this was the central problem for her at this time and the main theme of this session. In the previous sessions, Mrs. A.H. had been discussing his death due to a gastric hemorrhage in con-siderable detail.

The context, then, was established by reference to the previous session and to the psychologically most important reality trauma at the moment. The richness of the material, the conscious reactions and the unconscious fantasies contained in these associations, now becomes apparent.

Briefly, in her manifest dream Mrs. A.H. puts herself in her father's place and suffers from his symptoms. Her subsequent asso-ciations (and those from the previous session) reveal the latent content of the dream and the intrapsychic conflicts and unconscious fantasies with which the patient is struggling. Thus, she longs to be with her father and to undo his loss, to die with him and as he did. She is also angry with him, and this is reflected in the displacement of her rage onto her husband and children.

Of particular note is her anger at her daughter for lying, because this led to one genetic factor: an unconscious source of the patient's rage at her father, and one of the unconscious fantasies related to her symptoms involved the fact that her father had deceived her by deserting her as a child and she had never forgiven him. The memory of the pregnancy test also touched upon unconscious childhood fantasies of wanting her father's child and of wishing to be one with him. Lastly, the patient fantasied impregnation by the therapist in terms of a father transference. She also put herself in her father's place and thereby expressed the unconscious fantasy that his doctor had been responsible for his death, and that she was similarly endangered in her therapy.

Contexts may be repressed or even consciously concealed, and without such knowledge the material forms into a hodgepodge without a central organizing theme. We then either recognize that we do not understand the material or fall into the error of interpreting aspects of the material in isolation. The latter will usually lead to intellectualizing and not to contextual, emotional insight.

A second vignette is relevant:

> Mrs. A.H. began this session by describing how her husband, a businessman, had had a lawsuit initiated against him in connection with his business dealings. She was in a panic, even though the suit was unjustified. She had stomach pains and dreamt on the previous night that her maid and babysitter were discussing her father, saying that he couldn't do all that he claimed he could do for others. She associated: her father had been an attorney and could have helped set the situation straight for her husband. She went on to recall some of her father's shady dealings in law and then his desertion of his family when the patient was an infant. Had she overheard her mother and aunt talking critically about her father? She reviewed the excuses he had later made for his absence and realized that they were really rather absurd.

This session seems prompted by the law suit and its intrapsychic repercussions for the patient: her longings for her father who could rescue her and her husband, her rage at her father for his desertion and dishonesty, and some implied concerns regarding her husband's honesty. There is little that is specific or revealing in regard to the unconscious fantasies evoking the gastrointestinal symptoms.

But in the following session the patient revealed that she had inadvertently not mentioned an incident which had occurred prior to the previous hour. Her husband had had an abortive grand mal seizure and had soiled himself the night before that session. In this context, the session described above had another focus and central meaning related to the intrapsychic conflicts and reactions evoked by the seizure. In fact, the patient had used her father to screen feelings and fantasies regarding her husband. The most active and meaningful conflicts and unconscious fantasies actually related to her spouse. Manifest associations in this second session were to fears of intercourse and to quarrels with him; they revealed her rage, her fears of being soiled or impregnated by her husband, and her fears that his illness would be discovered by others. The maid in the dream cleans their laundry and might see that her husband's underwear was stained. The stomach symptoms actually related to fantasies of being urinated into and harmed or impregnated by him. In the correct context, the unconscious conflicts and fantasies become clear and specific.

I will crystallize some tentative, but pertinent, inferences drawn from these observations and the many others of which they are typical.

1. *Specific communications of both a verbal and behavioral nature within a given session can be properly understood on all available levels—conscious and unconscious, past and present, and reality issues and intrapsychic conflict—only if the correct context is ascertained.* Context is defined as the central problem with which the patient is dealing, the primary adaptive task. Context in regard to neurotic problems, as distinguished from those that are real, refers most often to some reality event (day residue) which evokes intrapsychic anxiety, conflict, conscious and unconscious fantasies, and efforts at resolution. More rarely, major intrapsychic reactions are evoked by biochemical, hormonal, and other inner changes.

2. *Context is the key to the detection of unconscious fantasies, since it provides the crucial information regarding the nature of the intrapsychic conflict and the task with which the ego is confronted.* It is therefore the major unconscious organizer of the material and provides the hidden focus of the associations.

3. *As with any aspect of the total intrapsychic conflict, the context may be repressed and kept unconscious in a defensive effort at warding off anxiety.* These defenses must be worked through. The context may then be directly revealed by the patient or may have to be detected from the latent content of the patient's associations. It is crucial to be aware of the lack of context at any given moment in treatment, and to seek it out or wait for it to emerge.

4. *In assessing the patient's ego functioning, context is also a crucial factor.* Only through such knowledge can we assess the exact defenses in use, the degree to which the intrapsychic and behavioral response is appropriate or a reflection of malfunctioning, and ascertain the cost to the total personality for a particular adaptive effort.

5. *Ascertaining the correct context may change a disjointed, confused session into a readily intelligible one, full of latent meaning.* Shifting contexts also play an important role in bringing new, previously repressed or unavailable fantasies and memories into the material on a manifest or latent level. Similarly, new contexts play a role in giving new meanings to familiar conscious fantasies and memories.

Detecting the correct context depends on an unblocked therapist, with a capacity for empathy with those experiences that traumatize people. It depends, then, first and foremost, on his qualities of human understanding. It depends, too, on his ability to abstract and think symbolically and multidimensionally; to listen with an ear tuned to the primary processes; and to suspend reality-oriented logical thinking in order to listen to the idiom of unconscious processes, only to return to reality when warranted. In feedback fashion. context determines the associations of the patient, while, conversely, the associational clusters reveal the context.

As I indicated briefly above, it is the appearance of new contexts (adaptational tasks) that is one means by which old material gains new meanings. For example, one patient described a memory of her mother's hospitalization in the context of the death of an aunt. At the time, it clustered with other material related to separation and loss, and the patient's depressive response to such losses, including the related intrapsychic conflicts and fantasies. Later in her psychotherapy, when a friend had a child, this same group of recollections emerged in the context of her frustrated longings for a son from her husband, which then led to expressions of such a wish from the therapist, itself traced to her father. In this context, her mother's hospitalization clustered with fantasies of replacing her mother and having a child with her father. Further, new versions of these recollections reported at this later time revealed additional aspects of these previously repressed fantasies. Thus, with shifting traumas and contexts, new latent meanings—repressed fantasies—contained in this set of early memories emerged. This is a most important process in developing and deepening successful psychotherapy.

It must be emphasized that the therapeutic work with more superficial and accessible levels of unconscious fantasy-memories, and especially with defenses and resistances, play a crucial role in the appearance of the new meanings latent in this material. The context (day residues) would remain repressed or would evoke defensive reactions were it not for this factor.

Interpretations based on a correct understanding of the main threads of the material, the primary context, and the psychopathological aspects of the patient's reactions, will lead to confirmatory responses from them, to symptom-relief based on inner change, and to a progressive revelation of repressed conflicts and fantasies which can then be worked through. In contrast, failure to establish the primary adaptive task will lead to an unproductive focus on reality problems, or to isolated, meaningless work with disconnected conscious and unconscious fantasies. An integrated view of the patient's conflicts and adaptive responses will not emerge.

It is apparent, too, that context helps organize thematic threads and sequences into figure and ground; that is, into stimulus and response. While Freud (1900) correctly pointed out that the importance of the repressed intrapsychic fantasies (latent dream content) far outweighs that of the reality precipitate (day residue), he also realized that we need to know the nature of the latter stimulus if we are to understand the former. It is context which provides the guiding light for the search for both.

Let us turn now to vignettes which reflect the failure to utilize context properly. I will comment as the session unfolds.

> Mr. D.D.'s first therapist had left the area and he came to his initial session with his new therapist. The context here, we can already anticipate, will be this change, whatever else has occurred in the meantime in the patient's life. At such a moment, it would take a major trauma to create a second context for this hour.
>
> The patient began the session by commenting that the therapist's desk was disorganized. He wondered: had she heard anything about him from his previous therapist? The fact that Mr. D.D. began his session with references to his new and old therapists tends to confirm the thesis that the change is a primary concern and adaptive task for him. From his comments, we may wonder too if he is anxious, concerned, or even suspicious about his transfer.
>
> Mr. D.D. went on to criticize his previous therapist and then praised him. He asked his present therapist about her vacation plans, since the former therapist had taken one soon after they had begun his treatment. Failing to get a response, he described some of his emotional problems, including homosexual fantasies about his first therapist. He then shifted to complaints about his mother, her seductiveness and her pressure on him to take on the role of his father, who had died a year earlier. He wanted very much to get away from her clutches.

This material, in sequence with the reference to the change in therapists, must cluster around this central axis. A budding erotized transference is detectable from the sexual references to the former therapist and the patient's mother. Its lack of disguise suggests poor defenses and a likelihood of unresolved conflict and anxiety. The therapist, however, failed to recognize the context at hand; she inquired directly about the patient's problem with his mother. This led to many trivial details about his relationship with her, and the session culminated with a sudden request by the patient to take two weeks off from therapy.

This is a typical outcome to an incorrect intervention (see Chapter 19), here based on the therapist's failure to recognize that as the manifest content shifted, the primary context remained the same. Derivatives of conscious and repressed fantasies were expressed and missed; they would not have been ignored if the therapist had kept the primary unconscious focus in mind. The therapist's questions about the patient's mother encouraged his defensive displacement, isolation and rumination, and a focus on a real problem; it shut off the emerging derivatives related to the intrapsychic conflicts evoked by the change in therapists. The acting out with which the session culminated was a final testimony to the therapist's failure to listen and interpret correctly, and an extension of the detrimental defensive avoidance promoted by the therapist. Its motives in unconscious rage and needs for revenge, and in flight from sexual wishes toward each therapist, had not been anticipated, identified or worked with in advance of the acting out.

Mr. D.D.'s conflicts with his mother may have an important bearing on his intrapsychic difficulties and symptoms. For the moment, however, no acute trauma is described, and the patient is using a reference to a real problem to communicate disguised fantasies about the therapist. This is evident both from his conscious preoccupation with the change in therapists and the other associational material that clusters readily about this element. At a later time and in a different context, such as after a specific seductive act by his mother, this relationship might become the context for the material in several sessions and the intrapsychic conflicts related to it would be illuminated. However, in this session, the main source of the patient's conflicts is in his relationship with his two therapists (see Chapters 20 and 21).

Another danger which results from a failure to establish the relevant context for the patient's intrapsychic conflicts is that of interpreting or exploring derivatives of repressed fantasies in isolation from reality and the rest of the patient's problems and responses. This error is relatively uncommon in students of psychotherapy, since they tend to avoid unconscious fantasies and to focus on real problems which do not, for the moment, relate to inner needs and conflicts. Here, however, is a brief illustration:

Mr. D.E. was a man with a borderline syndrome in therapy for serious work inhibitions and social difficulties. In the two preceding sessions, he had been in a rage over the therapist's repeated lateness to his sessions. He had thought of quitting therapy and the material had revolved around themes of having anal intercouse with his girlfriend, quitting his job, and fantasies of bending over for others who would then penetrate him.

In this session, he described having his girlfriend perform fellatio on him and his thoughts of leaving her; feeling stared at by his parents; reading psychology books; and a quarrel with his boss over a mechanical job that the patient had done poorly. He wished that he could speak up to his boss.

The therapist intervened here, stating that the patient envied men who used their hands better than he did, and that he was afraid to talk up because of his anxiety about losing relationships.

Mr. D.E. said that he didn't know—it wasn't clear. He had had a fantasy that two men attacked his girlfriend; he went to rescue her and was stabbed. He was dying and she comforted him.

The therapist said that for the patient, closeness brought death. The patient asked why, and why he feared loneliness. His father irritated him, but there was nothing homosexual in it.

I will add a few comments that the patient made in the next hour: he spoke of a movie about deaf and dumb people, of yelling at some friends, and of women's black pubic areas that he wanted to have intercourse with and kiss. The therapist commented that the patient wanted to do a lot to women, and the patient said that it was love, not harm.

This therapist has worked entirely without context and has attempted to define some rather blatant fantasies in isolation. There is no confirmation of these interventions from the patient (see Chapter 19). Further, this random approach has aggressive and seductive (homosexual) overtones that the patient unconsciously perceives and he responds with disguised, rageful fantasies of revenge toward the therapist (see Chapter 22). Finally, the patient unconsciously seems to decide that the therapist is deaf and dumb, and the assaultive fantasies persist.

Working without context is indeed tantamount to not understanding the patient, and often results in interventions which he experiences as sexual and aggressive thrusts. They create a therapeutic atmosphere in which the patient's reactions to the therapist's errors dominate treatment.

In this vignette, the most likely context for this material is the patient's rage at his therapist for his lateness and insensitivity. The material organizes readily into a series of derivative fantasies related to these issues, which form, then, the main latent content of the communications.

I will add one last example of the search for the primary adaptive task:

> Miss D.F. was in her early twenties, and had asthma and a severe character disorder; she lived at home. She had been in therapy over a year and was faced with her therapist's vacation. She had not, as with past separations, begun to wheeze, but was struggling to find substitutes for the therapist to whom she could attach herself. She had recently explored and worked through sexual longings for an older, single brother that had strong incorporative and guilty dimensions to them.
>
> In this session, she described feeling very well, and then suddenly depressed and physically ill with a cold; she felt as if she had a fever. Her boyfriend came over and she was remote, picked a fight, and was unresponsive to his appeals to her; they then shared some amphetamines. She went on at some length.
>
> The therapist recognized a lack of immediate context, and detecting no special clues to the precipitate of the patient's somatized depression in the material, he asked what might have prompted it. The patient then realized that her boyfriend had kept her waiting and that she had

been furious with him. She described how she had sat away from him, feeling sick, and had waited for him to take care of her. The therapist related this to her anger at his leaving and also pointed out her use of somatic illness for withdrawal, revenge, and as an appeal for better care. This, he pointed out, was a low-key equivalent to her wheezing. Somehow, though, he felt that there might have been more to the events that had precipitated this intense reaction (the principle of overdetermination); he asked Miss D.F. is she could think of anything else.

Miss D.F.'s thoughts went to her mother, who had been nagging her about her general lackadaisical attitude. If she (Miss D.F.) had infectious mononucleosis or hepatitis, her mother would let up and even take care of her, nursing her as she once did with the asthma. She now recalled that she had been wheezing a little at night, and had taken pills to prevent it from getting worse. These pills and the amphetamines were interpreted in the context of the pending separation as the magical "good" mothers that the patient demanded by wheezing, which was itself a dangerous, somatic form of pressure.

Miss D.F. then remembered that she had dreamt of an asthmatic attack. In the dream, she was then in a hospital room and her boyfriend was with another girl. The room reminded her of one where a particular nurse had taken very special care of her; she was always there with the right pill to ease her symptoms.

In this vignette, we see a layering of contexts. The background adaptive task for the patient is the therapist's pending vacation. Turning to the patient's symptoms (the therapeutic context), the therapist sought additional proximal contexts which would help to organize the specific associations. First, one repressed day residue, of the quarrel with her neglectful boyfriend, and then another more intensely repressed one of her quarrel with her mother, emerged. With these events now in the patient's awareness, a previously repressed dream was recalled; its manifest and latent content, along with the rest of the material, revealed further unconscious fantasies related to the patient's separation conflicts and its genetics.

The search for contexts is never-ending. We work through each major trauma over a series of sessions, but always keep an ear alert for the next problem and its repercussions. The instinctual drives mobilized for adaptive purposes, and the fantasies related to them, are the crucial intrapsychic aspect of context. Outer context for neurotic reactions is echoed by an intrapsychic context, and both must be known.

Among the most commonly repressed primary adaptive tasks are those related to anniversaries of past events and traumas such as the death of a parent or sibling, divorces, illnesses, and birthdays (see Pollack, 1970 and 1971). Especially when these anniversaries stem from early childhood and are related to experiences that had evoked considerable anxiety, depression, and intrapsychic conflict, they may be repressed. Despite this, there will be evidence of disturbances and conflict in the patient's life and behavior during the weeks surrounding the anniversary date. Often, the current difficulties and the material in the sessions will relate in some direct or disguised way to the original trauma and to the conscious and unconscious fantasies evoked by it.

Periods of inexplicable disturbances should invite the suspicion of a repressed anniversary. Sensitive listening to the patient's associations may provide clues to this missing past event. I will illustrate:

> Mrs. D.G. was a depressed woman whose father had died when she was four. She had little to say about his death. After several months of treatment, she reported that she was "spotting" vaginally and detailed multiple fears of anesthetics. She had imagined her husband telling her children that she was in heaven and had an intense fear of dying. Despite resolution of the gynecological symptom, she spoke of fears that her children would be killed and described a fantasy in which one of her daughters died of leukemic hemorrhages despite her own prayers. In the next few sessions, Mrs. D.G. reviewed her sexual promiscuity as a teenager; there was a seemingly endless and hopeless search for a gratifying partner. She

then reported a dream of a fire in the basement of her house; in it she attempts to rescue her son as the floor collapses and she barely does so. Associations were to her fears of fires, the death of a cousin in a fire, and to the recent death of her father-in-law.

In the absence of current day residues and contexts for much of this material, the therapist explored a hunch and asked Mrs. D.G. the date of her father's death. The anniversary of this event, it turned out, had occurred during the first session described here, and the patient's reactions to this catastrophe provided the basic context for all that had followed. The following year, at the same general time, there were additional reactions to this death. For example, Mrs. D.G. reported a dream in which she shot herself and was afraid that she would get lead poisoning. Associations now led directly to fantasies of the way her father had died (e.g., poisoned, perhaps by the doctors) and to suicidal fantasies of joining him, and then to the recall of early childhood fantasies of being in heaven with him. During this period, there was no evident outer stimulus for these concerns, though she worried greatly and without apparent reason about her children's health.

In all, anniversaries may generate powerful unconscious fantasies without immediate external provocation. Similarly, the work of therapy may stir up powerful unconscious and conscious fantasies that are important contexts for later material. These inner contexts, ultimately related to external realities, are not to be overlooked in our focus on outer primary adaptive tasks.

THERAPEUTIC CONTEXT

One last means of organizing the material of sessions remains to be discussed. This I have called the "therapeutic context," the report of symptoms, acting out, and other manifestations of psychopathology in a given hour. Since one of the ultimate goals of therapy is resolution of the conflicts, fantasies and memories at the roots of such psychopathology, the therapist should make the occurrence of such dysfunctions a fulcrum for all other material in the session. When such a symptom is reported, the entire manifest and latent content of the hour, and of one or more previous and subsequent hours, is to be viewed as illuminating its precipitates (adaptive context) and unconscious meanings. Allusions to psychopathology are among the prime contexts and indications for interventions (see Chapter 17).

Briefly, to illustrate this aspect, which will occupy us later in great detail (Chapters 11-19) we can return to the next-to-last vignette (Miss D.F.). The therapeutic context there was the patient's depression and somatic illness, as well as her argument with her boyfriend (characteristically, when upset, Miss D.F. tended to be argumentative and provocative) and drug usage. The interpretive work in the session centered upon these manifestations of her psychopathology.

With Mrs. D.G., the therapeutic context was her acute depressions and multiple anxieties. Similar contexts will be found in the other vignettes in this chapter.

One final vignette crystallizes concepts offered in this chapter and points up the crucial importance of context.

> Mr. J.L. was in therapy for about a month because of anxieties in meeting people in his sales job. He had been exploring these anxieties and his concerns about being successful in business, linking his sense of insecurity to his father's remoteness, when the following session unfolded.
>
> The patient began the hour by saying he hated smoking cigars, as he was doing; they made him sick. His business partner took a long weekend vacation and the patient was terrified of making his calls to their clients; he wanted to sleep. It was a test that had been set up by his partner, and he had failed to make an important call. His partner would pick up the pieces when he returned; the patient would feel safe again.
>
> His father had been over to repair some cabinets; the

patient is so helpless with such things. It's as if his father were taking something away from him though. He can't talk to his father and even tell him about therapy—his father would see it as another failure.

His cousin saw a psychiatrist for a drug problem and it didn't go well. He had thoughts of leaving treatment; the therapist shouldn't allow him to do it. He's too dependent on others—without them he'd be a bum.

In supervision, I was at a loss to formulate this material. The separation from his partner did not seem sufficient context for the patient's sense of despair and the disillusionment with treatment. Somehow, the hour did not seem to fall into place and I stated this, recognizing that such hours are inevitable. As I concluded my discussion of the session, the therapist mentioned in passing that he would have only one hour to present the following week—the next scheduled session fell on a legal holiday. With that information and context, the entire hour could be organized and understood. It contained a multiplicity of latent fantasies and reactions to the pending separation from the therapist, including incorporative fantasies (the cigar), suspiciousness over being left, a sense of helpless dependency, rage over his need for the therapist, doubts about treatment with thoughts of leaving it, and depression and anxiety. Without knowing the primary adaptive task facing the patient, the key latent context was undecipherable.

With this, I have completed my study of the framework for the therapist's listening to the material from the patient. Having established the means of recognizing neurotic problems, and the importance of the adaptive and therapeutic contexts in organizing and understanding the patient's communications, we can now move on to an exploration of the form and manner in which these communications are conveyed to the therapist.

10 The Specific Communications from Patients in Psychotherapy

Patients communicate to therapists both verbally and nonverbally by a variety of means, some of which I shall explore here.* My focus will be on the manner in which each specific form of expression provides surface and in-depth information to the therapist.

NONVERBAL COMMUNICATIONS AND BEHAVIOR WITHIN AND OUTSIDE OF THE SESSION

Such behavior constitutes a relatively important, although infrequently directly useful, source of data. It includes, for example, in-session rhythmic movements, playing with or pulling hair, biting or picking at fingernails, smoking, getting up from the chair, pacing, sitting away from the therapist, not looking at him, and unusual

---

* This chapter is a revised version of my paper, "A Psychoanalytic Study of Material from Patients in Psychotherapy," which first appeared in the *International Journal of Psychoanalytic Psychotherapy*, Volume I, 1972. The interested reader may refer there for additional details of this paper, which was based on an analysis of the contents of thirty sessions from each of ten patients in psychotherapy.

forms of dress. It may also take the form of silences and instances of acting in—disturbed behavior directed toward the therapist. Such matters as requests for matches or kleenex, leaving the session to go to the bathroom, and the offer of a gift include major nonverbal dimensions, as do many neurotic symptoms.

In addition to these behavioral expressions, the patient gives the therapist many nonverbal cues in his associations. This includes his tone of voice, mood and affects, phrasing, language and idiom, richness or shallowness of thought, and other such dimensions. Such communications may reflect subtle and more blatant nonpathogenic or pathogenic fantasies; they may also indicate inner progress and the establishment of new, positive levels of adaptation. To illustrate briefly:

Miss A.D. wore an outfit which strikingly resembled a maternity dress. In the context of her grandmother's death and hints in the verbal material that she had responded in part with pregnancy fantasies and wishes to replace the lost person, this apparel was referred to in the interpretation of these fantasies to the patient. While the dress fit the rest of the material, its meaning was not specifically confirmed by her subsequent responses and associations.

Miss A.F., who was asthmatic, sucked on or ate something in several sessions early in her therapy. Questioning and listening revealed nothing meaningful in regard to this behavior at the time. Sometime later, however, when she described a dream of being swallowed by a fish and associated to fantasies of swallowing someone up or being swallowed up herself, the eating habit helped relate these fantasies to the transference.

Mr. D.H. was a phobic young man and quite inhibited. One signal of his new freedom of functioning and lessened anxiety was that he began to smoke in the sessions. The therapist did not comment regarding it.

Miss D.I., as her therapist's vacation approached, spent long periods in her sessions in silence. Her verbalizations were hollow, routine, and related to superficial realities. There was a distinct air of withdrawal. Later, associations were to being close to someone and at one with them. The silence served both defense (withdrawal) and impulse-wish (silent union). It is this kind of situation which merits a nonverbal or more primitive verbal response from the therapist (see Chapters 11 and 17).

In all, while nonverbal communications in sessions are difficult to modify and often not crucial for intervening, they may also be extremely important. This is especially true with patients functioning on a relatively primitive, two-person level for long or brief periods of time. They require special listening and nonverbal sensitivities on the part of the therapist. Adept listening for the context and associations to these pre- and nonverbal expressions can lead to considerable understanding of the problems for which they serve as indicators, and their often primitive latent content (see Chapter 9). Further, their prominence in a therapy session often means that other kinds of behavioral expressions, especially acting out and somatizing, may follow. Interpretation of these in-session actions often provides the necessary insights to help the patient avoid such disruptive behavior and regressive somatizing.

The other kinds of communications from patients in the session are mainly verbal, though they may refer to nonverbal responses and behavior outside the sessions. Contained in these verbal reports are a multitude of nonverbal nuances and implications. Their prominence in the material suggests primitive functioning, and conflicts related to early disturbances. It is well to isolate them in listening to the patient, since their structure and meanings are distinctive. To illustrate:

Mr. D.J., a young man with a moderate character disorder, had been transferred to a new therapist when his first one left the area. He was infuriated and anxious. In an early session with his new therapist, he reported thoughts of quitting treatment, and that he was reading

books on new therapies, for instance, *The Primal Scream.*
He remembered waking with nightmares as a child, and
screaming and being refused access to his parents' bedroom; until he was sixteen, he kept the light on in his
room. He had left his bedroom light on the other night.
He then mentioned how angry he would get when his
friends turned against him.

The use of the books and lights as always-available, albeit non-
human, supports, highlights this patient's sense of loss and demand
for a parental type of closeness and constant care. His past screaming and present threats to act out by leaving treatment also have
important nonverbal elements to them. In response to such needs
and such ways of expressing them, a stance that is understanding,
on the proper level, and empathic is an essential supplement to the
therapist's verbalized interventions.

One last example:

Miss D.K., a depressed young woman with a severe
character disorder, was faced with her therapist's vacation. She began her session by jokingly asking if she
could take his ash tray home with her; or maybe he had
an extra picture of himself that she could look at when
the going got rough and she wanted some support. She
had the impulse to become promiscuous and was frightened by it. This was one reason she had sought therapy;
she paid for such nights of intimacy with guilt and
depression afterwards. She recalled being frightened
when she began nursery school and insisting that her
brother sit with her. Next, she thought of a friend who
had refused to borrow a record that she (Miss D.K.) had
offered to lend her because the former liked the singer
too much and probably wouldn't return the recording.

In addition to detailing to her the intensity of Miss
D.K.'s longings to possess him or any part of—or substitute for—him, and her insistence that this be concrete
and real, her therapist asked if she fantasized giving him
a gift. The patient had indeed thought of such a parting

gesture. If not that, she added, he could take her along with him instead.

REFERENCES TO CURRENT EVENTS AND BEHAVIOR

References to current events and behavior on the part of the patient and others, excluding for the moment acting out or acting in, which are treated as separate categories, constitute a substantial part of the content of most sessions. In my previous study, more than half the time, the content of these descriptions, understood in proper context, appeared to be meaningful either as surface indicators of emotional problems and ego dysfunctions or less significantly, as reflectors of important latent, repressed unconscious fantasies.

The frequent use of this kind of material to communicate unconscious fantasies should alert the therapist to listen carefully to descriptions of routine events for such derivatives, as well as for reflections of aspects of the patient's ego functioning. It warns him, too, to be wary of simple-minded listening to reality events and problems, without searching for latent meaning by considering both the broader context of the communication and the sequence of associations in which it is embedded. For six of the ten patients in the study on which the material in this chapter is based, this type of communication was a major source of insight. This was particularly true of patients who were prone to shut off their inner fantasy life and dreams, and who preferred to focus on actions and behavior. The therapist must, with such patients, tune in on the unconscious derivatives expressed in their descriptions of life events.

For some patients, descriptions of daily events are strongly immersed in reality, and are described in a manner, sequence, and context that reveals virtually no latent content. These patients defensively seal off their inner life and focus on real problems and conflicts without their intrapsychic repercussions. The derivatives of their repressed fantasies are well hidden. The therapist must be particularly alert to detect latent implications in their material, and the interpretation of such content is quite difficult and usually meets with strong resistances. Other patients, in contrast, communicate available latent content through many channels, including daily events. Derivatives of their repressed fantasies are readily detectable and interpretable, their availability shifting largely with momentary resistances and fluctuations.

In all, then, references to reality events, the concerns of others, and real situations which confronted the patient, are communications that may serve a variety of purposes and to which the therapist must listen in a variety of ways. These descriptions may define the current primary adaptive task (day residue) which is central for the patient's intrapsychic conflicts. They may convey indications as to how well he is handling such stresses and the extent to which ego dysfunctions and unconscious fantasies are interfering and causing maladaptive, neurotic responses. They may convey derivatives of repressed unconscious fantasies in their thematic content and sequences. Further, they may serve as realities sought after by the patient's ego as a response to the primary adaptive context, or they may be utilized defensively to avoid expressions of intrapsychic conflicts. Outside events may also be used as a vehicle for conveying displaced-disguised reactions to, and fantasies about, therapy and the therapist. Only a clear understanding of the central current context will place the material in the proper light (see Chapter 20). To illustrate:

> Mrs. A.A. was upset by an anticipated move of her therapist's office; it would be inconvenient and was prompting feelings of vulnerability. In one session, in this context, she spoke at length of the sudden move of a woman teacher who had helped her daughter. Mrs. A.A. was angered by this unexpected loss. This material, a displaced indicator of unresolved feelings about the therapist's move, served to provide clues as to her underlying unconscious fantasies of rage.

> Mrs. A.J.'s son was receiving psychological tests in school. In the context of describing her dread of her own fantasies and impulses, she spoke at length of her son's current problems, of her fears for him, and of a newspaper article on children in state hospitals. Her own

anxiety and fears of going crazy were the main latent, unconscious content.

This same masochistic patient, for the first time in her life, spoke up when a woman tried to get in front of her in line at a movie theater. She felt no guilt in telling the woman off. This was a significant indicator of major intrapsychic changes in this patient, who previously suffered all indignities and hurts in silence.

Mrs. A.J. also described a time when her husband was talking at length at a party in the presence of exhibitionistic women, alluding to how all women want to be prostitutes. In context, this reflected the patient's unconscious, but emerging, struggle with her own seductive and prostitution fantasies.

Mrs. D.L., a woman with a severe character disorder, had responded to her husband's sudden wish for a divorce with acute anxiety and disorganization. In one session, she described in some detail an incident in which a friend's husband had deserted her without warning; the friend had been infuriated and crushed. The patient went on to describe a newspaper article which she had read over and over; it was about a woman who had committed suicide. Next, she described having been to a dinner where a woman was present who had been divorced recently; somehow, Mrs. D.L. had not realized that such things happen so often.

There are a few central threads to guide us to the possible latent content in these descriptions of daily events. Mrs. D.L. was apparently attempting to deal with her possible divorce (the adaptive context), and with the real and intrapsychic conflicts and anxieties this was evoking in her. There are direct references to being deserted, damaged, and feeling depreciated by someone else. These describe aspects of the patient's inner feelings in response to the real, external hurt; they are appropriate, adaptive reactions to a real conflict with another person. In contrast, the reference to the woman who committed suicide is undoubtedly an externalized (projected?)

representation of the patient's own suicidal impulses and fantasies. It may also be a layered communication in which murderous fantasies toward her husband are conveyed in a disguised, self-directed form; further associations are needed for clarification. In any case, this reality reference is a displaced-disguised representation of fantasies arising from a neurotic response to the reality at hand and is clearly based on intrapsychic conflict.

In the session, the therapist asked the patient directly if she was feeling suicidal. She replied in the affirmative and detailed vengeful fantasies of taking her own life to expose and humiliate her husband. On the side of her ego, her worry about losing control over these impulses was explored, and her controls reinforced. The patient concluded the session by recalling a night when she had been mountain-climbing and had been lost on a mountain ledge; at the height of her despair, a young man had rescued her. This may be viewed as a transference fantasy and unconscious perception that confirmed the value of the therapist's intervention, conveyed through a recent recollection (see Chapters 18 and 22).

ACTING OUT AND SYMPTOMATIC ACTS

There is, of course, a vast literature on acting out and considerable discussion of symptomatic acts. Here, the focus will be on the frequency with which these serve as indicators of problems and vehicles for the expression of unconscious fantasies, and the manner in which acting out often reflects some degree of ego impairment, though one must not forget the important role that adaptive trial through action plays for some patients. Briefly, acting out may be defined as any alloplastic living-out of an intrapsychic conflict that involves an extended piece of behavior. Such behavior expresses unconscious fantasies and is usually detrimental to the patient and others. Symptomatic acts, on a continuum with acting out, are generally more circumscribed pieces of behavior, less consciously rationalized and more ego-alien than acting out, and usually, though not always, less harmful to the patient and others.

In my original study, such behavior constituted a rather frequent mode of expression. Since the patients were mainly borderline and adolescents, they were especially prone to such behavioral expressions of problems and fantasies. Four of the six symptomatic acts identified in that study revealed unconscious content related to neurotic symptoms; about half of the acting out served as indicators of problems, and another third yielded unconscious fantasies. Thus, acting out served as a prominent indicator of difficulties, particularly ego-impairments, and was a less useful immediate source of unconscious material.

In dealing with acting out, the therapist must not only search out the unconscious meanings through an understanding of the context and content of the behavior, but also address himself to the impairments in controls, capacity to delay, and difficulties in handling sexual and aggressive impulses. Acting out also often reflects major resistances to the uncovering work in therapy. To illustrate briefly:

> Mrs. A.A. had only daughters; she spent the day with a friend who had recently borne a son. In this context, she forgot to take her birth-control pills. This proved to be a reflection of her unconscious wish for a son.

> Miss A.B., in response to her mother's hospitalization and the resultant uncovering in her therapy, began to recall childhood primal scene experiences and her repressed sexual fantasies regarding her father. At this point, she stole a man's shirt for her own use. This overdetermined act had many latent meanings. Briefly, it was, in part, an acting out of an attempt to disrupt therapy and possibly have her parents remove her from it. It was also an expression of her hope to be found out by her parents and to evoke their anger, creating distance especially between herself and her father. Her poor controls were also apparent. On a deeper level, the central unconscious fantasy which subsequently emerged was that she viewed the primal scene as one in which her father attacked and damaged her mother (she dreamt of a monkey clawing at her own head). Her own wish was to be attacked by her father and to attack him in return and steal his penis. Guilt over this wish evoked the need for punishment also reflected in her behavior.

Mr. A.E. felt ill and left his school, knowing quite well that his absence would be discovered and reported to his parents (he was a chronic behavior problem and on the verge of suspension). The context was his therapist's pending vacation, which he was experiencing in terms of his mother's tubercular illness; this had taken her away from him for a year when he was about two years old. He fought bitterly with his parents after they had indeed been notified by the school, and he left home for several days. As is true in most cases of acting out, the patient denied that he was at all affected by either his therapist's vacation or his mother's past absence. Associations indicated that he was determined to prove his capabilities to survive without his therapist or his mother, in the face of a panicky and suicidal response to their leaving him (he had also tripped on LSD and became momentarily acutely suicidal). This complex sequence of acting out expressed rage and denial, and hinted at important unconscious fantasies. It was also an acting out of transference fantasies, since it was evoked partly by the therapist's vacation; it was directed against both the latter and the patient's mother.

Acting out quite often expresses reactions to the therapist. It may also relate to other types of unconscious fantasies, as this vignette shows:

Miss D.M., an adolescent with school and drug problems, began a session by describing how she had provoked her mother into a furious battle that ended with her mother threatening various punishments. Her father was away and he could not serve as a buffer between them, as he often had in the past. Her mother would get sloppy and not dress until quite late when her husband was not around. The patient was thinking of several boys she would like to go to bed with, and was having trouble controlling herself.

I will stop here and consider the material. We see indications of impaired controls and the patient's struggle to maintain them. Can we also detect a latent thread? The key stimulus (context) for the acting out in arguing with her mother (the therapeutic context and neurotic problem) appears to be the absence of the patient's father so that Miss D.M. was thereby left alone with her mother. The sequence of associations that follow this information is: fighting with her mother—noticing her lack of modesty—thoughts of being promiscuous with boys. We can suspect from these threads that some underlying repressed homosexual anxieties and fantasies regarding her mother are the key to the patient's intrapsychic conflict. This was confirmed in a subsequent session when the patient dreamt of a friend who was said to be a lesbian.

References to Therapy and the Therapist: Acting Out Related to Treatment and Acting In

In this category, I have isolated all allusions to the therapist and treatment, and all acting out that is primarily evoked by, and directed toward, the therapist. Not included here is material from patients which takes other manifest forms, such as day and night dreams, and serve as vehicles for displaced conscious and unconscious fantasies about the therapist.

This kind of acting out includes absences, living out of fantasies related to transference- and reality-based reactions to the therapist, and attempts to disrupt treatment. In my original study, it was not a major mode of communicating latent content and unconscious fantasies for any patient. However, it did serve rather often as an indicator of neurotic problems. As one would expect, such behavior most often reflected serious resistances against therapy and disruptions in the therapeutic alliance, and reactions to pending vacations and terminations.

Absences

Absences from sessions is one form of behavior directly related to therapy. It is often an indicator of serious problems in treatment and of tendencies to act out and communicate nonverbally. Some examples will serve to clarify:

> Mr. A.E. used absence twice to express his response to his therapist's pending vacation, indicating unconscious anger and the wish to desert him first, though more specific unconscious fantasies could not be developed from his associations. Previous material suggested that this behavior reflected his unresolved unconscious conflicts and fantasies, including rage, regarding his mother's absence in his childhood, but exploration in the context of these absences did not produce new data. His tendency to act out and deny inner fantasies at such times was a recurrent pattern.

> Miss A.G., an adult in therapy because of severe depression, was consciously doubtful about treatment and strongly resistant. Her nine absences (several due to illness) described in my previous study were a poorly controlled reflection and acting out of her wish to terminate her therapy; they were also used to express some displaced rage against her boyfriend. Beyond this, however, the specific unconscious meanings of these missed sessions did not unfold at that time, despite the necessary focus in her hours on them. Much later in her therapy, through material related to other situations that this patient avoided, the phobic aspects of her absences became clearer—that is, she avoided situations that evoked anxiety related to possible bodily damage; beyond this, however, the unconscious meanings of these situations were not clear.

VERBALIZED COMMUNICATIONS: REFERENCES TO THERAPIST AND THERAPY

In my previous research, direct references to the therapist and the therapy were a relatively common type of content in sessions.

They centered around allusions to termination, vacations, and absences. They proved to be frequent indicators of resistances, but did not lead to unconscious meanings unless the context was detected and used to understand the material.

The focus of psychotherapy is usually on the life problems of the patient. The relationship with the therapist in its real and transference manifestations is, one hopes, set in a positive tone through a strong therapeutic alliance, providing a relatively silent background to the treatment (see Chapters 20 and 22). At times of vacations, termination, some unusual event related to therapy, major resistances, and technical errors and countertransference problems, this relationship will tend to come into focus. Beyond these moments, work with the therapeutic relationship is usually confined to negative transference problems and disturbances in the therapeutic alliance that impede treatment; a true transference neurosis generally does not appear during psychotherapy (see Chapter 20). The therapist must be on the alert for such material and the resistances and unconscious fantasies it reflects. It is crucial to ascertain the context in which such communications appear, in order to correctly interpret and resolve the relevant unconscious transference- and reality-based fantasies and resistances. Such work may be vital to the continuation of therapy and to the resolution of the patient's neurosis.

RUMINATION OR FLIGHT

In my previous paper, I included all indications in sessions of rumination, avoidance, and flight from the affect- and conflict-laden content of sessions in this overall category of manifest material. Such indicators cut across the specific content of the patient's association and are so designated through the clinical judgment of the therapist. Rumination is a common defense-resistance and must be assessed for underlying content. If the context in which the rumination occurs, and the underlying meaning or latent material it covers, are not discernible, the therapist may confront the patient with it; this often enables the patient then to modify this defense and reveal both the underlying fantasies on which it is based and the material that it covers (see Chapter 13).

The study on which this chapter is based showed that rumination or flight were common occurrences in these sessions. Although they served always as general indicators of resistance, they seldom were very specific, and only rarely were they analyzable in terms of underlying fantasies. Clearly, these are major roadblocks which merit direct confrontation in an effort to get the patient either to explore the underpinnings of his resistance or to get back to his central anxieties and conflicts.

One clinical vignette will serve to illustrate:

> Mrs. I.O. was a depressed woman in therapy who had been ruminating over several sessions about whether to divorce her husband or not. The context was the pending termination of her treatment, necessitated by clinic regulations, a topic that she was avoiding. The therapist pointed out her remoteness to her and she immediately revealed a dream in which a teacher is criticizing her for being a bad mother. Associations led to the patient's anger at the therapist for forcing her to leave treatment prematurely.

TRANSFERENCE AND REACTION TO THE THERAPIST

To briefly illustrate such material here (see Chapters 20 and 21 for a more detailed presentation):

> A common indicator of resistances to treatment was acted out by Mrs. A.I., a woman with a severe character disorder, who, instead of leaving work and driving toward her therapist's office for her session, headed toward her home. She was having thoughts of leaving treatment, and a dream she reported in the session (to which she was late) readily revealed the unconscious fantasies that prompted this behavior and a discussion of her doubts about treatment. She dreamt that she was looking at her mother's ugly vulva. The context related to Mrs. A.I.'s work in treatment with her feelings of bodily impairment and disfigurement. She had revealed her use

of padded bras, felt humiliated, and sought to flee these revelations and their implications for her.

In response to his therapist's coming vacation, an adolescent who tended to act out, Mr. A.E., came to his session under the influence of marihuana. He had dreamt that someone wanted to kill him, directly revealing some of the unconscious anxieties involved in his behavior. Further associations indicated that he was attempting to provoke his therapist, to keep his distance from him, and to prevent the emergence of unconscious fantasies and memories of being deserted and destroyed, and of murderous revenge on the therapist with its consequent talion punishment for him.

Also in response to her therapist's pending summer vacation, Miss A.F., who was in the first month of her therapy, asked if she was permitted to get to know his other patients. This was an indicator of transference fantasies and longings, but exploration produced no further workable associations and latent content. A month later, as the separation drew closer, she left her purse in the therapist's office (a symptomatic act); again, nothing developed in her associations, though her longings to remain with him seemed clear. Lastly, in the session preceding his vacation, she was wheezing. Associations related to her seeing other doctors in the therapist's absence and exposing his failure to help her. She would make him suffer somehow. She had fantasied being hit by a car and saw it as a bloody massacre. This provided one of the first opportunities to interpret this patient's asthma as expressing the unconscious wish to hold onto others—here, the therapist—and as an expression of fantasies of revenge for being abandoned. It also reflected unconscious fantasies of destroying her therapist and herself—the latter both as punishment for her forbidden instinctual wishes and to evoke guilt in the therapist for leaving her.

Mrs. A.A., who had an hysterical neurosis illustrates a type of transference fantasy that is apparently not evoked by the therapist's behavior, arising primarily out of inner need and traumas outside of treatment. She had been wishing for a son; her husband had failed to give her one. She reported a fantasy of meeting her therapist at a party and said that she had developed anxiety coming to her session. She wondered why her therapist saw other patients on the couch. She had asked her dentist if he had any sons. She was depressed and thought of suicide. Interpretation of her wish for a son from her therapist, based (from other material) on a father transference, was amply confirmed.

ACTING IN

Acting in refers to the living out of feelings and fantasies directly toward the therapist in the session, and often has both verbal and nonverbal aspects. It may take the form of direct attempts to seduce or attack the therapist, leaving a session, and pacing about. It usually indicates some kind of neurotic problem, and may convey latent content when viewed in proper context. Such behavior is not uncommon among borderline patients and when disruptive to treatment and the therapeutic alliance, merits prompt exploration and resolution. Nondisruptive forms of this behavior may require both verbal and nonverbal tolerance and response by the therapist.

To illustrate:

Mrs. D.N. was a woman with a borderline syndrome who was in psychotherapy for acutely disruptive anxiety, and a period of mental disorganization after an accident in which she carelessly fell from a ladder and injured her back. Early in her therapy, it emerged that one unresolved area of intrapsychic conflict for her related to the scars left by her father's abandonment of his family for several years when the patient was an infant. She had repressed and denied almost everything connected with this trauma, and split off the entire constellation of feelings and fantasies related to it.

Her accident had occurred when her father had taken ill and in the context of her exploration of the factors in her injury, material related to him slowly began to emerge in the first months of her therapy. Her attitude toward these disclosures was one of enormous terror and primitive anxieties: if she spoke of him, he would die and God would punish her; she should have her tongue cut out. Massive denial alternated with realizations regarding her childhood and present feelings of hurt and rage, and her primitive fantasies of destroying or devouring her father, and of being united with him. The therapist's main work in this phase was directed at strengthening the patient's capacity to tolerate and accept these feelings, memories and fantasies; helping her to recognize the very costly to herself "magic" that she was using to deny them; and assisting her in seeing the inappropriateness of her fears of remembering and of talion punishments.

In one session, Mrs. D.N. recalled that when she was about eight years old, her father gave a gift to a cousin and she (Mrs. D.N.) responded by feeling deprived and neglected. As the feelings of hurt and rage mounted, her fears of being struck dead by God intensified. She suddenly denied having felt hurt at all, shifted to a slightly altered state of consciousness, and got up to leave the session. The therapist pointed out that she seemed totally terrified of the simplest human feelings of resentment toward her father and that she resorted to extreme kinds of flight in response to them, such as going into a remote, altered state and wanting to leave. The patient felt reassured and returned. She then spoke a little more about her confusion regarding what she could allow herself to feel about her father. She left the session and the next patient, on coming to the therapist's office, found his usually open outer door to be locked.

In the next hour, the patient could not remember locking the door, but exploration of her fear of the therapist and her rage at him for the feelings and memories about her father which were emerging in the therapy, led her to recall locking his door several times before—in spiteful revenge against the therapist and with the thought: he's dangerous, everybody stay out!

The latent content inherent in the patient's attempt to leave the session and in her locking the therapist's door is revealed by the context of these actions. Both behaviors also reflect major pathological defenses and ego dysfunctions, and represent a critical disruption in the therapeutic alliance. There are therapeutic pitfalls in over- or underemphasizing this type of communication, but these will be discussed later (Part VII). I will conclude, however, with one reminder about the latent content of such material:

Mrs. D.O., a depressed woman, was furious with her therapist: he did not understand her; he was a man and prejudiced against her; she should seek out a woman therapist. After berating her therapist in this fashion, she went on to describe her husband's supposedly joking remarks at a dinner party regarding her thin, unfeminine body and her refusal to go along at times with his sexual wishes. This was, for her, a very sensitive area, with many conscious and unconscious idiosyncratic meanings, and she had been deeply hurt (and, as it turned out, infuriated).

There had been no detectable insensitivity by, or hurt from, the therapist in the previous session. Thus, this material regarding him is clearly displacement of rage and revenge from Mrs. D.O.'s husband onto the therapist; an interpretation which actually resolved her fury at the therapist when it was made.

The therapeutic principle, then, is to recognize that, at times, manifest content related to the therapist may have latent meanings essentially related to, and displaced-disguised from, someone else. Only detection of the correct context for the material will enable an accurate understanding of the latent aspects of the communication.

SLIPS OF THE TONGUE

My general experience has been that these phenomena—while fascinating, sometimes useful to the therapist in understanding the patient, and interesting structurally as compromise formations (Yazmajian, 1965)—are seldom useful in producing insight for the patient in psychotherapy and often may not be worth pursuing. For instance, in the original study, slips of the tongue were quite rare; only three were recorded, and each of these reflected unconscious fantasies. Several others were not recorded since they led nowhere, though they were indicators of some kind of disturbance.

A good rule of thumb is that slips to which the therapist can readily associate, whose unconscious meanings he can understand, and which he feels will prove truly meaningful for the patient are worth exploring and interpreting; the others are best left alone and not brought into particular focus. If subsequent material clarifies the meaning of an unclear slip, it can be referred to by the therapist when making an interpretation of the relevant material. Often, however, pursuit of slips of the tongue leads to intellectualization and speculation, which detract from the main themes and problems of the session. To exemplify how slips of the tongue can, however, reflect important unconscious fantasies, consider these examples:

> Mrs. A.A., in the session described above, spoke of buying a new couch—uh—mattress for her bedroom. The slip alluded to fantasies of her therapist's couch as her bed.

> Mr. A.E., whose mother had been deathly ill in his childhood, had not taken care of his own penile discharge for some time. He finally had it checked out and also brought his fiancee to his doctor for an examination. The physician placed her on birth control pills which the patient, in describing this event, three times called "diet pills." His associations clarified the slips; birth control pills were known to cause fatal hemorrhages. He could not tolerate either the thought of another loss like that of his mother or any expression of his recent resentment toward his fiancee.

AFFECTS AND NEUROTIC SYMPTOMS

Affective disturbances and inappropriate affects are a type of symptom, and they are an important potential dimension of each session. Most often, these references are to anxiety, rage, and depression. In my study, such expressions were of average frequency and served entirely as indicators; patients tended to report consistently a specific single kind of affect during the period of study. Two patients in the study often utilized reports of affect as indicators of problems; for the rest affect was an aspect of self-experience which either was seldom described or infrequently led to insight into unconscious material. Of course, reports of overwhelming panic or depression are crucial indicators and often reflect impaired or even collapsing ego functioning. These rare experiences serve as a reminder that even infrequently used indicators or vehicles of unconscious content may, in a given context, be the critical communication from the patient.

Non-disruptive and signal affects such as mild anxiety or depression are also reported in sessions and may refer to experiences during or outside of the hour. They are not uncommon indicators of neurotic problems and their latent meaning is clarified by the context, and content and sequence of the rest of the material. As nonverbal responses of varying maturity, they may touch upon both the early and late phases of experiencing intrapsychic conflict.

Other neurotic symptoms were rarely reported by the patients during the period of the study. Mrs. A.A. experienced hysterical throat symptoms, and reported phobic symptoms. While these symptoms were all ultimately analyzed to some extent, during the period of the study they served almost entirely as indicators of regression or, through their diminution, of improvement. The understanding of the unconscious meaning of symptoms came, of course, from other sources.

I will illustrate briefly:

> Mrs. A.A. reported anxiety and throat tightening. The context was the birth of her friend's son and a visit to her. She fantasied that she was driving with this friend and that they had an accident in which her friend was killed.

She then thought of her sister who had a son. The anxiety had been evoked by her unconscious rage at her sister for having a son, and the death wishes this evoked. The throat symptoms led back to her mother's vocal cord surgery when the patient was a child, and to death wishes directed at her mother and punishment for them.

Mrs. A.I., in exploring her bodily anxieties in her therapy, recalled her fear of heights. She dreamt of an old boyfriend who stood on a bridge; as she approached him, the crowds nearly pushed her off. Over several sessions, she linked this man to her father and recalled showers she had taken with her father as a child. She had, of course, seen his penis. She had thoughts of getting pregnant and also dreamt of floating in the air and letting herself down slowly. Associations led to repressed derivatives of primal scene experiences. This overdetermined symptom related, at this time, to fantasies of her own body as a phallus in danger of being destroyed, as she had once wished to destroy her father's penis. Heights related to falling and bodily destruction, which included the talion punishment for her incestuous fantasies. Fantasies of impregnation and consequent bodily damage were also involved.

PHYSICAL SYMPTOMS

We do not abandon our principles for listening to manifest and latent content when physical symptoms are reported in a session. As symptoms, they merit utilization as therapeutic contexts for our thinking about the material of the therapy hour. This is true of physical symptoms that are generally thought of as somatically-founded (e.g., a sore throat, fever, bronchitis, etc.), of those generally conceived of as psychosomatic (e.g., asthma, colitis, peptic ulcer, headaches, etc.) and those generally conceived of as hysterical (e.g., nonneurological numbness, paresis, etc.). Sound therapeutic work with each of these often primitive, nonverbal communications can be accomplished with all such manifestations if the therapist listens in depth to their context and to the content of the rest of the material in the session. Such symptoms usually require repetitive working through which can be successful only if both the choice of somatic channels of expression, and the unconscious fantasies and conflicts which they express, are analyzed. In the earlier study, references to fleeting physical symptoms were common, while more critical physical symptoms were rare, except for the asthmatic patient and Mrs. A.H., who was prone to psychophysiological gastro-intestinal symptoms. I will present two condensed vignettes:

> Mrs. A.H. had gastrointestinal pain and diarrhea. Material over several sessions led to a dream of a cave in which fat was melting off a hamburger. Associations were to the birth of her sister, and the diarrhea was interpreted as related to fantasies of being pregnant and getting rid of the fetus. This was verified when she recalled that her pain was in her lower abdomen and that she had thought of calling her gynecologist (a confirmation via a previously repressed fantasy; see Chapter 18). Her fear of these fantasies and her tendency to express them somatically was also noted to her.
>
> Miss D.P. was asthmatic and had a severe character disorder. In one session, she reported wheezing. Her father had left on a trip and she had been panicky. She interrupted her train of thought and asked for a match from the therapist. Her boyfriend had jilted her and she was furious; she stole his cigarette lighter before he left. Based on this and earlier material, the asthma was interpreted as being a somatic expression of fantasies of taking into self and possessing her missing father, in fear that she could not survive without him. She then recalled having stolen her father's belt just before he left, and hiding it in her room.

Asthma is a highly overdetermined symptom, as are most physical symptoms; this fragment has been oversimplified to demonstrate one latent fantasy reflected in the symptom.

CREATIVE WORKS BY THE PATIENT AND OTHERS

Patients unconsciously seek out or generate such creations at times when specific unconscious fantasies and conflicts are especially active. Some will write poems and stories as they attempt to communicate derivatives of their fantasies and to adaptively resolve within themselves the related intrapsychic conflicts. Or they may make references to story lines from movies, television, shows, books, and persons they know. As a rule, such material is inherently layered and rich with latent content, though it may serve defensive purposes as well. In all, these creations should be handled much like dreams, since their structure resembles them in many ways (see below). These references are a relatively rare form of expression, but, when they are referred to, they almost always have been selected to express important, repressed unconscious fantasies stirring within the patient.

I will illustrate:

> Miss A. F. was in a relentless battle with her parents, whom she unconsciously wished to destroy and who similarly wished to destroy her. She wheezed as she described provoking her parents in various ways. She had "killed" her own creative powers in order to hurt them. She had once begun wheezing when she saw a film of atrocities in Vietnam. The mutually murderous dimensions of her own unconscious fantasies and her struggle with her parents were reflected in this precipitate. This was further elaborated when a movie in which a "speed freak" was blown to pieces prompted a second asthmatic episode.

> Mr. A. E. reported after about six months of treatment a story of a man who dies when left by his son. Associations revealed that it was a derivative of his fears of dying when his mother left him as a child. This then led to his first actual recollection in therapy of his previously repressed childhood separation from his mother.

Later in the therapy, after his therapist had taken a vacation, he reported a dream, which, in part, was about a garage door that he opens over and over because it keeps falling back. He had decided not to go back to college—a self-destructive and vengeful act. Associations linked this behavior to his father, who was, among other things, a garage door salesman who had never achieved much in his life, and who had failed repeatedly in efforts to educate himself. The dream reminded the patient of a myth which he had recently read. In it, someone kept pushing a huge rock up a hill, and, just as he reached the top, it rolled back. As a reflection of hell and of this patient's unconscious need to fail as his father had, this myth served admirably as a derivative and expression.

RECENT MEMORIES

Memory material related to both recent and childhood events and fantasies turns up fairly frequently in therapy sessions and both are major sources of unconscious fantasy content. Recent memories are also not uncommon indicators of resistances and neurotic difficulties and, therefore, are an important source of meaningful data in sessions. For half of the patients in my original study, they served as major reflectors of unconscious fantasies; and virtually every patient used this material to convey repressed fantasies at one time or another.

Often, recent recollections that contain important derivatives of unconscious fantasies are repressed and emerge after the working through of resistances, or they appear after additional traumas heighten the conflicts related to the events recalled. Such remembering often serves to confirm an interpretation and to enhance insight through further, meaningful revelations. In addition to their utility for ascertaining unconscious fantasies, these memories reflect, and can be used to assess, the patient's recent levels of ego functioning. The following vignettes indicate how such material can reflect manifest and latent content, depending on the context in which they are embedded:

Mr. A.E. had delayed attending to his penile discharge until he had developed insight into his need to repeat, in the present, various aspects of the period when his mother was ill, and until he had worked through part of his need to hurt his mother by harming himself. The details of his recent urological illness, his handling of it, and his thoughts about it, all confirmed aspects of this unconscious and unresolved conflict with his mother.

Mrs. A.J. was a depressed woman whose daughter was going to marry and leave the New York area. After working through early resistances to therapy, she produced material indicating that her tie to her daughter was a current version of an unresolved, ambivalent tie to her mother. Interpretations of this led to the recollection of many relatively recent experiences with her mother—such as the patient's appendectomy, which led to a battle between her husband and mother—and of occasions when her mother had abandoned her. She also recalled a time when her mother stopped talking to her because she had moved out of her mother's neighborhood. The patient had been enraged and had wished that her mother would drop dead; similar unconscious fantasies regarding her daughter prevailed.

In the last session of her therapy, Miss A.D., a depressed adolescent girl who had been denying any sense of loss or anxiety over the termination, reported a dream. In it her best girlfriend returns from her vacation, only to leave suddenly again; the patient is upset and looks for her. Associations were to her friend's trip and to the support she got from her friends, with whom she could discuss her problems. The manifest dream in this context was directly interpreted to the patient as reflecting her upset about termination. She then reported a second dream in which her father was ill in the hospital and she wanted to visit him; her boyfriend left her because of it. Her father had bled internally and had had surgery, and

only later she learned that he had nearly died; the doctor
had been blamed for the downhill course. She denied any
feelings about these events. The unconscious equation
between separation and death, the unresolved negative
transference—the unconscious fantasy that her therapist
had harmed her in some way, and her own unconscious
anxieties about herself and termination were all reflected
in these dreams and memories.

EARLY CHILDHOOD MEMORIES

Early memories are complex communications which are comparable in structure (with some differences) to dreams. They convey
genetic information about the patient's childhood experiences, the
nature of his early relationships, and the traumas he has suffered.
These are all important contexts for the development of his neurotic
problems. In addition, such material appears in a given session or
series of sessions embedded in a current context and in association
with other material, and thereby conveys specific latent meaning and
unconscious fantasies which relate to the patient's current emotional
problems. Listening to such material is therefore always multi-
leveled and complex, and the therapist will use one dimension in a
given session, and other dimensions in other hours.

Recollections of early childhood experiences and, more rarely,
childhood fantasies and dreams were a major source of unconscious
fantasy content and occasionally served as indicators of problems
in my previous study. In the example below, note how various types
of material follow upon one another and build sequences through
which expressions of the unconscious fantasies are conveyed; each
element of a given fantasy is expressed in a different form of communication:

Mrs. A.A. was working through her wish for a son,
which had been traced back to her longings for her
father and his penis, and to her desire to give him the son
her mother never gave him. At this time, she dreamt of

being in bed with her girlfriend's father, who wants to have intercourse with her; she decides it is wrong and leaves. It was clear to her that the manifest dream was one of renunciation, and she felt that it was an expression of some resolution (after considerable working through) of her incestuous longings. Associations confirmed this and its basis, in part, in anger and disappointment in her father. She then remembered a previously repressed childhood memory of seeing her father in the tub and being frightened and stimulated by the sight of his penis. Working through this experience, and its current effects on her relationship with her husband, led to a series of sessions in which she related a dream that her father and sister were dead, and vented rage at her father for past and present hurts. During this period, the patient shared a hotel room with her children and remembered doing this in her childhood with her parents. She recalled her mother's terror of a mouse in the hotel room and realized that this probably related to observations of her father's penis and intercourse. A dream of eating celery led to fellatio fantasies and wishes to devour her husband's-father's-penis. Her view of intercourse as a mutual attack unfolded next, and then a long series of early childhood fantasies, in which the patient is raped and abused, and in which her rescuers are beaten, emerged from repression. These guilt-ridden fantasies were related to punishment for her desires for, and against, her father and led to a conscious fantasy (in the present) that she would develop cancer. Working through this rich network of material, at this crucial point in her treatment, enabled this patient to resolve her anxiety and hysterical throat symptoms.

CONSCIOUS FANTASIES (DAY DREAMS)

Conscious fantasies are not to be confused with unconscious fantasies. The former are in awareness and the latter are not, though they may (and should) become conscious to some extent during treatment. This is, in fact, one goal of therapy. Conscious fantasies may, therefore, contain disguised derivatives of unconscious fantasies, though they are by no means the only such derivatives, and may serve as the starting point for the search for unconscious expressions. They are another kind of manifest content that can be either meaningful or defensive, depending on the context in which they appear and the structural balances which went into the creation of the fantasy. Thus, early in therapy, they are largely manifest screens, which are well disguised, though they reflect underlying fantasies which are themselves unconscious. Then, as the therapeutic work proceeds, the patient becomes aware of less-disguised derivatives of these repressed fantasies. In this way, previously unconscious fantasies become conscious. The degree to which a given conscious fantasy reflects relatively disguised or relatively undisguised unconscious content can only be assessed through an understanding of the context of the material, the moment in therapy, a knowledge of what has been previously repressed, and an understanding of the patient's intrapsychic conflicts, symptoms, and genetics.

In my original study, conscious fantasies were among the three most frequent types of communications from the patients. They were used only moderately often as indicators, although they proved to be the single largest source of latent, unconscious fantasy content.

In this group of patients, these fantasies served as a primary vehicle for communicating unconscious material for seven of the ten. The three exceptions were Miss A.D., who primarily utilized dreams for expressions of unconscious fantasies (both manifest dreams and their latent content reached through associations); Miss A.G., whose conscious fantasies were highly defensive and who revealed more of her unconscious thoughts through her behavior and her recent memories than through any other means; and Mr. A.C., who mostly utilized his current behavior and acting out to reflect his strongly guarded and rarely revealed unconscious fantasies, and with whom conscious fantasy material was highly repetitive and defensive. Later work with Mr. A.C.'s defenses and resistances led to the emergence of considerable unconscious material, primarily through the vehicle of manifest dreams (and less so, because of some continuing degree of defensiveness, through his associations to them). This uncovered previously unreported, repressed fantasies.

I have already alluded to many conscious fantasies, particularly in the last vignette regarding Mrs. A.A. One additional example follows:

> Mr. A.C. avoided leaving his house for any extended period of time. His manifest dreams seldom led to meaningful associations, but they hinted at frightening, incestuously tinged sexual impulses toward women and homosexual fantasies toward men. As efforts were being made to define these fantasies by modifying the repressive barriers, so that he could bring them into consciousness, the patient began to report conscious fantasies that intruded into his awareness. These were prompted by his first efforts to sleep at a friend's house. They included a fantasy of having intercourse with his friend's mother and of his friend's brother playing with his penis. These fantasies for the first time gave specific content to the instinctual drives which prompted his phobic stance. At the same time, their latent content related to still repressed memories and fantasies regarding his own mother and two brothers.

The therapist must remember that conscious fantasies are layered and may, at a given moment, reflect the breakthrough of a previously repressed fantasy—this last vignette offers a good example. At another moment, they may convey highly disguised derivatives of a repressed unconscious fantasy; and still later, reflect a massive defensiveness and covering for other repressed fantasies. In listening to such daydreams, then, we treat them like night dreams, and, in context, search out their implications. Since the layering of what is revealed in one session and covered up and defended against in the next, is never-ending, the therapist must recognize that these newly emerged fantasies undoubtedly also served as a derivative and cover for still deeper, repressed unconscious fantasies. Thus, later sessions revealed that Mr. A.C.'s libidinal fantasies toward his mother and brothers covered destructive and murderous fantasies that were terrifying in nature.

To illustrate this point further, Mrs. A.A.'s daydreams of having cancer, alluded to earlier, proved to have as their latent content repressed fantasies of being made pregnant by her father and being devoured and destroyed by the forbidden fetus. Another level of latent content was related to her fantasies of eating her father's penis, and being eaten and destroyed by it in talion punishment. This emerged, as I noted, through her dream of eating celery, which was followed by associations to a friend who had gotten food poisoning; the thoughts about cancer and pregnancy came next.

DREAMS

The discussion of conscious fantasies is applicable to dreams. Manifest dreams are, in a sense, conscious fantasies experienced in an altered state of consciousness and remembered in the waking state (Langs, 1969); they are not unconscious fantasies. Failure to understand the implications of these facts has led to confusion in conceptualizing the role of work with manifest dreams in psychotherapy. Associations to dreams, and the context in which the dream is experienced and reported, are also important in understanding the latent meaning of these communications. Dreams can serve as indicators of problems and as reflectors of both unconscious fantasies and ego functioning.

There are three levels of possible work with dreams. The first is with the manifest dream alone, devoid of context or associations. This level is an experimental one and has merit as such (Langs, 1966, 1967, 1969). It is virtually never used clinically, however, though it may be resorted to, if context and associations are lacking, at a time when the manifest content of a dream indicates some inexplicable, but important and urgent, conflict or problem. For example, the unexpected and seemingly inexplicable appearance of suicide or murder in a manifest dream calls for inquiry and comment at any time, even if associations and context are lacking, though we virtually always should have related material from the patient on hand with which to work.

The second level of work with dreams is with the manifest

dream within the specific context in which it is reported. Some patients, such as Mr. A.C. and Miss A.G., referred to above, for long parts of their psychotherapy simply do not associate to their dreams or do so sparingly or with little enlightenment. Almost all patients do this at some time in their treatment. In such sessions, the therapist attempts to ascertain the crucial content of the dream through the context which is often determined through the detection of the day residues of the dream—the reality events that precipitated it (Langs, 1971b), and through his previous understanding of the patient. The therapist can thus rightfully interpret such a dream, if an unconscious fantasy has been revealed in this way. At times, the manifest dream in context directly reveals a previously repressed fantasy or memory, which can be pointed out to the patient without additional material. At other times, by using the context and day residues, the therapist can detect a latent fantasy expressed in disguised form in the manifest dream, which can also be interpreted to the patient. Further, manifest dreams in context (as is true, also, of conscious fantasies and memories) are important reflectors of conscious and unconscious superego promptings and derivatives and of various aspects of ego functioning, including object relationships and defensive operations. Dreams in context can therefore be used to work with many aspects of functioning and fantasizing. However, the therapist can justify interpretive utilization of the manifest dream in context alone, only when every effort has been made to obtain all possible associations.

The third level of work with manifest dreams includes the associations to the dream and is directed toward an understanding of the dream work and associated latent content. These associations are of two kinds: direct and indirect. The former refers to the thoughts which come to the patient's mind as he thinks of the whole dream and of any of the elements of the dream. These, which may be quite revealing or quite defensive, are assessed in context and in light of the day residues. The latter consist of all of the other material of the session, which is not directly derived from responses to the manifest dream. This material may provide clues to the context of the dream and the conflict with which it deals. On the other hand, this material may reflect strong defenses against the unconscious, latent content of the dream and a flight from it on all levels.

Associations to dream elements are among the most important avenues of unexpected insights in psychotherapy. Often they lead to latent content that could never have been anticipated by the therapist from the manifest dream alone or in context. Yet, more often, the associations are specific and essential elaborations of unconscious trends to which the therapist has already been altered from the manifest content of the dream in context, and which lead then to specific interpretations of the currently pertinent unconscious aspects of the material.

Thus, we can expect that manifest dreams with, and at times without, associations are important sources of insight into unconscious dimensions, major sources of confirmation of interpretations, and vital contributors of new threads and avenues in the work of treatment. In my original study, they were a relatively frequent source of meaningful material and, while they served only occasionally as indicators of problems, they were a major source of unconscious content. This was equally true of manifest dreams understood in context and of the latent content of these dreams as revealed through associations.

For half of these patients, both manifest and latent dream content served as a primary vehicle of unconscious fantasies. For all, at some time, these communications proved meaningful, and for most, use of dreams and the report of conscious fantasies unrelated to the dreams went together. As already illustrated, meaningful work with dreams also often led to the lifting of repressive barriers and to the emergence of previously unreported, early recollections and other significant unconscious material.

Since work with dreams and their associations is demonstrated in the previous vignette, I will add only a few examples here:

> Mrs. A.J. dreamt of coming to her session in a negligee. Termination was approaching, and she had recently described her husband's sexual problems. She had no direct associations and the rest of the session was filled with trivia. We can be certain, in this context, that sexual transference fantasies were stirring. Later sessions revealed genetic aspects of the latent content of this dream; she had shared her father's bed in the morning

well into her teens and had never worked out her sexualized attachment to him.

Mr. A.C. was anxious about sleeping at his boyfriend's house for the first time. In connection with his job, he also spent time at an attractive girl's apartment. He then dreamt of showering with a man with a huge penis. He went on to ruminate about his feelings of sexual inadequacy. Despite inquiries, there were no direct associations to the dream, nor did he relate the dream to those two events. Yet one could make the valid interpretation, from the context of the manifest dream and the sequence of material, that the patient fled contact with women by turning to men homosexually in search of a seemingly indestructible phallus, and then in turn feared such wishes.

Mrs. A.I. dreamt that something was wrong with her hand; she had cut it off with shears and had replaced it with a false hand. She had been discussing her displeasure with her body. The dream was prompted by her having cut her nails; she had also attended the bar mitzvah of a friend's son that day. She remembered having a friend who shot off her hand. She then thought of her small breasts, of her unattractive nose, which she had had fixed surgically, and of her distress over the manner in which she had lost her virginity. She recalled seeing her father's penis and her childhood fantasy that conception occurred when the man dropped something from his anus which reached the woman's anus. She denied seeing her parents in intercourse, but recalled childhood dreams of being bitten by a dog. She added that criminals used to have their hands cut off. In the next session she spoke of capping her teeth, of her menstrual period which had come that week, of feeling damaged, and of wearing padding in her bras.

This is a complex network of manifest dreams, associations, and latent content (Langs, 1969 and 1971b). One can detect many unconscious fantasies in this material, all relevant to the patient's neurotic disturbances related to her body image. The early traumas that evoked some part of these disturbances are revealed, as are later consequences. The main unconscious fantasy seems to be her unconscious image of herself as a woman damaged and punished because of her incestuous wishes for her father. She sees herself as a "castrated man" and fantasies reparation of her "lost penis" through surgery. In fact, she later acted out these pursuits in a manner anticipated by the dream and her associations to it.

LYING AND DECEIVING; CONSCIOUS CONCEALING IN SESSIONS

Lies to, and deceptions of, others, including the therapist, and conscious concealing from the therapist in the sessions (a form of acting in) deserves separate consideration, even though they overlap with other categories, because they are indicators of serious psychopathology and of a major disruption of the therapeutic alliance. The therapist, therefore, must be alert to any direct or indirect clues as to their existence (often, themes of concealing, hiding and dishonesty, or actual contradictions, will appear in the manifest material), and be prepared to explore and resolve them. It is important to demonstrate in such work the disadvantages of these ego-syntonic symptoms to the patient and to his therapeutic endeavors, and to relate this behavior to ego defects and current unconscious conflicts and fantasies. I will illustrate this category with a brief clinical example:

> Miss D.Q. was a young woman with a severe character disorder and psychopathic trends. Faced with her therapist's vacation, she expressed intense wishes to replace him, either with a new boyfriend or one of her brothers. In one session, she expressed her love for her new boyfriend and reviewed at length an anticipated separation from him. She was determined, however, not to simply use him to replace the therapist, nor to go to bed with him for that reason alone. She was not going to discuss

the reasons for this attitude with him, nor discuss her problems with him either. She spoke further of her feelings about him, and then said that he had been upset and confused when she explained why she would not have relations with him.

The therapist picked up the contradiction inherent in her saying that she would not discuss with her boyfriend things which had come up in therapy and the indication that she had actually done so. Miss D.Q. said that she had lied to her therapist because she felt he would criticize her for what she had done, and she did not want to mess up her relationship with him when he was leaving. She went on to describe how, when under pressure with her boyfriend, she also had lied, as she had done so often in the past with her mother.

The focus of the recent therapeutic work had been on the patient's search for magical means of being close to, and one with, others, and the cost to her of such illusions, since realistic avenues of resolving separation anxieties were not fostered and the related conflicts were never resolved. Thus, the therapist's intervention focused on her lying as a self-defeating attempt to create magical fusions, and related it to her past habit of lying to her mother, who indirectly sanctioned it.

It is important in detecting such manifestations not to be angered by them or condemnatory. Rather, the therapist should work with the material at hand in the usual manner, ascertaining their context and latent meanings, and focusing on these deceptions primarily because of their serious consequences to the patient and therapy.

INDIVIDUAL DIFFERENCES IN STYLE OF COMMUNICATING

Each patient tends to have his own style of conveying unconscious material. Some patients, primarily defensive and resistant, reveal very little of their repressed, unconscious fantasies. In my original study, such patients tended to communicate more through reports of their behavior, current life events, and acting out, and less so by other means. In contrast, those patients whose material was richest in detectable unconscious content tended to report many dreams, along with their associations to them, and many conscious fantasies and childhood memories. They were more oriented toward their inner fantasy life and early childhood. With one exception, these patients tended to avoid acting out of all types.

Most of the patients in this study, however, showed mixed styles of communicating, affected in part by consistent interpreting of acting out and other detrimental behavior. Thus, they would act out, then dream or report a conscious fantasy, and then shift to an early recollection as insight developed. An overall, long-term trend toward diminished acting out and increased communication of inner fantasies, dreams, and early memories tended to occur as treatment went on and resistances were analyzed. This occurred, in part, because the patient's controls were enhanced and his tolerance for anxiety and unconscious expressions was increased. In the main, however, a patient's style of communicating remained relatively stable for long periods and was modified only slowly over the course of treatment.

Thus, in addition to learning to listen in depth to the various communications from patients, the therapist should be alert to the specific pattern and types of associations characteristic for a given patient. This reflects his cognitive style of communicating, which relates to his character makeup, defenses, and modes of discharge. It also directs our attention to the need to analyze and resolve disturbed and pathological modes of communicating, such as symptoms and acting out, and to help promote more adaptive means of working through conflicts, such as through day and night dreams and realistically constructive behavior. Such modifications can come only from the resolution of the intrapsychic conflicts and unconscious fantasies which perpetuate such disturbed means of communicating. The resultant inner-based shifts in communicating describes one dimension of the resolution of psychopathology.

CONCLUDING COMMENTS

The therapist's task of listening is complex and multidimensional; that is now quite evident. I have already organized it in a number of ways, according to specific contents; on manifest and latent, conscious and unconscious, levels; as related to real and neurotic—intrapsychic—problems; and by the detection of adaptive and therapeutic contexts. In concluding, I want to summarize the multiple frameworks for the therapist's listening in a more complete manner as a set of basic reference points which may be used to organize the material to which he attends.

In brief, the therapist listens to every communication from the patient on a manifest and latent, conscious and unconscious, level. Within this dual framework, he organizes the material from the patient around the following areas:

1. *The patient's current reality situation and problems.* From these emerge his reality conflicts and the primary adaptive tasks which evoke his intrapsychic conflicts.

2. *The patient's intrapsychic conflicts and fantasies.* This includes: id derivatives which reflect the instinctual drives— aggressive and sexual—evoked by the current events or intensified inner needs. Next are: the related superego expressions such as guilt, needs for punishment, and self-criticism on the one hand, and narcissism, ideals, goals, and self-esteem on the other.

Finally, there are the multiplicity of ego reactions which reflect it autonomous functions and dysfunctions, its role as mediator and synthesizer of the demands of reality and the other agencies of the mind, its defensive functions, its tendencies to regress or progress, its capacity to find adequate channels of instinctual discharge, its tolerance for frustration and capacity for delay, its facility for relationships and its main identifications—and considerably more. Especially important is the assessment of the final adaptation and resolution, or maladaption and symptom-formation, which the ego effects in the total current conflict situation.

3. *The patient's ongoing relationship with the therapist.* His transference reactions, the status of the therapeutic alliance and other nontransference aspects of this relationship must be con-

sidered. The patient's perception of the therapist's errors and human failings, when present, must be accounted for.

4. *The flow of the material from session to session, and within each hour.* The detection of resistances and the expression of repressed fantasies related to the patient's central intrapsychic conflicts.

5. *The genetic basis for each of these areas of reacting and communicating by the patient.*

While this is therefore a complex and elaborate task, its essentials lie in the determination of the most pressing day residues and their intrapsychic repercussions—mainly in drive and defense, and in assessing the total synthesis—adaptive or maladaptive— evolved by the ego. In any given session, one small part of this totality may be in focus, and the therapeutic work will center on it. This will depend on the main adaptive and therapeutic contexts, and the extent to which the patient responds openly or defensively to them.

However, the therapist does not react entirely randomly or catch-as-catch-can to the material from the patient. There is a general order of preference as to which areas are dealt with first and which take less precedence. These will be developed throughout the rest of this book. To state them succinctly and as a general policy to which there will be specific exceptions, the following is a list in order of highest to lowest preference for intervening by the therapist:

1. Reactions to errors by the therapist, and acute symptomatic crises—especially suicidal and homicidal impulses.

2. Disturbances in the therapeutic alliance arising from sources other than the therapist's errors.

3. Other resistances.

4. Current intrapsychic conflicts and the unconscious fantasies related to them.

5. The genetic basis for the patient's reactions to the therapist and for his present symptoms and inner conflicts.

6. Reality issues and problems.

With these as our guides, we can now turn to the entire problem of the therapist's interventions.

THE THERAPIST'S

INTERVENTIONS

11   Silence

Among the repertoire of interventions available to the therapist, paradoxically, silence is undoubtedly the most basic, the most under-valued, and the most misunderstood. (See the recent paper by Blos, Jr., 1972, and his references to earlier discussions of silence in the patient and in the psychoanalyst.) I consider it to be fundamental intervention.

There are at least two major ways in which the therapist uses silence: to listen; and as a nonverbal communication that can convey many meanings to the patient, ranging from acceptance to rejection. Both the positive virtues and the pitfalls of silence concern us here; in all, I hope to demonstrate that it is a major therapeutic asset with specific indications and principles for its use. Only when this is mastered can we understand the specific indications for verbal and other nonverbal interventions, and the potential risks of speaking out.

SILENCE AND LISTENING TO THE PATIENT

The therapist should begin every session with silence, since it is the patient's privilege to set the tone for and direct the focus of the session; it is his problems, impulses, and defenses with which the therapist must deal and the patient must lead him toward. To know what is on the patient's mind and the major adaptive tasks with which he is confronted, to determine a context for what is to follow, the therapist must be silent. Look to the realities that he describes and, at the same time, assess his intrapsychic state and response: Is there a central neurotic problem and major resistance in the session? Is the patient communicative, or are there frequent silences or periods of ruminations, rambling and empty or reality-oriented talk? Are clear or well-disguised derivatives of unconscious fantasy, or indications of important ego dysfunctions, discernible in the material?

The therapist, while silent, is very busy. If he is doing his job properly, he is recalling the last session; the recent material with its context and the patient's reactions and intrapsychic conflicts and fantasies; and his recent interventions and the responses. He is marking out and filtering through the patient's initial communications and probing the current flow of his associations. The therapist is silent, then, until he knows the manifest and latent content of the session, the resistances at hand, and formulates and confirms the intervention which will either enhance the unfolding of the material or lead to insight through interpretation. Simply put, he is silent until he must speak. He does not interfere with material that is moving in a meaningful direction. He learns to recognize when defenses have been modified and new, previously repressed fantasies and dimensions of intrapsychic conflicts are unfolding and when new perspectives, connections and genetics are coming through; at such times, he "intervenes" with silence to permit their full expression. Speech will usually interfere with such moments, deflecting the patient's focus and flow, and encouraging the reinstitution of defenses. It will convey the nonverbal implication and unconscious message from the therapist to the patient that he should stop revealing his unconscious fantasies; the patient will generally comply. Remembering this likelihood will help us to realize the specific risks and goals of intervening.

The therapist also listens silently when he does not understand the material in the session. Questions and confrontations under these conditions are often haphazard, distracting and detrimental, especially when the context is unclear. While there are constructive interventions which may be utilized during these periods of notable resistance, the therapist's basic stance should be to maintain silence and probe for clues to what is going on. Unresolved unconscious conflicts and disturbing unconscious fantasies evoke in the patient strong needs for resolution; if the therapist is willing to wait it out, the patient will of inner necessity get around to letting him know about it. If the therapist talks prematurely or guesses, he risks encouraging further flight and, in effect, often unwittingly offers a defense to the patient by focusing on some reality or irrelevant issue and blocking the revelation of the central unconscious conflict. In my experience as a supervisor, this outcome is typical, and enhancement of the material rare, when such uncertain comments are offered. Above all, respect the value of silence as the primary therapeutic tool for understanding the patient.

The following vignette will exemplify the use of silence in permitting the emergence of increasingly obvious derivatives of repressed material as a session proceeds. Notice how there is initial chaos, but then an eventual crystallization around a central theme. While a favorable development will not characterize every session in which the therapist is patient and silent, this will happen more often than not. If the material is not coalescing, the therapist can interpret the defenses at hand or make a confrontation (see Chapters 13 and 14); but first he must accept the patient as he is and listen.

> Mr. D.S. was a young man with a borderline distur-
> bance, who was struggling against becoming an overt
> homosexual. His therapist went on vacation. Before the
> separation, the patient had almost arranged job hours that
> would have led to difficulty in coming to his sessions. This
> turned out to be an attempt to act out his rage over being
> deserted by the therapist, a rage his associations linked to
> rejection by his father and brother. This had not been
> interpreted at the time.
>
> In the session after the vacation, the patient spoke of
> keeping his treatment a secret from his father and brother,
> and of his situation at home where he was referred to as
> "The Queen"—a term with clear homosexual overtones.
> He spoke of arguing with his father, of some problems

with his job, and of feeling that girls took advantage of him. His brother also used him. At parties he felt that people were talking about him and calling him a queer.

The context of this hour appears to be the therapist's vacation, and the patient's main unconscious fantasy-response is expressed with clearer derivatives at the end of the session. It would appear that Mr. D.S. had responded to his therapist's vacation with a fantasy of this kind: "You are like my father and brother; you use me and leave. I long to be closer to you in some homosexual way and fear that these wishes will be detected and I will be ridiculed." In the adaptive context of the therapist's vacation, and with the therapeutic context of mounting homosexual anxieties and the appearance of undisguised homosexual fantasies, a general interpretation upwards toward the less threatening aspects of the patient's reaction to the separation—referring primarily to his anger, his feeling used and deserted, and his longings to be close—was in order, but was not made by the therapist (see Chapter 16).

Let us continue with the vignette:

> In the next session, Mr. D.S. described in detail a party where he had smoked large amounts of marihuana and became (in his own words) "paranoid." He imagined that he was naked, defecating, and being talked about, and that he had made homosexual advances to someone, so that his father had been called to take care of him. In the session, after ruminating about his job, he added that he had also imagined while "high" that he had impregnated a boyfriend, that he had wires in his head so he could hear the thoughts of others, that he was laughed at because of his small penis, and that the police were coming to hospitalize him. He then described a dispute with his father.
>
> In this session, an acute regressive episode has been prompted, in part, by the therapist's failure to interpret the patient's separation reaction both before and after his going away (see Chapters 19 and 22). The fantasies in response to this event are now both clearer and more primitive; they include indications of defecatory rage,

longings for care, wishes for union through impregnation of the therapist, and a feeling that he was rejected because of his small penis. The patient seemed to be in an acute homosexual panic. More specific material is clearly available.

Again, the therapist had been silent in the session, and this, while clearly not the sole factor, contributed to the expression of more open derivatives of the intrapsychic conflict. We may also suspect by now that the therapist's silence had become a less appropriate response, and more a failure to intervene properly.

In the session that followed, Mr. D.S. recounted his relationships with men, including teenage homosexual fantasies in which he wished to grab and capture men's genitals. He described this in sequence with his feelings about his father's disinterest and occasional sudden desertion of the family, and his aloofness from the patient. Finally, the therapist broke his silence and interpreted the homosexual, father-related fantasies and longings evoked by his own vacation, and the accompanying anxiety and rage, and the patient's anxiety lessened.

This vignette reflects the complexities of the therapist's use of silence. On the one hand, it fostered the unfolding of clearer derivatives of the patient's repressed fantasies until they were relatively undisguised. There was an intense need in this patient to adapt to the intrapsychic conflicts evoked by the therapist's vacation and to let the therapist know of his anxiety-provoking unconscious fantasies about it. Had the therapist intervened prematurely with questions or other interventions, he might have unduly bolstered the patient's defenses and prevented his more blatant fantasies from emerging, thereby limiting possibilities for insight and inner change.

On the other hand, it would appear that the prolonged silence was inappropriate and anti-therapeutic, fostering an acute regression and disruption in the patient's functioning. Interpretations of the early material once it had emerged probably would have fostered better controls and adaptation to the situation. This is supported by the fact that the regression was predicted in supervision. Silence may reflect countertransference problems and must not be maintained when an intervention is indicated (see below).

The value of silence on the part of the therapist is seen most clearly in those sessions where an unexpected clue to the hour comes near the very end of a session. This is not uncommon when either the adaptive context or the main intrapsychic conflicts and unconscious fantasies are unclear, and the material does not coalesce around a central theme. I will illustrate:

> Mr. D.T., a young man with a depressive character disorder, tended to be quite defensive in his sessions. For several hours he had been ruminating about his job and about various reality-based arguments with his mother. His girlfriend had lost her job and, in one session, he raged against her boss. Some of the material implied unexpressed anger at the therapist.
>
> In the following session, he reported having watched a medical television show that had reminded him of his tonsillectomy, an experience that he had not recalled in years. He had seen his parents afterwards and raged against them in great detail for various ways in which they were hypocritical regarding money and religion. He had been anxious, without knowing why. It was near the end of the session that he reported for the first time in his treatment that he had a penile discharge and was worried that he had veneral disease. This turned out to be the main source of his recent anxiety and of many repressed fears and fantasies of bodily harm.

This unanticipated denouement to a confusing session, foreshadowed only remotely by the reference to the tonsillectomy, was possible only because the therapist remained silent, recognizing that he lacked both a context for the session and a central theme. Since these keys were unavailable, questions would have proven distracting, while a confrontation with the lack of focus on the part of the patient had not proved useful in the past; further, it did not seem advisable since the patient was manifesting expressions of affects, which was something he rarely did.

A final illustration of the value of silence follows:

Mr. D.U., a young man with a borderline syndrome and homosexual problems, was in his first month of psychotherapy. He felt considerable anger at not being able to manipulate and control his present therapist as he had previous ones. In the week before the session to be described, he had made several attempts at acting out in response to confrontations with his poor controls and his wishes for license to gratify his impulses without regard for others. This behavior had been interpreted to him as part of his ruthless quest for power and control; dreams which expressed intense anxieties about bodily deformity and disintegration followed and were explored.

In the session under discussion, Mr. D.U. was ruminative, describing how he broke off with a girlfriend, detailing visits to various friends and relatives over the weekend, describing several experiences which had brought him close to homosexuals though he avoided any overt sexual experience, and reviewing a family celebration which he had attended with his siblings and parents.

The therapist kept silent. Nearing the end of the session, the patient mentioned that while with his brother, he suddenly had the fantasy of being penetrated anally by him, and that he had thought of taking some tranquilizers, but had not done so.

In this session, the therapist was silent because he did not detect a central context or theme, and felt that the patient's acting out was under reasonable control for the moment—there was no therapeutic context. He did not interpret or confront the rumination because he was interested in seeing what was emerging and felt that the topics, while diverse, might have some importance. He also wanted to see what manifest and latent content would follow, and preferred not to guess at the important aspects of the material. As it turned out, the emergence of terrifying bodily anxieties in the previous week proved an important context for this hour, creating in the patient pressure toward homosexual fantasies and behavior as maladaptive efforts to reassure himself regarding his bodily integrity. The final communication in the session conveyed this with great impact.

The therapist's silence creates a pressure for the patient to search consciously and unconsciously for further associations and to communicate more meaningfully. When this leads to the revelation of important repressed material, as it did here, we may consider silence confirmed as the appropriate "intervention" (see Chapter 18). Often, only the therapist's silence can permit or foster the revelation of conscious and unconscious "secrets" toward the end of the hour. On another occasion, for example, this patient unconsciously concealed until the end of a session the fact that he had taken unprescribed medication in a context that emphasized rage at his therapist. Again, the therapist had remained silent.

The choice between judicious silence and a confrontation with the patient's rumination depends on the therapist's clinical hunches and knowledge of the patient. Often, either tack proves valid, as opposed to pursuing trivial manifest content, and will be confirmed by the revelation of previously concealed or repressed behavior or fantasies and memories.

These are the basic principles and indications for silence, and they are to be applied with only judicious exceptions:

1. *The therapist is silent after greeting the patient and escorting him into his consultation room.* That is, he allows the patient to begin the hour and the material to unfold.

2. *He remains silent until he has accomplished the following:* He must understand the material and its implications for the patient's neurotic conflicts and ego dysfunctions, and especially some aspect of their unconscious roots; or ascertain that there is a specific need for an intervention (see Chapter 17); or sees that there is a relevant and important question to ask, or a comment to make which he believes will modify resistances and develop the material further. This is to be used sparingly.

3. *He is silent while he formulates and identifies the primary adaptive task, the resultant intrapsychic conflicts, the therapeutic context, the patient's level of ego functioning and adaptive responses, and the key unconscious fantasies and memories.* After forming

his hypothesis, he waits for confirmation from the ongoing material before speaking out.

4. *He is silent if the patient is working well, unraveling his thoughts and conflicts, and allowing the derivatives of his unconscious fantasies to emerge.* Whenever possible, he wants to support his patient's autonomous, constructive functioning; silence at times of such adaptive, positive work during the session is ego-building for the patient, and interventions may be infantilizing.

5. *He remains silent if he does not understand what is going on and there is no urgent indication for comment; he does not offer isolated comments or formal interventions gratuitously, but waits until he can offer the most integrated, interpretive statement possible.*

6. *He may choose to be silent even if the patient becomes silent.* While he may ask the patient what he is thinking about, or what his thoughts are about the silence, his primary focus should be on the meaning and usage of this silence and on understanding the context in which it occurs.

SILENCE AS A CONSTRUCTIVE NONVERBAL COMMUNICATION

The therapist's silence actively communicates fantasies and feelings of which he should be aware, and which should be distinguished from the patient's own fantasies, correct or incorrect, about that silence. It is important for the therapist to determine whether the patient is correctly in tune with the implications of the therapist's silences or whether he is distorting, projecting, and misconstruing them according to his own inner needs, conflicts, and fantasies. He can only do this if he is in tune with himself, and understands his true usage of silence and its implications.

Silence cannot, of course, convey the specific insights that verbal interventions can. Nonetheless, it conveys many important ego and superego-building communications from the therapist to the patient, such as: "I accept you" and "I am (one) with you." It may also, in a given context, mean "I sanction or will not criticize you or your behavior"; "It is you (the patient) who must accept responsibility at this time"; and, "I can tolerate your impulses toward me or others without having to strike back or defend myself." This benign usage of silence is integral to the therapist's role as a good mothering figure who offers a good "fit" or "protective hold" to the patient, and it is an important nonverbal enhancement of the therapeutic alliance.

The nuances of silence as a tool of good therapeutic care, comfort, acceptance, and support are difficult to teach; it must be accompanied by inherent warmth and natural sincerity. Further, there are so many different kinds of silence and settings for silence, that I can only illustrate some of the more common meaningful uses here. They range from ignoring direct questions to moments where the patient simply wants to share a mutual period of silence and peace with the therapist.

SILENCE AS SANCTION OR ACCEPTANCE OF THE PATIENT

As I earlier indicated (Chapters 8 and 9), the therapist is constantly assessing the patient's adaptive responses for their cost to himself and others, and the extent to which they seem appropriate and realistic, or neurotic. Thus, when a patient describes an important decision or piece of behavior that appears sound to the therapist, it is generally best not to express direct approval since it tends to create undue control over the patient, promotes subservience, and infantalizes him. The resulting detrimental responses in the patient will disturb the therapeutic alliance and process. Silent acceptance, on the other hand, emphasizes the patient's own responsibility for his behavioral adaptations, while implying a benevolent air of approval. It is not a manipulation of the patient and yet it is a conscious response, since the therapist has no choice but to assess and respond to the behavior or ideas of his patient. If these seem inappropriate and neurotic, he will, of course, endeavor to eventually interpret the unconscious fantasies that account for them; to be silent under those circumstances constitutes a sanction of acting out or of the patient's neurotic and maladaptive responses (see below).

This kind of silence on the part of the therapist can be illustrated with any session in which the patient had acted adaptively and constructively, or is endeavoring to work out an intrapsychic conflict on his own, and is being permitted to do so. I shall illustrate briefly, selecting a vignette where other uses of silence are also included.

Miss D.V. was an asthmatic young woman with a severe characterologic disturbance who had been in therapy a little over a year. She was approaching one of her therapist's vacations. In the past, these had prompted considerable regression, including blatant sexual acting out, provocations of others, intense fantasies of incorporative union and of murderous vengeful rage, and episodes of asthma.

In the session under consideration, it was becoming clear that her separation anxiety and maladaptive incorporative needs had lessened considerably. While still concerned and anxious, she expressed her needs in a controlled manner and through minor unconscious bits of acting out and acting in. For example, she forgot her matches and asked to use some from the therapist. This was interpreted, from her associations, as a reflection, relatively benign in quality, of her fantasy of being incomplete without the therapist. She developed her first lasting and relatively stable love-relationship with a new boyfriend, who was far different from the destructive and promiscuous fellows to whom she had previously attached herself. Lastly, she responded to her parents' provocations, which were strikingly intense when the therapist was going away, with patience and control, and was not drawn into their usual bilateral battles.

In one session at this time, the patient was pensive, calm, and silent for long periods. The therapist, in turn, was also silent. Miss D.V. described her thoughts about having relations with her boyfriend. She recognized her need to replace her therapist and was weeding out these feelings from her genuine feelings of love for her new friend. She had been working this over for several weeks and wanted to sleep with him soon, but would not act impulsively as she had done in the past. She was planning to arange for contraception rather than risk impregnation as she had before, and she was feeling quite content. The therapist did not speak and the session ended.

In this hour, the therapist's silence implied that he accepted her exploration of her fantasies and review of her anticipated behavior as nonneurotic, as far as was detectable, from the material. It also had other implications, to which we can now turn.

SILENCE AS ACCEPTING THE PATIENT'S WISHES FOR APPROPRIATE ACCEPTANCE AND CLOSENESS

In responding with silence to the implicit wish for closeness, and even a sense of oneness, conveyed by Miss D.V.'s silence, the therapist offered a benign gratification of the patient's wishes. He felt that an intervention, such as an interpretation of the unconscious wish for closeness with him, would be experienced as a harsh rejection, and would disrupt the therapeutic alliance (see Chapter 17), create conscious and unconscious rage, foster regression, and undo the ego-building and structural changes developing within this patient. This gratification could be interpreted later if it continued unduly or if it appeared in the context of blatant resistances. In the meantime, the patient could feel accepted and continue to organize her thoughts and feelings in a positive way. The fact that she did not subsequently act out destructively confirmed this use of silent acceptance by the therapist.

There are obvious dangers in gratifying wishes for closeness expressed through silence. The therapist must be clear that the context is benign and that verbal interventions would be disruptive or lead nowhere. Patience on his part is always ego-building for the patient, who will identify with it and feel accepted and reassured by it. It should not be overdone or it will become seductive and disrupt therapy. Moreover, the patient may be using the silence as a resistance to gain distance from the therapist and the material at hand. Here, the patient's silence is a reflection of a disruption in the therapeutic alliance and it must not be shared with him by the therapist; ultimately it must be interpreted. The context of the silence and the associations from the patient before and after it will enable the therapist to understand its meaning and deal with it accordingly.

SILENCE AS A REINFORCEMENT OF THE PATIENT'S AUTONOMIES

The therapist's silence in this session with Miss D.V. also conveyed to her that she is, indeed, responsible for herself and her life decisions, and for her moral code, ideals, and behavior. When applied judiciously and wisely, this use enhances both ego and superego.

SILENCE AS AN EGO-BUILDING FRUSTRATION AND AS NECESSARY DISTANCE

Appropriate and reasonable doses by the therapist of frustration and distance as an object (person), aid the development of autonomous functioning in the patient. A useful tool is silence, including failure to answer direct questions, or to respond to direct or implied requests for verbalizations from the patient. While the therapist must ultimately answer those questions that are realistic and demand an answer, silence is the appropriate response to many queries.

In this context, silence generates pressures toward regression, followed by new integrations, and toward individuation. It communicates to the patient that the therapist is not immediately available to him, is waiting to hear more, is necessarily remote, can be justifiably and nonhostilely cruel, and that the patient must tolerate his inability to control or possess the therapist. The momentary loss of the therapist at a time of need, when appropriate, aids in developing the patient's capacity for mature object relationships and frustration tolerance.

SILENCE AS A TOLERATION OF THE PATIENT'S HOSTILITY, SEDUCTIVENESS, AND/OR PATHOLOGY

At times a patient describes primitive or potentially repulsive fantasies, behaves destructively with others, attempts verbally to attack the therapist, or is openly seductive with him. Such communications merit ultimate confrontation and interpretation, but the therapist's initial silence expresses tolerance without criticism, defenses, and responsive seductiveness or hostility. When confronted with such material or behavior, many therapists respond morally or defensively or otherwise out of their own needs, and become too active too soon, reacting before the material unfolds and appropriate interventions are possible (see Chapter 22).

Such initial silence and acceptance fosters the therapeutic alliance and the patient's capacity to tolerate and face his own impulses without fear of retaliation or adverse comment from the therapist. He can then accept the pathological aspects of his behavior and work toward modifying himself through insight.

Let us now move on to some technical problems in the use of silence by the therapist.

PITFALLS IN THE THERAPIST'S USE OF SILENCE

Technical errors in the therapist's use of silence tend to fall into two groups: excessive and insufficient usage. Let us study both.

INAPPROPRIATE AND EXCESSIVE SILENCE

It has been my experience as a supervisor that therapists-in-training are only rarely inclined toward repetitive periods of undue silence. While they may, often enough, fail to respond to the patient's need for an appropriate intervention, they will, more often than not, speak up in some distracting, irrelevant, or otherwise detrimental way. Their inappropriate periods of silence are, therefore, rather selective and occur at moments when they are in a long-term dilemma or caught up in a specific countertransference problem. The following factors may be involved:

THE THERAPIST'S SILENCE AS AN EXPRESSION OF ANGER

The use of silence—"the silent treatment"—to express conscious or unconscious hostility is well known. Therapists are not immune to such uses of silence. Thus, when they feel provoked, annoyed, or enraged by a patient, they may fall silent either to punish the patient directly, or defensively and primitively to withdraw from him. Caught up in this rage, fearful of expressing it, unable to resolve it, and maladaptively defending himself against it, such a therapist loses his clinical perspective. With his silence, he deviates from his role as a therapist and acts out against the patient. I am not suggesting that anger at the patient need always be inappropriate. But such anger must ultimately be controlled and become a source of insight into the patient's conflicts and need to be provocative, and if necessary, the occasion for self-analysis (see Chapter 22). Otherwise, the patient will consciously or unconsciously detect the therapist's silent fury, and respond to it maladaptively in turn, thus generating a cycle of provocation and response on both parts—a misalliance without conscious insight in either party.

Since this kind of "silent treatment" is so often utilized without awareness by the therapist, it is difficult to detect in supervision. It may be picked up from the patient's response to the silence, in which his unconscious, or sometimes conscious, understanding of the therapist's silent anger and its sources is reflected in his associations. The alert therapist can be directed toward self-awareness and self-analysis with resolution of his own countertransference problem by a similar scrutiny of, and tuning in on, the patient's material (see Chapter 22). Often, the inappropriate silence is strongly rationalized and defended by the therapist. We may suspect its presence in situations where the patient has clearly been provocative toward the therapist, and where silence prevails when interventions are clearly indicated (see Chapter 19). This brief vignette illustrates:

> Mr. D.W. was a homosexual young man with a severe character disorder, who had been in therapy for about a year when his therapist went on a three-week vacation. In the session upon the therapist's return, the patient initially spoke of how well he had done during the interruption in treatment, but then went on to describe a series of homosexual experiences that he strongly rationalized as gratifying and harmless. The last one, however, he actually described as a total, infuriating loss of control and hostile seduction, which had led the patient to feel terrible about

himself and his behavior. He referred to similar guilt-ridden homosexual episodes in reaction to an earlier separation from the therapist which had had aspects of vengeance against the deserting therapist-parent. As the session ended, the patient spoke of his father, who had promised to be home to lend him his car, but had disappeared for the day instead; the patient had been furious.

This session is one in which the therapist remained silent despite the patient's blatant acting out, the presence of material which lent itself for interpretation, and even an unconscious appeal for helpful intervention. The session begins with a not-uncommon form of flight into health (see Chapter 21), but then regressive responses to the separation, including acting out, anxiety, and guilt, are reported. This is a strong therapeutic context and a clear indication for an intervention (see Chapter 17); failure to intervene—remaining silent—is both destructive toward the patient and a sanction of this behavior (see below). The associations indicate that the patient was seeking help with his losing battle against his inappropriate and to him painful homosexual ways of "resolving" the intrapsychic conflicts evoked by his therapist's absence. The final comments about the patient's deserting father offered specific transference links from the therapist to this parent (see Chapter 20). Yet the therapist ignored it all.

When confronted in supervision with his failure to intervene here, the therapist expressed resentment regarding the patient's tendencies to act out so repeatedly. Later, he also spoke of his own anger at having to end an idyllic vacation. His specific and general anger was expressed in his silence with this patient. Further, he was aware of repeated difficulties on his part in dealing with homosexual fantasies and behavior.

This formulation was confirmed to some degree in the following session through the latent content of the material. The patient there spoke at length of feeling hopeless and misunderstood by his friends and parents, of being turned down by many prospective employers who destructively turned coldly and silently away from him and seemed afraid of him, and of wanting to vanish silently from his present lifescene.

SILENCE AS AN UNNECESSARY AND INAPPROPRIATE DEPRIVATION

The aggressive meanings of undue silence on the part of the therapist are varied and overlapping; each has a different source within him and may evoke different responses in patients. Some patients, depending on their pathology and past experiences, are especially sensitive to certain kinds of silence in their therapist, and relatively unmoved by other types.

Excessive, repetitive silence, especially when an intervention is indicated (and this will inevitably occur within a session or two in almost all psychotherapies), is an unnecessary and inappropriate deprivation for the patient. It constitutes a failure of the therapist to function adequately in his role of promoting insightful inner change, and a lack of sensitivity to the patient's most basic needs for communication and expressions of concern.

While unnecessary deprivation through silence is somewhat difficult to define precisely, it can nonetheless be picked up by a sensitive supervisor or patient. The latter is, of course, the ultimate gauge for this assessment which must be made in the specific context of the patient's needs. In general, when the therapist has been silent for a while, and in response, the patient regresses, acts out, or develops symptoms, we may suspect that the use of the silence has been incorrect (see Chapters 19 and 22). This has been illustrated in the vignettes with Mr. D.S. and Mr. D.W. Eventually, the patient will, usually unconsciously, address himself to the overly frustrating silence in his therapist. This is best seen with Mr. D.W., whose reference to his disappearing father may have been directed toward the deprivation constituted by the therapist's uncalled for silence, in addition to his ongoing reaction to the recent separation. In his second hour, the derivatives are more apparently related to the therapist's silence, and the latent content of the hour can best be understood in that context. In our therapeutic work, we attempt to reverse this process: we allow the thematic threads of the material (here: hopelessness; not being understood; being rejected; people afraid of him; and wanting to vanish silently) to direct us to the context so that we recognize that the patient is reacting to our aloofness and that it may, indeed, have been destructive.

In all, if silence is the prevailing intervention, the therapist must constantly assess the patient's response to it. Limited regression, the development of new material and of new revelations, and fresh insights, all confirm the use of silence; disruptive regression and marked resistances suggest that it is technically incorrect and may well be the result of countertransference problems.

I want to isolate one group of patients where the therapist's use of silence is especially hazardous and generally incorrect. These patients, from the very first session, complain or fall silent themselves if the therapist does not ask questions or talk. They are both terrified and enraged at even a relative silence, and enormously mistrustful of him for it. These primitive demands for words and nurture, more than for insights, must be considered seriously, and efforts made to respond. The therapist must demonstrate a capacity to tune in on the patient's primitive needs and offer reasonable and appropriate gratification of them through verbal activity. Without such gratification, the therapy will not unfold and premature termination will occur. Only the offer of an environment suited entirely to the patient's needs and to the creation of the sense of a "harmonious mix-up" (Balint, 1968) for him will enable the development of a therapeutic alliance with such patients. Silence creates for them an objectless world in which they feel terrified and deserted, and vulnerably alone; or it is seen as part of a hostile, nongratifying, enemy-world.

While this problem is seen in some regressed, narcissistic and borderline adult patients, it is especially common in adolescents and young adults. I have already alluded to Miss C.J. (Chapter 7), an adolescent who demanded that her therapist talk actively from the outset of her meetings with him, as did Miss C.N. (Chapter 8) who was also in her teens. With the former patient, this demand was overdetermined: she did not want to reveal her own very serious and terrifying inner conflicts; she had severe separation anxieties and conflicts, and could not tolerate the gulf between herself and a relatively silent therapist; she was orally insatiable and devouring; and she had been severely and irrationally punished with silence as a child. Miss C.N., on the other hand, revealed only one main determinant for her demands for words from her therapist, though undoubtedly more existed: she had intense separation anxiety of a kind that promoted regression and panic, and needed to be constantly bathed in, and filled by, words. A therapist who was silent even for a few minutes was viewed as being no longer present or as actively attacking, and as a deserting mother-figure who wanted her to perish.

An active, nurturing, participant-like stance is essential with such patients, and their dread of silence demands focus early in their treatment, even in the initial hour if possible. As an indication of the serious threat such a dread of silence in the therapist poses for the therapeutic alliance, both of these patients terminated treatment soon after it began. While other factors were involved, intolerance of silences, even momentary, on the therapist's part and the failure both to respond directly to it with useful comments and to adequately analyze the unconscious fantasies and ego-defects on which it was based, were major contributors to this event.

Silence as an Inappropriate Sanction of the Patient's Maladaptive Responses

It must be remembered that if the therapist does not speak, the patient may feel that the behavior or symptoms that he has described have received his approval. Patients often state this quite explicitly: "You have nothing to say about what I did, so I must have handled the situation well; you would have said something if I had been destructive in any way."

While this does not mean that the therapist must always speak when the patient has acted out or regressed in some other way, it does imply that most of the time he should do exactly that, based on an understanding of the material of the session (see Chapter 17). Even delaying an indicated intervention for one session is experienced by the patient as a reinforcement and approval. If the associations do not lend themselves to an interpretation of the pathological behavior, a confrontation with it is often indicated (see Chapters 13 and 14). At times, a comment may be postponed pending further exploration, but the therapist must recognize this delay and take care to eventually analyze the acting out presented by the patient.

Mr. D.W. (see above) viewed his therapist's silence in just that way. He continued to act out homosexually, in part precisely because his therapist failed to intervene when such incidents were reported in treatment. This was true despite the fact that the material lent itself to interpretation and that the patient often indirectly asked for help. We may suspect a serious countertransference block here. The therapist has become similar to the mother who ignores her child's destructiveness to himself and others; it must gratify fantasies within her and will surely continue. In therapy, this leads to an antitherapeutic alliance that undermines the treatment.

SILENCE AS A DEFENSE FOR THE THERAPIST

Silence may be used by the therapist as a defense against his own sexual or aggressive intrapsychic conflicts and fantasies about the patient. These may lead to a fear of closeness—represented by verbal interventions with the patient, and to the defensive use of silence to create a barrier of distance and as a provocation. This may be reflected in prolonged periods of silence that occur especially when the communications from the patient have stirred up the therapist's particular countertransference problem area. It is also reflected at times in the therapist's failure to answer realistic questions from the patient, even after they have been fully explored. Silence may also be used defensively whenever a therapist consciously or unconsciously wants to avoid a particular aspect of the material from the patient in an effort to let it pass by unnoticed.

OTHER MISUSES OF SILENCE

Silence on the part of the therapist may also be used inappropriately to draw the patient closer and involve him or her in intense seductive fantasies about the therapist. It may also be used to undermine the development of a strong therapeutic alliance and the concomitant intimacy (mixed with necessary deprivation; see Stone, 1961), or to foster premature termination by the patient for a multitude of countertransference-evoked reasons.

In all, then, while silence is one of our most fundamental therapeutic tools, its misapplication can derail the therapy.

TALKING TOO MUCH

While excessive silence is not to be underestimated, talking too much is the far more common difficulty. There are many obvious countertransference reasons for this, and I will briefly mention a few. Therapists who speak too soon or too much do so out of their own unresolved, pathological narcissism—their love of their own thoughts, ideas, and concepts. They also do so to be consciously or unconsciously seductive or aggressive, controlling, and manipulative. They may do it to push the patient away or as a defense used to avoid unconscious fantasies or other material that is anxiety-provoking for them, and to keep the patient close to the surface, where his associations pose little threat. They do it because they are confused and want to pretend that their empty words shed light on the material when they only add to the chaos; and they speak too often because they do not want to hear clearly, owing to their unresolved conflicts about listening as a form of auditory voyeurism. They do it also out of an unresolved need to feed the patient and out of conflicted fears of appropriately depriving him by maintaining an optimal level of frustration and distance in the therapeutic relationship.

Each therapist has his own style of speaking out or remaining silent, and his countertransference difficulties tend repetitively toward inappropriate silences or excessive talk. It is well for each therapist to know his propensities and to analyze and work through any problems along these lines so that they are, as a rule, not disruptive to the therapy (see Chapter 22). Here, too, the therapist can be guided by the material from the patient. Confirmation of his interventions (see Chapter 18) indicates that the timing and context was correct, while nonconfirmatory responses suggest that he is incorrect or talking too much. If the latent content of the material from the patient refers to themes of excessive talking, nagging, being controlled, or being overwhelmed by words or word-equivalents, the therapist should be alert to this problem. Patients seldom allude to the therapist's overactivity directly. One exception that I recently observed followed about twenty minutes of silence by a therapist who had previously been prone to talk out repeatedly and was now attempting to control this behavior after it had been discussed in supervision. The patient suddenly interrupted his flow of associations and said that he had just realized how peaceful the setting was; the therapist wasn't coming at him with interruptions and comments like he usually did.

This next vignette, while perhaps a bit extreme, illustrates the consequences of talking too much.

> Mr. D.X. was a young man with a borderline syndrome who had been in therapy for a year. The session to be described preceded the therapist's vacation. The material from prior sessions suggested tremendous rage at Dr. S., the therapist. This had two main roots: the desertion represented by the vacation and this overactive therapist's repeated failure to listen to and understand the patient. Genetically, there were links to experiences that the patient had endured with his father.
>
> The patient began the session by saying that he was still bothered by the pending separation. Dr. S. immediately asked for further thoughts. The patient said that he was confused by the question, and then went on. Dr. S. had told him in the last session that he felt unworthy and he did not know what had been meant by that. Dr. S. quickly interrupted and told the patient, "You also said that you felt I didn't understand you." Mr. D.X. went on to speak of fears of losing control of himself and Dr. S. said that maybe the patient felt that he couldn't control him (Dr. S.).
>
> Despite the condensation of the material here, we can see that Dr. S. was intervening in an arbitrary, haphazard, and incorrect manner. No central theme was permitted to emerge, nor were the derivatives of unconscious fantasies allowed to develop; no insight was possible. I will not belabor this point, but simply add that nothing became clear in this session. The patient's specific fantasies and conflicts regarding the therapist's vacation never developed.
>
> In the latter part of this session, the patient con-

sciously and unconsciously indicated that he was aware that he was not given the chance to express himself. He spoke of how he and Dr. s. never got to the point; he directly disagreed with many of Dr. s.'s comments (and correctly so); he even contradicted Dr. s. several times; and he wondered out loud why Dr. s. said many of the things he did. Mr. D.X. said near the end of the hour that he had had a daydream that Dr. s. did not return. This may well have come, in part, out of his frustration and rage at not being considered as a separate person by this therapist, and at not being heard by him. Dr. s.'s response to this fantasy was to suggest immediately that possibly Mr. D.X. was planning not to return himself. The patient ended the session by saying that maybe Dr. s. was right, but that he had no such plans and besides he really thought that something else was bothering him and that somehow he had not discussed it in the session.

We can suspect that overactive therapists like Dr. s. are angry, controlling, not interested in their patients' associations—or in the patient, and afraid of what is inside the patient, such as his unconscious fantasies. Such therapists are a totally disruptive influence on a session. Dr. s. seems to have been in conflict about his pending vacation and was apparently attempting to avoid exploring the patient's responses to it.

This vignette can serve as a reminder to be silent unless there is clear and good reason to speak; to listen to the patient and not confuse your thoughts with his; and to allow your own thoughts to follow from those of the patient and not from your own, idiosyncratic, countertransference-based notions. The antitherapeutic, sadomasochistic alliance that prevailed in the session with Mr. D.X. demonstrates how detrimental, on so many levels, talking too much on the part of the therapist can be. The patient's denial of so much of what the therapist said stemmed from his need to maintain a grasp on reality (here, the patient had a better grasp than the therapist), to maintain his own identity and autonomy and not be inundated by the therapist, and to defend himself from the therapist's verbal assaults. The nonverbal dimension of ververbalizing by the therapist creates an atmosphere of pressure, danger, and terror. Flight from treatment is a common outcome.

Dr. s. not only spoke too much, but also intervened quite incorrectly most of the time. These two problems commonly go together. Since such overactivity is a reflection of the therapist's own inner problems and pathology, it takes the form of excessive talk, while the deviant content is derived from the therapist's unresolved conflicts and pathological fantasies.

In essence, silence is essential so that the patient may express himself and be understood on all levels. Its appropriate usage contributes to a warm and accepting therapeutic atmosphere and alliance, and to a reasonable separateness between the patient and therapist. As an intervention, in the special sense of that term, it communicates the need for more and clearer derivatives of unconscious fantasies and conflicts from the patient, and an acceptance of his constructive behavior. Pitfalls in the use of silence relate to excessive or too little usage. In all, the therapist's silence is a complex, multi-leveled, conscious and unconscious communication reflecting its use as a tool to further the therapeutic process; deviant applications reflect unresolved conflicts in the therapist. Some patients are excruciatingly sensitive to its use, while all patients will react on some level to an inappropriate use or to what is probably more common, a failure to use it sufficiently.

12 Questions and Clarifications

There are two basic groups of verbal interventions available to therapists—questions and clarifications—that are not as simple as they might appear to be. Here, I shall discuss their appropriate and inappropriate use and specific indications, but I shall reserve most of my comments about their nonverbal aspects for Chapter 17 (see also the pioneering papers by Bibring, 1954; and Olinick, 1954).

Questions by the therapist may be broadly defined as efforts to resolve ambiguities and uncertainties in the patient's communications; to investigate all pertinent omissions; and to further develop the derivatives of latent content and unconscious fantasies in his associations. In all, they serve to promote fuller expression and understanding of the many communications from the patient.

There are two kinds of clarifications: first, those that restate the patient's communication to him much as he made it or with minor changes; the therapist may add a particular emphasis not used by the patient. This is done primarily to sharpen the latter's awareness of certain conscious thoughts, fantasies, affects, conflicts, or behavior in an effort to explore its meaning and implications further. It may also, in a given context, suggest a different appraisal of the material than that implied by the patient or hint at latent meanings inherent in the communication (see Bibring, 1954). Such interventions form a continuum with both questions on one side and confrontations on the other (see Chapter 13); all of these deal basically with the surface or manifest content of the material from the patient, though they are utilized at times to promote expressions from deeper levels. They may even contain implicit interpretative aspects when the manifest content of the associations is reiterated in the hope that the patient himself will realize the latent content. Because clarifications overlap in this way, they will be discussed sparingly in this chapter.

A second type of clarification, which I will delineate briefly here, refers to the therapist's explanations of his own communications, either in response to questions from the patient, or because he becomes aware himself of ambiguities in his own remarks.

INDICATIONS FOR QUESTIONS

There are some general indications for questioning by the therapist. While many questions occur spontaneously to the therapist, often will clear conscious or intuitively correct justifications, the therapist cannot interrupt the patient to direct each query to him or the therapy will lose its spontaneity, and the revelations contained in the sequence of the patient's flow of associations will be lost. Thus, in asking questions, these basic considerations should be kept in mind:

1. *By and large, a question should be directed toward the development of the major problem and theme, the context or adaptive task, of the session.* It should not distract the patient from this train of thought. Questions should not be random, nor should they be too frequent in any given session. In sessions where the major theme is not clear and the therapist senses the possibility of developing meaningful associations, exploratory questions which specifically derive from the patient's own associational material are in order. They should be asked only if the material lends itself to them, and they should not be forced.

In sessions where the patient is ruminating and his defenses are strong, questions are seldom useful, and will only tend to promote further rumination. In such hours, a question may imply nonverbally that the patient is communicating meaningful material that the therapist wants to develop further and both parties find themselves actively sharing obsessive defenses: the patient ruminates and the therapist encourages it. The proper intervention under these circumstances is either silence or a confrontation of the patient with his defenses, pointing out that he is remote and ruminative.

2. *When an important and clearly incomplete group of associations appear, allow the patient to continue to associate by himself; wait and see how he deals with the material and whether the latent content becomes clearer.* If he does not clarify the area in doubt, the therapist can later refer back to these associations and ask his question. If defensive avoidance is evident, this can be pointed out to the patient at that time.

Do not be hasty with questions. After the report of a dream or the breakthrough of a previously unreported fantasy, the therapist will usually have many questions. Do not ask them immediately— let the patient explore and struggle with the material first. With dreams, when the associations are scattered or avoided by the patient, ask: what does the dream, or a specific element which you suspect will lead to fruitful associations, bring to mind? Do not ask: what do you think the dream—or dream element—means, or other questions which will promote intellectualizing, rumination, and other defenses in the patient.

3. *Be prepared to tolerate ambiguities; do not be in a hurry to resolve them with questions.* Remember that in raising questions, you focus the patient in a particular direction and at a particular level, and tend to exclude for a while all other material. It should be worth doing, or not be done at all.

4. *If you find you are asking too many questions (three, four or so in a given session), stop and listen; you can be certain something is amiss.* It may be that you do not understand the material at all and should sit back to reformulate. It may also reflect the fact that the patient is immersed in deep resistances which you have failed to recognize and interpret. Or the excessive questioning may reflect a variety of countertransference problems. Frequent questions, and too-frequent inerventions of any kind, lead the patient to confine himself to the surface of his mind and to realities, and to a superficial, isolated, unintegrated type of "therapy" that I call "trivia therapy."

5. *Remember that questions may have a powerful influence on the patient and the material from him.* They have many nonverbal implications and can convey to the patient that he is not proceeding clearly enough on his own, that he should allow himself to be directed by the therapist, and that he should focus on one area rather than another. Good questions may, on the other hand, communicate to the patient that the therapist is encouraging him to forego his defensive resistances and thereby reveal derivatives of unconscious fantasies. Whatever the implications may be, it is important to be aware of them on every possible level so that the effects on the patient are clear to you. These effects extend beyond his direct responses to the inquiry, and include fantasies about why the question was asked, about being guided by the therapist, about being penetrated or controlled, and about being interrupted. Especially when a question proves to be ill-timed or poorly directed, these reactions in the patient will require analysis and working through. In contrast, where the meanings of the question are facilitative, the patient will unconsciously appreciate it and respond accordingly.

6. *There are many indications for silence rather than questions.* If we recognize the unmatched value of permitting the patient to communicate on his own through the flow and the manifest and latent content of his associations, we will, correctly, be more inclined not to ask questions than to do so.

Some clinical vignettes will illustrate the consequences of ill-advised questions and the rewards of those that are well timed and necessary.

> Mr. D.Y. was in psychotherapy because of homosexuality and a lack of direction to his life. In the light of recommendations made in supervision, Dr. Q. had shifted from his extensive, disorganized, and unproductive activity and questioning to relative silence. Over the next few sessions, the patient said nothing directly about this change in the therapist, but the latent content of his associations reflected his many fantasies about the change in the therapist.
>
> In the next session, this pattern continued: Mr. D.Y.

spoke of a psychology teacher who had been extraordinarily nice of late, and then briefly referred to a favorable discussion of his therapy with a friend. He mentioned a near-fight with a man who had been cold and nasty, spoke of a fellow whom he wanted to seduce but who was playing hard-to-get, and then described a girlfriend who was proving difficult to get involved with—he wanted to live with her, but did not know how to approach the matter.

To briefly formulate the material to this point, in the context of the therapist's recent inactivity, we can safely consider that these associations reflect derivatives of the patient's fantasies about the therapist's silence and his reaction to it—both longings and anger. We must decide whether an intervention is indicated. The disguised expressions of the unconscious fantasies and conflicts related to the therapist's silence are probably not sufficiently direct or available to the patient's awareness to merit interpretation. They are what I term "remote derivatives" (see Chapter 9). While they are becoming more open and to the point, and undoubtedly will soon be ready for interpretation (see Chapter 14), silence is indicated for now. This will give the patient the opportunity to develop his responses and fantasies further until he is on the verge of direct awareness of them, and interpretation will be feasible.

Dr. Q. thought otherwise: he felt that he had an opportunity here to explore Mr. D.Y.'s difficulties in relating to women, and he asked the patient what came to mind about his problems with this girl.

This appears to be a simple question, but it is not. In supervision, I predicted that this would only lead to rumination and intellectualizations. The question was asked without regard for, and understanding of, the central context of the session: the conflicts engendered in the patient by the therapist's silence. It can only divert the patient away from this context and reflects the arbitrary selection of one element in the patient's associations for further exploration, while ignoring the rest. It is much too focused on manifest content and will interfere with the unfolding of the actual concerns of the patient. Even if I were in error about the specific context in this session, the proper intervention here would still be silence, to permit the primary adaptive task and central intrapsychic conflict to unfold more clearly. Let us see if this formulation was borne out.

> The patient responded to the therapist's question by ruminating about the girl and his relationship with her in vague and general terms. He went on to intellectualize about his confusion regarding sex in a very remote way, and spoke too of his problems in being honest with women and his ideas about love. The session ended on this hollow and pseudophilosophical note; nothing specific emerged.

The therapist's intervention apparently did not in fact allude to the central intrapsychic problem with which the patient was dealing. It related to an incidental issue, one which, at another time, might be more pertinent. It therefore promoted intellectualization, isolation, and rumination in the patient and was unproductive. The development of the latent transference theme was broken off, and the defenses of displacement and rumination which the therapist offered were welcomed and used defensively by the patient.

Among the most unfortunate defenses against the unfolding of anxiety-laden associations are those offered by the therapist to the patient. We may conclude too that incorrect questions prompt defensiveness, and not insight; and that we must therefore attempt to restrict questions to those that are pertinent and relevant to the main context and central issues of each session. To conclude this vignette:

> In the next session, the patient's rage at the therapist erupted quite openly and without disguise. His silence proved indeed to be the source of intense anxiety and intrapsychic conflict and fantasies within the patient, and the rage at this "desertion" was reinforced by the therapist's failure of understanding.

Having sampled some of the consequences of an inopportune question, let us consider the consequences of correctly used questions.

> Mr. D.Z. had been in therapy for about a year. He was depressed, relating poorly to women, and unable to hold a steady job. He had been talking rather vaguely about his sexual problems and had mentioned fantasies of raping and impregnating young girls. In the session to be discussed, he repeated these fantasies and then described a date with his present girlfriend. He mentioned, in passing, that he had masturbated after the date, and then went on with further trivial details about this relationship.
>
> The context here seems clear: it is the patient's sexual conflicts and his related conscious and unconscious fantasies. The therapist, making this deduction, decided to ask about the masturbating. He did so because the associations had become repetitious and the material was not developing or deepening, and because the patient had so quickly gone on to other matters after mentioning the masturbation. He therefore had good reason to suspect suppressed and probably repressed material here, and there was a clear indication to inquire in that direction since the patient had become defensive. A reasonable alternative would have been to confront the patient with his defensive avoidance. Such an intervention would non-verbally imply an inquiry into what had been left out.
>
> In the session, the patient was therefore asked what he imagined while masturbating. In response, Mr. D.Z. described a series of unreported fantasies, most of them related to anal intercourse with women, during which he abuses and demeans them. This then led in two directions: first, that he was not using contraception when having vaginal intercourse with his girlfriends; and second, to previously unreported memories of his father taking his temperature rectally from infancy into his teens and his erections in response to this procedure.

The pertinence of this question was strongly confirmed here; new avenues were opened up. There emerged previously unreported acting out and a repressed childhood memory that conveyed important genetic material related to the patient's sexual conflicts. Good questions, properly timed, can be the crucial intervention in a session and can alter intrapsychic defenses in a manner similar to proper confrontations.

With a patient who acts out, questions are one means of promoting a necessary split in his "ego" (i.e., self) so that he begins to stand apart from and observe his behavior; this is a first step toward the development of controls and insight. Even if not productive of deeper material, then, such inquiries have value as a model for identification for the patient, and as a means of querying rather than sanctioning such behavior. Such questions are on a continuum with confrontations (see Chapter 13), and are utilized when interpretation of the acting out is not feasible from the material. Consider these clinical illustrations:

> Mrs. E.A., who was well into therapy, had spoken of her longings for a son; she had two daughters. In the next session, she mentioned, in passing, that she had forgotten twice to take her birth control pills. Later in the session, the therapist simply asked her what came to mind about not taking the pills, and she immediately connected it to her wish to get pregnant in the hope of having a son.

> Mr. E.B., a teenager, was prone to repetitive acting out, and was slowly realizing it in his therapy. During the month which marked the date of his mother's major surgery some years before, he finished working in New York City and impulsively drove all night to visit a friend in Washington, D.C. There was no mention of the considerable dangers involved, but instead, the patient detailed the visit. The therapist asked what occurred to the patient about the fact that he had driven all night. Mr. E.B. then reviewed this aspect of the situation with considerable thought, recognizing the risks that he had taken, and ultimately acknowledging the suicidal impli-

cations of this behavior. He then confirmed his own insight by connecting it to his mother's surgery and to the fact that, while driving, he kept thinking of putting on his safety belt and shoulder strap, but had failed to do so. In a subsequent session, he remembered his suicidal-depressive response to her surgery at the time in his childhood when it had been done.

Compact, well-directed questions are amply confirmed through sudden insights and the recall of previously repressed material (see Chapter 18). They are in keeping with the central context of the hour, and are attempts to lift the repression directed against important derivatives. When they are well designed, they are often made with an interpretation in mind, and afford the patient the opportunity to work toward conveying, and then understanding, the unconscious meanings of his behavior or conscious fantasy.

The main principles underlying the use of questions can be summarized thus:

1. *Ask questions wisely and in context, not at random nor too often.* Try not to deviate from the central theme at hand.

2. *Ask questions when some piece of material (a fantasy, dream, or odd behavior) hints at far more than the patient has revealed.* This is particularly telling when it is followed by defensiveness and a lack of developing associations. Also, consider questions into gross and important ambiguities and distortions.

3. *Use questions to provide a model for self-exploration with patients who act out and deny, and are not inwardly oriented.*

4. *Listen to responses to questions as you would to any intervention.* Confirmation consists basically of the development of new and meaningful associations; failure to confirm is usually reflected in rumination and intellectualization (see Chapters 18 and 19).

PITFALLS IN USING QUESTIONS

EXCESSIVE QUESTIONING AND COUNTER-TRANSFERENCE-BASED QUESTIONS

Some therapists disrupt many, if not almost all, of their sessions with their patients by asking repeated, inherently unnecessary and antitherapeutic questions. In these "questioners," I have detected evidence of a strong fear of unconscious and primitive fantasies (frequent questions generally will keep the material from deepening and confine the therapeutic field to the surface); a great need to control and manipulate their patients; considerable anger and destructiveness which is expressed in what often becomes a barrage of questions, overwhelming the patient; a great deal of unresolved narcissism which leads them to believe erroneously that their thoughts and questions take precedence over the patient's productions; and a marked confusion regarding the nature of psychotherapy—to name a few of the most apparent countertransference problems reflected in this style.

Countertransference-based questions include many that are consciously rationalized, but actually serve seductive and defensive needs in the therapist. The former is most often reflected in appropriate questions regarding the therapist himself that promote an anxiety-provoking and nontherapeutic focus on the person of the therapist, and tend to evoke erotic and erotized fantasies about, and sexual desires for, him (see Chapter 22). Unnecessary and excessive questions about the patient's sexual experiences and fantasies constitute another form that this problem takes.

The defensive use of questions is seen when the patient is developing his associations around a particular central theme which is creating anxiety in the therapist. Under such conditions, he may turn to a question which is related to peripheral associations of the patient, thereby shifting the focus of the material away from the theme that is disturbing to the therapist to something relatively innocuous for him. Out of his own anxiety, the patient will usually welcome the offer of the defensive displacement away from the emerging central theme, and will veer away from it. Often enough, he will eventually get back to his main problem, since he wants to deal with the anxiety it is evoking; thus, the therapist who is capable of perceptive listening has an opportunity for self-analysis and correction, and nondefensive exploration the second time around.

The therapist's specific motives for the error of asking too many or ill-timed or disruptive questions are matters for self-exploration (see Chapter 22). I will briefly illustrate countertransference-based questions which were unconsciously detected by the patient and referred to in the latent content of his associations. They were also seen as erroneous in supervision, and nonconfirmation was predicted. In addition to attention to reflections in the material from patients, the detection of such errors by the therapist is based on subjective awareness and insight. A good guide is to explore your motives and fantasies regarding your questions and your relationship with the patient, when the following occurs:

1. *You are asking too many of them, more than a couple a session.*

2. *Your question does not help promote the development and unfolding of the material.*

3. *A session which seemed to be going well was somehow derailed after you had asked a question.*

4. *You have been asking questions and the patient has been regressing, acting out, and developing symptoms.*

5. *You have been asking questions and there is an apparent problem in the therapeutic alliance.* This could range from major resistances in the sessions, to acting out of transference fantasies, to threats of (and sometimes actual) termination.

I have observed many misapplications of questions, and shall illustrate with a single excerpt from the work of a seldom-silent questioner-therapist:

> Miss E.C. was a young woman in therapy for a couple of months. She was depressed, dated men who abused and demeaned her, and tended to act out in self-defeating and self-destructive ways. I will describe a fragment of a session during a period when the therapist had been actively questioning the patient.
>
> Miss E.C. began the hour by describing how she had absented herself from her job for several days to go off with a boyfriend. The business was located in a very dangerous neighborhood, and he wanted her to change her job but she did not really like the pressure from him. The therapist asked why the patient had not looked for a new job. Miss E.C. responded with superficial excuses and rationalizations, and then spoke of an occasional fear of

traveling on the subways. The therapist asked about this fear and the patient described how she worried that she might miss her station or be pushed onto the tracks while waiting on the platform. She then spoke of a robbery at work which had happened some time before and of her fear of horror movies, which sometimes prompted bad dreams. The therapist asked about these dreams and for any other dreams that the patient could recall. The latter then remembered a dream of returning to her home, which was out of town, and seeing her old boyfriends. Associating, she recalled that her mother never liked these friends and the therapist asked why. This led to a host of details about the young men Miss E.C. had dated and her general relationships with them. She then went on to describe the annoying and constant pressures that her current boyfriend put her under; he did it to irritate her. Somehow, she just complied with his demands, and hid her anger. The therapist asked her why she did such a thing; once again, the patient rationalized and ruminated.

This patient was bombarded with questions, some of which were unnecessarily directive and aggressive in tone. The therapist's questions were random and aimless, and in supervision, it was predicted early in the presentation of this session that the patient would feel controlled and attacked, and respond accordingly on some level. This was confirmed toward the end of the session when the patient spoke of her boyfriend's excessive pressures on her, her submission to them, and her hidden anger. A possible earlier expression of the way this patient responded to the therapist's excessive questions was the reference to her fear of being pushed in front of a train.

The net result is a sadomasochistic therapeutic misalliance in which the patient's need to be attacked and abused is gratified by the therapist; this is incompatible with the production of insight and inner change. It is, instead, a mutual acting out of transference and countertransference fantasies and impulses. On the part of the patient who continued at a most dangerous job and with a destructive boyfriend, it reflects an important aspect of her psychopathology and unresolved intrapsychic conflicts and fantasies, and it was being repeated rather than altered in her treatment. As for the therapist, her need to dominate and attack her patient is gratified by her excessive questioning; further, her questions seemed based on a fear of, and a wish to, perpetuate the patient's masochism. Her comments in her discussion during supervision seemed to confirm these impressions.

A further consequence of this questioning is that no central theme develops in the session. The associations become scattered, though they eventually revolve around the patient's conscious and unconscious response to the therapist's actual and technically incorrect behavior (see Chapter 22). No deepening of the material occurs, nor is consistent therapeutic work possible; isolated fragments prevail. Frequent questions will most certainly delay, if not prevent, the emergence of derivatives of repressed fantasies, as it did in this session. The result is a form of "trivia therapy," and not effective psychotherapy.

HYPOTHETICAL QUESTIONS

I have observed a number of therapists who ask theoretical or hypothetical questions of their patients and I have never seen a confirmatory, material-developing response to these questions. Theoretically, this makes sense: asking an unreal and therefore intellectualized question regarding something that does not constitute an active adaptive task or source of anxiety for the patient is bound to promote defensive and hollow ruminating and intellectualizing. Such questions should not be used by the therapist.

Actually, hypothetical questions are often far more than empty queries; they may convey, in their content and manner of presentation, anxiety-provoking and traumatic dangers to the patient, and disrupt the therapeutic alliance and treatment itself. I will offer two vignettes. The first relates to a minor hypothetical question which served as a brief distraction and was quickly dropped, while the second is far more complex and will enable us to establish a number of important additional principles of technique.

Mr. E.D. was a depressed man who had just begun

therapy. He called to cancel his fourth session ten minutes before it was to begin, stating that his car wouldn't start. His therapist offered a later session and the patient said he didn't think that the car would be ready in time.

The patient began the next hour by asking if he was responsible for the fee for the missed session since he had called and it was the car that was at fault. The therapist responded that he was, indeed, responsible for the fee, reminding the patient that he had offered a later hour. He then asked the patient how he felt the matter would have been dealt with if he had gotten his car started right after the call cancelling the hour.

The patient ignored this last question; said that the therapist was right; and went on to talk about how much his wife criticized therapy and psychotherapists. He also spoke of the strict upbringing of his childhood, and his guilt over his excessive drinking and cheating on his wife. She treated emotional problems as if they were crimes.

The hypothetical question here was pointless and distracting. It appears that the therapist was confused and even disturbed over charging Mr. E.D. for the missed session and in some fumbling, hypothetical way, endeavoring to cover his tracks by confusing the issues. It led nowhere directly, though it may have contributed to the patient's subsequent rage at the therapist.

The central issue here is the therapist's handling of the cancelled hour. In Chapter 5, I pointed out the ground rules for dealing with such issues: never offer substitute sessions before exploring the cancellation with the patient; and never defensively justify such a stance to the patient nor quibble over his basic responsibilities for his sessions, once established. Explore the patient's reactions instead. In this vignette, the patient cannot help but be confused by the offer of a substitute hour and then the charge for the missed session. Why should he not also be offered a later make-up session? The inconsistency contributes to a potential rupture in the therapeutic alliance, and to the patient's anger and guilt. Further, it is compounded by the therapist's too-quick answer regarding the fee and his failure to explore the patient's feelings and fantasies regarding it.

While more could be said regarding this vignette, let us instead move on to consider this clinical situation:

> Mrs. E.E. was a severely depressed woman who sought therapy when the oldest of her three living sons became a teenager and she felt that she could not handle him. A younger son had died three years earlier in the following way: the patient had been playfully wrestling with him on the floor of their living room and this had led to a quarrel with her husband, and considerable shouting. The son had run out of the house frightened, and was hit by a bus and killed. Added sources of guilt and depression were Mrs. E.E.'s many affairs, and the likelihood that her oldest boy was not fathered by her husband; as he grew older, he resembled one of her lovers more and more closely.
>
> In the first weeks of her therapy, she reviewed these and other facets of her life and her depression. The session to be discussed occurred immediately before the therapist's winter vacation. Mrs. E.E. began the hour by describing an intensification of her feelings of depression, hopelessness, confusion, and wishes to die. She eventually focused on her fears that the illegitimacy of her oldest son might be revealed; this thought made her feel worthless and bad. She sometimes thought that she would be better off if he were dead and gone, but that idea upset her still more. She viewed these uncertainties and her difficulties with him as punishment for her contribution to the death of her other son; if she had not played so wildly with him, the accident would never have occurred.

The therapist intervened here. Before considering what he said to the patient, let us attempt to formulate the material to this point.

It seems likely that the context here is the pending separation from the therapist and that the themes of loss, guilt, shame, and anger relate in some way to Mrs. E.E.'s fantasies about his departure. From this, it appears that the proper intervention might have been to remain silent in the hope of detecting a bridge, or even some direct reference, to the therapist and the pending separation. In the absence of such a linking element, should the session be approaching its end, the therapist might intervene by relating the material to the vacation and demonstrating its link to the death of her son and her rage over being left; he could then attempt to explore why the vacation was evoking fears of exposure, and feelings of guilt and worthlessness.

> The therapist in fact told Mrs. E.E. that she was using her worries about the possible exposure of the paternity of her son as a decoy and a cover, and as a reality through which she was protecting herself from her real and deeper feelings of worthlessness, which were there long before this child was conceived. He then proposed his hypothetical question: after all, he added, what really would happen if she actually told her husband about her son, or if it were known? (His tone implied that it would be of little consequence.)
>
> The patient immediately panicked and said that she could not let her husband or anyone know about her oldest son; it would be too upsetting. How could it possibly help therapy to reveal this and get it out of the way so she could work on her real feelings of worthlessness? She went on in this vein, quite upset. The therapist said that he was not suggesting that she tell her husband, but merely that she explore it in the sessions. While still guilty and upset, she became calmer and the session ended.

There is much to be considered here; I will confine myself to commenting on the effect of the hypothetical question, and a few important additional issues:

The hypothetical question was experienced, with some justification, as a directive and a trauma. Instead of the pending vacation which should have served as the context for the hour, it became the central problem of the session. It evoked intense conflict and anxiety in the patient in the following ways:

It created a direct conflict between the patient and the therapist regarding whether she should reveal her secret to her husband even though it would cause her considerable suffering. If she did not do so, she risked the disapproval of the therapist and, according to him, the failure of the treatment.

It evoked rage at the therapist for his hurtful suggestion, and intrapsychic conflicts regarding the expression or control of this anger, for fear of permanently losing him.

It is likely that the patient also felt misunderstood and condemned by the therapist, since he completely missed her worries about his vacation and implied that she was a bad person for many secret reasons. The consequent guilt, self-condemnation, and anger undoubtedly all contributed to her panic.

The suggestion that she confess, and reveal her secret badness, must have touched upon a host of intrapsychic conflicts and guilt related to her sexual acting out, her seductive fantasies regarding her dead and her oldest sons, and countless other guilty secrets. The panic response is quite understandable in light of all this.

The therapist seems to have a countertransference-based need to have the patient deny and avoid her guilt over the death of her son, despite the fact that it was an important source of neurotic problems for her. He also needed to avoid all references to his pending vacation, and to condemn the patient and even suggest that she do a penance for her "sins." Therefore, the patient had real cause to be frightened by him (see Chapter 22).

The hypothetical question was the crux of the therapist's expression of his own difficulties and the trigger of the patient's panic. It cannot, in any way, be viewed as a harmless error. It was devastating to the patient and derailed the therapeutic alliance and treatment. These questions may contain powerful implicit communications and reflect antitherapeutic, personal fantasies of the therapist. They therefore can be destructive or seductive, and seriously disturbing to the therapy.

Technically, this is an example of the therapist's interpreting the patient's use of reality as a defense long before the reality trauma itself has been detoxified and resolved by her. We must learn to make interventions on the surface, and that guilt may stem from real experiences and the fantasies they evoke. Only after the guilt and intrapsychic conflicts evoked by the death of her son and the illegitimacy of her other boy had been worked through over several months, could we justify labeling these as defensive covers for other sources of guilt; and we could do so only when the material from the patient pointed to another specific unconscious reason for the guilt.

Actually, the defensive use of this material deserved interpretation first, since it was primary. This follows an important principle of intervening: interpret and deal with defenses, their content and usage, before interpreting the content of the unconscious fantasies that they cover (see Chapter 14). Thus Mrs. E.E 's references to anger, guilt and a sense of loss regarding her two sons was a compromise: a defensive avoidance of her fantasies regarding the therapist's vacation, and a derivative expression in displaced form of these very fantasies. A correct interpretation would have alluded to both of these facets of the material.

In conclusion, then, the use of hypothetical questions is ill-advised and is to be avoided. They are, in general, a vehicle for countertransference-based aggressions against, or seductions of, the patient; defensive rationalizations by the therapist; or an invitation to the patient to intellectualize and move away from the central context of the session: the intrapsychic conflicts and sources of anxiety with which he is dealing.

FAILURE TO USE QUESTIONS WHEN INDICATED

Often enough in supervision, I have observed sessions in which the patient has reported a clearly significant but obviously incomplete communication and the therapist has not inquired into it. This failure to ask a question led to the prediction that the material from the patient would not develop and, at times, that a significant regression would occur; these predictions were almost always confirmed. Among the more common untapped communications avoided by both patient and therapist were allusions to some kind of serious acting out that merited specific investigation, and the report of a dream. Less frequently, it was a conscious fantasy or a childhood memory.

Avoidance of questions about, or a confrontation with, acting out may express a sanction, conscious or unconscious, of the maladaptive behavior of the patient (see Chapter 11). It reinforces the use of action instead of thought in dealing with inner conflicts and can create an antitherapeutic alliance in which acting out prevails both during and outside the sessions, and insight and inner change do not occur.

Avoidance of dreams is striking in some therapists who defensively ignore fantasy material of all kinds and who, I suspect, fear their patient's unconscious fantasies. While manifest dreams may, indeed, be reported for largely defensive purposes, they often provide crucial, otherwise unavailable avenues for associations and the development in depth of the material of the session. If the patient ignores such a dream—and most are potentially of this kind—or associates only briefly to it, it is incumbent upon the therapist to inquire further. If not, valuable material is lost and the session usually will not jell. The same principles apply when a previously repressed event, memory, or fantasy is reported. The therapist should allow the patient to develop and associate to it, but if he does not do so fully, a question is essential.

To reiterate, the therapist's motives for avoiding inquiries are most often those of a defensive nature; they reflect a poor understanding of the session and of psychotherapy, a preference for staying on the surface or working with realities rather than intrapsychic conflicts, a need to promote acting out and regression in the patient, and fears of unconscious fantasies.

Failure to ask appropriate questions may indicate a basic failure in technique. The therapist should be interested in obtaining additional, much needed associations to manifest threads which are suggestive, in a given context, of considerable latent content. Without such inquiries, the material of the session remains flat or unclear. This failure to explore may be based, first, on the therapist's impatient and overvalued urge to make interpretations, often without sufficient material from the patient. Many therapists are so eager to do this that they utilize fragments of associations from the patient and fill in the gaps themselves—or not at all. Second, such therapists do not value properly the associations from the patient, preferring their own thoughts and fantasies. Third, they lack a faculty for sensing when associations are ripe and likely to be rich in latent content. Finally, they are inherently impatient and hasty, and have difficulty in giving the patient sufficient time to develop the material, and work coldly with his associations in an over-intellectualized way. The outcome is virtually always nonconfirmatory and regressive responses in the patient (see Chapter 19).

These therapists teach us to listen at length to the patient and to value the associations which he can bring to bear on a particular topic, event, dream, or fantasy. These associations will often be quite surprising, and convey manifest or latent content otherwise totally inaccessible to us. On the other hand, properly timed and stated questions acknowledge that the patient is the exclusive source of the material and the associations out of which we build our formulations and interventions, and reflect interest in exploring the ramifications of material that appears meaningful and that he has not sufficiently associated to directly.

We must, therefore, balance the two aspects: we should learn when to let the patient roam about verbally, and when to bring a manifest element into focus for direct associations. The therapist must not be too hasty; a good general rule of thumb is first to let the patient associate freely, while assessing the nature of the associations—as to whether they are defensive and ruminative, or full of manifest or latent content related to the central theme of the session. In the first case, a well-timed question may redirect the patient to the possibly important material, and result in more open, less defensive associations. If the patient then continues to be defensive, confrontation can be made.

In returning to a piece of behavior, a dream, fantasy, or any focal element, do not promote intellectualizing defenses by asking: "What do you think about this?" Rather, questions like: "What does this bring to mind?" encourage free associations and direct expression of experience, and are to be preferred to those that lead the patient toward detached self-observation rather than self-expression.

A brief vignette illustrates some of these points:

> Mr. E.F. was a young homosexual with a severe character disorder who had acted out homosexually during his therapist's vacation. His therapist, obviously annoyed, had, upon his return, at first ignored this behavior and

then commented upon it critically, without interpretation, stating out of context to the patient that once more he had gotten revenge for being left by finding self-destructive replacements for his therapist. Confirmation did not follow; instead, the patient justified his behavior.

Mr. E.F. was late for the next hour. He described how he had completed a lot of unfinished business at work, and then reported two dreams. In the first, his mother was yelling at him about a marihuana-smoking friend whom she did not like. The patient could not get her to stop, though she was yelling at him for the wrong reasons. In the second, a monster was trying to kill him.

In association, he mentioned having had a pleasant conversation with his mother the evening before the dream. Earlier, he had been with a girlfriend, who was a "pain in the ass" and a know-it-all; the dream could have been about her. He had been to a friend, a priest, and had had a long talk with him. Other ruminations followed.

The therapist asked the patient what he thought about the first dream. The patient talked at length about the difference between his mother in the dream and in real life. The therapist then asked the patient if he thought that the dream and his lateness were due to a worry that he would be nagged by the therapist because of his behavior during the separation. The patient said that he did not think so, denied concerns about his behavior during the therapist's vacation, and blamed himself for not doing enough about everything. He then talked at length about failing to take care of an aspect of his job for which he was not actually responsible.

In the next hour, the patient ruminated anxiously and without focus.

The context of this middle session appears to be the therapist's hostile remarks in the previous hour (cf. the yelling mother and the monster). Both dreams deserved inquiry since the patient largely avoided them and they were undoubtedly related to the main theme of the hour. Asking the patient what he thought about his first dream prompted rumination, as we would expect. Any question which might have led the patient toward a tie between the manifest dream and latent fantasies about the therapist would have been preferable. The therapist could also have made the general query: "What more do your dreams bring to mind?" The mutual avoidance of the dream of the monster was especially unfortunate. As a result of all of these errors in technique, the session ended in confusion and was followed by an anxious, regressed, and chaotic hour.

Another brief vignette will illustrate a simple failure to inquire and its consequences:

> Miss E.G. was a college student with a moderate character disorder, and complaints of depression and lack of involvement in her work and relationships. She had similar difficulties in associating meaningfully in the therapy, and the therapist had responded to this problem entirely by asking her extra questions to encourage her to be more productive. While he learned a little more about her life, little had changed within the patient.
>
> She began one hour by mentioning that a boy with whom she had had a casual affair some years earlier had just been married. She dreamt that she was dancing with him while his mother watched. She went on to relate fantasies of marrying this young man and then discussed a conflict between her new school hours and the time for her sessions. She spoke of a tough professor with whom she had elected to take a course and ruminated about school. Then she spoke of not liking to be stared at by the therapist, of not liking to feel like his patient, and of how depressed she became when nothing happened in her sessions.

There are two main points to be made here from this vignette. First, the therapist's failure to investigate the patient's dream contributed not only to an unfocused hour, but to the patient's eventual depression and complaints. This mutual avoidance of potentially meaningful material undoubtedly was a significant factor in the patient's generally hollow sessions. Second, it is technically inadvisable to attempt to deal with resistances such as ruminating by asking many direct questions. The unconscious motives and fantasies on which such defenses are based must be analyzed and resolved if such a patient is to communicate meaningfully. The therapist's positive capacity to detect meaningful derivatives and bring them into focus for exploration also can contribute to the favorable development of therapy in such patients. With Miss E.G., the dream and her eventual associations to the therapist hint that erotic transference fantasies were one motivating factor in her defensive remoteness. Questions relevant to this impression might have furthered the analysis of the roots of this resistance, and helped to modify it.

From this chapter, it is clear that questions are an important intervention in psychotherapy and are not to be taken lightly. Everything that the therapist does, or fails to do, in his relationship with the patient is significant for both of them. He must aim to be both spontaneous and correct in his use of questions; to ask them usually after consideration if they are necessary in the context of the session; but to feel free to use them quickly when pertinent.

CLARIFICATIONS

CLARIFICATIONS OF THE PATIENT'S ASSOCIATIONS AND BEHAVIOR

Clarifying statements by the therapist overlap with questions, confrontations, and interpretations, and may be used in a manner comparable to any of these. Thus, there are few principles that apply to clarifications alone; most are adapted from the other interventions to which they are related. The main technical principles regarding this intervention are:

1. *Clarifications may be part of a question or by themselves imply a query.* The therapist may ask the patient to clarify something which was difficult to hear or which was ambiguous or confusing. He may also make a direct request to the patient to clarify further a particular event, fantasy, dream, or any communication.

The emphasis here is on the patient's conscious thoughts and associations, and on additional facts and fantasies related to the area in question. In using clarifying inquiries, the therapist should follow the principles already established for the use of questions; they must be relevant to the central theme and not an expression of countertransference problems. Clarifying important ambiguities is a valuable therapeutic tool when indicated. On the other hand, do not become a "clarificationist" through excessive use of this intervention. With patients who are repetitively vague and ambiguous, and who often avoid mentioning important details of fantasies and experiences, the therapist should analyze these defenses; do not be seduced into too many inquiries.

2. *Clarifications may imply a confrontation (see Chapter 13).* The therapist repeats what the patient has said or done in an effort to confront him with it, and to promote further consideration and associations. He may do so, for instance, in the hope of developing the unconscious meanings or ego defects reflected by a piece of acting out, or to develop the material regarding the conflicts and unconscious fantasies related to a dream or conscious fantasy. The principles related to confrontations apply here and will be developed in Chapter 13.

3. *A clarification may also be a subtle form of interpretation, of special importance because it is designed to involve the patient actively in formulating the interpretation or insight.* The clarification itself may be worded with new accents which will lead the patient to detect the unconscious fantasies latent in the manifest material. Thus, when a sequence of associations in an identified context reflect an unconscious connection or fantasy which is rather clear to the therapist, he may choose simply to repeat or minimally modify the patient's comments in the hope that the latter will, himself, identify the latent content therein contained.

Without defining interpretations more fully here (see Chapter 14), I shall briefly illustrate this type of clarification:

> Mrs. E.H. was a depressed woman in once-weekly therapy. Her father had died during surgery when she was five and his loss had left its mark on the rest of her life. In one session, she began by detailing a dilatation

and curettage that she had had the previous week. She had been very upset, and feared the need for major surgery. The nurse had removed the nail polish which her daughter had painted on her nails, and she had become acutely anxious. She was frightened of not being able to breathe under the anesthetic and recalled that while she was actually anesthetized, she had dreamt of tumbling through heaven and of her father being there somewhere.

When some rumination followed, the therapist clarified the sequence of the associations by repeating the main elements in it, noting the apparent sources of her anxiety, wondering about the meaning of the loss of the nail polish, and emphasizing the culmination of the sequence in the dream about heaven and her father. The patient responded by clarifying the meanings of the ambiguous elements in her communications and by a crystallization of some insights. Thus, she quickly realized that her fears of surgery were related to her father's death and to her repetitive fantasies of dying and joining him in heaven. As a child, she had imagined many versions of his death, including one in which he was smothered by the anesthetic. The nail polish was a link to her daughter, without which she feared that she might die and never see her child again—much as her father had done to her.

In this vignette, the therapist's clarification of the sequence of the material only hinted at the unconscious content that he had in mind, and was made in an effort to see how much the patient could develop and bring into awareness on her own. The intervention was confirmed by the addition of previously unreported fantasies and memories, and much heretofore latent material became conscious. The patient's defenses were readily bypassed by the intervention.

CLARIFICATIONS OF THE THERAPIST'S COMMENTS AND BEHAVIOR

This form of clarification may come spontaneously from the

therapist or in response to a question from the patient. Once again, a matter that seems on the surface to be relatively simple is often the source of considerable confusion and difficulty for the therapist; I shall briefly outline a few principles.

1. *If the therapist states something to the patient that is, upon reflection, ambiguous, he should feel free to restate it at an appropriate moment, assuming that it is important to the development of the session.* If the patient goes off into other important directions, however, he should allow his unclear comment to pass. If relevant, the matter will come up again and can be handled more precisely and correctly at that time.

2. *If the patient asks the therapist directly to clarify part of his intervention, it is in general best to do so, while at the same time making note of the area of his confusion.* However, repetitive questioning of interventions suggests either that the therapist cannot express himself clearly, either in general or to the particular patient, or that the patient is resisting listening to his interventions. Both must be analyzed and resolved, the former as a countertransference problem for the therapist and the latter to be worked through from the patient's material.

3. *In the matter of therapist-initiated changes in hours, vacation plans, and the like, simple non-personal clarifications of relevant questions are in order.* However, questions that are made about plans already well defined to the patient are usually indicative of conflicts about the change. Thus, at times, the therapist may delay any direct response and, instead, ask the patient to clarify and explore his own question and its implications. After the relevant conflicts and fantasies are developed and analyzed, he may then make the clarification.

4. *In response to queries from the patient, there are several things to keep in mind.* Do not be harsh and unnecessarily frustrating in responding to realistic and appropriate questions from the patient. Too many therapists mechanically react with the pat, easily caricatured: "Why do you ask?" or "What does your question bring to mind?" Often, such a response serves the therapist's defensive and hostile needs, rather than the patient and the therapy.

On the other hand, do not lose sight of your role as a therapist who must listen in depth and respond therapeutically. Because a realistic question is asked, it does not follow that the therapist is obliged to respond on that level, especially if deeper implications are evident. In all, maintain a reasonable and human balance between a direct answer and the need, when indicated, to delay responding in favor of analyzing.

5. *At times, a patient will ask the therapist to clarify an intervention from the previous session.* Almost without exception, I recommend that such requests be analyzed and not answered. There are many reasons for this, including the fact that this is much like dealing with a hypothetical question. It is not real for the moment; it leads to intellectualizing instead of work with current issues, and constitutes a sharing of defenses with the patient. Further, it shifts the focus in the session from the patient to the therapist, at a time when the patient's continued associations should prevail.

13 Confrontations

THE CORRECT USE OF CONFRONTATIONS

Confrontations, and clarifications that also confront, constitute the most important intervention arising from the manifest content of material from patients. They are critical in assisting the patient to modify and correct ego dysfunctions such as impairments in controls (acting out), or in thinking, reality testing, and object relationships. When properly selected, they further the development of the material and central theme in a session, and foster the revelation of derivatives of unconscious conflicts and fantasy. They are thus a preliminary step toward interpretation.

Confrontations are used to bring into focus conscious thoughts, real situations and conflicts, and realistic choices open to the patient in a given situation. Properly used, they help him to resolve these problems so that intrapsychic conflicts and unconscious fantasies may then be analyzed. They are especially useful in directing the patient's attention to surface resistances and defenses manifested in the session, thereby enabling him to modify them. They do not develop the links to the specific unconscious fantasies that lie below the surface, although they may shade off into unconscious elements by helping the patient to become aware of apparent implicit meanings in his associations or behavior.

By definition, then, confrontations are interventions in which the therapist directs the patient's attention to a piece of behavior or a thought that is evident to both parties. By saying, in effect, "Take a look at what you are doing," or "Consider what you just said," the therapist fosters a split in the patient's ego (actually, in the self or total personality), so that he is better able to stand aside from himself and observe his own thoughts and actions (see Devereux, 1951; Bibring, 1954; Corwin, 1972; Buie and Adler, 1972; Adler and Buie, 1972; Weisman, 1972; and Adler and Meyerson, 1973).

Confrontations differ from interpretations in this greater surface emphasis and stronger relation to real rather than neurotic and intrapsychic conflicts; in the failure to delineate specific unconscious fantasies; and in the frequent absence of genetic reference because of the emphasis on current problems and defenses in confrontations, although past facts and fantasies may be referred to (see Chapter 14).

Acting Out and Repetitive Patterns of Behavior

Let us begin with this vignette:

> Mrs. E.K. was in therapy because of depressive episodes caused, on the surface, largely by her husband's several affairs. In one session, she described how she had read a note from her husband's mistress that had been left on his dresser, and she went on to rage against the two of them. It became clear as she continued, and the therapist eventually pointed this out to her, that she had ignored the existence of the note and had never mentioned it to her husband, even though it was left in a place where she would inevitably find it. The patient responded immediately to this intervention by realizing that she had unwittingly promoted the continuation of the affair by her failure to confront her husband with the note, and went on to explore the implications of this sudden insight.
>
> In a subsequent session, Mrs. E.K. described how her husband was telephoned at home by a girlfriend who was in acute distress with an emergency. The patient agreed

to her husband's going to see this other woman and proceeded to rationalize: she feared that harm would come
to the woman; this was an exceptional situation; and so
on. The therapist repeated these latter excuses back to the
patient in a questioning tone and this led her again to
recognize at once her own participation in, and promotion
of, her husband's affairs.

The first intervention was a confrontation, while the second was
actually more in the form of a clarification with confrontational
aspects. Both related to the behavior of the patient and the surface
implications, albeit unconscious ones, which the patient had failed
to recognize. Confrontations of this kind enabled this patient to
recognize her own unconscious encouragement of her husband's
behavior, though they did not indicate the unconscious motivation
and the specific fantasies and genetic experiences on which it was
based. This is, however, the first step toward such discoveries.

Confrontations of this kind also foster improved ego functioning.
Here, the patient was helped to observe and consider her own
behavior, something she was not especially prone to do. Acting out,
of which this behavior is one form, is most often accompanied by
defensive denial of the true implications of the behavior and by a
related failure in self-scrutiny, which is an important aid to the
development of impulse controls and the curtailment of destructive
acting out.

These particular confrontations also inherently demonstrated to
the patient her defenses of denial, avoidance, and rationalization.
They also alluded to aspects of her failure to resolve her real conflicts with her husband, and pointed toward the basis for this in her
own intrapsychic conflicts and unconscious fantasies. Thus, we see
that confrontations may serve to bring into awareness repressed
aspects of surface behavior that the patient has failed to recognize,
but not unconscious fantasy systems, to which they can, however,
prepare the way. Unfortunately, many therapists confine their work
to this confrontational level, and fail to go beyond it; effective inner
change can occur only if the underlying specific unconscious fantasies are reached and resolved.

Mrs. E.K.'s failure to confront her husband with his behavior may serve as a model for the therapist to avoid. Failure on his part to confront his patient with dangerous or destructive behavior constitutes a sanction of the action; it will promote acting out and acting in, and generally poor controls. Thus, confrontations must be made when indicated; failure to do so nonverbally supports the patient's disturbed behavior. However, certain dangers must be kept in mind: such confrontations must not be made too quickly, intolerantly, or in a morally condemning tone. The patient must be allowed freedom of behavioral exploration; confrontations must not be used to control or direct the patient. It is essential that the therapist be aware of the implications of maladaptive behavior and explore them with the patient tactfully. The outcome will be comparable to that with Mrs. E.K.; both interventions made to her were confirmed through sudden, freshly discovered self-awareness (see Chapter 18). Correct confrontations modify the patient's defenses and permit new, meaningful material to enter consciousness.

I will now illustrate another confrontation of acting out, which is one major indication of a need for this intervention, whether or not it is accompanied at the time by any interpretive comments.

> Miss E.L. was an adolescent with a strong propensity to act out through poor school work, drug-taking, and the repeated choice of sadistic boyfriends. In one session, she alluded for the first time to the fact that she was having sexual relations with her current boyfriend. She then recounted previous sexual experiences, and, in light of her pathology, the therapist asked if she had used contraception. The patient replied that she used a kind of rhythm method, and the therapist pointed out the obvious risks involved. The patient then reviewed these herself and subsequently insisted on proper contraception.

In this instance, the patient was actually aware of the risks inherent in her behavior, but repressed and suppressed them. At times, confrontations may be part of an educating process with stress on thinking things out and controlling behavior that is destructive to the patient or to others. The therapist must question such behavior through confronting the patient with it, in contrast, for example, to Miss E.L.'s parents, who constantly ignored clues of this kind and thereby fostered her acting out. The value of this surface, reality-oriented work is not to be underestimated, though it must always eventually be supplemented by interpretive interventions.

Often, a patient begins a session by describing a piece of acting out. The therapist's job is to listen to the material *before* confronting the patient with the surface implications of his behavior. In this way, he may detect the context of the behavior and its unconscious meanings, and be in a position to also interpret aspects of it when he makes his confrontation. Premature confrontations focus the patient on the surface and prevent deeper material from emerging, offering to the patient a defense that fosters the repression of relevant unconscious fantasies. The therapist must learn to use confrontations only when it becomes clear that deeper material is not at the moment available.

A good illustration of this comes from a therapy where the patient was in the process of acting in and deciding to quit therapy. This is an anxiety-provoking moment for any therapist, and all the more calls for proper technique. He must listen before intervening, in the hope of understanding the unconscious basis for the flight. Only when this is not discernible, is it justifiable to turn to a simple confrontation of the consequences of prematurely ending therapy (see Chapter 25).

> Mrs. E.M. had been in treatment for some time for severe characterological problems. She had mentioned termination occasionally throughout her therapy. She began the session under study by stating that she was thinking of leaving treatment. She went on to describe some recent quarrels and serious problems with her husband, and still other problems and anger with her children. She thought of running away. Her husband was losing interest in her sexually and she was frustrated and enraged. She imagined herself cutting up the sheets on the two beds in her bedroom. Other men seemed far more considerate and understanding than her spouse.

Let us pause here to ask what the therapist could have done at this point. I see two choices: first, he could search out through questions, or directly interpret in a general way, the sexual fantasies hinted at in the transference, based on Mrs. E.M.'s associations to sexual frustration and the attractiveness of other more understanding men. Such an intervention would be made on the hypothesis that the central adaptive and therapeutic context in the session must be the wish to terminate treatment—a potentially disastrous resistance that must take precedence. In addition, there are indications that the patient has a severe problem with her husband, which seems to be evoking intrapsychic conflicts, and both conscious and repressed fantasies related to her spouse and the therapist. These conflicting impulses were probably evoking considerable anxiety and were one factor prompting the thoughts of leaving the therapy.

But we must decide whether the derivatives of these underlying conflicts and fantasies are clear enough, and whether we anticipate that an interpretation of them would diminish or heighten Mrs. E.M.'s anxiety and defenses (see Chapter 17). I suspect that these expressions of the repressed fantasies were actually far too disguised and much too strongly defended to be accepted and confirmed by the patient. Thus, any reference to them probably would have increased her anxiety and risk the possibility of mobilizing added defenses through an actual decision to terminate.

The therapist could also interpret the wish to terminate as a displaced expression of her rage at her husband; if she did not lash out at him, she would at least destroy therapy. This intervention certainly could be made, but it seems to relate to a secondary set of unconscious fantasies and motives, and does not touch upon the central issues. Nonetheless, it could serve as a first step toward dealing with this material. I believe, however, that a confrontation is also indicated here.

This takes me to the second possible way of dealing with this situation, namely, confronting the patient with the inadequacies of such methods of dealing with her problems in life. As in the situation with her husband, running away resolves very little—nothing changes internally, and external change is effected at great cost to all concerned. If necessary, the therapist could also remind the patient of the ground rules pertaining to major decisions, and point out the advantages to her of exploring at length such a critical move as termination (this is, of course, a direct suggestion; see Chapter 16). Only if all this fails to alter the patient's decision regarding termination, would I recommend interpretation of the context and the unconscious fantasies and motives regarding the probably erotic transference. Thus, confrontations with the consequenses of potential or actual acting out may permit the patient to establish sufficient controls to forestall maladaptive behavior, and allow for added time in which derivatives of the repressed fantasies that are active at the moment can be expressed and interpreted.

Actually, Mrs. E.M.'s therapist chose this latter course because he felt that termination was actually not imminent and he hoped to gain sufficient time for less disguised derivatives to unfold in the sessions. This did, indeed, occur in a subsequent session when the expressions of the patient's sexual fantasies about the therapist appeared openly, and he was able to interpret their unconscious meanings and their relationship to the patient's thought of leaving treatment.

DEFENSES AND RESISTANCES

Confronting the patient with his manifest defenses as they are used by him outside and within the sessions constitutes an important initial step in the analysis and modification of these mechanisms. This is always ultimately supplemented by an in-depth analysis of the unconscious uses and meanings of such defenses so that lasting structural change is achieved (see Chapter 14). In the clinical material presented earlier in this chapter, we can identify several confrontations with defenses and recognize their consequences. Thus, when Mrs. E.K.'s therapist confronted her with her failure to mention her discovery of the note from her husband's girlfriend, this defense of denial and avoidance was promptly modified by the patient, who recognized the unconscious sanction that it implied, and later discussed the note with her spouse. Confrontation with her permission to her husband to go to another girlfriend had a similar outcome. With Miss E.L., the therapist's confronting question regarding contraception also immediately modified her avoidance of the risks she took in utilizing a questionable rhythm method; her behavior in this matter was also subsequently changed. In the material presented there, none of the underlying unconscious fantasies on which this behavior was based was unearthed. In later sessions, however, derivatives of this patient's repressed wishes for a child were expressed in her associations and analyzed.

Lastly, with Mrs. E.M., a confrontation with the hazards of premature termination of her treatment assisted her in controlling her impulses to quit therapy and fostered the eventual expression of the fantasies underlying this behavior.

In all, confrontations with defenses promote both their scrutiny and modification by the patient, and facilitate the revelation of the unconscious fantasies on which the defenses are based, as well as the repressed material covered by such defenses. Let us now turn to a vignette that illuminates the use of defenses as resistances within the session, and the effects of confronting the patient with them.

> Mr. E.N., a young man in therapy for moderate characterological problems, had been vaguely alluding to fears of becoming involved in homosexuality and said that he would somehow be humiliated because he had a small penis. At a party, he had been self-conscious and anxious. He described the party in detail and then spoke in even greater detail about his job. The therapist confronted the patient with his discomfort at the party and his shift away from it into rumination. The patient responded by describing at length his fears of becoming a homosexual, his attraction to men, his homosexual masturbatory fantasies, and several early adolescent homosexual experiences.

Here, a correct confrontation with the patient's use of the defences of isolation and rumination led to prompt modification of these defenses, with the revelation of many repressed memories and fantasies, which subsequently were analyzed and yielded a number of still deeper unconscious fantasies and memories. Such modification of defenses in response to direct confrontation is a remarkably frequent outcome. In principle, then, unless there is a specific reason to do otherwise, the therapist should confront the patient with his use of such defenses whenever they are prominent, especially when, he has reason to believe that readily available and important repressed fantasies lie beneath them.

The therapist should recognize the need to be alert to the defenses that his patient uses in his life, and in his sessions—the resistances that interfere with the unfolding of the latent content of the material, and the revelation of the patient's unconscious conflicts, fantasies and memories. On the whole, we interpret defenses before latent content or unconscious fantasies related to intrapsychic conflicts (see Chapters 14 and 17). Often, it is not necessary to wait to ascertain the underlying fantasy-content of resistances; direct confrontation with them is indicated whenever they are apparent and interfering with the development of the material. If we have enough material to understand the underlying fantasies, we include an interpretation when intervening. If not, confrontation alone is indicated for all kinds of defenses serving as resistances, including displacement, projection, intellectualization, rumination and more broadly, defensive acting out and flight.

A final, brief illustration of a confrontation with a resistance will complete this discussion:

> Mr. E.O. was a depressed young man with moderate characterological problems. He had difficulties with his school work and had to be sent to a private high school. He was quite guarded in his sessions, and began one of a series of ruminative hours by describing how his parents were pestering him about his school work. He lied to them about it and then felt guilty. In the session, he fell silent for a long period, occasionally speaking to describe the details of his quibbles with his parents and his lack of concentrated school work. The therapist confronted the patient with the flatness and emptiness of his thoughts, and Mr. E.O. spoke of his general forgetfulness. It reminded him that on the previous night, he had dreamt of hitchhiking. He recalled a girlfriend who had hitched a ride in Germany; the driver had attempted to attack her and she had fled. It had all happened near a concentration camp. The therapist pointed out that this must reflect the patient's fears of treatment and of himself, and must

account for his flight into silence. The patient agreed and the hour ended.

This is a typical sequence: silence and rumination—confrontation with these defenses—response by modifying the defenses and revealing new material which often contains derivatives that can be interpreted.

EGO DYSFUNCTIONS

One of the most common applications of this technique is to confront behavior and thinking which reflect ego impairments of all kinds. Because of this, such interventions are relatively frequent in the treatment of borderline and other severely disturbed patients. To prove effective, however, treatment of such patients cannot be confined to this level and must include interpretations of the unconscious fantasies which perpetuate such ego dysfunctions. Nonetheless, confrontations direct the patient's ego resources toward dealing with the dysfunctions and building new and effective structures. Nonverbally, they contribute to the atmosphere of a good, concerned, therapeutic milieu that promotes ego-development, and they can be used to focus on superego defects such as dishonesty, unrealistic ideals and punishments, and lacunae.

A brief illustration will enable us to discuss this type of confrontation further.

> Mr. E.P. was a young man who was in therapy because of depression, and failures in high school and college. He responded to any anxiety-provoking situation with acting out that reflected an intense use of denial, poor impulse controls, and impaired capacities for delay and internalizing conflicts. An example is his response to his therapist's pending vacation after six months of therapy. This experience was linked for him to his mother's illness and hospitalization when he was four, although almost all of the memories, fantasies and conflicts related to this event were strongly repressed. Thus, he began taking "downs" in large amounts, provoked a fight with his parents, and

left home, all within a few days that fell two weeks before
the separation from the therapist. Verbally, in his sessions, he was entirely unaware of any feelings and fantasies related to the pending interruption in therapy, or of
any connection between his behavior and that coming
event. Lacking derivatives of unconscious or even conscious fantasies and memories, the therapist elected to
confront the patient with the manner in which his behavior reflected ego impairments detrimental to himself and
others. He told him that he responded to stress, and
specifically to the pending separation, with silent anxiety
that prompted the search for immediate expressions of
his rage at his therapist through his actions at school and
at home. All of this was done, the therapist added, while
he denied every possible aspect of the matter that was
disturbing him and the dangers entailed in his behavior.

I will not detail here the patient's response, except to note that
this intervention evoked reflection on his part, improved controls,
and a budding sense of concern and conscience. In addition, in
subsequent sessions, some genetic material and derivatives of
repressed fantasies began to emerge. Throughout this treatment, this
sequence was repeated in one form or another many times, and the
outcome was favorable.

In this confrontation, the therapist introduced elements not in
the awareness of the patient, such as the connection between his
behavior and the therapist's pending vacation. Confrontations often
include the addition of such general and relatively simple unconscious elements, and therefore shade into interpretations. The distinctions here are not especially crucial; we must learn the use of
each of these interventions and mix them freely according to the
material available.

Confrontations of this kind promote healthy indentification with
the therapist, and with his ego-enhancing concepts and controls. They
are supplemented by a patient, thoughtful, analyzing, relaxed but
controlled, stance on the part of the therapist. Through these
avenues, considerable growth is generated in the patient.

Mr. E.P. was typical of the acting-out patient in that he began to report his dreams and conscious fantasies (daydreams) only after long periods of confrontational work. This, then, is an important role of confrontations: they are essential in helping the patient to bring destructive acting out under control and in promoting the shift to verbalized expressions of intrapsychic conflicts and fantasies. Put another way, they are important in moving the focus of therapy in these patients from real conflicts and problems, to those that are intrapsychic. The therapist can then recognize the derivatives of such inner conflicts, and develop and analyze them.

One last brief example of this kind of confrontation will conclude my discussion.

> Mrs. E.Q. was a widowed woman who sought brief therapy because she was acutely disturbed by a series of problems with her friends, neighbors, and co-workers. She described in some detail how one of her co-workers, a young and popular girl, was spreading malicious rumors about her, especially that Mrs. E.Q. was promiscuous at work and in her neighborhood. Her boss knew; the patient could tell from the way he looked at and spoke to her, and from discussions of his dislike of the color red and of a loose girl he knew. All of this must refer to her (the patient) as a whore. She was certain that she would be fired and was hard-pressed to explain why this had not happened.

> There were many other similar details. Her conclusions regarding the plot against her were based on inferences and the personal application of impersonal comment; they were full of inconsistencies. The therapist, in the few sessions he had with her, confronted her quite directly with these facts. Painstakingly, he picked up many of the inconsistencies and flaws in her thinking, and emphasized its inferential aspects. He told the patient that this was a sickness and encouraged her to get it under control, and not permit herself to think along such lines. The patient responded with considerable relief. At first, she was not convinced, but within three sessions, she began to report detecting her own illogical and inferential

thinking, and she did not succumb to it. While several lapses did occur, by and large, she maintained herself better, kept her job, and settled down at home.

Confrontation was the only intervention available to the therapist with this decompensating paranoid schizophrenic woman. Had the patient been able to continue her treatment, the unconscious fantasies and conflicts related to the delusions undoubtedly would have unfolded and been available for interpretation. Confrontation was directed toward the healthy and rational part of the patient's ego (self), which recognized that the therapist was concerned, and trusted him. Through confrontation, the therapist "lent" the patient his healthy and sound capacities for judgment so that she could identify with them and reacquire such facilities for herself. Subsequently, she took over these functions herself. Thus, the therapist promoted a split in the ego (self) so that the healthier part assessed the disturbed sector. The intact assessing part of the self was strengthened until it became dominant, and logical, secondary-process thinking, not overwhelmed by her drives, became the main mode of functioning for the patient regardless of the anxiety, stress and underlying fantasies. These particular confrontations did not contain prominent elements of unconscious factors. In essence, the therapist told the patient: "This is a sickness; it is an illogical, inferential, inappropriate, unrealistic, and emotional way of thinking and has no basis in fact. Recognize the signs of such thinking and get it under control; do not let it influence you." The assured, trustworthy, concerned, and helpful manner in which this was conveyed fostered the patient's acceptance.

STALEMATES AND CRISES IN THERAPY; RUPTURES IN THE THERAPEUTIC ALLIANCE

There is one use of confrontation that overlaps with those already discussed, but that constitutes a special and most important application. That is the use of confrontations at times of stalemate and crisis in therapy. Often, this is the only intervention available to the therapist at such moments in treatment because they are usually accompanied by strong resistances and defensiveness in the patient, making the detection of unconscious fantasies especially difficult. Because of the sensitive nature of such situations for both the patient and therapist, this type of confrontation poses special problems. The therapist must be particularly alert to countertransference problems, and must also be careful to express himself clearly and in the interests of the patient. Proper timing and a correct assessment of the situation is also essential. I will confine myself here to a single illustration (see Chapter 25 for a further discussion of this topic).

> Mr. E.R. was a phobic young man with a borderline syndrome, who was in therapy because he had been unable to leave his home to attend an out-of-state college. Initially, his treatment unfolded well, revealing an intensely ambivalent, sado-masochistic tie to his mother, who had alternated periods of excessive seductiveness with outbursts of murderous rage, even physically attacking the patient. The patient refused to leave her—it unfolded in his therapy—out of fear of her being destroyed in his absence (an unconscious wish of his), out of the need to remain with her in order to make her life miserable, and because of overdetermined fantasies that he would perish without her. There were many other dimensions to his clinging to his mother and home, of which homosexual anxieties were particularly prominent, though they were not clarified at the time. There was improvement in Mr. E.R.'s functioning as these conflicts were analyzed, and he began to attend a local college. He avoided girls, and never slept away from home, but managed to control his repetitive battles with his mother and father.
>
> Mr. E.R. then settled rather comfortably into his treatment situation. He would come to his sessions and discuss many real problems and the anxieties related to them, but he reported virtually no dreams or fantasies; little that was related to his neurotic problems appeared. He went along contented and unchanging.
>
> After six months of this, Mr. E.R.'s therapist decided to confront him with the stalemate. He told the patient

that he was using therapy only to maintain his present equilibrium and not to resolve his symptoms and emotional difficulties further. Many denials and rationalizations followed, and then a vague acknowledgement that the therapist was right; but still no fresh material emerged. The therapist then made a further confrontation: the sessions could not continue indefinitely on such a basis; either the patient began actively to attempt to change or he would have to accept his present gains from treatment and consider termination. He emphasized that therapy was no longer serving the patient's wish to resolve his inner difficulties and that this was actually detrimental to him.

This is a difficult and complicated group of confrontations; however, they proved critical to the resolution of the stalemate. The patient had been avoiding both anxiety-provoking life situations and his inner fantasy life. Confrontation with a realistic choice of stopping at this level or moving on, actually led to a completely different line of behavior and associations on his part. Briefly, expressions of the underlying homosexual fears and wishes began to emerge for the first time in treatment, and he slept away from home for the first time in his life. Previously repressed sadistic fantasies toward women also appeared. The intrapsychic dangers and sources of anxiety were related to these inner fantasies and impulses, and to his fears of losing control of himself.

Confrontations of problems in therapy should be relatively rare, but do occur in many areas: stalemates; misuses of treatment; attempts to manipulate, seduce or attack the therapist on some level; serious misconceptions about treatment; and the persistent use of defenses and resistances which derail the therapy (see Corwin, 1972). It is imperative that the therapist detect such major problems; however, he should think through a confrontation for some time before presenting it, all the while listening for the unconscious basis of the difficulty. When he makes his confrontation to the patient, he should couple it with as much in the way of interpretive comments as the material permits. All too often this is overlooked and omitted; the outcome under such circumstances will be more in doubt. The therapist must be certain not to resort to a confrontation where the material permits an interpretation.

OTHER COMMON TYPES OF CONFRONTATION

I want briefly to allude to some other common types of confrontation which supplement interpretative work.

The "Cost" of a Particular Maladaptation

Whenever possible, the therapist should include reference to the cost of a given maladaptation on the part of the patient to himself and to others—the toll in restrictions, limitations, loss of relationships, self-criticism and guilt, condemnation and hurt from others, and the pain to others. As I have discussed in Chapter 8, every adaptation to real and intrapsychic conflicts entails a cost to the patient and others. Some are made at great expense to him and those around him; these are maladaptive. Others are less costly and even rewarding; these are adaptive. Confrontation with the undue consequences of a given adaptation awakens the patient to the possibility of less destructive means of handling problems, and motivates him to seek other, less detrimental solutions to his conflicts.

Here, too, the therapist should not fail to recognize the contribution of repressed, unconscious motives, conflicts and fantasies to repetitive maladaptions. Interpretation of these underlying facets are often themselves complemented by a confrontation of the price the patient is paying for his particular resolution of these intrapsychic problems (see Chapters 14 and 16).

The Patient's Own Contribution to His Suffering

I have already, in the case of Mrs. E.K., illustrated this type of confrontation. This is an important application of this intervention, demonstrating to the patient, when true, the ways in which he unconsciously arranges his own difficulties with others and creates the very things he wants the least, protests most against, and feels persecuted by.

Reality Problems and Possibilities

The therapist does not want to forget reality and the patient's surface problems. Often, confrontation with choices and real conflicts are indicated as interventions, especially when the patient, for whatever reasons, obliterates awareness of such possibilities. This borders, at times, on direct suggestions, which should be avoided, since the patient should maintain responsibility for his life and his decisions (see Chapter 16). However, these confrontations often help the patient to resolve his real conflicts so that the underlying intrapsychic contributions and conflicts become available for exploration and resolution.

Gross Corruptions Outside and Within Therapy

Detection of dishonesty or corruption of any kind is an indication for an intervention by the therapist, particularly since material for interpretation is often not available. Failure to confront under these circumstances usually constitutes a sanction of such behavior in the patient, and promotes his superego pathology. If the dishonesty relates to the sessions and the therapist, it constitutes a major impairment in the therapeutic alliance which must be explored and resolved. Likewise, such behavior in the patient's outside life reflects major pathology which will also require full study and resolution. Such confrontations must be made, however, without moralizing or criticism of the patient; they are offered solely in terms of the detrimental consequences to the patient and others.

Manifest Dream Elements

A common form of confrontation which often shades into general interpretations occurs with manifest dreams in context and with certain types of associations (see Chapter 10). These latter are generally reiterations of the manifest dream elements, ready translations of them, or repetitions of apparent implications of the dream, rather than associations which lead to repressed and displaced latent content. An illustration will clarify this very common intervention:

> Mr. E.S. was a college freshman in treatment for several months for school problems and general aloofness; he had a moderate paranoid-like character disorder. He began one session by reporting this dream: he is on the campus of his school. There is a dog standing between

himself and one of the buildings. He is afraid of the dog, but it does not attack him. Then, as he goes toward the door, he falls and the dog begins to go after him. Another student comes along but refuses to help.

A long silence followed the report of the dream and the therapist confronted the patient with his fears of revealing anything more. The patient described his absence of further thoughts and ruminated about his way of withdrawing from the therapist. The dog in the dream was an animal who lingered around campus because a bitch owned by one of the students was in heat. Being attacked like that reminded the patient of his frequent complaints against his father, who was critical and unreasonable. The student, he added, must be the therapist, but he had no idea why no help was offered. The therapist concurred with this last connection, adding that this mistrust was reflected in the patient's silences and guardedness in the sessions, whatever its underlying roots might be.

Here, most of the associations are a translation of the manifest dream. The thematic content related to being attacked and not helped was connected with the patient's father and therapist, and this was part of the confrontation made by the therapist at the end of the session. In contrast, the reference to the bitch in heat, which suggests unconscious conflicts and fantasies related to possible homosexual anxieties and a feminine identification, are a clue to well-disguised latent content. This association, which could lead to an interpretation, was not pursued by the therapist, apparently because it was early in the therapy. It might well have been interpreted in displaced form (so-called "upward interpretations"; see Chapter 16) through a reference to the patient's feelings of helplessness or passivity in the treatment situation.

Confrontation with implicit meanings of dream elements is often used as a means of identifying conscious fantasies, apparent resistances and defenses, and realistic conflicts and fears. It is to be distinguished from the interpretation of dreams that deals with idosyncratic associations, latent content, intrapsychic conflict, and specific unconscious fantasies. It may prepare the way for interpretative work, but should not be substituted for it.

INDICATIONS FOR CONFRONTATIONS

I want to summarize and integrate my discussion of confrontations by delineating the major indications and principles related to these interventions. They are:

1. *Confrontations are called for when there is evidence of acting out, other ego impairments, resistances to therapy, acute symptoms, and other surface problems; the patient is either unaware of them and their implications, or has not sufficiently explored their meanings.* Technically, we endeavor to split his ego ("self") into an experiencing part and an observing part, and thus promote better self-observation and controls, and the eventual development of insights.

2. *Confrontations should be made when the patient's associations do not provide sufficient derivatives for an interpretation.* Interpretive comments should supplement and supersede confrontations whenever possible.

3. *Confrontations are also used to bring into focus behavior or associations which will lead to the expression of further derivatives of important intrapsychic conflicts and the unconscious fantasies-memories that relate to them.* In principle, this may seem easy: all the therapist need do if some material seems to be unfolding is confront the patient with an unfocused aspect or sequence. In practice, however, this is a dimension of technique filled with pitfalls. Often, silence is to be preferred to confrontations of this type, because premature focus can either be erroneous or mobilize strong defenses, and not, as hoped, lift repressions. This is a matter of timing, which the therapist must learn through experience and feedback from patients.

4. *While confrontations generally demonstrate surface phenomena, they shade into general interpretations when they are used to direct the patient's attention to connections between events or fantasies, or to apparent implications of behavior or thoughts, of which the patient was previously unaware.* Suggesting to the patient that

there are latent connections between the manifest contents of a sequence of associations, and doing so in plain language, is an example of this type of confrontation.

5. *Confrontations should be utilized with a full sensitivity for therapeutic and adaptive contexts, timing, considerations of the patient and his associations, and all of the important means of good technique* (see Chapter 17).

TECHNICAL ERRORS AND PROBLEMS IN THE USE OF CONFRONTATIONS

We are now ready to discuss the misuses and the technical problems connected with confrontations: failure to use, overuse, poor timing, and other errors such as the use of a confrontation when an interpretation is indicated. There are therapists who may be described as "confrontationists"—they seldom interpret and generally confine themselves to surface interventions.

OVERUSE AND UNDERUSE

Too frequent use of confrontations may reflect a host of countertransference problems and technical errors. These include fears of unconscious and primitive fantasies; insensitive narcissistic needs to interrupt, dominate and control the patient; seductive and especially aggressive needs and impulses toward the patient (confrontations can be especially nasty, hostile, and manipulative); and the need to condemn and criticize the patient, owing to the therapist's own problems with his conscience. They may also serve other defensive and avoidance needs of the therapist, and encourage the patient to discuss reality issues rather than intrapsychic ones or to become obsessed with material that is not related to the key context of the hour.

On the other hand, the relative failure to use confrontations when they are indicated may arise out of countertransference needs to sanction acting out and other regressions, such as ego dysfunctions and symptoms. Such silence nonverbally represents a looking-away, permission-implied response on the part of the therapist. It contributes to an antitherapeutic alliance and fosters the patient's pathological use of nonverbal responses to traumatic situations. It thus constitutes a failure to educate the patient and to assist him in the revision of his ego dysfunctions. Confrontations are often missed by therapists who themselves have corrupted superegos, ego dysfunctions and maladaptive responses similar to those used by these patients.

The patient will respond to misuses of confrontations with non-confirmatory reactions, including regressions of all kinds and difficulties within the therapy (see Chapters 19 and 22).

The following vignette illustrates the failure to intervene in this manner when indicated.

> Mr. E.T. had been in psychotherapy for two months because he was depressed and not functioning in his job or with friends; he was divorced. He began one session by describing how he had finally seen his former wife and son after months of avoiding them. His wife had remarried and told the patient that her present husband wanted to adopt his son. The patient felt that he was an outsider and described a great sense of relief at no longer having any responsibility for his child. He could now move to California and be free; there were no feelings to leave behind, just empty memories. He asked the therapist for his opinion about such a move; he wanted something to lean on. It was a chance to be reborn; maybe he would join the army and fight.
>
> He began the next session by describing a call from his parents, which he welcomed—an unusual reaction for him. He had gotten high on drugs. He then ruminated about moving and that he did not feel guilty about his son; no one existed for him. It was haunting being around them anyhow; he was going west. He withdrew from everyone and felt afraid that he would crack up. He felt stupid and mad right now, a waste.
>
> In the next hour, he asked for medication and complained about possibly losing all he owned because of his debts. He fantasized about killing himself and ruminated

about his aimlessness. He had nothing else to say. The therapist told him that he was holding back because he had not been given the medication. The patient said that he was thinking about many things and launched into a painful self-accusatory tirade as a destructive father who had damaged his son; he did not want to be punished by losing him.

The therapist, here, missed the context of this material almost entirely; namely, that Mr. E.T. had been severely disturbed by the threatened loss of his son. He was reacting to it with denial, detachment, anxiety, ideas of flight, guilt, depression, and suicidal thoughts. In the therapeutic context of his regression and failing defenses, a confrontation was in order. This could have led to the general interpretation of his various reactions, and fostered the expression of derivatives of specific unconscious fantasies related to the intrapsychic conflicts evoked by this trauma. It would also have conveyed a sense of empathy and understanding. The therapist's failure to confront this patient with the focal point of his distress constituted a lack of sensitivity. In response to the total failure of the therapist to intervene, the patient's regression intensified and he asked for alternative gratifications from the therapist. The therapeutic alliance had been disturbed, but was quickly directed along proper lines when the therapist recognized that the patient was holding back something painful.

Poor Timing

While I shall discuss the timing of interventions of all kinds in Chapter 17, I want to discuss here selected problems related to the timing of confrontations, since there are distinctive technical issues involved. Confrontations may be premature, overly delayed, unnecessary, or incorrect in their timing and content. It is often not realized that erroneous confrontations, rather than innocuously failing to enhance the flow and unfolding of the material from the patient, can actually interfere with the development of the session. This is particularly true when repressed material is emerging. Incorrect confrontations usually prompt the patient to break off this unfolding and to shift to other topics that virtually always serve defensive needs, and that are then obsessively discussed.

I shall illustrate:

> Mr. E.U. was an older adolescent with a borderline syndrome, who had been in therapy for about six months. He had reacted to his therapist's recent vacation with an acute regression, with obsessive fears that some minor action on his part would lead to an accident or to someone's death. He also heard again a voice in his head which criticized and condemned him. His therapist, upon his return, had been discouraged by this new symptom and other difficulties that he was having with this patient, and indirectly communicated this to him in various ways, even openly considering a reduction in the patient's sessions.
>
> At a time when some of this had been dealt with and corrected (the therapist had regained his perspective and interpreted the patient's murderous rage over his vacation and various negative feelings toward him), the patient came to a session ten minutes late. There had been an accident on the highway and Mr. E.U. went on to ruminate about his trouble sleeping, his difficulties in school where his work was inconsistent and erratic, and his parent's annoying critical pressures on him. He then spoke of his father's therapy and how the latter needed to scrutinize his own problems instead of attacking and blaming others. He wondered if therapy didn't fail some people; his cousin had been in and out of psychiatric hospitals many times.

The therapist chose to make what was basically a confrontation here, though the general interpretation of an unconscious displacement was also involved. He told the patient that he seemed angry that treatment was not helping him more quickly.

What is your assessment of this intervention? I would suggest that this intervention is somewhat premature. The major adaptive problem—the context—of the session is not established, and the confrontation may not help clarify it, since it directs the patient's focus and limits it. Further, it is not quite correct: derivatives of anger and impatience with the therapist are not in clear evidence. It would have been preferable to be silent and wait. If the therapist's hypothesis, as reflected in his statement, is correct, silence on his part would permit the emergence of confirmatory material, less disguised and more easily understood by the patient when pointed out to him.

> In the session, the patient agreed offhandedly with the therapist's words, and then went on to talk about how he felt like two different people when he took examinations. He was breeding flies for a biology laboratory and found it disgusting. The variants were weird; at times he felt like knocking them off the table.
>
> This intervention was not clearly confirmed. In fact, this is a good illustration of a nonconfirmatory affirmative response since it is followed by no development of the material, nor supportive manifest and latent content (see Chapter 19). Nonetheless, the therapist went on to state that the patient was furious with him, and wanted to destroy him. This time the patient said he just did not know, and became annoyed that the therapist kept saying that he was angry. He then complained again about his school problems and his parents.
>
> Briefly, in the next session Mr. E.U. reported a dream of a policeman and a house, to which he did not directly associate. He was silent a good deal and spoke of his fears of ending up with a menial job after college. The therapist confronted him with his feelings of hopelessness and worthlessness, and again told the patient that he was angry with him.

This confrontation is, I believe, now repetitive, out of context, and directionless, a fact borne out by the patient's response to it in the session. He went on to ruminate at length about the real danger that he might fail in school and how he was at loose ends. This was a nonconfirmatory response.

In the last session of this series, Mr. E.U. reported having the same dream again. Things seemed to be going a little better in school, but the voice in his head continued to disturb him. It interfered with his concentration on his work and created considerable indecisiveness. He then spoke of the onset of these symptoms some years earlier, but was unclear as to the circumstances and about his fears of doing wrong or being immoral. The therapist pointed out that his conscience was working overtime.

Unperturbed by this ill-timed, and interfering confrontation, Mr. E.U. went on to describe a series of current strange anxieties and rituals which included rocking and sucking his fingers, and nail biting which led to bleeding. The therapist again intervened, stating that the patient saw a lot of his own behavior as infantile.

What is involved here and what might you expect? As I predicted in supervision, this last confrontation—an intellectualization and a second unconscious attempt by the therapist to deflect the patient away from describing his symptoms, anxieties, and unconscious fantasies—finally pushed the patient off the subject. After all, he had been avoiding these disturbing symptoms for several sessions, and recounted them now only with great difficulty; he therefore, unconsciously welcomed the displacement and defense offered to him by the therapist.

Thus, Mr. E.U. went on in the session to ruminate about his parents and how they had fostered infantile attitudes in him. They feared his disturbed behavior (it would appear that the patient had correctly and unconsciously detected his therapist's countertransference problem; see Chapter 22) and would tolerate his destructiveness without reprimand. He was now suffering because of their foibles. The therapist closed the session with a final, poorly timed and poorly worded confrontation: the patient's parents neither stimulated nor regulated him and he therefore had to form his own conscience.

While many problems in technique are illustrated here, I want to use this material to highlight difficulties related to the use of confrontations. These confrontations were poorly conceptualized, premature, apparently incorrect at times, and did not enhance the flow of the material. They served the therapist's apparent need to avoid the patient's description of disturbing, primitive symptoms and the underlying unconscious fantasies related to them. They were presented without clear context and without a central focus. There is a failure here to listen to the patient and to allow the material from him to unfold. The therapist also appears to be using these confrontations to condemn and goad the patient, a facet that may be reflected in Mr. E.U.'s dream of the policeman. Further, there is an aggressive quality to these interventions. In all, it suggests that this therapist is a "confrontationist" who has misused this intervention in many ways. A sense of chaos prevails in the therapy, along with a rupture in the therapeutic alliance. Actually, several of the following sessions were occupied with the patient's responses to his therapist's difficulties which, while disturbing to therapy, were eventually worked through when the therapist recognized his problems and got them under control.

Technically, if the therapist recognizes that he has failed to obtain confirmation of a confrontation and that he has actually sidetracked the patient, it is generally best to remain silent for a while; the patient will usually return to the main threads of the hour. Should this not happen, the therapist can bring the patient back to the main context, if he can detect it, through a question or some other surface intervention.

INCORRECT USE AS AN INTERPRETATION

In principle, whenever material is available for interpreting, this intervention must take precedence over all others. The therapist may confront at such times, but this must be coupled with the proper interpretation. An alert observer can find countless examples of errors in this regard, particularly on the part of less experienced therapists and those who fear or do not understand unconscious fantasies.

The following vignette dramatically illustrates the consequences of this kind of error:

Miss E.V., an adolescent with a severe character disorder, had been in therapy for over a year. She had responded to her therapist's long summer vacation with considerable open rage and indirect indications of intense erotic fantasies about her therapist. These feelings were heightened by the therapist's persistent and aggressive interventions through confrontations. The problem was further aggravated by the therapist's lateness to several sessions, which were left unexplored, and the patient's first vaginal examination, done for a suspected infection (she was a virgin), which prompted the expression of derivatives of intense but repressed fantasies of being raped. For example, she reported that her half-brother was being very seductive and wild, and she recalled past times when he had fought with her and locked her in a room or cornered her, attacking her physically. She added that she was beginning to be sexually stimulated by him and wanted him jailed. It appeared at the time that these references conveyed in displaced and disguised form Miss E.V.'s fantasies about the therapist.

As this unfolded over several sessions, the patient let the therapist know that she was concealing her conscious fantasies from him; she spoke of trivia and of terminating. She also talked directly about her attachment to the therapist and her hatred for him because he was so austere and distant, but would not tell him her sexual thoughts which, she said, were quite intense. She then missed a session with a poor excuse and in the next hour she reported a dream: she sets fire to all of her house except her own room. (The reader may recall that Freud's patient Dora reported a similar dream that introduced her plans to terminate her analysis; see Freud, 1905.) Associations were sparse, but included a fantasy of setting fire to the therapist's office.

Two sessions later, Miss E.V. reported another dream: she had a baby in the rear of her car (sic!) and is driving over a bridge. They go off the bridge and into the water. As she tries to save the baby, an ocean liner bears down on her, threatening to chop her up. She tried desperately to get out of the water. Associations were to her seductive half-brother, who was still after her, and to her fears of bugs. The therapist suggested that the dream had a sexual meaning and the patient responded with denial, anger, and threats to leave.

These disruptive feelings intensified in the following session, and the patient reported that she had hallucinated dead bodies in cars after her last hour. She felt that the therapist was staring at her in the session, much like her mother often did. The therapist suggested that Miss E.V. was reacting to him with the same feelings that she had toward her mother. The patient responded that therapy was becoming a farce and that she felt like screaming; she left the hour early.

In the next session, the patient described a new group therapy program at school. After observing one session in which the participants spoke freely and confronted each other openly and honestly, she decided that she wished to join it. She asked the therapist if he would permit this and when he did not respond, said that she was thinking of quitting treatment anyhow. The therapist pointed out (confronted) that this was a continuation of her behavior in walking out angrily the previous session, but Miss E.V. interrupted him in a fury and demanded an answer to her question. The therapist confronted her more directly: group therapy would interfere with her treatment with him. She became enraged and questioned this statement. The therapist pointed out that she was disagreeing with everything that he said. She became sarcastic, said that all he could do was beat around the bush, and stood up, saying that she was leaving for good. The therapist suggested that she not leave and she refused. She said goodbye and never did return.

This is a dramtic segment of a psychotherapy which brings up many issues in technique, including the handling of the relationship between the patient and therapist, of acting in, of threats to terminate, and of major disruptions of the therapeutic alliance (see Chapters 20-22 and 25). For our purposes here, I want to note that the therapist repeatedly missed opportunities to interpret this patient's resistances and unconscious fantasies; chose instead to make superficial and even erroneous confrontations, many of which were simple repetitions of the patient's statements, not included in the above summary; failed to confront the patient early in this sequence of sessions with her more than apparent and intensifying thoughts of termination, and did not interpret their underlying basis in intrapsychic conflicts and fantasies.

There are many factors that led to the ultimate termination, and I shall here briefly allude only to those that are pertinent to this discussion. To what extent failures to interpret and incorrect confrontations contributed to the abrupt manner in which the therapy ended cannot be definitely stated, but they certainly played an important role. I will discuss this latter point in the next chapter.

It would appear from this material that the therapist was afraid of this patient, and drew back from both her rage and her sexual fantasies. Because of his countertransference problems, he may have wished to see her leave treatment. He missed many opportunities to confront her with the specific expressions of her rage at him and with the derivatives, fearful to her, of her sexual fantasies about him. This failure to intervene, coupled with his lateness and his disregard of the patient's reaction to this added hurt, promoted an acute regression (acting out, acting in, and acute symptoms), and intensified Miss E.V.'s erotic feelings toward the therapist and her fear of them. Apparently, her dread of these feelings and fantasies, and some unconscious sense that the therapist could not deal with them either, as well as her vengeful rage, caused this patient to terminate.

Let us now focus on the last session. Correct interventions in the previous sessions undoubtedly would have helped this patient analyze her disturbing, partly conscious and largely repressed, fantasies and impulses; she might not have brought her treatment to the brink, and over it. Therapy became a sado-masochistic exchange and misalliance, rather than an opportunity for insight and inner change. Yet, much might have been done in the last hour to set matters straight. It is here that I want especially to demonstrate the

inadequacy of confrontations when material is available for interpretation. The therapist's confrontations were relatively correct in
the last session: the patient was, indeed, continuing the flight she
had begun by leaving the previous hour early; she would indeed
undermine her treatment if she entered the group situation (see
Chapter 6); and she was certainly refuting everything that the therapist said to her. His last suggestion, that she not leave the session and
treatment prematurely, was, however, insufficient. The proper confrontation at the end should have been with the patient's repetitive
acting out of her impulses and fantasies; with her past flights from
her home, which had failed to resolve any of her problems; and with
the failure of such behavior in general to resolve her inner conflicts:
only the external situation was altered—and at great cost to herself.
The therapist should have made clear the advantages of staying in
therapy for at least a while and exploring this critical decision,
compared with the clearly detrimental consequences of not doing so
—not in an angry or threatening manner, but with a strong tone of
concern for the welfare of the patient.

However, the whole sequence and context of this decision to
terminate, and the many fantasies reflected in the patient's associations and behavior, was open to interpretation. This massive acting
out of a resistance which ruptured the therapeutic alliance and led
to termination reflected the patient's conscious rage and unconscious
fantasies of wishing to destroy her therapist. The derivatives of these
partly repressed fantasies included the fire and the association to his
office, the hallucinated dead bodies, and the relentless and dangerous
boat, which was in part, a projection of her own fury. This rage was
evoked largely by the therapist's interventions and behavior—his
lateness and his vacation. Further, the patient was taking flight from
her dreaded fantasies-wishes to be seduced and raped by the therapist and to have his baby. This is reflected in the patient's conscious
rape fantasies, and in the dream of the baby in her car and the boat
which is bearing down on her. Much as she fantasized jailing her
seductively attacking half-brother, she lived out her need for an
artificial protective barrier from her therapist.

This abbreviated discussion should make it clear that many interpretations were necessary and available here to supplement the confrontations made in the final session and earlier. The therapist must

learn to delay his confrontations as long as possible, though this is difficult when termination is threatened, in an effort to get at the much-needed, critical, unconscious fantasies which underlie the behavior or resistance which is the potential subject of the confrontation.

"CONFRONTATIONISTS"

The two illustrations of the techniques utilized with Mr. E.U. and Miss E.V. serve as useful examples for a brief discussion of therapists who confine themselves largely or exclusively to confrontations. There are two major, interrelated factors in the persistent use of confrontations to the relative exclusion of interpretations. The first is based on lack of knowledge—the failure to understand the structure of a symptom and the unconscious aspects of symptom formation and their resolution; the second on countertransference problems, especially the fear of unconscious fantasies and primitive material from the patient. This latter includes the need to battle with patients, the excessive need to make patients submit to the therapist, and his own inappropriate need to become their conscience.

1. *Three things go hand-in-hand*: *failure to understand the structure of neurotic behavior and symptoms, failure to recognize unconscious factors in symptom formation and maintenance, and an improper concept of the nature and use of correct interpretations.* As a result, confrontations are used as alternatives to interpretations; indeed, they are often put in the guise of interpretations, though they are not that at all. For example, "You see me (the therapist) as your mother," was an intended interpretative statement that the therapist made to Miss E.V. But she had already said this herself many times in her therapy; nothing truly unconscious was alluded to. Comments by therapists such as: "You are angry"; "You are having sexual fantasies about me or someone else"; "You are avoiding"; "You are behaving self-destructively"; or, "You are destroying your therapy", are all on the surface of the patient's scope of awareness. They do not touch upon truly repressed and unconscious aspects of the patient's intrapsychic fantasies, and are not specific; they are general interpretations at best (see Chapter 14). Such interpretations can be used in an erroneous and defensive way in order to avoid the depths

of specific unconscious fantasies; confrontations serve this purpose even more effectively.

In essence, then, confrontations may be used by the therapist to deny the role of unconscious factors—motivations and fantasies —in the creation of a symptom, and to deny the essential need to modify these unconscious facets in order to resolve symptoms through intrapsychic change. Confrontations adhere primarily to the surface, shifting back and forth with conscious sequences and links; real, not neurotic, problems; and reality in general. They are used to manipulate this surface and to direct the patient's attention to it, and thereby tend to exclude unconscious elements.

2. *The countertransference aspects of the near-exclusive use of confrontations are complex, but are probably the major determinant of this style of intervening.* Briefly, to elaborate my earlier remarks on this topic, confrontationists fear unconscious material, with its intense instinctual-drive derivatives and primitive, anxiety-provoking fantasies. These potential disturbers of the therapist's own intrapsychic equilibrium are avoided at all costs by these therapists. Repeatedly, they make a confrontation at the moment when the patient is moving toward the depths and unconscious fantasies are beginning to emerge. They thereby insure a shift back to reality and the surface.

A secondary and related factor is the therapist's need for aggressive control of the patient, and his excessive need to make him face his behavior and resistances in a manner that is hostile and, at times, punitive. Confrontations become the rationalized vehicle for such inappropriate aggressions, and are to be distinguished from the more appropriate and necessary, that is, neutralized, confrontations related to efforts to help patients to face the detrimental consequences of their disturbed behavior. There is a fine but crucial line here between the appropriate and inappropriate utilization of confrontations, and the primary guide is the patient's response (see Chapter 19). Confrontationists use this technique as a weapon against their patients, not as a tool to help them, however painful the process may be.

In concluding this chapter, I shall now briefly summarize my discussion of confrontations, their definition, the indications for their use, and the major pitfalls in their application:

1. *Confrontations are interventions in which the therapist, in context, directs the patient's attention to selected, pertinent aspects of his behavior or his associations, including sequences and other surface relationships between the parts of his communications.*

2. *Confrontations are used to bring into focus for exploration acting out, ego and superego dysfunctions, and dangerous or neurotically meaningful behavior; resistances in treatment and disruptions in the therapeutic alliance; and major crises or stalemates which interfere with the work of therapy.* They demonstrate important surface connections between aspects of behavior or fantasies, and bring into focus material which may, upon further association, lead to the understanding of repressed fantasies.

3. *The goal in using confrontations is to encourage self-scrutiny of detrimental or maladaptive behavior and to foster better controls, improved ego and superego functioning, and, in the sessions, the exploration of potentially meaningful associations, thereby fostering the expression of derivatives of unconscious fantasies.*

4. *Confrontations should never take precedence over interpretations and should be supplemented by the latter whenever possible.* Confrontations are used alone only when an interpretation is not possible and an intervention is required.

5. *Confrontations should be timed to enhance the flow of associations and not to interfere with this unfolding.* They should be made when the patient is blocked and the derivatives of unconscious fantasies are not developing. Generally, they should not be made when such material is in abundance or when a clear context is not in evidence, unless they are utilized to demonstrate this last fact.

6. *Overly repetitious or near-exclusive use of confronting reflects ignorance of the structure of neuroses and of the technique of psychotherapy, and indicates major countertransference problems, which are usually based on the therapist's fear of unconscious fantasies and instinctual-drive expressions, and on an aggressive need to control the patient and to represent a condemning conscience to him.* Failure to utilize confrontations when indicated often reflects a countertransference-based need to sanction acting out and corruption in the patient. Both of these difficulties create serious impairments in the therapeutic alliance and must be resolved.

14 Interpretations

THE NATURE OF INTERPRETATIONS

There is a brief and deceptively simple definition of interpretations: that they are verbal interventions through which the therapist makes material previously unconscious in the patient, conscious for him in a meaningful and affective way. Interpreting is no simple matter, and it requires much effort to understand what this intervention is really like, to define the different kinds of interpretations, and to delineate the pitfalls in their usage. In this introductory section, I want to offer some examples to give the reader a feeling for what interpretations are, before beginning my discussion of them by dealing with the distinction between general nonspecific interpretations and those that are specific and definitive.

INTERPRETATIONS IN PSYCHOTHERAPY

Many therapists lack a basic understanding of the nature of interpretations, their sources and indications, and the responses from patients that constitute their confirmation (for some basic references, see Freud, 1905, 1909a, 1909b, 1918; Kris, 1951; Loewenstein, 1951 and 1957; and Greenson, 1967). There is a sequence here that is critical to our methodology: material from the patient—interpretation—confirmation (or lack of confirmation). Only with a grasp of this whole process can we establish the distinction between valid and invalid interpretations.

Let us begin this study with the following much-abbreviated vignette:

> Mrs. E.W. was a married woman with hysterical symptoms who was well into her therapy when the bar mitzvahs of a number of her friends' children led to the exploration of her disappointment and rage that her husband never gave her a son. In this context, in the session to be described, the patient spoke in detail of her longings for a son and of some of the surface real and fantasied reasons for this intense wish: a son would take care of her; he would please her father who was also sonless; and he would give a sense of completeness to her family structure. She then described a fantasy of meeting her therapist at a party and of feeling embarrassed by it. It was toward the end of the session and the therapist made this interpretation: Mrs. E.W. wanted to meet him socially because she imagined that he could give her a son. She responded that she had not mentioned it, but she had experienced a good deal of anxiety on her way to her session, and had been thinking of the couch in the therapist's office and what it might be used for. She went on to describe a discussion with her dentist in which she had gone out of her way to find out if he had a son, and learned that he had two.

The intervention made here was a transference interpretation of an unconscious fantasy related to the therapist, with probable genetic ties (not alluded to in the intervention) to the patient's father. The session began with expressions of the patient's conscious but frustrated wish for a son. In this context, the sequence, in which the next set of thoughts related to meeting her therapist socially, provided the clue to the patient's currently central unconscious fantasy and intrapsychic conflict: Mrs. E.W.'s wish for the therapist to impregnate her and give her a son, and the anxiety this evoked. This fantasy, of which the patient was not directly aware, was interpreted to her and confirmed through the recall of the previously repressed thoughts of the therapist's couch, and of her displaced interest in her dentist's sons.

Notice these aspects of the interpretation: it utilized derivatives expressed in various communications from the patient in the session and crystalized them around a central context in terms of a fantasy not entirely conscious to the patient. It was formulated from these indirect and disguised associations and not from a directly conscious thought or fantasy from the patient. It is also specific, based on the material of the session, and is put simply, in the patient's idiom. The level and content is in keeping with the material at hand (many additional fantasies related to having an affair with the therapist and having intercourse with him, for example, are not touched upon since they are not active at the moment and would detract from the intervention), nor does it go beyond the current associations. For example, the wish for a son from the therapist had its basis in an earlier similar wish connected with Mrs. E.W.'s father; this was not clearly in the material at this time and was not referred to until later when the derivatives of this genetic factor were present.

The patient's response indicates that the fantasy interpreted to her was truly unconscious and repressed; it was confirmed indirectly, with meaningful new material. What emerged from repression in this instance was not the conscious wish, but derivatives that were less disguised than before, and references to the anxiety it was evoking.

Let us look at another clinical example:

> Mrs. E.X. had been in therapy for over two years when considerable material slowly and very painfully emerged, conveying an image of her self and body as deformed and mutilated. She responded to this by activating her long-considered plans to seek out a plastic surgeon for a number of cosmetic procedures, and with thoughts of terminating her psychotherapy. The therapist interpreted this as an attempt to concretely repair her damaged image of herself by external measures rather than through

anxiety-provoking inner change, and to flee these emerging awarenesses by leaving her treatment. She responded over several subsequent sessions with two dreams: in the first, she is in her session with a cousin who has (in fact and in the dream) muscular dystrophy and leaves with her. In the second, she sees her mother's vulva; it is ugly and repulsive. Her associations related to her upset over having discussed in treatment her feelings about her body, and to memories of seeing her mother nude and feeling repulsed. The therapist interpreted one unconscious meaning of therapy for her through this last dream and her associations; it was experienced as a confrontation with her body, which she found ugly and defective, much as she had responded to the sight of her mother's genitals. Further genetic material related to frightening primal scene memories, and expressions of her negative feelings about therapy and her body followed.

The therapeutic problem and context for this material was the patient's desire to terminate treatment, a crucial resistance and rupture in the therapeutic alliance. The adaptive context for the resistance was the patient's growing awareness of her defective body-image and the consequent anxieties, intrapsychic conflicts, and fantasies, evoked, in part, by hurtful remarks from Mrs. E.X.'s husband. In fact, the flight from the therapist was to some extent displaced from her husband. This interpretation was not made at the time, but may serve to remind us of the overdetermination of symptoms and acting out, and the need to make many different specific interpretations to resolve a symptom or piece of disturbed behavior.

The patient's proposed adaptation to the resultant intrapsychic conflicts was to alter her body physically and leave treatment. The "cost" for this effort at resolution would include the likelihood that the surgery would fail to achieve its intended end, and the loss of the psychotherapy and consequent opportunity for inner change.

The specific interpretations were made because the therapist found in the material from the patient derivatives of the unconscious fantasies upon which her wish to terminate was based, and conveyed them to her. In essence, she unconsciously experienced therapy as a confrontation with her defectively viewed body; her resistance-defense against this was flight and plastic surgery. With these initial confrontations and interpretations, the material deepened and the derivatives became even more explicit. The therapist then selected for interpretation the repressed fantasies that related to these resistances, in keeping with the principle of dealing with resistances first.

Here again we see that the crux of an interpretation is to make conscious for the patient repressed, unconscious motives and fantasies on which disturbed behavior and thoughts are based. The specific current fantasies (latent content) reflected in the material are used in the intervention and, as in this instance, past memories and fantasies (genetic aspects) may be interpreted as well. For an interpretation to be meaningful, the therapist must correctly detect unconscious content that is currently charged with affect.

Once this material is available to the patient, he is in a position to reconsider the intrapsychic conflict and his adaptation to it, and to perceive the primary-process, illogical and unrealistic aspects of his thinking and fantasizing, the genetic connections, and current motives. This is a complex process in which awareness of many dimensions of unconscious processes is achieved. Without awareness of repressed fantasies, the old maladaptions will continue, fed by these needs and fantasies, and new adaptions will not be possible.

We can now offer the following general description: Interpretations take as their starting point a current adaptive context (reality). They deal primarily with mobilized unconscious fantasies which contain expressions of id wishes and needs, ego responses such as defenses and object relationships, and superego reactions such as expressions of conscience and ideals. These fantasies also contain memories of important past experiences and reflect aspects of the patient's self-image and current functioning (see Chapter 8). Interpretations, then, are the heart of the psychotherapeutic intervention. They bring into the patient's conscious awareness the nature of his intrapsychic conflicts, the sources of his anxieties and guilts, and the motives for his symptoms. They are constructed by recognizing the context of the patient's communications and by synthesizing various manifest elements in his associations into a latent fantasy.

Unconscious fantasies are complex and varied in nature, and there are many ways of categorizing interpretations. Here I shall use those that are particularly relevant to psychotherapeutic technique.

SPECIFIC AND GENERAL INTERPRETATIONS

The distinction between specific interpretations, which refer to definitive unconscious fantasies, and general interpretations, which are both more superficial and ill-defined, is an important one clinically. In the two preceding vignettes (Mrs. E.W. and Mrs. E.X.) the interventions used by the respective therapists included specific and personal interpretations. They referred to the details of the two patients' repressed fantasies in an idiom borrowed from the exact derivatives through which each had expressed, in disguised form, the unconscious content. The repressed wish is expressed in content that is verbally defined and is linked to specific affective, defensive, and conscience reactions which are also part of the total unconscious fantasy. The interpretation of genetic factors derives from concrete past experiences of the patient, and for each intervention there is a specific adaptive context. In all, the unconscious content that is revealed clearly arises from a particular individual matrix of past and present experiences. Of course, specific interpretations for different patients do have common features; all people share in the human condition, and symptom-evoking, traumatic situations of childhood and adulthood are rarely entirely unique. Beyond this, however, interpretations must be specific for a given patient at a particular moment.

This distinction will be clearer if I present some general interpretations for comparison. The following vignette includes interpretations of both kinds:

> Mr. F.P. was a college freshman in treatment because of tendencies to withdraw suspiciously from others, to be depressed, and to do unusually poorly in school; he had a moderate character disorder. As I have described before (Chapters 6 and 9), he came to one session report-

ing that he was under pressure from his parents to enter group therapy as a supplement to his individual treatment, a matter not discussed with his present therapist. He spoke at length of his fears of a loss of his own sense of privacy through this move and described some difficulty in refusing the offer; his response had been indefinite. His parents, and especially his father, pressured him directly and indirectly through criticism of the way he was doing at school despite his present therapy. Mr. F.P. alluded to ways in which his parents had betrayed his confidence in the past; he was uncertain what would prove best.

When Mr. F.P. fell silent for a long while, the therapist pointed out to him that he seemed to welcome the opportunity to dilute their own closeness in his present therapy, perhaps out of some sense of mistrust. In addition, he noted that the patient had kept his associations to this whole problem rather superficial. The patient agreed and said that during the silence he had thought of a baseball player who had recently been traded from one team to another. The therapist said that Mr. F.P. must know that a ball player cannot play for two teams, and that his thought of entering group therapy is, indeed, a flight from his individual therapy.

The patient agreed and subsequently refused to enter the group. In the next hour he reported that he had dreamt that he was about to go into a building at his school when a dog came after him. As he went for the door, he fell and was attacked by the animal. A boy came along and refused to help him.

After reporting the dream, Mr. F.P. fell silent. He could not understand the dream, it brought nothing to mind. He withdrew when he was confused at school. The dog could be the therapist, though he was not sure. Silence followed.

The therapist agreed that the dream seemed to reflect some view of the therapist as unhelpful, but that this was all a bit too pat and hollow. The patient then said that the dog was one that loitered around his dormitory because his room-mate's dog was in heat.

In the next session, the patient reported being ill and nearly missing his session (as he had done after several other meaningful hours). He described a long search for his old medication for his stomach upsets, which he found and used. He spoke again of entering the group therapy situation. The therapist said that in some way Mr. F.P. saw himself in therapy much like his room-mate's dog—he took things in from the therapist but it frightened him and he had to push the therapist off to protect himself. The patient then recalled that the dog had actually gotten pregnant, and had been given an injection and aborted. He went on to describe his father's ways of prying and getting to secrets which the patient kept from him.

There were two general interpretations: of the patient's wish to interfere with the closeness between himself and the therapist, and of his possible mistrust; and of the patient's view of the therapist as unhelpful. Neither of these broad fantasies had been directly verbalized by the patient. They were repressed and outside his scope of direct awareness, and he only vaguely acknowledged their presence. In calling them to his attention, therefore, the therapist was making interpretations that used feelings and fantasies which were implicit in the patient's associations, but lacked definition, specific content, and clues as to their exact sources.

In contrast, the interpretation of the unconscious fantasy that group therapy was like going to a new ball club has a unique and specific quality, as does the interpretation of the patient's passive-feminie wishes to be entered by the therapist, and his reactive fear of these desires. This was not immediately evident from the reported dream of the dog, and could only be developed out of the specific associations to the bitch in heat, the patient's thoughts of leaving therapy, and his search for his pills for his stomach ailment.

The following principles regarding specific and general interpretations can be developed from these observations:

1. *General interpretations are ill-defined, relatively evident, and amorphous or lacking in specific content.* In contrast, specific interpretations allude to highly individual, well-disguised but definitive and rich in content, unconscious fantasies. They can be stated only in terms of the patient's current adaptive tasks and past life history.

2. *To modify symptoms, the therapist may use general interpretations in a preparatory manner.* However, these must eventually lead and give way to specific interpretations of unconscious fantasies, in a current context and linked to highly individual memories of past experiences and fantasies (genetics).

We can now look more carefully into general interpretations. Consider this clinical material:

> Mr. E.Z. was a young man in professional school who had moderate characterological problems. He was in treatment with a therapist whom he did not know personally, although he did know many of his colleagues. Early in his therapy, in a session before the one I shall study, he wondered aloud about whether he could trust his therapist: whether he knew him well enough, or should continue therapy; he then spoke of the aloofness of his father.
>
> The therapist began the session under consideration fifteen minutes late and apologized. The patient ruminated about school and his need to discipline himself so that he did not sleep through his classes. He had dreamt that he had blown up his school. There were some people there, but he did not know who they were. In association, he recalled a television show: some people were angry at another group of people and blew them up. He then ruminated about quitting school for a menial job. He asked the therapist if he was boring him. A girlfriend of his had been divorced; she felt she could not trust anyone; they were all bad. Mr. E.Z. felt that he was like her. Asked by the therapist for an example, he went on to describe a date with another girlfriend and then some minor details regarding school. As the session ended, the

therapist told the patient that he seemed to find it difficult
to talk to him because he did not trust him.

The therapist here made a general interpretation to the effect
that the patient, without being fully aware of it, was being vague
and having trouble communicating to the therapist (i.e., was in a
state of resistance; the therapeutic alliance was impaired) because
of his mistrust of him.

This intervention is an attempt to make the patient aware of his
difficulty in talking and of its basis in uncertainties about the therapist. Thus, it is an interpretation, but a general one, and contains no
specific fantasies. Such general interpretations may serve as preliminary interventions pending more specific material, but they
must be recognized as nonspecific and superficial; the therapist
must be prepared to go on from there. Many therapists, however,
fail to penetrate further into specific unconscious fantasy content.
The outcome of their work is not unlike that of the confrontationists
I described in Chapter 13. It is incomplete, intellectualized, superficial, reality-oriented, only minimally intrapsychically and conflict-
oriented, and results in little if any true readaptations and lasting
inner change. General interpretations should not be used when the
material from the patient lends itself to more specific interpretations. This brings us back to the vignette; what additional interventions might have been made? The following seems pertinent to this
question:

The context of this session seems twofold: the ongoing problem
with the therapeutic alliance (the resistance) and the immediate
reaction to the therapist's lateness.

The prevailing tone of the hour is anger and explosive rage, to
which the mistrust could have been related. There is an implicit,
unconscious criticism of the therapist's lack of discipline, expressed
in the derivatives related to the patient's self-criticisms of his own
lack of discipline (a defensive turning against the self), and in the
dream which manifestly and by association indicates murderous
rage and the presence of mutual warring parties. It is not clear from
the material whether the primary fantasy relates to the patient's
wish to destroy the therapist or to a fear of being destroyed by him.
Although both undoubtedly are present and interrelated, one must

be more central at this time, and for reasons that are also unclear. Two courses of action are indicated:

- The therapist should ask questions about further associations to the dreams and its sources (day residues). The thematic threads are too barren and the immediate context too unclear.
- The patient chose to ignore the therapist's lateness and his own response to it. Once the sources of his rage were clearer, I would have asked about this omission. After all, the disturbance in therapeutic alliance is central at this time, and such an exploration might prove fruitful. Further, to ignore this lateness, which undoubtedly was provocative, is to foster and sanction avoidance of direct discussion of the patient's feelings regarding this real hurt. It can only contribute to a further rupture in the already tenuous therapeutic alliance (see Chapter 22).

The main interpretation in this hour undoubtedly should have related to the problems in the patient's relationship to the therapist and to the most affectively-laden and meaningful communication— the dream and the patient's associations to it. Had the therapist's queries made the context of the rage clearer, this would have been easy to do. Without this, the therapist could have pointed out that the patient had been talking in the previous session about his mistrust of the therapist and is now talking about two factions at war, one destroying the other. He must be concerned with something of this kind in treatment—perhaps more so in this hour because of the therapist's unfortunate and inadvertent lateness.

This would be a general interpretation with some specific content, presented to the patient in the hope of eliciting still more specific derivatives of the repressed fantasies related to those intrapsychic conflicts that were producing the patient's resistances and thoughts of terminating. It is at the level of the material and as specific as possible for the moment.

The interpretation of mistrust was too repetitious of past manifest material from the patient. It is not focal in the material of the session, though related to the probable central issues. Once pointed out, however, it should have been linked to recent references to being in therapy with a therapist who knows friends of the patient. This would at least indicate a specific source of anxiety and point to a specific cluster of repressed fantasies.

One last question remains to be posed, even though it anticipates a later discussion (see Chapters 18 and 19): were the interventions made by the therapist in this session confirmed or not? It was predicted in supervision that nonconfirmation would prevail and that the next session would contain derivatives of the patient's reaction to the somewhat erroneous intervention and to the fact that the therapist's lateness was ignored; this was borne out in the session already described and in the following one.

In that hour, the patient first mentioned not wanting to be seen entering his therapist's office. He said that he had forgotten a long dream and then complained about a girlfriend, a socialworker who was overly dependent on him; she ignored his request for a favor, so he stopped seeing her. He recalled that in his dream he was looking out windows and could not see anything. He feared that inside of himself, he was different and weird. The rest of the hour was quite ruminative.

In essence, the patient's resistances and anxieties about his therapy continue to be expressed. The derivatives also indicate that he felt ignored and was having further fantasies of revenge by terminating therapy. The inability to see, and possibly his fears of his weirdness, probably refer to the patient's unconscious perception of the therapist's blindness, and may be a sensitive and correct assessment. Self-accusations and self-criticisms are a frequent means by which patients express negative fantasies about, and unconscious perceptions of, their therapists.

The following brief vignettes will illustrate other kinds of general interpretations:

> Mr. F.A. was a young homosexual man. His therapist had been on a long vacation and in the first session upon his return, the patient spoke of wanting to get away and travel for a year. He feared being sexually impotent and had picked up a young man at a bar to reassure himself that he was attractive and liked by others. He wished he had closer family ties, and recalled the death of a favorite uncle. The therapist pointed out his confusion regarding sexuality and the patient ruminated.
>
> Mr. F.A. was fifteen minutes late for his next session,

saying that he had missed his train connections. The therapist said that he must be angry about his recent vacation and the patient said no—he just was tired of his sexual hang-ups—and he ruminated more about them.

It is especially common for therapists to use general interpretations when patients are reacting with various specific fantasies and behavior to their vacations. Resistances are often strong, derivatives well disguised, and acting out common. While a general interpretation is better than none, it is too superficial and incomplete if specific latent content is available; in essence, it is incorrect and the patient will respond accordingly (see Chapter 19).

In this vignette, the specific fantasies hinted at in the first session relate to longings for closeness with the therapist in terms of a past closeness to a favorite uncle; the vacation of the therapist may have been equated with the death of this uncle. The loss is repaired through a homosexual replacement and the patient thereby reassures himself that the therapist has not left him because he is repelled by him. The cost to the patient is, of course, the homosexuality and the guilt which followed the acting out.

These missed interpretations have some degree of specificity; in contrast, the interpretation of concealed anger made by this therapist is quite general and, what is more unfortunate, made out of context and without derivatives to support it. It is a premature interpretation which subsequently was not confirmed. I suspect that only after the patient's longings for closer ties to the therapist had been analyzed would his rage over having been left emerge in a form that would permit interpretation.

General interpretations are characterized by such phrases as: you are angry; you are sexually aroused; you see this person much as you saw your mother or father; you don't trust this or that person. They are useful, but their value is limited. While touching upon unconscious elements, they are insufficient for insight into specific intrapsychic conflicts. The main therapeutic pitfall is the failure to reach specific repressed content and the stalemating of therapy on a general and superficial level. We should keep this distinction between general and specific interpretations in mind as we investigate the main uses of interpretations. Also we should recognize that overall, a sound interpretation begins with a therapeutic context (a symptom), moves on to the adaptive context, then touches upon the patient's intrapsychic responses and includes the instinctual drives involved as well as the patient's defenses, and then traces out the genetic dimension. While this may be done over several sessions, it is the ultimate, specific interpretative goal.

RESISTANCES

In essence, all measures utilized by the ego to master anxiety and resolve intrapsychic conflicts are termed "defenses." They may be adaptive or maladaptive, conscious or unconscious, used by the patient in his daily life or in therapy. It is the last that are termed "resistances": all of the devices used by the patient to interfere with the progress of his treatment and to prevent the affective expression of the potentially disturbing derivatives of unconscious, conflict-related fantasies in the sessions (see Greenson, 1967). While usually referred to most succinctly with terms such as "repression," "denial," "projection," and "isolation," these defenses are actually complex mechanisms with unconscious meanings and motives, rich in latent content. Thus, a complete interpretation of a defense or a resistance will go beyond the general intervention that simply alludes to a mechanism of whose use the patient is unaware; the latter is akin to confrontations and to the relatively contentless interpretations described in the previous section. They are important preliminary interventions, but are limited in effect. A full interpretation of a defense or resistance will allude to the context of the defense (its reality precipitates), to the impulses and wishes against which the patient has erected the defense, to the superego contribution—in terms of such things as guilt or self-condemnation and self-punishment—to the genetic links involved, and to the latent meanings (fantasy representations) of the defense itself. Such a complex analysis calls for many well-timed interventions and is usually done piecemeal.

I have chosen the interpretation of resistance as a starting point for the exploration of types of interpretations because of the well-known, basic, sound dictum that the therapist should interpret resistances first and foremost among therapeutic problems (see Chapter

22); only when these are resolved or under control should he interpret the fantasies related to the patient's symptoms or disturbed behavior. Correct interpretations of resistances lead into and blend with those related to nuclear, pathogenic, unconscious fantasies. Technically, to the very last moment of therapy, the therapist should be on the alert for expressions of resistances. They are ever-present and related to important aspects of character and symptoms, and must be the object of interventions whenever they impede the flow of therapy or their meaning becomes clear from the context and material at hand. Often, there is an overall sequence in which the analysis and resolution of resistances is followed by the uncovering of repressed material, in turn followed by new resistances. These latter take countless forms, including mental blocks, attacks on the therapist or on treatment, thoughts of terminating, confused sessions, shifts from neurotic to real problems, and rumination or doubt. They must then be interpreted and worked through so that further uncovering can follow. Sometimes, a real event or incident will prompt strong resistances in therapy, and the therapist's job is the same: when significant resistances are in evidence, they must be brought into focus and interpreted, not ignored in the hope that they will pass.

Thus, whatever evokes resistances, the therapist must be constantly alert for them. Even when repressed material is emerging, we look for the resistances that are active for the moment, and at times interpret both the emerging unconscious fantasies and the unconscious resistances when we intervene. Where resistances prevail, the therapist must listen to the material and understand its context and unconscious meanings as expressed in the patient's derivatives and behavior.

Technically, the therapist must first recognize that a resistance exists and is interfering with therapy. Then, he must determine the nature of the resistance, and assess what is prompting it. Lastly, he must detect the unconscious fantasies on which the resistance is structured—its unconscious meanings and genetic history. The specific and complete interpretation of resistances unfolds out of all this. Usually, interpreting a resistance includes two main steps:

1. *Confronting or interpreting to the patient that he is resisting, using plain language and not technical terms, in an effort to make*

him aware that he is being defensive and blocking the work of treatment in some way. The therapist should make the patient aware of how he is accomplishing this blockage, pointing out that he is ruminating, acting out, avoiding a specific topic, remote, producing many confused dreams, or avoiding his inner fantasies—to identify a few of the forms of unconscious resistances. From the sequence of the material and the context, the therapist should, if possible, also make conscious for the patient the general setting of the blockage. For instance, he may be able to point out that since the topic of his father or mother, or of sex, or of his rage at his wife has come up, the patient has been remote, unclear, or otherwise unproductive.

This level of confrontation and general interpretation should often include some indication to the patient of the "cost" to him of the resistances, including the disruptive effects they have on the therapy. Thus, the therapist may point out that the patient is getting nowhere in his sessions, or that his symptoms remain unmodified because of his resistances. This is done noncritically to help motivate the patient to take a look at his resistances, so that he may both consciously modify them and unconsciously produce derivatives that will illuminate the repressed aspects of the resistances.

In all, then, this first step is generally a matter of helping the previously unaware patient realize that something he is doing is interfering in the sessions, that it is taking a certain observable form, and that it is occurring in a particular context.

2. *The second step is for the therapist to establish and interpret from the patient's associations the specific repressed fantasies that determine the nature and form of the resistance, their unconscious meanings, and their genetic roots.* This is the crux of the therapeutic work which leads to the resolution of resistances. It also enables the patient to understand his character and the ways in which he deals with his anxieties: his on-going defenses. It establishes both the history of these adaptive and maladaptive maneuvers and their present use, and enables the patient to replace ineffective or destructive defenses with those that are more effective and appropriate. The pathology reflected in resistances must be modified if treatment is to be successful.

In psychotherapy, consistent confrontation with and interpretations of resistances has two major functions: first, within treatment, the resolution of the resistances and defenses related to it, and second, the subsequent revelation, and ultimate working through, of the critical, pathogenic, conflict-related unconscious fantasy-memory material on which symptoms and characterological disturbances are based. Thus, analysis of resistances leads to the heart of the neurosis; and in and of themselves, they reflect important characterological disturbances and maladaptive defenses. They form the basis for secondary symptoms and contribute to primary symptoms as well (e.g., phobic avoidance is related to the resistance of avoidance in therapy; and obsessiveness in life will go with comparable distancing in sessions).

In analyzing resistances, then, we are exploring important character traits, defenses, and aspects of symptoms. Further, when the unconscious fantasies-memories related to resistances are explored and analyzed, they will merge with the unconscious fantasies-memories on which the presenting symptoms are based. One last point: resistances are complex in structure and serve reality, the id and superego, as well as the ego. Thus, they may be motivated by needs for self-punishment or by the desire to gratify sexual and aggressive wishes. They are, then, not to be viewed in a simplistic way.

The following vignette serves to illustrate these concepts and demonstrate both the general interpretation of resistances and that made in terms of specific unconscious fantasy and memory content.

> Mr. F.B., a paranoid character with a borderline syndrome, had been in once-weekly psychotherapy for several years and had shown considerable improvement. As he approached termination, he alluded to a previously unreported symptom: an irrational fear of getting his own urine on himself or his clothes. He was afraid that the contamination might cause some kind of ill-defined permanent harm to himself. He did not want to discuss the symptom; it disgusted him to mention it. Initially, his therapist confronted him with this avoidance and its consequences: nothing would be worked through if he maintained his stance.

In subsequent sessions, Mr. F.B. spoke of his rage at
others and of fantasies of destroying them. His fear of
contamination was, in this context, interpreted as a fear of
talion-punishment for his murderous rage (a general
interpretation of a symptom-related fantasy). Following
this, the material became vague and repetitious, and was
filled with details regarding the symptom and minor
events in the patient's life. These resistances were pointed
out, and the patient then spoke of how much worse he
was getting and how he would probably need therapy
indefinitely. The therapist now interpreted an unconscious fantasy on which the patient's conscious and
unconscious avoidance—the lack of relevant derivatives—of working with the symptom (the resistance) was
based: the patient did not want to resolve this symptom
since it meant leaving treatment and his therapist. This
was confirmed in three ways: first, Mr. F.B. directly
acknowledged that the therapist was actually one of very
few people he could talk and relate to; second, he spoke
of his fears of losing control of his impulses, alluding to
the protection and safety he felt he gained through his
relationship with the therapist. Lastly, the resistance was
modified and the patient turned in the next few sessions
to the symptom. Now he associated it with homosexual
masturbation fantasies in which he imagined himself
grabbing at the buttocks of men and ejaculating into
their anuses. He recalled knowing a woman who had
developed a purulent vaginal infection from a hospital
bathroom.

Next, Mr. F.B. reported that he had dreamt of throwing an object into the air and stabbing it with a bayonet
as his mother watched. He went on to say that he felt
suicidal and had fantasied shooting himself in the therapist's office. This was interpreted as an attempt to flee
what was emerging in the sessions (i.e., initially, from the
vantage-point of its adaptive use as a resistance rather
than from the aspect of its uncertain unconscious meanings). This led to the immediate recall of another dream,

repressed until then: he is sitting at work on a dirty chair. An elevator in the center of the area opens and people come out of it. In associating, he recalled that a co-worker had fainted and wet himself with urine in that location. The object he stabbed was like a piece of fruit; the thoughts of his mother evoked rage. He suddenly recalled having heard her urinating in the bathroom throughout his childhood and into his later years; on the night of the dream, she had left the bathroom door open. This led to the recall of sexual fantasies about her that intruded into his mind and to a dread of being enveloped and controlled by her.

In the next session, he reported a dream of coming to his therapy session with toilet paper in his hand and slipping in the hall. In the dream, the therapist tells him that his sister is on the phone and the patient responds that the therapist is lying; he has no sisters (a fact). He goes to the phone and a man speaks. Associations were related to his feeling that treatment was "crap" and to his view of the therapist as out to destroy and betray him. The toilet paper was used by his mother after she urinated. When rumination followed, the therapist pointed out the patient's own attempt to destroy his therapy by devaluing his therapist in order to protect himself from the anxiety related to the emerging memories and fantasies. The therapist then inquired about the reference to a sister. The patient reported for the first time in his treatment that his mother had had two miscarriages when he was an infant. He now remembered that he had read an article on chemical abortions on the day before the dream, and another on congenital and acquired diseases that develop in utero.

At this point the vignette provides suffient material for my main points—and much more. Here, I want to emphasize the following:

1. *Resistances are ultimately based on multiple unconscious fantasies and memories; they are overdetermined.* In this vignette,

several of these fantasies emerged. The patient avoided discussing a symptom and this was based on a fantasy (need) of wanting to hold onto the therapist. This fantasy was primarily unconscious and had deeper roots in that it related to unconscious wishes for a homosexual union with the therapist via anal intercourse. A further level of meaning emerged when it was revealed that Mr. F.B.'s mother had had two miscarriages; termination was unconsciously perceived as a miscarriage that would destroy him. For these unconscious reasons he opposed termination.

I have not attempted to detail the entire structure of the unconscious fantasies related to the patient's various resistances. But I do want to note the enormous sense of anxiety and dread of annihilation involved. The resistances in Mr. F.B.'s treatment—his avoidances, defensive rage, and clinging—were motivated by the same kinds of terror that prompted his symptoms. Further, the analysis of these resistances did indeed lead to deeply repressed core fantasies and memories on which the patient's symptoms were based. In all, then, the same unconscious fantasies that motivated the patient's resistances were also the basis for his neurosis.

The relationship with the therapist and the therapy situation itself unconsciously took on meanings, related to conflicted unconscious fantasies and memories connected with his parents, that evolved out of his reaction to the trauma of the miscarriages. This demonstrates how transference fantasies evoke resistances that merge with the genetically determined fantasies evoking symptoms. In the terms used in Chapter 8, the patient had made a regressive assessment of the treatment situation.

2. *Technically, these unconscious fantasies must be analyzed if the resistance is to be resolved.* The derivatives of the repressed fantasies underlying major resistances must be worked through if the patient is to deal with his central anxieties and conflicts, and resolve them. Instances of this kind serve to emphasize how ineffective confrontation without adequate specific interpretation will be.

Notice especially that the therapist correctly interpreted the derivatives of the repressed fantasies in terms of their adaptive uses as resistances when they emerged. He did not prematurely attempt to relate them to the patient's symptoms, nor did he ignore these resistances. He searched for understanding of the unconscious meanings of the resistances at each turn, and used the material to this end whenever possible. In this way, the resistances were clarified and resolved, and the patient's defenses modified. Only then did the derivatives expressing the unconscious meanings of the symptoms unfold. If we keep in mind the principle of interpreting the defensive and resistance aspects of fantasies first whenever possible, and that we do so within an adaptive framework (i.e., their role in resolving intrapsychic conflicts), we have the main tenets for style of interpretation.

Thus, for example, when the patient reported a fantasy of murdering his therapist, the interpretation offered was that he wanted to interrupt therapy and avoid the memories and fantasies that were emerging. This was the adaptive-resistance function of the fantasy, and it was stated first. Later, links to the patient's own unconscious fear of being destroyed by the therapist and to his guilt that he had in some magical way participated in his mother's miscarriages—the fantasied murder of the fetuses—emerged and were interpreted (this was not detailed in the report of the vignette). Here, once again, the fantasies related to the resistances merged with those related to the patient's neurotic problems, including his paranoid character structure.

3. *To reiterate, the finding that the unconscious fantasies on which resistances are founded tend to merge with those upon which the symptom is based is most important, since it indicates that there are at least two rewards to the patient and therapist in analyzing resistances: first, a resolution of obstacles to the therapy; and second, an insight into the unconscious meanings, dynamics, and genetics of the symptoms themselves.* Actually, analysis of symptoms and characterological problems proves to be impossible without analysis of resistances, which must be valued as another "royal road to the unconscious." Patient working through of resistances and the unconscious fantasies and memories on which they are based is the key to effective psychotherapy.

In this vignette, we can see that as the patient approached some of the deeper meanings of his resistances (for example, the fantasy that to be terminated is to be miscarried and be destroyed), he was also involved with versions of the unconscious fantasies related to the symptom—to be urinated upon is to be destroyed as the fetuses were. Once more we see that the same repressed fantasies and memories determine the symptom and the resistance, and undoubtedly, the form of each.

To apply these concepts and principle of technique to another clinical situation:

> Mr. F.C., a borderline young man who feared becoming homosexual, responded to a prospective separation from his therapist with the breakthrough of fantasies of a homosexual encounter with him. The therapist made this interpretation and, from other material, linked the fantasies to experiences with, and fantasies about, the patient's father. Over the next two sessions several previously unreported, repressed childhood and adolescent homosexual experiences and fantasies emerged. In the session following these disclosures, the patient spoke of how difficult psychotherapy was for a girlfriend of his. He also described a series of petty job problems in great detail and then speculated on his feelings about his father, referring to things he had read in books on homosexuals.

At this point, material for an intervention can be formulated as follows: This sequence begins with the therapist's announcement of his vacation and the patient's reaction with homosexual fantasies. A pending separation has evoked transference fantasies that become the vehicle for the unfolding of a series of memories, and conscious and unconscious fantasies related to the patient's homosexual problems (see Chapter 20). Here then, we see that transference is, on occasion, another road to the unconscious in psychotherapy.

With the unfolding of the memories and fantasies related to his homosexual impulses, the patient apparently became anxious and conflicted. In a familiar sequential pattern, he then became resistant: he expressed, in a displaced form, using a girlfriend, the derivatives of his concern about treatment, ruminated about real and trivial problems, and spoke in an intellectualized manner.

Technically, the therapist should intervene here and demonstrate to the patient that the homosexual memories and fantasies that he had been describing had apparently evoked some anxiety, and that he was now remote and avoiding this subject in any meaningful way. This would constitute the first type of intervention I outlined above: making the patient aware that he is resisting and of the possible motives. The specific fantasies underlying the resistance are not apparent from the material for the moment. It may be that another, anxiety-provoking repressed experience or fantasy was on the verge of emerging, and was being covered up. Or a new, disturbing transference fantasy may have been developing and this was being actively repressed. The therapist must listen to the material from the patient for derivatives of such fantasies, which would then be specifically interpreted.

Lastly, the resistance itself may have an unconscious meaning, such as: "I (the patient) will not give you (the therapist) anything more of mine to touch"; or "I will not expose anything more—my genitals—to you." This is, of course, speculation, but we may expect the specific homosexual transference fantasies to become the source of resistances and flight, and should be prepared to interpret this development, should it be reflected in the material.

In fact, a reference in the following session to Mr. F.C.'s fear that his brakes would fail on his way to the session indicated in this context that unconsciously he feared losing control of his homosexual impulses. His description of his attraction to a man at work highlighted this fear, but further specific material did not, as it happened, unfold.

This vignette has brought us back to fundamentals: the technique of confronting the patient with his resistances in plain, descriptive language, and the general interpretation of the context in which this is occurring so as to indicate the nonspecific, unconscious motives. Another vignette explores further the interpretation of the specific unconscious fantasies upon which a resistance is based.

> Miss F.D. was a very resistant patient who had sought treatment because her fiancé had left her for another girl and then returned to her. She blamed him for her suffering and focused on the reality issues involved, rather than her inner fantasies and conflicts. After the therapist con-

fronted her with the indications that she had actually encouraged the relationship between her fiancé and the other girl, she missed a session. In the next hour, after ruminating and rationalizing about her absence, which was without realistic cause, she spoke of a girlfriend who had run out of her dentist's office in a panic when a tooth was being drilled.

Since Miss F.D. further ruminated, and since the acting out through the absence from the session was a clear indication (therapeutic context), the therapist elected to intervene at this point, and to do so in two steps: a confrontation and superficial inerpretation, and an interpretation of a specific unconscious fantasy. Thus, he interpreted first Miss F.D.'s absence as a flight from the therapy and suggested that the motive for it was her fear of her own inappropriate (neurotic) participation in creating her suffering. To help to motivate her toward therapeutic work, he also pointed out her fear of the implications of this behavior—that she herself had emotional problems. Secondly, he interpreted a specific fantasy on which the resistance was based: her unconscious view of treatment as a dangerous and painful penetration and attack upon her integrity. While this latter intervention was based on a minimum of clinical material, it was offered because the therapist had confronted the patient with her general fears of therapy on many occasions, with little result. This interpretation actually led the patient to report phobic symptoms and bodily anxieties not previously described.

Let us now move on to additional vignettes to clarify further how we detect and interpret specific unconscious fantasies related to resistances.

Mr. F.E. was a young, depressed man with school problems and a tendency to form destructive relationships. He had been severely traumatized by his mother's illness and hospitalization when he was three years old. He tended to be very resistant and oriented to external reality in his sessions. Some of his associations indicated a great dread of reviving the childhood trauma which had, on some level, prompted suicidal and other terrifying fantasies.

One set of fantasies underlying his resistances was expressed in several recurrent dreams in which he was pursued by hoodlums or a Negro, who were out to murder him. The genetic meaning of this latter attacker, a man, was not clear from the material, though the patient's associations pointed to his father and to the basis of his fears of him in sexual longings for his mother. This appeared disguised in his dreams. For example, in one dream, Mr. F.E. was with his fiancée and a Negro man attempted to break into the patient's house to murder him and to rape his fiancée in his mother's bedroom. Associations made it clear that the dream was an expression of angry sexual fantasies toward the patient's mother and of punishment for these impulses. These fantasies were also one unconscious basis for his symptoms.

At a time when Mr. F.E.'s insurance coverage for treatment was about to end, he reported that he had dreamt that someone was attempting to break into his car and steal his expensive tape recorder; he then realized that the recorder was not in the car and he had nothing to fear. In the session in which the dream was reported, the patient next spoke about his therapist and their recent discussion of his remoteness which had been initiated through a confrontation. He had given his car to his uncle for repairs and had removed the recorder so that it would not be stolen.

At this point the therapist intervened; he interpreted the patient's unconscious view of therapy as an assault on his privacy and an attempt to steal what was inside him, and added that he was protecting himself from this danger by hiding within himself the things that were important to him. Thus the therapist defined both the form of the resistance, and the specific repressed fantasies on which it was based. The patient responded by speaking of his therapy as being like a museum trip; he immediately recognized that this reflected his detachment and lack of involvement in treatment. He next said that something else was on his mind, and spoke of his insurance running out and his dilemma about continuing without it—he had little money of his own. He then described the details of this problem.

The therapist made another interpretation; he pointed out to the patient that apparently the insurance had also served as a protection against involvement in treatment. It helped him to feel that he was not putting himself "on the line" or in danger, and to insure that thoughts and feelings dear to him would not be stolen from him.

In this session, the patient's resistances, undoubtedly mobilized by the pending loss of his insurance, are the central adaptive and therapeutic contexts. From the material, we learn that, unconsciously, the insurance had made therapy unreal for the patient; he had nothing of value to lose (see Chapter 5). We see again that insurance may in reality support strong resistances in the patient and actually nullify or significantly lessen the therapeutic outcome. The issue must be analyzed, and the fantasies and realities related to it deserve interpretation whenever possible.

In the following vignette, we can study the role of the circumstances of external life in the development of resistances in therapy:

Mrs. F.F. was a woman with a borderline syndrome who had been in treatment for two years when her husband became ill and began to neglect her. Over a month, derivatives of fantasies of turning to her therapist for care and sexual gratification emerged. For example, she described fantasies of meeting a man who would listen to her and accept her in every way. She dreamt of living near a doctor friend and meeting him at an affair, and of surprising the man who was doing repairs on her house at his office. She also dreamt of a man with urinary problems and of a urinary blockage of her own—themes previously related to sexual fantasies. As this unfolded, the patient spoke of terminating her therapy prematurely, complaining that she was getting nowhere. She expressed

open annoyance at the therapist for his smugness and
failure to help her.

The resistances here were apparently prompted by the patient's
erotic fantasies about the therapist. The therapist here chose not to
interpret the fantasies motivating the resistances or their specific
latent meanings, such as: "I must flee because I wish to be seduced
by you and fear these impulses." He waited because of the very
sensitive nature of these fantasies, the patient's borderline pathology, and the lack, as yet, of reference to him that would define
their transference nature in a way meaningful for the patient; he
felt that she would not terminate for the moment (see Chapters 17,
20 and 21).

In subsequent sessions, the derivatives of the transference fantasies became clearer, and the patient finally
said that she thought that her therapist wanted her to say
that she had romantic thoughts about him. He interpreted
the defensive projection here, and then alluded to the
recent expressions of Mrs. F.F.'s fantasies toward him.
The patient responded by describing how she admired
the therapist. Then she defensively criticized him and,
afterwards, told her husband about the problems she was
having in the sessions. In response, the therapist interpreted the patient's unconscious need to bring her husband into the sessions as a protection against her own
sexual fantasies and impulses. The patient then revealed
a fantasy that the therapist had discussed her with his
wife. This (resistance) unconsciously served a similar
defensive purpose, the therapist pointed out, namely, to
bring others into her sessions as protectors, and further,
to justify her need to conceal her conscious fantasies and
ultimately their unconscious roots from the therapist.

Mrs. F.F.'s resistances took several forms, ranging
from the abrupt desire to terminate to discussing her sessions with her husband. They were initiated by frustrations with her husband that evoked a series of erotic
fantasies and wishes directed toward the therapist, along

with anxiety and intrapsychic conflict. The resistances themselves were compromises with contributions from each of the psychic macrostructures. For example, telling her husband was an expression of her anger, guilt and defensive need of protection.

In general, then, resistances have many unconscious meanings; each must be heard in turn in the latent content of the patient's associations and specifically interpreted to him. Remoteness may be based on defenses against attacking the therapist or seducing him. Other resistances have specific genetic roots in early experiences and relationships. One patient would not talk to her therapist because his silence was equated with that of her parents, who would not talk to her for weeks when angry with her; it was her unconscious talion revenge. Another was remote in order to frustrate her therapist, whom she saw as a seductive brother, and with whom she was at the same time teasing and provocative; she was also frigid with her husband.

The following clinical incident illustrates work with defenses and resistances early in therapy. Such work is of prime importance in the opening phase of treatment (see Chapter 23).

Mrs. F.G., a woman with a severe character disorder, in her third session of therapy, began the hour by saying that she had just learned of the sudden death of a friend from a brain hemorrhage. She then asked if she could refer to notes she had prepared before the session because she had so much to discuss. The therapist said that everything was "grist for the mill," including her use of notes. In turning to them, she spoke in detail of a recent evening out where the chatter was inane and everyone avoided painful topics. Other trivia followed. The therapist intervened here: he pointed out that while the patient could not have anticipated the specific use to which she was putting her notes in the session, her remark about avoiding painful topics was the clue to her use of them to bring up stale thoughts instead of permitting her upsetting feelings about her friend's death to come through. Mrs. F.G.

then put her notes aside and described the circumstances of her friend's death and her great distress; her own anxiety some years earlier when a friend had died of Hodgkin's disease; her daughter's fantasy that people are buried everywhere; and the upset and chagrin that she experienced during a series of serious illnesses in her husband and children. She then went on to refer to something she believed that she had already mentioned: she was spotting vaginally and had been called by her gynecologist the previous week; she was to be hospitalized for a dilatation and curettage. It recalled for her a miscarriage she had had several years earlier. Pointing out that the patient had not mentioned this to him, the therapist asked if this was in her notes (the use of these notes for resistance purposes had led him to believe it might not be), and the patient said it was not. Now he interpreted the original purpose of the notes as a vehicle through which she hoped to avoid this distressing news. The patient agreed and added that she had actually been bleeding for several months. The therapist asked when it had begun, and she suddenly realized that it had been four months earlier when her anxiety had started. She then, as the session ended, recalled a dream: she and her daughter are being attacked; she tries to protect her daughter, but the child disappears.

This vignette demonstrates a number of principles; I will list the major ones:

1. *The therapist interpreted the written notes initially as a general resistance, using as his model the derivatives offered by the patient, along with his observations of her behavior in the session.* This is a living example of the defensive use of isolation, where both the surface use (the friend's death) and the deeper use (the danger to the patient herself) are apparent.

The interpretation of the resistance was confirmed through the appearance of affectively meaningful associations, and then through the emergence from repression of the patient's concern about herself (see Chapter 18). Interpretation of the attempt to avoid this latter trauma led to further removal of repressive barriers, and to the recall of the precipitating event for this patient's symptoms, with a related dream.

2. *This vignette provides a good model for the operational definition of repression: keeping out of awareness a psychically active fantasy, memory or experience—a process that is prompted by the attendant conflicts, anxiety and guilt.*

3. *Here, early in treatment, the interpretative focus is on the patient's defenses and resistances.* Pointing these out properly, using material from the patient, in itself leads to modifications of the patient's defensive alignment and the emergence of critical, that is, core, disturbing events and their intrapsychic echoes.

Early work with defenses leads to relatively superficial, but genuine and meaningful, insights and, at the same time, provides the patient with a model of how psychotherapy proceeds, thus setting the tone for a strong therapeutic alliance and for work toward insight (see Chapter 23). Since consistent work with resistances and defenses is the major route to central intrapsychic conflicts, the therapist should not wait too long in the face of significant resistances, nor allow opportunities to pass without comment. If he is in tune with the manifestations of such resistances, he can, if he so elects, wait for further material from the patient before intervening.

Another vignette demonstrates why the therapist must thoroughly explore resistances before other fantasy-laden material is brought into focus. Briefly:

> Mr. F.H. was in thrice-weekly psychotherapy for various behavior problems, depression, and suicidal attempts; he was an ambulatory schizophrenic. He was in his first month of treatment after working with several previous therapists and being hospitalized after a serious suicide attempt with his car. At this juncture in his therapy, he was infuriated by his present therapist's efforts to help him set limits on his behavior and the confrontations with his acting out, manipulativeness, and corruption.
>
> In this session he reported a dream: a drug-sharing girlfriend is with him and his family at a hotel. Then the

friend is pregnant; they have a girl. Associations led to a homosexual attempt to seduce a hotel manager and to his mother's wish to see the therapist, to which he had responded angrily. After some rumination by the patient, the therapist decided to intervene: he asked what came to the patient's mind about his mother's request and his response. This proved fruitful, since it led to thoughts about disrupting his therapy by putting the therapist "on the spot" with his parents. His wish-fantasy was that the therapist would betray his confidentiality as a previous therapist had done. The therapist interpreted the unconscious, adaptive resistance aspects of this fantasy: such a corruption on the part of the therapist would undermine his entire stance, provide implicit sanction for the patient's corrupt ways, and thereby enable him to perpetuate and justify them. Mr. F.H. responded by remembering another fantasy: that of calling one of his previous, more permissive, ineffectual therapists. He realized that this fantasy entailed similar disruptive and corrupt goals.

The therapist wisely did not pursue the enticing dream offered by the patient, but dealt with defenses, resistances and acting out first. He knew that core fantasies would follow, as they did in subsequent sessions. It would have been technically unwise for him to explore this pregnancy fantasy while the patient was quietly busy attempting to disrupt and destroy his therapy. In fact, he might well have left his present therapist if his acting out had not been analyzed; the therapist might have explored a fantasy-system but lost a patient. The dream may well have been offered to deceive the therapist, as a smokescreen for the patient's avenues of acting out against therapy; in other words, it constituted a seduction and deception, rather than an avenue to the resistances. If time permitted, associations to the dream might have been explored. It hints that homosexual fantasies toward the therapist were motivating the resistance, but this could be specifically adduced only after the forms of the resistance were clear and the derivatives could be interpreted.

This patient was endeavoring to create with his therapist an antitherapeutic, corrupted alliance, so that he could perpetuate rather than revise his pathology. A therapist must not be seduced, consciously or unconsciously, into doing this. The indications are that this patient's previous therapists had done so; the patient's suicide attempt may well have been the outcome.

Dreams and fantasy material are inherently attractive to dynamic therapists. They must never be so interested in such material, however, that they overlook resistances and defenses; gentle, persistent interpretation of these first is a sine qua non. If the session and material permits, the therapist can analyze the resistances first, and the dreams afterwards.

Let us now summarize the basic principles for the interpretation of resistances:

1. *Resistances are among the most important therapeutic contexts. Their interpretation is a primary and ever-necessary task and the search for their current and genetic basis, their unconscious motives, and the unconscious fantasies that determine them is of the highest priority for the therapist.*

2. *Interpretations of resistances are of two kinds:* General and superficial ones that make the unaware patient aware that he is in fact resisting and of the general, unconscious reasons for this. Unconscious defenses involved in the resistance may be identified in simple language. Specific ones in which the unconscious fantasies evoking the resistance are dealt with, and the specific unconscious meaning of the resistance, including its genetic basis, is pointed out.

3. *Problems in interpreting resistances include:*

• The failure to interpret the resistances specifically in terms of the individual life experiences and fantasies of the patient, a tendency to utilize only general and superficial interpretations. The failure to recognize that the therapist must be constantly alert for resistances and their basis, particularly later in therapy and when repressed material is emerging.

• The failure to recognize that wherever possible resistances should be interpreted as quickly as feasible. If, however, they are based on anxiety-provoking fantasies, the therapist must be tactful and wait for clear expressions of these fantasies in the material.

• A tendency not to listen to the material from the patient for latent content reflecting unconscious meanings of resistances. This kind of listening is essential for the proper use of interpretations.

 • Too great an interest in deep material and repressed fantasies, at the expense of understanding defenses.

4. *The resistance aspects of latent content should be interpreted before those related to core conflicts and symptom-evoking fantasies.* This enables the therapist to utilize the adaptive framework, and, in context, demonstrate the adaptive and defensive purposes of unconscious fantasies. The unconscious fantasies related to resistances tend to lead to, and merge with, those related to the patient's ongoing symptoms and intrapsychic conflicts.

DEFENSES

Not every defense is expressed as a resistance, and the therapist does not wait for defenses to be expressed as resistances, in transference reactions, or toward therapy to interpret them. Defenses are an essential part of the resolution of all of the patient's intrapsychic anxieties and conflicts, and of the unconscious fantasies that reflect their use and their contribution to symptoms. Defenses, like resistances, often have a complex unconscious structure of their own and can be fully understood only through a comprehensive view of the unconscious conflict and fantasies, and the genetic roots, to which they are related and on which they are based.

The following vignette will exemplify a group of unconscious defenses of the ego and their interpretation:

> Mr. F.I. was an acting out adolescent. His mother had nearly died of a bleeding ulcer when he was a child. His fiancée, with whom he recently fought, had decided to take birth control pills and he three times referred to them in his session as "diet pills." The patient finally focused on his slip and realized that he had read that birth control pills could cause fatal hemorrhages. He did not mention his mother, but her illness had been referred to in several recent sessions. When the patient shifted to rumination, the therapist intervened. He pointed out that Mr. F.I. could not bear the thought of his fiancée endangering herself and suffering his mother's fate, particularly at

a time when he was furious with her, and so he denied the nature of the pill she was taking.

It is important to not use technical language in such interpretations; this promotes isolation and intellectualization. It is also vital that the therapist constantly allude to defenses in his interpreting and not confine himself to id material such as the patient's murderous rage at his fiancée and his mother. Unconscious fantasies are best approached from the defensive and adaptive aspects of the material first. In this instance, the defenses implied in the interpretation are those of repression (of the fear that his fiancée might die; of the genetic links to his mother; and of his own murderous wishes), some degree of denial (that his fiancée was on the dangerous birth control pills, and of the threat of losing her); and some degree of reaction formation or undoing (stating that his fiancée was on harmless rather than possibly harmful pills). Each defense has its own underlying fantasy structure and a specific relationship to the patient's central, ongoing intrapsychic conflicts, and the repressed fantasies related to them and to his symptoms. Genetically, Mr. F.I. had used defenses similar to those he applied here in his past struggle with the inner conflicts evoked by his mother's illness. Adaptively, these defenses serve to spare the patient from his fear that his fiancée might die and from fantasied fulfilment of his rageful fantasies toward her. The slip of the tongue gives him momentary inner peace, but it is far from a lasting or effective means of resolving a conflict.

Let us consider another clinical example:

> Mr. F.J., a young man, with a borderline syndrome, feared sleeping away from home at his college dormitory. He had recurrent fantasies of being attacked and knifed there. In one session, he reported a dream of seeing his mother in a bathroom; there was blood on the floor. Associations related to fears of hurting his mother and his anger with her. Interpretation of this rage and his unconscious fears of talion punishment if he should leave her, led to the previously unreported recollection of an incident where his mother threatened to kill him with a knife.

> With this, the therapist pointed out that the danger of being murdered existed in reality at home and that the patient had defensively shifted it to the outside in order to maintain his ties to his mother.

We see here first an unconscious projection of the patient's own rage onto strangers; then the lifting of a repression after a correct interpretation, revealing a new recollection; and finally a displacement and projection of the danger of being murdered by his mother onto strangers. There is also the implicit denial: his mother is not dangerous, though others are. Less explicit for the moment is the displacement onto his mother of Mr. F.J.'s own fears of bodily harm. These defenses were interpreted in simple terms and with reference to their specific fantasied basis. They were confirmed by the further unfolding of the material.

We can also see here how one source of anxiety and the related unconscious fantasies can defend against awareness of those on another level. Often, the fantasies that have been most recently worked through are stubbornly and defensively maintained in order to avoid new material; they are used as a resistance which requires its own working through (see Gill, 1963).

Interpretation of defenses, in context, most often forms part of the total interpretation of an unconscious fantasy-memory complex, though it may be done independently. These interpretations depend on a full understanding of the intrapsychic mechanisms of defense, their unconscious use and structure, and their adaptive roles.

Many interpretations of defenses are facilitated by models offered by the patient in his associations. Two brief examples will illustrate:

> Miss F.N. was in therapy for depression and social problems. Her therapist had cancelled an hour because he had been ill. In the following session, the patient spoke of a friend whom she had visited and who had ignored her; she had cried while going home. She had been afraid that she had been followed and would be attacked. She detailed the negative changes in her relationship with her friend. The therapist asked her if she was also upset about

the cancelled session (a poorly stated general interpretation that was made in too tentative a manner, without alluding to the derivatives in the patient's associations). Miss F.N. said that she had not cared about it and spoke further about the hurt from her friend. She had hidden her distress and tears from her father when she got home. She then discussed other people who had deserted her, and became angry with her therapist for taking notes during her sessions.

While we can ascertain from this vignette that weakly stated interventions invite negation and denial, the matter probably could have been corrected if the therapist had detected the model of the defensive denial offered in Miss F.N.'s associations: the allusion to hiding her tears and distress from her father could have been taken as an expression of her need to deny her rather obvious distress regarding the therapist's absence.

Mr. F.O. was in therapy because of his unhappy marriage and depression. He had recently revealed a series of masturbatory fantasies in which he was humiliated and hurt by the woman he was engaging in intercourse. In the hour following, he was ruminative and spoke mainly of his anger at his wife, who had had an accident with his car. He mentioned very briefly an old fantasy of being tied up by a woman and tortured, but quickly shifted to details of trivial problems at work.

In the next hour, the patient was again remote. At one point, he spoke of how he knew of many things that need fixing around his house but was the kind of person who avoided such problems. He then spoke of wishing to be an actor and of leaving therapy.

Here, the defense is one of avoidance, and the model offered by the patient in his associations is that of not doing the necessary repairs around the house. This should have been related to the patient's avoidance of the emotional problems that had recently emerged in therapy, perhaps with an added reference to the "price" involved for the patient: nothing would be fixed or resolved.

The possible interpretations of defenses are virtually unlimited, and I shall not try to illustrate even the main variations (see the Index of Clinical Material). The principles of interpretation are comparable to those for resistances and will not be repeated here. If the therapist has recognized the need to watch for manifestations of defenses and to understand that they cannot be thought of in simplistic terms, but are to be understood in depth, he is well on the way toward working effectively with defenses, either seeking to modify the varieties of maladaptions, or silently or actively supporting healthy and adaptive defenses.

REACTIONS AND FANTASIES TOWARD THE THERAPIST AND THE THERAPY

Here again we are dealing with a complex and difficult topic, one which will occupy us at some length in Chapters 20, 21, and 22. In this section, where the focus is on the technique of interpretation, I shall only very briefly define the most important problems and then exemplify them.

Reactions to the therapist, in behavior and in conscious and unconscious fantasy, range from those that are primarily determined by relationships and experiences with past significant persons in the patient's life—transference reactions—to those that are primarily determined by the actual behavior, communications and attitudes of the therapist—nontransference responses. In almost all situations, the patient's reaction is based on a mixture of both, in which one tends to predominate.

These reactions are always precipitated by some current experience or trauma inside and outside therapy. Within therapy there are, first, those that are inherent and inevitable in the therapeutic relationship, such as the "tilted" aspects which favor the therapist, other realistic aspects of the relationship, the correct interventions the therapist makes, and his vacations; and second, those that arise out of the therapist's errors and such countertransference problems as aggressive and seductive interventions, missed interventions, incorrect interpretations, and attempts to control the patient. This distinction is important because in the first type of precipitate the therapist has not erred or behaved inappropriately, and the patient's reactions and fantasies are in focus and interpreted. On the other hand, with the second type of precipitate, the therapist has played an active, to some degree inappropriate, and sometimes damaging, role that must be recognized in making an interpretation. In this case, the responsibility for the patient's reaction must be shared, and the true role of the therapist acknowledged, though not belabored. At times, a patient's reaction to a situation where the therapist's countertransference problems predominate may be quite appropriate and adaptive, even though it results in criticism of the therapist or termination of therapy. Leaving an unhelpful or destructive therapist is hardly unsound or maladaptive, especially if the therapist proves unable to get his problems with the patient under control.

Both types of current precipitates (contexts) generate reactions with genetic roots and an intrapsychic basis in conscious and unconscious fantasies. There are reality-based conflicts between the patient and a realistically traumatizing therapist, and in addition, intrapsychic, neurotic conflicts, transference fantasies and reactions based mainly on past relationships: this is an important distinction. The therapist must be in tune with the manifest and latent meanings of his interventions and failures to intervene, and with his actual attitudes toward, and fantasies about, his patient in order to decide whether the latter's action is realistic and adaptive, or neurotic and maladaptive. For purposes of this discussion, I shall label neurotic reactions determined largely by past figures, as "transference"; and realistic, adaptive and appropriate reactions as "reality-based" or "nontransference."

We must also realize that transference and realistic reactions and fantasies toward the therapist may serve multiple purposes and functions, much as any other communication. Depending on the context and the central reality-based and intrapsychic conflicts, these responses may serve as resistances and defenses or as the conveyors of important unconscious fantasies and repressed memories related to the patient's emotional disturbances.

Reactions to the therapist and treatment may form the basis for serious resistances to therapy and disruptions in the therapeutic alliance; they are almost always one facet—sometimes crucial—in the premature interruption of therapy. The therapist must be especially alert to such fantasies, and their derivatives and expressions. Not every resistance has as its central and primary source the reality-based and transference reactions to the therapist; they may stem from fears of unconscious fantasies, and the anxiety and guilt they evoke, or from a need to suffer. Nonetheless this relationship is a factor in the structure of virtually every resistance, and when resistances appear, the therapist must always examine the patient's relationship with him for any fantasies, transference or appropriate, that are contributing to the resistance.

As pointed out earlier, in the section on resistances and defenses, transference and, at times, reality-based resistances, tend to merge into core transference fantasies that reflect unconscious fantasies related to the patient's neurosis.

Technically, we must learn that in psychotherapy:

1. *Many reactions to, and fantasies about, the therapist are primarily realistic and secondarily of a transference nature.*

2. *The main focus of psychotherapy should be the patient's life problems.* Only when the patient or the therapist in some way introduces the relationship between these two parties into treatment, should the patient–therapist relationship be explored and interpreted.

3. *This is a most sensitive area of interpretation for both patient and therapist.* The latter must proceed with accuracy and caution.

Now, let us look at some clinical vignettes (see also Chapters 20–22 for more clinical material):

> Mrs. F.K. was a severely depressed white woman who was infuriated by her daughter's engagement to a Negro. When the wedding date was set, the patient came to her session in a rage against therapy: it had not helped and nothing had changed, she was getting worse, and she wanted shock therapy or medication. The therapist listened silently. After raging for a while, Mrs. F.K. went on to describe the setting of the wedding date and then stated that she had been angry with one of her other children, a son. She had had a fantasy that he was killed in a car accident. The therapist then intervened: he told Mrs. F.K. that she was in a murderous rage against her daugh-

ter because of her marriage plans, and that this rage was partly displaced onto her son and partly turned against herself, in a talion-like fashion, leading to her wish for punishment through shock treatment—a move also calculated to evoke revengeful guilt in her daughter. Further, her fury at the therapist was based in large part on her unspoken fantasy that the therapist was going to prevent her daughter's marriage; this had not turned out to be the case.

Material in the following sessions confirmed these interpretations and led to an interpretation of some of the genetic factors operating at this time. Thus, Mrs. F.K. dreamt that she was in a wheelchair; everyone was nice to her except her daughter. Associations were to a cousin who had attempted suicide when her husband had left her. Mrs. F.K. then described her relationship with her mother, now making it clear that she was deeply attached to her, but also that, because of her mother's angry aloofness and tendency to be hurtful, she was also intensely infuriated with her. The patient's longings for closeness and union with an idealized mother, and her murderous rage against her mother for not gratifying these longings, a rage turned against herself, were the genetically founded unconscious fantasies upon which her reaction to her daughter and therapist was based; it was this that was interpreted and confirmed here.

In this vignette, we can identify the following:
1. *These reactions to the therapist may be considered as primarily transference fantasies since they are largely determined by reactions to a past figure (the patient's mother).* Notice, however, that there is also a realistic factor here: a current hope that the therapist could prevent her daughter's marriage. In all, the unconscious transference fantasy appears to be something like this: "You are a bad, destructive, unhelpful mother who has failed to magically change the situation with my daughter. I want to destroy myself to destroy you and to make you feel guilty"—this was a technique also used by her mother against the patient. The central precipitate

is clearly the marriage plans of the patient's daughter, and there is also a displacement of rage and fantasies from her daughter onto the therapist.

2. *The resistance aspect of these transference fantasies refers manifestly to the desire to leave psychotherapy and undergo electroshock treatment, and to the request for medication.* The specific underlying fantasies have been noted already.

3. *The repressed transference fantasies lead into unconscious fantasies related to the patient's depression.* Here too, as with fantasies related to other kinds of resistances, the same unconscious fantasy complex ultimately determines the transference fantasies and the symptoms.

From this it is clear that interpretations must be as specific as possible; and those related to the transference should be tied to the intrapsychic conflicts prevailing in the patient's life, and to genetic material when possible.

The therapeutic context here was a major resistance and a serious rupture in the therapeutic alliance that called for interpreting. There were ample references to therapy and the therapist. In general, it is wise for the therapist not to introduce himself into the interpretation without such references from the patient.

A second vignette will illustrate another kind of interpretation related to treatment. This example derives from a countertransference-evoked error which led to a kind of acting out by the therapist, and was compounded by his failure to detect and understand the patient's reaction to his mistakes. The material is condensed, but should be adequate for the reader to formulate and time his own intervention. Since no interpretation was offered at this juncture by the therapist, any confirmation of a proposed intervention must be derived from the subsequent development of the material.

> Mr. F.L., a young man with a borderline syndrome, had been in treatment for about a year, and was having difficulty talking about his masturbatory fantasies. He finally told his therapist that when he masturbated, he imagined "screwing women up the ass." He then recalled that when he was a child his father would take his temperature rectally when he seemed ill, and did so well into

his teens. This gave him an erection and led to his masturbation with objects inserted into his anus. His mother for her part gave him enemas and he later gave them to himself to arouse himself sexually. In the context of working on this material, the therapist inadvertently ended one session ten minutes early. The patient began to leave, noticed the error, and pointed it out. The therapist apologized and the patient returned, suggesting that the therapist get himself better organized, and then berating himself for being so openly critical. When the therapist pointed out Mr. F.L.'s obvious annoyance, the patient brushed it aside and joked that he might skip a few sessions himself—but it did not matter.

In the next hour, the patient ruminated about his efforts at finding a new job and being turned down at several places. He felt like leaving the session early since he had nothing more to say, and the therapist pointed out that he seemed to want revenge for what he had done the previous hour, which the patient flatly denied.

The therapist was about a minute late to the following hour, and the patient pointed it out and then went on to ruminate again about his job and how therapy seemed headed nowhere. The therapist said that the patient was using his hurt feelings to avoid discussing the matters he had recently brought up in therapy. Mr. F.L. responded by describing fantasies of having sexual relationships with adolescent girls, and how distant he had once felt from people after a vaccination for polio. The therapist at this point once more ended the session ten minutes too soon, caught the error himself, and called the patient back. Another apology and questioning of the patient regarding his feelings led Mr. F.L. to say that he did not know what to say; somehow he felt just as he used to when he was being drilled by his father, at times when they did his school work together.

In the following hour, the patient said that his father had asked him and his brother to move out of the parental home (they were both young adults). He wanted to quit treatment; the therapist suggested a revenge motive to him. He agreed; it was like wanting to break up with his girlfriend. Mr. F.L. felt that the therapist should talk to his parents, and ruminated about the way he blamed himself for things that went wrong and that he had been masturbating a good deal lately, thinking of anal intercourse. He was, he felt, telling his therapist off for the first time and it felt good. With this, the session ended.

At this point, we can criticize the work of this therapist and offer several specific interpretations that should have been made to the patient. I would make the following comments:

I chose this clinical interlude to highlight the way in which the therapist, in reality, can provoke quite strong and disruptive reactions in patients through countertransference-prompted errors. Such behavior or interventions, while unfortunate, can often (though not always; see Chapter 22) be corrected and used toward insight and inner change if the patient's responses and their realistic basis are correctly understood and interpreted.

An interpretation is strongly indicated here for a number of reasons, briefly: to ameliorate the effects of the countertransference-evoked errors—the actual hurt to the patient; to produce insight and inner change out of hurt and chaos, a most rewarding experience for both parties. Without reparation of the therapist-evoked disruption in the therapeutic alliance, the entire treatment could be undermined. The patient's threats to terminate constitute another reason to intervene, because the patient was experiencing regressive symptoms. Finally, intervention was indicated because there were interpretable derivatives of repressed fantasies and intrapsychic conflicts available.

These indications for interventions are among the most common we have, though not all that exist. They offer an informative sampling, and convey the complexity of this issue (see Chapter 17).

In this instance, the therapist deceived himself in thinking that his comment that the patient wished for revenge on him was specific and sufficient. Such "global" interventions as these are virtually never especially effective, and they lack the specific content, and personal and genetic referents, that make an interpretation meaningful for a given patient. At best, they are preliminary and rather like confrontations.

What, then, using the material at hand, should have been added to give the interpretation a content-laden, specific reference? I would suggest one integrated interpretation that should have been made at this time, to the effect that Mr. F.L. was experiencing his early dismissals as rejections and even invitations to leave treatment, much as his father had asked him to leave his house. Further, Mr. F.L. was finding these dismissals stimulating and sexually arousing, much as he felt when his father inserted a thermometer into his anus; this was prompting his masturbation and fantasies of anal intercourse. These experiences with the therapist had, for him, the quality of an actual repetition of those disturbing, assaultive-penetrating episodes with his father.

Such an interpretation aims at making conscious for the patient both the specific context of the material and the particular repressed current and genetic meanings of this episode, determined by his own life experiences. This would enable the patient to understand the deeper significance, for him, of what the therapist had done. Only through this could the therapist's errors and the patient's responses be sufficiently worked through to enable therapy to resume a reasonable course. Without these interpretations, which acknowledge both the therapist's contribution to the patient's fantasies and the patient's responsibility for his behavior and fantasies, the unconscious gratification in the repetition of the sadomasochistic ties to this patient's father would derail treatment, and would constitute an antitherapeutic alliance and mutual acting out.

Later, I will discuss this patient's response as a type of therapist-caused syndrome, "iatrogenic masochism" (Chapter 22). Here, I want to focus on the problem of interpretations of material deriving from the relationship between the patient and the therapist. I chose this example to show that patients respond to actual errors and countertransference problems on the part of the therapist, and that these must be interpreted specifically and in depth from the patient's associations, if insight and the return of a proper therapeutic alliance and atmosphere is to be achieved. Such work may be described as dealing with transference (more precisely, nontransference) resistances, but this hardly does justice to the complexity of the matter.

In this particular situation in supervision at this juncture, I had suggested to the therapist interpretations along the lines I have described. It is of predictive and confirmatory interest to add the material from the session that followed these formulations.

> In this hour, Mr. F.L. began by saying that the thera-pist was right; he did blame himself for everything. He then went on to describe for the first time another form of his masturbation, one in which he masturbated while defecating, and then smeared the feces over his back. It was extremely exciting for him. He also mentioned how his girlfriend was, for the first time, giving him the things he wanted.

I will refrain from diverging into a discussion on the many fascinating aspects of this latter material, especially, this remarkable lifting of a repressive barrier with the revelation of a previously unreported masturbatory practice, in response to, of all things, a series of countertransference problems and technical errors. The added material, however, confirms the masochistic gratification that the therapist's behavior was affording this patient and indicates that this continued when the therapist failed specifically to interpret these aspects of the situation.

To summarize:

1. *Interpretations related to the relationship between the patient and his therapist range from those that are primarily transference-based responses and fantasies, through those that are evoked either by appropriate or inappropriate and erroneous behavior of the therapist.* The patient's behavioral response, and the fantasies and recollections evoked by the particular interaction with his therapist, must be understood and interpreted in the relevant context and traced out into the specific unconscious fantasies and memories stirred up by the situation.

Such interpretations, then, should in general, take the reality that is prompting the patient's response as the starting point for the intervention. From there, the therapist should use the specific derivatives in the material to interpret the particular unconscious conflicts, fantasies and memories active at the moment. Interpretations which ultimately lack instinctual drive elements are seldom, if ever, complete.

2. *Fantasied responses to the therapist, which may have elements of resistance in them, merge into, and ultimately blend with, the unconscious fantasies and experiences that are central to the patient's symptoms and neurosis.* The example with Mr. F.L. is typical: his sexual perversions and masochism had, indeed, arisen in part out of his disturbed relationship with his father. This was repeated in reality in his relationship with the therapist. It is likely that such gratification precludes the ultimate working through of these problems with a therapist who has participated in them (see Chapter 22). Even afterwards, however, interpretation of the unconscious meanings of such an experience can lead to clarification of the patient's basic neurotic problems and promote the resumption of a workable therapeutic alliance.

Often, such realistic and fantasied responses to the therapist are evoked by correct or appropriate behavior and interventions. Such fantasies and their ties to the past may be interpreted directly—without the complications involved in dealing with those related to therapeutic errors. These experiences with the therapist unconsciously correspond to, or facilitate the projection of, repressed memories and fantasies related to the patient's anxieties, traumas and conflicts, and thus readily lead into these important areas.

3. *Interpretation of transference and reality-based resistances and fantasies in general should not, and generally do not, become the central work of psychotherapy.* They should be analyzed and resolved, to allow the return of the therapeutic work to the life problems and consequent intrapsychic conflicts of the patient.

NUCLEAR UNCONSCIOUS FANTASIES

Much as all roads led to Rome, all of the therapeutic work related to the crucial unconscious factors in the creation and maintenance of neurotic symptoms leads to the interpretation and working through of the major nuclear repressed fantasies on which they are based (see Arlow, 1969). This, in all of its complexities, is pivotal in the resolution of symptoms, a sine qua non for the achievement of true inner, structural change (see Chapter 17). In introducing this concept, I want to emphasize these points:

1. *Interpretation of nuclear unconscious fantasies includes the delineation of the specific, relevant genetic experiences (traumas), the central anxieties or other affects involved, the key intrapsychic conflicts, and the role of instinctual drives (the id), of conscience and ideals (the superego), and of defenses, controls, object relationships and other adaptive measures (the ego; see Chapter 8).*

2. *Such interpretations rendered piecemeal as the material permits provide insight into the unconscious motives, meanings and origins of symptoms.* This, in turn, can lead to the adoption of new solutions to the conflicts involved and to the resolution of the symptoms and maladaptive character formations. Such a resolution is, by far, the most stable avenue for lasting change. Most other interventions provide means of inner change that are far more limited, or relate to outer environmental manipulation without stable inner change at all.

3. *While in psychotherapy these interpretations are, as I noted in Chapter 1, much more limited than those possible in psychoanalysis, they are feasible and necessary.* Interpretation of selected, but crucial, unconscious fantasy clusters and a limited working through of related material is the most common occurrence at the peak of such therapeutic endeavors.

4. *Such interpretations are built over a series of sessions through derivatives expressed through a variety of largely disguised communications.* They touch upon different facets of the symptom-producing intrapsychic conflicts in some kind of sequence, and are finally woven into a totality through a series of interpretations and confirmations which provide previously repressed, additional material for the ongoing work.

In this work, the therapist must painstakingly move toward the interpretation of the symptom-producing unconscious (core) fantasies through a repetitive analysis of resistances. Further, the defensive and adaptive dimensions of these core fantasies are to be explored first, and their depths and instinctual content subsequently. Many therapists settle for far less, and achieve far less in the bargain. One must therefore become familiar with such work—the reader will find helpful examples of this type of interpreting elsewhere in this book (see Index of Clinical Material). I shall now illustrate further:

> Miss F.M. was a college student who came into psychotherapy with a history of severe asthma since childhood and problems with her school work, drug use, and promiscuity; she also had a severe character disorder. The material to be presented here is drawn from a period toward the end of the first year of a thrice-weekly psychotherapy.
>
> In the previous weeks, the patient had explored the death of a close relative during her childhood, which had evoked guilt over murderous wishes toward each of the members of her immediate family (two younger siblings and her parents) and, by talion punishment, was a factor in the onset of her asthma. In this context and on this level, the asthma represented her own death sentence for these murderous, guilt-ridden fantasies. Several related experiences and fantasies had been worked through during this period of the therapy, and it brought considerable symptom-relief, including a diminution in the asthmatic episodes, and contributed to recent positive character changes. On the other hand, visits at this time to her home on weekends had led to battles with her parents, reflecting their relentless mutual rage; much work still remained to be done.
>
> In the first session of this sequence, Miss F.M. described fresh arguments with her parents and then spoke of her new boyfriend, a fellow from college who was quite in tune with her moods and thoughts. She had taken drugs with him and then driven her car while she was high, though her licence had been revoked. Later that night, she had a brief period of wheezing, but was able to control and limit it. She reported a dream: she is on the floor of the bathroom, nude, and among people who are making remarks about her. She went on to say

that the dream reminded her of one of her hospitalizations for asthma, which she then described, and of an old boyfriend who had admired her body. Her therapist asked her what prompted the dream and she then recalled an incident that she had forgotten to mention: a fellow, Ed, whom she knew, had committed suicide by hanging himself. He had been living with a friend of the patient, a girl whom the patient thought was his sister, but she had recently learned that they were actually cousins. Miss F.M. had the impression that the two were having an affair. She had been told that another girlfriend of his had rejected him and that this led to the suicide. She then commented that he had smothered himself and linked this to her brief asthmatic episode, which had actually occurred soon after she had learned of Ed's death. She often sat in the bathroom when she wheezed.

The therapist then made this comment: Miss F.M.'s asthma was her own attempt at suicide by asphyxiation in punishment for her murderous rage against her parents, who had rejected her.

In the next session, the patient reported having left some drugs at home, their being discovered by her parents, and their subsequent battle. Two dreams were described: in the first, Miss F.M. was riding a racing motorcycle which fell apart; as the patient fell, she bled. The second had occurred on Thanksgiving night several weeks earlier: she was on a stagecoach or in a convertible with many wounded Civil War soldiers, whom she was nursing. Associations were to dangerous motorcycle rides she had taken in the past and would avoid now; to falling apart; to thoughts of becoming a nurse; and to her feeling that an asthmatic attack was coming on, for which she would blame her therapist. She did not believe that Ed had really committed suicide; the therapist connected this to her own repeated denial of the seriousness of her asthma (an interpretation of a prominent defense used by this patient). The therapist also sensed for the first time, though he did not as yet state it to the patient, that she was trying to give up some of her self-destructive behavior, as represented in her thought of no longer riding on motorcycles, and was turning to more constructive outlets for her conflicts and feelings; instead of continuing the civil war with her parents, she was thinking of helping—nursing—those who were injured by such wars.

In the next session, in the context of the patient's description of her improved controls—she had refused an offer of drugs and had not resorted to stealing in a situation where she had done so in the past—the therapist alluded to the recent changes in her behavior and fantasies. She again discussed her strong reaction to the suicide, now adding that she had once slept at Ed's house, in his bed, though he was not there at the time. She then recalled how she would go into her father's bed and shared it with him when she had nightmares as a child, and reviewed various beds that she had shared with boyfriends. The therapist reminded her that she had also done this with both her brothers and sister. This confrontation, based on past material which contained implications that the patient might develop further, was made because of Miss F.M.'s earlier comment that she had thought Ed was having an affair with his sister. It prompted a recollection that had not arisen in several years: when the patient was about ten, she had been told about intercourse by some friends and had gone home and attempted several times to seduce her brother; she had felt guilty over these incidents.

The following hour, Miss F.M. described a chaotic weekend in which she had taken drugs, stolen money from her parents, inadvertently allowed more drugs to be discovered by them, and carried out other corrupt and provocative actions. In the ensuing disagreement with her parents, she had confessed many of her recent misdeeds. The therapist intervened: he interpreted the patient's behavior as a response to her recollection of the attempts at seducing her brother. She was committing other crimes and confessing to them in an effort to be punished, as a cover for those she had committed against her brother, and for which she really wanted to be made to suffer. The patient responded with a thoughtful pause, direct agreement, and the comment that her boyfriend had blamed treatment for the recent mess and had told her to quit; she had hung up on him.

In the next sessions, the patient took drugs before and after her hours in what was interpreted as her attempt to provoke the therapist and avenge herself on him for his confrontations and interpretations. At the same time, Miss F.M. reported fantasies of being among the most wanted criminals and of ending up dead of an overdose of drugs on the bathroom floor. For the first time in years, she cried over her plight, and over her guilt and her self-destructiveness, and realized that in the past, it was at times of crises such as these that she had developed asthma. Her fear that her brother would blackmail her also emerged.

To bring this vignette to a close, in the next session, Miss F.M. described settling down and making peace at home. She dreamt that she was in a car between two of her friends, Al and Fran, and that she fell back and couldn't breathe. The dream was prompted by two things: a newspaper story of a woman who asphyxiated herself in a car after her husband had died, and a short story she had read about a brother and sister who committed incest. She pointed out that Al was currently trying to seduce Fran, who is a virgin.

The therapist finally made an important specific interpretation to the patient, one which perhaps should have been made earlier though he had decided to wait until the derivatives were incontrovertible. He stated that the patient's wheezing initiated by Ed's suicide was her punishment for both her attempt to seduce her brother and her murderous rage against him. He reminded her in this context of an incident in which she had tried to choke him when he was an infant. This intervention was confirmed in the next session when the patient reported sleeping excessively for the past five days. Associations linked this to her asthma (as a more adaptive substitute) and finally to the death by an overdose with sleeping pills of a girlfriend who had been promiscuous. She then recalled a male cousin's attempt to seduce her that had occurred in his bathroom.

I have presented this rather lengthy vignette to illustrate not only the general technique of interpreting, but also the way interpretations should be developed, expanded, and made more specific as the material unfolds, and how, when material is unfolding, the therapist can wait for increasingly open and less disguised (close) derivatives of the patient's unconscious conflicts and fantasies before intervening. Briefly, I will emphasize these points:

The therapist intervened for two main reasons: first, the therapeutic context—the patient was both symptomatic (asthmatic) and acting out; second, the initial material lent itself to interpretation of aspects of the patient's central intrapsychic conflicts and the unconscious meanings of her asthma. Subsequent material deepened the insight into the conflicts which formed the basis for her symptoms and acting out, and the interpretations could therefore be expanded.

Once any vignette of this type has been completed, we should be able to define a salient part of the structure of the patient's symptoms, including the central unconscious fantasies most relevant to the intrapsychic conflicts and their genetic basis. The reader should be able to formulate this material accordingly. To select the major highlights: the suicide of Ed was viewed unconsciously by the patient, through her own inner set and conflicts, as self-destruction out of guilt over incest with his sister, and this event rekindled her own unconscious guilt over her attempts at incest with her brother— an area of conflict that she was also moving toward at the time in her therapy. Thus, a current trauma reawakened an earlier, neurosis-producing trauma, at a juncture in treatment when the patient's defenses had been modified sufficiently to permit a relatively full working through of the relevant conflicts.

Self-punitive asthmatic symptoms followed, as did criminal behavior of the classic type that is prompted by intrapsychic guilt in which one crime is committed to obtain punishment for another, deeper crime. The dreams of lying nude on the bathroom floor and of being unable to breathe reflected nuclear unconscious fantasies related to this theme. On another level, Ed's death gratified her unconscious wish for her brother's death, for which Miss F.M. also sought punishment in fantasy and reality.

Beyond this, I leave it to the reader to formulate the material, particularly the role that interpretations of unconscious fantasies, genetic factors, and intrapsychic conflicts played in resolving the patient's symptoms at various levels.

The interpretive work here illustrates some of the most basic principles of interpretation being developed in this chapter: interpretations must be specific and individualized, relevant to the patient's particular patterns of neurotic behavior; interpretations should deal with latent content that clusters and coalesces, and not with isolated fragments; interpretations should generally begin with the reality precipitates (context) for the unconscious fantasies, should be stated within an adaptive framework, should identify the specific repressed fantasy, and should link all of this to the symptom in focus (the therapeutic context); interpretations, if correct, will be confirmed (see Chapter 18), lead to additional insights, and ultimately to symptom-relief. Interpretation of defenses and resistances comes first. We may expect a sequence of alternating resistances, working through, insight and further resistances or acting out. This is well illustrated here.

In preparing interpretations, a stance of listening to the material loosely and openly at first, and then precisely and specifically, aids in formulating the intervention. It is best to develop hypotheses silently and to speak only when subsequent material supports them, unless there is a pressing reason to interpret (see Chapter 17). Further, stay in tune with the crucial content of recent sessions in order to utilize it for later interpretations. This is most important for deepening and widening one's interpretive work.

Note how important the interpretations of guilt and the need for punishment (superego derivatives) was in this material. This patient's asthma was overdetermined, and in this vignette one complex root of this symptom, related primarily to her intrapsychic conflicts and fantasies regarding her brother, was analyzed. Part of the patient's attempt to readapt to these unresolved conflicts took place in her therapy, and with the therapist's help, led to new, non-neurotic adaptations in place of the costly asthmatic and self-destructive, punishment-inviting behavior. In all, then, the interpretive work touched on many aspects of the total conflict situation and the complex repressed fantasies and memories related to it. Anxiety and guilt motivated this process and both were alleviated through it.

Interpretations are valid interventions in psychotherapy of any weekly frequencies.

Miss F.M. was in thrice-weekly psychotherapy, but interpretive work of this kind may be used in less frequent treatments, including once weekly (see especially the vignettes of Mr. F.B., pp. 467–469, who was in once-weekly therapy, and Mrs. K.T., in Vol. II, who was in twice-weekly treatment). It is carried out within the limits imposed by the frequency of visits on the relationship between the patient and the therapist, and on the derivatives available in the material. These limiting factors do not, however, preclude vital work with interpretations of all kinds.

In general, another good rule of thumb is to interpret derivatives of relatively recent intrapsychic conflicts and fantasies before dealing with those that are from earlier periods. Usually, the patient's associations will develop in such a manner. In any case, premature genetic interpretations made before connections to current symptoms and conflicts can be established will usually lead to isolation and nonconfirmation.

To emphasize two of these points further: interpretations of resistance-related, transference, and nuclear unconscious fantasies should begin with the adaptive context, the reality evoking the fantasied responses. They should be phrased within the adaptive framework so that the patient is aware of what he is coping with, and how. Interpretations of isolated unconscious fantasy content are generally best avoided; if the context is not clear and has been repressed, the therapist should wait for derivatives related to it or confront the patient with the absence of a clear precipitate for the material. This also applies to genetic interpretations, where it is best to include in the interventions references to the adaptive problems in the patient's childhood which evoked the early fantasies and responsive behavior. With Miss F.M., for example, the therapist, in a later session, based on additional material, interpreted the context of the patient's attempts to seduce her brother to be her sexual and bodily anxieties evoked by her pubertal development, and her guilt-ridden incestuous desires for her father, which were stimulated by his overseductiveness.

I have attempted, then, to illustrate the interpretation of core unconscious fantasies related to neurotic and psychosomatic symptoms, and to disturbed behavior. Once more, it is fair to say that the possible variations are infinite, although the basic principles are relatively constant. I shall now move on to some final comments about the technique of interpretations.

CONCLUDING COMMENTS

I will close this chapter with a review of the indications for interpretations (see also Chapter 17). In addition, I will briefly discuss some of the problems of using this intervention.

INDICATIONS FOR INTERPRETATIONS

Applying the principles governing indications for interpretative interventions depends largely on a thorough understanding of the nature of an accurate, meaningful and well-timed interpretation. The therapist must develop an instinct for listening for the derivatives of unconscious fantasies, for recognizing their differentiation from conscious fantasies, for the proper time to intervene and the readiness of the patient, and for the appropriate language to use in interpreting these unconscious fantasies to patients. With this in mind, I will briefly suggest the main indications for interpretations:

1. *The therapist interprets, most obviously, when the derivatives of an unconscious fantasy, or an unconscious memory, motive, mental mechanism, or other unconscious mental expression, are clear and sufficiently developed in the material for him to believe that an interpretation at that moment will be accepted, confirmed, integrated, and worked through by the patient.* The therapist should learn to think in relatively simple fantasy-terms, as does the patient unconsciously and indirectly through derivatives, using plain language and drawing the key words and phrases from the patient's

own associations. If his initial formulations are correct, subsequent associations will add to his insight, and clarify and elaborate upon the unconscious fantasy he is planning to interpret. At an appropriate juncture (e.g., when the patient adds a vital link, is on the verge of stating the fantasy, reaches a point when the fantasy will fill a gap in the material, shifts to defensive avoidance, or if the hour is drawing to a close), the therapist interprets, using language that is appropriate to the age of the patient at the time when the major part of the fantasy was constructed, or the age that is most relevant to the memories and conflicts reflected in the material. Then he listens for confirmation or failure to confirm (see Chapters 18 and 19).

Depending on the patient's style of communicating, the therapist may choose to interpret derivatives of nuclear repressed fantasies based on hunches or undeveloped leads, or to wait for further material. He will decide on several grounds: first, whether the patient generally tends to continue to develop unconscious threads from one session to the next, or instead, to drop themes quickly so that they do not soon return again in the material. Secondly, whether the patient has responded to such interventions with confirmation and development of the material in the past. Thirdly, whether the situation is somewhat urgent with a strong therapeutic context such as acute symptoms, acting out, or other regressions, or whether there is time to wait. Fourth, there is the strength of the therapist's hunch and the degree to which he feels that the interpretation is important. And lastly, there is the extent to which the patient is resistant or accessible at the moment.

It is a complex decision. As therapists, our capacity to be in tune with the patient's material quite well or rather irregularly will also prove important, as will our general clinical skills. If we decide to intervene, we should do so explicitly or tentatively as the material permits, and then wait for further developments (confirmatory elaboration or failure to confirm). Experience in careful listening before and especially after such interpretations will enhance the therapist's skill in making tentative interpretations when they are necessary.

2. *Whenever there is a need for an intervention of some kind, and the material lends itself to an understanding of unconscious*

facets, the therapist interprets. Thus, whenever resistances, acting out, and other crises and regressions occur, interpretations are the interventions of choice. Too many therapists settle for confrontations and attention to surface ego disturbances, and ignore clues to unconscious factors. If ego dysfunctions such as acting out, not delaying, and poor reality testing are present, the therapist should certainly point them out in an effort to promote ego development. But he must, at the same time, scan the material for derivatives of the unconscious fantasies related to these impairments. The key to symptom modification and lasting structural change is the interpretation of as many aspects as feasible of the diverse elements in, and genetics of, major unconscious fantasy complexes. A constant, though relaxed, alertness to such derivatives is a prime task for the sophisticated psychotherapist.

PROBLEMS IN THE USE OF INTERPRETATIONS

Countertransference difficulties and the failure to comprehend the structure of neurotic symptoms are the main contributors to misapplications of interpretations. I will discuss different aspects of these errors briefly here (see also Chapters 19 and 22).

Underuse of Interpretations

The failure of many therapists to make specific interpretations and to analyze unconscious fantasies may be due to a lack of knowledge, to fear of unconscious and primitive fantasies, or to unresolved personal conflicts in a particular area. Thus, some therapists repeatedly miss primal scene material, others avoid oedipal conflicts of one type or another, while still others ignore pregenital derivatives. Such blocks generally must be modified through personal analysis or astute self-awareness.

Specific Errors Regarding Interpretations

I shall discuss in some detail the technical errors in the use of interpretations in Chapter 19. Incorrect interpretations are operationally defined as those for which no validation follows, and we will be in a better position to understand them after a full study of the patient's responses, confirmatory and nonconfirmatory, to interpretations. Here I shall only briefly list some of the most common misapplications of interpretations and conclude with a brief discussion of their basis.

Superficial and Nonspecific Interpretations

These have already been alluded to in several sections of this chapter. General and superficial interpretations are often related as much to real conflicts and problems, as to neurotic ones. They are necessary at times as first-stage interpretations, but must be followed by, and not substituted for, specific and deeper interpretations. Therapists who fear the depths and those with unresolved conflicts in a specific area are likely to confine themselves to this level of general interpreting.

Too Deep (So-Called "Id") Interpretations

Some therapists counter-phobically, or because of an insensitivity to the anxieties and conflicts that deep interpretations can stir up in their patients, plunge into the depths of primitive fantasy material quite early in therapy or do so later on before the patient is really prepared to deal with such material. Until now, I have emphasized errors related to excessive superficiality because it is far more common than excessively deep interpretations in therapists who are learning. But the latter is a disruptive error, as well. The level of an interpretation must be in keeping with the material from the patient and deal with content that he can handle and elaborate upon, rather than be panicked by. Therapists who are always in hot pursuit of instinctual drive-laden fantasies often interpret such material without proper context or an adaptive framework. They seem to be stimulated by such content or to select specific aspects of it for interpretation that is repeatedly too deep because of unresolved voyeurism, seductiveness, and other conflicts within themselves. As a result, their patients either flee treatment or deal with such interpretations in an isolated or otherwise defensive manner; a few join in a mutually seductive misalliance. In other instances, such interventions are experienced as assaults which disrupt the therapeutic alliance or convert it to an antitherapeutic sadomasochistic one. Gradually, deepening interpretation should, by and large, characterize the therapist's work in psychotherapy.

Premature Interpretations

These are ill-timed interpretations which may be prematurely too deep or simply offered before sufficient derivatives are available for a sound interpretation. They may heighten defenses and impair the unfolding of the material, or prompt regressions and premature termination if offered too often. The therapist must generally wait for workable latent content before offering interpretations of unconscious fantasies.

Incorrect Interpretations

As I will demonstrate in Chapter 19, incorrect interpretations are far from innocuous (see Freud, 1937). They usually stem from countertransference problems in the therapist and are based on his own unresolved conflicts and fantasies. As such, they reveal a great deal about the therapist to the patient, much of it unconscious for both parties, though usually the patient's material registers the problems on some level. This will often lead to reactions by the patient to the therapist's countertransference fantasies and complicate therapy considerably. Further, the patient will sense that he is not being understood. His inner conflicts and fantasies do not move toward proper clarification and resolution, and regression and acting out often prevail.

Erroneous interpretations are made by every therapist. If they are detected through reconsideration based on the failure of the patient to confirm and/or his subsequent regression, they can be corrected through confrontation and analysis. Undetected, they will often be repeated in varying forms and seriously disrupt the therapeutic alliance and therapy. Therapist-induced resistances will prevail and premature termination may follow. The therapist must, therefore, be on the constant alert for indications within himself of countertransference problems and interpretative errors or reflections of these in the material from, and behavior of, the patient (see Chapter 22).

Incomplete and Inexact Interpretations

It was Glover (1931) who first described these two kinds of errors in interpreting and pointed to their possible potential value under special circumstances. An incomplete interpretation deals with only part of an unconscious fantasy and conflict. It may serve as an initial step, but the completion of the interpretation then depends on the therapist's awareness that more must be covered. The material from the patient will often lead the way. The therapist's need to avoid certain aspects of the material often accounts for lastingly incomplete interpretations.

Inexact interpretations are sometimes used to support defenses in the patient, though they more often are partial errors by the therapist and lead to consequences similar to erroneous interpretations.

Missed Interpretations

Awareness of having missed an interpretation depends on the therapist's capacity to successfully reassess his work, especially when he senses that something is amiss. It is not uncommon early— or later—in one's career as a therapist to discover that an interpretation has been missed after a session is over, with the lessening of the therapist's anxiety and the establishing of some further distance from the patient and his associations—all of which may modify the therapist's own defenses. If the therapist is correct, the material of the next session will usually confirm his evaluation. This missed interpretation can then be made using the added derivatives in that hour. The situation is more difficult if resistances follow, since the therapist must then decide whether this is due to his omitted interpretation or to other factors. In such situations, the therapist may sometimes go back to the previous material and interpret it. The danger here is that this will be stale and isolated; the advantages are that the uninterpreted fantasy may be the key to the resistance.

If the therapist is unaware of a missed interpretation, subsequent material from the patient may direct him to it if he listens properly. When the interpretation is discovered, he should be able to recall the earlier, missed derivatives as support for his formulation, and refer to them when interpreting. We can be sure of one thing: the patient will express derivatives of unconscious conflicts and disturbing fantasies with a great deal of repetition until the context which has evoked them passes, his defenses are finally reinstated, or the problem is analyzed.

Missed interpretations are also a common topic in supervision.

In essence, if a supervisor proposed a missed interpretation, the subsequent material from the patient should confirm and support it if he is correct. In addition, regression and acting out will often occur specifically because the interpretation was missed.

Interpretations are missed primarily because of countertransference problems, in which defenses of all types are used by the therapist (see Chapter 22).

The main errors in the use of interpretations, then, stem primarily from the therapist's unresolved intrapsychic conflicts, his disruptive fantasies, his instinctual drive needs and superego pathology, his defenses and other disturbed ego functions, including at times, gross distortions of perception, reality testing, and relating. In essence, they stem from the therapist's psychopathology, and are best resolved through personal therapy (or insightful self-analysis after such therapy); rarely are such problems mastered without help.

15 Reconstructions

DEFINITION AND IMPORTANCE

Reconstructions, or as they are alternately termed, constructions, deserve a separate chapter, not only because they have certain distinctive characteristics, but also because they are relatively neglected and misunderstood, especially by psychotherapists. In fact, except for a recent monograph by a Kris Study Group (Fine, Joseph, and Waldhorn, 1971), there has been little systematic study of this kind of intervention even by psychoanalysts (for that matter, there are few systematic studies of any of the basic interventions in psychotherapy and psychoanalysis; regarding constructions, see also the pioneering papers by Freud, 1905, 1918, and 1937; Kris, 1956; Reider, 1953; and Rosen, 1953). Reconstructions seem particularly alien and even frightening to many therapists, who find them difficult to comprehend and to use. They thereby neglect an important, and at times crucial, type of interpretation.

In this chapter, I will briefly define reconstructions, discuss their importance and the indications for their use, and illustrate their application. If the therapist values and bears in mind this intervention, he is quite likely to find opportune moments for its use; if not, he will probably never use it and miss those exquisite moments in therapy where reconstructions are the key to the therapeutic work and lead to dramatic lifting of repressive barriers, and the consequent remembering, working through, and symptom alleviation.

A reconstruction is an attempt based on what is both present in, and missing from, the patient's material to fill an apparently important gap in his recollection of some event in his life, along with its actual outer and inner repercussions—a gap that must be bridged for the full understanding of a particular symptom and the anxieties, conflicts and fantasies related to it. A reconstruction, then, is an attempt by the therapist to build a vital missing link that has been so effectively repressed by the patient that it remains absent from his direct awareness despite all other interpretive efforts. The need for construction arises when the therapist senses that an explanatory event or fantasy is lacking. This occurs, for example, as material unfolds around a particular theme or context, and yet the patient's history or conscious memories and fantasies lack something which could account for his current behavior and fantasies, and for the derivatives and latent content of his associations.

Reconstructions derive their importance from the fact that real events and experiences have implications and consequences for patients that differ from fantasies (see Greenacre, 1956, and Chapter 8). In essence, real traumas evoke a multiplicity of behavioral and fantasied responses within the child or adult. While these responses themselves have important second-order repercussions and contribute to intrapsychic conflicts and symptoms, no analysis of a pathological fantasy-system is complete without tracing it back to the childhood or adolescent events to which it was related, as part of the patient's attempts at adaptation. Neurotic symptoms and most ego dysfunctions will not develop out of conscious and unconscious fantasies alone, but out of real traumas and their intrapsychic meanings to the patient.

Therapists need clinical experience and sound intuition to develop an ear for the kinds of pathology that must be traced back to actual disturbing events, and further, for the significant absence of references to such experiences in the associations of the patient. Well-disguised clues to the missing incidents, or to missing but crucial segments of known traumas, may be present in the patient's associations or conveyed in his behavior; the therapist must be especially alert, however, to identify the ultimate source of such derivatives. In time, the therapist learns that certain symptoms and fantasies are often related to particlular kinds of traumas, or that certain kinds of early events and fantasies are often associated with particular types of current (adult) reactions and fantasies. Such hints lead him to search for missing material at the specific moment in treatment at which they occur. Constructions depend on the therapist's knack of sensing what is missing and on a good sense of timing. This in turn depends on the therapist's wish for a total understanding of a given symptom in terms of current conflicts and fantasies, as well as those from the past, on his ear for incongruities, and on his ability to sense, for example, that something more traumatic than known to that moment had to have occurred for a particular reaction or symptom to have evolved in the patient.

Another important source of data which both suggests reconstructions, and gives clues as to the nature of missing events and relationships missing from the patient's direct recall, is the therapist's direct observations of the patient in the sessions, and especially their interaction. If the patient's recollections are not sufficient to explain his reactions to the therapist and his interventions, the therapist will begin to consider constructions to fill in the missing genetic links, which will be in accord with the patient's behavior with him.

The first step, then, lies in sensing that something is missing, and then listening to the material for unconscious derivatives (expressions) related to the missing link. If the therapist's hunch is right, the material from the patient will provide him with relevant clues and will interdigitate well with the proposed construction. While repression will be maintained and the event or fantasy not directly recalled, there will be evident disguised expressions of its content. And it will be out of these derivatives and his own perceptiveness that the therapist will offer the reconstruction.

Thus, reconstructions fill voids and refer to an event or fantasy that once happened and is essentially totally forgotten (repressed), while interpretations refer to derivatives of available memories or fantasies that are unconscious at the moment, but potentially conscious and understood once brought into awareness. The two actually form a continuum and blend into each other. Technically, confirmations of constructions may be comparable to that for interpretations, though often they take a different form and emphasize the more complete establishment of what actually happened.

Reconstructions may be classified in a number of ways. Temporally, they may be divided in those that refer to relatively recent events and those that refer to more remote, childhood events. They may be classified according to major content into those which reconstruct parts or all of a crucial life event, those which reconstruct missing affective responses, and those referring to important missing fantasies. Most often all three content types are ultimately included in a given construction. They may also be divided into those related to a single, acute, traumatic event and its consequences, and those related to continuing situations such as household climate, and especially to on-going disturbances in important childhood relationships.

Constructions are always offered because they are vital to understanding the symptoms of the patient and provide one necessary but missing key to them. Some writers refer to reconstructions upward, that is, from childhood events to present ones (Lowenstein, 1957; see Chapter 16). I prefer to not use this term in this way since it may obscure the concept, whose essential characteristic is the filling in of an important missing link in the history of the patient.

The indication for a reconstruction is, then, a critical void in the patient's life story (childhood or recent), and in his real and fantasied, conscious and unconscious, responses to it. The void is felt when the known history and fantasies of the patient do not offer sufficient explanation for the patient's behavior and symptoms; when these symptoms are not resolved by working through a relevant trauma-fantasy network; or when aspects (derivatives) of the missing material are communicated through dreams, symptoms, acting out and other indirect channels.

Major reconstructions are made when there has been sufficient indirect material from the patient to give the therapist some idea of what probably happened and, further, when the acuteness of the symptoms requires an interpretative intervention and the therapist believes the critical factor to be a missing historic event. Reconstructions of a minor nature ("You must have felt such and such a way, or thought something of this or that kind, or this or that must have happened.") are fairly common in psychotherapy; those related to major, repressed traumas are more rare, though not infrequent.

Clinical material is especially useful in comprehending this intervention. The endeavor to render conscious material missing from consciousness for the patient may lead to direct recall of much or fragments of the event in question or to later events related to it. Its relevance may be so convincing to the patient that he may integrate it into his understanding of his symptoms without directly remembering the event in question. In such instances, though, indirect supportive memories and insights will occur and serve as confirmation. In all, inner, structural change should eventually evolve on the basis of correct constructions (see Freud, 1937). I shall now illustrate some of the main types of reconstructions.

ASPECTS OF RELATIVELY RECENT EXPERIENCES

The therapist is quite often, perhaps without realizing it, able to sense, and is called on to fill in, important voids in the patient's recollection of recent traumatic events and experiences that are related to unresolved symptoms. This is especially so for borderline patients or for acute and severe traumas in any patient; here, denial and extremes of repression may eradicate crucial aspects of the event.

Consider this vignette:

> Mrs. F.R. was a seriously suicidal ambulatory schizophrenic woman who was in once-weekly psychotherapy; she had been on the verge of killing herself a number of times. She had improved clinically until her older brother was found to have a malignancy of the colon. In the past, he had been the main figure of support for her, and his threatened loss evoked a serious, near-psychotic depression and much displaced rage onto her husband and only child. Her parents and other siblings were also intensely disturbed by this news, and much chaos followed, especially since there were differing professional opinions regarding the management of his illness.

In a session about six weeks after the news regarding her brother first emerged, the patient reported an amnesic episode which culminated in her finding herself on her bedroom floor with a knife in her hand; she remembered nothing prior to that. Associations were to her rage at her husband and child, and nothing more specific emerged; there were no references to her brother's illness in the hour.

The following week, the patient was more controlled. In her session, longings for closeness with her husband and therapist, unusual feelings for her, were expressed openly. The therapist asked what had prompted these feelings and Mrs. F.R. responded that there had been considerable family turmoil regarding her brother, who now had to consider specific treatment, including possible surgery and hospitalization. The patient, to whom he turned for advice, was in the middle of many family disputes regarding these decisions. She went on to recall that she had also dreamt of her therapist standing too high above her.

The therapist asked when the specific decision regarding her brother's care had first come up (this question was based on a reconstruction that the therapist was formulating); the patient stated that it had happened two weeks earlier. The therapist, whose hunch was confirmed, then offered a specific reconstruction: he suggested that the events, feelings and fantasies related to her brother's illness and the recent controversies regarding his care had evoked Mrs. F.R.'s amnesic episode of near self-destruction. The patient quickly confirmed this and now filled in more of the gap: her parents had called that day just before the episode; they had fought with the patient over her brother, attempting to blame her in some strange way for his illness. Once this was further detailed and clarified, the therapist offered an interpretation of the reference to his standing high above her in her dream, using the now revealed context of the material. He said that he suspected that this was an expression of her fantasied long-

ings to join her brother in heaven should he die. The
patient said that she had actually thought of that too,
but had not mentioned it. Her murderous rage at her
parents, which she had turned against herself by taking
the knife in her hand, was then pointed out to her (the
final therapeutic context). It was interpreted as another
meaning of the desperate efforts on Mrs. F.R.'s part to
dissociate herself from these realistic conflicts, their intrapsychic repercussions, and the consequent nearly uncontrollable rage toward her parents and herself. It protected
her from possible suicide, though at great cost to herself.

This is an example of the reconstruction of a recent, strongly
repressed trauma and its consequences. The gap was clearcut—
amnesia—but the events with which it was connected (context) and
the inner fantasies and conflicts related to it were not apparent until
derivatives began to appear in the second session after the event.

The indications for the reconstruction can be readily seen and
were even rather urgent. The patient was suicidal and lacked conscious awareness of the trauma which had provoked her amnesia
and her holding onto the knife; there could be a fatal recurrence of
this kind of episode if the precipitates and fantasies were not determined and worked through. The need to reconstruct must be balanced, however, against the availability of derivatives with which to
formulate it. There must be sufficient disguised latent content on
which to base the intervention, lest it be too much the product of
the therapist's own fantasies and too remote from what is accessible
to the patient.

Confirmation also came quickly: the patient immediately filled in
a number of missing and relevant events and fantasies in direct
response to the intervention. Subsequent diminution of her dissociative tendencies and suicidal depression also confirmed the correctness of the reconstruction (see Chapter 18).

Reconstructions can be far more difficult to sense, to make, and
to confirm. Consider this example:

Mrs. F.S. was a woman with a borderline syndrome
who was in twice-weekly psychotherapy, which she began

after the following incident: she had been standing high on a ladder when the ladder seemed to sway; she panicked and jumped from it, falling back to the ground. The ladder itself did not fall and in retrospect the patient realized that it had hardly moved. While she was not seriously injured, hypochondriacal symptoms and depression followed.

She had made considerable progress until after about a year of treatment, when her mother took ill with a seemingly minor malady. This led to an acute separation reaction on the part of the patient, who was very closely tied to her mother, particularly since the latter had been seriously ill a number of times when she was a child. This separation anxiety, and a series of related somatic symptoms were explored in Mrs. F.S.'s treatment, and connected with her longings to be cared for by her mother and to die with her if need be. More deeply, there were fantasies of swallowing her mother in order not to lose her, marred by additional fantasies of being attacked in return from within by her. During this time, there were peripheral references to the ladder incident, but they did not seem to develop in the material manifestly or latently, nor did they point in any consistent direction.

Then her mother took a turn for the worse, and appeared to be seriously ill with leukemia. The patient then reported that she had found out that this illness had actually been first diagnosed some two years earlier, a few months before the episode with the ladder. With difficulty, Mrs. F.S. then recalled that after her panic on the ladder, at another time when she had had an anxiety attack, she had overheard the members of her family wondering if she had been told that her mother was seriously ill. The therapist offered a reconstruction, which he put in the form of a question: did the patient actually know about her mother's illness before the incident in which she jumped from the ladder?

Let us pause here and ask why the therapist made the reconstruction. Firstly, he felt that there was something missing regarding the patient's leap from the ladder. While Mrs. F.S. was a borderline patient, he nonetheless felt that it would, as a rule, take some acutely upsetting trauma and/or related instinctual wishes to precipitate such a sudden panic and loss of control. Therapists who appreciate the role of reality in the development of severe pathology in general and of specific disturbed behavior will acknowledge that this is likely to be valid. Actually, Mrs. F.S.'s therapist had been watching since her treatment began for some acute precipitate that had created the context for her behavior on the ladder. None had appeared for a long time and this void had become quite intriguing to him. Then, as the information about her mother's serious illness emerged, the therapist listened to the sequences of the associations from the patient for manifest and latent themes: the fact that the diagnosis of leukemia had actually been made before the accident and not long after, as the patient had maintained previously; the reference to overhearing a discussion about something related to this subject; the externalized question as to whether Mrs. F.S. already knew of her mother's illness; and the fantasies of remaining united with her mother. All of this pointed to the probability that the patient had some knowledge of her mother's illness, to severe separation anxiety, and to suicidal impulses related to fantasies of remaining united with her mother in death.

As the therapist reconstructed to himself the possible events and fantasies that led to the leap from the ladder, he found support for his thesis in the unfolding material, and from his review, in this context, of earlier material, which I shall not detail here except to note that fantasies of joining her mother in heaven were in evidence; they had heretofore been largely related to depressed-suicidal fantasies in response to the childhood separations from her. Now, they seemed to have been rekindled by the mother's present and serious illness, and the whole constellation of the patient's childhood anxieties, conflicts, fantasies and pathological solutions were remobilized and possibly acted out. All this divergent material and the patient's behavior seemed to fit together better with the reconstruction offered to her. Further, feelings of guilt and self-punishment were hinted at in the earlier material. A major source appeared to be childhood and current fantasies of murderous, devouring rage at her mother for deserting her when she was ill during the patient's early years, and for her present and final "desertion" as well.

To return to the vignette:

> Mrs. F.S. responded to this reconstruction by directly denying any such knowledge, and immediately dropped the topic. She did, however, develop acute anxiety and physical symptoms in the session in which it was offered, and went on to ruminate in a somewhat dissociated state—a defense that she often used under stress—that she must have leukemia too. She then recalled a forgotten dream; in it, her girlfriend has leukemia, but no symptoms. To the patient, this was a denial that her mother was ill at all.
>
> In the following group of sessions, the question of when the patient actually learned about her mother's illness was avoided entirely. The therapist could detect no indirect evidence for the correctness of his reconstruction and became rather uncertain of it. Instead, these sessions focused on an elaboration of the patient's earlier fantasies of dying with her mother, hating her mother for deserting her, the guilt, the gastrointestinal symptoms and their unconscious meanings in this context, and related material.
>
> Some two months later, Mrs. F.S.'s mother died. The patient had an acutely disturbed and pervasive reaction to her loss, of which I will present only one aspect. Several sessions after her mother's death, Mrs. F.S. was struggling with her fears of developing leukemia herself, as both a fantasied punishment for her rage against her mother and a continued expression of her longings to be united with her. She reviewed some of her fond memories of her mother and mentioned, for the first time in her therapy, a surprise sixtieth birthday party she had given for her mother a couple of months before the patient's own jump from the ladder.
>
> Once again, his suspicions rekindled because the event had been repressed and because it was sequentially

related to the death of the patient's mother, the therapist asked Mrs. F.S. if she had known anything about her mother's illness at that time. She once more denied any such knowledge, but then recalled a disturbance that had occurred during the party. It was something about her mother refusing to take some kind of medication and something about doctors not knowing what they were doing. She heard the commotion from a distance, and came over to inquire, but was put off. She then remembered seeing that her mother was quite upset and sensing that something was amiss.

The therapist then presented a full reconstruction of what probably had happened: the patient must have overheard the nature of her mother's illness, reacted with an acute, guilt-ridden, suicidal depression, and lived out her fantasies of self-punishment and union with her mother in her leap from the ladder.

This time, Mrs. F.S. listened carefully and in her direct response was more willing to accept the reconstruction. She went on to talk further of her guilty feelings that she had somehow contributed to her mother's death, and of her own fears of dying. There was as yet little in the way of clear confirmation of the reconstruction, though it was gaining support.

The following session was replete with lengthy dreams of being with her mother and replacing her with a substitute. She had fantasized that her mother was in hell, and this helped the patient and therapist crystallize her anger and condemnation of her mother for being ill and deserting her. She reported that her stomach pains had gone away after the previous session. When the therapist related this relief to his reconstruction, the patient added that she had talked to her brother about the incident: they had indeed been discussing her mother's illness at the time of the commotion at the party, and she might well have overheard something more specific. Further new material and working through of the patient's reaction to her mother's death followed.

We can now briefly review this vignette and its implications: The reconstruction was related to a relatively recent event and focused on an experience and a fact that seemed to be a missing link in understanding the patient's disturbed behavior (symptoms), and its attendant panic, intrapsychic conflicts, and fantasies.

Indications for the reconstruction included, firstly, the observation of a critical gap in the material—the immediate reasons for such a grossly disturbed behavioral response. Secondly, and of considerable importance, was the need to understand and analyze thoroughly the circumstances and specific fantasies surrounding this dangerous behavior so that it would not occur again. Thus, life conditions comparable to the original adaptive context might occur again without the patient's awareness and lead to a similar sequence of behavior—unless the true nature of what had happened was understood.

What appeared superficially to be perhaps simply the result of the patient's impaired ego functioning—poor judgment and controls—became especially suspicious to an already alerted therapist when he learned that the patient's mother had actually become ill before the ladder episode. The coupling of a reference to this incident with the other information put him on the track.

In this instance, the patient responded initially to the construction with denial, flight, and virtual failure to confirm. The therapist, for his part, tucked the issue away in a corner of his mind and was prepared to raise it again if the material warranted it. While therapists must be prepared to drop or revise unconfirmed constructions, this therapist's knowledge of Mrs. F.S.'s frequent and massive use of denial prompted him to adopt a wait-and-see stance.

With the next incident in this traumatic series, the death of the patient's mother, there was a modification of the repressive barriers with which the patient had blocked her recollections of the time when she first realized that her mother was seriously ill. We can only speculate why the initial reconstruction failed to produce the intrapsychic shifts that her mother's death and its consequences accomplished. It may be this patient was terrified of her death wishes toward her mother and the enormous guilt they evoked. She was strongly inclined toward magical thinking and may well have feared the power to wish—or even think of—her mother dead, with the consequent fruition of these wishes in light of her mother's then potentially fatal illness. The intense need for the patient to deny any possible loss of her mother also played a role. In addition to all these internal factors, we must wonder whether the timing and the form of the reconstruction were proper or whether the therapist had erred in some other way. We must, as a fundamental principle, learn to question ourselves and our technique as therapists first, when things go awry in therapy, and only afterwards explore the possible contribution of the patient. In Chapters 19 and 22, I shall show how the material from the patient can serve as a guide for both sources of difficulties.

As a source of real and intrapsychic danger rich in genetic implications, the knowledge of her mother's illness was bound to create panic and chaos for Mrs. F.S., and in keeping with her primitive defenses, she obliterated all memory of it. Only her behavior on the ladder betrayed her secret knowledge, but without other clues, the latent content was not detectable, at least by this searching therapist. Only as the patient attempted to work through the anticipated and then the actual loss of her mother was she willing to provide clearer derivatives of what happened, though she did not recall the incident directly. It was at this point, however, that the reconstruction could be offered to her again with a more successful and confirmatory outcome. At times, the therapist must be quite patient; cajoling or pressing the patient could not have produced the necessary recall, though it might have caused panic and rage. The therapist had to wait until the patient let him know, by nonverbal means, that she was ready to work through the repressed experience; then his construction became a critical, effective intervention, resulting in the alleviation of symptoms.

CHILDHOOD EVENTS, FANTASIES, AND RELATIONSHIPS

I shall begin with a lengthy vignette, as an illustration of some basic principles of this technique.

Miss F.T. was a young woman in psychotherapy

because of tendencies to act out and a moderate character disorder. During the first six months of her treatment, she had worked effectively and developed new controls and insights leading to notable improvement in her problems. At the turn of the year, her therapist informed her of a vacation he planned for the end of February. She became depressed and angry, thought of stopping treatment, and dreamt of sleeping with an old boyfriend. When this was interpretively related to the pending separation, as reflecting a sexualized way of holding on to the therapist, she remembered that the dream had an additional part: she and her sister were having an affair with an older man, someone the age of her therapist.

Over the next few sessions, she went on to speak of feeling slighted by the therapist's leaving and of how her father favored one of her two sisters over herself. Her mother's neglect—because she had worked when the patient was a child—was also described. Other, specific memories from her early childhood followed: an accidental fall in which she bloodied her head and a vaginal infection that a woman doctor painfully probed—it was like being impregnated with a bullet (both from about age eight); trips with her parents throughout her childhood during summer vacations; and being accident-prone—catching her leg in the spokes of a bike when her parents were away, and often being bruised from falls. She did not recall masturbating at that time, she added, in discussing the vaginal infection.

She then reported this dream: she is in a shoe store, waiting. Two of her friends get pointed shoes; she herself does not get what she wants. There is a saleslady— then she is a salesman—and he had three pairs of shoes, two brown and one blue. In the session, she went on to ruminate about one of her sisters who had recently been a bridesmaid, about waiting to hear from her father (the patient did not live at home), reading a book about sex and wanting to have intercourse with someone, and that her girlfriend's psychiatrist had said that a sock in a shoe represented intercourse. She then remembered that she had masturbated before going to sleep the night of the dream, and wondered if masturbating had actually caused the vaginal infection she had as a child; she felt guilty about it.

The therapist in turn wondered aloud to the patient about the wish in her dream. The patient said: maybe it was to have a penis. The therapist agreed; he suggested that as a child she had probably seen her father's penis— possibly when they had traveled and shared a room—and that she had wanted to have a penis herself, and to be a boy.

The patient was uncertain, though somehow she knew that she did not feel fully feminine. Her father had always wanted a son (he had instead three daughters) and she was the one who had most shared his activities and worked with him on his job. One of her greatest wishes as a child was to own toy guns.

In subsequent sessions, she related this wish for a penis to her promiscuity and added other confirmations to the reconstruction. A dream in which she had two high-balls while in a bedroom with an older man was notable among these: she wanted her own set of balls. After some flight which was analyzed as a resistance, she then reported a recurrent fantasy of being a popular male singer. Further, a dream of her aged, senile grandmother led to an exploration of her view of women as helpless and endangered. When this was interpreted to her, she recalled seeing her mother's bloody menstrual pads as a child, and her fantasies that her mother had been damaged and penetrated by her father. She now remembered fantasies of wishing she could get pregnant without ever menstruating. In later sessions, her wish to bear her parents—especially her father—the son they wanted also emerged.

During these few months after the reconstruction, nothing more was said regarding possible primal scene experiences and seeing her father nude. Her functioning was so much improved and her acting out so well controlled that she began to plan to terminate her therapy with the end of her college year in June. Soon after, her mother took ill and required a cholecystectomy.

At this point, Miss F.T. dreamt of being in a movie theater and seeing *Love Story*. She went on to recall past hospitalizations of various family members. She had had sexual relations with an old boyfriend and dreamt that she was "balling" (having relations with) a famous male performer. She was anxious about her own bodily integrity; associations also focused on the past illnesses of her mother and father, particularly a near-fatal illness of the latter.

She then dreamt of a movie theater in which a monkey was clawing at her head. Associations were to her mother's then-pending surgery, and to an older man she knew who owned a monkey. She then ruminated a good deal. Here, the therapist again offered a reconstruction. He had not forgotten the patient's missing allusions to observing parental intercourse. He also felt that an element needed to account for the fantasies evoked in Miss F.T. by her mother's pending surgery was missing, and detected hints of its nature in the material. The reconstruction seemed necessary to help the patient work through her anxieties about her mother's surgery and the termination of her treatment.

In the material were references to movies (and observing, looking, and death), to movie stars (and admiring), to intercourse, and to her head being attacked (often this is a displacement upwards from below and from the genitals). It suggested two interrelated fantasies and sets of memories to the therapist: experiences of observing parental intercourse, and accompanying unconscious fantasies that it represented a powerful, handsome, man—father—attacking and harming the woman—mother; related to this were unconscious fantasies of her mother's need for surgery—and possibly the surgery itself—as a result of, and comparable to, the sexual attack.

Thus, when the patient spoke again of the clawing and then related it to the planned surgery, the therapist suggested that it also seemed to refer to some ideas about intercourse that were based on earlier observations of her parents having relations.

At first, Miss F.T. denied any such memory, though she reviewed again the occasions when she had shared motel rooms with her parents. One of her sisters had had her first menstrual period on one of these trips and was afraid that her father would notice it. Then the patient suddenly, but vaguely, recalled waking up herself one time—she was already a freshman in college and still shared a room while away with her parents—and hearing movement of some kind. To a direct inquiry, based on a hunch of the therapist's that used previous material (this was a reconstruction of a later sequence of events), the patient recalled that just three weeks later she had first had intercourse; it had indeed followed that experience in the motel, as the therapist's question had suggested.

In subsequent sessions, a great deal emerged. First, memories of overhearing and seeing her sisters in bed with boyfriends, one of whom was very hairy, like a monkey. Then she recalled for the first time in therapy that she would consciously fantasize about her parents in intercourse; it was quite upsetting and she linked it to their many daily quarrels. Dreams of being unattractive followed, as did acting out (including stealing) calculated to anger her father with whom she was now living at home while her mother was in the hospital.

Then, a dream of a cold, gray forest with felled trees led to memories from early childhood when Miss F.T. shared a room in a cabin with her parents; she had awakened during the night to noises there too. Other even earlier similar experiences were then recalled, as were the nightmares that accompanied them—of tidal waves and drowning. Masturbatory fantasies, including conscious sexual wishes for her father, also emerged, and further material related to her view of intercourse in terms of her mother being attacked, damaged, and bloodied. While all of this was analyzed, her mother's surgery was successful and the patient handled it well.

Then, in the final session of her therapy, Miss F.T. remembered for the first time in many years an early childhood fantasy: she would imagine an alligator under her bed and feared that it would bite off her foot if she stepped on the floor. She also recalled a frightening image she had had at age six or so while in the first motel room that she could recall having shared with her parents: something small was getting large. She thought of a penis, of her mistrust of men, and of her fantasies that her father had done something to her mother. Fantasies of having had a penis, of her father having bitten it (and her mother's) off, and impulses of revenge-in-kind against her father, were all in evidence.

I have presented these two main reconstructions, of the patient's penis fantasies and of primal scene experiences, and the patient's response to them, in some detail, in order to enable the reader to sense the nature of an early genetic reconstruction, the reason it is made, and the patient's response (see Chapter 19). From this material, I shall emphasize these main points:

1. *Genetic reconstructions tend to relate to early traumatic experiences and relationships that have been entirely or partially repressed and are no longer remembered.* Derivatives and consequences of these experiences are nonetheless reflected in the patient's behavior, fantasies, and other communications. The reconstruction is essential in filling a gap in knowledge of the genetic aspects—the real traumas—that laid the foundation for the patient's symptoms. Without it, an important void is felt and the symptoms are not fully resolved.

Among the most frequently reconstructed childhood experiences, then, are deaths of family members, births of siblings, primal scene experiences, seductions, sudden abandonments, and other specific acute traumas. Another type of reconstruction relates to repressed, long-term, chronic exposure to hostility, detachment, seductions, recurrent separations and even more subtle traumas at the hands of important childhood figures, especially parents and siblings.

In these two types of reconstructions, the content depends upon what has been repressed and obliterated by the patient. Thus, the therapist may reconstruct the actual fact that a specific traumatic event did, indeed, occur, and allow the patient to elaborate. Or he may reconstruct a particular unconscious fantasy or fantasies related to the childhood events in question. At times, the focus will be primarily on the reconstruction of a specific unconscious fantasy (e.g., Miss F.T.'s wish for a penis), and the patient will then, if the reconstruction is correct, add related unconscious fantasies (Miss F.T.'s fantasy that her father had bitten off the penis that she once had) and the specific traumatic events that prompted these fantasies (Miss F.T.'s parents' wish for a son, their fostering of a masculine identification in her, and Miss F.T.'s observations of parental sexual behavior). One might also suspect from this material observations of fellatio; unfortunately the therapist did not offer this specific idea to the patient so we have no way of validating it.

Thus, depending on the material at hand, the therapist reconstructs events, atmosphere, or fantasies in the hope of providing a starting point from which the patient will fill in the missing material, be it further events, aspects of on-going relationships, or fantasies. These constitute confirmation of the construction.

2. *Genetic reconstructions are also made when there is lacking in the historical picture of the patient as revealed in his therapy a specific experience or unconscious fantasy that would sufficiently explain his current reactions and present fantasies.*

In listening to his patient's material and in fathoming the intra-psychic conflicts and fantasies evoked by a given current event, the therapist is constantly generating a picture of the patient's intra-psychic responses and their connections to known fantasies and conflicts. After the therapist and patient develop new insights through interpretations based on available derivatives, they will explore new fantasy-memory clusters, and the therapist will scan the biographical sketch the patient has afforded him. He will ask himself if this biographical sketch of events and major fantasies is sufficient to explain, and relates adequately to, the emerging inner conflicts, fantasies, and behavioral responses of the patient. If there appears to be a major void, he then searches the material from the patient for hints of derivatives of this. He will then base a reconstruction on these clues, not only bacause he had an interesting hunch, but because full understanding of the patient's neurotic reaction to a particular situation absolutely requires it.

Sometimes, the therapist does not have enough clues to make a reconstruction to the patient on the first occasion that he senses a lack of genetic foundation for the understanding of an aberrant response. At such moments, several reconstructions may occur to him—an event, a fantasy, a part of a different event. It is usually best to hold off until further current life experiences evoke additional responses in the patient, and the material begins to support one particular reconstruction more than any other. Then it can be offered to the patient, usually in a session where a relevant link to the reconstruction is available.

3. *The material from patients on which reconstructions are developed is no different from that on which any intervention is based.* It includes dreams and their associations, conscious fantasies, acting out, and all of the different kinds of communications available to us as therapists.

For example, the reconstruction of Miss F.T.'s penis fantasy was based on her reaction to the therapist's pending vacation, including her dreams and associations; her acting out; and a series of conscious childhood memories. It was built up in the therapist's mind over a number of sessions and presented to the patient when she dreamt of wanting shoes and expressed a wish for a penis in an isolated response to his question. A review of the material by me in supervision, incidentally, indicated that the therapist might well have reconstructed at this time the related fantasy that she had once had a penis and felt somehow that she had been injured or damaged and lost it. Subsequent material, of course, confirmed both of these fantasies, and related them primarily to the patient's wish to be the son that her parents never had and to her fantasies in response to primal scene observations (e.g., that the man was not damaged).

4. *The reconstruction that Miss F.T. had witnessed sexual relations between her parents was not confirmed initially.* Only when her mother became ill and needed surgery did the present life experi-

ences of the patient evoke intrapsychic conflicts and fantasies that further stirred up such recollections and modified the barriers to their recall. These repressed memories were well disguised, but hinted at in her conscious recollections of the patient's own and other family members' illnesses and injuries, and in her acting out.

5. *In principle, if a therapist formulates a reconstruction that is valid, but does not present it to the patient immediately, subsequent material should support it (as did the sequence before each of the reconstructions made to Miss* F.T.*).* This supportive material enables the therapist to feel some security regarding the reconstruction and he will readily find a session which invites the presentation of his thesis.

6. *Once a reconstruction has been made, the therapist sits back and listens.* The validity of the reconstruction rests upon the material from the patient that follows it. An initial denial may or may not be valid; only subsequent associations hold the answer. If little new material emerges directly or indirectly, the therapist must consider himself in error either in content or timing. He then listens openly to the ongoing material from the patient either for indications of a different reconstruction or for hints as to why the patient had to deny it at this time.

On the other hand, if fresh recollections, fantasies and insights follow, the therapist has been correct in what he offered to the patient.

7. *In considering this and other vignettes in this chapter, we see that recognition of the role of reality in the evolution of neurotic symptoms and behavior is essential in the resolution of these disturbances.* Therapists who do not realize how important single and repeated traumas are to the development of symptoms will fail to see the need for reconstructions and will, as a result, fail to tie many fantasies and conflicts to specific contexts and adaptive tasks. The resultant therapeutic work will be incomplete.

Two reconstructive efforts will conclude this presentation. The first is drawn from the opening phase of therapy, while the second was made near termination.

Mr. F.U. was a young man who sought treatment for recurrent depressions, a failure to organize his life or to hold a steady job, and multiple somatic symptoms; he was diagnosed as having a narcissistic character disorder. In his first session, he reported what he considered, correctly, to be the major disruptive experience of his life: the death of an infant brother in a fall from an unattended carriage when the patient was five years old. After detailing the episode, he wondered if he was not using it as an excuse for his problems and doubted that it could have wrecked his life.

In the early weeks of his therapy, the patient largely ruminated and appeared disorganized. Occasionally, a dream of a bleeding animal or an explosion in which people were killed led to thoughts about his brother, but nonpsychotic confusional thinking would quickly follow and nothing developed. Then, an uncle who was relatively young died. The patient denied having any feelings about it and turned to written notes he had made before that session to describe in detail a dream of an attack by a dog, which he nearly kills. For the patient, the notes meant that nothing was real or could be remembered. When the notes and the recurrent confusional periods were interpreted as part of a massive flight from the painful, recently re-evoked memories of his brother's death, Mr. F.U. slowly began to recall the details of this event. With the therapist focusing on defenses as they appeared, the patient himself reconstructed the experience bit by bit, recalling aspects that he had forgotten for many years. The therapist only occasionally offered constructions of aspects of what had happened when they seemed evident in the latent content and relevant to the patient's current symptoms. I will not detail the months of difficult but deeply meaningful and expanding work involved, but will confine myself to a single illustration of the constructions made by the therapist.

In one session, after several hours spent in recalling painful details of the circumstances before and after the death of his brother, the patient was acutely remote and confused. He spoke of seeing dead animals in the street and of how upset this made him; he linked this to seeing the body of his dead brother. He had never looked at a dead person again. He ruminated about how confused he felt, and the therapist suggested that he must have been very confused when his brother died. He then remembered the chaos after the child's body had been found, and the details of the period immediately after. This included his rageful fantasies against God and his being shuffled off to a neighbor's house without being told anything. Next, he remembered his mother's agitated depression, which lasted for months, probably until another pregnancy was well along. The hour ended as the patient described the death of other relatives and his intensely furious and dazed reactions.

When a patient reports an acute trauma from any period in his life, and especially from his childhood, the therapist should anticipate that this will be a focal point of therapeutic work, especially in the opening phase (see Chapter 23). Included in such work will be efforts at reconstruction on the part of both the patient and therapist, the latter fulfilling his responsibilities to fill in important missing (repressed) dimensions reflected in disguised derivative form in the patient's associations. As you can see, such work can begin in earnest quite early in treatment, and need only wait until the traumatic event has been actively mobilized for the patient; this may be the result either of modifications of defenses against recalling the trauma or of a current event that serves to bring up the past experience (see Chapter 8).

Readiness to offer reconstructions is part of the therapeutic stance of the therapist to the very end. I will describe in Chapter 25 a last session of treatment in which the patient herself, in response to the therapist's inquiry regarding a dream, recalled for the first time the acute trauma that had actually prompted her to seek therapy (see Miss K.Y., Vol. II). Here, I will now describe a reconstruction made in the terminal phase of a successful psychotherapy that lasted about a year.

Miss F.V. was a young woman who became acutely

disorganized while in her late teens and had to leave school. There were episodes of confusion and suicidal thinking, and outbursts of rage. The diagnosis was that of a decompensated schizophrenic reaction, but she recompensated strongly within a few months of beginning her treatment.

Most of the early months of the therapy centered upon Miss F.V.'s intensely and primitively ambivalent relationship with her mother. As the patient improved, she returned to school and began to see boy- and girl-friends again. She dated and petted, and explored her sexual anxieties and conflicts. She began to think about her father and how aloof he was. Material related to being repulsed by seductive old men emerged and dreams of attempted seductions by such men were reported. She spontaneously denied having sexual fantasies about her father, and said that her parents did not have relations—they were so at odds. She recalled early childhood bed-wetting and nightmares associated with it. In these, her father's face is torn off; someone eats bread; one of her brothers is electrocuted; and she is ill and the bed is spinning—a doctor gives her an injection through red drapes. Many of these dreams were associated with trips she had taken with her parents during which she had shared their room with them. Memories of being beaten up by a brother and of throwing feces were also tied in. The therapist suggested that she may have seen her parents having intercourse or viewed her mother's menstrual pads.

Miss F.V. began the next hour by recalling that her brother had recently called her a whore. She remembered further nightmares from her childhood: in one, her father is exposing his genitals to her and she pulls at his face and then eats bread; some doctors have solved the mystery of life. When the patient's associations became diffuse, the therapist asked if she had ever seen her father's genitals (a reconstructive query). The patient denied it at first and then directly recalled an experience when she was less than five and had had a nightmare; she crawled into bed with her father who was nude and saw his huge thing. Her associations then went on to fantasies about the births of her two younger brothers and her childhood fantasies that intercourse entailed the woman being defecated upon or torn apart. She felt dizzy (a recurrent symptom) as she spoke in the hour, and the therapist wondered if this symptom was not related both to these fantasies and to her reaction to actually witnessing her parents in intercourse.

In the next hour, while not directly recalling the primal scene, the patient said that her mother, in a discussion, hinted that she—Miss F.V.—had seen her parents having relations; the patient was certain that she had. In this connection, the patient worked through her repulsions regarding physical contact with men. Her fears of being damaged and her own need to maintain an excessive distance from her father were also explored. She became more relaxed with her dates. She recalled being exhibitionistic as a child and walking around nude at home, and then feeling at that time that her leg or something inside her was damaged. New recollections of her father's seductiveness emerged and after working through these issues, the dizziness stopped and her relationship with her father improved dramatically.

This vignette, involving a patient who was an ambulatory schizophrenic with multiple anxieties and disturbed relationships, indicates that reconstructive work can be used to great advantages with such patients. Miss F.V. found considerable relief in understanding some of the real and fantasied sources of her conflicts with her father and her anxieties about dates. In a sense, aspects of her ego dysfunctions were based on a series of early sexual traumas and her father's ongoing seductiveness. Reconstruction of these experiences proved vital to symptom resolution and improved ability to relate.

This work was done in the last month of the therapy and the memories were later linked to fantasies and feelings related to termination. The experience of ending therapy is one that often mobilizes previously repressed, traumatic and symptom-related experiences. Constructions of a kind generally unfeasible during any other period of therapy can be made at this time.

In concluding this discussion, I shall emphasize one obvious implication of this material: valid reconstructions are sometimes vital to the progress of psychotherapy. Further, there are, indeed, in the associations of patients in psychotherapy sufficient derivatives of these missing events in the life of the patient to build constructions, and sufficient material in the patient's responses to assess reliably the correctness of what has been stated and to promote crucial intrapsychic changes in the patient. In essence, then, a therapist should be ready to offer reconstructions where they are needed. They can be an exciting and important intervention in insight psychotherapy.

16　*Supportive Interventions*

The use of supportive techniques during insight-oriented psycho-therapy constitutes one of the most misunderstood areas of intervention. Empirical observation has led me to a careful reassessment of the frequently used concept of "supportive therapy," for all too often a patient's response to a so-called "supportive" move reveals that instead of promoting reassurance and ego-integration, the maneuver has prompted regression and disintegration. Many so-called "supportive" interventions reflect primarily countertransference problems, theoretical misunderstandings, or misguided technique on the part of the therapist. But setting aside these blatant and often erroneous efforts to be directly supportive, there are appropriate means of supporting patients, especially at times of acute crisis. It will be my main goal in this chapter to distinguish between these two classes of interventions, and to establish the principles by which interventions that are actually nonsupportive may be avoided and truly supportive interventions properly applied. I shall also attempt to establish a repertoire of appropriate supportive interventions for psycho-therapy; some of them, to my knowledge, have not been clearly defined previously.

ACTIVE SUGGESTIONS AND MANIPULATIONS

I shall ask the reader to study a clinical vignette before I offer any discussion or attempt to formulate any principles. I suggest that the reader attempt to formulate the clinical material, to make his own assessment of the support offered to the patient, anticipate the patient's response to it on as many levels as possible, and attempt to assess these hypotheses in light of the material emerging after the therapist's critical intervention.

> Mr. F.W. was a young man with a severe character disorder who sought therapy because he was unable to establish a sound career for himself and because he felt insecure and inadequate with women. Quite early in his treatment, it became clear that his main reason for seeking therapy was a great fear of becoming an overt homosexual. After several months, it emerged that he had many homosexual fantasies that strongly stimulated him and that he feared he might live some of them out. In the first session in which the patient alluded in any detail to these fantasies, there were references to fantasies of seeing the therapist socially—though no mention of homosexual thoughts about him; fantasies that Mr. F.W.'s father had been killed in a car accident; and indications that the homosexual fantasies centered upon thoughts of men's penises. In the next session, he reported masturbating excessively and that his mother was sharing a bedroom with himself and one of his brothers, because his father preferred to have the windows open all night and his mother could not tolerate it. His parents often fought. He recalled childhood memories of messing up his room and making his mother angry, and of wanting his mother's care and love.
>
> Over the next few sessions, he spoke of being favored by his mother over his siblings and his father, and of his fear that his friends saw him as homosexual and used him. An acute regression followed: he took LSD and believed, delusionally, that he was nude, that he had

made a series of homosexual advances, and that he was being talked about and humiliated. He recovered the next morning and in the next few sessions, described his fear that his penis was too small and was inadequate, and reported that he had masturbated with fantasies of touching men's genitals. Several latency and adolescent homosexual experiences were then recalled—essentially those of mutual voyeurism and masturbation. At this point, the remoteness of his father and his longings for greater closeness with him emerged. He felt attracted to a male friend at work; there were expressions of fears of losing control; he was becoming more anxious.

In the next session, he reported that his brother had gone to live in a college dormitory and that his mother was now sharing the bedroom with him alone. He recalled sharing his parents' bedroom until age seven and that he often heard noises and frequently joined them in bed for part of the night—in effect, as he put it, coming between his mother and father.

At this point, the therapist, who had offered only minor interventions throughout this period, made a "supportive" intervention. He indicated to the patient that much of his problem arose from sharing a bedroom with his mother, and suggested to Mr. F.W. that he change his sleeping arrangements.

Briefly, to clarify the basis for this intervention: the therapist had determined that sharing the bedroom was one major source of the patient's homosexual fantasies, which, in this context, were a complexly structured defense against openly incestuous wishes and fantasies toward his mother, and also possibly a fantasied effort to appease his father and rob him of his power to punish. The therapist reasoned, with some soundness, that as long as the patient slept in a room with his mother, with his father's permission, there would be little that could be done in therapy to modify this aspect of his fantasies and pathology. The reality of the sanctioned intimacy with his mother would generate them over and over as part of his adaptive responses, and there would be few other alternatives available to him.

Let us follow for a while the patient's reaction to the intervention:

> Mr. F.W.'s immediate response to the suggestion was that this would be hard to do without insulting his mother. Also, she might suspect he was a homosexual because of it. He did not want to change therapists, he continued, and he feared becoming too dependent on therapy through something like this. He sometimes made his therapist's words into God's words, and had to refute them because of that. Yet he was glad his therapist had spoken in that session.
>
> These were the highlights of the following hour: He had not changed the sleeping arrangements. He had dreamt that his father had died; he associated that it might therefore happen. The therapist seemed to know what dreams meant. He then described how he had lied about his job to get a better job. He was, indeed, once again separating his parents sexually. His house was so open that people walked into the bathroom and felt that they could intrude; there was no privacy. He felt conscious of his small penis for a moment as he spoke. His father came into the bathroom as if to look at his (the patient's) pubic hairs; it was annoying.
>
> By the next session, he had left his mother's bedroom. He spoke of clandestine mutual exhibitionism with one of his sisters; she got away with things forbidden to him. He ruminated, and finally expressed a great fear of being dependent on the therapist, who could be missing part of the story; yet the therapist's words would affect his (Mr. F.W.'s) whole life, and the therapist could, after all, be wrong.
>
> In the following hour he mentioned a homosexual attraction to a co-worker and then resentment about the time set for the sessions. He felt sexually attracted to the therapist and jealous of the family he must have.

He also felt angry with his therapist and wanted to be condemned by him for his homosexual thoughts.

I shall condense the next few sessions. They included anger at his father for telling him what to do; and a dream in which someone was murdered, and the patient knew the killer, who is killing everyone and was about to get the patient, too. Mr. F.W. directly connected the dreams to his therapist's "intruding on me," and referred directly to his advice, though it was now a couple of weeks later. He also felt that homosexuals were in another part of the dream. Associations were to his father and brother, and to a feeling that the advice from the therapist was somehow like a homosexual advance. He was upset that he was still preoccupied with the "incident" of the advice-giving in therapy and he felt that he was getting into something very disturbing.

The homosexual fantasies then became more open and the patient feared that they were intensifying. They became consciously directed toward the therapist, whose penis Mr. F.W. wanted to see and touch. He felt incurable and panicky, and fantasied an affair with the therapist in which the latter attempted anal penetration and was impotent. He then recalled for the first time in therapy overt homosexual experiences of mutual fellatio which occurred in his teens.

He turned to a promiscuous woman he knew and "fucked her because you can't fuck your therapist." In the midst of this desperate attempt at self-reassurance—it was now some two months after the therapist's suggestion to him—Mr. F.W. spontaneously dated his homosexual fantasies about his therapist and his mounting anxiety to the days after this specific advice had been offered. He now revealed, in response to an inquiry, that he felt that his therapist, by his counsel, was asking him to give up women and accept him; he thought that the therapist wanted to have an affair with him. The therapist then confronted the patient and crystalized his distortions and misconceptions in this matter, and in the next sessions, for the first time in weeks, the patient reported a sense of relief and diminution of anxiety.

I have presented this vignette in some detail because it is, and this may surprise many readers, typical of the response in patients to direct and active "supportive" comments, advice, and manipulations. In this case, the therapist was faced with a situation in which Mr. F.W.'s anxiety was mounting; the patient had experienced an acute regressive episode under LSD and was not functioning well in general. It was clear to the therapist that Mr. F.W. was in a panic resulting from homosexual urges and fantasies evoked largely as a defense against incestuous fantasies toward his mother that were threatening to break through into direct awareness, or may have done so without the patient's reporting it. These latter, incestuous needs were being gratified on some level in reality because the patient's mother was sharing his bedroom in preference to his father's and with his permission. This current situation was, according to the patient, a repetition of more subtle indications of such a preference for him on his mother's part in the past, and of the blatant sanctions that he had received as a child to share his parents' bed.

In the face of the patient's mounting disorganization, the therapist felt that an intervention was clearly indicated; this was an urgent therapeutic context (see Chapter 17). There can be no doubt as to the validity of this assessment; at issue, then, is the form that the intervention should take. The therapist chose to attempt to alter one major reality stimulus for the regression and for the homosexual fantasies and impulses: the sleeping arrangements. Again, from the material from the patient (confirmed by general clinical experience), it would appear that this is an important contributor to the patient's conflicts. My discussion focuses on the way the therapist chose to help the patient modify this disturbing reality.

The therapist, observing the intensification of symptoms and the lack of any effort to change the sleeping arrangements, chose to intervene with a direct suggestion. Its validity and effects can be assessed by what followed, in both the short and long run.

Briefly, I would point to the patient's immediate lack of

appreciation or relief, the general lack of a positive response on his part, and the further regressive qualities of his reaction to advice that was intended to relieve his tension. In fact, his response to this advice is so typical of the fantasies and behavior evoked by such measures that I shall list each aspect separately. Thus:

1. *Patients usually respond to direct advice, suggestions and manipulations with some degree of mistrust and resistance, and a rupture in the therapeutic alliance.* Rather than appreciating the directive and following it with relief, they resent and feel threatened by it. Mr. F.W. even verbalized an immediate fantasy (as a negation) of changing therapists, apparently preferring that to changing his relationship with his mother and fearing the implications for his relationship with the therapist in the advice-giving. Often, patients will, indeed, leave treatment because of active therapeutic interventions of this type. As we will see, the underlying reasons or fantasies for such a response are complex, but they are critical in determining the patient's overt responses. These measures appear to be of little direct and immediate help to the patient and seriously disrupt the therapeutic alliance. On the surface, they tend to create a dominant-therapist and submissive-patient misalliance if the advice is accepted by the patient.

2. Mr. F.W. *fantasied that the therapist was playing "God" and feared submitting to this "God." Thus, advice from the therapist fosters anxiety-provoking passivity, submissiveness, and helplessness in the patient, related of course, to this patient's own passive-homosexual wishes and anxieties.* For any patient, however, it will evoke anxious unconscious fantasies and repercussions on some level, and these will be played out in keeping with his prevailing personality structure and psychopathology. On this level, the therapist is viewed as omnipotent and feared.

Advice from the therapist also deprives the patient of the opportunity actively to resolve his own intrapsychic conflicts and to modify anxiety-provoking reality situations and related inner fantasies. The loss of autonomy and the forced dependency seriously undermines the entire structure of the patient's adaptive resources.

3. *Associations, including the recognition that the dream occurred in the context of the therapist's offer of advice, indicated that the manifest dream reflected latent rage at, and murderous fantasies about, the therapist.* Fury, instead of gratitude, has been evoked. There are many underlying reasons for this rage; it is a fairly typical response to this type of intervention.

4. *The advice by the therapist was seen by the patient as an intrusion on his privacy, and probably his bodily integrity, as we can see in the derivatives concerned with the lack of privacy in the patient's house.* To put it another way, such interventions violate the patient's rights, especially his right to determine his own life as he best sees it. Such intrusions often parallell the behavior of members of the patient's family, especially his parents, including that of the patient himself with his parents. As a result, they repeat a pathogenic interaction rather than offering an opportunity for a new, maturing, and insight-giving experience with the therapist. They become a form of mutual acting out between the patient and therapist, and generate an antitherapeutic alliance in which the patient is unduly controlled and infantalized.

Unconsciously, the patient also sees the therapist at such a juncture as inappropriately voyeuristic and prying—a further meaning of the bathroom material.

5. *In adopting an active, advice-giving role, the therapist takes another unnecessary, and destructive risk.* He attempts to direct the life of his patient on the basis of partial information, and he could be quite wrong. It is one thing to be in error regarding an interpretation, which is directed toward understanding and not immediate behavior. Such an error can be corrected and also has relatively less, though considerable, influence—unless it is repeated —on the patient's behavior because it lacks inner resonance and response in him (see Chapter 19 for a discussion of the complexities of this issue). On the other hand, a directive must either be obeyed or opposed. It assumes great powers of judgment and control on the part of the therapist, and hints at omnipotence, and by contrast, at the patient's weakness and helplessness. Through such interventions, the therapist takes on a risky burden of responsibility. Such a stance is almost never necessary or justified.

6. *Directing the patient to give up one form of acting out will almost always be followed by other forms (e.g., a promiscuous woman was readily chosen to replace Mr. F.W.'s mother).* No intrapsychic change has been effected, unless it is the unfortunate one of lessening the patient's sense of responsibility and self-reliance, and intensifying his conflicts.

7. *Such advice, as portrayed in Mr. F.W.'s later dreams and fantasies, is unconsciously perceived as an assault and a homo-sexual—or heterosexual—seduction.* Mr. F.W. consciously came to feel that his therapist wanted to have him as a lover, and this accounted in part for the patient's acquiescence, his fear and rage, and his flight to a nondescript woman.

In effect, the offered advice, experienced as a seduction ("Come sleep with me, your therapist, and not your mother"), served to weaken the patient's defenses against his homosexual fantasies and impulses. As a result, they became more intensely blatant, and frightening. Further, they prompted a homosexually-tinged antitherapeutic alliance between the patient and therapist. Granted the obvious distortions in the patient's perceptions and fantasies, and the contribution of his own psychopathology, other clinical experiences indicate that such fantasies, often quite unconscious, are among the typical responses to this group of interventions. Thus, direct advice, rather than enhancing intra-psychic defenses and efforts at conflict-resolution, often tends to weaken the patient's defenses against repressed, forbidden impulses and results in increasing anxiety.

8. Mr. F.W. *also expressed fears of going crazy and of being in a mental hospital, where he could be protected from losing control over his impulses.* This is another common response to suggestions from the therapist, and is based on many unconscious fantasies. For example, there is the feeling that the therapist fears so strongly for the patient that the patient himself should not feel safe outside of a hospital. The advice is a directive and a restraint, in the sense that hospitalization is, and the patient feels that one implies the other. The latent nonverbal message (fantasy): "You (the patient) can't handle your impulses or the daily problems in your life," enhances his anxiety and generates thoughts of flight to a hospital. The advice is, as we can see, anything but reassur-

ing. The intensification of the homosexual fantasies and anxieties that resulted from the intervention in this instance contributed both to the fears that the patient had of losing his mind and his wish for a safe haven.

9. *Fantasies of revenge on the therapist are another common consequence of his giving advice.* Mr. F.W. expressed this rather dramatically and very much in accordance with the ever-present talion principle: he would seduce his therapist into a homosexual tryst in which the therapist attempts anal intercourse and is impotent. The advice, then, is unconsciously experienced as an anal penetration and castration—a feminization.

There are many variations on these themes and the conscious and unconscious fantasies which unfold in response to this type of intervention; those from Mr. F.W. are typical. The impotency wished on the therapist is both revenge on him and self-protection for the patient.

Inappropriate interventions offered under the guise of being supportive, then, tend to evoke negative and regressive responses —iatrogenic syndromes (see Chapter 22)—rather than alleviating symptoms and promoting inner growth. The specific form of the response will, of course, depend on the nature of the ill-advised manipulation, the patient's personality structure and psychopathology, and the nature of the ongoing relationship between the patient and therapist.

Before delineating some general principles of technique that evolve from these and other observations, I want briefly to discuss additional aspects of this material.

1. *The question of whether it was reasonable to consider the therapist's advice as a supportive intervention at all is an issue of definition that can be correctly answered only after we have studied a variety of interventions with supportive intentions or goals.* I shall postpone the full discussion until later. Here, I shall simply make the following comment:

The therapist's conscious intention was to help the patient leave a situation that was generating intense anxiety and promoting a severe regression, which threatened to become even more disruptive and to lead into homosexual behavior. The material clearly indicates, however, that a conscious intention to be supportive is not enough to define an intervention as supportive. In fact, intended supportive interventions may be very disruptive. However, those of us who inherently question such directives must realize that many therapists do indeed consider them an aspect of support in psychotherapy. Many types of active manipulation and extra-interpretive (nonneutral) maneuvers are used daily by therapists and rationalized as supportive; this vignette demonstrates one not uncommon type. Further observations will actually demonstrate that such interventions are almost universally nonsupportive and disruptive for the patient and the therapy. Truly supportive interventions enhance the patient's ego and his adaptive capacities and do not demean him. Further, they are confirmed by a subsequent improved capacity to function and an opening up of the material in the sessions.

2. *In supervision, I made a series of predictions about the consequences of the therapist's interventions; they did in fact support the formulations offered here.* The disruptive effects on behavior and the fantasies which followed were anticipated as soon as the advice to the patient was reported.

3. *What other interventions might the therapist have substituted for his direct advice to the patient?* If we all agree that the patient was regressing and that sharing a bedroom with his mother was fostering the regression, then we must agree further that an intervention is indicated by this therapeutic context. What form should it have taken? I would suggest that the therapist should have seen the sleeping arrangements with the patient's mother as the critical adaptive context of the material of the session in which they were mentioned, and have been prepared to interpret to the patient the intrapsychic conflicts and the fantasies—the needs and fears—that were being stirred up by this sharing. This might have been best revealed by exploring Mr. F.W.'s masturbatory fantasies which were prompted in part, by this arrangement; such an exploration probably would have led to quite meaningful material. The ultimate interpretation could have emphasized how much this situation was stirring up for the patient, and how actually and potentially disruptive it was for him. Associations undoubtedly would have then indicated that the patient's intensified homosexual fantasies were related to

sharing the bedroom and were part of the patient's maladaptive flight from the erotic fantasies about his mother, whom his father had "given" to him. Thus, the homosexuality could have been interpreted to him as a defense and denial of his wishes for his mother. Pointing out how disturbing and emotionally costly this arrangement was to the patient, might have motivated him through insight to change the situation himself.

Further interpretations would have elaborated upon these basis themes, adding as the associations permitted, the genetic basis and forerunners of this overt mutual seduction and the patient's responses to it. This facet emerged quite clearly in the sessions and deserved full exploration and interpretation. The gratifications for the patient in the arrangements, many of them quite inappropriate and worth conscious repudiation (mobilizing the patient's healthy superego) could also have been explored and interpreted. In addition, if the therapist had missed the implications of the material initially, confrontation with the sequence of events—i.e., sharing the bedroom with his mother and then regressing acutely with specific defensive and homosexual fantasies —could have been a starting point for a subsequent interpretation of the implications and consequences of the sleeping arrangement.

The point to be emphasized here is that correct interpretations are inherently supportive and are the intervention of choice in any situation where the patient's associations permit. In addition to clarifying unconscious fantasies and conflicts, interpretations can confront the patient with the consequences for him of a particular reality or behavior (see Chapter 14). With Mr. F.W., this is the sleeping arrangement; at other times, it may be a particular situation that the patient has placed himself in, or a specific, though maladaptive and costly, attempt he has made to resolve his anxieties. In principle, we confront the patient from his associations—his fantasies and behavior—with the consequences for him when such realities exist, and thereby motivate him to alter the situation.

Thus, the therapist need not tell a patient to modify his life situation or realities, thereby depriving him of his autonomy, ingenuity, self-criticism, and capacity for change. He need not promote passivity and helplessness, inadequate functioning, and a poor and disturbed self-image—all of which the patient, unfortunately, will later exploit, and which will haunt the therapist. The therapist need only interpret to the patient, and confront him with, what he sees and understands; he can and should expect the patient to then act according to the insights he attains. In so doing, the patient grows and matures. And in fact, if he fails to act, the therapist should then explore and analyze this critical failure to use what he had learned, or the patient's failure to learn in the first place. This is a major dysfunction, which must be modified through insight so that the patient becomes optimally adaptive in his life. Bypassing the issue through directives deprives the patient of work toward the essential kind of change necessary for emotional health: an ability to take in, learn, understand, and modify his inner self, and to make the necessary changes in his reality situations to promote inner and outer adaption.

I have detailed Mr. F.W.'s responses to his therapist's advice so that there can be no uncertainty about the principles that follow from these observations. They are:

1. *Direct advice and manipulation are generally to be avoided in insight psychotherapy.* Exceptions relate only to extreme emergencies when the patient is suicidal or homicidal. At times of crisis, active interventions that are not directive, but will enable the patient to maintain his own autonomy and alter his life situation as necessary, are indicated.

2. *No intervention in psychotherapy can be viewed naïvely; instead, the therapist must recognize that a myriad of conscious and unconscious fantasied and behavioral reactions follow from the patient after every intervention.* Carefully listening will permit an assessment of the consequences of each intervention (see Chapters 18 and 19).

Specifically, an intention to be supportive to a patient need not be experienced as that by the patient, and often is not.

Attempts to be supportive by directing the patient's life and behavior are threatening on so many levels that they are bound to be disruptive to the patient and to the therapeutic alliance, rather than enhancing adaption and treatment. Given the different past histories, problems, and therapeutic relationships that exist, no two patients will necessarily respond alike to such an intervention. However, all will react negatively and in keeping with their personality and genetic history.

A patient may welcome being manipulated on some level, though he usually objects for other reasons. These patients form antitherapeutic, sadomasochistic or dominant-subjected alliances with the therapist, which then undermine constructive therapeutic efforts. Such misalliances must be detected from the material from the patient and modified by the therapist through both a change in his behavior toward the patient and correct interpretations (see Chapter 22). Often, countertransference problems play an important role in the misapplication of interventions that are intended to be supportive.

I shall now exemplify these principles through a discussion of directive measures which are used in the name of support, but which, in reality, are disruptive and antitherapeutic. I shall then discuss those rare situations, as in the case of potentially suicidal patients, where directives may be needed as a last resort after interpretations and confrontations have failed. Finally, I shall consider truly constructive and supportive interventions that may be used at times of crisis or when the patient requires direct assistance in the face of his own ego failures.

Among the most commonly used and supposedly supportive interventions are: offering advice, directives, and sanctions to the patient; arranging to see someone who is creating difficulties for him; directly reassuring him; answering anxiety-ridden, latently meaningful questions; offering to hospitalize him; offering him an extra session; and prescribing medication. Many of them relate to environmental manipulations; all are directed toward some kind of outer, superficial change. The possible list of such maneuvers is, of course, virtually endless; here, I shall present representative vignettes, from which we can establish some additional principles useful for interventions of this type.

The first vignette demonstrates some errors in technique that also bring to light new factors in a therapist's offer of inappropriate support.

Mrs. F.X. had been in twice weekly therapy for four months with Dr. O. because of phobic symptoms. In the midst of exploring her fears of being with groups of people and her anger at various family members, she began a session by saying that she felt anxious coming to the hour. She spoke of a neighbor who could tell what her moods were, and how she avoids this neighbor. The therapist related this to a fear of himself—rather prematurely, for he had not allowed the theme and related associations to develop sufficiently. The patient responded by asking him if he was going to miss one of the sessions in the following week to observe a Jewish holiday (she had good reason to believe that he was Jewish). Dr. o. pointed out that Mrs. F.X. was concerned about separation. This constituted a gratuitous confrontation to a legitimate question; the therapist did not wait for further material. When this session was presented in supervision, it was predicted at this point that the patient would become angry and react negatively.

Mrs. F.X. did, indeed, go on to complain bitterly that her husband was cold and indifferent, and never answered her questions; she was ready to pick a fight with him. She recalled his business trip right after their honeymoon (the therapist had gone on vacation two weeks after Mrs. F.X. had begun her therapy). She spoke of feeling anxious again and ruminated. Dr. o. said that he would in fact be missing next week's session, and suggested, in view of her anxiety, that they make up the hour on the day after the religious holiday. Mrs. F.X. did not know if she could arrange it and would let him know.

Dr. o. responded to this patient's increased anxiety by offering a make-up session. He considered this to be a supportive intervention. In supervision, it was predicted that Mrs. F.X. would see the "gift" of the added hour as a seduction and as a reflection of the therapist's anxiety about her capacity to function adequately on her own. There might also, it was added, be some gratification for her in the offer, since this phobic woman wanted a protective mother, but the negative aspects would predominate.

In the next session, Mrs. F.X. stated that she was feeling better. She had experienced an acute fear of her pediatrician when she took her daughter for an unnecessary consultation; she had only a minor cold, but the patient had taken her to the doctor out of her own irrational fears. Her thoughts went to a friend with a facial scar, whom everyone derided; she had ended up in a state mental hospital. Mrs. F.X. then spoke at length of her own fears of going crazy. She was not able to arrange to make the alternate session and asked whether Dr. O. thought she could not make it for a week on her own.

From the vignette, I want to emphasize these points:

Many of the regressions and exacerbations of symptoms to which therapists respond with active, inappropriate, support-intended measures are the result of countertransference problems and incorrect technique on the part of the therapist; they are largely iatrogenic (see Chapter 22).

In this instance, Dr. O. failed to allow the patient's conscious thoughts and feelings, and the indirect associations that would lead to unconscious fantasies, to unfold. He was too active with too little material, and too general in his comments, since he lacked specifics. His failure to respond properly, to explore and analyze the patient's responses to the anticipated missed session, set the stage for Mrs. F.X.'s mounting anxiety.

There is no substitute for correct technique and, ultimately, correct interpretations. Further, in assessing a regression in a patient, the therapist should always examine his own possible contribution on every conceivable level (see Chapter 22).

In this case, the intended supportive intervention was the offer of an additional hour in response to the patient's increased anxiety. All we need do is to delineate the patient's response to this offer and we will know if the measure was in fact supportive. In essence this response was: decreased anxiety while in the next session, though an acute anxiety episode occurred elsewhere. The patient alludes to an unnecessary consultation, prompted by her own undue fear; the unconscious message to the therapist is clear: Mrs. F.X. saw the offer of the extra hour as gratuitous and as a reflection of the therapist's irrational anxieties.

There is reference to a person who was humiliated and who ended up in a state mental hospital. Here, the unconscious communication alludes to the patient's own humiliation in being seen by the therapist as weak and helplessly defective, and to her concern that her therapist fears her ability to function and handle stress on her own. She seems to be worried that he fears that she may need hospitalization (this is the ultimate in so-called support; this patient unconsciously equates the offer of an added hour with the offer of hospital care).

Her own fears of going crazy reflect an anxiety set off by the therapist's clear, though indirect, communication of such concerns on his part to Mrs. F.X.; they are, then, iatrogenic. The patient refused the offer and reassured the therapist regarding her ability to function. The patient responded by a kind of flight into health —actually, this was more a temporary countertransference "cure" (see Chapter 22)—in reporting, in the session after the therapist's offer, that she felt better and had functioned well. This served to deny any special need for the therapist and to alleviate her anxieties about any kind of decompensation on her part, as it was evoked by the therapist's offer. It was for the patient, a constructive and adaptive response in this context.

To summarize, the patient consciously and unconsciously felt that the therapist had made an unnecessary, humiliating offer out of undue fear for her capacity to function on her own. In part, she responded by pulling herself together; and in part, she expressed her fear of the therapist in a displaced manner, through her reaction in her pediatrician's office.

As already suggested, true support in this situation would have come from correct interpretations after proper listening and the therapist's expressing (or implying) a belief in the patient's ability to function. This would offer her insight and implicit support, which she could incorporate into herself and which would aid her in properly modifying her behavior. This contrasts with the self-deprecatory consequences of the actual intervention.

The correct interpretation would enhance the therapeutic alliance on many levels, while the erroneous one disrupted it, creating an antitherapeutic alliance—in this case, one of mutual fear and possibly of dominance and the struggle against submission. One method infantilizes the patient, while the other promotes maturation.

I want here to underscore a fundamental therapeutic principle: many incorrect "supportive" interventions (and many other technical errors) arise out of a particularly unfortunate therapeutic stance that is characterized by a need to infantilize the patient and, especially, by a failure to believe in his own integrative capacities. This attitude fosters regression in the patient and an undue belief on the part of the therapist that he must be directly manipulative and supportive to bolster the patient's failing ego. If, on the other hand, he expects the patient to handle whatever happens, and to adapt and function, the therapist communicates a kind of trust and implicit support that creates an ego-enhancing tone for the entire therapy.

I will continue now with another clinical example:

> Miss F.Y., who had a moderate character disorder, was jilted by her boyfriend. She was furious that her psychotherapy had not helped her avoid such hurts, and she described at length her feelings of helplessness, despair, and anxiety. There were also references to her sister's falling apart and being hospitalized for it. All of this occurred about two months before the therapist was due to leave the clinic in which he was treating the patient; at that point he was to terminate the treatment. Miss F.Y. was also reacting to this pending termination with considerable distress.
>
> The therapist intervened as the patient's anxiety mounted. Miss F.Y. could continue her treatment in the clinic for at least another year, he told her. She would do better than she realized, he added.
>
> In the following session, the patient spoke of despising people who need reassurance, and who behave as

others wish in order to please them and not be rejected by them. She then described how her boyfriend became enraged whenever she made noises; she cannot stand that.

Here, we have another direct attempt by a therapist to reassure a patient. The unconscious message as sensed on some level by the patient actually seems to be: "Don't be sick, be well." The therapist made no interpretation of Miss F.Y.'s reaction to the pending termination. Instead, the symptoms became the basis of a self-imposed manipulation of the therapist: he added a year to her therapy because of them. While this may be a realistic basis for such a recommendation, to do so without a full analysis of the separation reaction is to foster an antitherapeutic alliance in which action rather than insight is predominant. Further, Miss F.Y. felt despicable and weak because the therapist had felt it necessary gratuitiously to reassure her, and she unconsciously (and probably correctly) sensed that he was infuriated by her regression. She, in turn, responded with anger and rage.

This vignette highlights the finding that a therapist's conscious belief that he is actively and directly reassuring the patient usually covers other countertransference-based motives and fantasies. We may rightly begin to suspect that those therapists who actively manipulate and reassure their patients are either frightened or angered by them, or threatened in some other way. Unresolved and inappropriate guilt, or appropriate but disruptive guilt related to mishandling of the therapy, may motivate such interventions. While we cannot validate these speculations here (I will not attempt in this book to explore to any extent the basis for countertransference problems; see Chapter 22), we must in any case orient ourselves toward self-investigation when we are inclined to use such measures.

In the present instance, the therapist seemed to use reassurance to diminish the patient's anger at him, to alleviate his guilt both over leaving her before the therapeutic work was completed and over having actually accomplished very little in her treatment, and to deflect the patient's focus away from himself. In addition, we may follow the clue offered by the patient, who was in a position to tune in on her therapist: he may well have been angry that she had regressed at a time when he was ending the therapy. Indeed, in the following week the patient openly expressed resentment against the treatment and vented anger over the therapist's coldness. She missed the session after this outburst without calling the therapist. Such acting out against therapy and blatant disruptions in the therapeutic alliance are very often the culmination of incorrect, support-intended interventions. Material from later sessions indicated that the patient also felt that the therapist had been seductive in making his remarks, and that she had fled (missed an hour) because of that, and to gratify her wish to be revenged on her therapist for his pending desertion. Non-manipulative, nonseductive, correct interpretations of the material related to Miss F.Y.'s responses to the pending separation probably would have forestalled such behavior and enabled her to control it, through insight.

Other vignettes point in the same directions. Briefly:

> Miss F.Z., a young woman with hysterical symptoms, began to describe to her therapist strange fantasies that she had been having of being trapped in his office and of merging with the walls. She was reacting to his mishandling of her treatment in ways that I shall not detail here. Rageful fantasies followed: tearing things to pieces and provoking senseless attacks upon herself. In response to these and other primitive fantasies, the therapist asked her a series of questions designed to shift the focus away from these disturbing images and thoughts.
>
> The therapist intended to use these distracting questions to halt the patient's regression by creating a different focus; in reality they constituted an antitherapeutic attempt on his part to avoid relatively primitive material and rageful fantasies directed toward him. In all likelihood, the intervention was prompted by his own

anxiety and countertransference response to the patient's fantasies and anger.

Miss F.Z.'s reaction to the intervention was to shift away from the anxiety-provoking material to empty rumination. The therapist had unconsciously suggested (offered) this defense to her and she readily used it; both shared the defense to the detriment of progress in the therapy (see Chapter 22).

Two brief vignettes will conclude my clinical presentation of the variations in erroneously conceived offers of support.

Mr. G.A. had been in treatment for about eight months because of anxiety and fears of becoming a homosexual. His therapy had been rather chaotic for a long period which led up to a time when termination, necessitated by the therapist's leaving the area, was a few months away. His anxiety mounted and dreams of poisoning someone, and of walking away from and not helping his brother who had been bitten by a shark, went unexplored. As the patient's anxiety grew, the therapist gave the patient his home telephone to call in case of an emergency. In the next hour, the patient spoke of how terrified his parents were of his symptoms and how hopeless he felt. The therapist had, for the first time, opened the door for him when he left the previous session and the patient felt upset and cut off by the move. He spoke of quitting school and of a friend who quit his job. He remembered sharing a bedroom with his grandfather, and seeing him nude and with a truss; the old man later died of cancer. He also recalled an earlier period in his childhood when he shared a bedroom with his sister. He would have pain in his heart, and felt that he was punished for having sexual fantasies about his sister's girlfriends. As the hour ended, the therapist reminded the patient that the next hour was cancelled.

Other factors contributed to this patient's mounting

anxiety and regression, but the therapist's offer of his home telephone, intended to be supportive and reassuring, proved to be far from that. The patient's associations indicate that he viewed it as a reflection of the therapist's fears of his pathology and as a blatant seduction—and he was probably correct in his unconscious assessment. The therapist missed the correct alternative of interpreting the patient's rage at him for his desertions and the patient's fears for himself once abandoned. Once again, so-called support was offered in the framework of a failure to understand the patient's communications and amidst strong evidence for major countertransference problems. A mutually seductive and fearful misalliance was the outcome.

Mr. G.B. was a young man, an ambulatory schizophrenic, who had been in therapy for six months because of episodes of confusion and general social withdrawal. In a pattern that he repeated several times, and which went uninterpreted, he had responded to his therapist's recent vacation with severe anxiety, the experience of criticizing ego-alien voices in his head, and suicidal thinking. While describing these symptoms, he also spoke of his parents' current vacation and his fears that he could not exist without them. However, he maintained his equilibrium and controlled his symptoms over the following week and was calm in his two sessions.

Then, the therapist cancelled the next hour by telephone because he was ill. In the session that followed, the patient began by referring to a conflict between his school hours and the following session. He said that he was depressed again and reported suicidal thoughts. He described a series of problems with his school work and said that he had been hearing explosions in his head. Treatment was not moving fast enough. The therapist related his suicidal thoughts to his poor school performance, and the patient ruminated about killing himself and about how little therapy was doing for him.

The therapist suggested that this was a serious symptom
and that if he could not control his suicidal impulses,
he should be hospitalized or put on medication. The
patient agreed, saying he did not really want to kill
himself.

In the next hour, the patient said that he had been
more anxious than ever at the end of the previous
session. He was having stomach upsets and complained
that everything was the "same old crap over and over."
He expressed rage against his teachers, who did not
understand him, and added that he even felt threatened
and scolded by them at times.

In later sessions, when his rage at the therapist for
his vacation and cancelled hour was expressed in still
less disguised form, through a dream of a plane that
crashed while taking people on a vacation, the therapist
finally interpreted the patient's hostility toward him and,
as a result, the suicidal fantasies were controlled and
resolved.

Once again we observe an offer of so-called support in the
form of hospitalization or medication at a time of confusion in
the therapist, evidence for countertransference problems, and
missed interpretations. The patient unconsciously sensed that the
therapist was actually angry with him, and in discussing this
material in supervision, the therapist acknowledged that this was
true. While the patient felt relieved for a moment in learning that
his therapist was concerned about him, this relief did not last
because of the form in which this concern was expressed (the
offer of medication or hospitalization). Further regressions followed
until correct interpretations were made.

The reader should keep this vignette in mind when he comes
to the next section, where I shall discuss direct offers of support
in true emergencies, made only after all interpretative efforts have
failed. In this vignette, these had not been offered to the patient
first and this made the supportive gestures hollow and rejecting,
rather than helpful.

Further vignettes would merely be repetitious, and I have

already established the essential nature of these repeated observations, to which I have not, as yet, observed an exception, except for dire emergencies. Before proceeding to these, I shall briefly summarize the main observations arising from this discussion.

1. *Directive interventions range from advice to the patient through manipulations of the therapy or of his environment to the prescribing of medication.* They are externally directed, rather than arising from within the patient, and are not aimed at creating insights and inner change.

2. *Such interventions have heretofore been called "supportive" because of the intentions of the therapist.* Empirical observations indicate that they almost always are actually prompted by lack of knowledge regarding proper psychotherapeutic technique or unconscious (sometimes conscious, though not acknowledged) countertransference-based motives of other kinds within the therapist, and do not have the intended ego-enhancing or ego-integrating effects for the patient.

3. *Such active manipulations are usually utilized at times of crises and regressions in the life of the patient and in the therapy.* Very often, the use of poor and incorrect technique by, and countertransference problems in, the therapist have significantly contributed to the occurrence of such crises.

4. *The therapist's motives for such active manipulations include:* a sense of helplessness and of not understanding the patient, along with an urge to do something; an inability to utilize interpretations effectively and a resort to other kinds of interventions; a lack of true belief in the unconscious and conscious repercussions of his behavior on the patient. "Active" therapists of this type seldom listen carefully to the responses of their patients and do not understand their full meaning.

Consciously or unconsciously, such interventions are also motivated by the therapist's undue anxiety, anger at the patient, or need to control, dominate or seduce him. On the other hand, fears of the patient's anger and seductiveness may play a role in evoking such maneuvers as defenses for the therapist. An attempt to avoid the unconscious stirrings of the patient is also a factor.

5. *Patients will respond to these active manipulations on two levels: in behavior and in fantasy.* The effects unfold in his life

and in his therapy. Among the most common responses are the following: Further regression and chaos in the life of the patient and in his symptoms, particularly more destructive forms of acting out. The patient correctly perceives the therapist's manipulation as an acting out, and uses it to justify (sanction) his own acting out. Disruption in the therapeutic alliance, with acting out directed against the treatment in the form of absences and even termination, or the formation of a specific form of antitherapeutic alliance.

Where some temporary (and it is always momentary) relief does occur, attention to the material in the sessions reveals that it is based on such factors as a fear of the therapist, a need to submit to him, or a need to show him how inadequate he is by contrast. This leads to one type of defensive flight into health or so-called countertransference cure (see Chapter 22).

The main feelings and fantasies evoked in the patient are those of humiliation, fear for his capacity to maintain himself on his own, fears for his sanity, rage at the therapist, feelings of being controlled and seduced, and feelings that his integrity and his rights have been violated.

6. *Overall, such manipulations reflect a fundamental failure on the part of the therapist to believe in the integrative capacities of the patient.* They are basically infantilizing, and serve as invitations to the patient to regress further and to be helplessly dependent on the therapist. Virtually no human being welcomes such a role; most bitterly oppose it. Such maneuvers, then, give therapy an atmosphere that is fundamentally antitherapeutic, one which fails to promote inner understanding and change, maturation and self-reliance, the development of new and more effective adaptive resources, and an adequate and positive self-image.

One final comment: This discussion of active manipulations has been related to their application in insight-oriented psychotherapy. The implications of these findings and resultant principles of technique for other types of psychotherapy are beyond the purview of this book, though I suspect that many of the same principles apply. It is a matter well worth further study. Careful listening in depth to the patient's responses to such interventions remains the essential tool for judgment and understanding.

THE EMERGENCY USE OF DIRECTIVES

Under what circumstances is a therapist justified in intervening in an active, directive manner; when are such interventions indicated and truly supportive? I shall attempt to answer this after presenting a clinical vignette.

Miss G.C. was an ambulatory schizophrenic woman in once-weekly psychotherapy. She lived with one of her three sisters and had a very destructive relationship with this sibling. Her life was quite empty, and her relationship with her parents was marred by their destructiveness; she was also constantly suspicious of, and battling with, her fellow-employees in her tenuously-held, unsatisfying job. When Miss G.C. was a child, her psychotic mother twice tried to smother her and had made one serious suicide attempt herself.

Throughout her first year of therapy there were periods when she had been seriously suicidal. These episodes were handled by a mixture of work toward insight and, more rarely, by directly supportive measures, of which I will give one example.

At the time of this vignette, Miss G.C.'s only brother was seriously ill. He had been responsible for her care as a child and was the one supportive figure in her life; his loss posed a tremendous threat to her on many levels. In response to this crisis, the patient became seriously and acutely suicidal once again, feeling that her life would be pointless without her brother around. A dream of allowing herself to be hit by an oncoming taxicab was one representation of these wishes; her serious intention of taking a mixture of pills or using her car in a variety of possible ways to kill herself was another. By now, she knew from her work in treatment that she was capable of losing her perspective, and would develop a dissociative state and truly want to die; but at the moment, she could not detach herself to any significant extent from these wishes. She wanted

to die, and the therapist directly pointed out that this
was a senseless flight, and later, from other material,
that it also was a pointless effort to remain united with
her dying brother and to avenge herself on her destructive mother by depriving her of two of her children at
one time. The therapist was seen by the patient, however, as a hated enemy who thwarted her wishes to die.
Despite this, she clung to him and her treatment—and
her life—by a thread.

To summarize the material from several sessions
during this period: in one hour, she reviewed several
psychiatric hospitalizations of relatives (including her
mother and another sister), making it quite clear that
any attempt to hospitalize her would result in her immediate suicide. This was communicated in a mixture
of direct and indirect affectively-laden ways that led her
therapist to believe her. In the past, too, hospitalization
had been seen as a total failure and humiliation, and
it brought up a devastating and rageful identification
with her mother that evoked extremely intense self-
destructive impulses. She refused medication; it also held
too many negative associations of failure and likeness to
her mother.

Miss G.C. went on to describe her mentally sick
sister's suicidal wishes. The latter suddenly opposed the
patient's treatment and suggested a dual suicide. The
patient was in a turmoil: to whom should she listen?
She really believed that her sister wanted to help too,
though she went on to detail how the sister obliterated
painful perceptions and denied so many things. Whom
should she believe, she asked.

The therapist directly used the patient's associations
to point out that Miss G.C.'s sister was quite irrational
(this was, to some degree a judgmental manipulation
even though it was reflected in the material from the
patient). In response, the patient spoke of her sister
as part of her family; she had to really care. References
to her mother enabled the therapist to remind the patient

of how unfortunately destructive the members of her family could be. At that point, the patient revealed several near-suicide attempts. She was confused and, as the session ended, the therapist asked, as he had done before, that she guarantee him with her sincere word of honor that she would not attempt to take her life, that she would call if her feelings got out of hand and her impulses were too intense, and that she would return the following week. The patient hesitantly agreed.

In the next hour, Miss G.C. had gained some perspective and was less acutely suicidal. She said that her therapist was the only sane one in her life.

Later on, when matters became acute again, the patient was on the verge of leaving therapy. She stated that she felt well, but associations hinted that this was a cover; for her, therapy meant living and termination was a prelude to suicide. This interpretation, which was offered to her, was confirmed by an angry but direct admission. When the patient would not modify her intention, the therapist made it clear that he preferred to continue to work with her, but that if she would not control her suicidal feelings, hospitalization to assure her safety would be the only resource remaining to him. She agreed to control herself and to return the following week. She did so, describing some relief from her symptoms and then reporting fresh material which led to further understanding of her suicidal wishes and enhancement of her controls.

From this vignette, we can derive most of the principles of technique we need regarding the timing and occasion for directive interventions in insight-oriented psychotherapy.

1. *Directives and manipulations are to be kept to a minimum and used only when absolutely necessary.* They are indicated, with caution and within proper limits, when the patient is unable adequately to utilize his own integrative and adaptive capacities, and when his life or that of someone else is also endangered—this is the crucial indication for such maneuvers. We may expand

it cautiously to include dangerous, acute regressions during which interpretative and confrontative interventions are not possible or have failed, though the therapist should always search out the reason for this. Here, one must use careful clinical judgment and flexibility, being neither unnecessarily controlling nor indifferent to acute crises.

2. *Directives are to be used only after every effort has been made to listen to and understand the dynamics and genetics of the situation, and the relevant ego dysfunctions and unconscious fantasies, and every attempt has been made toward correct confrontations and especially correct interpretations.*

3. *Lifesaving, direct manipulations are justified in principle because they are, in such circumstances, ego-enhancing.* They provide the patient with critical controls and perspectives that he is lacking at a time when every effort to help him to generate them on his own has failed. The patient is, indeed, subservient and passive in this situation, but he has made this a necessity and has not been so placed by the therapist. Still, helplessness in the patient is not in itself an indication for directives.

The communication to the patient that the therapist wants him to survive is another crucial aspect of active manipulations under these circumstances. This intervention is ego-enhancing to someone who is so turned against himself and who has such a terrible self-image that he wants to destroy himself. Secondarily, the intervention strengthens what is often, with such patients, a very tenuous and difficult therapeutic alliance.

The ultimate validation of the life-preserving, maturing aspects of these interventions lies in the patient's response to them. While he may refer to his dislike of the pressure from the therapist, he usually does so in a relatively benign tone. Primarily, however, the responses are much like those of Miss G.C.—patients are reassured, relieved, respond with improvement clinically, and often move into new areas of material as a reflection of their renewed sense of hope.

4. *Once the crisis has passed, directives, since they are parameters of therapy (see Eissler, 1953), must be analyzed and undone as far as possible on several levels.* To clarify this aspect:

I find it useful to define all noninterpretive interventions in psychotherapy, except for expressions of human concern (see Greenson, 1967), as parameters, and to apply in general the principles described by Eissler. This means that manipulations such as these must subsequently be explored, analyzed, and resolved to whatever extent possible, to insure that the patient will not be especially prone to regress so as to invite such interventions, which are sometimes gratifying, later on, and so that he will become actively responsible for his behavior himself.

In doing this, the therapist should be cautious and wait until the crisis has passed and the patient has shown indications of a renewed or new capacity to handle matters for himself. Premature undoing of the parameter can undermine the sincerely intended effects it has had for the patient. On the other hand, delay, both in detecting the patient's readiness to re-establish and secure his own autonomous functioning, and in assisting him by exploring the meanings of the parameter with him, will also prove detrimental. The key, as always, lies in being sensitive to the patient's communications.

Such manipulations are commonly viewed by patients as reflecting the therapist's genuine concern for and positive image of the patient; as placing the therapist in the position of a strong protector against the forces (inner or outer) that seek to destroy the patient; and as gratifying intense longings for a good parent, usually never before available. Negatively, these maneuvers, despite their lifesaving value, may also be seen as infantilizing, aggressive and seductive. In this context, however, the therapist has a crucial intervention (confrontation) available to him, one that is not justified if he has unnecessarily manipulated the patient. He can demonstrate that the patient's pathology made the active steps necessary, that they were quite realistic under the circumstances, and that they did not serve countertransference needs, but instead, the needs of the patient. In fact, failure to intervene actively when a patient's life is endangered would itself indicate countertransference problems and human failings in the therapist, as, for instance, that he was tired of such a very trying patient and eager to be rid of him.

A therapist, then, is justified in being actively manipulative when the patient's or someone else's life is clearly endangered, and interpretative and other nondirective interventions have not enabled the patient to establish the necessary controls. Such interventions should be sincerely made and kept to a minimum. Once the crisis has passed, the meaning of the intervention for the patient should be explored, analyzed, and resolved. In all, the result will be the preservation of life and ultimate maturation for the patient. If the therapist is uncertain, it is best for him to bend toward caution when a life is at stake, and to err on the side of temporarily overprotecting the patient rather than unduly risking a suicide.

APPROPRIATE SUPPORTIVE INTERVENTIONS IN PSYCHOTHERAPY

This topic merits a very broad study that could well touch upon every important aspect of psychotherapy, and I shall of necessity be selective and at times quite brief. This discussion is organized in two broad groupings: the generally supportive aspects of psychotherapy and interventions, and specific supportive interventions.

THE GENERALLY SUPPORTIVE ASPECTS OF PSYCHOTHERAPY

This is familiar territory to many readers, and I shall, therefore, simply summarize the main ways in which the therapist is implicitly supportive in psychotherapy:

The Therapist's Stance

Through his general tone and the positive ways in which he relates to the patient (see Chapter 17), the therapist is basically supportive. Included here is the proper establishment of the therapy and the therapeutic relationship, and acceptance of the patient, his communications and his pathology, with warmth, understanding, and all that goes into creating a suitable therapeutic atmosphere and alliance. Also important is the relative absence of countertransference problems in the therapist—so that he does not use the patient to gratify his own nontherapeutic needs, and the therapist's competence. In all, then, the therapist's ability through concern and empathy to establish a proper "hold" or "fit" in which the patient feels secure enough to explore his inner conflicts and fantasies, and to venture into new adaptations in reality, is the essence of this supportive dimension of psychotherapy.

> Mr. G.D., a young man with a borderline diagnosis, alluded to this aspect of the therapist-patient relationship as his treatment was nearing a termination necessitated by his therapist's move to another city. The treatment had been characterized by few interpretations, and many confrontations, only sometimes correct. Despite this, the patient was demonstrating a strong attachment to the therapist and intense regrets over the pending separation. He had been talking about his mixed feelings about the end of his treatment when he began a session with this dream: he was playing on the railroad tracks with trains buzzing all around him; he was nearly hit and reached out toward the third rail. He associated to childhood walks with a friend on rail tracks; the friend would warn him when a train was coming—he had felt safe and protected. Trains referred also to the power that the therapist had to assist him in the face of his own sense of helplessness. Other associations related to the patient's depression and suicidal feelings in response to the pending termination. The therapist's role in safeguarding the patient from harm and from losing control over his own aggressive impulses is clearly portrayed here.

The Timing of Interventions

Correct interpretations, properly stated and timed, are in many ways the most supportive intervention available to the therapist; properly timed confrontations have similar though less powerful effects. Such insight-producing, inner-strengthening measures are supportive in that they are ego-enhancing and maturing for the patient; they are the interventions of choice in almost all therapeutic situations. Communicating both an understanding of the patient, and a specific insight into his inner conflicts and fantasies, carries supportive values on many levels.

Supportive Bypassing

Tact and timing are critical. Knowing when, for example, not to interpret or not to stir things up is one aspect of this kind of support. There are times when focusing on a certain area of conflict for the patient or on particularly disturbing fantasies can be disruptive, and the therapist must either wait for clearer derivatives, which would indicate both that the patient is prepared to deal with the material without regressing and that expressions of it are readily at hand to demonstrate its validity to the patient, or allow the material to pass until later in treatment. At such times the therapist must first work on strengthening the patient's ego, especially his capacity to tolerate anxiety and maintain controls, before dealing with a particularly sensitive area.

This technique constitutes, essentially, support through the therapist's temporarily sharing with the patient the defenses of isolation and avoidance. In doing so, he must be certain that such bypassing is indicated by the needs and hypersensitivities of the patient and not by fears of his own; in the latter circumstances, he will be creating an antitherapeutic atmosphere. In fact, such a supportive technique should be used quite rarely, with the therapist's full conscious understanding of his reasons, and with full preparation to deal with the avoided issues at a later point in treatment. This technique merges into the general policy of waiting for the emergence of meaningful and clearer derivatives of an intrapsychic conflict before intervening.

Its use is illustrated in the following two vignettes:

> Mrs. G.E. was a woman with a borderline syndrome in her second year of therapy. At a time when many of her problems had been resolved, she brought up the prospect of terminating her treatment. There was considerable anxiety regarding this eventuality and some regression to behavior and reactions until then con-

trolled; for instance she permitted herself to become helpless, felt overwhelmed, and dissociated herself when anxious. Dreams and fantasies reflecting anger at her husband and interest in other men began to appear. Their manifest content and the associations to them suggested that they reflected sexual fantasies about the therapist. They were of the house of a doctor, a relative of the patient, in which she was at peace; of someone strange, dressed in white, in her bedroom, threatening to attack her; of nearly being hit by a train and going to a hospital; and of running off to a tropical island with someone. Mingled with these themes were references to uncontrolled urinating and defecating, to becoming pregnant, and to eating strange foods.

The therapist had found in his previous work with this patient that interpretations of sexual fantasies were particularly disturbing to her, as was any suggestion that she felt inclined to be unfaithful to her husband. Further, disguised expressions of fantasies, when interpreted directly to her (here, there were no direct references to the therapist as yet), had tended to make her anxious, defensive and suspicious of the therapist. She did not tend to act out such impulses and was not regressing further, so the therapist did not address himself to these derivatives in his remarks, but waited for them to become even less disguised. He was fully aware of their context—the possibility of terminating her therapy. He did, however, help the patient muster courage to express her feelings and fantasies more directly by confronting her with some of the themes in the material, such as her searching for a protector, or her longing for something she felt was missing (these were supportive confrontations).

In this way, then, he consciously and deliberately shared a direct avoidance with the patient in order not to foster an unnecessary regression, or extreme defenses, which could be expected to develop if the underlying fantasies were interpreted too soon. He was prepared also to interpret the material if a need (a therapeutic context) arose, and when the derivatives became clearer.

After about a month, the patient dreamt directly of writing to the therapist, and her associations related to her erotized longings for her dead father. The therapist was then able to demonstrate the patient's many communications of similar longings for himself and to link it both to her father and the termination. While she was briefly upset initially, the patient was struck by the many expressions of these fantasies and went on to describe how she had actually been having occasional conscious thoughts of going off with her therapist. She was able to maintain sufficient distance from these ideas to recognize them as fantasies that she could understand and not dread; she did not regress, but worked them through over the next few weeks.

The second vignette is somewhat different, though related:

Miss G.F. was a teenager with an ambulatory schizo-phrenic syndrome and a history of excessive drug use, poor functioning at school, and promiscuity. She tended to regress to a disorganized paranoid state when under stress; this impaired her judgment and functioning and often led to uncontrolled outbursts of rage and destructive behavior at home.

In her second year of therapy, through which aspects of her functioning had improved considerably, Miss G.F. was faced with her therapist's pending midwinter vacation. Before his previous summer vacation, she had regressed and had been particularly destructive toward her parents. Dreams and fantasies at that time had revealed many unconscious fantasies related to this behavior, including a paranoid-like rage at her therapist for deserting her, much as her mother had done in a very destructive manner in her childhood. Also evident in the material at that time were relatively undisguised dreams of seducing the therapist sexually in order to possess him. In the past, she had had conscious sexual fantasies about her father and had seduced one of her brothers, but then defended herself against these poorly controlled impulses by subsequently suspecting them of wanting to seduce her and nearly believing that she had been raped in her sleep by one of her uncles when he had visited with her family.

The therapist had attempted at the time of the summer interruption to show the patient that she wanted to hold onto him sexually primarily to be mothered (an interpretation of a displacement; see below). His aim was to provide the patient with insight with which she could maintain her sexual controls, which had markedly improved during the therapy, and to forestall paranoid outbursts at home, based on projection of these sexual fantasies or renewed sexual acting out. Miss G.F. responded to these interventions, which were based on obvious dreams and associations, with blatant denials and paranoid rages directed at the therapist. There was a rupture in the therapeutic alliance, and the patient became quite suspicious and mistrustful; she acted out at home, though not as destructively as before, but did not act out sexually.

At the time of the midwinter vacation, the same kind of derivatives appeared in the patient's dreams and associations. There had been little change in the patient's fragile, projective-denial defenses, and the therapist elected not to pursue these themes as long as there was no destructive acting out, unless the patient indicated some readiness to explore these transference fantasies. This did not occur, and since the patient's reaction to the separation did not approach psychotic proportions, and regression did not occur, the material in question was left untouched. The therapist believed, based on his earlier experience, that any attempt to explore it would have been severely disruptive for the patient.

Instead, several nonsexual transference interpretations were offered to the patient when other aspects of the material were being interpreted. For example, the therapist pointed out Miss G.F.'s rage at her mother for leaving her alone one evening, reviewed facets of it, and gently noted her excessive sensitivity to any separation—including those from himself.

Actually, with this last intervention, we have come to two specific supportive aspects of interpreting: that of "sharing the focus" or "sharing the transference," i.e., interpreting a disturbing fantasy about one person toward whom it is relatively unacceptable in terms of similar fantasies toward someone with whom it is more acceptable; and interpreting upward or through a displacement, i.e., alluding to the patient's rage and general separation anxieties—and earlier, to her wishes for mothering and care—instead of her sexual fantasies. In these ways, the therapist emphasizes readily acceptable aspects of the material and then may add a comment regarding something more anxiety-provoking when the patient is better prepared (see below).

In deriving from these and other clinical experiences the principles for the technique of avoiding certain aspects of the patient's material, I would emphasize these points:

1. *Proper interpretative technique requires tact and timing, waiting for the proper indications to intervene, and allowing a blossoming of the derivatives at hand.* Beyond such general tact, it is supportive when derivatives relate to especially painful and anxiety-provoking material, to allow time for relatively undisguised, easily interpreted derivatives to appear before intervening. In most instances, this will be the trend as the patient endeavors to deal with or adapt to the intrapsychic conflicts and unconscious fantasies related to the material.

2. *With borderline and schizophrenic patients, such waiting is particularly useful, since it enables the patient to become familiar with the fantasies that are disturbing him, and the evidence for the interpretation becomes clearer, so that it is less likely to be denied.* It is, then, out of respect for the regressive potential of these patients and their tendency to react defensively that the therapist uses the utmost caution. On the other hand, the therapist must not be threatened by such regressive potentialities and avoid in-

dicated interpretations that will ultimately strengthen the patient. In the last analysis, correct interpretations must prevail.

3. *Among the more common areas of excessive sensitivity in patients are incestuous or homosexual fantasies, primitive murderous fantasies toward beloved family members, and erotic transference fantasies.* The therapist must move cautiously, too, with any material known to create regression in a particular patient, slowly dealing with it as the associations and the patient's ego permits.

4. *In most instances, interpretations upward, interpretations of other displacements, undercutting or devaluing, and sharing the focus of the interpretation are preferred supportive interventions when dealing with especially terrifying material (see below).* However, when it seems likely that further regression will follow from any attempt to deal with specific fantasies at such times, the therapist is justified in avoiding them entirely, unless regression and acting out increase.

5. *The decision not to confront or interpret should be weighed carefully, so that it is used sparingly and only at times of crises and of clear indicators that interpretations, though correct, would be disruptive (e.g., the primitive guilt evoked by Miss G.F.'s erotic fantasies toward the therapist).* It must also be clear from the material that such a step is in the best interest of the patient and does not reflect countertransference anxieties. The expectation should be that, as the patient's ego is strengthened, such material will then be analyzed and worked through.

SPECIFIC SUPPORTIVE INTERVENTIONS

Of many, the sometimes subtle, supportive interventions, I shall discuss these: directly supportive though not directive comments added to interpretations; supportive confrontations; interpreting displacements (so-called interpreting upwards); and depreciating or devaluing.

Supportive Comments Added to Interpretations

At times of crisis, or when making an interpretation that has painful and potentially disturbing aspects to it, the therapist can add supportive comments to his intervention. These should not be in the nature of direct reassurance or comfort to the patient, but are dictated by the nature of the past and present material, and require some creative skill. I shall illustrate with a few examples.

Mrs. G.G. was a woman with a borderline syndrome who was being seen in treatment twice weekly. She tended to use dissociation and flight, and would even get up to leave the session when confronted by herself or the therapist with disturbing memories, thoughts, fantasies and feelings. This was especially so with negative references to her father, who had left her several times as an infant and child. Repeated working-through of these experiences and their repercussions on her life had enabled the patient to tolerate far more peacefully the recall of painful memories connected with his absences and the terrifying fantasies they evoked.

As termination of her treatment drew near, the material hinted at an erotized father transference with fantasies of holding on to the therapist sexually. Dreams related to doctors with whom she ran away, and to a builder whom she surprised at his office and seduced. She was also angry at her husband and apparently saw her therapist as her rescuer. The therapist allowed this potentially upsetting material to build since it was becoming less and less disguised, and previous work in this area had been quite difficult for the patient. Finally, she hesitantly and with a half-retraction reported a conscious fantasy of leaving her husband to go off with the therapist. The therapist then intervened when the patient responded to her own revelation with the thought of leaving the session prematurely. He pointed out to the patient that these fantasies had been building for some time, and delineated the material which reflected them, their specific nature, and their links to her father. Seeing that the patient was quite distraught and beginning to alter her state of consciousness as he completed his interpretation, the therapist continued: Mrs. G.G. had faced distressing thoughts of this kind in therapy before, particularly regarding her father. She certainly must realize that dissociating herself and attempting to disappear or run out did not help her resolve these feelings, and she must have learned by now that she could face them and cope with them directly. The patient was upset, but acknowledged that she could do so and went on to add further material. She did not dissociate or leave the session.

In this situation, the therapist used a supportive confrontation to bolster the patient's ego as she began to regress in the face of the focus on her anxious and guilt-ridden fantasies about the therapist and her father. The reminder of her past positive functioning and of the benefits of facing rather than attempting to obliterate such fantasies helped her muster her ego strengths to deal with this material. She did not resort to her old, relatively primitive defenses of dissociation, flight and denial, but held the line, so to speak, and further explored her fantasies and anxieties instead. The confrontation proved supportive in that it helped the patient control the regression and deal with her fantasies on a more mature level.

A more abbreviated example is this one:

Miss G.H., a young woman who had a severe character disorder, alluded several times in her therapy to incestuous fantasies and possibly actual sexual experiences in her childhood with one of her brothers. Each time they came up, however, she fled them. Then, the suicide of a young man who was the cousin of a girlfriend of the patient, and who was living and sleeping with this friend, evoked anxiety, guilt, and self-destructive acting out in the patient. A dream alluding to her brother and to self-injury led the therapist to interpret this reaction as linked to her sexual fantasies and resulting guilt about her brother. This time the therapist also confronted the patient with her past flight from these fantasies and the self-destructive acting out which went along with it, and he suggested that it was "high time" Miss G.H. faced these fantasies and worked them out. She confirmed the value of this added comment by now revealing actual guilt-ridden incestuous experiences with this brother and by then exploring the entire matter over a number of sessions, and without acting out.

Here, the therapist again addressed himself to the ego strengths of the patient and added to his interpretation a confrontation with a maladaptive defensive flight that she had used to deal with her sexual fantasies and experiences with her brother in the past. This undoubtedly helped the patient to reveal more about these experiences and work through her guilt, while the interpretation alone might only have heightened the patient's anxieties and defenses. Certainly, these defenses could then have been confronted or interpreted if they appeared; it is a matter of one's style of working whether he prefers to wait for this eventuality or to anticipate it. Often, once a strong repression-supportive defense has been utilized by the patient, it proves difficult to modify; anticipating and thereby preventing its operation if possible is advisable.

Addenda to interpretations, then, are not made routinely, but are indicated and are of value if it is a case of anticipating from earlier similar experiences the patient's defensive or disruptive reactions to a particular interpretation. They are intended to bolster the patient's ego resources, and his capacity to tolerate the intervention and to work with it further. Such comments should not be made defensively, reflect any insistence by the therapist that his intervention must be correct, nor depreciate the patient. They are useful in letting him know that the therapist realizes that his interpretation is potentially disturbing, while emphasizing, usually through references to positive past experiences in treatment, that the patient has the capacity to handle it.

Supportive Confrontations

Most confrontations have a supportive element, and many are directed specifically toward such ends. This type of confrontation is designed to help the patient face such things as his self-destructive and outwardly aggressive behavior, his unnecessary pathological defenses, and dangerous reality situations. Confrontations with various alternative solutions to realistic and even neurotic problems, and with the consequences of different avenues of possible action, also have supportive aspects to them; but these must be based as much as possible on the patient's own ideas and material.

Consider this clinical example:

> Mr. G.I. was a teenager with a moderate character disorder who was in therapy because of school and acting-out problems. In one session, he reported confusion regarding the date that day and showed other evidence of a slight memory impairment. He alluded to heavy marijuana smoking. In addition to dealing with the dynamics of this self-destructive behavior—I will not detail this here—the therapist confronted the patient with the dangers of excessive use of the drug and the reports of organic mental syndromes caused by such use.

Here the confrontation was intended to convey concern on the part of the therapist. This is both something with which the patient can identify, and a means of enhancing the patient's own controls and search for less costly ways of handling his anxieties.

Such confrontations should not be used too often, and should not replace interpretive work. They should always be directed toward enabling the patient himself actively to consider and deal with the critical problems at hand, and should not promote undue subservience.

At times, and always in keeping with the material from the patient, a very useful form of support through ego and superego building comes from confronting the patient with alternative adaptions to inner and outer conflicts and problems that he himself has consistently overlooked. This must be done with the utmost sensitivity and care, in a way that avoids directing the patient—though obviously some degree of suggestion is implicit

in the technique—and only after the patient has clearly and repeatedly failed to recognize on his own rather obvious maturity-
promoting alternatives.

To illustrate:

> Mrs. G.J., a woman with a borderline syndrome, was
> working toward termination of her therapy. In one
> session, she reported that she had dreamt of a group
> of women sitting in the street. Her mother lay on the
> ground and then, at the patient's suggestion, sat in a
> chair. Associations were to her son's bar mitzvah (his
> entry into manhood), to her father's funeral and sitting
> afterwards in mourning, and to her son's dread of going
> to a sleep-away camp. The patient then recalled a series
> of incidents from her own childhood at camps; they
> revolved around illnesses, accidental injuries, and death.
> She also remembered how her mother always sat with
> her until she fell asleep as a child.

Among comments related to the patient's fears of termination
and "coming of age," with its links to the loss of her father and
her lifelong dread of separation and consequent harm to herself,
the therapist pointed out that Mrs. G.J. had virtually no concept
of the growth-promoting potential of inevitable separations and
aloneness. She had been deprived of such positive opportunities
as a child and now had difficulty both in offering them to her
own children and accepting such opportunities, like termination,
for herself.

The therapist here went beyond the interpretation of the
context, dynamics, conflicts, and genetics of this patient's reaction
to termination, in an effort to promote ego growth and adaptation.
Often, patients do not realize that such positive alternatives exist;
pointing them out fosters their use and enhances the patient's
capacity to resolve the related conflicts. In keeping with this,
the therapist should reinforce new constructive adaptations when
the patient discovers them himself.

Another vignette demonstrates the consequences of missing
an opportunity to confront the patient with these adaptive alterna-

tives, and introduces a related topic: confronting the patient with the consequences of poor controls, inadequate limits, and ill-defined or overly-open boundaries.

> Mr. G.K. was in therapy because of fears of becoming a homosexual. After he had been in therapy for ten months, his father died. Among other reactions, he began to describe conscious sexual fantasies about his mother, with whom he was now living alone. These were described to the therapist in a vague manner and had to do with seeing her nude in her bedroom. In the session in which he described this, he went on to mention overt homosexual fantasies regarding his fellow-workers. He then said that he wanted some advice from the therapist, but felt that the latter was strong enough not to offer it. He recalled that in the past, the therapist's advice had accomplished nothing.
>
> In the next session, Mr. G.K. described how his mother had been leaving the bathroom door half-open when she bathed; he would rush by, trying not to look in. In sequence, there followed references to other exhibitionistic practices of his mother, to seeing a woman-neighbor nude, to being called a fag, to putting on his mother's underwear as a child, and to fears of developing fantasies of having relations with his mother.
>
> The therapist did not intervene in this session. The incestuous fantasies were overt, and direct reference to them would probably have increased the patient's anxiety and guilt. Interpretations of a displacement did not present themselves in the material; sexual wishes were primary, and while underlying dependency longings no doubt existed, they were not central. Such an interpretation would, in fact, offer the defenses of denial and displacement to the patient, rather than produce insight.

In deciding on a correct intervention here, we must focus on the key problem here (the adaptive context): the mother's actual seductiveness and the patient's responsive participation. It is, therefore, in their mutual failure to establish boundaries and privacy that the confrontation should be made. The therapist could have pointed out to the patient that he was being overstimulated by his mother, that he had not confronted her directly or implicitly with her behavior, and that he was thereby participating in it. He could have added a supportive confrontation-interpretation to the effect that the failure to establish adequate boundaries was generating not only frightening incestuous fantasies, but also troublesome flights into homosexual fantasies and even thoughts of becoming a woman. In this way, the price that the patient was paying for his incestuous interaction with his mother would be made clear, and a necessary internal conflict generated within the patient. Through this, the development of proper boundaries and of mature superego and ego functioning, would be enhanced.

To confirm in part the validity of these formulations, I shall add the fact that in the next session the patient described how he had masturbated with his bedroom door half-open; his participation in the seductiveness was now explicit. Once the therapist had worked on these problems in the manner discussed here, the patient developed a greater degree of privacy with his mother and there was a distinct diminution of his blatant incestuous thoughts and his homosexual fantasies.

These supportive confrontations, then, endeavor to point the patient toward healthier adaptations to inner and outer conflicts. The therapist attempts to promote ego and superego development, and the development of reasonable renunciations and appropriate channels for the discharge of instinctual drives. Such interventions must not be made in a moralizing, judgmental or manipulative manner, and the patient's autonomy must be preserved.

One last illustration of this type of confrontation follows:

> Mr. G.L. had previously attempted suicide after a homosexual affair in which he was the recipient of anal intercourse; he was diagnosed as borderline. Exploration revealed previous homosexual experiences such as fellatio, but not anal intercourse; Mr. G.L. based his denial that he was a true homosexual on the fact that he did engage in the latter practice.

The disturbing episode had been prompted by his parents' vacation and his terrifying sense of loss, aloneness, and rage, which he sought to alleviate and express through a homosexual encounter.

The therapist interpreted these aspects of the homosexual behavior as they unfolded from the patient's associations and, in the context of other associations, related the material to the patient's use of denial and his feelings of being overwhelmed by reality. He then pointed out how such denial rendered him vulnerable to this kind of inundation and promoted frantic behavior on his part.

The goal here was to interpret the dynamics of the situation and to confront the patient with the maladaptive aspects and "cost" of his current defenses. The price paid for the denial was emphasized, so that the patient could be more alert to his use of such mechanisms and their disadvantages, and combat them.

SUPPORTIVE INTERPRETATIONS OF DISPLACEMENTS

The technique of interpreting displacements is an important general intervention, though difficult to master, and can often be used as a supportive measure. In essence, the therapist interprets the patient's use of associations and fantasies on one level as a displacement from, and screen for, affect-laden material at another level. He does so in a supportive way at times of acute regressions and anxiety, by demonstrating to the patient less primitive uses and meanings that the terrifying relatively blatant impulses and fantasies convey, or dealing with a kind of intellectualized defense in which the patient ruminates using seemingly deep and primitive fantasies, in order to avoid more superficial, meaningful, and affect-laden material. One intervention of this kind is the reconstruction of the more recent consequences of a former event, described in a pioneering paper by Lowenstein (1957).

Let us begin with a clinical vignette:

Mrs. G.M. was a woman with a narcissistic disturbance who sought therapy after an affair had not helped

to resolve her anxiety and her many feelings of dis-
satisfaction with herself. She was confused and flooded
by intense sexual fantasies that she had trouble controlling. Early in her therapy she experienced strong
sexual feelings for her therapist and was disturbed by
them. She began one session by reporting that she had
dreamt of sitting like a child in the therapist's waiting
room with his other patients. An older woman said that
she loved the therapist; then Mrs. G.M. was in his consultation room, reading a book and feeling how warm a
person he was; she began to cry.

Mrs. G.M. recalled that in the previous session the
therapist had correctly interpreted several until-then
repressed fantasies related to a conflict that was plaguing
her, and that she had felt good. She had read about
therapists seducing patients and had felt frightened. She
had never had any sense of independence, and had clung
to her father and then to her husband. She had read
a short story; a husband gives love-gifts to his wife
and destroys her through them. She had been reading
another book and had fantasied having intercourse with
a strange man. The woman in the dream looked like
her mother and had breasts like her. She felt sexually
aroused by the therapist and felt angry at herself. With
her husband, she was most gratified sexually when sucking on his penis; she had not had enough of that as a
child, she guessed, referring to nursing at her mother's
breast.

The therapist intervened here, using the material of
the session and that from recent sessions in which the
patient had expressed her rage at the deprivation experienced with her cold, distant, martyred mother. He
pointed out that Mrs. G.M. had intense longings for
closeness and care, which she expressed through any
means available to her including sexual longings and
fantasies, and that she sought such care and feeding
from him as she did from so many others. His understanding of her in the previous session had intensified

these longings, which she once more expressed in sexual ways, just as when she felt that he did not understand her, she was hurt and enraged.

Mrs. G.M. responded that it was so childlike and so true. She had been eating excessively and drinking lots of milk. She had inadvertently left out the end of the dream that she had reported earlier in the hour: in it, she had actually attempted to seduce the therapist. She thought of her father and of how she had shared her parents' bedroom for many years, often going into his bed. The therapist pointed out how confused she was about the meaning of closeness, and how sexualized her view was as a result of the experiences of her childhood.

In this session, the therapist interpreted Mrs. G.M.'s sexual fantasies and longings as representing a not specifically sexual desire for nurture. Mrs. G.M. confirmed the validity of this intervention by recalling a repressed part of her dream and by developing one specific additional genetic root of this response—sharing her father's bed.

To conceptualize this intervention in more technical terms, we could say that a sexual fantasy was interpreted here in terms of primarily oral dependent needs. Specifically, the unconscious sexual fantasy offered by the patient was that of sucking at the therapist's penis (implied by the dream and associations to it); beneath this fantasy, condensed with it, and also more relevant and meaningful at this time, was the patient's wish to be fed at the breast of her mother—to be cared for and loved by her. This wish was then displaced onto the patient's father, who was the warmer, more giving, mothering parent.

There are other ways to describe this intervention correctly. A seemingly sexual-genital fantasy is here the cover for an oral-pregenital fantasy; what appears as a three-person, oedipal rivalry is a front for a two-person, pre-oedipal, early "oral" wish for union and care. Characteristic of this later level is the wish that only the patient's needs be recognized and gratified in some total, continuous way (see Balint, 1968). The patient's instinctual-drive fantasies related to sucking at and incorporating her mother's breast are at the root of the sexual fantasies which are expressed in the guise of heterosexuality. In this sense, we have interpreted "downwards" here—from the oedipal to the oral level; yet in stating it in terms of care and love, we have spoken in the language of a less primitive and less instinctive functioning and experiencing.

Thus, a careful analysis of interventions which are referred to as "interpreting upwards" show that their structure is complex. At times, they move clearly upward from deeper, more primitive and usually pregenital fantasies and interactions to more superficial oedipal and post-oedipal levels, but at other times, they contain both elements. I have termed these interventions "interpretations of displacements."

Interpretations of this type are based on our understanding of the development of the child, and of his instinctual drives and ego (see Chapter 8). I shall here merely recall as an illustration the oral, anal, phallic and oedipal stages of development. The oral stage encompasses the first year or so of life, the child's budding instinctual drives and derivative fantasies, as well as the budding defenses of this period—e.g., projection and introjection, the developing autonomous ego, and the primitive lack of the self-not-self distinction. As the child grows, new instinctual drives and modes of ego functioning develop, centering upon other erogenous zones and means of relating; during these periods, the earlier modes of functioning and fantasizing are reworked at the newer level of concepts. An earlier fantasy of devouring an amorphous mother can later be expressed as anally incorporating her breast, still later as caressing her breasts, then as being affectionate to her, and when older, as being affectionate to or having sexual intercourse with another woman.

There are many complexities to this kind of layering; instinctual-drive derivatives are organized in a hierarchy from those that are primitive, blatant and primary-process-dominated to these that are socialized, reality-attuned, modulated, and secondary-process related or sublimated. It is these expressions of instinctual drives, and the level of the ego and superego functioning with which they are handled, that we explore in dealing with our patients' conflicts and symptoms.

With this as a brief background, we can now more intelligibly describe "interpreting upwards." In its simplest form, the therapist responds to primitive instinctual-drive expressions from a patient, in context and with proper indications, by pointing out their less primitive, more derivative, sublimated and socialized meanings and uses. In this way, the therapist offers meaningful support to a patient who is terrified by his primitive impulses and fantasies, by pointing out that they are in the service of very basic, human and social needs. He says to the patient, for example, "Your wish to suck on a penis is related to wanting care and love"; and this is both a correct adaptive use of the primitive fantasy and reassuring to the patient.

A second, related intervention is actually an interpretation of a displacement with a downwards slant, though without the use of primitive language. Here the therapist tells the patient that his seemingly adult needs serve different and more primitive ones. He may say, for example, "Your wish to have intercourse is related to your wish to be taken care of and fed." The sexual aspect here is related to oral needs. Of course, all sexual longings are a mixture of displaced pregenital and genital longings. The goal here is to interpret that aspect of the fantasy that is most relevant from the material and to do so from a correct understanding of the patient's adaptive efforts. This reassures the patient as well.

The therapist should not offer this type of intervention as a defensive displacement to the patient, but as a correct interpretation of displacement that the patient himself is using. He is not saying to the patient: "Don't fear your wish to suck, think of it as a wish for care," but "You really want care and express it in a primitive way."

These interventions also apply to aggressive expressions, which form a hierarchy from primitive and explosive world-shattering impulses to more controlled, modulated and specific anger.

Let us now turn to a few more examples of this technique.

Miss G.N. was an asthmatic young woman who had

a severe character disorder, and was prone, as she began
to explore her repressed fantasies, to blatant incestuous
dreams and fantasies. This carried over into her past
and present behavior with her brothers and her father,
which was seductive and sexually exhibitionistic. When
the actual seductive experiences with her brothers
emerged, her guilt was very intense, and she had an
asthmatic episode—an unconscious punishment of herself
(the asthma, of course, had other unconscious determinants as well) and also acted out self-destructively.
Much of this was analyzed and worked through.

Several quarrels with her father, and related associations, indicated that her repressed fantasies and experiences (memories) with him were now emerging in the
material. In one session, she reported a dream in which
she had relations with a Negro. Associations readily
pointed to sexual fantasies about her father, who em-
ployed Negroes in his business, for instance, but also
related to her father's hostility and coldness toward
her, and to her wishes for closer and more communal
living with him.

At this juncture the therapist directed his interpretations not toward the blatant sexual wishes about her
father, but toward her wishes for a better relationship
with him and her anger at his aloofness. The patient
then discussed this without undue guilt, and afterwards
slowly produced derivatives related to her sexual fantasies and experiences with her father; these were then
specifically analyzed and interpreted.

In this condensed vignette, the therapist, rather than prematurely interpreting the patient's undisguised incestuous sexual
desires for intercourse with her father, elected to interpret two
displaced and related sets of fantasies. The first was an interpretation upwards to less instinct-laden wishes for closeness with
her father. The second focused on the patient's more acceptable
aggressive feelings of anger with her distant and frustrating father.
Since the therapist was aware of what lay beneath these two levels,

he could later interpret the directly sexual aspects of the material when the patient was better prepared for it. These interpretations of displaced derivatives of the deeper, more primitive and anxiety-provoking fantasies are truly ego-supportive. They also make the depths eventually more understandable, their adaptive aspects clearer, and strengthen the patient's ego in preparation for the more disturbing material.

Notice that this material contains a common type of supportive interpreted displacement: conflicts over aggressive impulses are interpreted as displacements covered by sexual fantasies. In general, aggressive fantasies and conflicts are better tolerated by patients than sexual ones. Thus, when blatant sexual material screens or contains elements of hostile conflicts, the latter should often be the initial interpretive focus. Displacements from primitive aggressive fantasies onto less threatening sexual fantasies also occur.

The therapist must be quite sensitive to the truly pertinent level of the material, since he must eventually also interpret not only the displacements, but the more primitive fantasies themselves. His own countertransference anxieties must not dictate his intervention. This is a delicate matter; in general, one deals with the more superficial levels earlier in therapy, although, if the patient can tolerate it and the associations are truly meaningful and in context, deeper material can be worked with and interpreted when there is a pressing need to do so even though it is early in treatment.

Another common displacement in which generally primitive fantasies and impulses are used to avoid more superficial, affectively meaningful material is that of homosexual behavior and fantasies. Overt homosexual expressions convey primitive longings for basic care and affection, and serve to express rage and hostility. Interpretation of these fantasies often includes references to displacements. For example:

> Mr. G.O., a homosexual young man diagnosed as borderline, responded to his therapist's pending vacation by picking up a professional man at a "gay" bar and having anal intercourse with him. He then panicked with

guilt and remorse, and came to his session quite
disturbed. The material in the session related to themes
of separation and revenge.

The therapist interpreted the homosexual behavior
as a displacement of the patient's longings for closeness to him, and as an expression of the vengeful wish
to "screw" the therapist, adding a reminder (confrontation) of the consequences to the patient of such acting
out. Later, more specific primitive fantasies emerged and
were analyzed; these included wanting to bore into the
therapist and devour his insides, and wanting to fuse
with him in various ways.

In principle, then:

1. *Interpretations of displacements are a common aspect of
intervention; they are specifically supportive when primitive,
blatant derivatives of instinctual drives, both sexual and aggressive,
are creating anxiety, and when the patient's associations indicate
that these relatively undisguised expressions are in the service of
more socially adaptive needs and fantasies.* Such interventions may
take the form of interpreting or reconstructing upward or downward in terms of the level of psychosexual and ego development,
and chronological age of the patient, but they always include a
shift from relatively primitive and undisguised fantasies to more
general, less primitive and better defended expressions if they
are to be supportive.

Upward interpretations include references to displacements
away from relatively simple longings for care, or expressions of
hurt and anger, to primitive oral and anal devouring and incorporative fantasies. The patient's anxiety-provoking, primitive fantasies
are, in context, interpreted as expressions of more affect-laden
human longings and feelings.

Downward interpretations—which overlap with those termed
upward—include the interpretation of blatant sexual fantasies and
behavior in terms of dependency; the interpretation of seemingly
genital-sexual material in terms of pregenital needs and wishes
which are conveyed to the patient, however, in socially acceptable
terms, and not through reference to the specific primitive

derivatives. Thus, supportive interpretations are always upward in the sense of shifting focus from primitive content to content that is more acceptable to the patient, regardless of the ultimate psychosexual level from which the derivatives are drawn.

Reconstructions upward include interpretations of the more recent effects of an earlier event; they are especially supportive when the earlier experience is surrounded by primitive anxieties and fantasies, and the later consequences are less disturbing. Reconstructions downward may also be used when recent events are anxiety-ridden, while earlier events are less so, and clarify the later ones.

2. *"Interpretation sidewards" is another form of interpretive support through work with displacements, in which primitive sexual fantasies are dealt with in terms of more general aggressive needs; contrariwise, primitive aggressive fantasies are interpreted in context as expressions of longings for love and care.*

With the techniques here enumerated, the therapist interprets anxiety-provoking fantasies and behavior in terms of less threatening derivatives, which are simultaneously being expressed and screened in this manner. The result is both a diminution in anxiety and the unfolding of meaningful and workable material.

Supportive interventions must be used carefully and with discrimination, and should be supplemented in time by interventions that ultimately clarify and work through the specific disturbing unconscious fantasies that are bypassed. The primitive aspects of the patient's intrapsychic conflicts and fantasies must not be neglected, but must eventually be explored and analyzed.

DEPRECIATING AND DEVALUING

As a specific supportive measure, and an essential confrontation throughout therapy, this is an extremely important intervention. It aims to motivating the patient toward positive inner change, and away from acting out and other symptomatic resolutions of his conflicts. By depreciating and devaluing patient's particular maladaptive resolution to a conflict and showing him its excessive cost, the therapist aims at something that is essential for inner change, and yet goes beyond the interpretation of dynamics and content, into an area that is important, yet rarely considered systematically.

The supportive use of this technique aims at making acutely disturbing fantasies and behavior less valuable to the patient and helping him place his thoughts or actions in more reasonable perspective, assess the consequences of his fantasies and behavior, and seek healthier resolutions of his problems.

With this brief introduction, I shall illustrate several variations of this type of supportive intervention.

> Mrs. G.P., a narcissistic woman, sought therapy after several disappointing affairs. Quite early in her treatment, it became clear that these quests had been desperate attempts to find warmth and closeness lacking in her relationship with her husband, and to gratify fantasies of incestuous reunion with her father, whose serious illness had prompted this behavior, and with her mother, who had subsequently moved away. In a session very early in her therapy, she dreamt of having relations with her therapist, and became terrified of her promiscuous impulses and the many sexual fantasies she was having toward him and several other men. In the context of associations related to a reduction in her fee made to ease her financial burdens and to being indulged by her father as a child, the therapist made two supportive comments: that she was being flooded by her sexual impulses and not maintaining sufficient distance from them (thereby offering her an ego-building model of controls); and that she tended to sexualize relationships, only to become disturbed about her feelings and further disrupted. Thus, he was devaluing these fantasies and, to some extent, this kind of sexual behavior; he was also demonstrating part of the cost she paid for these maladaptations.
>
> In a later session, the therapist, in the context of new material, demonstrated that her affairs disrupted her relationship with her husband and son, and generated guilt and self-punitive behavior as well. He also then

interpreted the use of these sexual fantasies and behavior to gratify longings for care, offering a supportive
interpretation of a displacement from sexuality to dependency. He linked this in a general nonsexual way to
her longings to be closer to her father and mother, thus
avoiding the blatant sexual fantasies toward her father
and primitive wishes toward her mother—at a time
when it was felt that such allusions would heighten her
anxiety and guilt. These measures supplied the patient
with both support and insight; her anxiety diminished,
as did her erotization of treatment.

Here is another vignette:

> Mr. G.Q. was an ambulatory schizophrenic young
> man who would not leave home to go to college out-of-
> town; he had in fact never successfully slept away from
> home. After a year of therapy, as he dealt with this
> problem and actively sought to sleep out, he revealed a
> series of homosexual fantasies and anxieties, related to
> impulses to grab at a friend's genitals and suck another
> friend's penis. Associations revealed a marked sense of
> impotence and femininity, and the fantasy of incorporat-
> ing a huge penis to replace his own inadequate phallus.
> This would also, further associations indicated, magically
> protect him from further attack by his mother and father,
> who had often threatened to kill and otherwise maim
> him.
>
> Much of this was quite disturbing to the patient. In
> interpreting these fantasies and memories, and linking
> them to the patient's fears of leaving his house (which,
> on one level, he equated with becoming a homosexual),
> the therapist questioned (undermined-devalued) his homo-
> sexual adaptation to his conflicts with his parents and the
> phobic stance that was designed to protect him from his
> homosexual impulses and fantasies. He pointed out that
> Mr. G.Q.'s handling of his bodily anxieties by seeking out
> another man's penis only added to his anxiety and guilt,

and provided at best an inadequate, fantasied resolution. The implication was that other adaptations would be more suitable, but the therapist did not suggest these to the patient; rather, he left him to search for them himself.

In addition, he explored the patient's use of the phobic defense, based on the fantasy that if he left home he might become a homosexual. The therapist devalued this use of external controls by showing the patient, in context and using added material, how much he paid for restricting himself and how such outer-directed reliance on external safety measures was a poor substitute for inner controls.

The therapist, therefore, not only interprets the repressed fantasies, memories and conflicts on which symptoms and defenses are based, but also, at judicious moments, devalues and undermines maladaptive resolutions to these conflicts. Minor comments of this kind may be appended to many interpretations (see Chapter 14); they are of special value when the patient has not mobilized himself actively to pursue new avenues of conflict resolution or is caught up in a regressive sweep, in that they help to motivate him to search for new and less costly adaptations, rather than passively accept an interpretation without seeking active change. The therapist mobilizes the patient's ego resources and lessens pathological guilt by these confrontations with the cost of a given resolution to a conflict. Let us consider another clinical example:

Mrs. G.R. was a woman with a borderline syndrome whose father had deserted her and her family when she was a child. While in therapy, she learned that he was seriously ill. Threatened with losing him permanently, she began to regress. Her dreams and conscious fantasies were filled with devastating, devouring rage and fantasies of incorporating his body or his penis in order to deny and undo the threatened loss, and to have a final revenge. She was suffering from stomach pains and terrified by her primitive fantasies. Any awareness of the least anger at her father frightened her terribly; she feared she would omnipotently cause his demise. This led to acute dissociative flights.

In slowly working through this material with Mrs. G.R., the therapist linked these primitive fantasies to her reaction to her father's sudden desertion of his family when she was three. He went on to explain to her that the blatant nature of her present reaction was due, in part, to the nature and level of her reactions at the time of that earlier trauma and to its severity (genetic interpretive reassurance and a confrontation upward). Thus, for example, he pointed out in context how terrified and vulnerable she must have felt then, and how her wishes and fantasies that he return to her —or had never left her—must have been imagined in simple, childlike terms, such as her being inside of him, or the reverse. He also helped her to understand her present rage in terms of the early hurt, and its expression in primitive language and images.

In another vein, he pointed out the anxiety-provoking aspects of these fantasies, which failed to resolve the pending loss of her father and even prevented her from working out her feelings of loss and becoming more independent of him. These comments referred to the cost to the patient of her maladaptive efforts.

When the rage toward her dying father mounted and became more overt, it was largely displaced onto her husband; the patient again became terrified and dissociated herself. Here, the therapist reminded her that altering her state of consciousness had not helped her to resolve previous conflicts, with which she had dealt more adequately in a direct manner when she had controlled her state of consciousness. At other times, he pointed out the senselessness of her present rage, challenged her sense of omnipotence and demonstrated how she was unnecessarily alienating herself from her father and husband because of it, and lastly, noted that all this was also generating unnecessary guilt and self-punishment, another aspect of "cost." All of these comments were added to specific interpretations of repressed fantasies and other confrontations of ego dysfunctions.

Here is still another illustration of these techniques:

> Miss G.S. was an ambulatory schizophrenic adolescent who, when provoked by her mother's manipulativeness, would have temper outbursts, break objects in her house, and threaten to kill herself. After several months of therapy, while working on the dynamic aspects of this behavior and the related primitive unconscious fantasies with which the patient was struggling, the therapist also pointed out that she could indeed devastate her mother by such behavior and threats, but that this would provide her with a pyrrhic victory at best.

This last type of devaluing is rather frequently used with acting-out adolescents. It confronts the patient with the fact that such acting out, directed, as it often is, against his parents, can indeed hurt and upset them, but that this can be done only at great cost to the patient in suffering and related consequences.

I shall now delineate the main principles for the use of these devaluing interventions, briefly illustrating certain other aspects:

1. *Depreciating and devaluing the patient's pathological fantasies and behavior, and demonstrating to him the undue or extreme cost he pays for a particular maladaptation to a conflict, are indicated when the patient is experiencing overly-primitive fantasies, is unable to gain distance from them, and is acting out aspects of them and showing poor controls.*

Such interventions should primarily be made through the use of models offered by the patient in his associations, although they can be offered de novo where indicated. In the latter case, the patient's material should be used where possible.

To cite a brief example: Miss G.T., a destructive, acting-out adolescent, in describing her temper tantrums, went on to talk of a girlfriend who was always angry, and consequently always lonely and forlorn. The therapist used this as one model of the cost to the total personality of the repetitive living out of angry impulses.

Models such as these are extremely common and easily detected if the therapist is aware of their value.

2. *Among the more common indications for depreciating maladaptations, uncontrolled impulses, poor defenses, and primitive fantasies are the following:*

HOMOSEXUAL PANICS. These are often accompanied by unconscious fantasies in women of having a penis, and in men of incorporative, primitively destructive fantasies, often associated with fears of the loss of their own penis. While discovering and working through the specific precipitates and conflicts involved, the therapist should, where material permits, devalue such fantasies as too-costly solutions to the patient's real and intrapsychic conflicts. For example, the disruptive consequences of a woman's near-delusional belief that she has a penis or a man's near-delusional dread that he will be castrated can be demonstrated to such patients from their associations, and their meager adaptive usefulness undermined by comments accompanying interpretations of the defenses, dynamics and fantasies involved.

SUICIDAL FANTASIES AND THREATS. Here, too, the empty quality and extreme cost of the triumph (the pyrrhic victory) over another person through self-destruction, its use to punish the other person, and its pointlessness as a "solution" to despair and loneliness deserve constant focus. The extreme cost to the patient cannot be overemphasized.

SELF-DESTRUCTIVE ACTING OUT OF OTHER KINDS, INTENSE INCESTUOUS AND INAPPROPRIATE SEXUAL FANTASIES, OR PRIMITIVE AGGRESSIVE FANTASIES. Often there is insufficient distance from these and poor controls over the fantasies and related behavior.

ANY SEVERE SYMPTOM, as it is being analyzed and understood, can be devalued at some appropriate point as a relatively poor resolution of intrapsychic conflict, thereby promoting the patient's search for more mature, sublimated, and less costly adapations.

3. *The therapist must not overuse these techniques; the main dangers are, first, being overcritical and exercising too much control*

over the patient; and secondly, stressing these interventions at the expense of interpretations of the specific anxieties, dynamics, and unconscious fantasies involved. The defensive aspects of such manifestations and behavior must also be dealt with. Without interpretive work, true renunciation and working through will not occur. Further, the therapist must not overlook the gratifying aspects of these maladaptions, and must clarify and analyze them. The techniques described in this chapter are designed to help the patient make such gratifications less valuable to him, but are not to be applied at the expense of the patient's right to experiment and adapt.

4. *The same caveats, of course, apply here as elsewhere: to guard against excessive use, and against countertransference-based uses.*

5. *In general, supportive comments tend to be more useful with borderline patients, or those with severe character disorders, or poor controls.*

These last chapters have centered upon the many and varied routes that a therapist may take to convey his understanding and to promote the working-through of psychopathological problems. One crucial issue remains to be tackled: that of validation—for without attention to confirmation, no therapist can assess the value of his interventions. But before tackling this difficult matter, I shall pull together the diverse conclusions of these latest chapters into some general principles, which take in both verbal and nonverbal, explicit and implicit, aspects of intervention.

17 Basic Considerations in Intervening

Delineating the basic principles of intervention, their timing and style, and their nonverbal aspects will help us to an integrated understanding of when and how to intervene, and when not to do so.

THE TIMING OF INTERVENTIONS

The therapist's task of listening to his patients has many dimensions. He searches the manifest content for latent material; he listens for reality precipitates and contexts, and their behavioral and intrapsychic consequences; and he attempts to define the sources of the patient's conflicts, anxiety and guilt, and to ascertain how the patient is dealing with them. This leads him to the search for unconscious fantasies and the reflections of id, ego and super-ego expressions and derivatives. Through it all, the therapist observes the ego's characteristic methods of adapting and the cost to these adaptions. All the while, he stays in tune with realistic and transference aspects of his relationship with the patient, and follows symptom-formation, regressions, and progressions in all of their nuances. He looks for therapeutic problems and contexts, and for symptoms and behavior that must be analyzed.

With so much to listen for, and on so many levels, the task is formidable, but manageable. I have already demonstrated how context provides a crucial framework for listening, and how we follow the line from reality precipitates to intrapsychic and behavioral repercussions (see Chapter 9), and shall review this briefly here. In principle, the therapist begins by listening silently, and formulating. He tolerates ambiguities and uncertainties, and while he is ready to crystallize his understanding into an intervention, he is patient and not premature in speaking. He listens further and tries to fathom, remembering the recent sessions, especially the last one, and the thread of the recent therapeutic work. He listens for new contexts and develops new hunches, always beginning at the surface and with the current realities and recent traumas, and observing the patient's adaptions or maladaptions; from there he follows the material into the depths or until he is met with strong defenses. Sometimes something seems to be missing or surprises him; he must attempt to understand it.

As the patient goes on, the therapist either finds that his budding formulations receive support or that clarifying threads are lacking. This is crucial: he should, by and large, take the time to test his hypotheses silently whenever possible, and do so before intervening. If he is correct, the continuing associations will enrich and deepen his formulation. If not, there will be no "fit," and he should reformulate.

The decision to intervene—therapeutic context aside, for the moment—is relatively easy if he has ongoing confirmation of his thesis. He then waits for an opportune moment—a key phrase, a nodal point, or an added link—and makes his interpretation, thereafter listening to the patient's responses, awaiting confirmatory material (see Chapters 18 and 19).

If the material does not in fact develop in the direction of his initial silent formulation, the therapist must rely on his clinical skills, knowledge of the patient, understanding of his defenses, and the specific clinical indications for intervention that he observes at the time, in deciding whether to intervene or not. In general, if there is no pressing need to intervene (therapeutic context), it is best to remain silent and reorganize one's ideas. If the therapist feels that the patient is avoiding a critical conflict or fantasy, he may decide to intervene in a tentative way and observe the consequences, but he should not do so too often. More often, he should, at such times, look for major resistances and defenses, and interpret or confront them if the material lends itself to such an intervention.

In principle, then, we listen, formulate silently, seek additional confirmation and deeper insight into our hypothesis, and then intervene if the material crystallizes. If not, we await further associations and pause to reformulate.

While this is the therapist's general stance, there are specific indications for interventions that go beyond the general principle of intervening (interpreting) when derivatives of unconscious fantasies become clear. Let us turn to this subject.

INDICATIONS FOR INTERVENTIONS

For many years, we have all been taught, in one form or another, that we interpret at a time when the patient's unconscious fantasies and their derivatives have become "preconscious," that is, when they reach a point of expression where an interpretation by the therapist will readily lift them from repression into the patient's awareness. This is not only extremely limited, but misleading. In fact, it is remarkable that we have so little in the way of well-established concepts and general principles for interpretation or intervention on any other grounds.

Actually, there are many specific and, at times, urgent indications for interpretations and other interventions that go beyond the intrapsychic criterion just alluded to, and that merit full understanding and mastery by psychotherapists. I have already alluded to most of these indications in discussing specific interventions; here, I shall pull them together in general, summarized form. In essence, we are dealing here with the role of the therapeutic context of a session in establishing reasons for an intervention.

ACTING OUT

I shall begin this discussion with a behavioral criterion for intervening that is based on an assessment by the therapist—acting out (see Chapter 10). This is one of the most common therapeutic contexts alerting the therapist to the necessity for an intervention. It is, at times, difficult precisely to distinguish acting out and adaptive, nondestructive behavior. This assessment should be based on the material from the patient, including the adaptive context in which it occurs, the tone of the associations in which the reference to the behavior is embedded, and the patient's conscious and unconscious fantasies. Findings that point toward acting out rather than suitable adaptation include: a strong basis for the behavior in anxious or guilty conflicts; indications of unconscious fantasies that are being lived out with some disregard for other realities; any strong unconscious basis for the behavior and lack of fit with outer realities; seemingly unnecessary harm and suffering for the patient and others; and any sense of poor controls or of an irrational basis for the behavior. The therapist's own values, needs and acting-out propensities, while inevitably factors in his assessment of the patient's behavior, should play a minimal, nondistorting role.

The principles of intervention in this situation are these: if the patient's behavior is assessed as acting out and associational material supports this evaluation, or if there are indicators of potential acting out, the therapist should actively intervene, preferably with an interpretation that begins with the reality precipitate evoking the behavior (the context), and leads into the unconscious fantasies, conflicts, and genetics related to it. If the material does not lend itself to interpretation, or if the therapist after careful listening fails to detect significant threads, then, toward the latter part of the session in which the maladaptive and destructive behavior has been reported, the therapist should confront the patient with the acting out and its apparent implications. To this, he may add, if the material permits, references to the price the patient is paying for the behavior—consequences for himself and others. Then, the therapist must wait for additional material, since the goal is ultimately to interpret the unconscious motives for the acting out so it may be controlled and renounced by the patient.

A nonmoralizing confrontation that stresses the cost to the

patient is generally advisable when an interpretation is not possible, because the patient will unconsciously perceive the therapist's silence in the face of acting out as sanction and permission; the confrontation disrupts such a silent antitherapeutic alliance. It is also an important intervention because acting-out patients almost always have had such misalliances with their denial-prone parents, and themselves often deny the pathological and destructive aspects of their behavior.

In all, acting out constitutes a prime therapeutic context for organizing the material of a session and reason to intervene. The assessment that a specific behavior is, indeed, acting out rather than a reasonable behavioral search for new expression, change and adaptation is, as I indicated, a critical factor. As to principles:

1. *The therapist himself, as the assessor of acting out, must have analyzed and worked through his own such tendencies.* He must find no conscious or unconscious gratification in this type of behavior nor have the need to severely condemn or moralize against it. Acting out is to be viewed as maladaptive behavior costly to the patient and to others, and a part of the patient's efforts to achieve pathological gratification while defensively remaining unaware of anxieties, dangers, and inner fantasies. The goal is to help the patient adapt more successfully.

2. *The therapist must constantly try to understand the attempt at adaptation in acting out; in defining any behavior as "acting out" he must be certain that it is, in the main, destructive to the patient and others.* In exploring acting out, the therapist must work with the patient's poor controls, his living out of fantasies, and the accompanying denial; all of these characterize this kind of behavior.

The therapist must always weigh the danger of adopting a critical and condemnatory role with the patient through repeatedly questioning his behavior, and running the risk of an antitherapeutic alliance in which the patient acts out to evoke punitive responses. A properly balanced approach is essential.

3. *In dealing with acting out, the therapist should always explore to himself—from his own self-awareness and the material from the patient—the possible role of his behavior and interventions in the development of this symptom.* Unconscious needs

along these lines on his part should be made conscious through self-exploration; these lead to realistic and countertransference-evoked reactions in the patient toward the therapist and therapy (see Chapter 22) and are among the most frequent causes of acting out. If undetected and unanalyzed in the therapist, the responsive aberrant behavior in the patient will often seriously disrupt treatment.

ACUTE REGRESSIONS AND SYMPTOMS

Acute anxiety, regressions and emotional symptoms of all kinds, including psychosomatic symptoms, form another set of therapeutic contexts for organizing the material in sessions and indications for interventions by the therapist. Briefly:

1. *Acute symptoms and regressions should be the therapeutic context, the focal point, of the session in which they appear or are reported; associations in the hour illuminate their adaptive context and unconscious meanings.* An interpretation is again the intervention of choice; if sufficient material for such an intervention is lacking, confronting the patient with those elements of the situation, in reality or fantasy, that seem most relevant to the disturbance is indicated. To foster the therapeutic alliance under these latter conditions, the therapist may add a comment to the effect that more work lies ahead in order fully to understand what is going on. This provides an atmosphere of concern and support in a nonmanipulative way. The main risk under such circumstances is that of speaking prematurely without waiting for the associations which contain the clues to the latent factors in the situation. All too often, the therapist is frightened by the sudden appearance of symptoms such as psychosomatic reactions, phobias, or anxiety attacks, and other regressive phenomena—sudden dissociated states, acute failures in reality testing, paranoid reactions, psychotic-like decompensations—and is prone to reassure himself by resorting to ill-defined "supportive" interventions. Such empty verbalizations or offers of medication, made without insight or understanding, only increase the patient's anxiety, since he is usually unconsciously, and even consciously, aware that the therapist is frightened and confused, and in a sense regressing too.

2. *The correct technique at these moments is for the therapist silently to review the recent sessions, including the recent events in the patient's life and the ongoing therapeutic situation, while listening to the material.* The focus must be on the regression, its meaning and causes (the therapeutic context). Almost always, dramatic life events or problems within the therapy—errors and countertransference difficulties—form the context for such regressions. Once the precipitate is identified, the unconscious meanings and fantasies that it has evoked, and the relevant conflicts, anxieties, and genetics will emerge. Usually, insight into these aspects of the regression or symptom will be available in the derivatives contained in the patient's associations. Thus, the therapist will be able to interpret, though he usually supplements his interpretation at such times by references to the cost of such maladaptions and by downgrading the importance of the symptom. Essential in this work is the conviction that regressions and psychosomatic symptoms are active attempts at adaptation, often represent attempts unconsciously to manipulate the therapist, and do not represent an aimless overwhelming of the total personality.

3. *If the therapist takes a firm interpretive stand and does not allow himself to be manipulated, blackmailed or frightened by acute symptoms or regressions, he provides both important insights and reassurance to the patient.* He will then recognize that the therapist is not deceived and is quite competent to deal with such disturbances.

The Appearance of Defenses and Resistances

In principle, as already discussed in Chapter 14, the therapist must give precedence to interpreting defenses and resistances throughout therapy over interpreting the content of the patient's unconscious fantasies, related to his central anxieties and conflicts. The therapeutic principle to be emphasized here is that the emergence in a session of any defense or resistance calls for interpretation and confrontation in context from the material at hand. Likewise, all disruptions in the therapeutic alliance take interpretative precedence over virtually all other therapeutic problems when they occur. The primacy of such indications for interventions deserves special emphasis.

EGO DYSFUNCTIONS AND SUPEREGO PATHOLOGY

The therapist must ever be alert for reflections of ego dysfunctions (e.g., impaired object relations, reality testing, and controls) and superego pathology (e.g., corrupt behavior, manipulations, lack of realistic guilt, and poor ideals and aspirations). Behavior and symptoms that reflect such pathology, and the fantasies related to them, merit interpretation in context whenever possible. When this is not feasible, queries and confrontation are indicated. With these dysfunctions, confrontation strengthens the weakened ego function and promotes the development of a healthy conscience and ideals. It does so through correct interpretations, the presence of the therapist as a noncorrupt model for identification, the development of realistic guilt, the refusal of the therapist to sanction corruption on any level, and the fostering in the patient of a healthy self-scrutiny, with realistic standards.

INSIGHTS INTO CRUCIAL UNCONSCIOUS FANTASIES

The therapist interprets derivatives of unconscious fantasies related to the patient's pathology (core fantasies), as they become meaningful and affectively available in the material from the patient (see Chapter 14). He is usually, at such times, aware of the current major themes and reality pressures, and the patient's intrapsychic responses and fantasies. As he formulates those aspects that seem most meaningful for the patient, he follows the material for confirmatory associations. If he finds them, he interprets the essence of the nodal unconscious fantasies from the patient's associations, and points out their relevance to the patient's symptoms, current conflicts and genetic past.

DISTURBANCES IN THE RELATIONSHIP
BETWEEN PATIENT AND THERAPIST

This category of indications for interventions overlaps with others already alluded to, but it deserves separate mention because of the special problems it poses. The single most important indication for intervening lies in the patient's reactions to errors by the therapist (see Chapter 22). In addition, any other disruption in the therapeutic alliance is an important reason to intervene. Beyond this, reactions to the therapist that reflect on any level, important facets of the patient's pathology or fantasies, constitute an indication for the therapist to speak out. In striving to maintain a positively-toned relationship and therapeutic alliance with the patient, the therapist intervenes whenever fantasies about the therapist are becoming disruptive or reflect major fantasy-systems related to the patient's symptoms. Not every transference fantasy should be interpreted, only those that are reflections of important resistances and core, pathology-related fantasies (see Chapters 20 and 21).

These are, then, the main indications for interventions in psychotherapy. There are other less prominent reasons to intervene, but the basic principles established here should guide the therapist as to when he should speak—and why. On the whole, the therapist will find that there is an order of preference for the reasons to intervene and the type of intervention to be used in a given situation. In most cases, the patient's responses to the therapist's errors take precedence; disturbances in the therapeutic alliance and major resistances come next, while acting out, neurotic symptoms, and acute regressions follow, and ego dysfunctions and detection of core unconscious fantasies come last. The order of preference for the type of interventions by the therapist is: silence first, selected queries next; interpretation, with or without a confrontational or supportive addendum; and confrontation alone when an interpretation is not feasible. There must be room, too, for variations in this basic sequence and order of preference, but I will not attempt further elaboration here.

THE STYLE AND LEVEL OF THE INTERVENTION

THE LANGUAGE AND IDIOM

In interpreting or confronting, the therapist should always attempt to use the patient's idiom and language. He should endeavor to be accurate and precise, and as concise and specific as possible, though he will occasionally go further and integrate several aspects or levels of the material; in all, he should remain within the confines of the patient's fantasies and behavior. If he adds his own fantasy on rare occasions, the therapist should acknowledge it as his hunch and explain its relevance to the patient's problems and fantasies. In essence, then, the associations from the patient are the data out of which we mold our interventions; we endeavor to not wander far from this basic foundation.

Once the therapist has intervened he should sit back and observe. It should only rarely be necessary to add anything to a well-thought-out interpretation. Such additions are most often defensive or represent attempts at pressuring the patient; they are antitherapeutic. Besides, there is too much to learn from, and gauge in, the patient's responses to an intervention to press the point at that time (see Chapters 18 and 19).

THE LEVEL OF THE INTERVENTION

Interventions should be at the correct level. This is a complex problem that requires considerable clinical skill. There are always blind leads and deceptions in the material, not necessarily placed there consciously and maliciously by the patient, but often part of his unconscious defenses. The following principles can serve as guides:

1. *Begin always with the reality precipitate and the patient's conscious responses in fantasy and behavior (his adaptation).* Stay on the surface and utilize general interpretations as long as they remain meaningful and fresh; then turn to deeper fantasies and become more specific as the material permits.

2. *Do not overvalue "deep" interpretations of "id material"*

and primitive unconscious fantasies. It takes much work with the surface of the patient's thinking and fantasies, and with resistances, to make these interpretations truly affective and effective. If the depths are approached prematurely, intellectual defenses or panicky acting out are bound to follow.

3. *Just as listening should be balanced (reality; surface responses; unconscious fantasy—id, ego, superego elements; genetics; and total adaptive response and cost), interventions should be balanced.* They should relate to the surface and ego responses initially, and then expand into these other dimensions as the material so directs. Many therapists tend to be biased toward one of these levels and type of material, and this creates a serious problem in technique. Thus, some are plungers into the depths, while others prefer the surface and generalities. Some moralize or condemn, and overemphasize themes of self-punishment and guilt. Others insist on focusing on the past, to the exclusion of much of the present, while still others almost never deal with crucial genetic factors. A balanced approach to the material, with sensitivity to all these dimensions, allowing the patient's associations to direct you, is a sine qua non for sound psychotherapeutic work.

4. *The therapist should learn to listen to the multiple levels in the material simultaneously and alternatively.* He should thereby be capable of constructing unconscious fantasies by taking one element from a particular communication and other elements from different sources. If he tunes in on the repressed fantasy that is unconsciously directing the selection of the material, he will indeed find various elements of the fantasy embedded in the sequences and the diverse manifest contents of the session. In this way, the crucial latent content will be detected and the correct interpretation made, at the right level and using the patient's own language.

Well-Disguised (Remote) and Clear (Close) Derivatives of Repressed Fantasies and Conflicts

Correct interpretations and timing are fostered by the recognition that a given conflict and fantasy network is expressed through derivatives that vary in the extent to which they are disguised or blatant, defended or not (see Chapter 9).

Well-disguised expressions of intrapsychic conflicts and fantasies are, for purposes of intervening, considered remote or weak derivatives; they point to the operation of strong defenses, and seldom should be interpreted, since they indicate that the fantasy is remote from the patient's direct awareness and that he is probably not prepared to acknowledge it. In addition, they are usually ambiguous enough that the therapist's attempts at specific definition, or at proving their immediate relevance, may lead to error. Silent waiting for clearer—close—derivatives is indicated at such times; as a rule, patients generally tend to become more involved in important and unresolved conflicts, and to express the fantasies related to them in derivatives of increasing clarity. There is a tendency spontaneously to diminish defensiveness regarding unconscious fantasy expression; if this does not happen, a confrontation with the most evident defenses will usually prove helpful.

In the meantime, the therapist should be formulating an hypothesis; if this is confirmed by the development of the material, and the expression of less-disguised (close) derivatives, he will be on firmer ground for interpreting. With the use of such relatively undisguised expressions of repressed fantasies, he is more likely to obtain a confirmatory response from the patient.

To cite a brief example of a very common sequence (see Chapter 9 and the Index of Clinical Material for additional illustrations):

> Mr. G.U. was in therapy for a severe character disorder when his father died. In the first session after this event, he was depressed, concerned about living alone with his mother, annoyed in petty ways at her and his siblings, and he expressed many feelings of weakness and inadequacy. Since anxieties over incestuous fantasies about his mother, prompted by her open seductiveness, had been a problem for the patient before his father died, the therapist intervened here with a general inter-

pretation to the effect that the patient seemed to be using his feelings of inadequacy to get away from his mother.

In supervision, this was assessed as a premature intervention based on weak and questionable derivatives.

In the session, the patient responded to this intervention by ruminating about himself, his mother and other matters in an indefinite way, failing to confirm the interpretation. In several sessions some time later, he reported conscious sexual feelings toward his mother and several erotic dreams about her. These less disguised derivatives proved quite meaningful and were interpreted with greater precision, and with clear confirmation and development of the material.

In principle, then, the therapist should if possible, wait for clear and strong derivatives of unconscious fantasies and conflicts before intervening. Weak or remote derivatives are highly disguised and well defended, and interpretations on such a basis are seldom confirmed.

THE ALTERNATION BETWEEN REVEALING AND DEFENDING

It is useful for the therapist to recognize that patients have a tendency to communicate cyclically, expressing derivatives of unconscious fantasies with decreasing defensiveness and then shifting to periods of defensiveness. Depending on many factors—life events, the point in therapy, the transference, the therapist's countertransferences, etc.—patients will produce relatively clear derivatives of unconscious conflicts and fantasies that, though disguised, are readily detectable and interpretable. They will do this over several sessions, only to shift to a defensive stance, creating a period when very little, if anything, of these unconscious fantasies can be detected. Without conscious awareness, patients do indeed control the extent to which they communicate expressions of crucial repressed fantasies.

When little that is latent is expressed in the manifest material, the therapist focuses on the analysis of defenses, their motives and the unconscious fantasies on which they are based. Working-through of these defenses can occupy many sessions, but should eventually lead back into core conflicts and fantasies related to the patient's symptoms; at this point the defenses can be further analyzed (see Chapter 14).

Sensitivity to these inevitable fluctuations in defense and revelation aids the therapist in being tolerant and patient, and in focusing his interpretive efforts correctly on resistance-defense or content. It leads him to anticipate and accept a cyclical course of therapy.

SPECIAL AND NONVERBAL CONSIDERATIONS IN INTERVENING

IMPLICIT HURTS IN INTERPRETATIONS

Many important effects of interventions, other than the promotion of insight, are nonverbally and implicitly contained in the content, timing, and tone of the therapist's words. These effects may be far-reaching, both for the patient and for the therapeutic alliance; they will occur to some degree both with correct and well-timed comments, as well as with those that are erroneous. Thus, interventions, proper or improper, may contain narcissistic blows; may enhance the patient's sense of depression, guilt, or anxiety for the moment (though they are designed to lessen it over the long haul); may lower his self-esteem; and may entail a sense of loss, be it of a prized fantasy, a self-delusion, an important defense, or a part of his tie to the therapist. Further, interventions may cause the patient to feel attacked or seduced in some way, even in situations where this is not the therapist's main intention and he has not intervened out of countertransference problems. Each of these "side effects" may evoke regressions in the patient or seriously disrupt the therapeutic alliance and therapy, so the therapist must learn to anticipate them and weigh their likelihood against the need for the intervention.

I have already discussed situations in which the therapist, apparently correctly, refrained from interpreting material that he felt would lead to regressive symptoms or a paranoid-like rupture in the therapeutic alliance as a price for the insight offered (see Chapter 16). I shall also in Chapter 22 discuss the effects of apparently erroneous interventions; some of these interventions might not have been made if the factors I raise here had been considered carefully. The decision about intervening can, at times, be quite difficult. Alertness to the nonverbal aspects of our interventions will, however, enable us to be prepared for adverse reactions; they can then often be avoided or can be explored and analyzed if they occur. Unfortunately, empirical observations indicate that such traumatic side-effects of intervening cannot always be entirely undone and worked through. Sometimes, permanent damage is done to the therapeutic alliance and the therapy, especially if these responses are missed or their true source not recognized. It is essential to consider these possible implications of an intervention beforehand; and it is wise to delay if possible, or to interpret in a supportive manner, when a strong adverse response is likely (see Chapter 16).

Let us look at two highly condensed clinical vignettes related to these issues; afterwards I shall delineate the main concepts and principles to be considered.

> Mrs. G.V. was a woman with a borderline syndrome who was in twice-weekly psychotherapy. When she was an infant, her father had abandoned her family for several years and he did so again in her early childhood. It became clear at the outset of her therapy that she had many extremely disturbing conflicts and primitive fantasies about him and what he had done.
>
> In the first months of her treatment, as Mrs. G.V. told her therapist about her father, she recalled his return to the family in her teens, and his open seductiveness with other women. She then spoke of his recent rather serious gallbladder attack and rather hysterically cried about his lack of love for her; then she quickly denied this, saying that she wanted to leave the session.
>
> In a subsequent session, the patient described her father's open dislike for her husband, and how he had waited up for her when she dated in her teens and

would even follow her part way on some of her dates.
The therapist confronted Mrs. G.V. with her father's
domineering and infantilizing behavior, in an effort to
focus on and explore further the patient's conflicts with
him, and her tendency to infantilize her own children
and husband. The patient responded by crying about
her love and need for her father; she then felt that the
room was spinning and she wanted to leave the session,
but did not do so.

In the next hour, she reported having been very
disturbed and quite sleepless since her last session; she
had been crying and asking to be hospitalized. She
went on to describe, with considerable distress, an actual
sexual overture toward her by her father when she was
a teenager. She had come to the present session with
her mother because she feared someone would attack her
in the building. She felt disloyal discussing her father
and was certain that God would strike her dead to
punish her for it. The therapist responded by emphasizing
how terrified she was of her feelings about her father,
and that she had never faced and resolved them. While
this was painful for her, he added, there was no other
way that she could make peace for herself. Mrs. G.V.
responded by settling down, and describing various ways
in which her parents had denied having done any wrongs
toward her and had developed in her an unrealistic
sense of guilt about them. She still somehow believed
that any criticism of them on her part would lead to
God's punishing her; "You must blindly love your
parents," was their credo. The patient's own adoption
of such unrealistic thinking was then pointed out.

Aside from illustrating a series of supportive interpretations
and confrontations, this vignette indicates how a therapist's confrontation can be one factor in evoking a temporary regression
in, and a mistrustful response from, the patient. For Mrs. G.V.,
the confrontational focus on elements of her father's attitude
toward her stirred up repressed rage and the repressed memory

of her father's attempt to seduce her, with accompanying guilt, anxiety, symptoms, and thoughts of flight from therapy. The therapist was alert to these repercussions of his confrontations, and was able to explore them with the patient and gain still further insight into her gilt-ridden fears of criticizing her parents.

Yet, despite this, if he had been more in tune with this patient's enormous and overdetermined sensitivity to the whole subject, he might well have sat back and not intervened, waiting for the patient to proceed at her own pace. There was no urgent indication to intervene for the moment. Further, he could not in any way know what lay beneath her surface complaints about her father, and therefore, what such a confrontation might prematurely stir up (e.g., her father's attempt at seduction). All of these risks had to be balanced against the need to begin helping the patient to resolve her intrapsychic conflicts regarding her father. With fragile and borderline patients especially, it is wise to go slowly, both because their delicate egos can handle only a little at a time and because the underlying repressed memories and fantasies are often quite traumatic, primitive and disturbing.

Now, let us review a clinical experience where the outcome was not so fortunate.

> Miss G.W. was a borderline adolescent who was brought for therapy by her parents because of outbursts of uncontrolled rage at home, promiscuity, serious drug-taking, and a poor school adjustment. She brought much of this under control with six months of therapy and reached a point where her therapist's summer vacation was about a month away. She then began to regress by attacking her parents, searching for drugs, and considering a return to her promiscuity.
>
> At this time, over several sessions, she reported dreams of being seduced, raped, and robbed by an old friend named Arthur (her therapist's first name). Associations avoided any reference to the therapist, though fantasies that her father wanted to seduce her did emerge. Most of the associations alluded to the patient's

mounting impulses to act out. At this point, the therapist intervened.

He rather plainly told the patient that her dreams had to do with her fury at him, her suspicions of him because he was leaving her, and her guilty wishes to hold onto him through some kind of sexual tie—something she was on the verge of living out. The patient became enraged and suspected that the therapist was trying to seduce, trap and control her in some way. The therapist had little success in exploring these fantasies and in helping the patient control her impulses to act out.

In this situation, we must conclude that the patient was unprepared for the therapist's interpretation, and that, rather than promoting insight and controls, it evoked strongly invested defensive denial and paranoid-like fantasies about the therapist who had, in the patient's eyes, truly hurt her with his comments. We might postulate that this intervention was made too early in the patient's therapy (see Chapter 23) and was too close to her directly incestuous fantasies about her father. Miss G.W.'s delicate, failing integration was further disturbed by the therapist's attempt to interpret these repressed fantasies; a more supportive type of intervention was to have been preferred. A paranoid-type of rupture in the theraputic alliance was the outcome.

Much of this discussion is hindsight. The therapist was attempting to help the patient reintegrate and control her impulses to act out sexually and with drugs. It is a moot question whether alternative approaches would have been more successful: these include a greater emphasis on the defensive aspects of this behavior (e.g., its use to deny the pending loss and to disrupt therapy); interpreting upward with a greater focus on the patient's feeling hurt and wanting care; or greater patience in interpreting the transference by waiting for the patient to refer to the pending separation and focusing on her defective controls in the meantime.

The therapist here may have failed to recognize his fragile patient's enormous sensitivity to interpretations related to himself and, in addition, to any links to sexual fantasies about her father.

These latter were relatively undisguised and poorly defended against; as he learned later, they were based on actual seductive experiences. Such material is exquisitely painful and guilt-provoking, and requires special caution and sensitivity, especially in dealing with an adolescent.

In any case, this vignette illustrates the consequences of interventions that prove to be ill-timed, too threatening, and possibly insensitive. It took the therapist many months to work through even a small part of the paranoid-like response generated in the patient during this period. Such experiences are strong reminders of the power of the therapist's interventions not only to heal, but to disrupt.

I shall now outline some of the more important nonverbalized implications of interventions that have potentially disruptive effects, and then the kinds of disturbances that may follow from them (see also Chapter 22). But with all the emphasis here on the negative side-effects of interventions, it is well first to recognize a number of positive nonverbal implications.

POSITIVE NONVERBAL IMPLICATIONS OF INTERVENTIONS

A correct confrontation or interpretation may convey some of the following nonverbal implications:

1. That the patient is strong enough to tolerate the insight offered or to face the material with which he is being confronted;

2. That, in the patient's quest for better functioning, the understanding offered to him will foster the development of more adequate adaptations. Thus, if he accepts the pain and loss involved, he will, in the long run, feel and function better.

3. That the patient has, with whatever pain and struggle, conveyed something that is meaningful to the therapist and that it can, in turn, be pointed out to him in a helpful way.

4. That the patient no longer need be "sick" or behave in maladaptive ways. He is expected to, and can safely, give up unnecessary and costly defenses and renounce guilt-ridden, anxiety-provoking needs and fantasies for something less disturbing and more gratifying.

5. That the patient is working with a therapist who understands him; someone whom he can trust, who accepts his pathological ways and fantasies, yet will help him to revise and resolve them. In all, that there is someone to whom the patient can turn for understanding and aid when upset.

This brief listing will be supplemented in the last part of this chapter. Let us now move to the potentially negative aspects of interventions.

NEGATIVE AND PAINFUL NONVERBAL IMPLICATIONS OF INTERVENTIONS

NARCISSISTIC BLOWS

Interpretations and confrontations made by the therapist often refer to behavior and fantasies in the patient that are humiliating for him and are the source of lowered self-esteem and painful narcissistic blows. There is no psychopathology and therefore no psychotherapy without such hurts, but they must be recognized and dealt with very tactfully by the therapist. Demonstrating to the patient his pathological behavior, his lack of controls, his primitive fantasies, and his failure to achieve successful adaptions and sublimations is painful for him. Major confrontations and interpretations which contain such hurts call for an assessment of the patient's tolerance for these wounds, and for proper timing, dosage, and wording. If these are lacking, the patient will feel assaulted, hurt, and disliked by the therapist, and will become mistrustful, angry and defensive—all with some justification if the therapist's remarks were ill-timed or too severe. Patients who are narcissistic and so especially vulnerable should be helped with these vulnerabilities before other therapeutic work is done.

INCREASING THE PATIENT'S SENSE OF GUILT, DEPRESSION, AND ANXIETY

We must not forget that the loss of a longstanding defense, be it denial, a specific repression, or a more complex defensive acting out or phobic avoidance, can prompt a period of anxiety for the patient. Similarly, interventions regarding previously repressed fantasies can bring into consciousness fantasies, memories, and behavior to which considerable guilt is attached. This is quite painful to the patient; the therapist must be sensitive to these effects and measure his comments accordingly. Neurotic— inappropriate—guilt can subsequently be worked through, while realistic guilt for past misdeeds cannot be bypassed, but can be worked through in terms of the patient's present renunciation and repudiation of the guilt-evoking behavior and fantasies if this has taken place.

There are also many sources of depression for patients in the therapist's interventions. Facing their inadequacies and their hates, and experiencing past and present losses and separations, are among them. In already depressed patients, this becomes a critical consideration in deciding whether to intervene.

THE LOSS OF FAMILIAR AND ACCEPTED ADAPTATIONS

Positive inner change and the development of better adaptations, while advantageous over the long run, entail many losses for the patient. Although actually disruptive to his life, many of these adaptations are considered to be safe and necessary, and even life-protecting, by the patient. Maladaptive emotional ties to past figures in reality and fantasy are among the losses to patients who effect insight-based inner and outer changes, and they should not be underestimated. Such a weaning process is often quite painful and terrifying; it is to be developed quite cautiously and slowly by the therapist. Also lost in the process of working through to new resolutions of conflicts are the patient's sense of inner balance and certainty; his treasured, but most pathological, defenses; his pathogenic but established, maladaptions including the resultant symptoms which become valuable to him; and his inappropriate ties to others in his present life who both gratify and disturb him. It is obviously necessary, but painful for him, to lose these. Any given intervention may affect any one of these valued, but pathological possessions. If it is not properly timed, the patient may choose to keep his pathological relationship or current, though costly, psychic equilibrium and leave treatment.

It is, therefore, important that the therapist recognize the anxieties entailed here, and consider them before and after intervening.

LOSSES AND HURTS RELATED TO THE THERAPIST

Every interpretation entails some loss of closeness with the therapist, and contains some blow to conscious and unconscious transference fantasies or wishes about union, mothering, admiration, sanction for pathology and acting out, or submission by the therapist to the patient (see Tarachow, 1963). For each patient, the specific fantasy-wishes that predominate are based on earlier life experiences and conflicts and his present psychopathology. Initially, positive longings and fantasies usually contribute to the therapeutic alliance even though they are neurotic and inappropriate. With some patients, these wishes are a major factor in entering therapy, and they can be modified and replaced with realistic expectations only slowly.

For any patient, direct interpretation of transference wishes and fantasies entails considerable hurt, frustration, and loss. But any correct interpretation may further separate the patient from the therapist and deprive the former of his neurotic hopes in therapy. The patient's unspoken plea: "Unite with me," is replaced by the therapist's implicit rejoinder: "I am separate from you. I will not gratify your unrealistic wishes, but will only help you understand yourself and enable you to change from within." Here too the patient may experience a great, though inevitable, loss.

These, then, are some of the necessary or at times unnecessary nonverbal implications of the therapist's interventions. If they are not considered and anticipated beforehand, they may actually overshadow the verbal content of the intervention and result in unexpected negative reactions of many kinds. Certain regressed and narcissistic patients will actually respond almost exclusively to these nonverbal aspects for long periods of their treatment (see Balint, 1968). They wish to be fed and gratified in some way or another, or at least offered a benign setting in which to regress and express their pathology. They want their therapist just to be there and to be available. Interventions may disrupt this atmosphere and the patient will be quite disturbed regardless of the content of the therapist's comment. It is important to recognize and deal with the narcissistic aspects of their pathology first.

I shall briefly point out some of the most common consequences of implicit hurts in intervention. Since I shall review in some detail in later chapters the consequences of incorrect and countertransference-based interventions (see Chapters 19 and 22), I shall merely list them with a brief comment here.

CONSEQUENCES OF ILL-TIMED, HURTFUL INTERVENTIONS

Ruptures in the Therapeutic Alliance

These constitute one of the most common consequences of failure to consider the hurts and losses entailed in intervening. Consideration of the effects of an intervention on the therapeutic alliance should be part of the therapist's thinking regarding every intervention; it is a crucial element and too often disregarded.

As I shall later show in detail, the therapist must constantly strive to maintain the therapeutic alliance in a quiet, positive state. He does not want to profoundly disrupt or corrupt this alliance. Momentary disturbances are, of course, inevitable, but he must attempt to anticipate and minimize them, and to analyze them should they occur. Making a correct, but too traumatic interpretation and losing the patient is certainly not a satisfying outcome to therapy.

Among the kinds of disruptions that can occur should the therapist be insensitive to the nonverbal, hurtful implications of his interventions are:

1. Premature termination
2. Paranoid-like and depressive feelings of being misunderstood and even attacked by the therapist. In response, the patient will withdraw emotionally, and will not reveal further derivatives of unconscious fantasies. The patient's mistrust and rage toward the therapist can be enormous and quite disruptive. It must not

be overlooked that some degree of anger and mistrust when the patient has actually been hurt by the therapist is justified (see Chapter 22).

3. Intense defensiveness. The patient quite understandably attempts to protect himself from further exposure to the therapist's insensitivities. This can prevent the unfolding of material and lead to remoteness from the therapist.

4. An antitherapeutic alliance may replace the healthy therapeutic alliance. It may take a sadomasochistic tone, in which the patient submits to the therapist's aggressiveness and even invites further attack, thereby gratifying his unconscious passive-feminine needs and his needs for punishment. Failure to detect such a development can derail the entire therapy. Direct and therapy-disruptive attacks on the therapist may occur; as a response to the therapist's aggressiveness, this constitutes a mutually sadistic antitherapeutic alliance. Protective, hostile, or seductive reactions to the therapist constitute another possible response. If these are recognized, the therapist can modify his technique, and work through and resolve the misalliance with the patient; if not, an unfavorable outcome to the therapy is inevitable.

5. Disruptive acting in. Lateness, absences, leaving sessions early, and seemingly senseless verbal attacks on the therapist are not infrequent during sessions.

Acting Out and Regressions

Destructive acting of all types, disruptive to the therapy and to the patient's life, are another set of indications that the therapist should search for errors of this type.

As I shall show in Chapters 19 and 22, responses of this type constitute a characteristic reaction to most technical and counter-transference-based errors by the therapist. Careful listening to the latent content of the patient's associations at the time of such hurts will indicate the patient's awareness of the therapist's errors and their meanings for him. Associations related to these hurts will virtually always be present in the material; the therapist must listen in depth, and subsequently correct the disruptive factors.

NONVERBAL CHARACTERISTICS OF INTERVENTIONS

There are many nonverbal dimensions in the timing and manner of the therapist's interventions. Each therapist has his own style of communicating and reacts to each particular patient, or to certain kinds of material, in a characteristic way. Conversely, each individual patient will react differently to these dimensions of his therapist's interventions; some are more sensitive to the nonverbal than to the verbal content of the intervention (see Balint, 1968). The study of this area of psychotherapy has a long road ahead of it. These aspects are difficult for the practicing therapist to define and identify; in the total interaction between the therapist and patient, they constitute a somewhat ill-defined and yet crucial dimension. My main purpose here will be to outline some aspects for the reader who can, through self-awareness and self-study, develop sufficient sensitivity to use them constructively in therapy without letting them disturb his effectiveness.

SELECTION OF INTERVENTIONS

Unconsciously, every therapist is especially sensitive to fantasies and intrapsychic conflicts in certain areas and on certain levels, be they oral, phallic, exhibitionistic, pregenital or oedipal, and less sensitive, even defensive about material from other areas. This affects his selection of interventions, including his interpretations. I shall not belabor the obvious point that only a personal analysis can insure that these nonverbal aspects do not seriously distort and impair the therapist's work. Without self-awareness, these unconsciously determined preferences will inevitably prove restrictive. They have a pronounced negative effect on the therapeutic atmosphere and alliance, and on the therapeutic outcome.

Patients quite unconsciously become sensitive to their therapist's idiosyncratic selectiveness. The result is a bilaterally distorted therapeutic alliance and a setting where some conflicts may be resolved, but many others are not.

Timing of Interventions

Some interventions are never made, others are premature, and others unduly delayed. This, too, reflects the therapist's personal sensitivities and biases, which are thus communicated to the patient.

Tone and Attitude

The tone of an intervention, be it sympathetic, seductive, angry or indifferent, is an important nonverbal communication, part of each therapist's stance. When extreme in one way or another, it can have considerable effect on the therapy.

Of course, such intonations are not inherently detrimental to treatment—often their absence where appropriate is destructive. The point is that the therapist should be aware of his tone and his feelings, and should recognize when they are appropriate and when they are not. Moments of annoyance or even anger, of anxiety or of concern, may be quite appropriate for a therapist and very much in the service of the patient's treatment. At other times, they may reflect the therapist's unresolved problems and be disruptive. The subsequent material from the patient will help the therapist to distinguish these two possibilities (see also Chapter 22).

The therapist's attitudes are another complex nonverbal aspect. The fears, condemnations, and permissiveness implicit in the therapist's stance vary; extreme or biased attitudes are all too common. The therapist may, within limits, like or dislike a given patient, but any tendency to favor him or not, or to be unduly involved with him, will be disruptive.

Autonomy Versus Dependency

Therapists vary in their needs to draw patients close and to make them dependent. Some go to the extreme of not permitting any real sense of security or reasonable dependency in the patient. Some are more inclined to promote autonomous functioning in their patients than others. Others behave omnipotently—an approach certain to disrupt treatment—while still others are passive and rather ineffectual.

LEVEL OF THE THERAPIST'S COMPETENCE

It is simply a fact that some therapists are brighter, more gifted, and more sensitive than others. Patients sense such things, some preferring to leave incompetent and insensitive therapists, while others prefer an inadequate therapy in which they will not have to face the greater pain of changing, or through which they feel superior to the therapist and therefore reassured.

ATTITUDES TOWARD ACTING OUT AND REGRESSIONS

Some therapists are permissive in this respect in order to create an atmosphere of acceptance and "hold" in which the patient's preverbal and nonverbal pathology can unfold and be revised. For others, permissiveness is a consequence of their own corruption and need to sanction disruptive and even dishonest behavior. Therapists who tend to condemn regressions and acting out may do so out of fear, inappropriate moral judgments, anxiety, and needs to be punitive. Some therapists respond actively to blatant acting out and less so to less destructive regressions. The variations are many; self-awareness and flexibility is essential.

THE CONSTRUCTIVE USE OF NONVERBAL INTERVENTIONS

There are periods in therapy when the therapist's nonverbal responses are more important than his verbalizations; at such times, silent acceptance and availability may be the correct and indicated intervention (see Balint, 1968).

Patients with disturbances in the earliest years, and especially with disturbances in their primary object relationships (e.g., poor and insensitive mothering), will at some points in therapy communicate their needs nonverbally. They want acceptance, and an opportunity to experience a facilitating relationship and to grow again. Some want incessant gratifications; they pose serious therapeutic problems (malignant regression; see Balint, 1968). At times of regression to these levels, the sensitive therapist will pitch his emphasis on nonverbal rather than verbal levels. An atmosphere of constructive acceptance, of toleration and empathy, is crucial. The therapist should be like an available, but not demanding, mother. Words can spoil the effect or must be used in a more global or primitive way. It is from such patients above all that we learn that our nonverbal stance is a major contributor to the inner change we seek to develop in our patients.

Verbal interventions and especially interpretations generate insight and structural inner changes. But the relationship with the therapist—the legitimate gratifications, the avenues of identification, and the facilitating aspects of the relationship—are the essential background and setting for such changes (see Chapter 8). Further, when used with sensitivity and proper timing, nonverbal elements can lead to dramatic and otherwise impossible changes in the patient.

I shall briefly illustrate this.

> Miss G.X. a teenager, was asthmatic. During fifteen months of therapy, with considerable therapeutic work, insight, and inner change, she had begun to control her use of the asthma to express a variety of pathological fantasies and maladaptions. The therapist's summer vacation was approaching and previously she had had major asthmatic episodes with each of several separations from him.
>
> During the weeks prior to his leaving this time, there was little indication of regressive trends such as wheezing, sexual and drug-oriented acting out, and crises with her parents. The separation was mentioned by the patient, and derivatives of her fantasies related to it were explored largely in terms of a desertion by an uncaring mother. Reports of dreams, fantasies, and events alternated in her sessions with long periods of comfortable silence. The therapist responded by being silent too, feeling that he was accepting the patient and

allowing her to feel a benign closeness to him in this way. He also intervened less often and less quickly than usual during this period, and allowed the patient to search things out more for herself.

The patient settled into a new job after losing several. Her relationship with a new boyfriend stabilized and was more comfortable than any such past relationship. At home, there was peace. Her responses to several acutely traumatic experiences, not caused by her, were worked through without undue disruption.

During the next to last week before the vacation, she decided to join a meditation group. She had confused the dates of the vacation and described some displaced anger. The therapist saw the meditation leader as a substitute for himself and a maladaption, an acting out in the sense that it reflected an unconscious fantasy of not surviving the separation on her own or with age-appropriate relationships. He therefore interpreted the turn to the meditation group along these lines, and the patient responded by rationalizing.

In the next session, she reported a dream: she was with two old friends who were heavy drug users. Then, her boyfriend threatened to drop her if she did not join him in the group. She in turn threatened to have an asthmatic attack if he did that to her. Her associations were ruminative; she spoke mainly of trivial reality problems and of some annoyance with therapy.

The therapist said that Miss G.X. had responded with rage to his questioning her use of the group as a replacement for him. It had ruptured the peace between them and had threatened her with a deprivation; and she was responding with a threat of blackmail: either he let her turn to the group or she would wheeze and go back on drugs. She was threatening to return to her old, self-destructive ways of control, denying separations, and taking in supplies (i.e., incorporatively gratifying her needs).

Miss G.X. acknowledged her rage at the therapist.

In the next hour, she reported stopping all illicit drug intake and advancing in her job. She had decided to forget about the group and had had several very unusual and happy experiences with her mother. She later withstood the separation without being asthmatic or otherwise regressing.

In this vignette, an accepting and peaceful atmosphere contributed to the patient's experiencing a kind of good mothering appropriate to the therapist's role in treatment. It helped the patient to renounce her use of asthma for the gratification of fantasies of fusing with a symbolic mother figure and for other neurotic needs. A quiet oneness prevailed, until the therapist made a frustrating intervention, which was, he felt, indicated since the patient was communicating a latent anxiety that she could not tolerate the loss of a mothering figure without a replacement or regressing. He was well aware of what he had done, and the patient's dream and associations indicated that she had, indeed, been hurt and frustrated by it. The correct interpretation of her reaction to this frustration provided for the patient another experience of being understood, reinstated the positive therapeutic alliance, and helped the patient to resume her movement toward better and less costly adaptations.

We see, then, the value of the therapist's being in tune with his nonverbal communications, and understanding their effects, their limitations, and anything that disrupts their positive tone.

This lengthy study of the interventions available to the therapist has entailed a complex and tortuous journey, but one I trust, filled with many profitable stops. My goal has been to describe the basic kinds of interventions available to the therapist and the basic principles related to their use in psychotherapy. With this established, we may now move on to the next step in the sequence of the basic session: the patient's responses to these interventions.

Bibliography

Adler, G. and Buie, D. (1972) "The misuses of confrontations with borderline patients," *International Journal of Psychoanalytic Psychotherapy,* 1: 109–120.

―――― and Meyerson, P. (1973) editors, *Confrontation in Psychotherapy,* New York: Science House.

Alexander, F. (1954) "Psychoanalysis and psychotherapy," *Journal of the American Psychoanalytic Association,* 2: 722–733.

Arlow, J. (1963a) "Conflict, regression and symptom formation," *International Journal of Psycho-Analysis,* 44: 12–22.

―――― (1963b) "The supervisory situation," *Journal of the American Psychoanalytic Association,* 11: 576–594.

―――― (1969) "Unconscious fantasy and disturbances of conscious experience," *Psychoanalytic Quarterly,* 38: 1–27.

Balint, M. (1968) *The Basic Fault,* London: Tavistock Publications.

Beres, D. (1962) "The unconscious fantasy," *Psychoanalytic Quarterly,* 31: 309–328.

Bibring, E. (1954) "Psychoanalysis and the dynamic psychotherapies," *Journal of the American Psychoanalytic Association,* 2: 745–770.

Blos, P. (Jr.) (1972) "Silence: a clinical exploration," *Psychoanalytic Quarterly,* 41: 348–363.

Boyer, L. and Giovacchini, P. (1967) *Psychoanalytic Treatment of Characterological and Schizophrenic disorders,* New York: Science House.

Buie, D. and Adler, G. (1972) "The uses of confrontation with borderline patients," *International Journal of Psychoanalytic Psychotherapy,* 1: 90–108.

Corwin, H. (1972) "The scope of therapeutic confrontation from routine to heroic," *International Journal of Psychoanalytic Psychotherapy,* 1: 68–89.

Devereux, G. (1951) "Some criteria for the timing of confrontations and interpretations," *International Journal of Psycho-Analysis,* 32: 19–24.

Eissler, K. (1953) "The effect of the structure of the ego on psychoanalytic technique," *Journal of the American Psychoanalytic Association,* 1: 104–143.

Erikson, E. (1950) *Childhood and Society,* New York: W. W. Norton & Co.

Fine, B.; Joseph, E.; and Waldhorn, H. (1971) *Recollection and Reconstruction: Reconstruction in psychoanalysis,* Monograph IV; Monograph series of the Kris Study group of the New York Psychoanalytic Institute, New York: International Universities Press.

Freud, A. (1946) *The Ego and the Mechanisms of Defense,* New York: International Universities Press.

Freud, S. (1900) "The Interpretation of Dreams," SE: 4 & 5.

———— (1905) "A Fragment of an Analysis of a Case of Hysteria," SE: 7: 1–122.

———— (1908) "Hysterical Phantasies and Their Relation to Bisexuality," SE: 9: 157–166.

———— (1919a) "Analysis of a Phobia in a Five-year-old Boy," SE: 10: 5–149.

———— (1919b) "Notes on a Case of Obsessional Neurosis," SE: 10: 153–320.

———— (1912) "Types of Onset of Neurosis," SE: 12: 229–238.

———— (1915) "Obesrvations on Transference—Love," SE: 12: 157–171.

———— (1918) "From the History of an Infantile Neurosis," SE: 17: 3–122.

———— (1923) "The Ego and The Id," SE: 19: 3–66.

———— (1926) "Inhibitions, Symptoms, and Anxiety," SE: 20: 77–175.

———— (1937) "Construction in Analysis," SE: 23: 255–270.

Fromm-Reichman, F. (1954) "Psychoanalytic and general dynamic conceptions of theory and of therapy: differences and similarities," *Journal of the American Psychoanalytic Association,* 2: 711–721.

Gill, M. (1963) "Topography and systems in psychoanalytic theory," *Psychological Issues,* Vol. III, No. 2, Monograph 10, New York: International Universities Press.

Gill, M. (1954) "Psychoanalysis and exploratory psychotherapy," *Journal of the American Psychoanalytic Association,* 2: 771–797.

Glover, E. (1931) "The therapeutic effect of inexact interpretations: a contribution to the theory of suggestion," *International Journal of Psycho-Analysis,* 12: 397–411.

Greenacre, P. (1952) *Trauma, Growth and Personality,* New York: International Universities Press.

———— (1956) "Re-evaluation of the process of working through," *International Journal of Psycho-Analysis,* 37: 439–444.

Greenson, R. (1966) "That 'impossible' profession," *Journal of the American Psychoanalytic Association,* 14: 9–27.

———— (1967) *The Technique and Practice of Psychoanalysis,* New York: International Universities Press.

Halpert, E. (1972a) "The effect of insurance on psychoanalytic treatment," *Journal of the American Psychoanalytic Association*, 20: 122–133.

———— (1972b) "A meaning of insurance in psychotherapy," *International Journal of Psychoanalytic Psychotherapy*, 1: (No. 4), 63–68.

Hartmann, H. (1939) *Ego Psychology and the Problem of Adaptation*, New York: International Universities Press, 1958.

Jacobson, E. (1964) *The Self and the Object World*, New York: International Universities Press.

———— (1971) *Depression*, New York: International Universities Press.

Kernberg, O. (1967) "Borderline personality organization," *Journal of the American Psychoanalytic Association*, 15: 641–685.

———— (1970a) "Factors in the treatment of narcissistic personalities," *Journal of the American Psychoanalytic Association*, 18: 51–85.

———— (1970b) "A psychoanalytic classification of character pathology," *Journal of the American Psychoanalytic Association*, 18: 800–822.

———— (1971) "Prognostic considerations regarding borderline personality organization," *Journal of the American Psychoanalytic Association*, 19: 595–635.

Khan, M. (1963) "The concept of cumulative trauma," *Psychoanalytic Study of the Child*, 18: 286–306.

———— (1972) "The finding and becoming self," *International Journal of Psychoanalytic Psychotherapy*, 1: 97–111.

Kohut, H. (1971) *The Analysis of Self*. The Psychoanalytic Study of the Child, Monograph No. 4, New York: International Universities Press.

Kris, E. (1951) "Ego psychology and interpretation in psychoanalytic therapy," *Psychoanalytic Quarterly*, 20: 15–30.

———— (1956) "The recovery of childhood memories in psychoanalysis," *The Psychoanalytic Study of the Child*, 11: 54–88.

Langs, R. (1966) "Manifest dreams from three clinical groups," *Archives of General Psychiatry*, 14: 634–643.

———— (1967) "Manifest dreams in adolescents: a controlled pilot study," *Journal of Nervous and Mental Disorders*, 145: 43–52.

———— (1969) "Discussion of dream content in psychopathologic states," in *Dream Psychology and the New Biology of Dreaming*, ed. M. Kramer, 397–403, Springfield: Charles C. Thomas.

———— (1971a) "Altered states of consciousness: an experimental case study," *Psychoanalytic Quarterly*, 40: 40–58.

———— (1971b) "Day residues, recall residues, and dreams: reality and the psyche," *Journal of the American Psychoanalytic Association*, 19: 499–523.

———— (1972) "A psychoanalytic study of material from patients in psychotherapy," *International Journal of Psychoanalytic Psychotherapy*, 1: 4–45.

Loewenstein, R. (1951) "The problem of interpretation," *Psychoanalytic Quarterly*, 20: 1–14.

———— (1957) "Some thoughts on interpretation in the theory and practice of psychoanalysis," *The Psychoanalytic Study of the Child*, 12: 127–150.

Mahler, M. (1968) "On human symbiosis and the vicissitudes of individuation," *Volume I: Infantile Psychosis,* New York: International Universities Press.

Olinick, S. (1954) "Some considerations of the use of questions as a psychoanalytic technique," *Journal of the American Psychoanalytic Association,* 2: 57–66.

Pollock, G. (1970) "Anniversary reactions, traumas, and mourning," *Psychoanalytic Quarterly,* 39: 347–371.

——— (1971) "Temporal anniversary manifestations: hour, day, holiday," *Psychoanalytic Quarterly,* 40: 123–131.

Rangell, L. (1954) "Similarities and differences between psychoanalysis and dynamic psychotherapy," *Journal of the American Psychoanalytic Association,* 2: 734–744.

Reider, N. (1953) "Reconstruction and screen function," *Journal of the American Psychoanalytic Association,* 1: 389–405.

Rosen, V. (1955) "Reconstruction of a traumatic childhood event," *Journal of the American Psychoanalytic Association,* 3: 211–221.

Schur, M. (1953) "The ego in anxiety," in *Drives, Affects, Behavior,* ed. R. Loewenstein, 67–103. New York; International Universities Press.

Searles, H. (1973) "Some aspects of unconscious fantasy," *International Journal of Psychoanalytic Psychotherapy,* 2: 37–50.

Sharpe, E. (1937) *Dream Analysis,* London: Hogarth Press.

Spitz, R. (1957) *No and Yes,* New York: International Universities Press.

——— (1965) *The First Year of Life,* New York: International Universities Press.

Stone, L. (1961) *The Psychoanalytic Situation,* New York: International Universities Press.

Tarachow, S. and Stein, A. (1967) "Psychoanalytic psychotherapy," in *Psychoanalytic Techniques,* ed. B. Wolman, 471–510, New York: Basic Books.

Waldhorn, H. (1960) "Assessment of analyzability: technical and theoretical observations," *Psychoanalytic Quarterly,* 29: 478–506.

Wallerstein, R. (1969) "Psychoanalysis and psychotherapy (The relationships of psychoanalysis to psychotherapy: current issues)," *International Journal of Psycho-Analysis,* 50: 117–126.

Weisman, A. (1972) "Confrontation, countertransference, and context," *International Journal of Psychoanalytic Psychotherapy,* 1: 7–25.

Winnicott, D. (1958) *Collected Papers,* London: Tavistock Publications; New York: Basic Books.

Yazmajian, R. (1965) "Slips of the tongue," *Psychoanalytic Quarterly,* 34: 413–419.

Zetzel, E. (1956) "Current concepts of transference," *International Journal of Psycho-Analysis,* 37: 369–376.

Index of Clinical Material

Index of Authors

Adler, G.
  and Buie, 419
  and Meyerson, 419
Arlow, J., 26, 28, 37, 242, 243, 244, 262, 282, 497

Balint, M., 28, 38, 181, 239, 247, 252, 253, 256, 586, 623, 625
Barkin, L., 28
Berchenko, F., 28
Beres, D., 242
Bibring, E., 34, 391, 419
Blos, P. (Jr.), 171, 367
Blum, H., 28
Boyer, L.
  and Giovacchini, 236
Buie, D.
  and Adler, 419

Coltrera, J., 28
Console, W., 28
Corwin, H., 419

Devereux, G., 419

Eissler, K., 34, 125, 566
Erikson, E., 239, 249

Fine, B.
  and Joseph, 512
  and Waldhorn, 512
Freud, A., 245
Freud, S., 28, 210, 242, 243, 244, 262, 282, 292, 317, 444, 451, 509, 512, 516
Fromm-Reichman, F., 34

Gill, M., 34, 485
Giovacchini, P., 28
Glover, E., 509
Goldberger, L., 28
Greenacre, P., 238, 513
Greenson, R., 28, 39, 43, 82, 451, 464, 567

Halpert, E., 95
Hartman, H., 237
Holt, R., 28

Jacobson, E., 236, 243, 247
Joseph, E.
  and Fine, 512

  and Waldhorn, 512

Kanzer, M., 28
Kernberg, O., 236, 246
Khan, M., 38, 241
Klein, G., 28
Kohut, H., 99, 103, 175, 236, 242, 246, 248, 251, 253, 255, 256
Kris, E., 451, 512
  and Fine, 512
  and Joseph, 512
  and Waldhorn, 512

Langs, R. J., 26, 37, 279, 282, 288, 295, 296, 356, 357, 359
Loewenstein, R., 451, 515, 583

Mahler, M., 239, 244

Neiderland, W., 28

Olinick, S., 391

Pollock, G., 323

Rangell, L., 34
Reiser, M., 28, 512
Rosen, V., 512
Rosenbaum, M., 28

Savitt, R., 28
Schur, M., 243, 244
Searles, H., 175
Sharpe, E., 282
Silberstein, R., 28
Sperling, M., 28
Spitz, R., 239
Stein, A.
  and Tarachow, 34
Stone, L., 207, 254, 255

Tarachow, S.
  and Stein, 34

Waldhorn, H.
  and Fine, 512
  and Joseph, 512
Wallerstein, R., 34
Weisman, A., 419
Winnicott, D., 238, 239, 240, 245

Zetzel, E., 82

647

Index of Subjects